Gold Medal Flapjack
Silver Medal Life

(The autobiography of an unlikely Olympian)

Alison Mowbray

Matador
9 Priory Business Park,
Wistow Road, Kibworth Beauchamp,
Leicestershire. LE8 0RX
Tel: (+44) 116 279 2299
Fax: (+44) 116 279 2277
Email: books@troubador.co.uk
Web: www.troubador.co.uk/matador

ISBN 9781783062232

British Library Cataloguing in Publication Data.
A catalogue record for this book is available from the British Library.

Typeset by Troubador Publishing Ltd, Leicester, UK

Matador is an imprint of Troubador Publishing Ltd
Printed in the UK by TJ International, Padstow, Cornwall

For my mum who taught me how to cook
And for Nell and Lily who are teaching me how to be an Auntie

Acknowledgements

In a way, writing this book negates the need for an acknowledgements section since most of the people I would have wanted to thank for the part they played in helping me achieve my dreams will find themselves written about at some point within these pages. What I have hopefully done therefore is create an immediate group of people who will rush out to buy this book to see if they can find themselves mentioned. This is a great plus for a book about someone of such little fame. It would therefore be wasteful of time and book sales to mention you all on this page. If you want to see if you are in this book, you are going to have to buy it and read it – in one case right to the end – to see if you can find yourself. Don't cheat and look.

What I will say is that sharing this book with some of those people has already made it worth writing. One of the first friends I showed any of this with was Jo. For Jo's 40th birthday a couple of years ago I printed out the chapters that tell the story of how we met and our time learning to row (and drink) together at Liverpool University. I tied them up with a ribbon, put them in an envelope and sent them on their way (this wasn't her only present; I'm from Yorkshire, but I'm not that tight). I was worried when I sent it that 1. Jo wouldn't like what I'd written about her, and 2. She wouldn't like my writing full stop. I didn't hear anything back for three days, by which point I'd convinced myself that she hated it, was too embarrassed to tell me it was rubbish, and that it would now forever be awkward with one of my very best friends. Instead on the fourth day I had a text telling me she loved it, had read it straight through three times without stopping, could not put it down, it had given her goose bumps and made her cry and she had had no idea that I thought all those things about her. Similarly when I sent my school friend Gail 'her' chapters I got a text back "You've made me cry, I had no idea you thought that about me". On re-reading this I would like to point out that I made her cry in a positive way – I've only said nice things. When people stand up and say nice things about a friend at their funeral I always hope that they also said those things to them when they were alive. It seems a bit of a waste otherwise. In a very non-morbid way (if there is a non-morbid way of talking about funerals), I hope this book prevents me having to stand up and speak at very many funerals, because they will already know.

However, there is a specific group I owe a great deal to, most of whom don't get a name check. With all my heart I would like to acknowledge and thank Penny Mavor, Tom Battye, Rachel Dulai, Nicola Moodie, Annie Thomas and Francesca Zino (and also Jo Shindler (nee Dowman) and Gail Hutchinson again) for being my practical help and positive-thinking posse in the production of this book. At the same time as I sent a first draft of this manuscript to dozens of literary agents, I fortunately had the back-up plan of sending several chapters to each of these very good friends and, using the bribery power of flapjack, got them to read chapters and give me feedback. So at the same point as I was getting dozens of rejection letters, basically telling me that I wasn't famous enough to write an autobiography (or famous enough for them to be able to sell it anyway), I also had calls, texts and e-mails from these friends telling me 1. How much they loved it and 2. Which bits they didn't love quite so much and I could cut out or change.

It's been about a year and a half to get from that point to this, the brink of sending a finished and much improved manuscript off to be published, and I really could not have done it without them. I didn't realise at the time but the seven years writing this book was the easy bit. In rowing terms all that did was get me to the start line. The hard bit was the endless sequence of things I never even knew I needed to do to turn my typed pages into an actual book. Practically these friends have helped me turn those pages into something I think I'm more proud of than anything I've ever done in my life (including winning the medal that inspired it). But emotionally I have turned myself inside out, both in terms of the effort of keeping going alongside a full-time job, and in committing to print much that I've rarely if ever told anyone before. Every time I've most doubted myself or what I've written and so nearly given up on the effort of taking it to the next stage, I've thought about their wonderful feedback or I've had another call or e-mail encouraging me to go on. They are my friends so they were always going to tell me they loved it, but they didn't have to tell me it gave them goose bumps, or made them cry, or made them laugh, or they couldn't put it down, or they'd been up half the night reading it, or could I send them more chapters.

Thank you to my editor Martin Cloake – my professional help and encouragement in the past year and a half for his sound advice and also his flexibility in letting this remain uniquely mine. Every time you read something and think it was really slick – that was probably a Martin edit. Every time you read something a bit clunky – that was likely a sentence where I ignored his advice.

Thanks to Peter Spurrier for the wonderful rowing photos that are more than the specks in the distance my parents took. And to Jerry Lebens and Tangobootcamp for the dancing pics.

Massive thanks to Olympic Gold Medallists David Hemery and Allan Wells for reading this book, writing such wonderful Forwards and for their encouragement and feedback. I will always remember waking up to a text on New Year's morning from David saying he'd just spent the last week of his holiday reading my book out loud to his wife and "Wow! We loved it!" and Allan taking the time to call me and spend about an hour on the phone after he'd read it. I feel honoured and thrilled that they have even read this book, let alone contributed to the text.

Thank you to my brother and sister, John and Catherine Mowbray. Most people who have read this have asked "What do your family think? Are they OK about you publishing all that?" When I gave my siblings the first draft to read (as their Christmas present two Christmases ago – yes I really am that tight), I totally expected that they would want me to revise some sections (particularly the sections about them) but they have been totally accepting and asked me to change nothing. In fact again, sharing this with them has already made it worth writing. As you read this story you'll see we've not always been close. John and I were already doing better the past few years but when I gave the draft to him I didn't expect that he would spend the next three days reading it, right in front of me, every spare moment, quoting sections occasionally in a teasing brother but totally appreciative sort of way. Or that when he'd finished he would say "I feel embarrassed, I never knew anything about you. I never even knew about the rowing really. I'm a PE teacher and I love sport and I never even asked. I don't know what I thought you were doing all those years." Catherine already knew pretty much everything but I'm glad to have been able to tell her story as well as my own. She is an Olympian in her own way.

Finally, thank you to everyone who has ever heard me speak and come up to me at the end, or e-mailed me afterwards, to tell me the impact this story has had on you and how it has helped you. Even if it was to say, as often happens, "I feel so inspired. I don't know what I'm inspired to do yet, but I'm going to do something!" The first few dozen of you gave me the confidence to start writing this down, but I've needed every one of the rest of you to keep me going to this end.

Foreword

I was pleased to have Alison Mowbray become one of our speakers and coaches for our educational charity 21st Century Legacy and the 'Be the Best you Can Be!' programme. Now, having read this book, I couldn't be more delighted.

With great pleasure, I highly recommend her autobiography. It is true that life can be viewed as a journey. Alison takes us on hers, allowing the reader to see what it takes to explore and fulfil some of our human potential. Her observational and descriptive powers enable us to see and feel deeply into her experiences. Most will be awed by the volume and intensity of an international rower's training regime.

With great humour and remarkable honesty, Alison allows us to travel through her life with her. Some of us will be able to clearly identify with the obsessive nature of an individual with a powerful dream. Some will find it incomprehensible that anyone would put themselves though so much. The extent to which Alison has driven herself is a remarkable testament to the human spirit.

There are many insightful 'lessons for life' woven throughout her story. She is a remarkable role model for 'Resilience'. Alison shares stories, insights and strategies for coping with what experiences life throws at us. She writes so well and graphically, it is impossible to avoid the feelings of injustice and pain or fail to identify with the joy and relief when effort and dedication finally pay off. Largely we get out of life what we put in and Alison has certainly put a lot in. What has come out is great self-understanding and much wisdom. I hope that you will enjoy the read as much as I did.

Dr David Hemery CBE
Olympic Gold Medallist 400m hurdles Mexico 1968

An Olympic medal can be the inspiration for any sportsperson's dream. This book is an in-depth story of Alison Mowbray's endeavour to win an Olympic medal and fulfil that dream. It is a sincere and personal account of a lifestyle of commitment to training and the psychological stamina needed to reach the very top in sport, but particularly in Alison's sport of rowing. Her single-minded determination to overcome personal family anxieties, balanced with her academic studies and the ambition to be an Olympic medallist, was of unbelievable proportions.

The book has great detail of the determination and perseverance she needed in competing against other athletes and also identifies the genuine support from some of the people she trusted most. She talks frankly of both her strengths and faults as a person and as an athlete, but in spite of this, she had the self-belief and dedication to overcome all barriers that were thrown in front of her. She refused to give up after a disappointing Sydney Olympics, driven to pursue an opportunity for an Olympic medal in Athens with renewed passion and four years later fulfilled her ambition.

Alison Mowbray's book is a passionate and humbling read.

Allan Wells MBE

Olympic Gold Medallist 100m Moscow 1980

Contents

'If you are careful', Garp wrote, 'if you use good ingredients and you don't take any short cuts, then you can usually cook something very good. Sometimes it is the only worthwhile product you can salvage from a day: what you eat. With writing, I find, you can have all the right ingredients, give plenty of time and care and still get nothing. Also true of love. Cooking, therefore can keep a person who tries hard sane.'

'The World According to Garp' by John Irvin

Prologue: Running to a standstill

There was only one thing I could think of to do so I put on my trainers. I didn't want to go for a run, but still I knew it had the power to make me feel better if I would let it.

I ran out of the house and onto my usual beautiful Chiltern field and woodland route. I pushed myself on but every so often I would just find myself walking. I'd walk for a while but walking didn't have the power to stop me thinking, so I'd somehow pick my feet up into a run again. I ran/walked out of the wood, over the style and into the last field and then on the side of the hill I just stopped. Absolutely where I was. Didn't move another muscle. There was nowhere I wanted to be and nothing I wanted to do so once I'd stopped there was no reason to move again. I was outside myself looking in and felt quite calm. My outside self was wryly amused and I thought I would have had very little sympathy for anyone else being this melodramatic, but still I didn't try and stop the self-pity or move myself on.

I looked at the grass and thought, quite calmly, that I could sit down – but that would have involved moving and I didn't want to do that. So I just stood. I don't know how long I stood for but it was a long time. A herd of bullocks came over to investigate, daring each other to come closer like the rebellious teenagers they are, then scaring each other and starting back. I let them come close in their semi-circle, the Yorkshire girl in me safe in the knowledge that for all their daring a single shout and gesture would send tonnes of beef fleeing. But I didn't shout and I didn't raise an arm. I just stood. The light faded and it got quite cold, but still I stood.

What do you do when you've achieved everything you wanted to achieve? Where do you go from there? There had always been a goal, something to drive myself on for next and I'd kept after them my whole life because I instinctively felt it was taking me somewhere necessary. I was never really sure where it was but I was sure I would get there at some point and that it would all be worth it. And I think I thought (although I'm not sure I thought about it in concrete terms – it was more an unspoken understanding with the world) that when I got there I would be happy just where I was and be allowed to rest.

I'd won an Olympic medal. It had taken me 15 years from a standing start after first getting into a boat at the age of 18. I'd not been a sporty kid so it had taken me a long time to find something I could be good at and then a long time again to think I could be good enough at it to be Olympic medal material. I'd rowed for 15 years, training almost every day, often several times a day. It had been hard work, desperately hard work sometimes and I'd got very tired, but I'd loved it. I was on the British Rowing Team for the last seven years of that, through five World Championships and the Sydney and Athens Olympics, and finally, at the last call, in Athens 2004 at the age of 33, I'd won an Olympic medal. Everything I'd wanted to achieve. More than I'd ever thought was possible. And I'd thought that that was the point. I'd reached the top of the mountain and now I'd be allowed to rest. For the rest of my life? I think I thought so.

And that is where the story usually ends, not where it starts. The athlete holds their medal high, cameras flash, dreams are achieved and all is well with the world. A full stop. And if I'd got my arse in gear and written this in the first few months or year or maybe even two years after that moment, that is probably where it would have ended. But I didn't. Because I didn't know then that I had a story. Or that I could write.

I stopped being a full-time athlete for a living and let go of ambition. That's what happened next for me. I'd always wanted to be a normal person – spent my life trying to be like everyone else. But now I was I felt so boring. It had taken me 33 years to claw and paddle my way to the top of the mountain so I didn't expect that when I let go it would take me less than two to ride the stream back down again. That I would lose the energy and excitement for life that had expanded my chest and surrounded me with a Ready Brek glow. That had got me to the top of every mountain. That made me, despite all the hard work, happy. And I didn't know when I stopped rowing and let go, that three and a half years later, I'd be stuck, standing in a cold dark field, staring at cows.

I actually started writing this, eight years ago, as a recipe book (most places food is mentioned in this book, there used to also be a recipe for it included). All my life I've collected recipes like other people collect autographs, antiques, or friends on Facebook. Some I've inherited, some I've acquired, some I've stolen and some I've just made up. All the time I was rowing, I'd cook and bake for friends and crew mates, and when they asked for the recipe I'd tell them that when I stopped rowing I was going to write my recipe book and they could have it then. I like recipe books that are more than just a list of ingredients. I want them to tell me stories about where they came from, how they are cooked, when they were eaten and why they are loved. Books that I'm as likely to keep under my bed as in the kitchen. This book just started life as my attempt at writing the type of recipe book I like to read. I know I'm not famous enough to sell an autobiography so I never thought to write one. I never had the raw power and stature of Steve Redgrave, I am not that legend, and it would be as foolish for me to try and compete in the same book market as it would be on the same rowing machine. But while I never even figure in the debate over the world's greatest olympian I really do have the world's greatest flapjack recipe and no one who's eaten it has ever tried to debate that point. So I thought I'd write a recipe book. I'm not famous enough to write an autobiography but you don't have to be famous to write about flapjack.

So this book started out as a recipe book with a few stories from my life… and then it just got a bit out of hand to be honest. It became really important to me to also write this as a history of British Women's rowing because I don't think many people outside it really understand what the journey has been and how incredibly self-motivated and tough those women have had to be to pull themselves up, often in defiance of the first fledgling attempts at some sort of system, to that first Olympic medal in Sydney and those first Golds in London. And as I wrote I also found myself answering the question that so many people who have heard me tell this story have asked "Where does your determination come from?" I never had an answer. But I think I do now.

When I'd finished, people who know about books got rather confused and said, "What is it? Is it an Autobiography or a Cook Book or a Motivational Guide? We can't publish it because we don't know which shelf to put it on. And anyway you're not famous enough to write an autobiography." Really, I've long known this was not a recipe book any more. But I kept the recipes in for a very long time because when I told people I was writing a book and they asked what it was, it felt so much easier to tell them lightly that it was sort of a recipe book than to have the arrogance to say I'd written my autobiography. But eventually, finally, I've taken out all but one recipe. Because if this story is about anything it's about the importance of pushing yourself forward in your own life. It tells me again and again that I don't have the right to expect other people to have more faith in me than I have in myself. That I cannot let fear of failure hold me back from a chance of success. That I have to be brave in my own life. And anyway, I'm no longer afraid.

I actually work as an inspirational speaker, telling at least some of this story out loud to an audience. I'm not always the best at getting started but I'm pretty good when I get going and I'm legendary for my big finishes. I have an unusual story that surprises most people who hear it and if you've never raced an Olympic final I can take you there. I know I won't have to use flapjack to bribe the people I've already spoken to to buy this story. Besides, they may never have heard of me when I arrive, but once they've met me I'm usually the most famous person they know. Do you know more people in Britain have won the National Lottery than an Olympic medal? Despite recent successes, we are still a very rare breed. And I will always be one of them.

But it surprises people, and certainly kids, that getting an Olympic medal is not an automatic ticket to fame or fortune. The kids ask what car I drive and how much money I won and from one very cute four-year-old girl, waving her hand in the air, desperate to ask a question, "Do you....do you... do you live in a castle?" By the time I finish telling them this story, they get that that's not really the point (which is a good job). So you may never even have heard of me. Helen (my agent) never says, but I'm pretty sure people ring her up to ask for Steve Redgrave with his five or Matthew Pinsent with his four Gold Medals and then, when she tells them the price, they say "HOW MUCH! Do you have anyone cheaper?" And I imagine Helen, in her best Welsh accent saying, "Well, we have Alison, you won't have heard of her but she is very good."

But even they have not heard what happens next. I stop the story with the medal held high. Because that is what people expect and I've never known how to tell the next bit. Besides, I was still busy living it and even I didn't know where it would go.

I never planned to be inspiring. So really this is just a story of how I did the things I love, the very best I could do them and how very far it took me.

But how did I get there? And what was beyond that? And what is beyond that again?

And as for the rest of the recipes? I'm afraid those of you that have been waiting will still have to wait. But once I've finished this, I really will write that book. Because through all of this, cooking has been the constant, and I think, although some people may well debate the point, it really has kept me sane.

Chapter 1: Baked love & missed catches

"A story of mindset not muscle"

What's your first Olympic memory? I've asked that question many times since I started telling this story and heard many answers. For most of us it was a particular race or athlete that really caught our imagination – something we saw on TV between the ages of about five and ten. And if you ask that question to most Olympians and certainly most Olympic medallists (and I've been fortunate enough to meet quite a few), they won't have a second's hesitation in recalling the moment they saw *that* race, *that* athlete, when the light bulb came on and they said, "That's what I want to do. I want to go the Olympics. I want to win an Olympic medal."

But … it wasn't *anything* like that for me.

I do remember watching my first Olympics – Moscow 1980. I was nine and jumping up and down on our big pink sofa in front of the TV, screaming at the likes of Seb Coe, Steve Ovett, Steve Cram, Allan Wells, Brendan Foster and Daley Thompson. The only sport I'd ever seen live was going to Gateshead Stadium with my dad to watch the athletics. I'd seen these guys right in front of me, I'd got their autographs and now I couldn't believe that they were famous enough to be on TV. So I shouted at the screen, convinced I was making them go faster, that I was somehow part of their success – but having no idea it would ever be anything to do with me. When I looked at those Olympians I didn't just think they were superhuman, I thought they were a different species.

And that was largely because I wasn't any good at sport, which seemed to be some sort of pre-requisite for going to the Olympics. I couldn't, and still can't really, catch anything, throw anything or hit anything – and I'm a pretty slow runner. I was also, as my mother kindly put it, a "well-built" child. Not how people usually imagine a future Olympian. So, there's not much sport going on for a lot of this story. If you expected this future Olympian to be out training all hours from the age of six, then lower your expectations. This is a story of mindset not muscle.

At the time, I was at a small village primary school in North Yorkshire where the only sport we ever played was rounders. I can't catch, throw, hit or run – so how good do you think I am at rounders? I looked forward to games afternoon, which was pretty much any sunny afternoon, with a mixture of dread and hopeful anticipation that somehow I would have worked it out and that this time I would be better. But I never was. Everyone else used to keep count of how many rounders they got per game. I kept count of how many I got per year. I think my record was three.

I was always last to get picked when the captains were choosing teams. And even at that age I was fiercely competitive and hated being bad at stuff. I tried so hard to hit that ball when it was thrown at my tightly-gripped bat, to catch it when it sailed towards my hands and to throw it more than a few feet when I eventually scrambled, red-faced, to pick it up. But I rarely did. As those of us who play any sport eventually find out: the harder you try, the more you worry, the less likely it is to happen. But aged nine I still had a lot to learn.

Having skipped ages nought to nine I've missed a vital ingredient. So to regress, I'm back in the exotically-named Midlands town of Ashby-de-la-Zouch where I lived until the age of five. We lived in a house with a sweeping staircase and a grand hall that took what seemed to be the world's largest Christmas tree; a pink sofa as yet unaware of its fate as an Olympic-watching trampoline and currently used to hide behind during the scary bits of Doctor Who; my GP parents (the second and third most important doctors in my life at this point); the world's largest playroom (the world has definitely shrunk since I was five), a pink and purple plywood castle Wendy house (made by my dad) complete with ladder, an upstairs and crenulations (that I could nearly pronounce); a best friend called Sarah, and a brother who was born when I was two and given the job of getting on my nerves until I started to like him about fifteen years later.

But mainly I remember my mum's flapjack. The world's best flapjack recipe – right up there with the all-time greats like Steve Redgrave. Mum baked it by the half hundred weight when we were kids (there was a reason I was so well-built). The cake tins contained a permanent supply and it was the first thing friends asked for as they came through the door. I think it was the main reason I had any friends and, if I'm honest, I still regularly buy friendship with flapjack. It works, by the way.

The oldest of three, I was not so much a child as a vehicle for practising model parenting and my mother raised me in the school of baked love. These

Baby me and my baby-faced dad.

A rare photo of my brother and I actually getting on – something not seen again for about another fifteen years. Photo taken on the big pink sofa as yet unaware of its fate as an Olympic-watching trampoline and currently used to hide behind during the scary bits of Doctor Who.

days, to sugar is to sin against your child, and model parenting means hiding the cakes and biscuits. Back then, in our house, to love your child was to provide tins full of homemade cakes and puddings every day. To bake was to care and for me the two are still inextricably linked.

When my brother, sister and I left for university and the big outside world we took this recipe, with its miraculous icebreaking and friendship-forming powers with us. Mum's flapjack has travelled the globe. It is temperamental, but that is also its beauty and why making it for someone is a mark of true friendship. It says that you care enough to take some time and put yourself to some trouble. People feel the love when they eat it. It is great for throwing into a kitbag on the way to the gym, and its virtual indestructibility and satisfying solidity make it the most perfect hill-walking and trekking food. It also goes down well while sat on the sofa with a cup of tea and a friend.

It looks straightforward enough but you should not expect to get it right first, or every, time. It was the first thing I remember being baked at the age of about three, and the first thing I baked myself at the age of six or seven. But still, even after all these years, my sister and I are likely to open a

Glam 60's Mum and her 70's child (already showing signs of having eaten a lot of flapjack).

telephone conversation with the words, "I made Mum's flapjack yesterday and it's not quite right."

It's right when it has a deep caramel colour and the taste and texture of oats suspended in sticky butter toffee. It is slightly gooey when warm (fresh out of the oven it makes a great hot pudding with custard) and when cool it is a bit crunchy on the outside, particularly round the edges, but moist and chewy on the inside. You can't buy anything like it in the shops, so it is the birthday, Christmas, housewarming or thank-you gift of choice. Bake it, share it and eat it with friends. It's legendary for a reason.

I feel like this recipe is both my inheritance and my legacy so I like to pass it on. Share the love…

My Mum's Flapjack Recipe

280g/10oz butter
280g/10oz sugar
3 heaped tbsp syrup (it must be Tate & Lyle's, other syrups don't taste the same at all)
3 tbsp water
280g/10oz porridge oats
175g/6oz self-raising flour
Set the oven to 160^{0}C/ Gas Mark 3 (lower for fan assisted oven or turn the fan off if possible).

1. Melt the butter, sugar, syrup and water over a low heat in a large pan and allow to bubble gently for a couple of minutes until the colour starts to turn (to start the toffee-making process).
2. Turn off the heat and add the dry ingredients. Stir with a wooden spoon to mix.
3. Grease a deep baking or roasting tin with a thin smearing of butter. To make sure you can get the flapjack out, add a handful of extra flour to the tin, tap the flour round until it is stuck to the whole buttered surface, then tap the tin upside down over the sink to remove excess flour.
4. Pour the flapjack into the prepared tin (leave plenty in the pan for scraping so you can stand in the middle of the kitchen and eat it raw off the spoon).
5. Bake at 160^{0}C for about forty minutes until deep golden brown (the cooking time is the crucial part, if it cooks too quickly it will be dry and cakey rather than soft and chewy).
6. Allow to cool slightly, but cut into pieces while still warm and leave to cool completely in the tin.

I've given this recipe to friends who've added various dried fruit and nuts and then been disappointed with the result. This is already the world's best flapjack recipe so by definition it can't be beaten. Don't try to guild the lily.

Me (left), my best friend Sarah (right) and Jemima (middle). We all ate a lot of flapjack.

The week before my fifth birthday we moved to Aldbrough St John, the aforementioned small Yorkshire village. Our big old Virginia-creepered house was set on the edge of the huge village green (aka the rounders field) exactly opposite the small village school. The big move was memorable for three things: I had to leave my best-friend Sarah behind; I was desperate to start school; and the new house had an Aga. I don't remember how many days it was before we made our first drop scones directly onto the Aga hotplates, but it wasn't many.

Our new house had a paddock out back. Dad had a tennis court built on half of it and rotovated most of the rest for what was practically a market garden. The last section of paddock was wired off and for many years we reared geese to kill for Christmas. My job was to run from the stables (where Grandpa was bleeding the geese to death from a slit in the top of their head) with the jugs of blood to the kitchen, where Mum and Gran were making black pudding (you have to run quick because otherwise the blood coagulates). Our young parents were living out dreams of *The Good Life* and this was self-sufficiency in more ways than one. Pre-mobile phones and GP out-of-hours service, an on-call doctor had to be within earshot of the house phone at all times. An extension bell on the outside wall gave Dad the crucial extra quarter mile of freedom for weekends and summer evenings on call. It took ten rings to run from the furthest reaches of the tennis court, through the old stables, across the cobbled yard and through two rooms of the house to get to the hall phone (Dad counted everything). It was another two or three rings if he was at the bottom of the paddock and running in wellies. The patients learnt to hang on.

To start with, the surgery was actually part of our house. The whole three-room set-up of consulting room, waiting room and dispensary/reception was housed in one subdivided room. When Dad moved the surgery out to a house across the green and pulled down the dividing walls, the entire old three-roomed surgery formed a single room just big enough to take a table tennis table (if you didn't hit the ball too hard or want to take too much back swing).

It was a pretty traditional set-up; two male GPs worked alternate surgeries and on calls. When one of the doctors was in surgery, their wife acted as receptionist; when they were on call and had to visit a patient, the wife sat by the phone and would call the patient's house to let the doctor know where to go next. A fully qualified doctor herself, our mother seemed quite happy with this role.

After a few years, Dad's senior partner retired and Dad took over the two-man practice – in theory with Mum because they drew two salaries, but in reality Mum was looking after three kids. The deal was that Mum acted as a receptionist in the evenings, ran a few well woman clinics and the odd surgery, and Dad did all the rest – all the surgeries, visits and on calls, including all the nights. He loved it but I think it's fair to say it was never really a long-term healthy life plan.

We were virtually self-sufficient as far as fruit and veg, and tennis, were concerned. What we didn't grow we bought wholesale or received as gifts from farmer patients. It was not unusual to come home to find Dad cutting up half a pig carcass, skinning a rabbit or plucking a pheasant on the kitchen table.

I developed my own skills. Practise is said to make perfect, but unfortunately while this didn't prove to be the case for me and tennis, it did for fruit-picking. Hours and hours spent in amongst the raspberry canes, blackcurrant bushes and strawberry sets, methodically picking my way through many a sunny afternoon either at home, or to earn a few quid at the local fruit farm, have left me with not a little talent in this area. When I was 23, I quit my job as a science research assistant for Unilever because it was too hot and sunny to be in the lab and went commercial fruit-picking instead. I picked so many strawberries in the morning that they kept me on for the raspberries and currents in the afternoon. Paid by the punnet, I earned top whack and more per week picking fruit in the sun than I did in the job my degree qualified me for.

I'm a little rusty now but I reckon I could still hold my own in any competitive raspberry, blackcurrant or strawberry-picking situation. Unfortunately these occasions arise far less often than one with such skills and competitive instincts would wish for. It's an unfair world where being able to hit a ball over a net can be rewarded with such fame and fortune, but the ability to strip a row of raspberry canes bare of ripe fruit in a matter of minutes receives little to no media attention.

So, it was the good life in many ways and I do have those classic happy childhood memories of endless summer days running half-naked under the sprinkler in the back garden, playing hide-and-seek, climbing trees and parading around in outlandish clothes and outsized shoes from the dressing-up box. Dressing up was always a high priority and Mum's dedication and creativity meant we were regular winners in the annual village fete fancy-dress competition (this will explain a lot to those who know me).

After a couple of years, the ultimate home produce arrived in the shape of my sister Catherine. She seemed no more interesting than my brother, but being less annoying she was easier to ignore and I took even less notice of

Me and my little sister. Just one of many wins in the village fete fancy-dress competition. Mum's enthusiasm and creative talents meant that no one else really stood a chance.

her than I did of my brother for even longer in our lives. We were a distant set of siblings and our interactions were mainly limited to teasing and bullying. I regret that now.

It was a productive life even then. I helped out in the vegetable garden, digging and sowing and weeding and cropping and burning and shelling (pretty slick at that job too), and in the kitchen, chopping and blanching and boiling and jamming and pickling and baking and freezing. And in the winter there were still the geese, the pet goat and the wild birds to feed and the fire grate to clean out and re-lay and the wood to chop. It is amazing to me now that I was let loose, on my own, with a proper size, 'swing it over your head', axe, well before all my fingers and toes had even stopped growing (which I suppose from a medical sense is the best time to learn, as apparently they do reattach better). I also always made Christmas cards from that year's Blue Peter design and colourful paste eggs by wrapping them in onion skins and hard-boiling at Easter.

Most of it was fun and it seemed important to please both my parents. I loved watching things grow and the competitive nature of seeing how fast I could shell stuff. Making and baking and chopping wood were definite favourites.

Despite having doctor parents, I don't remember there ever being much spare cash around. At the tender age of 23, Dad bought a big house and a

Top: Spring and early summer with Snowy the pet lamb. We met a farmer carrying her on a cold wet walk in the Dales and he sold us an orphan sob story, that he already had too many to look after and that this one would probably die unless we took her. Then he charged Dad a fiver. Bottom left: Three kids, Dad and the geese (they didn't have names because we were going to eat them). From our interest this may have been the first year, but it was the first of many. Bottom right: Me, Catherine and Gordon, the first of two pet goats. We brought him back from a village car boot sale. It was our Mum's birthday so we cunningly bought Gordon for her rather than for us so she'd feel obliged to keep him.

few years later invested heavily in the practice and savings and pension plans for family security and his fantasy retirement. There were some fun holidays to various less touristy Greek islands and cottages in pretty places in Britain, but we made and made do with everything else. I remember every item of clothing and every record I ever owned until the age of about

16 because, as they were things we didn't spend money on, there weren't many.

To all intents and purposes we were the exaggerated, stereotypical, perfect family our parents so desired. They lived their lives (and ours to start with) to the formulaic middle-class script. School + university + marriage straight out of uni + wait two years + kids + husband brings home the bacon (or in our case buys half a pig from the butcher) + wife keeps house = everyone lives happily ever after. What they don't tell you is that there are no guarantees that the equation will add up, but for a short while at least it looked pretty idyllic.

Dad did mainly manly stuff. He worked more than full-time and maintained the vegetable garden, the lawns, the house, the geese and the fires, played tennis and chess, ran half-marathons and the primary school football team. He looked after anything to do with money, bills and cars, answered all official typed letters on his typewriter, made beer and carried all the passports, tickets, suitcases and responsibility when we went on holiday. Dad taught us our times tables and that shouting, losing your temper or arguing was not to be tolerated because the most important thing was to be liked by everyone and not to create a scene.

Mum did mainly womanly stuff. She worked part-time and maintained the flower garden, the soft furnishings and the children, sang in choirs, read novels, sewed, knitted and napped in the afternoons. She looked after anything to do with cooking and clothes and made potted meat (from the pig's trotters our father sawed off the carcass) and curtains and proper puddings for dinner every day, answered all handwritten letters from family and friends in beautiful handwriting, and carried the tissues and sweets

Me and my pretty curly haired baby sister in an olive grove in Greece. Mowbray girls doing what Mowbray girls do best – after dressing up and baking flapjack.

when we went on holiday. Mum taught us how to say "Bonjour" and count to ten in French and about old churches and that it was best not to argue or create a scene as it would upset your Dad.

This was perfect segregation of roles and ultimate co-dependency. They rarely spent a day, let alone a night, apart and despite earning at least some of her own money all her life, when Dad died, my sister had to show Mum how to read a bank statement.

So, I am the child of both my parents. I've kept hold of nearly all of it with the result that I'm a kind of hyperactive cross between All Action Hero and Victorian Housewife. To paraphrase a great Eddie Izzard line – I'm your sort of running, jumping, climbing trees, bake a cake while I'm up there sort of girl. That's where it's at.

Chapter 2: Getting to Grips with the Basics

"If you practise at something you get better"

Aldbrough was a traditional village with a traditional school sports day. While not a sporty child I was a smart one and as I hated to lose, sports day could be pretty painful. Alongside the much-desired but totally unachievable Winners and Runners-up cups at sports day, there was also the lamely named Tryers Cup for someone who tried hard but was still rubbish. This cup had my name on it in all but the most important, literal sense. No one tried harder and no one was more rubbish, but the Tryers Cup eluded me year after year. Despite the lame name, I still really wanted it. It seemed unfair to create some formal way of recognising what I was putting into this yearly nightmare of humiliation and then not reward me for doing it.

What I needed was a strategy. What I worked out (being a smart kid) was that the adults who awarded the Tryers Cup were not actually that smart (this was a common realisation about adults and not one that made me desperately popular). They couldn't spot the signs of someone really trying and needed more obvious clues. I would finish somewhere in the middle of the line-up and was not obviously the most useless. Upfront would be the sporty kids, the natural athletes who tried hard and battled it out against each other. At the back would be those either with or without sporting ability, but without life-threatening competitive instinct who trotted or walked their way down the course. And in the middle would be me, battling as hard as I could but to no avail.

So I probably didn't look rubbish enough to win the coveted Tryers Cup. Also, I didn't fall over. This, I noticed, was the crucial factor that worked right up to Olympic level (it was, after all, the Mary Decker-Slaney/Zola Budd era). If you came first you got the medal, but apparently the rules were that if you wanted all the attention and people to say how great you were, it was more important to fall over (preferably with a bit of a dramatic roll and scream), then get up and finish the race (preferably with a bit of a limp and a large grimace on your face). And I noticed that year after year the longed-for Tryers Cup went to someone who had fallen over. It was the clue the not-so-smart adult judges were looking for.

I remember my young brain coldly calculating my chances as the flat race approached. It was hard to give up the hope that maybe this year I would be faster and maybe I could miraculously win outright. I felt I was balancing the odds of running flat-out and winning the race, against a deliberate fall to throw the race but stand me in good stead for the Tryers. I remember it vividly enough to know this was a very serious decision and I was wrestling with it pretty hard. Standing on the start line I'd decided to go for the fall, but on the 'go' my competitive instinct took over and I sprinted (or rather lumbered) down the course to finish... my usual fourth or fifth. And the Tryers Cup was again awarded elsewhere.

Hence Plan B. One should always have a Plan B.

The important thing here was that alongside the 'serious' flat running races, in which I was never destined to shine, we also had the usual sack race, egg and spoon race, three-legged race and the slow bicycle race in which you competed to take the longest to complete the course (not as easy as it sounds especially on the uneven village green surface, but I was OK at this one – I've always been pretty good at going slow).

By the age of about nine I'd noticed three things about sports and sports day.

1. If you practised at something you got better.
2. No matter what I did and how much I practised, my legs would just not work fast enough to win the straightforward running races.
3. No one ever practised for the novelty events.

This then was my gap in the market, my chance of sporting glory. I would practise for one of the novelty events and wipe the floor with the amateur opposition. It was just a choice of which to specialise in.

With a revelation mirrored much later in my career, I realised that if you want to make the most difference to your performance then the team events are the ones to go for. An individual, even without practice, will always have a certain level of performance, especially if they've got the guts to just go for it. But once you get into a team of even just two people, the effects of non-practice can be disastrous even with maximum effort – in fact, often the harder you try, the worse it gets. To get a team to work well you need elements of strategy and co-operation that you can do without on your own. This means that in a team there is just more to work with, there is further to go, the difference between basic and exceptional is greater because there are more variables. Think first-time ballroom dancers stepping on toes; relay runners dropping the baton; too many cooks spoiling the broth and amateur three-legged racers falling flat on their faces.

I'm not sure I'd worked all this out by the age of nine but I somehow knew that the one to go for was the three-legged race. There may also have been an element of self-protection. It was one thing to practise running up and down the green *with* a friend; quite something else to spend that time jumping up and down in a sack by myself or running around with an egg on a spoon. Besides with someone else, it was just more fun. Especially if that someone else was my new best friend Kay White.

Kay and I practised hard at break and lunchtimes for weeks leading up to the big day. It's a complicated sport three-legged racing, not just a matter of speed, co-ordination and fitness. For starters there is the highly technical matter of selection of appropriate equipment, aka 'the tie' or 'binding'. Left to chance on the day, you would end up with the length of string or baling twine provided, and you might just as well sit down right there and then and attack your own leg with cheese wire. Winning with string – it's not going to happen. I've never been one for suffering unnecessary pain in the name of sport. All my rowing life I sat on seat pads to protect my bum and wore gloves when it was cold. To those who laughed at my softness I would just shrug my shoulders and then pass them in the final lactic-acid-legs-screaming sprint for the line.

Some brought their father's old ties or mother's scarves and we experimented with these options, but it was always hard to get a really reliable join. My parents being doctors, we had access to a secret weapon – the crepe bandage, flexible yet firm, soft on the flesh yet of good tensile strength. Binding selected, there was then the further issue of how and where to tie the knots and how far apart our legs should be. Many further summer afternoon hours were spent experimenting with this range of options (we didn't have to do much 'work' pre-SATs education) until the perfect combination was selected. Just in case you ever need to do this, it was a cross between a wrap and a knot – the bandage was wound round our ankles several times about an ankle-width apart and then several times around the middle of the loop to protect our ankles from clashes. This bandage system had the advantage over the dads' tie system of enabling the ankles to be further apart without risking the binding falling off mid-race (aka 'equipment failure').

We then devised our own training programme, which basically involved the time-honoured method of starting slowly and building up speed as our confidence and competence grew, getting the mileage in (round and round the village green), start practice and sprint practice. I think we were even advanced enough to discuss race tactics and contingency plans in case of falls or equipment failure (unlikely as this was with such high-tech equipment). All in all the underprepared opposition didn't stand a chance, and Kay and I were three-legged champions at least two and maybe three years in a row – glory days.

Despite my non-participation in formal sport, three-legged racing certainly wasn't my only exercise. Growing up in a little Yorkshire village,

Not being a sporty kid I have very few photos of me doing any sort of sport. This is the little known sport of lawn roller pushing. I'd be eleven here, just before I went up to the comprehensive school. You can tell that because I've already shot up and got skinny. Pushing the other roller are Emma (short hair) and Kay (long hair). Who knows who my teammate is and anyway, as you can see, I'm pretty determined that I can do this by myself. I am, as usual, coming second.

we all took for granted the most extraordinary freedom. We vaguely told our mums where we were going and vaguely said when we'd be back, and that seemed good enough. It was generally accepted that we'd be back in time for tea. There were no mobile phones to keep tabs on us, no limits or any rules bar the Green Cross Code and "Don't talk to strangers", and the radius of our adventures gradually increased with the length of our legs and the size of our confidence.

All this running around in the fresh Yorkshire air obviously required adequate fuel. I'm sure I did eat a good supply of fresh vegetables and quality savoury dishes as neither my mother nor the school cook would have even know what a convenience meal was but, unsurprisingly for a nine-year-old, these are not what I remember. Again what I remember is the sugar and the glory of cakes and puddings.

Mrs Botwright, the school cook from our little two-class village primary school, gave me the first recipe book I ever owned. She collected enough Be-Ro flour labels to get two tiny soft backed freebie recipe books for myself and Kay. I think it was a reward for helping with the washing up occasionally, but really we only hung around the kitchen to be sure of getting first choice of anything that came out of the oven. Having got this, my first recipe book, I set about trying all the recipes and used to spend whole Sundays starting at the front of the book and baking my way through until there was a film of flour on every kitchen surface, leaning towers of pots and absolutely no room left in our cavern of a cake tin cupboard. My original Be-Ro book is still just about intact but now very brown, caked in... well cake mixture and held together with sticky tape. Having just had a count up, I've worked out that I have, at some point in the last thirty or so years baked seventy of its 120 sweet and savoury recipes.

This was a time to get to grips with the basics of cooking and also of life. Despite all the baking I didn't really do much, if any, cooking until I left home. But Mum believed it was important to teach me certain life skills, so along with ironing, sewing, knitting and darning socks, she taught me one essential cooking basic – how to make a white (roux) sauce. Mum told me "If you can make a white sauce you can make anything" and this has proved to be very nearly true.

One exception to this, and therefore the other cookery basic that used to be in this chapter, is how to make perfect pastry. I make the best short-crust pastry. A skill I learnt not from my mother, who actually doesn't make great pastry, but from a cookery lesson at my secondary school – which is where the eleven-year-old me went next.

Life in a small Yorkshire village pre-computer and video games.
Top left: in theatrical mode with Stuart and Nicki Moodie. Our parents were all at medical school together and whenever we met up, us kids would spend the weekend writing and rehearsing a play to perform to the grown -ups. I think I'm a dog here (in Mums university gown).
Bottom left: another village fete fancy dress competition and another Mum Mowbray slam dunk. Catherine - bird, Alison - bird (political correctness not yet having reached Aldbrough), John - (jail) bird and my friend Emma - bird watcher (working on the theory that if you can't beat the Mowbray's you join them). The other kids look on in envy and despair.
Top right: maypole dancing. Yes really. We used to practice in PE lessons when we weren't playing rounders (same year as the bird fancy dress obviously – I didn't always dress like that). I also did a bit of clog dancing and my brother was an award winning junior Morris Dancer. Yes, that's a real thing, they went to competitions and everything. I was actually very proud.

Aged eleven, I was filled with excitement and dread at the thought of moving up to the big comprehensive school seven miles away. Excitement at all the new sports, because I thought I was just bad at rounders and was yet to find out I could be equally bad at everything else; at all the new subjects, because I could never learn enough; at the musical opportunities because, thanks to the vision of A.J. Bull (a frankly slightly scary old man by the time I knew him), all children in North Yorkshire state schools had the opportunity of free music lessons and free instrument hire (I wanted to play something big and brassy) and at the thought of new friends – which was also where the dread thing came in.

By the age of four and my first playgroup interactions, I'd worked out that I was not naturally blessed at this making friends thing. Despite acute awareness of this and valiant efforts all through my childhood, by eleven very little seemed to have changed.

It's not so surprising really. I still have the same thoughts and thought processes I've had since I was three or four years old, but it's taken a lifetime to moderate their outward effects and takes constant vigilance. More recently I'm referred to as 'individual', 'independent', 'driven', even 'inspirational'. But as a child you'd be more likely to hear 'loner', 'awkward', 'impatient' and, of course, 'bossy'. On a bad day I'm still all of those things in spades.

The most difficult thing to deal with is that I just want to be good at 'stuff' and I can't remember a time when I didn't want to be 'the best' at something. I'd watch Wimbledon and think tennis could be it, but having a court in the back garden and still not being able to beat the other village kids was an early indication that this wasn't to be. I'd watch Torvill and Dean and think ice skating could be it, but after going to the ice rink for my birthday treat and mainly hanging onto the side I'd realise it probably wasn't. I'd watch Young Musician of the Year and think that could be it and go and do extra piano practice and still really struggle with my Grade 1 pieces, and realise… maybe not.

I don't do things by halves, my world is black and white – there is no grey. In or out, up or down, my enthusiasm and scepticism know no bounds. I think this is where the early attraction to sport came from and the excitement of trying some new ones. I'd noticed the weird discrepancy whereby if you were first in a race or made the team then everyone wanted to be your friend, but if you were first in a test then for some reason the opposite happened. At school I worked hard and did well at the academic stuff and it made me unpopular. In sport you can work hard, do well and still be cool. I wanted some of that.

I love learning; there always seems to be so much to learn and do that if I live to be two hundred I'll never fit it all in. Every minute of every day is still an active choice between the three or four things I would most like to be doing with that time. Then, when I've chosen, it gets my full unwavering attention. Even if what I've chosen to do is chill out on the sofa for half a day and watch DVDs, I do it properly. Work will be out of my mind, I don't answer the phone and I have good snacks. I am never bored. So I've just never been good at hanging out, which is what kids in my village and kids the world over like to do. I had my first tango lesson a few years ago and after ten minutes the guy I was dancing with said, "In tango you sometimes have to do nothing. You're not very good at doing nothing are you?"

And last but not least, there is the need to be by myself. I'm not sure where it comes from. I thought for years that it was a result of an often rather isolated childhood and there's probably some truth in that, but it may be the other way round.

My mother swears I was born independent. She was a full-time mum, wanting nothing more than to do the full-time mother thing. If you looked at a cross-section of my mother, she'd have CARING written through her like a stick of rock. She wanted to cuddle and care for me but apparently I wasn't that interested. I played on my own and did my own thing and she tells me that she began to think this was just how children were until she had my brother and sister to prove otherwise. Apparently, some child psychologist came round when I was less than two to assess me as part of a study. When my mother made to leave the room and leave him to it, he expressed surprise and asked if she didn't want to stay, wouldn't I want her to stay? Mum said no, I'd be fine, and she'd just be in the kitchen if *he* wanted anything. Apparently that in itself was an unusual result for his study. I think my mother tells me this to prove it really wasn't her fault. I wasn't made odd, I was born odd. If I was being very deep, I'd say that my mother probably felt I'd cheated her in some way and I don't think she's ever really forgiven me.

It wasn't that I didn't have any friends. There were three lovely girls my age in the village and we played together in and out of school, but I was always aware it was a fragile and difficult thing that I had to work at. When I was about nine, a girl a year older than me had a birthday party and invited the whole of our primary school class except me. As she handed round the invites and came past, she lied very pleasantly that she was sorry but her mum had put a limit on numbers and she hoped I didn't mind. I smiled and said I understood and tried not to let her realise how rude she was – which bizarrely seemed like the most important thing. And then everyone came back telling party stories and my friends asked why I hadn't been there. I was too embarrassed to tell them I'd not been invited so I mumbled something about not being able to go and I saw the sideways glance that said 'she's weird, she never wants to do anything'. I didn't tell my parents because I was embarrassed that I couldn't do the friends thing. They wanted me to be happy and I would be letting them down if I wasn't happy. Things like that used to happen.

I can't remember a time when I didn't feel responsible for being happy. There was never a point when I was too young not to be telling myself that I was one of the lucky ones. I lived in a big house (I saw that it was bigger than a lot of my friends' houses); I knew we weren't rich but we had enough money for food and clothes and summer holidays to Greece (which I knew from watching the starving children on the news was not always the case); I was intelligent and I wasn't disabled in any way (unless you could count my chronic mal-coordination); I was at a good school getting a good education (which I understood to be one of the great advantages in life) and I had two parents who loved me, were obviously trying to do their best for me, and just wanted me to be happy. All of this had been given to me by chance without doing anything to earn it. So if I wasn't happy it was my fault because surely the rest was up to me to sort out. I've always felt it's rather a character flaw and actually just plain lazy not to be happy. I think I might have been quite an intense child.

So usually it was easier, less stressful, to be by myself. I baked, went out walking in the fields and watched a lot of old films on TV. But often I stayed in my room by myself, or Catherine, my sister, says if ever they couldn't find me I'd be sat on the style at the bottom of the garden reading a book. I loved reading and read a lot. Enid Blyton's *Famous Five* served me well to start with but was quickly outgrown, and then I devoured anything Dickens or Bronte or Austen, but always at the top of the list was *Little Women,* which I read at least twice a year for years and years. I've heard it said recently that pretty much all you need to know to understand a woman is which *Little Women* character she identified herself with as a child. I was, of course, Jo.

I also played board games, by myself. I didn't have imaginary friends; I never thought of the doll and the teddy bears as people, they just stood in for people. Typically, I'd position them round the other three sides of the board and play for hours. I'd be playing four games against myself and the toys helped me remember which of my selves' turns it was next. I was quite competitive but always scrupulously fair. After all, I'd only have been cheating myself.

I got pretty good at being by myself and could be very content. I always had a lot of thinking to do, which took a lot of time. I certainly would not have described myself as lonely. I just didn't like that the other kids, other adults and even my parents thought it was odd that I was by myself. I noticed even then how people think there must be something wrong with someone on their own.

It was tough, but I don't think particularly tough. I'm not claiming any particular hardship. Just that it shaped me in a certain way. It seems that for the most part, for most of us, being a kid and trying to work out how to get on in the world, while the adults who control your life are still trying to work out the same thing and fix the mental scars of *their* childhood, sucks. If self-preservation kicks in occasionally and makes a kid a little mean, or even a lot mean, it's not so surprising. And I was no saint. Probably my only real regrets in life are the couple of times I turned from bullied to bullier in a child's fairly typical attempt at seeking acceptance. It didn't work of course. It's hard work being a kid. Everyone has bad stuff to get through growing up and I don't expect the kids who made life difficult for me found it any easier. And maybe it's simplistic and I've never suffered enough to really know but I've always thought, "Do I want to get to eighty and think my life has been rubbish but it's not my fault, it's someone else's fault for what they said to me or did to me when I was five, ten, twenty or thirty?' Or do I want to *do* something to make my life awesome?" I choose *doing*. I choose awesome.

So I found ways of making it work. I would probably only have been about seven or eight when I devised my first bit of Al Philosophy and worked out that whatever else I could and couldn't choose about my life, whatever else was and wasn't making me happy, I could, if I worked hard enough at it, choose to think happy thoughts. I called it "The grass is not always greener."

I'd noticed that people said, "If only I'd done that instead of this, everything would have been so much better." And then someone else would joke, "Yes, the grass is always greener on the other side," and they'd both laugh. But they would still continue to think that the grass would have been greener and torture themselves about the bad choice they'd made and how much better it all could have been. I realised pretty early on that this was fundamentally flawed as a thought process because the only way you can ever know how anything will turn out is to do it. In every other case you are just making up what might have happened. If you choose to think that if you'd done something else then life would now be better, then you will never be happy with where you are now. Since you can't go back and change what you did, there is really no point in making yourself miserable about it. Plus, if you'd done something else, then it's actually just as likely that the result would have been worse not better.

I used "The grass is not always greener" alongside my second strategy "Don't worry, it might never happen," which works almost in reverse. Again it was based on a common phrase I often heard repeated and yet I noticed that people did worry, a lot, about things that might never and often did never happen. In fact the full mantra went, "Don't worry, it might never happen; if it does I can worry about it then and if it doesn't, then I'll have wasted this whole time worrying about nothing when I could have been happy." Again I was very strict with myself and made myself live by the mantra.

Learning to use these two mantras together made me a very positive and optimistic child. Aged thirteen, I think I helped my worret of a younger brother acquire a bit of the skill. In my first ever bit of mental toughness/personal resilience consultancy, I took my eleven-year-old brother to task on his obsessive worrying about things that might never happen. At times he could be a rather anxious child and I noticed he had a tendency to think of the most elaborately disastrous future-focused scenarios. One day, as he did this, I said, "John, don't worry it might never happen." He stopped and looked at me puzzled, and asked, "What do you mean?"

I gave him the mantra in full. We walked on and he kept quiet while he thought about it a bit, because kids are good like that they will think about new things. Then he said, "I've never thought about it like that before, but you're right. I'll try and stop worrying." And he did try and he succeeded quite a lot and worried a lot less, because kids are good like that – they will try something new.

But back to being eleven. I was in the middle of a growth spurt that shot me up 6 inches in under a year and briefly turned me from a well-built and frankly rather hefty kid into a sylph. I grew so fast my bones ached and my joints screamed and I could burn calories for Britain. And I rocked up on day one in my completely regulation school uniform, chosen specially from the recommended regulation uniform shop, so there would be nothing special to draw attention to myself, wanting only what every child of eleven wants – to be the same as everyone else.

This was such an obsession that I lost sleep over (in fact cried myself to sleep over) the fact that my mother had chosen to knit rather than buy my 'capstan blue' PE jumper. It wasn't quite the right blue – it knit up bluer and thicker and I lost the ability to use "Don't worry, it might never happen". I was terrified that I'd be on the playing field and everyone would be pointing and laughing behind their hands because my jumper was different. I couldn't talk to my mother about it as she had done such a nice thing to knit me the jumper and I didn't want to seem ungrateful. Also she never seemed to have been a child because she kept saying things like, "You don't have to be like everyone else" – so because "Don't worry, it might never happen" wasn't working, I tried something else. I lay there thinking that they (the imaginary kids I'd never even met) might be laughing at me, but my jumper was warmer, and on a cold day at least I would be warm when they were cold and then they would stop their (still imaginary) laughter. Now, I know that this ability to turn threat to opportunity is a common mindset in elite athletes and high performers in any field but then it was just a way I made up to get to sleep at night.

Being the same as everyone else was also difficult because I was already over 5′ 8″ tall, quite literally head and shoulders above the rest and still growing fast. And I was rather awkward and shy. Shy is not something you are allowed to be if you are eleven years old and heading towards 6 foot. Small little blonde girls who can't talk to new people are shy and it's cute. Everyone knows that tall people are naturally confident and therefore if they don't talk to you, they are obviously really stuck up.

And with all this new stuff to learn and do, I loved the lessons and I loved the work, and even though I knew it was uncool I couldn't help but throw myself into it all. I did all my homework, was the first to put my hand up in class, revised hard and got good marks in tests (getting full marks in the first-year science test on sexual reproduction was possibly the most awkward). So I was also a swot.

And – and this is the biggest AND – I was the only child in totally regulation school uniform. A fact I was made to realise a dozen times in the first hour and then repeatedly until the damned well-made stuff finally wore out. So many of the other girls had bought their navy skirts and white blouses from Topshop and Dorothy Perkins that I don't know how the school uniform shop stayed in business. Again I kept quiet because I would have felt dreadful asking for new stuff when I had chosen these. I knew my parents didn't have much spare money around and weren't buying any clothes for themselves at the time. Anyway, I knew it shouldn't matter what anyone wore. I just wished it felt like it didn't matter, because apparently you are one of life's losers if you wear an A-line skirt and a stiff-collared shirt. That's something I would like to remind those same girls when I see them now still walking around the same town looking fat and fifty. I would… but I'm not bitter.

Ironically the only thing no one teased me about was my homemade PE jumper. I had been worrying about something that had never happened, so that went into my information bank for next time.

So I was not the same, I was different. I was a sylph-like, stuck up, swotty square. Admit it, even you don't like the eleven-year-old me. I didn't like her very much either. So I got the skinny, regulation sock-clad ankle kicking I deserved for daring to be different and again I took it because I felt it was bad manners to point out that they were being rude. And anyway, it is always best not to create a scene.

But I wasn't the only kid with swotty square tendencies, which made me if not the same as, at least more similar to, some of the other swotty square kids. And it just so happened that they were the nice ones and the interesting ones and despite everything I did make some good friends.

And as for sport, with those legs, if you were a PE teacher which team would you put me on? Yup, they took one look at me and put me on the first year netball team.

Chapter 3: French horn rules

"The funny thing about luck is that it rarely, if ever, happens to the people at the back who can't be bothered"

It's 1982 and I'm eleven. I've arrived at secondary school and been spotted for the first year netball team. I am very excited. I was the tallest, which obviously meant I was goal shooter. And because I was closest to the net, for a while the law of averages meant I got the ball in more often than anyone else. It was fantastic for most of the first term. Until everyone else learnt how to play netball, and they worked out that I couldn't catch a ball or throw a ball or even run anywhere very useful. Apparently these skills are pretty useful for netball as well as rounders.

I remember getting on the bus to go to our first big competition, excited that this was it. I was finally part of a team, finally part of something and it was so important to get it right. But when we got there, even if I caught the ball I missed every shot on goal, was subbed out and finished the competition sat on the bench. On the bus back I was rather quiet, already thinking that it was over. And it was. They never asked me to play again. And that was all quite hard aged eleven.

But I'm over that now.

They didn't have three-legged races or raspberry-picking on sports day so I ran the 1500 metres. Not because I was any good at running 1500m, but because it was the only thing left when everyone else in my form had had their pick. The distance was too long and too painful even for most of the good runners. I knew I couldn't win but I have never been one to sit out and watch, so I signed up and set my own goals – I would not be lapped and I would keep running no matter what. And I remember the feeling of satisfaction in achieving those things and the pleasure of the mental battle to keep going. I learnt to run with my head rather than my unfit, chunky legs (being sylph-like didn't last long once I'd stopped growing upwards).

But I had one moment of unexpected glory in our year group cross-country when I was about fifteen. As usual it was held on the coldest and bleakest of winter days. We all stood shivering in our white Aertex shirts and little navy gym knickers for the route briefing and then we were off. Richmond is built on a hill; therefore, by definition, any Richmond run is a hard-core affair. We set off running and very soon the usual pattern emerged. Disappearing off in front were the girls who could actually run. Disappearing off the back were the girls who couldn't be bothered. And in the middle, well strung out, were a small group of the rest of us who were desperately bothered but couldn't run.

I ran the course leading that middle group, past the waterfalls, the castle and the old ruined abbey, through the woods and alongside the river (as well as being hilly, Richmond is also ridiculously pretty). I ran past the route monitor teachers who were checking we didn't cheat, up icy Lombards Wynd (surely the steepest paved road in the country) in my slippy Green Flash tennis shoes and back through the gate at the top of the school playing field to enter the finishing straight. I ran past the teachers and girls who were sitting out and there was a weird silence followed by a smattering of what I can only describe as confused applause. Then I saw it – the finishing tape *still intact* and held in place by two of the sitters-out. I was confused for a moment and then excited as I ran full pelt down the hill to take the tape and victory for the first time ever – closely followed by more jubilant 'non-runners'. The whole world turned on its head.

Staff and pupils were confused and trying not to doubt me while they offered congratulations, and I basked in my moment for less than a minute. Then the real runners appeared. They ran down the hill to yet more confusion until it was revealed that the leader had taken a wrong turn onto a longer route and they'd all followed. Except me. I'd been too far behind to see them so had kept to the correct, shorter route and taken the rest of the field with me. No one ever really mentioned it again, but I'd like to take this opportunity to point out that I STILL WON!

Maybe that's when I learnt that it's not good enough just to be fast and follow the crowd. You have to be fast and smart. And sometimes if you are smart enough, you will beat fast. And no matter how bad it looks, how far down you are, you should never give up, because sometimes crazy things happen and if you are in there close enough, often enough, you might eventually get lucky. And the funny thing about luck is that it rarely, if ever, happens to the people at the back who can't be bothered.

Fortunately school-life wasn't all about sport. On my first morning, as my mother straightened my regulation school tie in the regulation stiff-collared shirt, before she pointed me in the direction of the bus stop, she said, "Your Dad and I were talking last night. When we were at school we weren't really allowed to do very much and we both want it to be different for you. Whatever you want to do, we'll do all we can to support you. We want you to do everything you want to do." And to this they always absolutely kept their word. I joined everything and did everything and they spent the next seven years driving the seven miles back and forth to Richmond to pick me (and later John and Catherine) up from some after-school club or other.

Halfway through the first term I was given a school French horn and free lessons. And that was it. For the rest of my school career, wherever you might have expected a future Olympian to be doing sport I was doing music. Mainly life was about trying to balance music with homework and revision and even from an early age I was struggling to get eight hours sleep around all of it. I dragged myself out of bed dog-tired every morning and propped my eyes open in afternoon lessons, but I just had to be doing it all. Then, as now, I didn't want to miss a thing.

I got up at 6.30 most mornings to do piano and horn practice before breakfast, then ran out of the house with my horn and all my bags as the bus drew up across the green. The driver got used to looking over his right shoulder to see if I was on my way.

I had brass section rehearsals or clubs most lunchtimes, and after school there was choir, orchestra, swing band and my favourite wind band on Thursdays with Mr Jones. On Friday nights for years and years I had piano lessons with the slightly crazy, doll-like Mrs Johnston in the big house on Frenchgate that used to have stone lions out the front (whose eyes she painted green). After about a year Dad got up every Saturday morning to drive me back to school where I took the bus with the rest of my musical friends to Northallerton for Area Band/Orchestra. Eventually there was also County Band in the holidays. I was also in the school musicals (never more than chorus), the drama club, the debating society… it goes on.

My first brass teacher was Mr Stanley. He started my first lesson by saying, "Are you up for this? You have to be brave to play the French horn. It's not like playing the flute or the clarinet where there will always be several on each part. With the French horn, there's only you. If you don't play your part then it won't happen, and whatever you play it will always be heard, even if you get it wrong." I really wanted to play so I said I was up for it and we got started. I also learnt pretty quickly that unlike the flute and clarinet, there is not a key for every note. There are only three keys and for every combination you can play a dozen notes. You just have to pitch the note in your head, blow with confidence and hope the right one comes out. If you don't go for it 100% you won't get it anyway, so you have to just go for it; but if you make a mistake; it will be loud and everyone will know. Once you realise that a lot of what I learnt about life I learnt from playing the French horn, you will sort of get me.

I kept most of it going all through school. I got stuck with the piano after I failed my Grade 6, but the French horn really seemed to suit me. And although I played second horn to Mark Hall's very superior first until my last year when he left, I did get Grade 8 distinction. It was a surprise at the time because I was just second horn and didn't know I was that good.

The Aldbrough Church choir practice on Friday nights doubled up as the village youth club and we were taught to sing by Sam Herdman, the organist and choirmaster – "Hold an imaginary ping pong ball on a jet of water in your head. Don't let it fall into your chest." At one point Mum, me, John and Catherine all sang in the choir (SATA). Dad didn't come because he was on

The Aldbrough Church choir, where I learnt all I know about singing from our choirmaster Sam Herdman (centre back). I'm fourth in from the left and as you can see being skinny didn't last very long once the growth spurt was over. Next to me are John and Mark Hall (1st horn to my very poor 2nd). Catherine is the tallest of the girls front right (just in front of Sam), and mum is fifth in from the right. I don't know how my brother managed to escape the picture.

call, but he once did a special guest appearance in our village hall production of Joseph as a rather hip Pharaoh/Elvis ("Well I was wandrin' along by the banks of the river when seven fat cows came out of the Nile, wah-ha-ha, bop-shawaddy-wah, bop-bop-shawaddy") to much critical acclaim. I was very proud. Apparently the village called us The Family Von Trapp.

Year book photo

And although the social side of school was always tough, it did get better. I made some new friends including a new best friend called Gail, who amongst other great qualities was nearly as tall as me. Gail also had the unique quality of being able to be friends with me and my swotty, square friends *and* the ankle kicking, smoking-in-the-bus-shelter bullies. She was bright but not swotty, beautiful but not vain, wore the right clothes and was definitely not square. Gail could be friends with anyone and she chose (and still chooses) to be friends with me.

I revised hard for every test and every exam using my Dad's chess clock, so I could time my breaks as well as the work periods and keep to my self-devised schedule. As long as I'd revised properly and covered everything I loved taking exams. I learnt and distilled all the work down to smaller and smaller pages of essential notes and last bits I couldn't remember until, the night before, I was down to a few coloured flash cards. I'd get up in the morning, test myself once more with the cards, then put them away and spend a good hour curling or 1980's french-plaiting my hair and doing the 'not so subtle, but can still just about get away with it for school' 1980's make-up. I didn't really talk to anyone. The feeling of going into the exam both confident and nervous, prepared and totally focused, of knowing I'd done everything I could, of bringing the hundreds of hours of work together into that final session of clear brain thinking and non-stop writing was a buzz.

In sport it's called race head.

It was not all straightforward though. I worked so hard for my O Levels that I had trouble coming back and refocusing for my A levels. That, plus the usual teenage angst over boys and parents, meant I went rapidly downhill in my lower sixth. I didn't know what was happening to me. I didn't seem to be able to talk about it without crying so thought it best not to try and started to really struggle with the work for the first time. I didn't revise properly, in fact hardly at all, and had the terrifying experience of walking into the lower sixth exams totally unprepared. I looked at the papers and they made no sense. My marks were appalling and the reports from my teachers were worse. For the first time I was officially in trouble at school and was called in to see the head of sixth form.

Tim Culkin had been my O Level English teacher, so he knew me pretty well. I sat down in his office and he asked me what was going on. I couldn't say a word because I would have cried. He just waited as I visibly struggled to hold back the tears and all he said was, "You don't have to worry Alison; whatever you choose to do in life you will make it work – you're that type of person."

It stopped me in my tracks because I'd never heard anything like that before. It helped somehow. Over twenty years on and I still remember that line as I summon up the courage to follow some new crazy path. It's made me realise how important what you say to kids is. When I work with school groups now, I try and single out as many individuals as possible to say a few, specific, encouraging words. And several times they or their parents have come back and surprised me by parroting back a comment I can rarely remember and saying how grateful they are and how motivated they felt and what a difference it has made. Each time it strikes me and scares me slightly how easy it is to make a difference and how careful you have to be. Because, of course, words work the other way too and the ones you demotivate and strip of confidence will never come back, and then how will you know what you've done to them twenty years on?

I pulled myself together again eventually – cut down on some of the music and going to the youth club discos with Gail in my yellow and white seersucker jumpsuit or fluorescent pink T-shirt; pink, orange and turquoise checked skirt; leg warmers and chunky plastic jewellery (really, failing my exams was a blessing) and I swore I'd never walk into anything underprepared ever again.

I got up to ten hours a day revision, learnt huge passages of the textbooks by rote even if I didn't understand them, learnt every single chemistry multiple-choice answer for the last eight years (I worked out there were only about eighty questions in rotation) and pulled back the biology and chemistry to A's. In doing so, I proved to myself that you can fake ability with enough hard work. In the end it was too late for physics, as you can't really learn maths by rote, and I got a D. But I'm over that now

So sport wasn't really my thing. But between those years of eleven and eighteen, I kept watching the Olympics. And although I never thought it was anything to do with me, it did show me it must be really good to be really good at something – and I decided I wanted to be really good at, even the best at, something. So I took every opportunity and worked hard and with enthusiasm, because if the Olympics and Olympians had shown me anything it was the passion and hard work it took to get really, really good. You don't have to watch many post-race interviews to work that out.

And what I was really good at was science. It wasn't the coolest thing. I'd much rather have been one of the cool kids on the school sports teams but I was more your lanky, academic, geeky kid who did band camp. But I did love science and, despite a degree of feigned indifference to get me through the day intact with the school bullies, I couldn't really hide it. It got me from the start. I loved the way everything made sense and it made everything around me make sense. It explained things that I hadn't even thought needed

Classic 80's Big Hair in a 6th form photo. My band friends and I were very cool. From left, Sue (flute), Debbie (clarinet), Gail (no instrument but a great perm), Evelyn (oboe), Heather (clarinet), Lizzie (clarinet and ribbons), Me (French horn, perm, Lady Di giant clip in hair bow, Rocky Horror badge and New Romantic trench coat and wing collar).

explaining, like why the sky is blue, sugar dissolves in tea, pipes bust in winter and how my eyes work to enable me to see all these things. Once you know a few scientific principles, you can pretty much work out everything else and don't have to take anyone's word for anything. "Because it just is" never got very far with me.

I loved biology best, particularly evolutionary theory and the way if you think hard enough about it, natural selection and survival of the fittest can explain just about everything. Not just what we look like, but how we think and feel and interact – everything. When I ask myself "Where did that come from?" or "Why did they do that?", I'm often going back hundreds of thousands of years to look for an answer. Up to a point, it was all about zoology and animals. Biochemistry was all irrelevant symbols and boring equations. Then in one biology lesson the teacher drew a big circle on the blackboard and said it was a red blood cell. Then he drew the symbols for a chain of chemical reactions inside it to show how the chemicals inside the blood cell pick up oxygen in our lungs and let it go again in our muscles, then pick up carbon dioxide in our muscles and let it go in our lungs. I looked at the board and for the first time made the connection that these reactions were actually happening now in every red blood cell in my body. Even as I write about it now, I find myself looking down at my arm as I did then and imagining all the cells I can't even see and all the DNA and chemical reactions inside them that are even smaller, and the incredible fact that they all come together and work without me even having to think about it. That is incredible right?

That's when I started to get excited by Small Science. Then Keith Barwell, fresh-faced and enthusiastic straight out of his microbiology degree and teacher training, taught us all things bacterial, viral and fungal, and the conversion was complete. We quite fancied him as well, which helped. Every teacher at least starts their career with the vocation that they can positively influence lives and by the time our adventurous twenty-four-year-old biology teacher had fallen to his death while climbing a French mountain that summer he had at least changed the course of mine. I'd already enrolled at Liverpool University to do a microbiology degree. I'd decided that what I was going to be great at was science. I was going to be an Olympian scientist.

So I went to university to play around with bacteria and loved it all from the start. It was like someone had turned the colour and volume up on my life and I finally found my place.

To find you a card which had a French horn,
We're sorry you also must take all this corn.
But think what <u>we</u>'ve taken for Eighteen Long Years
And how many times we've been driven to tears.

———

"Her bedroom's a tip; you can't shut the door,
But she's lying and reading a book on the floor:
In the bathroom, the clothes and the towels piled high
And everything's covered with bright orange dye.
The drawing room's littered with musical mess
<u>She</u>'s doing her make-up and hair, we would guess:
It's twenty past eight, she is late for the bus,
But Alison's feeding the birds. Why the fuss?"

———

You cost us a fortune – Bovril and hairspray
Wear our clothes, take our car, but what can we say?
We're just glad we have you; it's all been worthwhile
For the love and the interest, the music, that smile.

———

And you've had to put up with your Dad and this Mother
And tolerance show to your sister and brother.
First of our three blessings, and eighteen years shared,
The rest is before you, the way's now prepared.
Have a wonderful life and a great and good time
May your songs be harmonious, <u>your</u> verses all rhyme
Yes, we know this is soppy, but at first we did warn
That a card with a horn on must be full of corn.

———

The ode my mother clipped to the inside of my eighteenth birthday card (she was legendary for finding just the right card). I think it's obviously where I get my literary talents from.

Chapter 4: Liverpool

"One should always have a Plan B"

Like many teenagers, I had outgrown home long before I left. I'd lived in a little village and commuted to a small town all my school life and whilst that set-up had given me the perfect amount of freedom as a child, I now felt restricted. I knew what I wanted. I wanted to go somewhere big and exiting. I applied to places that sounded big and shunned campus universities and places that marketed themselves on their friendly, community, sheltered feel. I didn't want to be protected, I wanted to be roughed up a little and see what else was out there.

Towards the end of sixth form, I got on the train to go to the interviews and open days. I'd always loved London and thought it was probably big enough. I had a good time in Manchester and Birmingham as well and came back from each visit with my eyes wide open and excitement coming off me like radiation. Then I took my first trip to Liverpool.

I got off the train at Lime Street Station and felt different, like something inside had flipped over and settled into a new place. This was Liverpool in 1989, just trying to sort itself and its image out after the Toxteth riots, but it still felt really friendly without smothering me. I had an interview with a really nice lecturer, toured the student union and they took us on a bus to see the sights (the only bits of which I can really remember were visiting the street sign for Penny Lane, painted onto the wall because metal ones were instantly nicked for trophies, and the street where they filmed Bread). The whole day I already felt like the cool independent student I imagined I would be. I walked back through Liverpool to the station, past the grime, the empty falling-down houses, the decaying decadence of another era and still I loved it. I got my first "All right Queen?" from a stranger on the street and by the time I got back on the train, I was never going to go anywhere else.

I spent my first week in the halls of residence bar (I wanted independence but student halls was enough for the first year) or my new neighbour's rooms, thinking "I can do this, I can make friends". The place was big enough and there were enough people that if someone didn't like you they just moved on and left you alone. It wasn't important to also make you feel miserable like it had been at school. I drank pints of beer, went out dancing in nightclubs and guys actually chatted me up. Cool, good-looking guys like the ones who'd been embarrassed to be associated with me at school because they still remembered me as the awkward eleven-year-old. Now however, I was no longer well-built or lanky, and it probably helped that my clothes sense had improved somewhat. Not worried anymore about looking like everyone else, my slightly dressing-up-box-influenced wardrobe, some of which I'd quite heavily embroidered myself, was definitely not square.

During the day, I wandered round the student union Fresher's Fair signing up for all the clubs and societies. The Orchestra, Gilbert and Sullivan Soc, Biochem. & Microbiol. Soc, The Chocolate Soc and even, as the only sport I could be halfway decent at due to years of Dad's coaching, Tennis Soc., to name but a few.

Then, on about day three I wandered past the Liverpool University and Polytechnic Boat Club stall (LUPBC). I'd never even seen any Olympic rowing at this point. My only knowledge of rowing was from watching the Oxford v Cambridge boat race on TV – but it came back to me that while watching one of those races, someone had said to me, "You'd be good at that Alison, you're tall." And I thought that it could be that whole netball thing again, but still I signed up. I paid just about the last of my term's allowance, sat on an ergo (the rowing machine) for the first time, pulled too hard, fell off the seat and landed heavily and embarrassingly on the rail (French horn rules). But that first Saturday morning I went down to the rowing club with about sixty other Freshers and got in a boat for the first time… and that was it. I just loved it. Here, finally, at the age of eighteen was the sport for me.

ROWING – You don't have to throw anything, catch anything or hit anything, and the relief when I realised you tie your feet firmly into the boat and no one was going to make me run anywhere… It was perfect. I finally realised that if I don't have to do any of those things, I'm actually a pretty good athlete. I'd got strong legs from walking and cycling up all those Yorkshire hills, a strong back and good lung capacity. Also, contrary to most people's expectations, you don't need strong arms for rowing, which is a good job because I've never been able to lift my own body weight or do even a single pull-up – and I had finally found a legitimate outlet for that quite vicious competitive instinct that made me want to beat everyone.

On Saturday mornings and Wednesday afternoons we put ourselves out in our rather beaten-up boats and rowed up and down our tiny 600m lake. We rowed one direction looking back at a field of cows and then turned round and had antelope and zebra on the other bank. This was rather a shock on the first day as no one had thought to warn us that the lake was in the middle of a safari park.

I wasn't even intending to go to the circuit training sessions on Tuesday and Thursday evenings because I had the Gilbert & Sullivan Society and everything else to go to. But by the time I'd rowed for the second time on Wednesday afternoon and been out for my first Athletics Union night out in 'The Raz' with all the other rowers, rugby players and hockey players and had the night of my life finally being one of the cool sporty people I'd always dreamed of… I turned up for circuits on Thursday evening and rarely missed a session for the next three years.

After a month or so, the original sixty was down to a hard-core dozen who loved it enough to go out on Friday night and still get up at seven on Saturday morning to get ourselves to the Student Union and into the rusty, rattly boat club minibus for the trip to the nearby Knowsley Estate. Sometimes I think that that was how I made it – by a process of elimination. I was just the one who kept turning up the longest and eventually there was only me left to go to the Olympics.

Rowing rewards persistence. This is a sport where if you can hang on in there long enough, smart might just beat fast. You engage every part your body from the pads of your toes to the tips of your fingers. You need to develop power for the sprint start and endurance to last through the rest of the race and, although every sport will stake its claim to being the most technical, rowing is certainly right up there.

Few people who don't row really get why rowing is so different. Firstly it's a whole body sport. Many sports claim to be full body, but with rowing you really do use and develop every muscle in its full range. You move your legs and arms from full compression to full extension (at opposite times to each other), your back and stomach move like you are doing a sit-up – and you are moving a weight (not just your own body weight) with every stroke. The closest parallel is probably a weightlifting snatch or clean and jerk. Secondly you have to co-ordinate that whole body movement with a piece of machinery that also has several moving parts. Now I'm really struggling to think of a comparison. It's like riding a bike if you also had to move your whole upper body and arms as well as your legs. Then the third factor is that you are moving your whole body AND the machine through water AND air. In swimming you move through water, but there is no machine to co-ordinate and no wind resistance. Also with rowing you are outside, so the water is constantly doing something different and the wind is constantly doing something different and affecting different parts of your boat and body in different ways at the same time.

The thing about rowing is that you have to do something slightly different every single stroke in order for each stroke to be the same. So you are constantly searching for the right way to take each stroke and using the sensitivity in every part of your body to give you information from all the variables as to what that might be. You can't switch off and go on to autopilot for one single stroke because each one is different. And then, finally, of course, you might have up to eight of you all trying to make each of those strokes exactly the same as each other.

SEPARATION is a big word in rowing because you have to be able to isolate different parts of your body to do totally different things at different times in the stroke cycle. CONNECTION is another because you have to connect your legs to the water via your back, arms and blades (technical talk for oars) and catch the sweet spot in the same way a tennis racket, golf club or boot connects with a ball. And BALANCE (as in "BALANCE THE BOAT WILL YOU!") because the boat underneath you may only be as wide as your hips and you have to keep your weight absolutely in the middle or the boat will tip, you'll catch your blades in the water and maybe fall in.

The search for the perfect stroke is relentless, addictive and totally absorbing. The feeling when you get another tiny step closer to perfect connection and the boat shifts underneath you in a whole new way makes your head sing and a fist of excitement expand in your chest. Golfers and footballers get that feeling of connection maybe once every 5 to 10 minutes, tennis players maybe half a dozen times a minute. Rowers get it eighteen to twenty-four times every minute for about an hour and a half in training and thirty to forty times a minute when racing. The levels of concentration needed are unparalleled by anything I've ever experienced. But when you get it, or even a little bit of it, it's incredible. I think maybe it's what other people feel when they think they've found God. And I think, maybe to answer the first question that anyone ever asks a rower, it's what gets us out of bed at those God-unearthly times in the morning.

You have to train so many parts of yourself in so many ways that even club rowers train most days and those with greater aspirations train three or even four times a day. Hours and hours for a few 6 to 8 minute races a year. It's an emotionally intelligent sport that's all about delayed gratification and learning to love the process.

So if ever there was a sport for a girl who had learnt to get herself up early every morning to do her piano practice, turn up every evening for rehearsals, feel a rhythm, take responsibility for her own part and yet be aware of and blend with others, revise for ten hours a day, and peak for and even enjoy exams... rowing was it. It's weird the lessons you learn when you think you are learning something else.

I also loved the circuit training (no throwing, catching, hitting or running here either) and very quickly came to love this sweating a lot, hurting a lot and getting fit thing. I'd been cycling all summer in a reasonably successful attempt to lose weight and arrive at university looking good, so I thought I was already pretty fit – apparently not. The day after that first circuit training session I'd never known such pain... until day two when it was even worse. Quads and glutes were hardest hit from all the squatting exercises and I appeared to have lost all ability to use my legs to lower my body. Surprisingly this meant walking downstairs was harder than walking up. Eventually I worked out it was easier to go down backwards. Lowering myself onto the toilet seat was totally impossible for several days, I just had to sort of position myself and fall. It was a period of bonding with my new club mates to spot each other hobbling round the university. We'd greet each other with tales of 'the bits that hurt most' and I shared my walking downstairs backwards strategy, which I saw caught on pretty quickly.

That first circuit was only thirty seconds per station – press-ups, sit-ups, burpees, star jumps, bench jumps... I paced myself and pushed myself but couldn't get all the way through any of them. Toughest though were squat-thrusts. Inspired by watching Brian Jacks squat-thrusting his way to glory every Friday night on BBC's 'Superstars', I thought I knew what I was doing but it proved harder than he made it look. I managed about eight. This became my marker for the whole circuit. Eight today, ten next week, twelve, fifteen, twenty until eventually I made it all the way through without stopping. Then the intervals went up to forty-five seconds and I started again. Once I could get all the way through forty-five seconds, it became a case of how many could I fit in – one a second, then more and more. By the end of the second term I was a squat-thrusts force to be reckoned with and if any of the guys were feeling feisty, they'd pair up with me to try and take me on… but always lose. Before the year was out, even if I wasn't quite Queen of the rowing (I wasn't even the best in my university) I was Queen of the gym and by my second year I was designing and running the circuit training sessions for everyone.

It wasn't long before I was fitting in extra ego and even running sessions and getting up at six o'clock one morning a week to cycle half an hour to the boathouse for an extra 'outing' (technical talk for going rowing), an Otty's Caf cooked breakfast, quick change in the loos and a last-minute dash to make it in time to sit gently steaming in my nine o'clock lectures.

There was no coach, no staff, no one to look after the boats, no one to organise transport or races – just us. Unlike any other boat club I've ever been part of, we were the rowers and we were the club. In a youth drama group I went to for a while at school, the ultimate insult was to call someone a handbag. Handbags have to be carried or they don't go anywhere. There were no handbags in LUPBC. The second and third year rowers filled all the committee positions and took turns to coach the new blood in the techniques that had been taught to them the year before. First years were expected to do the same the following year and did. I was secretary in my second year, organising kit and race entries, and women's captain in my third year responsible for training, coaching and selection. We had our committee meetings every Monday evening in the pub over a pint and still to this day they remain the most productive and co-operative meetings I have ever been part of.

Occasionally, a guy would turn up who had rowed before at school, who had actually received… coaching. It was like introducing fresh genes into the LUPBC pool of inbred technique. Anyone who had rowed before was considered a God. Shane was a God. When I say, as I usually do when I introduce him, that Shane taught me everything I know about rowing, it's now a little exaggerated but at the time it wasn't far from the truth.

A hefty Irishman, Shane coxed us in our first novice Eights race on a canal in Manchester after only a few weeks. Through my entire career racing always scared me sick. Mostly the fear was of not being able to do well enough, but in those first few races I was just scared I wouldn't be able to finish. I'd never raced before, not properly like this. I'd always paced myself in individual activities like cycling or running but had never put myself through serious pain, and even though I rarely stopped I needed to know I could if I really had to. Here I was going to be in a crew with seven other rowers and would have to row at the same speed as everyone else. What was going to happen in the race if it hurt too much and I couldn't go on? I'd let everyone down, that's what. I had no previous experience of anything like this from which to plan strategies or draw confidence and I was terrified. I was so terrified of not being able to finish that I was in danger of not even being able to start. But I really loved rowing and if I couldn't do this race today then I couldn't row any more, so I had to find a way. So I hatched a Plan B.

One should always have a Plan B.

I decided that if it happened and at some point in the race I just really couldn't keep going and I had to stop, I'd pretend I'd got cramp in my leg. I'd still be letting people down but no one could help it if they got cramp, so people couldn't get too cross with me. It wasn't a good plan but it was the only one I could think of. Holding tightly to Plan B relieved the fear enough for me to be able to get into the boat with the other girls, and with Shane nicely weighing down the stern, we set off paddling rather spider-like up to the start of our first winter head race.

The rules for a winter head race are as follows:

1. All boats of the same class row up to the start at the same time, queue up in order and then race down one at a time about 10 seconds apart. Your position in the race is determined by the time you take to complete the course, not by how many boats you overtake.
2. It must always be raining (unless it is snowing).
3. It must always be freezing.
4. Your warm-up row to the top of the course must be so impeded by all the other crews that by the time you reach the start, you must be much colder than before you started warming up.
5. All crews must arrive at the top of the course at least thirty minutes before the start of the race and sit absolutely still to ensure the regulation reduction of core body temperature.
6. All rowers must be desperate for the toilet before you are allowed to start. Boys may stand up in the boat and piss over the side. Girls must hold it in.
7. Ten minutes before the start of the race, a horn will sound and all rowers must remove all clothing except for shorts and singlet top. Spare kit must be soaking wet, weigh the equivalent of an extra crew member and be

stored in the bottom of the boat to provide appropriate ballast. When all the above conditions have been satisfied, the race may start.

8. For the first half of the race you must be so cold that you think you will die, then, within 3 strokes, you must become so hot that you think you will die.
9. All but one of the plasters coving the existing blisters on your hands must fall off during the race. If you chose to keep the remaining plaster on, it must ruck up so as to cause another blister.
10. You must always have some part of your hand in contact with the oar handle. Even after you've gone home.
11. The cox must shout continually all the way down the course.
12. The crew must totally ignore the cox.
13. The cox must take the widest route round all corners. If rowing with a stream or current the cox should avoid the fastest flowing part of the river.
14. Coming into the home straight, the cox must shout "last ten" at least five times.
15. Once the finish line has been crossed, everyone must collapse over their oar handles, gasp loudly and groan a lot to show how hard they have worked.
16. Everyone should continue to ignore the cox even if they get quite frantic.
17. Your boat must drift onto another crew or, if another crew is not available, onto the centre arch of a bridge.
18. Within one minute of finishing the race, everyone must say that that was amazing and they want to go up and do it again straightaway.

As you can see, there are a surprising number of regulations. But rowing is a very fair sport and cheating is rare; the rules are almost universally adhered to. We followed the above regulations and started to race. We were pretty damned good for novices and rowed really well. Sometimes we even had all eight blades in the water at the same time. I didn't even think about stopping; I didn't even think about Plan B let alone wonder if it was time to use it. I rowed hard and it hurt, but I finished my first race and gasped that it was amazing and I wanted to go and do it again. So I did, many times.

Despite, in fact possibly because of, being introduced to exercise, I put on a lot of weight that first term. This is not atypical of first year students or first time exercisers. Like many first time exercisers I was not fit enough to really do very much in the way of burning calories, but still thought I now had to do a lot of 'refuelling'. I lived in Roscoe and Gladstone halls of residence in my first year and mainly I lived on cooked breakfasts, scotch eggs, pork pies and huge Bakewell tart slices from the university bakery for lunch, and the cheese and ham sandwiches, crisps and club biscuits I got in my packed tea (because I missed dinner almost every night of the week due to training). This diet was supplemented most nights by a pint or two of bitter in the hall bar.

The only mirror in my bedroom was a tiny make-up mirror above the sink, so I didn't ever really see myself properly and there were no scales. I thought it was strange that I stopped being able to get into most of the clothes I'd brought with me, but if I thought about it at all (which wasn't often) I thought it was due to all the unaccustomed training I was doing and that I must be changing shape and getting more muscles. I thought this was a good thing. My best friend Jo and I went to a student production of *The Rocky Horror Show* and I won first prize for the audience fancy dress (years of training) wearing a micro-mini, a quite see-through black lace and velvet bodice that was really underwear, fishnet tights, above-the-knee black suede boots, my unbuttoned lab coat, red backcombed hair and fabulous painted-on make-up. We went there on the bus and I got up on stage to receive my prize and thought I looked great.

I went home for Christmas and got on the scales and saw I was nearly a stone and a half heavier than when I was last on them. That was a bit of a shock. I knew muscle weighed more than fat but that seemed like quite a lot. I stood in front of the full-length mirror in my underwear and tried in vain to get into the clothes I'd worn a few months ago and had left behind, and something began to dawn on me. I got my photos back from Boots and there was one of Jo and me posing in our *Rocky Horror* gear, and then it hit me. I'd got fat.

For the first time in my life, my female brain began to uncouple the words *thin* and *happy* and *fat* and *unhappy* that I had somehow, somewhere, picked up always went together. I was happier and more self-confident than I had ever been in my life and the guys still chatted me up in the bars and nightclubs, but I was definitely fat. I decided I'd better do something about it. I didn't really diet but just stopped being quite such a pig. I stopped supplementing my packed tea with chips and Chinese takeaway on the way home (I might have forgotten to mention those) and crucially, if I went to the bar, I drank squash and saved the alcohol up for one big blast on Wednesday nights. I was also starting to train properly and that helped too. Anyway, the

LUPBC after a winning day at Runcorn Head. Shane (who taught me all I know about rowing) is second in from the left (in the incongruent jumper). Jo, three in from Shane (looking down and laughing). I'm two more along from that. Everyone else can spot themselves. I promise I remember all but two or three of your names.

Women's Head of the River Race, 1992

Number up from Bow (right-hand side of the picture). Bow: Kerry, 2: Moyna, 3: Cath, 4: George, 5: Big Al, 6: Jo, 7: Siobhan, Stroke: Aisling, Cox: I really don't remember who this guy is (sorry!).

extra weight seemed to slip off without any drama and the extra money I saved from my new regime went to buy a very fitted cute lilac dress for the summer ball that even the photos said I looked pretty good in. I ripped up the *Rocky Horror* photo, which is a shame now because I'd have put it in here.

Fat or thin, I was having an unstoppably good time. This was the only time in my fifteen-year career where rowing created, rather than destroyed, my social life. Wednesday nights became a glorious, unmissable, alcohol-fuelled ritual; much enhanced by the presence of Jo – a real live Jo this time, rather than a fictional character from *Little Women*.

I first met Jo in the hall bar in that first crazy week and we quickly established that we were both doing Microbiology. Jo's microbiological conversion had been as rapid as my own and was apparently catalysed by examining the various moulds growing in her mother's fridge (Jo's mum is never too keen on her repeating that fact). I was pretty impressed by Jo on that first meeting; she made my first faltering attempts at cool independence seem rather pathetic by comparison.

Jo was like me, only more so. Taller (by half an inch – she had actually made 6 foot), more intelligent (she'd been put ahead a year at school), more well-travelled (she'd caught up the extra year by taking a year out travelling and had spent the last few months working on a Kibbutz in Israel – I didn't even know what one was), more glamorous (all tanned and long, slightly wild hair with a few braids and beads from her travels), more confident (when she wasn't talking to me she was holding the attention of several rugby club guys) and well… more drunk. I mentioned I'd just joined the boat club and Jo said she'd been thinking of joining. I said: "Oh, you should, apparently being tall is an advantage." She said she would and wandered off to rejoin the rugby guys. I was rather in awe.

Jo did join the boat club but didn't show up that first Saturday or the following Wednesday, having slipped on a wet disco floor that night and sprained her wrist. She turned up the second week, got in a boat for her first time and loved it as much as I did – although she was obviously more talented. The friendship wasn't immediate, we just happened to be living in the same place and doing all the same things – so we did them together. It took a while and, as it often does, the beer helped. The Wednesday night-pub, Trader Jacks, Raz-boat club ritual was well established long before we got there, but we definitely played our part in maintaining the tradition.

We drank… quite a ridiculous amount really. Pints of bitter to start with, then Jo and I would order quadruple vodka lime and lemonades, two at a time each… several times. Or sometimes we'd set ourselves to a ten pint a night challenge to see if we were up to it yet (determined not to be left behind the guys any more than in the squat-thrust competition). Eventually we made it. It's not something one is really supposed to admit, but I just loved going out and getting drunk. I loved the freedom and feeling of it. Is this the Olympic medal rowing story you were expecting? But it was usually just this one night of the week. And Jo and I would drink as much as possible in the pubs until the point at which we walked into The Raz nightclub and then we'd stop drinking. Because dancing was more important and we'd feel sick if we drank any more. It was a ritualistic night and we followed our own rules.

At 1.22 exactly every week, the selection of 1980's and early 1990's music (must include *The Only Way is Up* by Yazoo; *The Whole of the Moon* by The Water Boys; *Love Cats* by The Cure; *Tainted Love* by Soft Cell and *Come on Eileen* by Dexy's Midnight Runners) would stop and the DJ would play the whole of Don McLean's *American Pie*. This was the signal for all the rowers to break up any other bonds they'd formed during the night and all join together in one big swirling, staggering, dancing circle. I'd never felt more part of anything or connected to anybody than at the end of those nights.

And while all of it was wonderful and exactly the kind of life I'd hoped to find, it was the unexpected 'what happened next' that really made those nights so special.

Alcohol and walking are both well known for loosening tongues and as Jo and I staggered the three miles home after our nights out (choosing to walk at first because we were too tight to pay for a taxi and then because I don't think you could have paid us to get home any other way), laughing and reminiscing about the night gradually turned to just general reminiscing. I'd never really talked before – not like this. I'd chatted, made conversation, repeated stuff I'd heard elsewhere, espoused opinions and cracked jokes, but this was different. Very gradually we started to talk about stuff that most kids probably talk about when they are still at school, but neither of us ever had. Difficulties with making friends, boys you'd fancied that weren't interested, parent trouble… general teenage stuff. I'd never been able to share any of this before because I'd been so embarrassed about my inadequacies, but it seemed Jo had been at least as incompetent as me so that made it easier. It was like that point when you're reading a book and the writer expresses a thought or a feeling you'd thought was unique to you, and with a jolt you realise that if one other person has thought or felt it, then hundreds even thousands of people must think or feel it every day. People like to say that everyone is different and everyone is special. I'm not so sure. It seems to me that we are all essentially very similar and really very ordinary. There is no thought or feeling that hasn't been thought or felt a million times before (this in itself is not a unique thought) and when we understand that we get a better perspective and stop taking ourselves so seriously and thinking that life is insoluble.

After a few weeks, we both got to a point where there was nothing we wouldn't share. I didn't have to hide anything anymore. I'd never had a friendship or any relationship like it. Our conversations were an amazing thing that I looked forward to every bit as much as the drinking and dancing, but could only ever happen AFTER the drinking and dancing. Sharing stories with Jo and all the craziness that was Liverpool student life was part of starting to take myself a little less seriously. Life just became more fun. I was a very adult child and now I'm a rather childish adult.

Jo and I would walk the last mile down the grand, wide, obviously once beautiful but now crumbling, burnt-out and neglected Toxteth main street, still talking but feeling a little extra nervous energy because this place was supposed to be dangerous. But mostly it was just eerily deserted at three o'clock in the morning. I'm not sure if it was our naivety, intensity of conversation, stature or luck that kept us safe, but I never had any trouble in Liverpool. We'd talk our way right to the door but not hug goodbye. We weren't the type to do hugging.

After a while, one or other or both of us would have boyfriends to go back home with and the three-mile walks became rare. If I was the single one at the end of the night I'd still walk the same route home by myself and be a little more scared, but still enjoy the tranquil and sobering end to the evening (these are the stories you don't tell your mother until twenty years after the event). I'm left with the legacy that I'll walk pretty much anywhere by myself as long as, on careful evaluation, I reckon it's safer than circa 1990's Toxteth. Not much gets ruled out.

But, no matter how late I stayed out and how many vodkas had been involved, I never missed a lecture or lab from our pretty solid 9-5, five-days-a-week schedule in the whole three years. I never missed training either if I could help it, but work came before rowing – and when, in our second year, they scheduled microbiology labs on a Wednesday afternoon, Jo and I had to miss rowing. Instead we poured agar plates and gels and grew broth cultures and streaked out to single colonies and practised our aseptic technique and grew fantastically coloured bacteria in Petri dishes, some of which were even supposed to be there.

We were incredibly diligent, conscientious, thorough and rubbish. We'd follow all the steps and always be the last to leave, frantically trying to finish up before they threw us out. And that wouldn't really have mattered except that while other people seemed to produce the cultures and chemicals they were supposed to, our experiments never worked. We mixed up cultures, dropped glass rods through the bottom of test tubes, and after weeks of careful isolation, threw the sample into the waste and carefully presented the last wash for inspection. Both of us went on to do lab-based PhDs. What were we thinking?

But although I was rubbish at labs, I generally did pretty well at the academic stuff. The microbiology units were only about a quarter of the first two years, so I could choose whatever else I wanted. Mostly I chose the very responsible options of genetics, biochemistry, organic and physical chemistry, and molecular biology that I thought would be most useful to my future career (although I didn't really know what that would be) – but I got to pick some 'fun' ones as well. Palaeontology and parasitology were my idea of a good time and it felt pretty good that I didn't have to be embarrassed about saying that.

I'd come to a place where everyone was a top-set swot. Learning and being good at stuff was not to be mocked but envied. At one point in a very difficult physical chemistry course, I was starting to lose the plot and put my hand up in a lecture to ask a question. On the way out, a fellow student commented: "How did you follow that enough to even ask a question? I was completely lost." Over two years later in the pub after we got our finals results, another guy said: "I'm not surprised you did alright, you were the girl that asked that question in chemistry. No one else had a clue what was going on." Both of them were having fun but neither was mocking me. It was the stuff of legends for all the right reasons. This was an environment where asking an intelligent question was taken in the spirit of interest and inquiry in which it was meant and not just assumed to be showing off. On a night out in my first week, one of the guys who was chatting me up told me he was here to get a First. I was too, so I said so. It wasn't bragging, it was goal setting, and here it was OK to set your goals high and say so. I was in heaven.

Chapter 5: Addiction

"Nothing will change, nothing will ever change"

I remember vividly, early in the first term at Liverpool, walking on my own down Hope Street past The Everyman to catch a bus back to halls. It was raining. It rained every day of my first term but I was walking down the street smiling and I realised I was happy, completely uninhibitedly, unselfconsciously, not caring what anyone else thought about me, happy. And I didn't think I'd ever felt like that before.

I was still not very good at the boyfriend thing and got myself dumped a couple of times. Although painful, it was only to be expected as this was pretty much the first time I'd tried it. Anyway, at that age there is still something rather glamorous and romantic about that particular type of pain. There were three tall blond first year guys in the boat club and towards the end of that first year I'd already got myself entangled with and been rejected by two of them. I'd never really noticed the third.

Then one particularly memorable Wednesday night I got carried away drinking and talking in Trader Jacks and left later than usual with two of the other boat club guys. The three of us found ourselves locked out of The Raz. It was full. There was no way we could miss a Wednesday night in The Raz, so we made our way round the back of the club down a small passage behind the roof terrace. We braced our backs against the passage wall and our feet against The Raz wall and wriggled our way up, much like climbers get up rock chimneys. Once within reach of our mates they pulled us over.

Exhilarated, I sat on the waist high wall with my back to the two-storey drop, kicking my feet and happily surveying my home turf. Most people went in to dance but I just stayed there. Then the third tall blond boy came over, stood himself between my knees with his hands on my legs and asked me how I was doing. With a shock I realised he was chatting me up. This was totally unexpected as we'd hardly even spoken before. I'd never really noticed him, but I noticed him now and I noticed he was rather nice. Bright-eyed and still exuberant, I related the tale of my adventure. As we chatted, I got the same feeling I'd had when I first arrived in Liverpool. Something inside flipped over and settled into a new place and I thought I would never want to go anywhere else.

After that first night it still took us ages to get together properly. Then we were together for about four years, then again a few years later, and then again a few years after that. And although I could never bear to think of being without him, it was always difficult and I couldn't ever see how it would work out and eventually, finally, it didn't. But for a while we created a lot of memories and it was all part of the general, wonderful craziness that was Liverpool.

I rowed hard, played hard and worked just hard enough for two years. But I wasn't joking when I said I intended to get a First-class honours degree, so the third year was a different matter. At the start of the year we had a lecture letting us know exactly what we had to do to get each grade that summer. Fortunately for me the practical exam was worth just a small percentage. They told us that if you wanted a First, you had to have learnt everything covered in the lectures *plus* the content of the five or six journal references given at the end of each lecture. I got down to work.

One night, early in that third year, I got out of bed to answer the phone in the hall of the big Toxteth house I shared with nine friends. It was Mum. The police had just knocked on the door, got them both out of bed, breathalysed Dad and charged him with drink-driving and a hit-and-run.

Mum went on to explain that they'd had a couple of friends over from the village (Mum and Dad were now living in Richmond) for the evening and no one had drunk more than a sherry. She'd driven the friends home in her car (about a 45-minute round trip) and when she arrived back home, Dad was already asleep in bed. She'd joined him. Less than an hour later the police had rung the door bell, got Dad up and breathalysed him. Dad had failed the breath test but she didn't understand how because she'd seen that he'd only had a small sherry all evening. Could I look through my textbooks and find out if there was any way that that could happen? I thought I'd heard somewhere that maybe there was some yeast infection thing that could turn sugar into alcohol in the stomach and said I'd look into it.

What Dad added to the story was that after Mum had gone out, he'd taken his car out of the drive to turn it round before putting it into the garage for the night. While he was turning the car round, he thought he might as well drive the half-mile into town and turn round at the roundabout. It was dark. He certainly didn't remember hitting anyone with the car.

What the police added was that while Dr Mowbray was driving back through town, his car had mounted the pavement, hit a girl, knocked her over and driven away without stopping. A passer-by had taken the registration, which was how they'd come round so quickly. The girl was not seriously hurt. She was a girl I knew from the year below me in school and her brother had been in my year. Her parents were doctors in a neighbouring practice.

What no one was adding, but what had certainly happened, was that as soon as Mum had gone out (and probably during the rest of the evening as well), Dad had gone to his secret gin supply and drunk liberally – before taking the car out, maybe to turn it round, but probably also to drive it into town to restock at the off-licence while no one was around. I never found out whether he really was too drunk to know that he had knocked someone over or just too terrified to stop and covered it with a lie he probably eventually believed himself. He lied all the time. He believed his own lies.

It's what alcoholics do.

The statistics on the high incidence of alcoholism in the medical profession are a fair warning, but I'm not sure Dad would ever have seen himself in them. I'm not sure we did either. Growing up we thought we were a special case, different, had unique challenges to get through as a family. What I realise now, and what might have helped us if we'd realised it then, was that we were just a very ordinary family of an alcoholic. We didn't realise it because typically the medical profession has a particularly strong culture of denial in this area. They present late for treatment and usually only under considerable pressure from their families.

There is nothing unique about what I'm about to write. I write it not because it is extraordinary, but because it is very ordinary and I think it would help if more people realised that. It's hard to write and I don't write to hurt or blame, it's just how it was. I am an ordinary child of an alcoholic parent but that is different from an ordinary child of a non-alcoholic parent, so maybe it helps to explain some of who I am and what is to come. It took me a long time to look into it, but it didn't take me very long once I started to discover that the textbooks say we were a textbook case.

Throughout my superficially idyllic early childhood, Dad would have been in the classic early stages of alcoholism. Here the tendency towards alcohol addiction is masked by social activity; people in this stage drink to enhance their mood, particularly at social occasions and gradually find more and more occasions or reasons where the mood-changing properties of alcohol are desirable. Winding down after work is a classic and an easier excuse for doctors to make to themselves than most. At this stage no one really notices. I didn't notice, but it doesn't mean it wasn't there. Dad was already an alcoholic and we were already being brought up in an alcoholic household. It was already different.

Even the adult child state is classic in children of alcoholic parents. My father was almost certainly a textbook adult child as a result of his own incomplete upbringing (he didn't talk much about it but I'm guessing from what I observed and a few dropped comments very late on in life). Adult children are so-called because although they grow up physically, they are often emotionally and psychologically stuck. Raised by people who never grew up themselves, they have no normal example to follow, no way to learn how healthy families relate to each other and therefore never learn normal ways of thinking, feeling and reacting. As long as things are going smoothly they're fine, but in situations of conflict, controversy or crises, they respond with less-than-adult-like reactions. They have to guess at what normal is, often lie when it would be just as easy to tell the truth, judge themselves without mercy, take themselves very seriously, overreact to situations in which they have no control, have difficulty with intimate relationships, constantly seek approval and affirmation, feel that they are different from other people and are either super responsible or super irresponsible. When I first read this description, I not only instantly recognised my dad, but a list of character deficits I've consciously been fighting against all my life – and have, through awareness that I don't want to be like my dad, often tried to take the opposite position. You might already recognise a few.

One definition of addiction that I came across states that: "Alcoholism and addiction represent a misdirected attempt to achieve wholeness, to experience inner completeness and satisfaction." This might also have been written as a description of my father.

Dad was totally absorbed with creating the perfect life. As many people do, he took the hurt and disturbing incidences of his childhood and inadequate parenting and buried them deep, never talked about them, never brought them out to deal with, just buried them and built a new life on top. The new life was to be the picture-perfect family created from the images he carried with him of what his own childhood should have been. So, straight out of university, he found himself a good respectable job, a good respectable wife, a huge grand house and started having children – all by the age of twenty-four. He never gave himself the chance to experience anything that might have helped him grow up emotionally and psychologically and learn what normal was before he started raising children of his own. He was always baby-faced and in the photos we have of him and me as a baby, he looks little more than a child himself.

Dad always had to be right and know everything. Playing Trivial Pursuit was a nightmare because he had to tell you he knew every answer even if it was your go – "I know this one, I know this one!"; "I knew that!"; "I could have told you that!" And both our parents had to be perfect parents, so we were never allowed to show we were hurt or upset by anything they did. I learnt very early on to be enthusiastically grateful for everything that was given to me, even if it was something I didn't want or I had hoped for something else instead – because otherwise my parents would be hurt and I would be an ungrateful wretch. I learnt very young to hide my feelings and not talk about stuff that hurt or upset me, so as not to disappoint my parents. Any appreciation of anything or anyone else was also taken as a personal slight, that what they did and what they were was not as good – not perfect.

All that responsibility and expectation of perfection built on such shaky foundations.

As the first child, I was that adored object upon which parents project the image of the child they've been designing and carrying round in their heads since their own childhood. I think my father's desire to create his fantasy family and his ability to deceive himself was so strong that he was able to hold onto this image much longer than most.

At one point, my brother and I overheard him bragging to some of his friends about the superiority of his kids. "Oh, Alison and John hate that sort of music, they never listen to pop, they listen to…. (and here he quoted a couple of Sixties bands and musicians that I'm guessing were favourites of his). When *Top of the Pops* comes on TV, they watch it with the volume turned right down because they can't bear to listen to it." None of this was even vaguely true. His real children loved pop music and we'd never even heard of the groups his fantasy children were supposed to idolise. I was a big Adam Ant, Kate Bush and Queen fan (again it was probably all about the dressing up). I used to buy *Smash Hits* magazine and devour it in my usual quest for knowledge. In one of my rare cool moments, I actually won a Youth Club pop quiz in which I was the only person to know the name of Simon le Bon's boat. It's fair to say we both still idolised our dad who had been exuberant, entertaining and loving throughout our childhoods. He was the fantasy father he no doubt thought he should be to his fantasy family. But if he created this family he also controlled it. It was the greatest honour to please and the greatest disgrace to disappoint him. His real children always watched *Top of the Pops* and always on full volume and it was a revelation to us that our father would value kids who didn't like pop music. That week John and I sat down to watch *Top of the Pops* and, even though he wasn't there, as the music started, we both said with one voice "This is rubbish" and got up to turn the volume down.

The real me also loves wild birds. I was transfixed from the age of about three by the owls in the nearby Twycross Zoo, and then by all the garden and wild birds I could see around me. I'm no twitcher but I was a member of Y.O.C. – the Young Ornithologists Club (junior branch of the RSPB) – and of course being me had a fine collection of bird identification, picture and information books from an early age. The real story my mother told and still tells with pride is of the Christmas morning when we woke up to snow and I ran past Santa's delivery and all my unopened presents to put on my wellies and go out to the bird table to feed the cold, hungry, fluffed-up garden birds lined up on the yard wall waiting for their breakfast.

The fantasy story I heard Dad tell his friends with pride was of how I was such an expert on and had such an interest in birds, that when we went on holiday I didn't pack any clothes because I filled my case full of bird books. This was untrue; I only ever took my Hamlyn guide, but I was a little ashamed that I was therefore letting Dad down. So, when we were packing for our next Greek island holiday, I dutifully left aside most clothes and filled the rest of my case with my bird books (over a dozen I think and most of them large hardbacks). I closed the case and waited for Dad to collect it. He picked it up, exclaimed at the weight and put it back on the bed. I remember anticipating the pleasure it would give him to open the case and how pleased and proud he would be of me, but when he did he exclaimed again, threw the books out, told me off for being stupid and to pack properly – apparently with no recollection of the story he'd told his friends. I was stunned and didn't defend myself or argue (because you didn't argue in our house).

There are many such stories. All just little things. But there were a lot of little things and I was just little.

Oh and Simon Le Bon's boat was called Drum.

White, middle-class children aren't really allowed to have a tough time growing up. I can almost hear the cries of "Poor little rich girl" and it makes me cringe to think they might be right. It will certainly be the pattern of many people's childhood experiences. Alcoholism is not uncommon and often goes unrecognised in the early stages, and of course there are many other addictions that have the same symptoms and patterns and are built on similarly shaky foundations.

As I grew up I gave Dad some pretty good real material to boast to his friends about and sometimes it was even difficult for him to find room to exaggerate. But the pressures of building and keeping up the fantasy, of always having to be right and keeping all that stuff buried must have been increasingly hard, and by the time I was 12 he'd moved into the classic middle stages of alcoholism.

These are characterised by a more intense desire to drink. Alcoholics in these stages will drink more than they used to and probably start earlier in the day. There will start to be a loss of control. Other people will start to notice, but any comments will probably be dismissed due to denial. The alcoholic may make empty promises about cutting down (usually in an attempt to pacify), but attempts will be short-lived. Classically they don't see the problem as being with themselves and therefore justify their behaviour as being due to all the things that are 'wrong' with their lives. Dad was pretty textbook, but we thought it was just our dad.

The first I really knew of it was after my parents came back from a dinner party in the village. I was woken by the sound of my parents arguing and shouting at each other in their bedroom. This was a very odd thing that didn't happen in our house. The six-year-old Catherine also woke up and came into my room, and in a one-off unaccustomed sisterly act (I really was a dreadful big sister), I let her into my bed and we listened to the shouting together. John slept through; he could sleep through anything. I gathered from what I could hear that Dad had got too drunk and Mum was not pleased. Dad was defiant and defensive. I was with Dad on this one. So what if he'd had a few drinks and got a bit drunk – he worked hard, he was unwinding. People got drunk sometimes, big deal. Mum was a nag.

I was still with Dad the second and maybe the third time I was woken. But then it became increasingly regular and it wasn't just dinner parties. It was some, then most of his off-call evenings at home, whenever they had friends to stay for the weekend, their college reunion, any and all of our parties and celebrations, whenever we all went out for dinner and he wasn't driving, eventually pretty much whenever he wasn't working or on call. That summer holiday in Greece it was really evident and I remember the friends we'd gone away with (their friends) laughing at him, not with him. He was still my dad enough for me to be uncomfortable and embarrassed for him, although he wasn't for himself. He always thought he'd been very entertaining, everyone had had a great time and we were all picking on him. That Christmas and every subsequent Christmas when he was off call, it was unbearable. So it didn't take long before I was with Mum and since she never told anyone else about what was going on, I was her ear, her advisor, her councillor and pretty much her sole support from the age of twelve. It made me feel pretty special for a while. For a while.

John slept through all of it, but I lay awake. Little Catherine took to creeping out of bed when she was woken by shouting downstairs and sitting on the top of the stairs to listen. She says one night Mum came up unexpectedly and found her there. "It's all right Catherine, nothing will change, nothing will ever change," Mum said, supposedly to reassure. Cath laughs grimly now: "That was the problem wasn't it, nothing would ever change and somehow that was supposed to be a good thing."

Dad wasn't a violent or abusive drunk because it wasn't in his nature to be a violent or abusive man. I guess we should call that a blessing, but the downside was that there was never anything critical enough to force it to stop. He wanted everyone to like him and he wanted to be loved, so he became a soft, soppy, overly-emotional and desperate-to-entertain sort of a drunk. He slurred his words; made inappropriate jokes and comments; was overly familiar and tactile with other men's wives; couldn't follow or contribute to a conversation (blurting inappropriate and often childishly smutty comments) and fell down stairs in restaurants. When he was like that it made me feel physically sick. I found it unbearable but whenever there were other people around we all just had to bear it, because the only thing to do was not to draw any more attention to it and try and get him away/home as soon as possible. Not that he ever wanted to go, of course. He was having a great time.

Pretty soon it dominated everything. Even when he was sober, every thought and every aside conversation between the rest of us was about whether he was getting too excited, had had enough sleep, would last the day/evening. Any sort of event or occasion involving other people was a banker and therefore something to be dreaded – but also carefully planned, because if we could just get him to sleep enough during the day, eat enough that evening, stay calm and preferably drive, then we would hold out some hope. Catherine and I decided pretty early on that we could never get married. Getting him through a wedding day would be an absolute farce. Of course all children become embarrassed by their parents at some point so I'm trying to keep this in perspective, but no one really gets it. They say, "But he didn't hit you or abuse you. He just got a bit drunk. My dad gets a bit drunk sometimes." It's not that it's any one particular incident or that any of it was violently awful. It's just that it became pretty much all I knew of my dad from the age of twelve until he died nearly twenty years later. It grinds you down and it was hard to hold on to very much else of him after all that time.

And through all of this we rarely used the word alcoholic or ever really thought it, which seems odd now. To start with, the drinking was overt, blatant and even defiant – but then under increasing pressure from all of us he made his show attempts to cut down and we rarely saw him drink anything except ginger and alcohol-free beer, ostentatiously poured from the bottle or drunk from a glass with the bottle beside it. But mysteriously he kept appearing to be drunk. He would be outraged by any suggestion that he'd been drinking. He was just very tired; he'd been working hard. He'd always been susceptible to migraines, so for a long while it was passed off as him having migraine-like symptoms caused by stress and maybe triggered by the one beer we'd see him have. My throwaway comment about the yeast infection was seized on as another possible rational explanation that was also never tested for. No one was looking to eliminate possible rational explanations, no matter how bizarre they might be.

My parents had a choice. They faced what was really happening and dealt with it or they denied it and hid it as best they could. They went for the later and started to shut down their lives. They stopped inviting friends to stay for the weekend and eventually even for dinner. I'm not certain but I think the friends stopped visiting anyway as Dad's behaviour became more regular and more extreme. The parties and dinner parties became a thing of the past. Eventually, under continued and sustained pressure from us all, he advertised for a partner and stopped running the two-man practice essentially single-handedly. We thought this would help as it would reduce the stress and workload he said his migraine-like symptoms were due to. It didn't help, in fact (as he probably anticipated, which was why he held out so long) it got worse as the only thing that kept him from drinking was the responsibility of working and being on call and now that was less of the time.

Eventually, my parents moved out of the village into Richmond. They said it was to get away from the practice and reduce stress, but I wonder now if it wasn't to stop neighbours and even patients from dropping by unannounced. When we invited friends round, we would usually warn them that Dad wasn't very well and could sometimes act oddly. Dad 'not being very well', or 'tired' became the code we all used to describe what we couldn't quite explain. When I phoned home from Liverpool, sometimes Dad would come on the phone and be slurry, but often Mum would say she wasn't going to put Dad on as "he's not very well tonight, he's had a hard day."

He was always twitchy and found it difficult to relax and sit still, so we found it annoying but not unusual that while watching television in the evenings, Dad would be up and out of the room every five to ten minutes. Sometimes he'd come back with odd things from odd corners of the house. He'd get more and more "unwell" as the evening progressed. I would have been about fourteen the first time I followed him out of the room. I walked in on him in his study drinking from a plastic tonic bottle hidden behind the curtains. I didn't really know what I was looking at, but his extreme and obvious guilt made it plain that this was not just tonic. After that I could find him drinking gin pretty much whenever I could be bothered to follow him. I might find him down in the cellar or with his head in a cupboard or wardrobe. Every time was followed by a big row, accusations, denials, overwhelming self-pity, disgusting slurry snotty blubbing into his hanky, excuses, justifications, lists of all the things that were wrong with his life, threats from both sides, exploration of avenues for treatment, offers of help, possible resolutions (AA, therapy, rehab etc.), promises to be different… and every time would culminate in huge, long, deep into the night Dad-focused sessions that were completely useless because even if he hadn't been an alcoholic and lying through his teeth, he was still drunk and therefore could barely remember anything that had been said, resolved or committed to in the morning.

He'd get up looking dreadful; tiny eyes in a fat, swollen, puffy face. Hung-over, ashamed, not able to look anyone in the eye, not really able to remember but remembering it had not been good, apologetic but never understanding what he should be apologising for. And then he'd go to work and be buoyed by the job he loved and was good at and by the adoration of his patients. He'd come home defiant and back in denial and no external help would be sought and it would start all over again. I don't think we ever really had a conversation with him about it while he was sober, because while he was sober there was nothing wrong – and therefore nothing to talk about.

It was only Catherine or I who would ever follow him and find him drinking, because we were the only ones who were remotely curious and in the end even we rarely bothered. Because, what was the point?

And then he got drunk and ran someone down with his car.

I picked up my brother, who by this point was also at Liverpool University, in the car our ever-generous Dad had given us to share while we were there (although it makes it easier, things really are rarely as black and white as I'd like to see them). We went home for a whole weekend of the usual follow-up session, except this time he was sober and we missed out the row and accusations stage (since the police evidence did that bit), and just got straight on with the denial and self-pity.

Then John and I went back to Liverpool and I had my finals. We were pretty disconnected from the rest of the very public trial (unlike my little sister who was at home for it all and did not come off unscathed). The police and the newspapers had a field day at the downfall of someone who was supposed to be a role model and Dad paid a very large amount of money for a very large amount of legal help and narrowly managed to avoid prison. He just lost his driving licence for a year. Whilst he was obviously deeply embarrassed by the public humiliation, he wasn't obviously repentant. In one of his only conversations with me on the subject, he managed to make it all sound like an injustice, "Anyone else would have got one of their friends to say we'd been down to the pub for a drink *after* I'd taken the car back and that's why I was over the limit. But I'm too honest." He had a very rich fantasy life. I don't remember him ever going down the pub for a drink with a friend and as for having one who would perjure themselves for him… He watched Mum stand up in court and swear he'd just had one sherry all evening. And you couldn't really say she was perjuring herself as that's what she really believed. Dad wasn't the only one with a rich fantasy life. But still, despite the denial, losing your licence is a big deal when you have to drive every day for your job. He employed one of John's mates to drive him round his calls that year, which had to have been tough.

And despite all the stress (the supposed trigger), he wasn't "unwell" for a whole year. I assumed until recently that the trial had actually scared him enough to stop him drinking, but I suspect now he was probably just more careful about his consumption. The guy who'd driven Dad around during his ban let slip (assuming we all knew) that he'd once called round in the morning to pick Dad up for his rounds and walked in on him with his head under the kitchen sink drinking from a hidden plastic bottle. So maybe even his work didn't stop him drinking. I don't think he ever drove drunk again though. He was terrified of the police and was scarcely able to drive sober, let alone drunk, when a police car was behind him. Both my parents talked a lot about how the police victimised him.

His lack of "illness" in this year gave Catherine and I all the evidence we needed to believe all future incidents were alcohol-related, but the family remains divided on this issue. His patients were very supportive and rallied round. It seemed no one really believed all the reports and allegations and still no one ever used the word alcoholic. To show their support, there were even more wrapped bottles from patients under our tree that Christmas. Friends and neighbours badgered him to have a drink, "Oh come on Martin, have a drink, it's Christmas/ the holidays/ you deserve it, you've got to have a drink, what's wrong with you?" until it really would have been impossible to refuse without admitting he was an alcoholic – which he wasn't about to do, even to himself. Even his brother bought him wine. That's how well we all kept it hidden. And it wasn't hard hiding something no one wanted to see. After that year he was back driving and started to get "unwell" again, and things were back to normal.

Actually they both drank a lot, but Mum had much better tolerance so it rarely showed. I'd always thought that alcohol destroyed their lives and relationship so I couldn't understand why they kept at it, but recently I've come to realise that it was probably alcohol that kept them together. Facing their lives and relationship sober was not something to be relished and neither was brave enough to go it alone and get a new life.

Like I say, we were a pretty ordinary family.

Children of addicts and alcoholics are four times more likely to become addicts and alcoholics than children of non-addicts and alcoholics. So maybe it was lucky that I discovered rowing at the same time as I discovered alcohol. You may have spotted slightly addictive patterns to my personality. Usually I joke about it, although to me the fear of ever losing control of my life to any addiction is so powerful that I'm pretty damned careful. Just once in our normal cycle of accusations and denial did Dad switch track and say, "Alison, you know if I was told I only had one year left to live, I'd just take myself away by myself and drink the whole time. I'd drink myself to death."

"But why? How could you want that more than spending the time with Mum or with us? It doesn't make any sense."

"Alison, drinking is all I want to do all the time. It's constant."

And for once I was floored. "But what are we supposed to do with that? How can we fix this if you are not even prepared to try?"

"I'm not telling you this to find a way to fix it, I'm just telling you to help you understand how I feel."

I had nothing. There was nowhere to go with that. But I did finally understand what it feels like to be so totally addicted to something that it is all you want and you have no control over the rest of your life. No freedom. And I know more than anything that I never want to lose my freedom.

I know from experience that the one of the best ways to spot when you are becoming addicted is when you start to tell yourself you are using your "thing" in an increasing variety of situations and to deal with an increasing number of emotions. I do drink sometimes but the only reason I ever give myself is the truth, and that's that I like it and if I ever started to like it too often or too much I'd stop for a while. I try never to lie to myself or to anyone else about anything because I've seen what happens when you start lying to yourself. Lack of practice makes me a rubbish liar anyway. Lying a little is a social skill though that helps to soften the edges, but I never learnt to do that either. I can be pretty hard on you, I won't lie to you and I won't let you lie to yourself. You might not like me. I'm not proud of that. I'm still my father's daughter in some ways and, like him, I like to be liked. So I'm blunt and hurt and annoy people, and then feel bad about it. That's how it is.

I don't think I'm addicted to exercise (sometimes it is really hard to get myself off the sofa), but I'm aware this is what an addict would say. If I am, then I'm just glad it got me before anything else did.

Addictive traits are useful sometimes though. Over the Christmas holidays of my final year I started my patented O level/A level revision system with Dad's chess clock. After Christmas I started cutting down on the social life. For a while I only went out on Wednesday nights and then even they stopped. Once lectures finished I cranked up to twelve-fourteen hours revision a day and even stopped going rowing. A run round Sefton Park was more time-efficient.

Jo also wanted a First so we shared the onerous task of tracking down all the references and spent hours amongst the shelves of the university library locating the bound volumes and photocopying the papers. We read and made our own revision notes from every paper. We're still pretty sure we were the only microbiology students who did all that.

Our revision schedules were much like our rowing. Jo had more power and I had more endurance. Jo has a higher IQ; she just learns stuff faster. Sometimes we'd pick a topic and power-revise it for a couple of hours, then come together to test each other. Jo had always learnt more. But then Jo would always go to bed by 11 o'clock or she'd be useless for the next day, but my most productive and creative hours are always between about 9pm and 2am – so I would just keep going. Generally, I'd work until about 1-2am, then get up at 8am and do an hour before breakfast to help break up the day. If we were working at home most of our house would break at the same time for lunch and, like 90% of the student population, watch *Neighbours* for a nice sociable half-hour lunch break (timed on my chess clock). That was my social life. When anyone tries to tell me that all students are dossers and have an easy life, I can get pretty annoyed.

I learnt everything, and I mean every single little thing from every lecture note, associated textbook chapter and scientific paper on the list. And then I practised with old exam papers until I could reliably answer any question that turned up. I enjoyed most of the exams once they started. The calculations paper was a nightmare though and I came out thinking I'd blown it, until I talked to everyone else and found they'd had an even worse time (except mathematically-minded Jo who had really enjoyed herself – I didn't always like her). Then we had about a week before the extended essay paper.

This final paper covered the entire field of microbiology and we would have three hours to write an essay in answer to one of six one-line questions under exam conditions. I'd have to carry enough information in my head to be able to write for three hours on any topic that might come up in much more depth than any of the lecture courses we'd done. When I was studying biology at school, I heard it described as a literary science and I love that description. While chemists and physicists may to a large extent be able to get away with describing their work with symbols and equations (I once went out with an astrophysicist whose PhD was essentially a 200-page equation, unintelligible to all but about three people), biologists are almost certainly at some point going to have to use words. It's probably why, with my love of reading and literature, I was drawn to biology in the first place.

But how to revise for it? The entire contents of all my lectures represented only a small part of the whole field of microbiology and realistically I was only going to be able to revise one topic in enough depth to write a First-class extended essay. I started by sitting down with the all the old papers I could get my hands on and very quickly I saw that every year for the last six years there had been a question about the application of microbial-biotechnology in industry. There didn't appear to be any other topic that appeared so blatantly in all the papers. This then was to be my First-class topic. It was my best option but I don't think I could have slept at night if it was my only option. Still haunted by sitting in front of meaningless exam papers in my lower sixth, I needed a Plan B. One should always have a Plan B.

I found a second topic that cropped up in about four of the six papers and I thought I'd have to be pretty damned unlucky if neither of them showed up. I spent about 70% of my time on topic one and 30% on topic two. I worked hard but it was no hardship. It was fascinating and I loved it.

By the time I turned up on the morning of the last exam, I'd pretty much had it. I was pale, exhausted and skinny (I'd been dieting to avoid overeating while revising), and had developed a small but hideous patch of infected, suppurating little blisters of impetigo down from one corner of my mouth from sitting worrying a zit for hours and hours while revising. But that morning I woke up wired and absolutely ready to go. I was nervous but not scared. I had never been more ready, more prepared for anything. I'd left no stone unturned. There were no thoughts in the back of my mind that said "You should have done this..." This was just the biggest opportunity I'd ever had to show anyone what I could do.

I remember the exam quite clearly. I went in, took a deep breath, turned the paper over and scanned the questions. There it was. *Describe the environmental advantages of using microbial biotechnology in industry.* I smiled and was off. Writing and writing and writing. I put my hand up twice for another answer booklet and I had my left hand up while I was finishing writing the last page with my right hand, so I didn't have to stop the flow of all that was in my head onto the paper. Every genus, species and sub-species name of bacteria, every statistic, even the names of some of the original researchers was there. I was writing so fast I was struggling to keep it legible, but still I structured it into a comprehensive essay. With ten minutes to go, I had downloaded everything I knew and I pulled it all together into a concluding couple of paragraphs. As they called time on the exam I stacked and clipped the pages together, put my head back and looked up for the first time in three hours.

I was done.

I tried to go out to celebrate that night but didn't last very long, plus I was rather self-conscious about having nappy rash on my face. It didn't matter. We had weeks to fill before the results came out and nothing to do but enjoy them. I started rowing again and raced the summer's local regattas. I was by now a pro at 'late stops' and after York, Sheffield, Nottingham and Chester, serious rowing was followed by serious drinking until they threw us out at closing time and we'd all pile back onto the coach to go home.

By our third year we were down to a hard-core five girls from the thirty or so that had come down that first Saturday (me, Jo, Siobhan, Aisling and Moyna). We were good friends by now and between us would put out a damned good coxed four that won many races. Plus there were some great girls we'd trained up from novices in our second year; we put out the best eight LUPBC had ever had (or so we liked to think) and won the University Athletics Union Championships. This was a first for LUPBC and as I was women's captain, it's still one of my proudest rowing moments.

Between our finals and our results, we rowed and raced and had house parties and went to house parties and I had several lovely memorable days with my tall blond boy – including a trip with his housemates to Blackpool. I was rather hungover and fragile from the night before and he was really lovely to me – which was unexpected at the time, but makes me think now that if I'd been a little more fragile a little more often, we might have got on better. Basically we all did everything we could think of not to think about results until the papers were marked. Which eventually they were.

The day arrived and everyone in our house got ready to go our separate ways to our different departments to collect our results. I got a lift in with Jo and as we drove there was something neither of us could talk about, so we weren't talking. Then, while we were driving down the same Toxteth Street we had walked and talked along so many times, Jo finally said, "I don't know how I'll feel if you get a First and I don't, and I don't know what I'll say to you if I get a First and you don't."

"I was thinking the exact same thing. What do we do?"

"I don't know."

"Let's just hope it doesn't happen."

Hoping doesn't really count as a Plan B, but sometimes, in the final moments, it's all you've got.

They posted the exam results up on a window in the department and we all crowded round. There were only twenty microbiology honours students, so the list wasn't long. I deliberately looked at the bottom first and worked my way up. Through the Thirds, the 2:2s, then only halfway up the 2:1s when Jo grabbed my arm. "We both got them!" My eyes followed her finger and flicked to the top of the list. We were both there.

There were only two First-class honours awarded to microbiology students that year, and Jo and I got them. Speaking to one of the lecturers later, he said it was the first time anyone could remember awarding more than one First – but this year, they couldn't separate us.

Jo and I having an unstoppably good time in Liverpool 1989-1992

Chapter 6: Red, white… and very blue

"No goal is too big and scary that we can't at least do the next small step before we give up on it, and no step too small that we can't feel good about having done it"

I left Liverpool in the summer of 1992. It was the Barcelona Olympics and my first opportunity to watch Olympic rowing since it became *my* sport. I walked in from an all-night party (held in a field at the fruit farm where I was working) and Mum called to me to be quick as there was some rowing on. I joined Greg and Jonny Searle at about 500m in their Coxed Pairs final and stood watching dispassionately, my hangover kicking in, as they slipped out of medal contention through the middle thousand. I was about to walk away when suddenly something changed and the boat catapulted forward. Legend has it that Garry Herbert called: "If not now – when! If not you – who!" and the full force of double Searle was unleashed. Their boat cut through the field to take an impossible Gold, while our household once again jumped up and down on the same sofa (now reupholstered in blue) screaming at the TV.

Years later, when I first made the GB team, I sat chatting to Greg over lunch at the Holme Pierpont rowing centre in Nottingham. He excused himself saying he had to go and talk to some school kids and when he came back, I asked him what he said when he was asked to do that. He told me he just gave them the "Ordinary people do extraordinary things talk". I didn't say anything but just looked at the lean, muscled, impossibly glamorous giant in front of me and could feel myself raise a cynical eyebrow – "You ordinary? Yeah right. You don't even know what that word means."

Back in 1992, fresh from picking strawberries and sleeping on a bouncy castle in the middle of a field, the Olympics were still something other people did. People like me could still be great scientists though. I thought that probably involved getting a PhD, which meant staying on at university. This was a good thing. I liked university. If I was going to be the best I thought I should probably go to Oxford or Cambridge. They had some pretty good rowing going on too, so that seemed like a good way forward. That was about my level of thinking on the whole subject. The plan was to go to Bedford for six months to work as a research assistant for Unilever, apply for a PhD, earn some cash and then go travelling with Jo for six months before starting the whole student thing again.

I'd worked in Bedford the summer before on a Unilever student placement, taught myself to single scull in one of the club boats and won my first sculling race at Bedford Quarts Sprint Regatta after just a few weeks. Going out for my first race someone told me: "Relax! This is novice sculls, if you don't crash and you don't fall in, you win." I took their advice and sacrificed a little raw power for careful steering. I was down off the start but then rowed through my opposition as they ricocheted from bank to bank. I made it through every round and eventually won the final in a similar fashion to receive the gigantic Quart tankard as my 'Novice Pot'. It felt incredible to race and win by myself like this. I was hooked.

Most weekends, if Bedford Rowing Club didn't go to a regatta, I'd send off my own race entries (LUPBC secretary training), strap my boat to the top of my car and take myself off to race somewhere in my single. If Bedford Rowing Club was going, then I'd also race in a couple of fours. There were often weekends when with heats, semis and finals in three or four categories, I'd race almost constantly, jumping out of one boat to run and pick up my single and row back up to the start again for my next race. One particularly hot day at St. Neots Regatta, I made the final in all four of my categories and rowed about 12 races back to back. It was all very good race training and I no longer ever had a shadow of a doubt that I would be able to finish any race I started.

As I got better and more confident, I didn't have to hold back anymore to avoid crashing or falling in, but still I'd always get dropped off the start. But I learnt if I just kept sculling solidly, inevitably I'd catch up and row through my opposition in the last stages of the race. In single sculls, you race the same people all summer so we got to know each other pretty well. After one race the girl I'd just beaten said: "It's always the same, I get ahead off the start and think I've got you, but then you come back and there is nothing I can do about it." And at another regatta I overheard a girl warning my opposition for the next race: "You can never think you've got her beaten. She always comes back on you at the finish." I guess this was about the point I started to become legendary for my big finishes.

I'd had a pretty good summer all in all, won a lot of pots, learnt a lot about racing and got a good tan. As a useful aside I did some work for Unilever in the immunology department, helping to clone the antibody proteins they use in their pregnancy test kits into bacteria. I was accommodated in a huge Bedford house with all the other students. Mostly they were engineers working on ice creams (getting the chocolate to stick to Magnums was a big thing that summer) or washing powders and they brought home production line samples and seconds of chocolate and washing powder for the house to share. I didn't have much to contribute. Possibly the most useless products in the history of the world are experimental and seconded pregnancy test kits.

A year later I was back and racing in Bedford Head that first weekend. Linton 'Gus' Guise, the women's coach, found me after the race. "You only row quarter slide. I saw you rowing up to the start and you were at quarter slide so I thought it was just a warm-up exercise, and then you turned round and raced like that the whole way down. You did OK though. If you ever decide to row full slide, you'll probably go quite fast."

Rowing is one of only two Olympic sports where you win by being the fastest at going backwards (you can think on the other one). In rowing at least, the reason for this is that it allows you to use your biggest muscle groups (your legs), specifically glutes and quads to move the boat. In skiffs and early rowing boats, the seats do not move so you sit with your legs flat and row just with your body and arms. But even with this fixed seat rowing you can bend your legs a little bit to get extra power (this is about quarter slide position). Inevitably, of course, people (men mostly, rowing not being a seemly sport for ladies) wanted to go faster because they were racing each other (obviously something the ladies would never want to do having far more gentle temperaments), so they elongated the seat so they could bend their legs more and slide further each stroke engaging more leg power. They'd wear leather shorts and grease them and the seat so as not to wear out their breeches and bums and probably get to about half-slide position. Then someone (almost certainly a man again, it's a bit difficult to do this if you are wearing a full length hooped skirt) designed a seat with wheels that went up and down in little tracks called runners so the rowers could get right up to full slide, shins vertical and calves pressed against the thighs. Apparently I was negating all that technological development.

And it wasn't just the sculling, my rowing was equally appalling. My self-taught Liverpool rowing technique was 'pull as hard as you can and see what happens' and something pretty dreadful was happening. I was very fit and very gutsy so I could shift a boat, but I didn't make it a very comfortable for anyone else.

So I set to work with Gus. Pretty early on he took me to one side and said that he wanted to consider me for selection for the winter head races, but he had to think about the more important summer races like Women's Henley and the National Championships and he needed rowers who were going to be around all the way through. We had a great group of girls that year with potential to win at the Nationals. Winning there meant we'd be able to go on to represent England in the Home Countries Regatta. So if I could commit to the whole year, I would have a chance at getting my England colours. Gus told me that: "Since that will probably be the summit of your career, you should think about it." He still remembers that line.

I did think about it and I thought he was probably right. I'd been to my first set of National Long Distance trials that winter and done surprisingly well in my single, so I also reflected on the fact that I would be twenty-years-old that summer and eligible for the Great Britain Under 23 team for the last time. I'd been rather cruelly denied the opportunity to compete at Junior (under 18) level because they have a rather strict entry qualification that states that all prospective candidates should actually have started rowing by this age. If I thought about it at all, I suppose I thought that if I could represent GB at U23 level that would be the summit of my rowing ambitions. I never really thought about where my rowing was taking me or where I could get to. I had a mantra I'd been repeating since I left Liverpool that went, "As long as I'm still getting better and still enjoying it then I'll keep going." I thought I could still get better (I didn't even try and think about how much) and I was still completely loving it, so was just looking for the next logical step.

Representing Great Britain in any capacity did seem a rather inaccessible dream, but I just wanted to know I'd tried. What would I feel like for the rest of my life if I didn't try? What would it feel like to look back and never know if I could have done it or not? It would be unbearable, that's what.

It took several glasses of wine over dinner with Jo before I finally plucked up the courage to say I was ducking out of our trip and staying behind to give rowing one last big push. So she went travelling by herself to Africa, Nepal and Australia and had fantastic adventures and I set myself the goal of making the U23 team and stayed behind to train and work all year. And Jo started to show that despite our similarities she has one more 'more'. She is definitely more balanced.

The Bedford women's squad trained four evenings a week and four more sessions over the weekend, but I felt I could do more, and would need to do more, to make National Selection. A couple of mornings a week I'd get up early to go sculling or running before work, or I'd cycle the ten miles to work and back, or get to training early and fit an extra sculling session in before everyone else arrived. On our day off on Friday I used to come down and row for sixty minutes as hard as I could on the ergo before going to my Friday night bar job. I tried to do at least one extra session a day.

I'd always be tired in the morning but the evenings, after I'd already got up early to train once and then worked a full day, were worse. Sometimes in the evening I'd have to go home after work to pick up kit and I'd make the mistake of sitting down on the sofa. I'd be so tired I wouldn't know how I'd even get off the sofa, let alone do the session. Your brain can play tricks on you when you are tired like that. I think that sometimes we have physical capability left but are just too mentally tired to access it and when we are sat on the sofa physical and mental tiredness feel the same. It is only experience that tells you that mental tiredness goes away when you exercise, but I've not found any level of experience that tells me, while I'm still sat on the sofa, whether it is my brain or my body telling me that I've had enough. And that is dangerous because if you want to be the best you have to access all your capability.

I'd be sitting on my lab stool at work with my head on the bench, my kit ready in the car so I wouldn't have to go home and face the sofa, or sitting on the sofa at home because I'd cycled and had to pick up more kit, and the voice in my head would say: "There is no way you can do this session, you are too tired today; it will do you more good to go to bed and get some extra sleep." And I'd have to fight the voice in my head, so I'd tell it two things. The first one was: "What will I feel like if I race at the trials and lose out on a place by a few feet and remember for the rest of my life that I skived this session?" And the second one was: "I don't think I can do this session but I can get up, pick my kit up and get in the car."

So I'd pick my kit up and get in the car.

Then I'd think: "I'm too tired to do this session but I don't have to do the session. All I have to do is drive to the club and sit in the car park".

So I'd drive to the club and sit in the car park.

And then I'd think: "I can't do this session but I can get my kit out of the boot and go and get changed. I can go home after that if I'm still too tired."

So I'd get my bag out, climb the stairs to the changing room and put on my kit. And often that would do the trick and I'd feel a new sense of purpose in my kit. But sometimes I'd still be too tired and I'd sit in the changing room with my kit on.

Then I'd think: "Now I've come all this way and I've got my kit on I might as well just get my blades and boat out and put it on the water."

So, I'd go down to the boathouse and get my blades and boat out and put the blades in the gates and tell myself: "Since it's all set up I might as well go out and row for 20 strokes. I'm not going to do a full outing, just 20 strokes."

So I'd get in the boat and push off and do my warm-up and row 20 strokes and then of course ninety-nine times out of a hundred I'd say: "Well now I've got this far I may as well finish". And I found I could. I think there has only been twice in my rowing career when I've used that tactic and still felt so dreadful after 20 strokes that I've turned round, put my boat away and gone home and slept a totally guilt-free sleep.

That is how I tell the difference between physical and mental tiredness.

Of all the stories I tell, it seems that this one resonates most with people. I've heard it quoted back to me months or even years later. People who have heard it have gone out and managed to restart doing some exercise after years, just a little at a time. And it's not just exercise; it works for pretty much anything. The first time I told this story when I came back from Athens, a woman came up to speak to me at the end of the session and said that she was in remission for cancer and I'd helped her because she realised that this was exactly how she needed to think about the next few days, weeks and months. How did I get to help a woman with cancer? My parents were doctors, they helped people with cancer. I thought I'd given up on that when I changed my career path. I was just a rower. It's amazing the things you do when you think you are doing something else.

It seems to me that sometimes we make life so complicated – we set our aspirations so high or make projects so large and difficult that we don't know where to start and scare ourselves into immobility. When that happens I do what I did with this book. I just begin and work out how to start later on. I stop worrying about how or where to get started and just do the most obvious next step. No goal is too big and scary that we can't at least do the next small step before we give up on it, and no step too small that we can't feel good about having done it. It seems to me that as long as we keep moving forward, these small steps can take us just about anywhere.

So I can't quite remember in what order it all happened, but I went to my

Bedford Women race Head of the River. Bow: Sharon, 2: Sue, 3: Danni, 4: Big Jo (rowing nicknames are not always that creative), 5: Me, 6: Little Jo (Nitch - we'll meet again in a later chapter), 7: Julie (Big Bav), Stroke: Yvette, Cox: Bryony

first National Championships in a Coxed Four and an Eight and we got silver and bronze medals respectively, which was good but not good enough to take us on to represent England in the Home Countries match. My winter trials performances had also been good enough to get me invited to the Under-23 selection trial in Nottingham. I loaded my boat onto the top of my car (Gus stayed behind in Bedford to coach the rest of the girls), drove myself up and

Bedford Rowing Club Women (Big Danni, Big Jo, Big Sue and Big Al) racing to a Silver Medal at the National Championships in Strathclyde. And (insert) dancing the Highland fling, because we are Scotland obviously, to the embarrassment of our cox.

raced in my single and won. Everyone was quite surprised about that, including me. I thought I'd been trialling for one of the crew boats but having won they offered me the chance to race the Single.

For both Gus and I, getting selected for the Under-23s was mission accomplished. Neither of us had experience past this point. The selection letter didn't really help. It came with a bill for travel and kit (there was no funding), a place and time to load my boat onto the trailer bound for Greece, and the flight times and that was about it. The letter didn't mention anything about coaches so I don't think we ever considered that Gus would come with me. I didn't even have a boat at this point. I'd been borrowing one from a very generous Bedford Rowing club guy but, understandably, taking it all the way to Greece was a different matter. Gus pragmatically suggested I take the old club training boat (an old Bergashell) and that seemed a good enough solution.

I raised the money through a combination of Unilever savings and Bank of Dad. At the appointed time Gus and I met at the boat club and strapped the big old Bergashell onto the roof of my car. I drove it down to the ARA (Amateur Rowing Association) headquarters in Hammersmith and a lorry drove into the back of my boat on the Hammersmith gyratory (a single overhangs a car by several feet), squashed it a bit and knocked the bow ball off. I stuck the bow ball back on with Gaffer tape (there's not much in the world that can't be fixed if you have enough Gaffer tape) and loaded it onto the trailer. I drove home, packed my bag, got myself to the airport and that was that. It was pretty much like going to St. Neots regatta really.

It was only when I got to the airport and saw that everyone else had their coaches with them that I realised this had even been a possibility. Then, as the journey progressed, I realised that everyone else knew each other because apparently they'd been training and racing together since they were about six (apart from a pair of guys from Ross on Wye rowing club who looked about as lost as me). When we got there everyone got out their shiny boats (which the coaches spent a long time adjusting and polishing) and had team briefings and talked about the foreign opposition by name as if they'd been racing them for years (which they had), and someone laughed (a little and not unkindly) at the carrying handles and gaffer tape on my Bergashell. For the first time I thought that perhaps it wasn't the thing to be racing in at an international regatta.

But everyone was really nice. The athletes and coaches alike adopted me as a rather strange outsider to their world, and one of the coaches replaced the gaffer tape with some glue. The kit was distributed and I put on my first ever red, white and blue Great Britain kit in the form of a badly fitting Lycra all-in-one with 'B' team diagonal stripes rather than 'full team' hoops to show I was good, but not that good, and a royal blue shell suit that would have done a 1990's Liverpudlian proud. It was about this point that I realised… "I don't think we're in St Neots anymore, Toto."

I raced my heat and semi and didn't make the final, but raced in the B-final (to decide places 7-12) and came about tenth. That didn't seem too bad for me.

And that was it. My goal had been to see if I was capable of representing Great Britain and apparently I was. I thought it should be easier from this point and someone would contact me and nurture my talent or something. But no one did. So I stayed on in Greece in lieu of the travelling I'd missed with Jo and had a fun week partying, drinking and sunbathing with some of the U23 rowers. Then travelled for a month on my own by bus and boat round places from my classical studies education (Athens, Olympia, Delphi etc.), ran out of money and was working as a waitress in a cocktail bar for a while (apparently just so I could write that line later in life). Then I came home, earned some more money, bought a second-hand blue Glyn Lock single, which I loved, and restarted my training.

Somewhere during this year I'd also been working for Unilever and applying for a PhD. It was a fabulous summer and I got rather bored of my lab job and looking out of the window at the sunshine, so this was the point I quit and went fruit-picking. I was still better at fruit-picking than lab work but still, rather strangely, no alarm bells rang about the whole lab research-based PhD thing.

I'd got as far as deciding that I should take my First-class honours degree in microbial-biotechnology and go to either Oxford or Cambridge. I visited both universities, read all the lab brochures, wandered round the colleges, met several supervisors, got more and more confused, and in the end made the very academic decision that Cambridge had won the last seven University Women's Boat Races so I'd go there.

I had the choice of a couple of labs on different projects with different supervisors. Both sounded good. The only information I had on doing PhDs came from a talk I went to in Liverpool where mostly they tried to scare you out of doing one. The opening line was: "50% of people who start PhDs don't ever finish." I registered this as nothing to do with me as of course I would be in the 50% who made it – that's who I was. The only other bit I remembered was them saying that the most critical factor to getting through was the relationship with your PhD supervisor, so we'd better pick one who looked to have plenty of time for us and had a good relationship with the rest of their students.

One of the Cambridge supervisors spent the best part of the day with me, walking me round the colleges, taking me to lunch and introducing me to his students, so he seemed like the best bet. I took up the offered PhD place in his lab in the biochemistry department with a three-year research grant. I should probably have done my homework a little more thoroughly.

Bedford was a strange year. I did some great rowing and met and rowed with some wonderful people. I shared a house with two brothers who were lovely to me and at 6′8″ and 6′6″ made me feel almost petite, especially on the occasions when my 6′4″ boyfriend (the same blond boy) came down and we all went out on the town. However, it wasn't Liverpool and it wasn't student life. Here everyone seemed to have settled into a coupled-up, family, 9-5 job normality that just wasn't me. I started to feel on the outside of life again. Even my boss at Unilever commented in one of my reviews: "Everyone likes you and you're friendly enough but it's like you are separate or something, I can't quite describe it." Spontaneously and rather embarrassingly I had to struggle to hold back tears at that comment. He hit some sort of nerve.

Plus I'd just left the most exhilarating and happiest part of my life behind and was now separated from my tall blond boy by a hundred miles and a boat club training regime that only enabled me to jump in the car at lunchtime after the second training session on Sunday for a few hours and a brief night, before jumping back in the car early hours to drive straight into work Monday morning. And it wasn't an easy relationship. Although he always said yes if I asked to visit and we had a great time when we were together, he never invited me up and wouldn't commit from one week to the next. I'd hold out all week, desperately hoping he'd call before giving in on Friday or Saturday night and picking up the phone myself. I seemed to forget the insight I'd gained in Liverpool about uncoupling happiness and weight and became pretty convinced that everything would be alright if I could just reach ten stone (I'm more normally around eleven stone). For most girls ten stone is big, but it would have made me very skinny if I'd got there. I nearly got there and I did get pretty skinny.

I think maybe rowing saved me from slipping down the anorexia-shaped hole that takes so many girls (including my sister). If I'd channelled all that relentless drive and determination (addiction?) into losing weight I have to think it's likely I'd have hit the ten-stone target and then gone for nine, eight, seven… Fortunately the primary requirement in my life was that I was able to complete my training programme so I got really good at being a rower instead. My little sister got really good at being an anorexic. We all need an identity.

Since my hardest training sessions were in the evening, I'd eat enough during the day to get me through. But then after training for about an hour and a half in the evening (burning around 1000 calories), I'd go home and eat a diet yogurt and an apple (containing around 100 calories) considering that since I'd already trained I could do without dinner. I'd go to bed starving hungry and obviously find getting to sleep and staying asleep very difficult, as it's hard to sleep when your stomach is eating itself. I think this is when my insomnia habit really started.

One particular favourite tactic was to do my sixty-minute 'hard as I can' ergo on Friday evening and then go straight to my bar job for the night and allow myself just a packet of crisps for dinner. One Saturday morning, our eight went all the way to Ely to do some long training pieces against the Cambridge University Women and after the first few minutes I found myself unable to do anything. I had absolutely nothing in my muscles with which to generate any power. Gus was calling to me from the bank to sort my stroke out but I could barely sit upright. We lost the pieces and I felt incredibly guilty.

I couldn't admit I'd not eaten as starving yourself when you are preparing for important races is just not the sort of thing you do, but I swore to myself all the way back down that river that if I could just make it back to the boat-house, I'd go and eat and never be so stupid again. Once in, I headed straight for the supermarket and loaded up with the highest calorie food I could find (I think pork pies featured somewhere) and felt better for the second session. After that, whilst still obsessively careful about how much I ate, I always made sure rowing, not weight loss, stayed at the top of my priorities.

I have an interesting relationship with my body. Maybe because it took me so long to discover what it will do for me, I feel removed from it. 'I' am what goes on in my head: my thought processes, my drive, my intellect, the part I've been conscious of and challenging and developing from my earliest memories. 'It' is this amazing vehicle (and I mean amazing–useful, not amazing–looking) that carries 'me' around. The part I'd not even begun to understand until I started rowing. The part I didn't trust in those first few terrifying races. The part I would now trust to carry me anywhere, through anything.

I'm continually grateful to it when it surpasses itself yet again to do something else I challenge it to do. Someone once told me a dog is so loyal it will keep running and picking up the stick you throw for it and bringing it back until it drops dead from exhaustion, rather than let you down. I think my body is rather like that. In other ways, it is a child. It is younger than I am and I can be proud of it when it performs well in a way I'm rarely allowed to feel proud of myself. I feel a responsibility to nurture and care for it.

People talk about our fragile bodies but I have noticed something very different. After all I have put mine through and the ways I continue to test it, it seems to me that our bodies are amazing and incredibly resilient. They are like that loyal dog and will put up with all sorts of abuse and still try and do their best for us. And it shocks me how people neglect and abuse their body with bad food and no exercise until it cannot repair itself anymore and bad things start to happen. And that they call that bad luck.

So when I look down at the legs I inherited exactly from my Dad and still think that they are too fat and chunky at the top, I also have to remember what they do for me and how far and fast they carry me and be grateful and treat them right. And when I'm unhappy and tempted down that road again (to starve myself to happiness), when I look at myself and dislike what I see, I remind myself of how ridiculously big and happy I was in Liverpool and how ridiculously skinny and unhappy I was in Bedford, and give myself a stiff talking to. I understand that if I'm unhappy I probably need to change my life, not my weight. Many sportswomen talk about how they were driven to anorexia through their sport, but I think it was the opposite for me. Sport has given me a value of my body above and beyond what it looks like. I wish more girls could have that.

I left Bedford and walked into my Cambridge PhD the following year with the same mentality that I'd taken to Liverpool. I decided that although they weren't graded, this was going to be an exceptional PhD. I was to be working with a strain of bacteria which naturally produces crystals of protein inside its cells that are toxic to insects but completely non-toxic to mammals, any other animal and plant life and in fact most other insect species (including the many beneficial strains of insect).

These protein crystals were already being used as natural biological insecticides in forestry and agriculture and our lab was working with the bacteria in various ways, including looking for new strains to kills different pests, trying to understand more about the proteins, and cloning the protein genes. Once cloned, the genes could be passed onto plant scientists who were working on introducing them directly into crop plants to produce naturally insect-resistant plants that didn't need to be sprayed with gallons of environmentally controversial pesticides. Believe it or not, when I started this PhD, it seemed like transgenic plants were an environmentally-friendly option. I was twenty-two and thought I was going to be a great scientist and save the world – like you do when you are twenty-two.

I knuckled down to start my PhD. I read the relevant papers and started following the recipes and methods in the textbooks and running the experiments. My experiments were in the 'finding out more about the proteins and how they fold' camp. There were some reported anomalies and my supervisor suggested that if we could find out what was going on in these cases, it would help explain what was going on in the normal cases. If that all sounds rather a vague basis for a PhD to you, then you are more switched on than me or my supervisor. I thought it all sounded a little vague because I didn't know very much about it and all would become clear. I was an optimistic little soul.

And of course there was also the rowing. I trialled for the Women's Blue Boat in my first year and although competition was fierce and it was never a forgone conclusion, I did make the crew. We got up at 5am most mornings to row on The Cam and get back in time for the undergrads to make their 9am lectures. In the evenings we did circuit training or 'Mad Mary Aerobics' (run by Mad Mary), both of which I loved. It didn't impede on my lab time too much, except that I had a bad habit of falling asleep at my desk in the afternoons.

My rowing continued to progress and it needed to. This was the first time I'd rowed every day and I found being able to pick up each outing with so little time in-between made a huge difference. My brain and my muscles could still remember from one session to the next what I'd done and what I was working on. I started to become a fan of doing something every day if you want to get good.

I'd been a bit of a 'strong arm rower' (which is not a good idea anyway but even worse for me as I have virtually no upper body strength) and coaches used to shout "RELAX" a lot. Then suddenly one outing, all at once, I did. After thinking about it and trying to do it for months but not really knowing what it was, all of a sudden I felt the tension go out of my arms and I was able to pick up the water with the back of my shoulder blades. My arm muscles were still working, but under a relaxed tension rather than a gripping tension. It was a revelation. I thought "Oh my God. This is it. This is what it's supposed to feel like. What have I been doing all these years?" I had to concentrate really hard at first to keep hold of it. Sometimes it would disappear for a bit, but once I'd felt it I knew anything else was rubbish and would just keep working at it till I got it back. And eventually it was there more often than not.

They were a great bunch of girls, most of who had learnt to row over the

Rowing with CUWBC. Like being one of the cool sporty kids at school – but with more gin. Boat Race crews 1994 (middle) and 1995 (top) and Sarah Winckless's Abba Gold party (Sarah is the tall blonde). Notice 1. I'm still great at dressing up and 2. The blister-covering plaster on my finger – a rower's essential badge of honour no matter how dressed up you get.

course of just a couple of years at Cambridge. I really enjoyed the experience. We all took it ridiculously seriously in retrospect, but it did feel like a really big thing to be involved in and the pressure to continue the winning streak was huge. We raced the Women's Boat Race in March at Henley (in my second term) and I got my first winning Blue. Being on any Blues team at Cambridge elevates you to a certain status. We were invited to all the right parties and made to feel rather special. It was what I imagined being one of the cool sporty kids at school would have felt like – but with more gin.

I was walking around Women's Henley regatta one weekend in June when I heard a rumour going round that my Cambridge coach (and long-time international coach) Ron Needs was recruiting and trialling girls to form an Eight to compete at the Commonwealth Regatta in Canada that summer. Rowing is not in the Commonwealth Games due to the relatively small number of Commonwealth countries that row, but rowing organises its own separate regatta. The Great Britain senior team do not generally attend, which leaves the door open for potential 'B' team athletes like myself.

I'd not heard anything about it, which I thought was a little odd as Ron had been my coach all year. I found him on the towpath and asked about it and received a bit of a confused response, which suggested Ron hadn't really thought I was good enough to consider. I don't want to denigrate Ron in any way though. As well as playing a part in getting me get selected for the U23 single the previous year, he has spent his life and career putting together scrap end boats with athletes that someone should be doing something with and no one is.

So, I talked him into letting me trial and went back to Cambridge with five days to prepare. Fortunately I did at least have a boat now and it was sat on a rack in Caius boathouse. Unfortunately, it was covered in dust, having sat there pretty much since I'd arrived. I was fit enough but I'd been rowing all year in an eight. Going from an eight to a single is rather like walking off a nice flat-topped wall onto a gymnastics beam. It all feels very insecure and twitchy. In fact, I sometimes liken being able to sprint flat-out in a single to being able to run flat-out across a tightrope. It's an amazing thing to get such a feel for the instability below you that your responses are so automatic that the little wafer of boat feels more like part of you than something to fall out of.

I was game to give it a go but understandably a little nervous. Fortunately, Simon Haines from one of the Town Rowing Clubs walked past as I was boating for my first outing. "Don't worry," he said, "you won't have lost it. It'll still be there once you get back in. Don't train too hard this week, stay fresh and just do a few top end bursts to get back up there again." I pushed off and started sculling and I *was* fine. I'd not lost it. Within twenty minutes I was paddling like I'd never been out of this sliver of a little blue boat. I often wonder what would have happened if someone else had walked by and told me what I was trying to do was crazy and impossible.

So after just a couple of outings I loaded my boat onto my car very early one Saturday morning and drove to the East London Docks rowing venue. It's a very confusing place and I drove around for ages before finding it at which point I was, unusually for me, running decidedly behind schedule. I screeched up, rigged my boat at top speed, ran to the loo, picked up my boat and blades and boated just behind all the other girls. It was only as I was paddling up to the start and had time to run through my race plan in my head that I realised I wasn't actually sure how long the race was.

All international rowing races are 2km long, but I had a feeling I'd heard this venue was too short for that. But how much too short? We were now nearly at the start and I was too embarrassed to ask, especially as no one had thought I was good enough to even be here. I didn't know much about sport's psychology at that point but I did think that not knowing the length of the race was the sort of psychological advantage one wasn't really supposed to give one's opponents.

Since I couldn't ask, I had to decide and I decided it was 1500m long. Once I'd decided that was fine. I turned round and got onto the start. "ATTENTION… GO!" and we were off.

I don't remember the first half of the race but I'm sure my standard pattern would have applied – dropped a bit off the start and then coming back. The 750m mark was halfway so I would have upped my rate at this point and started to push it on a bit more. Passing the 1000m mark with 500m to go, I know I went into my patented last 500m wind for home (I *am* legendary for my big finishes). In a single there are just over 65 strokes left so my race plan was always 'lift the rate, 10 strokes and one for luck, (50 left) lift the rate, 10 strokes and one for luck (40 left), lift the rate, 10 strokes and one for luck (30 left), lift the rate, 10 strokes and one for luck (20 left), through the roof now, wind for 10 (10 left), last 10 up, up, up don't count just keep winding for the line.' Somewhere in this last 500m, I drew level with and then overtook all the other girls and moved into first place. Up, up, up for the line and it was as I was heading into the last few strokes, just hanging on in there, that I was aware something wasn't quite right. I took another couple of strokes and then another couple and no one called "Down" (the call to stop rowing, short for "Wind Down"). I passed the 1500m marker (THE END?) and still no one called "Down". A simultaneous realisation and look over my left shoulder told me that this race was 1750m long and the finish line was at least another 25 strokes away.

And then a weird thing happened that changed not only how I see racing but also how I see life. I had been hanging on for the 1500m finish; lungs and legs screaming; desperate for the end and not quite sure if I could make it. I was genuinely, completely and utterly spent. Then I found I had to keep going, and within one stroke... I found I could. I dropped the rate a little and lengthened back out a bit, but I held up pretty well, maintained my boat speed and kept my place in the lead. I won and everyone was quite surprised about that.

And so I learnt that you always have more in you than you think you are capable of (it's your brain that stops you, not your body), that once you are ahead people tend to give up a little because they think you are cruising when actually you may be dying, and finally that just because someone is ahead in that moment doesn't mean they haven't killed themselves to get there and might be about to die themselves.

If you hang in there long enough and hard enough you might just get lucky.

Five years after that getting into a boat for the first time, rowing still had the power to surprise and delight me. It wasn't so much the rowing as the fact that rowing was the vehicle I'd found for testing the limits of my body and letting it surprise me. I was like my own ongoing science experiment to see what else my body might be capable of. If I'd been good at sport when I was growing up, I'm not sure I would have felt like this. I think I might have taken my body more for granted and have been less excited and exhilarated by discovering the things I could make it do. I loved rowing for many reasons, but this at least was a large part of its power. Every race was like an extension of that first ever race. I sat on every start line scared half to death, facing the unknown, not even knowing what question I was asking until I crossed the finish line and had yet another answer. "Oh my God. My body will do THAT!" And through my whole rowing career, I never grew out of it. I never stopped being surprised, delighted and exhilarated – just like I never stopped scaring myself half to death. Scientifically speaking, from my empirical experiments, the strength of one is in direct proportion to the intensity of the other.

Following the singles trial I had to come back and seat race in fours a bit to prove I could row as well, but I made it in. We were all working, so trained together at weekends in either Marlow or Cambridge and did our own training the rest of the week. I got a selection letter through the post that started "Dear Athlete," and still remember being more surprised by the fact that someone had called me an athlete than by the fact I'd just been selected to row for England in the Commonwealth Regatta.

We went to Canada (self-funded again – this time I was part-sponsored by a very generous local Richmond Garage) and got a Bronze medal which sounds pretty impressive until I tell you that there were only four Women's eights competing and the only crew we beat was Scotland. It was a good, if not totally enjoyable, experience. I'd had such a positive time in my Liverpool, Bedford and Cambridge eights that it knocked me rather sideways to encounter my first rowing bullies. It was only a couple of them, well one really, and actually I was by no means on the worst end of it, but it certainly took the shine off the experience. It was kind of like being back at school again. Up until this point I'd assumed everyone just grew out of needing to behave like that, but apparently not.

I came back and got on with my PhD and trialled for the Blue Boat again – this time as president. I decided it was time to stop being so passive and waiting for someone to spot or nurture 'my potential' and made a proactive move. I went to ask the Cambridge Men's squad coaches (both highly rated international coaches) if they would coach me in my single occasionally if I went out to Ely where they trained with the men. They said they'd be too busy. It had been a long shot and I wasn't offended – until I found out a few weeks later that one of them (the legendary Harry Mahon) had later walked into the gym and seen 6ft 3 Sarah Winckless on an ergo, and even though she'd just started rowing and had no results to her name, had been so overawed by her potential that he'd *offered* to coach her personally. They were right about Sarah's potential – she is a fantastic athlete and went on to get an Olympic medal – but I was starting to get a little frustrated that no one could see past my smaller frame to find anything worth working with, despite the fact that I was actually producing results. In the outside world I'm somewhat of a giant but in the international rowing world I'm somewhat of a waif.

It was a crazy, tough time. It took me over a year to work out that the research my PhD was based on was wrong. There were no anomalies to explain, they were experimental errors in the original research. It took me a ridiculously long period of time to work this out because I was so totally out of my depth in this world. The quote "You get promoted to the level of your incompetence" kept coming back to me and I felt I'd promoted myself to my level of incompetence. I'd thought I'd been a good scientist at school; I was top of my year at university, but that meant nothing here. I kept hearing the line "50% of people who start PhDs don't finish them" from the Liverpool lecture and cursed myself for my complacency. I repeated the methods and experiments but nothing made any sense, and instead of doubting the original research I assumed I was making mistakes in the protocol and just went back and did it again. This was nothing like being an undergrad and I didn't know what I was doing. Supervision would probably have been useful, but I found myself effectively on my own and just asking the other students and post-grads for help. I should probably have asked for more help but I just thought this was how PhDs worked. And my friendly supervisor was starting to scare me.

It soon became evident that the time he had allocated to me on my interview day had been pretty much my full allowance and that the bonhomie on display between him and his students had been for the benefit of the interview. The trick was to introduce the new student to us all on mass during a coffee break, and laugh and joke and play the part I'd seen him do so well in my interview – but never leave them on their own with any of us. We all played along because he held our fate in his hands and apparently rowing teams aren't the only place where bullies don't grow up. As he walked away with yet another candidate, we'd all feel rather guilty about the part we'd just played and someone would say "One of these days I'm going to tell them what it's really like", but we never did.

He didn't really check in with me at all until the end of the first year when I had to write a report that all first year students had to produce to be allowed to progress. I was unaware of quite how badly I was doing until this point. I pulled together what I'd done and for the first time he told me it was nothing. He also said how disappointed in me he was. Apparently he'd "left me alone" in my first two terms to row in the Blue Boat, but had then been really annoyed when I'd rowed in the college bumps. This was the first I knew of any of it, although it explained a lot. "Left alone" was pretty much how I'd felt but had assumed this was just how PhDs worked. I felt shocked and slightly sick. I'd always pursued at least two things in my life and succeeded in both – it was how I worked best. It had never occurred to me that my supervisor would think I would do just one at a time. What he didn't even know at that point, and what I was certainly now too scared to tell him, was that I'd committed myself to a second boat race by getting myself elected as CUWBC President. It hadn't seemed too big a deal when I'd signed up for it, unaware of the hidden wrath of my supervisor. It felt like a big deal now and of course it didn't take long for him to work it out.

He communicated mainly by leaving notes on my bench when I was out and I was too scared to go and talk to him when I was in. His lack of confidence in my ability meant that whilst I became increasingly sure over the next few months that all was not as it should be with my PhD, he thought the errors were mine. To be fair, I didn't do much to convince him otherwise as my own self-confidence was completely shot and I didn't trust my results either.

The rowing was also a nightmare. I probably shouldn't have done it again, but as not many of the girls were returning for a second year, there had been no one else to stand for president and I'd felt it was my job (never be a handbag). It shouldn't have been as bad as it was. I would have been all right with just the training, but I hadn't really recognised how much I was going to have to do for the presidency. All the other committee positions were filled by girls who didn't end up rowing, so they just weren't around. Also this wasn't like Liverpool Boat Club where everyone ran their own lives, assumed responsibility and made things happen. This was Cambridge where the undergrads lived in college, lived by college rules, had tutors and cleaners and were used to being looked after. It wasn't like the Men's CUBC system either where there was a professional group of coaches and support staff to sort them out. On the women's side in CUWBC we had a couple of voluntary coaches in the legendary team of Ron Needs and Rodger Silk who had worked their own kind of magic with CUWBC for years, but it was by no means full time. Most of the rest of the responsibilities for organising coaches and training and everything else that goes into running any sort of competitive club fell to the committee – which this year seemed to be me.

In the days before mobile phones I found it really difficult to track anyone down, and when anyone wanted anything done, they called me on the lab phone because that's where they knew they'd find me if I wasn't rowing. I co-ordinated and ran a squad of three crews (about thirty athletes) and over a dozen voluntary coaches and trainers for seven months from a wall phone in the lab ten paces from my supervisor's office – and he knew about it.

On top of the PhD and rowing nightmare, I was at a pretty low ebb personally. I'd finally broken up with the tall blond boy after the best part of four years. I think now that we were both Adult Children, him for a rather more traumatic and tragic reason than myself (that is not mine to tell). Neither of us really knew what normal looked like and in the whole time we tried to be together, we rarely if ever had a real adult conversation about what was going on. I'd tried everything I knew (which wasn't much) to make it work. I really hadn't wanted to finish it but eventually, after four years – when I still wasn't allowed to fix a next time to meet because I might actually think we were in a relationship and he still wouldn't introduce me to a lot of his friends in case they thought the same – I knew I had to. The hardest part was that I'd had to do it. The second hardest part was that he was going out with someone else within a couple of weeks. It was taking me a little longer to get over.

And finally... my relationship with my father had just about bottomed out. I didn't get home very much but I couldn't remember the last time it had been even vaguely all right. There were long telephone conversations with my mother about how bad she was finding it and what she was going to do about it, but never did. I was worried about her and would help her make extensive plans for how she could leave him – many times.

They visited me more often than I visited them as Dad found it easier to stay sober for a few hours at a time before they went back to their hotel, and I didn't have to see what happened next. But even then, he was starting to look like the physical wreck it was turning him into mentally. He was overweight, grey, puffy, swollen and droopy-eyed. I found being around him very difficult, but the more I pulled back the more he pushed forwards. There was a false heartiness and cheer in his greeting and conversation, in defiance of the reality of our relationship and the situation. He'd bowl up and chat loudly for a few minutes and crack a lame joke, and when I didn't join in with the game, he'd spit out a: "Give me a chance, I am trying."

"It's going to take more than staying sober for a couple of hours to turn things round, Dad. This has been going on for over ten years. If you can stay sober for the next ten years we might gradually get back to where we were."

"I can't wait that long Alison."

"Well then."

I tried to maintain a relationship with Mum and invited her down a couple of times by herself for choral events we could both enjoy on Thursday evenings, which was always Dad's night on call. Both times she turned up with Dad after he'd swapped his on call rota.

"I was hoping just to see you Mum."

"Oh I couldn't leave him at home Alison, it wouldn't have been fair."

He ruined both evenings because there was no way he could sit still for five minutes, let alone an hour. And instead of the relaxing evening off that I'd planned, I had to sit next to him twitching, shuffling and snorting. In the second concert, where there was more room, everyone around us moved seats for the second half to escape and I sat there feeling isolated and exposed. When I mentioned it later, both my parents had managed not to notice. Apparently on my parent's planet they not only spoke a different language but also saw through different eyes. I was starting to realise that this planet was Denial and it was where they had to live to live at all. Denial is not the same as lying because Denial world is a genuinely different place with its own truths. And I still find it scary to think of that now because how would I know if I was there?

All in all it was a very tough year. Then one day in the middle of it all I was hidden round the corner in the lab (I had a great bench and desk for hiding, which was maybe not a good thing) with my head in my arms on my desk feeling exhausted and completely defeated. I listed in my head all the things that were getting on top of me. I heard the language I was using, heard myself blaming everyone and everything around me. I thought I needed a good kick. If I'd had any energy left I'd have given myself that kick, but I didn't. It was all just too much to deal with, which was why for the first time since my bad A level year I wasn't dealing with any of it. I'd stopped working again and was going through the motions with everything else. But as I broke it all down in my head and listed out the sources of what was really bothering me, the fog of hopelessness began to resolve and I started to see things more clearly. There were four things in my life: PhD failing, Blue Boat failing, relationship failed, Dad drinking. The picture in my head was of me juggling and desperately trying to keep everything in the air.

And as I looked more deeply, I realised that these problems were not all equal. PhD, rowing and relationship were about my life and Dad drinking was about his life. PhD, rowing and relationship had been a problem for a few months and Dad drinking had been a problem for over ten years. And finally, finally I had a moment of clarity as I realised that sorting out PhD, sorting out rowing and getting over the relationship were things within my control, but stopping Dad drinking was not. I had tried, I really had tried, but it just was not mine to fix. And yet it had been thinking about Dad that took most of my focus, drained most of my energy and kept me awake at night. Every night and every spare waking moment I played out various scenarios and conversations that had happened or could happen or should happen – over and over the continuous circle of words that never had any effect and never reached a resolution, even when I did get to say them out loud.

I'd been in there fighting for so long I was completely drained. And nothing had changed except that it had got worse. Why was I in there fighting? What was he doing while I was fighting for him? Drinking – that's what. I'd had enough. My sister, the nurse, calls it compassion fatigue.

I'd also just heard a radio interview with Billy Connolly's wife, Pamela Stevenson. She'd written a book about her life and his and so had been talking about Billy and his alcoholism. She's known as a comedian now but she's actually a qualified psychiatrist, so when she talked about how she'd had to leave Billy to let him hit the bottom and give him a chance to recognise his problem and recover, she used the words co-dependant and enabler that I'd never heard before. I recognise that I was just one of many enablers who thought they were helping, but were actually creating a world where Dad could drink but never have to face the consequences. If they actually have to choose between you and the drink, there is at least some hope they might choose you. If they don't have to choose, they will continue to have their cake and eat it. They're drunk, not stupid. It felt like a relief to realise that what I was thinking of doing might actually be good for him and gave strength to my resolve.

But, as always, I wanted to be certain and know I'd done everything. And I thought I wasn't quite there yet. I'd never actually told my father how I felt about all of this, about the impact on me – not while he was sober anyway. So, I got out some paper and I wrote him a letter. "Dear Dad…" I told him how I was feeling; what it was doing to me and stopping me doing; how I'd felt over the past ten years; the specific instances of shame and humiliation; the hurt and frustration. The hours and hours I'd spent trying to help him and Mum with nothing to show for it and no action on his part. I told him I'd had enough, warned him that if he didn't change then I would – that I was preparing to disengage and leave him to it.

I kept the letter for a day and re-read it, just to be sure it wasn't heat of the moment stuff I'd regret. Then I put it in an envelope, sealed it, addressed it to him and sent it on its way. I felt the relief immediately and didn't even think about it much over the next day or so until Mum called while I was in the lab. "Alison, it's all right. I've got the letter." Her voice was calm and compassionate.

"What do you mean you've got the letter, it was addressed to Dad?"

"I know but I saw it first and thought it might be something like this so I kept it. It's all right, he's not read it."

I was confused. Why was that a good thing? "But I want him to read it. I want to let him know how I feel, that's why I wrote it."

"I couldn't let him read it Alison, it would destroy him. He can't read it now anyway; I've thrown it on the fire." I don't remember the rest of the conversation. I don't think I said much but I remember Mum's tone. It was one of forgiveness. The tone said: "I understand why you've done this and it's all right I forgive you, we don't have to mention it again." If I'd had any energy left, that in itself would have made me very angry. This was a new and unexpected development in the whole complex denial thing that I couldn't quite get my head round.

It could have been a whole new thing to expend energy on, this new frustration, but I didn't have that energy so I was prepared to call it a day and check out of the whole father/daughter thing (and probably a little more from the whole mother/daughter thing too). It was much easier. I didn't have to try any more. I didn't disappear physically, just mentally. I didn't argue with him any more. I didn't fight with him or for him. I became civil and polite in my interactions and kept them to the minimum necessary to maintain contact with and not put any more pressure on Mum. He was who he was and I would just let him be. I couldn't get my head round how my parents wanted to live their lives, but I finally realised it was their life. The important thing now was not to let it mess up my life. If I let that happen, it would be my fault not theirs. Their life is their responsibility. Mine is mine.

So, I dropped one of the four things and that gave me space to get my head round the three others. I kicked myself into touch around pining for the tall blond boy and started going out with another tall blond boy (the astrophysicist). He was actually nice to me for the couple of years it lasted (until I realised that nice wasn't really enough). He did radical things like actually arrange from one time to the next when we would meet and didn't seem to think that was too restrictive. And I can still remember exactly where I was in Cambridge marketplace when, after only a few weeks, he casually talked about going on holiday together later that year. I couldn't answer and had to fight the urge to run away and remind myself that this was probably quite normal for normal people – committing to each other for more than the moment you were in. It was going to take some getting used to and I don't think I ever really did, but mainly it was nice.

And I just had to knuckle down and play the whole Boat Race thing out again as best I could. I pretty quickly felt trapped in CUWBC and the presidency. It wasn't proving to be good for me or my rowing but there was no way out without letting a lot of people down. I'm sure I was less essential than I felt, but it never feels like that at the time does it? I tried to keep moving on with my rowing outside of CUWBC and stay connected to the international path I'd started with the U23s and the Commonwealth Regatta but again I was on my own. I went to the two sets of winter long-distance trials at Peterborough in my single to race the squad, just to find out if I was anywhere close. I didn't know what would happen if I did prove to be any good and did get myself selected as there was no way I could do it all, but I decided that wasn't worth worrying about now. It was a long shot anyway and I'd worry about that if it happened.

The trials were on Sundays and since this was the one day we didn't row with CUWBC, I could fit it in. I was stuck for transport as my car had died and there was no trailer going from Cambridge. I was sure there was a way to get there – there's always a way – but I was very tired and it felt like one step too far to organise. My parents must have picked up on this from a phone call and after I put the phone down, Mum called me straight back and said that Dad had said they were going to come down for the weekend and would love to drive me to the trial and see me row. Two hundred miles away and they were still living up to the promise they made to that eleven-year-old to support me in whatever I wanted to do. I didn't feel good about it, but I let them come down and help me out and was genuinely grateful. Sometimes Dad made it hard to dislike him quite as much as I needed to.

So they drove down and we strapped my boat and blades to Dad's roof rack and drove back up the A1 to Peterborough. My parent's job done, they went off to explore and find somewhere to watch from and I rigged my boat and got ready to race. It was a crazy windy day and the direction of the course meant it would be a head wind. One of the decisions before any race is to decide what gearing to race with because, unlike a bike, there is no way of changing it once you are out there. These days the blades are adjustable and you can shorten them to lighten the gearing for a head wind, but back then you had to 'bring the span in' which meant loosening bolts on the riggers moving them in towards the boat and then tightening them up again. It was a bit of a job.

All around me coaches were getting out their tools and adjusting the rigging. I didn't have a coach so I got out my tool kit, made a guess at a good gearing and made the adjustment. I got myself boated, rowed up to the start and started to race. All was going well and I'd overtaken quite a few girls when I noticed something didn't feel quite right. One of the pins had come loose – I'd not tightened the bolt up properly. I stopped and tried to finger tighten it a couple of times, but it kept working loose. With no tools in the boat (a major error I would never repeat) and no coach following me on the bank, I was stuck in the middle of bleak winter Fenland. I spotted someone else's coach, sculled into the side and called them over. He tightened up the bolt while the girls I'd overtaken sculled past me. I set off again and overtook them back.

It would probably have been wise to tighten up the other bolt at the same time though, wouldn't it?

So I had to find another coach with more tools. It was a farce. I wasn't last though. I wasn't nearly last. I'd not beaten any of the squad girls, but I still beat several others. In fact, even if you hadn't known about the whole rigging incidents (and the fact that I was doing all my training in an eight and had just hopped into my scull), you could still look at the results sheet and think I'd not done half bad. Enough for me to think it was worth another go.

The second trial was a few months later. This time I managed to convince one of the other girls in the Blue Boat, who had also rowed U23 in her time, and importantly had a car, that she really ought to go to trials too. We strapped both boats and both sets of blades to the top of her Morris Minor and headed off up to Peterborough.

This time is wasn't windy. It was raining. It had been raining for some time and there was snow melt. It was possibly just above freezing. The Fens were flooded but not flooded enough to stop us rowing. There really are not many days when the weather is considered too bad to go rowing (I remember a particularly windy day in the last few days of training before the Athens Olympics when we heard that all sailing had been cancelled because it was too windy. All the rowers had already been out on the water that day, twice).

This time, there was no need to adjust my rigging, but I went round everything and tightened it up again just to be sure. I boated (with a spanner taped to the foot well of my boat), rowed up to the start, turned around and started racing.

I was going pretty well. I overtook several girls and was strongly into my race. I was sculling well; I was really fit from the hard CUWBC training and it felt good. The water was flat and beautiful. All the insecurities and problems of the past months melted away. This was where I was in control. This was why it was worth the tiredness and the effort and stress of juggling my crazy life and upsetting my supervisor. This was why it was worth getting up for those cold, 5am winter training sessions on a half frozen river and half killing myself in the gym and on the ergo.

For *this*... For *this* feeling...

And then, suddenly, the world turned blue.

Doesn't it always happen that when things are going really well, you take your eye off the ball and it all goes horribly wrong? More specifically, in my case, I'd taken my eye off the bank. I couldn't actually see the bank because of the flooding, so rowing up over it was easier than it sounds. I don't know how long I'd been sculling over a field rather than down the river, but I knew exactly the point at which my blade hooked itself behind a tree stump rather than a wall of water. It was the point at which my boat did a sideways somersault and bucked me in. It's a shock and disorientating to go within a split second from head totally in racing to head totally underwater like that. I fell in once at Bedford so quickly that it took me several seconds to work out that the reason the world had suddenly gone green was that I was looking at it through a murk of algae and goose excrement. That registered before the fact that I was no longer in my boat

This time I thrashed around blindly for a few seconds panicking that I was going to drown, before re-enacting the comedy classic of putting my feet down and standing up in water that made it just past my knees. It was rather embarrassing, but fortunately there were just miles of bleak empty Fens to the left and miles of bleak empty Fens to the right and a few girls sculling down the river (the ones I'd just overtaken), who were rather absorbed in racing and remembering not to run up over the bank. Once I'd got over the shock, I realised that I was OK and my boat was OK. I was soaking wet though and starting to get rather cold. There was about another fifteen minutes left to race and after that there were another couple of miles to row back to the landing stages and boathouse. I thought my race was over and that it was safest to get somewhere warm as quickly as possible, so I got back into my boat (still half full of water) and paddled a couple of minutes down to the marshal and aid station.

I pulled into the side and explained what had happened to an old guy who was positioned there to help. He helped me out of my boat and then spent what felt like several minutes trying to open and unfold a silver emergency blanket while I patiently started to freeze. Eventually I could bear it no longer and, as courteously as I could, took it off him, shook it out in my freezing fingers and wrapped it round me. Then I looked at him and waited for him to tell me what happens next. And he looked back at me and said nothing. "What happens next?" I said eventually. Trying to remember that this guy was a volunteer and losing my temper was not appropriate.

"Oh, I don't know."

"Well, what's the plan when someone falls in? This is the rescue station, what's the rescue?"

"I don't know."

"I'm going to freeze if I stand here any longer, I'm soaking."

"Well I suppose I could give you a lift back in my car."

"That sounds good. What about my boat?"

"Oh, I don't know. I can't take the boat." I looked at him and he looked at me and then I lost it (just a little bit honest). "Well if there wasn't any way to get me or my boat back, why have you let me stand here and freeze? I was quite warm while I was rowing and now I'm going to have to get back in anyway."

"Oh."

So I took off the silver blanket and gave it back (very gently) and jumped back in the boat (still half full of water) and set off sculling again. I was pretty angry and worked up, so before I knew it my rating was back up to race rate and I was racing again – I sort of couldn't help myself. The water in the bottom of the boat sloshed round my ankles on every stroke and I thought it would have at least been a good idea to empty that out, but it was too late now. I was warming up – hell, I was on fire. I overtook people again. I raced down the rest of the course and crossed the finish line in fine style.

I stopped just past the finish to let them know I'd fallen in, as I didn't want my time up on the results sheet as if nothing had happened. I rowed back to the boating area, got changed, de-rigged my boat and hung around for the results. Not for me actually, but for the girl I'd got a lift with. There was a fair bit of banter with people I knew as word got round I'd fallen in. There was more ribbing than sympathy but I deserved it, and now I was dry, warm and safe, I could see the funny side.

The results came out and I had 'Fell in' written next to my name, but I wasn't last. I wasn't nearly last. I'd not beaten any of the squad girls but I'd beaten several others including the girl who gave me a lift, which is why I don't mention her name here although we are still friends and she knows who she is. As we drove home, the optimist in me took over and I thought that it was probably a good thing that my boat had fallen apart in the first trial and I'd fallen in in the second. What I'd done at those two seemingly disastrous, waste of time trials was enough to prove to myself, if not to anyone else, that I was fast, that I did "have potential".

As we drove home I reasoned that if I'd had flawless races, I might have done enough to be invited to final trials and actually face selection. I would then have faced an impossible decision. I had to get the PhD but I couldn't have turned down a selection opportunity, and it was impossible to do both at this point. People say that life is short, but I have a different view. I think that if you look after yourself and with a bit of luck, then life is long and you can fit so much in. You can do everything you want but not necessarily all at the same time. You just have to work out what won't wait.

I was already twenty-four, but I was still getting fitter and faster. I still thought the rowing would wait. Getting my PhD and winning our Boat Race though – I had to do those now or not at all.

In the final run-up to the March Boat Race, it was not looking good and Oxford beat us in the Head of the River. I was terrified we would lose for the first time in nine years during my presidency and the stress of the responsibility of feeling like I had to single-handledly make us go faster (not really a great team tactic) had wrecked any progress I had made with my rowing. Ron tactfully took me aside and showed me a video clip of us racing where I was rowing just about as badly as I'd ever seen, and I was moved (with my total consent) from the influential, technical number seven seat in the stern of the boat (where I'd raced the previous year) to the place where I could do the least damage – the cruelly termed "donkey" seat in the middle at number three. This helped the crew and took some pressure off me.

Just as I was about to go away for the last few days' boat race preparation in Henley, I finally managed to convince myself enough to convince my supervisor that my PhD was fatally flawed and built on rubbish science. We didn't really talk much but he was good enough not to lay into me as I disappeared off to row for the week. I was to take some papers with me and decide what I wanted to do next. I was already one and a half years into my three years' funding.

We raced. We were down off the start. We rowed though Oxford. And won.

I felt tired and desperately relieved. That was it. I cried on the landing stage when we got out of the boat, but they weren't tears of joy. I smiled for a few hours and there is a photo of me holding the trophy aloft beaming, but I was going through the motions. I never really got much, if any pleasure from that win. The previous year I'd trained just as hard and got the same result and loved it but this year I'd taken on far too much, even for me. It was an important lesson in not putting in more than I could hope to get out.

But at least I was able to put one more ball down safely. Only one left, my PhD. And I wasn't about to drop that one.

To leave, or stay and restart my PhD? It was never really a decision. Despite what my supervisor may have thought, the two winning Blues were nothing to me without the PhD. The whole point of Oxbridge Blues is that they demonstrate that you are someone capable of achieving sporting excellence *alongside* academic excellence – to get the first without the second seemed pointless. My aspirations had dropped from getting an 'exceptional' PhD to just getting the thing and I no longer had ambitions to be a great scientist, if a scientist at all, but I knew part of me would forever feel a failure if I didn't sort this out. You finish what you've started.

And a final strong motivator was that if I got the PhD, I'd be Dr Mowbray. It wasn't that I particularly wanted the title or any title, I'm happy to be just Alison. But a surprising number of situations demand a title (usually to tick a box on a form). I already knew I didn't ever want to be Mrs Anybody; I hated the sound of Ms Mowbray and was already at twenty-four feeling too old to be a Miss. Mrs Somebody, Ms Mowbray, Miss Mowbray are all different people you picture in your head even if you've not met them/me and I didn't want to be any of them. But I thought then that Dr Mowbray was someone I could be if people wouldn't let me be just Alison.

Whatever the reason, I was finishing this PhD, no question. I'd decided I wanted to work with one of the unstudied strains of the bacteria and clone, sequence and understand a new toxin gene. My supervisor suggested a new strain and protein and I had read up on it while I was away. Now I was back and full of enthusiasm. I set up the first bacterial cultures and got going. I should really have talked to my supervisor first. I sort of knew this somewhere in the back of my mind, but the little talking we did was never pleasant and this was just easier. Denial and avoidance are rarely good long-term strategies.

I was summoned to his office and he let loose. It seemed like everything that had been saved up from all the conversations we should have been having over the past eighteen months came out. Whilst I'd known I was no favourite, it was a real shock to hear just exactly what he now thought of me and how I'd conducted myself over the past year and a half. He was furious and literally spitting with anger. I didn't really have anything to defend myself with and the conversation finished with: "You've been taking the piss. I'm done; I wash my hands of you. If you want to go and find another PhD somewhere else, I'll not get in your way. I'll write you a note saying it's just not worked out here, but that's it."

We were a large lab with many PhD students and mainly the way we all coped with the difficulties of our PhDs and the tricky relationship with our supervisor was to sit around in pairs or small groups bitching and violently agreeing with each other about how bad it all was. Usually one of us would have been reduced to tears by a latest supervisory intervention and it was kind of essential therapy to get it out and know we weren't the only one to be on the receiving end. I reached for this as my first reaction, but it was hardly a positive way forward. I didn't have a way forward. I was completely stuck.

I found help from an unexpected source. Alistair had been our cox that year and I was round at his house that Friday night for dinner, sympathy and more mutual sharing of PhD woes. He was doing a history PhD, but apparently the feeling was much the same. We'd eaten and I was lying on the living room floor reading a magazine I'd found down there. There was an article entitled something like "Machiavellian women at work". I don't remember all the details, but the important bits to me at that time were that 1.) people like to be liked and are therefore more likely to like you if you show them that you like them. 2.) Male bosses can find it more difficult to relate to women that work for them and therefore treat them differently. 3.) If the woman responds to this behaviour badly, it can set up a vicious cycle of more and more negative behaviour. 4.) In this situation the boss always 'wins' because he's in the position of power so, if you want to break the cycle, you have to actively change how you behave towards him rather than wait for him to change his behaviour towards you. 5.) This may feel like 'giving in', especially if you really feel you have been wrongly treated, but the Machiavellian principle applies. *The end justifies the means* because if you get what you want out of it at the end, then you both win. *Both win* is the only other outcome to *he wins you lose*. 6.) If you persist in trying to get *you win he loses* then you will always lose. It's his show.

This magazine article was probably the first bit of workplace psychology I'd ever come across. It made me think and it made me feel... rather embarrassed actually. I'd been so busy defending and fighting and blaming and excusing, I'd never actually stopped to think how he saw me? How much of his behaviour is a response to my behaviour? For the first time I got out of my own head and my own misery and stepped into his shoes to view me. It started to explain a lot and it wasn't pleasant viewing.

He must have expected a lot when I'd arrived with a First-class degree and a letter stating I was top of my year, but then I had singularly failed to generate any results. I balanced my busy life as always. I arrived in the lab at 9am after my morning rowing session and left at 5pm to go training, but came back several evenings a week and at weekends to make up the time and try and make my PhD work – but all he must have seen was a student who was not there at 8.30am when he arrived and left before he did. I became resentful he never helped me but he thought he was giving me a break by leaving me alone to focus on rowing in the boat race for a year.

Then, having no real idea how bad my PhD progress was, I'd rowed with my college crew for the Bumps races and signed up for a second boat race year by getting myself elected as president. He must have been furious that I'd reneged on the unspoken agreement he'd made in his head that I would row for one boat race but then stop and concentrate on my PhD. I cringed when I thought of all the boat club calls I'd taken and made within earshot of his office, completely unaware of his wrath. As I'd floundered and panicked and failed, he'd just assumed I was focused on rowing and didn't care about my PhD. As I withdrew, more and more scared of him and his response, he'd become more and more aggrieved that I didn't come to him for help.

Oh my God! It was MY FAULT! Well, at least some of it. I had given him no reason whatsoever to trust or respect me. I'd been incompetent and unreliable. I didn't like him and I showed it. I showed him no respect, either in how I worked or how I talked (or didn't talk) to him.

I was sitting around feeling hard done by waiting for him to understand me and change the way he behaved and yet HE was the successful one. The facts were: he was well-established, internationally respected and running one of the largest labs in the university. Many, many students had got their PhDs under his supervision. If I didn't get mine he'd lose no sleep over it, no one outside the lab would think anything of it (50% of PhD students don't finish), I would be forgotten within the year and he would continue his successful career and become a professor. I on the other hand had no results to show for eighteen months work, would forever consider myself a failure if I left and would have a permanent eighteen-month hole in my CV: "So I see you were at Cambridge for eighteen months and won two boat races, what else did you do there?"

The bare fact of the matter was he had no reason to change. If I didn't change then he wins, I lose. I finally, finally got it. I had to give up trying to beat him into submission and working out how to make him lose. I had to concentrate on how I win, on how we both win.

It seems so simple but I see it so often, and not just in female/male boss relationships. I saw it in sport and I see it in business. We sit around whingeing and waiting for our coaches, our bosses, our superiors (our parents even) to be better people than we are and change the way they behave because they should, because they're paid more, because that's their job. And when they don't, we let ourselves fail and feel validated in doing so.

But I thought, "Do I want to get to eighty and think my life has been rubbish, but it's not my fault – it's OK because it was my supervisor's fault for what he did to me when I was in my twenties? Or do I want to *do* something to make my life awesome?"

So I did several things. The first was to make chocolate puddle pudding, a legendary recipe acquired from Janet Mowbray (my cousin's wife), for Alistair, since he wasn't coxing us anymore and could actually eat. That didn't do much to help my relationship with my supervisor, but it definitely made us both feel better.

Next I called Mum, who is good when anyone is feeling lost and low and asks for help (it's when I'm happy and independent that she has no idea what to do with me). She suggested that I could start by apologising for those things that I had done wrong and maybe I could write a letter if I couldn't talk to him. So over the weekend I wrote a letter and apologised reservedly and ashamedly for all the things I had been guilty of in the last year and a half. This wasn't about being two-faced or compromising my values. The apology was reserved for the areas where I recognised I had been out of order and felt genuinely sorry. I slid the letter underneath his office door on Sunday evening. Monday morning I went in and walked past the open door of his office. I said "Hello" and he said "Hello" back. Neither of us mentioned the letter, but he let me get back to work so I assumed he'd read it. It hadn't done any harm and it hadn't cost me much either.

Next, I stopped living in avoidance land and plucked up the courage most days to drop by his office and respectfully update him on what I was doing and any progress or lack of progress. It was hard at first, but got easier. I also did a bit of research. I spoke to Vishna, a Malaysian student and one of my best friends in the lab. She had been reduced to tears on occasion by our supervisor, but did seem to have a better relationship than most of us. I'd noticed she didn't call him by his Christian name like the rest of us but called him Dr ______. She said this was because it was the culture in her country to give their teachers this level of respect. Respect was good. I couldn't genuinely do 'like' so I wasn't doing that, but I could genuinely do 'respect' so any tips on how to do that better were gratefully received. I switched to Dr ______ too and it actually felt better and didn't seem to do me any harm.

And finally, while I was still trying to work on the credibility thing and get some results, I could at least do reliability and I started keeping his lab hours as a minimum, making sure I was in before he was and around until he'd gone. Previously, I'd belligerently told myself that I wasn't going to be one of those people who hung around even when there was no work to do just to brown nose – but now I decided I was, if that's what it took. Being a smartarse only really works if you actually are smart.

I changed. I was trying and he could see that. He responded and got a bit nicer, just like the article said he would. We both had a nicer time and I got to continue working on my PhD. We were both winning and it didn't feel like I'd lost anything that was really important to me. I'd swallowed my pride and it wasn't choking me. I've always thought pride is a rather weird and not very helpful or healthy emotion. Dad was very proud he'd never missed a day's work; it didn't matter how sick he got at home, as long as he got to work.

I'm quite proud I managed to swallow my pride though, so I don't know where that puts me.

So, after a false start and a first and final warning, I set off again on my new PhD project with officially just one and a half years left. Rowing was relegated to an hour a day of sculling or gym work just to keep my body healthy enough to keep my brain working and I buried myself in the lab. I was re-energised, I was enthusiastic, I was working hard. I deserved success.

I was still rubbish.

Chapter 7: Survival of the fittest & cooking for cash

"Success is the ability to go from failure to failure without losing your enthusiasm"

I'd never failed before, not like this. A year, then a year and a half spent on the new PhD project. Two, then nearly three years spent on this PhD and still no results. I was desperately frightened of having to walk away with nothing – and actually just pretty desperate. The repetitive nature of the failure was wearing and soul-destroying.

I'd sit in the lab computer room, late into the night, early morning sometimes, long after everyone else had gone home, desperately looking through my sequences… and there'd be nothing. I'd get on my bike and cycle home and I'd be at the bottom, telling myself, "No really, that's it. I've done everything I can. I can't waste another week… another day of my life doing this. I'm going to quit tomorrow." I'd get home, crawl into bed and literally cry myself to sleep that I'd just wasted so much of my life. And then I'd wake up in the morning and before I'd even opened my eyes I'd be thinking, "You know what I could try is…". And I'd jump back on my bike and cycle back in and set it all up again… and again… and again…

But in the midst of it all, something started to happen. I was in new territory and it was testing me in new ways, but I found a way to cope that was almost pleasurable. I set up my own routine involving long lab hours, every evening late into the night and pretty much every weekend, but always getting out at some point to do some exercise (after my supervisor had left for the day). I'd do ergo or weights on my own in Lady Margaret Boat House (the college CUWBC trained out of) and as the evenings began to lengthen, I went sculling again. I alternated ninety-minute ergo sessions one night with forty-minutes sculling and a forty-minute weights circuit (that I designed myself) the next. I took one day off a week and then started again. I put at least some of the weights up every time I did the circuit and got a personal best, even if it was only by a few metres on most ergos. I recorded and charted the exercise carefully and colourfully in a little notebook. Getting fitter and moving on in at least some area of my life seemed to help me bear the stalemate in the other. The explosive weights circuit I designed made me strong in a way I'd never been before and have never replicated since, despite years of squad training. It was the best and most efficient training I ever did.

I wasn't sculling very much because it's a time consuming way to exercise, but when I did it was going well and again I was efficient with my time. I was still taking advice from Shane. He told me that the important thing about sculling was not to stop until you got to the end of the river, not for anything. In a crew boat you don't stop because you don't want to annoy the others, but when you are on your own you'll tend to stop for the smallest thing. And stopping leads to more stopping. I sculled when I could, didn't stop and concentrated hard because I didn't have long and every stroke was precious. I was still concentrating on keeping my arms relaxed and picking up the water with the back of my shoulders, then all at once, pretty much within one stroke, I felt the tension go out of the back of my shoulder blades and I was able to keep my arms, shoulders and upper spine totally relaxed and pick up the water with those large wing-shaped Lat muscles that get so developed in swimmers and rowers that we can never wear normal clothes. It was a revelation. I thought, "Oh my God. This is it. This is what it's supposed to feel like."

It felt like a beautiful way to scull. I was starting to move the boat faster with what felt like less effort. But what was interesting was that when I got it right and picked up the water in this new relaxed way, my heart rate went up. I'd made it easier to work harder and I could keep going at this new intensity for longer without feeling physiological discomfort. It wasn't until I stopped the boat to turn round at the ends that the extra effort caught up with me and I'd gasp for air.

It's a weird thing about rowing but just because you look like you are working hard and even feel like you are working hard, it doesn't mean you are. In order to row harder you can't just go at it harder, you actually have to pick up a more solid wall of water on the end of your blade and that can be a surprisingly difficult thing to do. You have to connect and time your blade entry and pressure with the movement of the boat and water, so you lock the blades into a fixed point in the water and lever the boat past. It's a tricky thing. It's a beautiful thing.

This was an Olympic year and the 1996 Atlanta Olympics loomed. They seemed a little less distant now as I knew girls on the squad facing selection, but it still didn't seem a realistic goal. I didn't really know what I was training for. I knew with my PhD work I couldn't actually DO anything with it, but exercise was part of my life now and it kept me as sane as cooking.

I went to the first set of winter trials in Peterborough (November 1995). The squad girls didn't have to go to the first trial because of its proximity to the World Championships, but Guin Batten raced anyway for a bit of a run out and set off with the men. This time my boat didn't fall apart and I didn't fall in. I came second to Guin, which effectively meant I'd beaten every female sculler in the country who wasn't already in the squad. Everyone was quite surprised about that, including me. I found the results sheet in an old pile quite recently and see that I beat several well-known names that would crop up again and again over the next few years: Lindsey, Raine, Springman, Grose, Gough, Woolf, and Laverick – some by quite a long way. I vaguely thought I'd be spotted – that someone might call me up and offer me some more coaching or something – but I went home and didn't hear from anyone and nothing happened. I sort of wondered what the trial had been for then, but just got back on with my PhD and training.

I heard about a trial for a Four that Ron was putting together to race internationally that summer. He already had three girls and was looking for a fourth. He thought he had found her, but I made him give me a trial. The trial involved paddling round the lake at Nottingham a couple of times with each of us to see which felt better. I thought my boat felt really good and I wasn't the only one. When Ron announced that the other girl (6 foot 1 and big ergo) was selected, the rest of the girls in the crew said they thought it felt better with me and actually argued my case. But Ron delivered the line I was getting used to hearing: "Well that might be the case now, but I think Helen has more potential."

But actually Ron was the only coach keeping even half an eye on me and in April 1996 he organised for me to go out to my first International Club Regatta in Ghent with Marlow Rowing Club. I took a rare weekend out of the lab and won the Single at Ghent, which again I remember being totally surprised by.

By early summer I hadn't raced for a while and was missing it. I needed something to set against the relentless, repetitive failure of my PhD experiments, so I decided to go and race Women's Henley in my single for the first time. I put my entry in and the draw came back. I was drawn against Sarah Springman in the first round.

A World Champion tri-athlete, Cambridge Don and general Wonderwoman, Sarah was trying to convert her triathlon fitness (a non-

Olympic sport at the time) into rowing prowess in the hope of going to the Olympics, even though she was already rubbing up against forty. Sarah had come to rowing through the '*Daily Mail* Girl' route. The *Daily Mail* had got together with an ex-squad coach frustrated with the lack of progress in women's rowing. Together they ran a campaign to recruit tall girls with a good pedigree from other sports to boost the talent pool. These girls would row and train together in London, so most of them had to give up their jobs and the *Daily Mail* gave them grants to facilitate this. It was this in particular that really upset existing female rowers. The current squad girls didn't get grants and had to balance work with training to live. They were passionate about rowing, had put their lives and careers on hold for years to follow their dreams and were desperately trying to improve and get to a level where they would be Olympic medal contenders, but it was pretty hard without funding. To see that money go to other girls who'd just stepped in a boat, and to have it written in the national press that this was because there was no existing talent in British Women's rowing, was rather a slap in the face. I'd been rowing at Liverpool at the time and I remember even Jo and I feeling rather slapped. We were tall, we were keen, we were fit – why were we being excluded from a scheme to develop women rowers by the fact that we already rowed?

When the *Daily Mail* girls didn't immediately trounce the squad girls at the first set of trials, the support and funding quietly slipped away. But Sarah Springman was self-driven enough to keep the dream alive a little longer and she hounded coaches and wrote her own training programmes. She never did make it to an Olympics (although she got far enough to silence most cynics), but at the point when I was drawn against her in the first round at Henley she was super fit, sculling well and going fast. I knew this because Sarah told me herself. This was pretty basic sports psychology for an international athlete like Sarah, but it was more than I knew – so, heading off to race her at Women's Henley I never doubted the truth of this and that she would whip me. I was so sure of this that I only took one set of rowing kit and two pretty dresses, so that when she knocked me out in the first round I'd be able to hang around with my friends for the rest of the weekend and have a long overdue break.

I left the lab on Friday evening, slung my single onto the roof of my car and headed to Henley. On Saturday morning I put my one Lycra on and went out to race Sarah. I won. I won my next round as well, washed and almost dried my all-in-one that night at my friend's house, then won my semi-final on Sunday in damp Lycra. The ex-Liverpool and Bedford friends I did have time to catch up with in my much-reduced social schedule all said (for the first and last time), "Oh my God, you look ripped!" Irish Shane told me I had a wild, mean look in my eye. I should have bottled that training regime. I lined up in the final against an American girl who'd been over for a few weeks winning at pretty high-class local regattas. Someone told me she'd been saying she thought she had it all sown up. I wasn't telling anyone anything. I didn't know anything. I just went out to race.

Racing at Henley is a unique experience. The start is on a narrow bit of river between an island and the bank and even in a single it feels like you are way too close together for safety. You can literally look over and see the whites of your opponent's eyes – so you try not to do that. If you manage to get off the start safely and not hit the floating wooden booms, the island or your opponent in the first 300m, then there are floating wooden booms all the way down the river marking the course. These booms signal disaster if you get too close and hit them, and trouble if you get too far away and stray into your opponent's path. Racing at Henley feels different. At Henley, more than anywhere else, it's a dual and it's personal.

The only part of the race I remember is being side by side with the American passing Upper Thames (about 400m to go). Side by side with your opposition it's always temping to think 'pull harder', 'work harder', but armed with my new more fluid technique, I thought 'relax harder' – and stroke by stroke I slid past. (What I didn't learn about life from playing the French horn, I learnt from working out how to move a boat through water). Topped off with a Mowbray big finish, I won the single sculls final at Women's Henley, which was a pretty big deal at the time. No matter what happened in the lab that week, I couldn't keep the smile off my face.

And you know it's not until now, as I sit down and record all these results together, that I realise I must actually have been pretty good. At the time I was genuinely surprised by each and every win.

Whilst in rowing I was learning the benefit of 'relax harder', I was having much more trouble outside of the boat. I was having trouble relaxing, sleeping, and sometimes even breathing. For all my Zen-like words now, back then what I mostly felt was just one small step away from blind panic. I was now nearly three years into my PhD and I still had no results.

In too deep to walk away, I kept cycling home in despair and cycling back in the morning to give it one last shot. I did get one thing sorted that year

On my way to winning the Single at Women's Henley 1996

though. PhD theses are generally big, boring books but there is one interesting page. Most people start their thesis like a novel with a quote that they feel sums up their PhD experience. The internet was just coming online and I spent rather more time than I should surfing through quotes to find the perfect one. I had the quote before I had any results. It was a tough decision, but I had it narrowed down to a final three.

No matter what happened in the lab that week, I couldn't keep that smile off my face

"People say I'm involved in tennis. I'm not involved I'm committed. You know the difference between involved and committed? It's like eggs and bacon. A chicken is involved in eggs and bacon. The pig… the pig is committed." Martina Navratilova.

I felt more pig than chicken and I liked it, but it wasn't quite right.

Second was an anonymous quote that goes: *"A clay pot will always remain a clay pot while it sits in the sun. It has to go through the white heat of the furnace to become porcelain."* That one I still love and use as a mantra for myself and friends when stuck in or facing yet another furnace. I've written it on more "You'll be OK, hang on in there" cards than anything else. I wasn't sure this experience was turning me into porcelain, but I was sure I was undergoing some sort of chemical change and would never be the same again.

But the clear winner was a Winston Churchill quote that simply says; *"Success is the ability to go from failure to failure without losing your enthusiasm."*

By this point, I really thought I knew what that meant. For me, just getting up every day and being able to go from failure to failure without losing my enthusiasm was something to be proud of. I had never been tested like this before and I hadn't known I would be able to keep going. I didn't know where the energy and enthusiasm came from each morning, but it kept coming and I was starting to rely on it. My nightly despair was now tempered by the knowledge of my newfound strength and woven in with the voice of doom was a new voice that said: "Quit your moaning girl, you know you'll be alright in the morning." It still felt just as bad when I looked at those empty sequences after all those weeks, but somehow I was just able to bear it better. Even if I never got this damned PhD (and the thought of that made me not able to breathe so I didn't think like that very often), learning that no matter how bad things got I would always be able to get up in the morning and I would always be able to go do it again was something I would now always have with me. I thought that, if nothing else, then knowing this about myself was my success.

I came to understand that sometimes we have to look outside the obvious to find success. You do get back what you put into life, but it's not a bank account. You don't always get to take it out when you want or in the currency you expected. Sometimes we need to keep our eyes open to notice where the rewards are coming from and they can come much, much later than we expected. It's a weird thing success anyway. I notice how many people, particularly sports people, achieve more than most peoples' wildest dreams and are still miserable – still think of themselves as failures. Why do that when it's just a flick of a switch in your head? Decide to think of it/yourself as a failure and be miserable, or decide to think of it/yourself as a success and be happy. If you have honestly put everything you can into something, then why not redefine success and allow yourself to be happy? Who else's decision is it anyway? Let those who would point the finger get up off their sofas and walk.

It's stretching it to say that I was happy at this point. But taking just that small morsel of pride and success out of what was otherwise the unmitigated disaster that was my PhD and focusing on every tiny thing I could that was positive, both in and out of the boat, got me to a night nearly three years on. I was sat in front of the computer yet again, staring at the strings of DNA sequence data. I remember exactly what night it was, because even though it was relatively early in PhD land (just about 9pm), I was on my own in the lab because everyone else was down the pub watching a crucial England v Holland football World Cup match (that guys of a certain age still remember). I stared at the DNA sequence data and there it was, a bacterial toxin gene sequence, and then just downstream from that *a second* toxin gene sequence. I'd done it. I'd cloned not one but two genes (bargain 2 for 1 offer on genes that day). I had my first result. I took the night off and went down the pub to join my lab mates. They cheered when I told them and bought me a pint or two and my cycle ride home that night was rather more cheerful (and wobbly).

And in that one moment, I moved from the 50% of people who don't finish their PhDs to the 50% of people who do. Winston Churchill would say: *"The only time you fail is the last time it doesn't work and you don't go back and do it again."* He did, in fact, say that. Dr Alison Mowbray, who is not quite as articulate and always needs more words, would say: *"No matter how bad it looks, no matter how far down you are, you should never give up, because sometimes crazy things happen and if you are in there close enough, often enough, you might eventually get lucky. And the funny thing about luck is that it rarely, if ever, happens to people at the back who can't be bothered."*

The summer of 1996 felt very different. I finally had something to show for my time in Cambridge and was able to make relatively quick progress for a while. Now I had some hard results to prove I was working, I took a bit of freedom back. I switched time zones for a couple of weeks and watched more Olympics than ever; hours and hours through the night of absolutely any sport that was on, before grabbing a few hours sleep and heading into the lab later than I'd dared for years. It's weird really, I rarely watch sport on TV – I'd rather be out doing than watching – but there is just something magnetic about the Olympics and I cannot look away. When I watched the women's rowing now, I was watching girls on TV that I'd not only raced but actually knew to talk to. That summer I'd trained a few weekends in Henley with a sculling group Ron had pulled together. Some of the squad girls had been there at the same time and I'd sat and chatted over breakfast with Miriam Batten, Guin Batten and Ali Gill, who before had been just distant legends. But it was a disappointing Olympics for all of them I think, except perhaps Guin whose place in an Olympic final was a first for a GB women's single – even if she did then come sixth. Some of these girls had been making this their life for many years and still there were no medals. No British Women's Olympic Rowing medal – ever.

Meanwhile I became totally immersed in my PhD and, apart from watching a few hours of Olympics on TV, my head barely left it. I stayed on for a fourth year at Cambridge to analyse and categorise the genes and express the proteins and determine their toxicity to different strains of mosquito larvae. When my grant ran out I made extra cash by baking cakes to sell through the biochemistry coffee bar and ran aerobics sessions on Sunday afternoons in the Gonville and Caius common room.

At the time I was lodging with a very house-proud landlady who would, quite rightly, have been rather shocked at my attempts to run a business out of her kitchen had she known. I didn't have a car, so once a week I'd leave the lab earlier than usual, cycle to the local supermarket, load up on ingredients, pack what I could into a rucksack and hang the rest in carrier bags from my handlebars to cycle the precarious mile or so home. Fortunately my landlady worked in the evenings so I'd have a couple of hours to bake unnoticed – a whirling dervish in the kitchen, two or sometimes three things on the go at once, always keeping the place as tidy as possible in case she came home unexpectedly (which she never did). I mainly made the flapjack recipe you already have, plus chocolate biscuit cake and a few other favourite tray bakes (you will obviously have to buy my next book now to get these recipes). When all the trays were full I'd carry them upstairs to my room to cool, and then go back and clean the kitchen until all signs of activity were removed. I'd be in bed asleep by the time she came back, with only the baking smells as evidence.

In the morning I'd fill old biscuit tins with the cakes, pack them into a holdall, strap it to the pannier rack on the back of my bike and cycle in to deliver them. As well as providing cash, baking probably helped preserve my sanity during that time (cooking can keep a person who works hard, sane). It has also had the lasting legacy of turning me into both a very tidy and very efficient cook.

I had to keep applying to the examining board for extensions to my lab time and despite my progress I was now desperately racing the clock. I still had days and weeks of despair where I thought I'd never get enough together to pass a PhD, but I kept going and started to write up later that year. I finally got to join in the "Which font?", "which point size?", "which line spacing?" conversations that dominate this stage of a PhD student's career (Palatino linotype, 12, 1½ – just in case you are at that stage yourself, in which case you will be interested) and I discovered a new rhythm and contentment within all the desperation and weariness that somehow, weirdly, I remember with affection.

I discovered (maybe remembered) that I loved writing. I particularly enjoyed writing sections comparing large numbers of toxin genes from different bacteria. I could see how my genes had evolved from insertions, deletions and swopping around parts of other toxin genes and I wrote the story of their evolution. I reconnected with what had first excited me about science all those years ago.

My new routine was to arrive just in time for morning coffee break and potter around all day running or rerunning the last few experiments. In between I'd re-read what I'd written the night before and tinker with it, trying to simplify the language and cut unnecessary words and sentences that had seemed so vital when first written. I couldn't really write anything new at that point, there were too many people around and too many distractions, but I was slowly getting myself into the right state. Around 5pm I'd leave the lab to do some exercise. Occasionally I went for a quick scull, but mostly I was running again as the most efficient use of my time. I'd come back to the lab, climb out of the second floor window and sit outside on a balcony (that wasn't really a balcony) and eat my dinner feeling unusually tranquil after my calm day and exercise. And I can still recall now the feeling as my anticipation rose and my focus narrowed into 'race head'. Then I'd go back into the now quiet lab with usually just one or two students or post-docs pottering around, start up the computer (which used to take ages in those days) and start to write.

It would take me a while to get going, but around 9pm something would start to kick in and the words began to flow. It didn't work if I started at 9pm; it took the whole day to work up to it. The longer I worked, the better it got;

so I'd work as late as I could possibly stay awake. 80% dark chocolate was often the caffeine fix that got me through to two or three in the morning. I'd then cycle home, get to bed and for the first and last time in my life not set an alarm. I'd go to sleep and wake up when I'd had enough, which was usually just in time to get back to the lab in time for morning coffee break. And then I'd begin again. The single best thing about my whole PhD was having that period in my life when I decided my own timetable, found my own rhythm and didn't set an alarm.

And it's funny but after all this time, when I think back to those four PhD years, I can remember the panic, the misery, the stress and the despair; I can remember that I did feel those things and I can still tell the stories, but I don't feel them anymore. Now what I feel is the sense of peace and tranquillity that came with the freedom of the last few months. My strongest mental image is of sitting on the lab balcony (that wasn't really a balcony) eating dinner, enjoying the remains of the sun and looking forward to the evening's work. So I wouldn't change any part of those four years because then I wouldn't have that. It seems to me that if we cherish the good bits of our life, then we can't regret the bad or difficult bits. Every choice we make and every act of luck or fate or whatever you want to call it takes us down a different path to a different outcome. And so the only way to get to those moments you cherish and wouldn't lose for the world is exactly the way you got there.

Don't get me wrong, this was not the exceptional PhD I had first aspired to. I didn't change the world, except perhaps my own. I didn't have very much new data, but I think I did some good stuff with what I had. I presented a poster of my research at a conference in Canada and people (including those whose papers I'd read and quoted in my thesis) came to talk to me and were interested in what I was doing. They asked if I was publishing any of it. This was a big shock. I'd completely given up on the hope that this PhD might have any value past just completing a personal battle. I'd not at any point had anything from my supervisor that mirrored those conversations and he'd never talked to me about publishing papers. Our relationship had not really improved beyond bearable. He left me alone as long as I looked like I was working and kept my lab bench tidy, and left me aggrieved, petty little notes when I did not. Those notes used to really hurt when I'd worked until the early hours, failed again and somehow managed to find enough enthusiasm to drag myself back. But you can't explain to a note that you'd forgotten to tidy up because you were so distraught at another three weeks' work wasted or you'd been engrossed in the magic of writing until two in the morning.

Once I'd cloned the genes he understandably defrosted a little and as I started to hand in chapters for proofreading and editing, he'd hand them back with a nod and a few comments. Although he never really said explicitly, there was a new tone of pleasant surprise and maybe even just a tiny little bit of respect. Here, finally, was something reminiscent of what he'd expected from the First-class honours student he'd interviewed four years previously. But he never went so far as to suggest my PhD might actually be any good. And I never did publish.

I existed in a bubble most of the time. Apart from three days at Christmas and a day off to go down to London to run the marathon in a time of four hours and a minute (I was aiming for sub-4 hours and was on track all the way round, except that I forgot about the 365 yards bit of the 26.2 miles – this goal-setting thing is quite incredible when you think about it), I was in the lab at some point everyday all year. I stopped competitive rowing totally and didn't go to trials or any races. Once a week or so I'd skip out of the lab in the evening to meet Morag, a Blue Boat friend, for a quick dinner in the pub at the end of the road. She was at a similar stage in her Geology PhD and every so often one of us would phone the other in their lab and talk them into taking a half-hour dinner break to save our sanity. We'd meet and eat and talk like crazy for an hour (never just half), before going back to our respective lab bubbles.

I was single at this point so there was no boyfriend to take up my time, although I was now communicating occasionally again with Liverpool blond boy via letter and phone. We'd both been out with other people in the interim and I think learnt a little bit about how this was supposed to work, so were wearily testing it out (couldn't live with him; couldn't live without him).

I called Mum once a week from the lab phone in the evenings and that was about the only contact with my family unless Mum called to offload Dad stuff. The situation had not improved. Apparently he was now going to Alcoholics Anonymous meetings. This could have looked like progress, but I think that was the point. It looked like progress without requiring him to actually stop drinking. Every so often it would get very bad and Mum would threaten to leave and he would have to do something that made it look like he was doing something about it. It was a game they played out once in a while that prevented either of them from actually having to change. At one point, Mum took a blood sample from him while he was "ill" to send in for analysis to supposedly find out once and for all if it was due to alcohol. The first I heard about it was when Mum called me in a state because the test had

With my mum (and I assume Dad is taking the photo) in Cambridge. I'm looking a lot more competent at this form of water transport than I actually ever was.

come back negative for alcohol and Dad was gloating and crowing like it was all alright then, we'd all been making it all up. Mum was confused. She had never really believed he drank but now she didn't like what the results of this test meant any better. It confused me for a while too until I probed further and Mum told me (not thinking anything of it) that after taking the blood, she'd then given the sample back to Dad to take to the hospital for analysis along with the patients' blood tests. He also picked up the results. "There was no way that was the same sample Mum."

"Oh, he wouldn't do that Alison." It was a game with interesting variations.

I couldn't keep going like this for very long, I'd run out of money and anyway my lab extensions had finally run out. That summer, after four years, it really was time to move on. I still had a fair bit of writing up to do, but I could do that anywhere. I'd done all the experiments I needed and got all the data. It would be enough.

And now – knowing I would get this thing, this damned PhD, now, as I wrote that Winston Churchill quote: *"Success is the ability to go from failure to failure without losing your enthusiasm"* onto the front fly page, now it meant something different to me. It meant: if you know what you are doing is right, if you have the courage to go from failure to failure without losing your enthusiasm, then eventually… success… happens. It was like a magic formula.

I was twenty-six by this point and you might be wondering when the Olympic rowing story's going to start. Most athletes have either done it or not by this stage and are hanging up their trainers and going out to look for a proper job. I'd not even started. I'd not been spotted, I had no funding, I had no coach, I didn't even have a real Olympic ambition beyond a vague fantasy, I'd not rowed competitively for over a year. In fact I'd barely had my boat out for months and exercise had dwindled to a sneaky thirty-minute run most, but not every, day.

So just in case you are getting impatient and wondering when the Olympic rowing story's going to start, I would like to point out – it has already started. The skills I'd learnt in that lab would be every bit as useful to me in what happens next as what I'd learnt on the water and in the gym. I'd left behind my ambition of being a great scientist – the PhD had shown me it wasn't for me. But for all its seeming pointlessness and misery, it is a part of me and my life I would never want to replace. It was worth its weight in, well, silver.

Chapter 8: The Thames

"Momentum gives you balance"

So started the busiest and craziest phase of my life to date. But through it all, I felt like I'd been released. Towards the end of the fourth year of my PhD I'd decided that although research science wasn't for me, science still was and I would be a teacher. They say teaching is a vocation and I'd always felt its pull. When I'd been bored in lessons at school, I'd sit there working out how I could teach it better. I remember also wanting to be, amongst other things, a doctor, a vet, an engineer, a *Blue Peter* presenter and, after watching a television documentary about submarines, the first ever female naval submariner. But I thought that teaching was something I could do and would enjoy and therefore it would be my back-up plan, my safety net for all the other crazy schemes I had for how I could live my life. And that's exactly what it's been. I still think I would have made an excellent *Blue Peter* presenter though (my friends think I am).

The summer of 1997 was an astonishing time for British Women's rowing. The universal disappointment of pretty much the whole British Olympic Team at Atlanta 1996 (barring Steve and Matt) signalled a change in British sport. It was obvious that the days of the plucky amateur were over. As a nation if we wanted our athletes to fund themselves and hold down jobs, we could not also expect them to bring home medals. If we wanted to be able to watch the Olympics with pride and see the Union Jack go up that flagpole, we were going to have to pay for coaches and equipment and training camps and give the athletes a grant to live off so they could train full-time and still afford to eat. As if by magic the National Lottery started up that year and Bingo! (or Lotto or whatever you call it), there was the source of money to do it.

For rowing this meant that for the first time athletes coming back from the Atlanta Olympics had grants and didn't have to work; it also meant British International Rowing could afford a full-time professional coach for the women's squad – enter Mike Spraklen. In the 1980's Mike had coached Steve Redgrave to the first two of his Gold medals before moving to Canada as head coach. There he took the Men's Eight to Gold at the 1992 Olympics and moved on to coach the US women. When their Eight came a disappointing fifth in Atlanta, Mike accepted a contract to come home as GB Women's Head Coach. At that point the squad was down to just three or four women who had not retired after their own disappointments in Atlanta. So Mike set up a training base out of the Longridge Scout camp just downstream of Marlow and welcomed any women who were prepared to come down and train full-time with him. They wouldn't be funded until they started to produce some results but still they gave up their jobs, rented out their homes, kissed their partners goodbye, suspended their lives and came.

One year on and it seemed to be working. Miriam Batten (already veteran of two Olympics) and Gillian Lindsey took Silver in their Double in the Aiguebelette World Championships, just over a second behind the legendary Germans. What struck me most about that race, and still does whenever I see it, is the fact that coming into the finish they were in Bronze medal place, well clear of the rest of the field. After not medalling all season and with British women having not medalled at all for years, even a Bronze would have been a celebrated result and lesser women would surely have taken it. But Miriam and Gillian kept pushing and took Silver from the Romanians by just 0.13 seconds.

Then on the Sunday, a totally new Eight containing no returning Olympians came through to take third place and a Bronze medal. What's more, half of this eight (Alex Beaver, Lisa Eyre, Libbie Henshilwood and Sue Walker) had already got a Gold in the Four the day before. The Four is not an Olympic class boat and therefore not as competitive an event, which is perhaps why I mentioned it after the Eight and with slightly less fanfare, but still… Britain now had four female World Champion rowers. This was a big deal. The whole 1997 World Championships was a very big deal for British Women's rowing.

I'd rowed with Alex and Sue in the Commonwealth Eight. Francesca Zino, (also from the Eight) had been in Blondie, my second Blue Boat year. I'd even, although I'd forgotten it by this point, beaten Silver medallist Gillian in November trials just a year and a half previously. And so I was able to look across at my friends and think: "I used to do that; I used to train with them and race against them and sometimes, in my single, I used to beat them." And you know what it's like when you look at your mates doing something you used to do? I just thought "Wouldn't it be a shame it I was capable of doing that and I never found out."

I was already twenty-six so I thought it wouldn't wait much longer. I decided I'd give it one last big shot (OK, really my first big shot) and see what happened. Thames Rowing Club seemed to be the place to be. More of the squad girls had Thames next to their names than any other club, Thames usually won the big Women's Eights Head of the River race and it was well known that this was one of the few clubs in the country where the number and quality of the female membership outranked the guys (Bedford Rowing Club being possibly one of the only others at the time). Also Jo was rowing there in a training group with squad ambitions of her own, so it all made sense.

I applied to Roehampton Institute so I could move down to London to restart my rowing. When I got there I found that Roehampton Institute is actually an historic and much respected teacher-training college, but that was really a coincidence. When I went for my interview, the last question they asked was: "So Alison, we have to ask this for marketing purposes. Why did you apply to Roehampton in particular?"

"Well, I want to row out of Thames Rowing club at Putney and you're the closest." If I'd learnt anything from my PhD, it was that it was best to be clear upfront. The guy permitted himself a little smile and then, straight-faced, turned to his colleague, "I don't believe we are using that in our marketing material, perhaps we ought to make a note." They took me anyway. My PhD was useful for something.

I hired a transit van, into which, at twenty-six, with the exception of my sculling boat, I could still pack my entire life (most of it in very large plants) and moved down to Putney. Working until the last minute and with my PhD still incomplete, I threw my lab books, photographic film and floppy discs into a box, swiped the lab goldfish (Bop and Comet) that I'd bought to fill a huge flat-bottomed, long-necked flask that belonged to another era of biochemistry, and escaped under cover of darkness. With nowhere to live in Putney, I stashed my stuff and my fish at Jo's and slept for a month on the living room floor (and only once in the bed) of one of those first blond Liverpool Boat Club boys (before THE blond boat club boy) while I looked for a room to rent, started my course, joined Thames Rowing Club and got back into serious training. That first night I drove straight down to join a party at Tideway Sculler's Boat Club and already I felt transformed.

With Jo already rowing at Thames, it was easy to get to know the training group down there and they were a good group of girls. In about week two I cemented the friendships with a large pan of my special recipe sausage casserole (as is my way), and I was in. College was great too. I was back in the formal education environment I loved and even joined the college choir.

And I started training properly again. It was September and the final selection trials for the GB team would be in April. I had seven months. My first 2K ergo test told me how much ground I had to make up. For any trial (even club trials), before anyone will let you get in a boat and race, you'll usually face a 2K rowing ergometer test – the coaches' favourite, as they can just line everyone up and get easy hard data. Obviously the quicker you complete the distance, the more potential you are thought to show for moving an actual boat. There is definitely some truth in that and the GB squad all have quick ergos times, but ergo rankings are rarely the same as on the water rankings.

It is commonly said that "Ergos don't float". You don't have to move your own body weight on an ergo, so heavier people are advantaged while the extra weight may be a disadvantage in a boat. Also "Ergos don't float" because if you are fit and can just pull very hard on an ergo handle, you will get a good score. Rugby players can get good ergo scores, but it doesn't mean they can move a boat any more than my ability to beat them on the water means I can play rugby. Moving a boat through water is a highly technical thing. Pulling on an ergo handle – not so much. But this lack of technicality means that in an ergo test there is nothing but pulling hard and the score; no part of your brain or body function that you need to preserve to keep yourself afloat and no part of your brain that you can distract with thinking about the technicality of the stroke or even with racing the opposition. Because there is nothing else except your own score and pulling destructively hard every single stroke. I rowed because I loved the feeling of moving a boat through water and it was worth the pain – in fact sometimes I hardly felt the pain, because the harder I worked the faster the boat moved and the more wonderful it felt. But on an ergo there is no wonderful feeling; there is just work and pain. Lactic acid legs seizing up and screaming at you pain, lungs gasping for dry air burning pain, can't get air in quick enough scrape the lining off your trachea pain (I couldn't sing for a week after an ergo test because my throat was so raw), psychological pain from trying to override the physical pain. Pain.

The cut-off for even attending the trials was 2K in seven minutes ten seconds, a score I'd been just about capable of while at my peak in Cambridge. Even that is not a great score and at that point it was generally accepted that you needed to be at least sub-7 minutes to have any chance. In my ergo test that first week I just about managed to scrape under a very painful 7.30.

I knew that the squad girls up in Marlow under Mike Spraklen were training two or three times a day, about sixteen sessions a week. With my teaching course it was going to be hard to match that, but I had to get as close as I could. My Cambridge rowing had taught me how important it was to go out on the water every day so I made a pact with myself that my priority was to get out on the water every day, no matter what. I'd get up at 5am about three mornings a week to go sculling before college, or in the evening I could usually fit in an extra session before the other girls arrived from their full-time jobs in and around London. We then did the club session together. That way, with the four big rowing sessions at the weekend (two on Saturday morning and two on Sunday), I managed about twelve sessions a week around my college schedule.

Mostly it was a treat to row on that great sweep of the Thames between Kew and Putney commonly known as The Tideway, and after four years of rowing on the narrow, windy, overcrowded little ditch that is the Cam, I loved it. It takes a bit of getting used to though. You have to be in different places on the river at different times of the tide and there are long sweeping bends with specific places to cross. These are all things that you have to learn and remember, as there aren't any signs telling you what to do like on the road. You have to keep an eye on the water and the other crews, and there's quite a lot of shouting to each other about whether the tide's turned or not and who is in the right place. In addition, there are the big commercial and pleasure boats to avoid which is tricky as we go backwards, remember? And in the winter at 5.30 in the morning and 5.30 at night it's dark, so we'd strap red and white bike lights to our boats to give other rowing boats and bigger craft half a hope of seeing us. You have to keep your eyes open and your brain sharp and are making decisions on a minute-by-minute and sometimes stroke-by-stroke basis about where you need to be to get the best water and the best of the stream. Some people hate it and avoid rowing on the Tideway as much as possible, but to those of us that grow to love it, it feels quite something to gain an understanding of that river. This, after all, is what rowing was meant for; it's mastery of the ancient Waterman's craft and it gets into your blood.

On a good day The Tideway is a joy – a long, wide, glass-like sweep of water on which to ply your trade for mile after uninterrupted mile. But the Tideway is like a little bit of trapped sea and on a windy day it can feel nearly as ferocious. The open expanse of water means the waves roll into each other and build in size. When the wind blows it gets really choppy, but when the wind blows against the stream, the water boils with waves and white caps. These are the days when it's really, really tempting to think that you'd be better off in the gym. But I'd made a pact with myself that my priority was to get out on the water every day no matter what, so I used my Bedford one-step-at-a-time technique and refused to write the session off by looking out of the boat club door. If I could carry my boat down the slip to the water then that was a start. Occasionally it was too windy to even do this safely so I would ask for help. Then, if I could actually hold the boat down onto the water long enough to get in it, that was the next step. Then it was just a case of building up the slide from a relatively stable 'backstops' position (arms and body only) to see how far I could get. Even if I could only stay out for ten-fifteen minutes and didn't get beyond ¼ slide (or on a couple of occasions fell in), I'd kept my pact. The next time it was rough, it would be easier both technically and mentally, and how easy would it feel when the water was like glass? I learnt several points that helped me to scull/row in rough water – and still use them both on and off the water.

1. Remember to enjoy it and keep your sense of humour. If you can think of it as a crazy adventure rather than scary trial, that definitely helps. If you feel yourself start to tense up and resent it, remember to smile. The process of smiling seems to trick your body and boat into thinking that they are enjoying themselves and they behave better.
2. Stay relaxed. Reference to point 1 helps here.
3. Think of yourself as floating over the top of the water/waves rather than ploughing through the middle. This is why, contrary to what you might expect, I reckon it's actually easier to row a single in rough conditions than a larger heavier boat.
4. Accept that a fair proportion of the strokes are going to be rubbish because you are doing something very hard. If you row a rubbish stroke, accept it and forget about it and just think about how to make the next one good. This is particularly important when racing. Then, for every rubbish stroke you do, remember that your opposition will be finding it just as tough and rowing at least as many rubbish strokes. The less time you spend worrying about the rubbish stroke you've just done, the more time you've got to think about how to make the next stroke not rubbish.
5. Crucially what I learnt was that no matter what happens, no matter how

much or how little water you pick up on the end of each blade, no matter if you get one or even both sculls stuck in the water, knocked by a wave or blown by the wind; never stop, not for a second, not for a fraction of a second. No matter what the wind and water does to me above the waist, I can and do keep my legs pushing down in the same rhythm. I think of my legs as a metronome. My upper body is relaxed and goes with the flow and rolls with the punches, but my legs are fighting, battling to keep me pushing over that water. Control what you can control and don't worry about the rest. Think about that tightrope. If it wobbles and you stop, you know you're going to fall off so you run to the other side. Momentum gives you balance so the important thing in rough water is always to keep moving.

What I didn't learn about life from playing the French horn, I learnt from working out how to scull in rough water.

After a few weeks I started my teaching practice and added into my day an eight-mile cycle across Richmond Park to my teacher-training school and eight miles back at the end of the day. And it seems strange, but despite putting myself through all of this, I still didn't have Olympic ambitions. I remember one of my friends saying: "You're 26 and training again, what for?" and I answered: "I just think I might be able to get into the Four (a non-Olympic class boat) and go to the World Championships once. If I could row for Great Britain once I think that would be as far as I can take my rowing and then I can retire." My mantra was still "As long as I'm still enjoying it and I'm still getting better, I'll keep going."

I didn't have any idea how life was going to work if I actually did make selection that year. My teacher training was full-time until July and would not be possible alongside full-time training with the squad in Marlow and international racing if I made selection in April. I decided to worry about that if and when the situation arose and repeated a dialogue from *Shakespeare in Love* whenever I thought about the dilemma.

"The natural condition is one of insurmountable obstacles on the road to imminent disaster."

"So what do we do?"

"Nothing, strangely enough, it all turns out well."

"How?"

"I don't know. It's a mystery."

I didn't leave it all to the mysteries of fate though and did what I could to control what I could control (if you hang in there long enough and hard enough you might just get lucky). This involved doing the opposite of what I did in my PhD and proving myself to be really, really good at this teaching thing while I still could, so if I needed to be cut some slack later on at least I'd have built up collateral. Despite the demands of training, I prepped my lessons well and worked hard on my coursework. I was obviously still learning and made plenty of mistakes, but I discovered I was right about me and teaching – I could be good at it.

I was on as steep a learning curve as anyone else though. The first lesson I ever taught was two hours on Genetic Engineering to an A level group. I was practically a PhD in this so I prepared detailed notes and laminates and talked at them pretty solidly for the first ninety minutes. I was exhausted. They were very well behaved and gave me the most generous margin for error, but I knew by the baffled looks towards the end of the lesson that they had understood little, learnt nothing and would remember even less. In fact, I'd probably just forced any knowledge they already had on the subject out of their brains. I discovered that day that although I knew a lot about science I had a lot to learn about teaching, including the Second Rule of Teaching: you're not supposed to be the one doing all the work.

Not all my classes were as well behaved. I never did quite get to grips with my cheeky GCSE Science set. I tried everything to keep them interested, occupied and quiet, but rarely managed it. At one point I despaired, set them questions and retired next door to the science prep room to regroup. Their real teacher was sitting there marking other work and laughing quietly at me. "Did I hear you shout "Shut up!" and stamp your foot?" he said without looking up.

"Yes."

"How'd that work out for you?"

"Not great." After a minute sitting with my head in my hands, I went back in to try again. At some points it can be pretty hard to remember the First Rule of Teaching: there's no such thing as a bad pupil, only bad teaching.

But at the same school, I was also doing probably some of my best teaching ever just down the corridor with a bottom set of thirty thirteen-year-olds. Their regular teacher was old school in the worst sense of the word. He said the class were one of the worst he'd ever taught and called them 'The Zoo'. Apparently the only way to keep them quiet was to keep them busy writing, so he made them copy notes off the blackboard all lesson and said that at least that way they had all the information and he'd done his job.

With the benefit of a youthful lack of cynicism and a healthy dose of optimism and naivety, I really thought it could be different. From observing the class and talking to them I noticed they were not stupid and lazy, just a little slower than some and therefore lacking in confidence and really, actually, bored out of their minds. So when it was my turn I didn't dictate science, I started by telling them stories. Everyone loves a good story. This time, teaching about DNA, I took them back to what first engaged me in science. I asked them to shut their eyes and imagine they were Superman with X-ray, magnifying eyes and that they were looking at one cell on their arm that was less than the size of a pin prick – but, because they were Superman, it looked huge to them and they could see inside it. I described what the inside of every cell in their body would look like if they had Superman eyesight and then asked them to draw what they had just visualised.

They wrote very little. Instead I gave them worksheets with words, phrases and pictures that they had to cut up, reorganise and glue into place to define and explain various bits of science. If they didn't know the answers, they could look it up in their books and find out for themselves. They had quizzes and word games and cartoons and colouring in and I got to use all my *Blue Peter* creativity. Third Rule of Teaching: if all else fails cut, paste and colour in. I had to prepare a fair bit in advance but I used it again for years, and in the lessons I did very little except set up the activities, time keep and wander round chatting to the kids, giving them individual help if they needed it. I had thirty of the most difficult kids in the school working. And I was by myself, as their regular teacher, who was supposed to supervise me, took the term off sick with stress.

It was hard work but one of the most rewarding things I've ever done. I used the last few minutes of each lesson to go round and ask the kids what was the one thing they had learnt from the lesson. They could usually remember something and sometimes still remember it at the start of the next lesson. One of the biggest, coolest lads with the worst absentee record and, when he was there, the one who was the most difficult in class, started turning up for my lessons and telling other pupils off when they misbehaved (he was much more effective at getting them to behave than I was). He told me that he never used to like science, but he thought it was really interesting now and his favourite subject. I nearly cried. He started doing his homework and doing it well. I could write how great it was at the bottom in bright red pen and I wondered if he'd ever had that before. He started revising for tests and his marks weren't bad. At one point, a kid who was being particularly disruptive in the next set up was actually moved *into* mine and he started working too. Some of the kids even revised for the end of term test and got questions right. They felt pretty good about that. When I told them I was leaving, several of them thanked me on their way out and said they wished I could stay. I didn't want to leave either. I have no idea if the effect lasted or went beyond that classroom. You know when you teach that you can only influence such a small part of their lives but you hope, somehow, it will be enough.

But I didn't get to all of the kids and this was another important lesson. There were a couple of girls who still would not turn up with any regularity and did little or nothing when they were there. This bothered me and I did feel I was failing them, but I know if I'd focused on these girls I'd have been dispirited and given up. I remember this now when I'm teaching or speaking to a group or running a workshop of kids or adults and it's tough going. I find and focus on the ones who are getting something from it and let them give me confidence and energy to stay brave and keep trying. And gradually, I hope I'll draw others in. I try and remember those I know I did help, because if I focused on all the ones I couldn't help, then I'd stop and get to help no one. Even though I know there is no such thing as a bad pupil, only bad teaching, I can only ever do the best I know how to do in that moment. And since I'm always learning, I will never actually know enough to help everybody. And sometimes, even though they're not bad students, it's just not their time or I'm just not the right teacher.

So, like everything else, I had to learn how to do it. But teaching is still one of the very few things in the world where I have enough confidence in my ability that if I don't have time to prepare, I don't get too stressed. Teaching is the only thing I know I can do better than most people in the world on less work; the only thing I've ever done that I feel I didn't have to fake a talent for by learning it step by step.

Still there was plenty of work to do, plus the rowing training, plus – I have to admit – rejoining the world and having at least a little social life. Something had to give and that something was writing up my PhD. It just sat there on my desk and in a corner of my mind bugging me a bit, but not too much. I knew I would finish it at some point.

At Christmas I took a few days out of the boat (but not out of training as there are always my running shoes). My brother flew into London from Poland where he was teaching and brought Maggie with him (the Scottish lass who would eventually be his wife) and I hired a car to drive us all up to Richmond. Christmas at home was a ritual nightmare and I'd long since given up on this being a special occasion except in the worst sense of the word. Driving up on Christmas Eve, I felt the familiar dread as I got closer. It was tempered by the fun of sharing the car with John and Maggie, but increased somewhat by the thought that this was the first time Maggie would meet our parents. I knew what she was likely to see.

By mid-morning on Christmas Day, Dad was "ill/tired" again and slurring and stumbling. The rest was a farce. We faked it through lunch, keeping up appearances, as ever never quite knowing how best to deal with this in company. Dad was ostentatiously drinking soft drinks and disappearing every few minutes. It was a normal enough Christmas. I kept quiet because letting them get on with it was my new thing. Later, when we were clearing up, it ended up with just me and Dad in the kitchen. He was being very hale and hearty and full of Christmas cheer, trying to engage me in conversation and acting all petulant because I wasn't having any of it. "You're just so hard and cold, Alison." This was my parent's thing when I refused to play the 'We're all one big happy family' game and had been for as long as I could remember. I decided to give him the wisdom of my newfound philosophy on his situation. "Dad, why do you bother hiding the alcohol and pretending? If you are going to drink you should just do it. It's fine if you want to drink, it's your choice, but please don't treat me like I'm stupid. I know you've been drinking."

"Alison, I have not been drinking. I haven't drunk anything for months. We've been having such a lovely day, why do you have to ruin it?"

"Dad, this is not a lovely day. No one except you is having a lovely day. You're drunk."

"I am not! I'm ill Alison. I'm just so tired. I'm always so tired." And he sat down at the kitchen table, put his head in his hands and started crying. I'd been here before so many times, but despite my resolve part of me still thought, suppose he's telling the truth? What if it's not his fault and he is ill? At least if he accepted he was ill, then that was something we could work with. Maybe there was something I could do to help fix it. I'm good when there is something that can be done – it's what I do. I just wanted to be certain – really, really certain – I'd done everything I could.

So he sucked me into the game one last time and for the next couple of hours we went through the whole cycle again. I listened while he told me how rubbish his life was. How it was all such a disappointment. How he'd always wanted to be a pop singer when he grew up. He named all the people he knew who were off doing the things he really wanted to do with his life, recounted bitter tales of all the things he'd done to help other people and how they never visited any more or did anything for him – with no understanding that they didn't visit because he was a drunken, embarrassing host. In his head he got drunk because they didn't visit and it was the only pleasure left in life. I listened while he wallowed and wallowed and finally sank in self-pity.

Occasionally I chipped in with "What's stopping you doing those things?" or "You are one of the lucky ones you know, you have an education and enough money, you can do whatever you want with your life" or "You don't drink because your life is rubbish, your life is rubbish because you drink – you do know that?", which were met by a blank stare or sometimes a "I can't, your mother wouldn't want to." When I talked about taking responsibility for your life to my Dad, the same look of utter incomprehension would come over his face as when you talk fast to someone in a foreign language. We lived on different planets. I'm aware I probably moved to mine as an act of rebellion. Sometimes I think that most of what I've done in life has been to try to show my parents that they could take control of their lives and live a different way.

Finally we got onto the "I'm ILL, Alison" bit and I started to explore avenues for fixing this. "Dad, I've been reading up on it and I think you've got Sleep Apnoea. You snore really loudly and Mum says you sometimes stop breathing in the night. It would explain the tiredness and your high blood pressure and probably even your low alcohol tolerance" (I really do think he had it; those are real symptoms – I really had read up). "Sleep Apnoea is treatable. It could help." (I still think it could have helped).

"Oh no Alison, the treatment is horrible. You have to breathe through a tube in your neck overnight."

"That's not the only treatment Dad."

"No, it's horrible. I'm not doing it and it's not that anyway. I just have to work so hard."

"Well, how about cutting down on work? You don't need the money."

"No, I can't do that."

"Why not?"

"It's just not the right thing."

"Well what is?"

"I don't know!" More crying. Then I said: "Maybe you need to find other ways to relax; how about yoga or thai chi?"

"Oh no, I don't have to embarrass myself like that."

So yoga was embarrassing; falling down stairs in restaurants and being arrested for drunk driving was not embarrassing? So I said: "Maybe you should have someone else to talk to. Counselling, therapy, see a behavioural psychologist who could help you change your behaviour patterns."

We talked about that for a while. He said he might look into it and thanked me "so much for listening". I was totally drained from two hours of being non-judgemental and nice – a difficult thing for me to pull off at the best of times. I went upstairs to the loo and when I came back to the kitchen Dad wasn't there. I opened the door to our long, dark pantry and there at the back was Dad drinking out of a small Tango bottle. The way he turned to me, the startled look and the "Oh hello Alison!" were diagnostic. That wasn't Tango. These black plastic Tango bottles were his latest thing. He could open them up, drink some of the Tango, top them up with gin and then store the opened bottles in plain sight at the back of the stash of new bottles. The black plastic hid the tampering and the fact that they wouldn't always be full.

"What are you doing?"

"I'm just getting a soft drink."

"There's gin in those bottles."

"Well, it's Christmas. I work hard. I should be able to have a drink." Defiant Dad had swooped in and taken over from Self-Pitying Dad.

"Fine."

"Are you going to tell your mother?"

"I don't know if I can be bothered."

"She knows anyway. She knew I drank when she married me. It was her choice." This was new; the latest lie he was telling himself. I did ask Mum later just to check and apparently it wasn't the case, but I'd given up trying to work out what was true round here (what she actually said when I once asked her why she had married Dad was "Well all I ever really wanted was to get married and have children and 'women like us' don't have many options"). I walked back out into the kitchen and eventually he had to follow me because there was no other way out of the pantry. I was done now, but I just had to say one more thing (it's a bad habit). "You let me sit there for two hours and listen to you and try and help you, and you told me again and again you hadn't been drinking. You tried to make me feel guilty for saying you had. You lied to me solidly for two hours when I was trying to help you. How could you do that?"

And he stood by the kitchen door (I can still see him exactly), looked at me square on and spat out with slow emphasis on every word as if he was talking to someone very stupid.

"Because that's what alcoholics do, Alison. They lie."

And finally I got it. The convoluted depths of his self-deception and the pathology of the lying and that he would never, ever, get better. It was quite a trick really. That he could stand there and believe that statement to be true – lying to me wasn't his fault, it was the disease's fault (at least he'd picked up something useful from the AA meetings). And – this is the clever bit – *simultaneously* not actually believe himself to be an alcoholic. Because I don't for one minute believe he actually thought that about himself. He wasn't like those sad other people who went to AA meetings, he was different. He drank because he had real stress and real pressures and a really unhappy life. It was a neat trick, but in his head he pulled it off.

I didn't visit again for over two years. It was for the best rather than purely petulance on my part. The anticipation of my visit and the thought of having to hold himself together had him in such a state by the time I got there, there was no way he could get through it without resorting to alcohol, and if he did last a couple of hours he celebrated with a drink. Catherine also stopped visiting around this time after she invited her boyfriend's parents (tee-total Methodists) round for tea for the first time. Dad was off his face when they arrived and pouring tea onto the floor by mid-afternoon. Everyone sat through the whole excruciating tea ceremony pretending everything was normal (which actually it was). John was still away teaching in Poland so didn't get back much. Through all of this I'm sure the rest of Dad's world still envied him his perfect, loving family. And really we were doing him a favour. It was easier to pretend to himself and everyone else when we weren't actually there to challenge him with reality.

They still visited me though and I encouraged it. I was still trying to maintain some sort of relationship with my mother and she still wouldn't go anywhere without him. We'd just meet for a couple of hours and Dad could usually hold it together for that long.

I called once a week as I'd always done, but Mum called me even less often now because, unless she was desperate, she was protecting him. Also, since she'd finally said: "I've decided that I'm not going to leave your Dad", there wasn't really anywhere to go with the conversations. He'd threatened to kill himself if she left. Defiant Dad told me this too. "I've told your Mum I'll kill myself if she leaves." Neither of us really believed he'd do it, although his favourite trick, if he felt he wasn't getting enough pity, was to tell Mum and sometimes Catherine: "I've brought the Insulin home tonight, it's in my bag, just one injection and it'll all be over. I'll do it you know." But actually he had a couple of heart health scares (arrhythmias) and had been so visibly terrified by the actual reality of dying, it was obvious he wasn't about to do it deliberately. Mum also said: "I don't really care if he does but I don't think he will. He's spent his life paying into those pension plans and life insurance policies and they won't pay out for suicide. He couldn't bear to let them take it." Still, the threat let Mum feel like she had no choice but to stay, which helped her. Dad didn't need to have threatened suicide, he could have just threatened Mum with having to sort out her own car tax and that would have done it. Neither could be on their own and they'd both done a good job of interweaving their dependencies.

I successfully managed to switch off the emotional connection and really thought very little about it. It was rare now to lie awake playing the circular conversations over in my head. It cut into all family relationships though, because with the three of us kids scattered and not going home, we rarely saw each other either. But, if anything, I felt the relationship with my family as an absence rather than a presence and I'd successfully filled the gaps with rowing and friends. For me, my Thames year was a really happy time.

Chapter 9: Within my control

"Never let perfection get in the way of a good performance"

Back to rowing. Focus please. This is the important thing here. With only three months left of my campaign, I knew I still wasn't fast enough to make the GB team. Despite all that Thames Rowing Club had to offer I was rather frustrated with the level of coaching, which didn't seem to give me anything new. I was doing everything I could but was going to need more help to get there. Then in February, about two weeks before the third open trial and ten weeks before the final invitation-only trial, in one of those strokes of luck that sometimes happen to people who hang on in there long enough, one of the girls I was training with went to lunch with her friend Miles Forbes-Thomas and managed to convince him to coach our little training group of three scullers.

Miles had previously coached triple World Champion Peter Haining when he became Lightweight Single Sculls World Champion and Guin Batten in the Single at the Atlanta Olympics. After a bit of a fall out with the GB system and maybe his athletes (I'm not really sure what happened), he was at a bit of a loose end. Miles started coaching us just before February trials and straightaway I felt the difference. This was coaching but not as I'd known it.

Miles has a very clear idea of how the stroke should look and is relentless in trying to get you there. He almost never stops talking *at* you while you are rowing. It's all very level and very calm but *very* insistent. To be coached by Miles is to be subject to an unending barrage of words that takes some getting used to and makes or breaks people. We'd go out sculling and the sessions would be even longer and even harder than usual. But the difference was that for the first time in my rowing career, my brain hurt more than my body. "The catch needs to be quicker; no, no, no, still no, yes that one was better, what were you doing there? That's still good but you have dropped your body, I can't see the change, still can't see it, that looks better, hold that, now what's happened to your catch, good you've got it back, remember what that feels like, no, no, no", and on and on until invariably at some point I would just stop and sit there with my head in my hands.

When I thought it was all too much, that there was too much to think about, he'd let me sit for a minute and sort it out and then we'd set off again. And slowly the running commentary would start and build up until I couldn't take it anymore and I'd have to stop.

But Miles also knew the Second Rule of Teaching and every time I'd stop to turn the boat or change the type of work, he would ask: "How was that?" To start with I really didn't know, no one had ever really asked me before. I thought that was the coach's job – to tell me how it was. I'd say something like "OK" or "better" or "rubbish" but those generalisations were not acceptable.

He'd keep on at me, "What was better? What was rubbish? You have to be able to tell me how it feels. I'm not going to be there when you race so you have to know. We're going to do it again and next time we stop you're going to have to tell me how it felt and what was different so you'd better be thinking about it." So, as well as listening to the commentary, I'd have to be thinking about how the boat and the water and my body was feeling so that I could report back exactly what was happening and eventually (after a couple of weeks) I'd be able to say something like: "I noticed that when I sat up more and held that position all the way forward the connection with the water was more solid. It felt like I got hold of it better and actually I also noticed that my stroke rate came up and I was able to take more time forward and get a better ratio." Or I might just say "My head hurts."

We also did a lot of exercises where I learnt what small parts of the stroke should feel like even if I couldn't get it all. I went to the last open trial and just squeezed myself up into the top twenty. Not good enough to make the team but good enough to achieve my first goal and be invited to the closed trials in Nottingham in two months' time. It wasn't long before Bethia and Kate, the rest of my training group, retired hurt with injuries and then it was just me and Miles, for miles and miles.

Despite the intensity of the coaching, forcing me to think about it and feel it for myself actually made me less dependent as we progressed. Miles couldn't be around every session but because I was more aware myself of what it should feel like and knew what exercises to do to get the feeling back if I was struggling, I was effectively able to coach myself.

I trained like this, on my own, in London, with Miles for two months in the lead up to the final selection trial. The squad girls were all training together over in Marlow with Mike so I had no idea how I was doing against them.

Training with Miles, for miles and miles.

Right from the start Miles had told me that in order to compete against the squad girls I would need to increase my stroke rate – a lot. He told me that a 2k race should be raced at 36 strokes per minute for the first 500m, 34 for the second 500m, lift back to 35 at the 1000m, then winding up to 38+ over the last 500m and that that was what all the squad girls would be doing. I was used to racing at about 28.

We spent most of the week rating about 18 strokes per minute – hours and hours building aerobic fitness and practising at a speed that enabled me to really think about what I was doing and improve my technique. But at the start of the two months Miles showed me a week-by-week plan for how we would gradually build the rates up. A couple of times a week we practised getting up to rates above 30 and every Saturday we'd do a 2k piece at a higher rating profile aiming for the final practise piece two weeks before the trial at 36/34/35/38+. In addition, once or twice a week we did pieces of work on the new, aspirational stroke rates. Not the whole 2km but bits of it, maybe just 500m at 34 and a separate 250m at 36.

This forced focus on ratings was very new. Every coach I had ever worked with up to this point (and since in fact) had only let me increase my stroke rate to the point at which I could still row well. The moment the stroke fell apart I was to reduce the stroke rate until I was rowing well again. Miles's philosophy was that I was to do the high ratings or as close to them as possible, almost regardless of how badly I had to scull to get them. "You have to have a go and just keep going; if you fall apart it doesn't matter, it's practice, this is what practice is for. If it falls apart then at least we will have something to talk about and something we can work on to get better. If you keep sculling within yourself and it all looks good, then what are we going to talk about?"

I developed a new mantra at this point. I'm not sure whether it came from Miles or I read it somewhere or I made it up, but *"Never let perfection get in the way of a good performance"* works for rowing, teaching, music, dancing and pretty much everything I've found in life. Because the theory is not the lesson, the notes are not the music, the moves are not the dance and the strokes are most definitely not the race. Practise hard, consciously and thoughtfully, but then in any performance you just have to let yourself be taken over and trust in your practice and that some of the new technicalities will stick. And for the ones that don't – you go back and work on them some more, but at least now you know what they are.

As the stroke rates go up, they become increasingly hard to achieve and maintain. Miles's regime called for achieving the highest stroke rates at all costs. I vividly remember getting crippling stitches right across my stomach the first time I did this, so bad was my technique and breath control. I'd never got a stitch rowing before – as far as I know, something about the position of rowing means it's relatively unheard of (one of the saving graces of rowing is that you can train pretty much straight after you've eaten without getting a stitch or feeling too sick). In a race pace piece, I had to hit the prescribed rate first and *then* I'd focus on trying to get the right boat feel. If I hit the rates *and* it felt good, *then* I knew I was going fast. Both pieces of information were necessary.

Miles also demanded that every increase in stroke rate should be associated with relative increases in boat speed. I was to keep my stroke shape and profile the same regardless of the rate and just row more of them as the rates went up. Again this would seem to be fairly obvious but it's not common practice or commonly taught. Many coaches I've trained with and many athletes focus on getting the maximum possible boat speed from the low rate 18 strokes per minute steady state paddling (we do hundreds of hours of this – thousands in our careers). They row huge, long, strong strokes at the low rates, but then get stuck as the rates go up and they can't maintain this profile and power per stroke. If you train like this then you either have to race at a lower rate or reduce the length of the stroke to raise the rate, which is a problem because it's now not the same profile as the stroke you've spent hundreds of hours grooving in.

We worked specifically on hand speed and rate – 30 to 40 stroke rate builds: 8 by 8 by 8 by 8, up and up and up and up and up to destruction, again stopping way past the failure point each time. I did a lot of failing in those two months, which is why it was a good job I already knew that *"Success is the ability to go from failure to failure without losing your enthusiasm."*

In case I'm painting a picture of some sort of super positive Superwoman, I'd like to point out that that really wasn't the case. I was very tired and sometimes rather grumpy. Along with Miles's increased technical focus and ratings came increases in both volume and intensity of training. Fortunately he respected the fact that I was also doing my teaching course (he'd done one himself) and was relatively realistic about what was possible to fit around it. We'd sit down towards the end of each week with Miles's ideal training programme for the week ahead and my diary of school and lectures and see what would fit where. Non-negotiable sessions went in first; the two or three fixed rate pieces, a thirty-minute ergo at anaerobic threshold (a new piece of work for me and vital for rowers due to the unique nature of a rowing race), a fifty-minute session at UT1 (high heart rate steady state training) and two heavy weights sessions. Then we'd fill up the gaps with 90-120 minute steady state training and short(er – this is Miles and miles remember) technical paddles. It was a heavier work load than anything I'd ever done.

By this point I was getting up pretty much every weekday at 5am and cycling down to the rowing club to do a ninety-minute session on the water in my little boat, quickly debrief with Miles and then from that moment on I'd always be rushing. I'd run up the stairs, get showered and changed, then jump on my bike and cycle eight miles across Richmond Park to my teacher-training school, wet hair streaming out the back, eating my breakfast out of my bike basket. I'd get to school, quick change, teach all my lessons, stay behind for a couple of hours to mark work and prepare lessons for the next day (the other teacher trainers used to come in saying they'd been up till two in the morning preparing their lessons but I'd say: "No time, gotta go training, bye!"), jump back on my bike, cycle eight miles back through Richmond Park to Thames (straight to the rowing club because if I went home I'd probably fall asleep), do another one, sometimes two, training sessions that night, finish about nine o'clock, jump back on my bike; cycle, back up the hill (very... slowly... now...) grab a quick dinner... get to bed... get up at 5am and do it all again. Except at the weekend when I didn't have to be at the club until about seven or later sometimes depending on the tide, so I got a lie in.

But mostly, throughout it all, despite it all, I felt invigorated, because it was new and different and finally something was shifting for me, even if I didn't know quite what and even if I didn't know if it would be enough.

I concentrated every stroke on how my body felt picking up the water. I still worked on keeping my arms relaxed and picking up the water with my lat muscles as I'd discovered in that moment of inspiration on the Cam. The feeling of relaxation even at pressure. Then one day, all of a sudden, virtually in one stroke, I felt something different. I was able to keep my lats relaxed and pick up the water with my lower back. My arm muscles and lat muscles were still working, but under a relaxed tension rather than a gripping tension. I felt the boat lift out of the water and run on in a new way. It was a revelation. I thought "Oh my God. This is *it*. This is what *it's* supposed to feel like. What have I been doing all these years?

But sometimes, I just got really tired and grumpy.

At least once out on the water on a cold, dark morning, the wind blowing and the wash from the pleasure craft bouncing my little boat up and down like a cork, my hands split and bleeding from the hours and hours of being cold and wet, in constant pain from raw blisters on my bum where the bones stick through and contact the seat (no one tells you about that, do they?), so tired I wanted to fall asleep while I sculled but still with a fifteen-hour day ahead of me before I saw my bed again. At least once I stopped, slapped my blades against the water, cried and raged at Miles: "What's the point? I'm trying to do this here, on my own, in the dark, in all this wash, around my school schedule and they're all over in Marlow, training together, on flat water, funded and not having to work (at this point I still believed they trained in Utopia), and I'm still supposed to beat them before anyone will even look at me. What *is* the point?"

See, I'm not Superwoman – I can't play "The grass is not greener" all the time. And sometimes I cry. Miles would just idle the launch engine and sit and say nothing while I huffed myself out, and when I'd done he'd say: "Are we ready to go again? OK, so rate 18, steady state, when you're ready." And off we went again. Always "we" – notice that? I'd never had a coach use that before and I know it sounds a bit corny but somehow it really was. Miles is not a perfect coach. I don't know if he's even a great coach, but he was the perfect coach for me at that time. Not everyone can work with Miles and I've spoken to several athletes who are as keen to credit Miles with the end of their careers as I am with the start of mine. But this was where the extra maturity from getting myself through my PhD really started to come into play. I did used to stop on the water and say: "No, that's too much, you have to be quiet now for a bit", and many won't. I did also say: "That's too much training, I can't do that today", and many won't. He seemed to trust me to do everything I could and only call a stop when it was a physical impossibility to do anymore, and I trusted him that if he said we had to do it and I could do it, then I had to and I could. I'd never had anyone be that hard on me before, but then I'd never had anyone spend that much of their time on me before, or so believe I could do it before, or bring me as many chocolate doughnuts, so he got away with it.

I felt this sort of total, unspoken assumption from Miles that I would be good enough. He never said anything like "I think you've got what it takes" or "I see Olympic potential in you." I don't even remember any conversations where we discussed what "it" was. He seemed to so totally assume that I would make the team that year that it wasn't even worth talking about. All I think we ever focused on was being able to race that 2k piece at 36/34/35/38+, which he said would be enough. Miles said that was how international scullers raced and I believed him. Miles talked to me about racing that piece like it was a forgone conclusion that I would be able to do it and mainly I just didn't argue. Miles didn't talk about potential and he didn't seem to care who he was coaching. He told his athletes what they needed to do and as long as they kept turning up and doing it, he'd keep coaching them and there would be no one more on their side. I noticed however, that as soon as someone started missing sessions or not making the technical changes fast enough, he'd very quickly lose interest and stop being supportive and then I imagine it would feel very different to be coached by Miles.

But with two weeks to go, I was now so tired and the hardest pieces were yet to come. I still had to submit a sub 7.10 ergo and then there was our final 2k training piece at 36/34/35/38+. The day of my final ergo test I didn't scull in the morning and took the train to and from school to save my legs. I tried to sit down as much as possible during the day, but unlike rowing, teaching is not really a sitting down sport. On the warm train back to Putney, I was practically comatose and slipping off the seat. I ate a malt loaf to try and feed myself some energy and then just felt tired *and* sick. At that point in my career, I generally didn't mind ergo tests. I'd always been one of the best at Liverpool, Bedford and Cambridge, so had little to fear. That evening though, the dread was almost pathological. I knew the pain that awaited me and didn't have the resilience to face it. I did my warm-up and started the test, but I knew I didn't have a sub 7.10 in me that day and I'm not sure I ever had any intention of finishing. You can't start an ergo test (or anything) in that frame of mind and expect a happy ending.

Miles was usually very unsympathetic about stoppages in any piece on or off the water – it's a bad habit to get into and not one to be encouraged (stopping leads to more stopping). However, that evening he must have sensed the trauma was real, and when I stopped about halfway through, he said it didn't matter – I was perfectly capable; I was just overtired. I was supposed to be overtired at this point; we'd been training hard. I wouldn't be tired by trials and then I'd be fine. That was the important thing to remember. The ergo test was never mentioned again and right up to this point, I just sort of assumed I'd got away without submitting one. But thinking about it now, I know that's not very likely. I suspect Miles may have either said I was ill (which I sort of was) or maybe even submitted the score he believed I would have done (Miles really believes his own truths, which is subtly different from believing your own lies), but maybe I'm casting aspersions.

I still had to do the final training piece though. I fought and battled my way up towards those dizzy ratings and although I finished the piece, I never quite made them. That was OK though. I was perfectly capable; I was just overtired.

Oh, and apparently the other important thing to remember was that I'd done everything I could to try and get to the rates. Physiologically it would have shifted my body into a better place for the trial in two weeks' time and technically we now knew exactly what we still had to work on. So we went back to work.

Over the next two weeks the training volume came down, but the intensity of the work increased and included more high rate pieces to sharpen my body for racing. I don't remember feeling any less tired. My technique at the high rates, despite all the improvements, was still very raw and the ratings still unobtainable. The weekend before final trials, I'd been invited to a wedding in Ireland. Not just any wedding – rowing legend wedding. Not because either of the rowers getting married, Siobhan McKenna and Adrian Cassidy, were particular rowing legends, great though they both were, but because the story behind this wedding and this marriage is a fairy story worthy of the movies (the type of film where you come out crying and saying that that would never happen in real life).

Siobhan and Adrian met, fell in love, got engaged and planned their wedding. Then on his stag do in Henley, Adrian dived from the pub bank into the Thames for a bit of a swim, hit some underwater construction, broke his back and ended up in Stoke Mandeville hospital without the use of his legs. They cancelled their wedding plans but Siobhan married him anyway on their original wedding day, in front of just their immediate family. Adrian still immobilised and flat on his back in hospital, his future still terribly uncertain.

Eventually though, after months laid out, many more in a wheelchair, and hours and hours and hours of physiotherapy, including light rowing on an ergo before he could even stand, he walked out of there. One of only two patients there at the time who did. He had exactly the same damage as a man in the ward above him who would be paralysed for the rest of his life. Lucky guy, we might say. But if you read more of the step-by-step mental and physical challenges he set himself from his first few minutes of consciousness, written in Martin Cross's wonderful combined autobiography and biography of other rowing legends *Olympic Obsession*, you might again wonder on the nature of such luck.

They planned their second wedding, a grand ceremony in Ireland which was also cancelled for the rather happier reason that Siobhan was pregnant. So Isabella was born and wedding number three was planned and by this point I think both families felt they had so much to be thankful for and so much to celebrate that they just went a bit wild. They hired a castle for the weekend and invited all their friends to come along and fill it.

So for all sorts of reasons I wanted to be there. But I was plagued by serious doubts. At 27, I felt that these trials were my last chance. I'd invested everything I could all winter and felt that the direction of my future rested on the results. If I didn't get through I would get a proper job and give up on any squad ambitions. What was I doing even considering taking time out of the boat a week before this life-deciding event and going off to Ireland for a two-day party?

But Miles said I should go. He said that we were ready. We'd done everything we needed to do bar the last few short pieces. There was really nothing significant to do this weekend anyway. I was supposed to be resting up so I might as well go and relax in Ireland. We could row Friday morning before I left and be back in the boat Monday so I'd only be two days out of the boat, it wasn't a big deal. It was actually more difficult to take Friday off school than it was to get the time off training.

I still had my doubts though. When a non-athlete asks you how you get up in the mornings or train day after day, you try to explain but they never really get it. Some of it is for the pleasure but, by this point in your career, mostly it's the guilt that gets you out of bed, back down the boathouse or into the gym. When you miss training you feel so wretched that the time off is miserable and you might as well just have gone and done it. It's a sickening, gut feeling that does not seem to have basis in any thought process, rational or otherwise. There have been times when I've woken up, full of cold or with pus in my throat from tonsillitis knowing I couldn't train, but still had to get up, drive to training and show my symptoms to my coach to get his official sanction to go back into bed, my guilt relieved enough to actually sleep. And I'm certainly not the only one.

Kate from my training group drove me to the airport. I was distracted by my doubts and guilt, so it wasn't until we were actually driving up the approach road to Luton and I saw the signs that I piped up with, "STANSTED, I SAID STANSTED!"

"Oh fuck, don't worry I can still get you there." I wasn't at all sure that was true and decided it was a sign I shouldn't be going at all. I rang Miles to tell him I was coming home and arrange training for tomorrow. He wouldn't let me come back and told me to get a later flight if I had to. Poor guy, *he* probably just wanted a weekend off. We got to Stansted late, but by some twist of the fate that I definitely do not believe in, the flight had been delayed. So I made the wedding, cried at the church (I was in good company), ate, danced, didn't drink and got a delicious lie-in on Sunday morning. I came home relaxed and refreshed, and jumped back in my boat on Monday a renewed woman. Sometimes Miles can be annoyingly right.

I did Miles's patented taper training that week. The sculling was still anything but perfect, but there were no more 5am starts and I started to feel a bit more human. Friday came eventually and Bethia (also from my training group) drove me up to Nottingham, even though she was injured and couldn't race herself. I put my boat together and in my last training outing something just clicked. All the technical changes I'd been battling to make suddenly seemed more natural. I could feel it and Miles could see it. I was ready.

Physically I was ready, psychologically being there was rather a shock. Miles and I had been so focused on the 2k piece and the trial that I hadn't really thought about who I'd have to be doing it against. I was surrounded by rowing legends who'd raced at the Olympics. Steve Redgrave and Matthew Pinsent were wandering around. Fortunately I wouldn't actually have to race Steve and Matt, but it was still rather intimidating to think that I was trying to put myself on the same stage. And I was going to have to race the female Olympians, those people on telly, and beat some of them – that is how trials works.

Fortunately for me the first race was a time trial, a 2km head race to get a ranking to seed us for the next round. I wouldn't actually have to see anyone I was racing. We were given a start number, rowed up to the start and then they sent us off one after the other about ten seconds apart. I sat at the top and waited my turn. Eighteen, go!… Nineteen, go!… Mowbray, go!… and I was off, straight into the race pattern Miles and I had been working towards all those weeks.

I wound up my start and then at about 250m settled easily onto 36 strokes per minute and it felt good. At 500m I relaxed even more, took more time and let the boat flow out to the required 34 strokes per minute. It still felt good and for the first time ever I managed to hold 34 all the way through the second 500. Coming into 1000m – halfway. This was the tough bit. I had to go up 1 to 35 and had never managed it before. I steeled myself, span my hands, pushed my legs harder and looked down at the rate – 35, bang on! I checked boat feel and it still felt good. I'm sure it was starting to hurt by now but it's strange how you never remember that. I just remember approaching the last 500m and bracing myself for the last 60+ strokes. Through the 500m, "10 strokes" spin the hands, push the legs, the rate lifted again. "10 strokes… and one for luck", "10 strokes… and one for luck", pushing the rate each time and as I went through the last 250m marker I was at 38+ and the boat was still running out and feeling good. Spin the hands push the legs; spin the hands push the legs; up, up, up every 12 or so strokes and each time the rate came up. Still with somewhere to go I span and pushed, span and pushed every stroke for the last few, crossing the line in the high 40's.

I paddled down and did my warm-down row feeling detached and slightly stunned. I'd hit the race pattern exactly, for the first time ever, and it had felt almost easy. Just as Miles had said it would be. He really can be most annoying.

I sculled in, took my boat off the water, strapped it to a rack and went and got showered and changed while they worked out the times. Then it was pretty much like getting my exam results. They posted them on a board and we all crowded round to take a look. Ever the optimist I started from the bottom again and worked my way up, disciplining my eyes not to jump ahead up the page. I got to about halfway, into the twenties and I couldn't find my name. Confused, I flicked my eyes down again to see if I'd missed myself. "I'm not there. They've missed me off. They've not timed me. What happens now?"

Then I heard Miriam Batten beside me (one of the scary people who had already been to two Olympics and World Silver medallist from the previous year). "Mowbray? Who's Mowbray?"

I looked at her. "I'm Mowbray."

She looked at me. "You're *second*."

I looked back to the list and flicked my eyes to the top and there I was...

1. Batten, G. (Thames)
2. Mowbray (Thames)
3. Batten, M. (Thames)

It was like reading....

1. Kelly Holmes
2. Alison Mowbray
3. David Beckham

It made about that much sense.

I went back to the friends of Bethia's that I was staying with to get some sleep and try to 'reassess my goals' for the next day. Everyone else was wandering around asking, "Who is she?"

And Miles... Well, you know what coaches are like, he was walking round saying "I discovered her... taught her all she knows."

The next day it was proper Olympic style side-by-side racing. And it wasn't a fluke. I raced really well in the heats and made it into the semi-finals. I raced really well in the semis and made it into the finals. And not just scrapping and clawing my way through in my usual style. I won't say it was easy because 2km rowing races are never easy, but I easily made it through each round. I was making it *look* easy.

We lined up for the final, six abreast. Already, whatever happens, I couldn't do worse than be in the top six, I'd already beaten several squad girls and secured a place somewhere on the team for that year. I can't actually remember my semi-final result, but I think I may have won it because I remember being seeded into one of the favoured middle lanes for the final. I was literally in pole position. So the starter called "Come forward to row" and we came forward to row.

And at this point, I have to explain about the start of a rowing race (this may just be delaying tactics as I know what happens next). This race is going to take us around eight minutes, give or take thirty seconds or so depending on the wind direction. So, if we think about it as something everyone can get their heads round, it's like running a couple of miles – very fast. So, if we picture the start of a middle-distance running race, what do we see? The athletes standing, one foot in front of the other, toes just behind the line, knees slightly bent, chest leaning forward; quite relaxed and groovy. And why do they stand like that? What do we know about the accepted tactics for a middle-distance race? What would you be shouting at the TV? "Keep it steady off the start", "Don't get too excited", "Pace yourself and save your legs for the finish". And why? Because working hard generates lactic acid and carrying that around in our muscles is painful stuff and literally causes the muscles to seize up. You want to save that pain for the end of a race.

And when we watch a middle-distance race in progress, who do we think is going to win? Where is the best position to be? "Tucked up in second or third position, just on the shoulder of the leader, letting them do all the pacing work and have the stress of wondering what's going on behind them." And what do we think about the guy who sprints off the gun and has a clear lead by 200m? "Is he crazy?", "What's he doing?", "He's going to blow so badly."

So, we all know how to race a middle-distance race. But this is rowing. As I've already mentioned rowing is one of only two Olympic sports where you win by being the fastest at going backwards. The other being backstroke. So now if you take your standard middle-distance race tactics and go off the start relaxed and groovy and tuck in just behind the leaders, the leaders are actually physically *behind* you. You can't see them. *They* now have the advantage of looking back, reading the race and matching your efforts stroke for stroke to stay ahead. In rowing, *staying* ahead is much easier than *getting* ahead.

So in rowing, the advantage is in being *first* off the start and to settle *in front*. This is not a secret – *everyone* is trying to be first off the start. This makes the start of a rowing race the opposite of relaxed and groovy. It's a flat-out, balls out, *sprint* start… and then you just hang on and hope you don't die. That's pretty much it. So the start is more like a sprinter getting into their blocks.

It's pin-drop quiet.

Even at the Olympics there are rarely spectators this far up the course. There are just the officials in the start tower, some kid hanging off the end of the pontoon holding onto the stern of your boat, and a huddle of coaches on bikes holding their stopwatches and quietly jostling for their own best position. On the "Come forward to row" call we tuck ourselves up into a compressed position and jam our blades into the water, like a sprinter tucking themselves into their starting blocks. The starter holds you there during the call over and you keep squeezing or tapping to keep straight against any side wind. In the pause between the call over and the start command, you stop tapping and use the power of prayer to keep the boat straight and squeeze the blades against the water to take up any slack like a sprinter pushes back against their blocks.

It's pin-drop quiet.

The start commands are "ATTENTION… GO!" and on the G of the GO you squeeze that first big stroke, then wind up and power up the next five or six hard heavy strokes to lift the weight of the boat and your own weight up on top of the water and sprint flat-out for the first minute or so to get in front… And then you just hang on and hope you don't die. People will try and tell you it's more complicated than that, but that's pretty much it.

This is where all those hours and hours of training come in. This is why rowers have to have it all. This is why we are in the gym interval training and lifting heavy weights, training like sprinters for a race that is five and a half to eight minutes long. The rower who can generate the most power off the start is most likely to get in front and have that advantage. This is why we are also on the water for 90-120 minutes every morning, then the same again on the ergo in the afternoon, why we ride bikes for four to six hours when we can't sit in a boat any longer without our back disintegrating, training like marathon runners for that five and a half to eight minute race. The rower who can carry the most oxygen to their muscles per heart beat will generate the least amount of lactic acid and be most efficient at breaking it down *while* they are still racing, ready for the sprint finish. This is also where those dreaded thirty-minute ergos at anaerobic threshold come in. Psychologically, you learn to live with the pain. Physiologically, your body gets very, very efficient at breaking down and recycling lactic acid while you are still working.

This is also why, at the Olympics, it's the rowers who are hanging on to each other still out of breath and unable to stand when they are interviewed some ten minutes after their races. It's just tougher for us, really it is.

So I'm pole position in the final, poised on the start, waiting for the "GO!" And I have to admit that at this point I'm thinking rather more about the Olympians on either side and rather less about the race plan. It's pin-drop quiet.

"ATTENTION… GO!" I take the first huge stroke.

And I turn round ninety degrees and am pointing towards the bank, which I quickly work out is not the quickest way to the finish.

And here, in case you do feel inspired to take up rowing, is a top tip from an Olympian. When you are there, poised on the start, ready and waiting, every muscle primed to fire… It really does help to have *both* blades buried in the water.

I'd been a little distracted and while my right blade was nicely buried, my left must have been out waving to the crowd. I'd taken one huge stroke with my right blade (how I stayed in the boat I don't know) and spun myself round, and then it took about six panicky little strokes with my left to get me back on course. So, *now* I'm straight, *now* I'm ready, but of course everyone else has sculled off and the coaches have all cycled off – including my coach who's now saying "I have *no idea* who *she* is". There's just me and the stake boat boy left. He is frozen, still hanging off the end of the pontoon and looking at me in horror.

It's all quiet again up at the start. There's tumbleweed blowing down the course. But I get myself quickly back into my own head and do my own start. And as I've said I'm pretty good when I get going and I am *legendary* for my big finishes. So, as we come into the last 500m, the last quarter of the race, I start to catch them up. I even overtake one of them. And I finish fifth.

And that was good enough to get me selected into the Quad for the World Championships in Cologne that summer. And so, all of a sudden, at the age of twenty-seven, two years from the Sydney Olympics, I find myself in an Olympic-class boat, with three other girls, two of whom I've just beaten and they're all training full-time and think they could go to the Olympics. So for me, at the age of twenty-seven, that's when my light bulb finally comes on and I think… "Maybe *I* could go to the Olympics."

In the same moment that going to the Olympics became a possibility, it suddenly became the thing I wanted most in the world. I try not to waste time wanting things or worrying about things that can't be, but once the door to the Olympics was pushed open that crack, I couldn't have stopped myself if I'd tried. I was grabbed by the scruff of the neck and pulled through. I was in there – 100% in there.

I still didn't really know if I could get to the Olympics. I was to learn that it doesn't matter how good you are, no one ever really knows. I was to learn that the most annoying question to ask an athlete is: "So, are you going to Sydney/Athens/ Beijing/ London 2012/ any Olympics?" It's annoying even a couple of months before the event and people start asking it years out. They still ask me now, eight years after I've retired. My answer (if I'm tired and grumpy) is: "No, I've been here working with you all day, not training. How can I be going to the Olympics?" and I laugh a little so it doesn't sound too offensive, but they get the message. What do they think it takes? People still insist on telling me someone they know who is "On the Olympic team for London 2012" even years before the event, and I have to smile and say "That's nice" and bite my tongue. No athlete ever describes themselves as being on The Olympic Team until the final selection letter a few weeks before the event. It's just not that easy and it feels annoying that people think it is – that they can have so little clue.

You don't choose to go to the Olympics. You lay out everything you have and let the Olympics take it – no deals, no bargains, no questions asked, no hope of return. You accept that maybe it will be enough and the Olympics will choose you… and maybe it won't. If you hold anything back for safety you won't make it anyway. It's a considered gamble. No matter how good you are, you have to fight repeatedly for selection every step of the way, until just a few months, a few weeks even, before the Olympics. Even when selected it's "subject to continued performance" and you know you could be dropped at any point and someone else take your place – and even after all that, even weeks, even days away, you could still get ill or injured, or there could be a terrorist attack or aliens could land. Asking an athlete to say that they are going to the Olympics is asking us to focus on things outside our control and that is something we spend our whole life trying not to do, just to keep hope alive, just to stay sane.

If you thought about the number of things outside of your control between yourself and your dream, you'd never start. If you thought about them every day, you'd have to stop. So, you don't do that. You just think about the things you *can* do, the things you *can* control, and you start doing them and then keep doing them until you get there or until control is forcibly wrested from you. That's what you do.

So I didn't really think about whether I could go to Sydney. I just thought about the things I could do to get there and I committed myself to doing everything I could to find out for sure if I could be an Olympian. "What would it feel like to look back and never know for sure if I could have done it?" It would be unbearable, that's what. I didn't so much care if I got there, but I wanted to be able to look back for the rest of my life and know that I'd done everything I could – that I had reached my limits. I never want to be an "I could have been but..." person.

Besides... I was still enjoying it and still getting better, so I thought I should probably keep going.

Chapter 10: A life stuffed full

"Never be a victim in your own life"

There was a lot to fit into the next two and a half years if I was to get to the Olympics and the pursuit of Sydney dominated everything. For the first time I wanted to put rowing first and give myself a decent chance, but there was still an unfinished PhD and more immediately an unfinished PGCE (teacher training) hanging over me. I had five months left to the World Championships and about three months left of my PGCE.

As I write I find it increasingly difficult to separate my story of the next few years from the story of those around me. So I think, before I start, what I'd like to say is that what I'm about to write isn't necessarily how it was, but it's absolutely how it was for me. This is the story from my perspective – not necessarily the whole story.

I was put into a quad with Rowan Carroll, Ali Saunders and Elise Laverick with Ron Needs as our coach. We went straight to Belgium for a squad training camp in Hazewinkle (which fortunately coincided with Easter holidays) and got into the Quad for the first time excited and with high hopes. Elise had been in the bronze medal-winning Eight the year before, but for the rest of us this was our first senior squad boat. But that first outing was not great and it didn't get much better during the camp. We couldn't balance the boat and so couldn't apply the work properly. It was very stressful but poor boat balance wasn't the only source of tension. The other girls, having committed themselves to full-time training, expected me to ditch the rest of my PGCE while I was adamant I had to finish. If I got to the Olympics that was great, but teaching was what I needed for the rest of my life and life is long (and definitely better if it's balanced). Also, I just didn't see the necessity of jacking it all in. I was quickly to learn that training in Marlow at the Longridge Scout camp (GB Women's only base at the time) under Head Coach Mike Spraklen was not the Utopia I had imagined it to be on my bleak Tideway days, and whilst they might have been dedicating their whole lives, my training plan and juggling act had proved more successful than many at trials. I held firm. I still think it was the right decision but I have to admit it was perhaps not the best way to ingratiate myself into a new crew. All in all, it was not the most comfortable ten days. My first exposure to squad training was all a bit of a shock and nothing like the ideals I'd held it up to be.

We came back and I was given five days out of the boat to fulfil my current teaching commitments while I worked it out with college and school. I met up with my lovely college tutor, explained my dilemma and waited to see how the mystery would resolve. Firstly (after congratulating me) he said that I was obviously a good teacher and someone they needed to make sure passed (all the hard work so far had not been in vain), that they could let me off the rest of the college days but teaching practice was a government requirement. Teaching practice in this last term was 70% of a full timetable and still more than I had time for. So I said, "What if I was ill?"

"But you're not ill."

"No, but presumably people do sometimes get ill during their PGCE, miss some teaching practice and still pass."

"Yes?" He knew where this was going.

"Well I've not missed anything so far. How much can you miss through illness before you fail? What if I missed those lessons and just taught the *real* bare minimum to legally pass?" He took a deep breath and looked at me like I was making his life very difficult, but still he said: "Yes OK, you can do that; I'll sort it out with the school." And he did, and somehow they managed to reschedule all my lessons into the mornings so I could make it to Marlow every afternoon. Plus once a week, on college days, I could be at Marlow all day and they'd even give me a week off before each of the three World Cup races. The mystery had been solved. It *had* all worked out. Or so I thought.

I typed up a timetable for the remaining PGCE weeks to show exactly when I was available and how many hours I could be at Marlow for every day. My pure intention was to show how committed I was. I sent it off to Ron and asked him to show the other girls. I thought I'd done a good thing. But when I turned up to row at Marlow that Saturday, the atmosphere was arctic – far worse than Hazewinkle. I didn't dare speak at all during the outing and again everything about the boat was uncomfortable.

We met during break and Ron said that we needed to talk about fitting the training around my school timetable. I was confused, "Did you not get my schedule? I've managed to sort it so I can be here every day." Rowan shot back at me that yes they got it and how dare I come down here telling them all when they should go training. And I could tell, from that one pent-up comment, that this had already been used in evidence against me in several heated conversations that week. My heady, carefree gesture of commitment had been interpreted as the new girl coming in and trying to call the shots. I felt a tension and a pressure in my chest not unlike that I'd experienced at school and it took me straight back.

I was to learn that these dynamics would be played out in various forms and to varying degrees all the time I would row in the squad. When I said goodbye to Miles and went off to join the squad (a bit like running off to join the Foreign Legion but without all the sand), I took him a baked cheesecake made from my mother's world's best cheesecake recipe as a 'Thank you' present (because we seemed to have gone beyond even the gratitude powers of flapjack) and he left me with a final piece of advice that seemed odd at the time: "Be careful what you say and to whom when you get down there. Don't say anything to anyone about anyone else, even if you think you are talking to a friend. If in doubt it's best to keep quiet."

This advice confused me at the time. I already knew several of the girls and did consider them friends, but still it was constantly in the back of my mind those first couple of weeks and I did keep pretty quiet. I was too scared to say much anyway and in fact at one point when I did venture to express an opinion, I was told by Rowan that they had to row with me but they didn't have to listen to me so I could just shut up and row.

Four days a week I went to school in the morning and the other three girls did two sessions in the gym while the rest of the squad rowed. Then, when I got to Marlow in the afternoon, we'd go rowing while the rest of the squad went to the gym. In the evenings I'd drive straight back to Thames Rowing Club to do one of the two land training session I'd missed in the morning. We had one full day a week together and I'd also try and fit in a couple of sessions on Sunday when everyone else had the day off. This way I was able to do most, but not quite all, of the training.

After one not so bad outing, the tension finally seemed to be lifting and just Elise and I were left in the tiny Longridge changing room. Elise is fun and friendly and as we chatted I let my guard down and innocently mentioned that I wasn't doing quite the full training and even went so far as to say that this wasn't such a bad thing as it was safest to build up to the new training programme gradually (Mike's training was very different to Miles's). This was true; many athletes fall foul of such transitions and quickly become long-term injured. It was true, but of course that didn't mean it had to be said. Oh for the skills of social lying.

The next day in the session debrief, I dared to venture another opinion about needing to make the stroke more dynamic. Rowan shot back with: "Well it's all right for you; you're only doing half the training". I shut up and again had a moment of clarity. I'd said something to Elise and just heard it back from Rowan's mouth. There had to have been at least one conversation in-between and from the tone of that comment it had not been a nice one. Miles's warning now made perfect sense and I took it fully on-board. From that point on for the next six and a half years, I would check and sensor pretty much everything I said.

Again, really truly, it wasn't about those girls. Rowan and I were already good friends, which was why it felt so weird. We'd rowed together in the Commonwealth boat and helped each other out with somewhere to stay for Regattas and got on really well. Rowan was best known for the contradiction of having long blonde curly hair, fabulous nails and wearing lots of girlie pink, yet being the one from all the girls in The Notts County Rowing Association to keep battling on until she finally made the squad and (like me) winning the single sculls at Women's Henley.

I'd also known of Ali for a while but this was the first time we'd rowed together. A qualified doctor (a proper doctor not a PhD) she had halted her training and moved down to Marlow to try and make the team. She would go on to row in the Olympics and to work as an A & E doctor, as well as go to further Olympics as a team doctor.

While we're on the subject of overachievers, there's Elise. Elise started rowing at a similar age to the rest of us but got her act together rather quicker, so was several years younger at this point. Elise had joined Thames Rowing Club and started learning to row and scull alongside her degree course at The Guildhall of Music. When I first met her at Longridge she'd already graduated from The Guildhall, got a bronze medal in the Under 23 singles (a few years after I raced and came tenth remember?) and, as I've already mentioned, was part of the bronze medal-winning eight in the 1997 World Championships. Every so often, when training permitted, she'd go and play her double bass in a professional orchestra somewhere. I went to see her play a couple of times and it was wonderful. How many people in the world get to *choose* between being a professional athlete and a professional musician? Elise chose rowing and in her second and third Olympiads (both medal-winning) she'd balance her rowing commitments with retraining in Law. She now works ridiculous hours in one of those high-flying companies in the City and spends her holidays cycling 120 miles a day across several countries at a time, for fun.

And we were just four out of about twenty girls training down at Longridge with Mike at that time and we were not atypical. There was a higher concentration of degrees, further degrees, PhDs, high-powered jobs and extraordinary talents sitting on hold in those rowing boats than you'd find almost anywhere else in the country.

The rowing talent identification system at the time did not seem to have been set up to ID us. The guys were much more likely to go to one of the public schools and start rowing there and be guided into the junior system by coaches who were used to doing that. Strangely there was no talent ID or support system for university rowing, despite the fact that most of the existing women's squad had come through that route. You had to go to National trials and beat squad people and you had to work out how to go fast enough to do that through a university or club system that had likely never met anyone quite like you before.

We'd had to be incredibly single-minded, ruthless, competitive and calculating to get this far. We'd had to put not just education and careers but often families and relationships on hold to get this far. The guys don't have to factor that in either. Many of the guys row and have kids, while even now in 2012 the women's squad have yet to set that precedent. We'd had to race against each other and fight against each other for years to get this far. We didn't suddenly stop being those women just because they put us in a room (in this case a scout camp self-catering kitchen) together and in boats together and called us 'The Squad'.

Add into that room and those boats the fact that we'd usually got into debt to get this far. Those of us in our first year knew there was no funding available until we'd actually proved ourselves by rowing at a World Championships. Those on the team from last year were perhaps not quite so broke but were worried they'd lose their place and funding to one of us newcomers.

Add into that room and those boats a head coach who openly stated that he didn't believe in trials and knew who was best from watching us in training. Add to all that a selection system that didn't stop at 'final' trials. Each year I'd get a selection letter that started with "Congratulations on your selection into the '*name of boat*'" and continued with the famous words... "Subject to continued performance."

Add all of that together and you know you'd better find a way of beating as many girls as you can on the water and on the ergo and in the weights room every single session of every day and of making Mike like you. Because I was to learn that it's not just PhD supervisors who like to be liked.

So, you've just put twenty of the most competitive and time-driven women in the country into one of the most internally competitive and manipulative systems imaginable (I may be exaggerating a little but I've built up to make a big point here so give me a little licence) and well... do you expect it all to be nice?

But what I've not said is that you've also got twenty of the smartest, funniest and not just intelligent but emotionally intelligent women in the same room and boats. Whilst we could not all be friends, mostly we grew to like and care for each other and each of us formed several deep, lifelong friendships. The breakfast banter could be vicious but more usually it was lively and funny. The competition was always intense, but there was always at least one of the girls you'd had to fight against on the water that would be there for you when things weren't going your way. And even for those you couldn't get on with, there was always a level of professional respect. No one skived, no one shirked and everyone turned up and fought hard with everything they had – every single session. So even if you couldn't like them all, there was no one you couldn't admire for that.

The season progressed and we rowed without glory in the three World Cup competitions that always precede the World Championships. Video showed us all leaning out of the boat to different sides. Every time I tried to sit straight, I'd feel like I had to row in a boat so unbalanced that my right side blade would be digging into the water and I couldn't get it out. I'd scull along like this as long as I could bear getting more and more frustrated, until finally I could take it no more and I'd lean to the left, the balance would shift, the blades would come off the water and everything would be fine except that I'd be hanging out of the boat twisted and in pain. We all felt uncomfortable and were each convinced we were the only one doing anything about the balance.

So, it was with a massive sigh of relief that I was finally able to put down at least one source of tension and finish my teaching practice. I went into Roehampton for the last day of term, met up with the other students from my year and had to explain why I'd suddenly dropped off the face of the earth, missed all my lectures and yet was now back to pick up my PGCE certificate. Finally, I could put all my attentions into the Quad and we could train with everyone else.

We trained abroad for the best part of a month before the start of the World Champs in Cologne. The men went to train at altitude with their coach Jürgen Grobler, but Mike didn't believe in altitude training so we went to Aiguebelette in France. Aiguebelette Lake is a little bit of rowing heaven set on three sides by mountains and all sides by green. We arrived before our rooms were ready and I don't just mean that the beds weren't made, some of the walls weren't made. The hotel set the four of us up in a half-built, wooden rooftop annex and to start with we were a bit disgruntled, but then, actually, we realised we'd got the best deal. We all but camped out in our tiny twin-bedded rooms with bare planks for walls, crates for bedside tables, naked light bulbs and exposed cables, but we also owned a huge balcony room with plate glass windows overlooking the lake. Again, the furniture was packing crates and sun loungers, but we loved it and everyone else came up to visit. I think setting up house here helped us to start feeling like a crew and even enjoy each other's company.

We went from Aiguebelette to the lovely town and lake of Varese in Northern Italy. Here we stayed in an old monastery (which might have been a hint from the management as to how they expected us to behave now the men's and women's squads were together). Unusually for a training camp we had single rooms and were within walking distance of the town. Having free time was a luxury and perhaps one of the main reasons for going on camp. Yes, you get better water and better weather and of course that helps, but you also don't have to cook or clean or go to work or college; you don't have to run around trying to find time to meet friends or family and the training water is minutes rather than miles from where you live. You have no option but to rest. I'd spent most of my free time in Aiguebelette sleeping to catch up, but now, for the first time in years, I found myself with an hour or two a day of real free time where I didn't have to feel guilty about what I was not doing.

Then we went to Cologne and at the age of twenty-seven, I raced my first World Championships. The weather was distinctly Northern Europe and there wasn't much let-up in the wind and rain. Grey is the colour of my memories of Cologne. But we'd finally sorted out the balance and had a much more enjoyable competition. We didn't make the final, which disappointed us, but didn't really surprise anyone – being the bottom ranked boat came with the advantage of low expectations. We were tenth, comparable to the women's Eight which failed to live up to the glories of the previous year and came eighth. With six of the same athletes as last year, it was rather a riddle as to what had happened in a year.

The Pair of Cath Bishop and Dot Blackie, who had been the only women's crew boat not to medal in 1997 after Cath had been taken ill just before their semi-final, took Silver. No German Double this year and Miriam and Gillian rowed another nail-biting final to become British Women's first ever World Champions in an Olympic boat class. Guin made the final again in the Single but was sixth for the third year running.

Neither our tenth place nor the grey dampened my spirits. I was still high on the fact that I was actually representing Great Britain at a World Championships. I got my first senior squad kit with the magic hoops and was rather 'kiddie in a sweet shop' when I went to pick up it all up. My excitement was apparently something else to be sneered at and glanced sideways about with raised eyebrows. It seemed that caring about the free kit was unprofessional, showed your focus was in the wrong place and was frankly just very uncool. That people were 'just there for the kit' and once they'd got it, they didn't care about the result, was an urban legend bandied round a fair bit. Apparently any excitement marked you out as one of those people (it was all rather Salem witch trials). I soon learnt to take my kit quietly and find the other girls who also got excited by new kit. We'd lock ourselves in a bedroom out of sight of the sneering hierarchy, get everything out of the plastic, try it on, parade around and laugh a lot. Quite shocking behaviour.

My parents came over for their first World Championships too, braving the wind and rain to sit shivering and cheering in the open grandstands with the rest of the British team supporters. They got to know the other parents and relatives and met rowing royalty (aka Steve and Matt) and shouted themselves hoarse. They loved it and it was good to have them there. But if they brought their devotion and support, they also brought the whole package. I met them after racing a couple of times and Mum couldn't resist pulling me to one side to confide. This was Germany, there was a beer tent, and Dad was very overexcited, so obviously… "Your dad was really embarrassing yesterday. I went to the loo and when I came back, he'd been to the bar and got a beer and I don't know how many he'd already had. He was all over the place all afternoon."

"Yes?"

"Well, he didn't have to do that Alison."

"Yes Mum, he did. That's kind of the point."

"Oh, yes, well I know." But she didn't and never would.

So the four of us raced our race. It felt pretty good and we were fond of each other and friends in the end I think. Elise kept us all young, Ali kept us all calm and Rowan used her manicure skills to paint Union Jacks on our big toe and thumb nails and all her own nails including her right ones using her left hand (she has a freakish talent, that girl). We'd come a long way in those five months but even as we paddled in after our final race, a shift was happening. We went to the Sunday night post-race party together and had a blast. Live music, dancing, free beer and sharking (Cologne set the standard by which I would judge all subsequent post-Worlds' parties and I would always after be just a little disappointed) but still the shift was happening. You fight against each other all year to get into the crew and then you have around five months to build yourself into a team that knows each other, trusts each other and will work with, rather than against each other. Then you race your final and somewhere on the paddle back to the landing stage, you realise that you are actually no longer a crew. The next time you meet you'll be back in singles going head to head in the start of the fight to get back in the boat. That's the shift. We had four weeks off before we were due back at Longridge to start training for the next season and the 1999 World Championships in Canada. The word 'off' is rather a misnomer as you are supposed to come back fit. I always did some training.

I didn't go on holiday, as I'd finally run out of excuses with my PhD. It was hard sitting down at the computer to get my head back into it after all that time. It was hard driving up to Cambridge and walking back into the lab when I would really rather be anywhere else. But hardest of all was picking up the phone after months of no contact to call my supervisor to ask him if I could come back, use the lab computers and start working again. Eventually, after I'd got a further PhD in prevarication, I picked up the phone, made the call and ate humble pie – again. It wasn't any fun but it was, after all, just a phone call. It was also rather satisfying to hear from my lab mates that he had spent the last year gloating that they'd never see me again and I'd never finish. *I'm* not gloating but… Ha!

I got cracking back on my PhD that month and was enough into it by the time the squad reconvened that I could hold the two side by side for a while. I was now commuting from Putney every day to train full-time with Mike and the squad at Longridge. Mike's training programme had Wednesday afternoons and Sundays free so I drove up to Cambridge after training on Wednesday and then again on Saturday. I still did my best writing late at night and found I really had to be in the lab rather than in Putney to do it as I was pulling files from everywhere. I got used to the late night/early morning two-hour drive back down the M11 and round the north circular to Putney.

I'd applied for and been granted yet another extension and had a final submission date that coincided with the week of December trials. This was not altogether a bad thing as there is less training to do in a pre-race wind down week. By this point I was totally sick of my PhD and was determined there'd be no more reprieves and extensions. Every chapter had been past my supervisor to check for accuracy and scientific content, and then my lab mates for proofreading until eventually, finally, it was ready for printing. We had a small, laser jet printer in the lab that laboriously printed one page at a time and I worked through the night, the three stacks of beautiful, pristine, acid-free paper pages growing and growing. Every so often there'd be pages where I'd have photos to stick in which was a moment of great excitement. I was determined to have them all ready so all I'd have to do was take them to the binders the following day.

Gradually, even the most desperate of PhD students left until it was just me printing and sticking. Eventually, in the early hours, I printed off the last page and added it to the last stack. I was going to have to leave my beautiful, pristine pages behind all day in the lab and still needed them to be beautiful and pristine when I came back. I cursed the fact that I'd not been down to supplies earlier in the day to get box files so I could store them safely. I hunted round for anything suitable but any boxes were all full of people's papers and I didn't want to disturb anything. At the bottom of the corridor, just past my supervisor's office, was a tall metal cabinet and on the top were at least ten used but empty and perfectly serviceable box files. I took three down, put a copy into each file and I even think I padded the spring clips so as not to dent the front page, such was my care. I took my three files and stashed them well out of the way under a desk in the computer room. You might wonder why I recount such fine detail but bear with me, as all will become clear.

Then it was back in the car and down the M11. I *think* I drove straight to Henley to save time and got a few hours sleep in the car before the outing, but it was December and it would have been very cold, so maybe I'm making that up. Either way, once I'd finished the morning's training, it was back in the car and back up to Cambridge. I arrived in the lab buzzing. Five and a half years after I'd started and my thesis was finally finished. I went to the computer room and looked under the desk and… confusion. No box files. I was so confused that for several moments I didn't even register the three copies of my thesis stacked naked, straight onto the floor. How could that be? I was giddy with a mixture of excitement, relief, shock and sleep deprivation and couldn't really compute what was going on. I picked them up and put them on the desk and checked them over. They seemed OK. There were a couple of people on computers so I asked after the files, but nobody knew anything.

Anyway… no time to think about it anymore… time was ticking on. I went down to stores and picked up some new files, packed my copies carefully again, arranged to meet a few friends in the pub later and began my walk of victory.

I didn't get very far. I turned right out of the computer room and was about to brave a cheery combined greeting, farewell and thank you into my supervisor's office when suddenly he was out and blocking my way. And then he spoke and gave me a present for which I will always be grateful, even though it wasn't immediately obvious as a gift.

"Would you steal my car?" I smiled at him bemused. This was obviously a joke. He was trying to make nice and tell me a joke. He was waiting for an answer and it wasn't obvious what the correct response was, like for a 'Knock Knock' joke, so I ventured, "I might, is it a nice one?" And I laughed a bit to show that I appreciated his humour. His face didn't shift. He looked very stern and tried again. "Would you steal my car?" I was rather confused now and actually slightly worried. This wasn't sounding like a joke any more but I didn't have the slightest idea what he was going on about. My smile stayed on but it was now a little forced. "No, of course not."

"Then why steal my files? You stole my files, would you also steal my car?"

My face cracked into a proper smile again and I actually laughed. Oh, it was a joke after all, well more of a tease really and not a particularly good one but I was in a good mood. I'd cut him a break and humour him – he liked to think he was funny. "Yeah, yeah alright, I borrowed your files."

"You didn't borrow them, you took them without asking and that's stealing." There was no reciprocated laugh, not even a smile. He was actually serious. This time my smile was of absolute incredulity and I spoke very slowly as if to someone about to lose all reason (subtext: "Please don't do this when we've been doing so well"). "It was three in the morning. You weren't here. No one was here. I needed somewhere to put the copies of my *finished*... (focus man, this is the important thing here) thesis. They were just old files, they were on the top of your cupboard and I just borrowed them for a few hours. Oh! – (it really only dawned on me at this point), did *you* put my copies on the floor?"

"I just took back what you had stolen from me." There was nothing left to say. I looked at him, shook my head and left. It was the last time we'd ever speak.

I was angry as I walked to the binders, but by the time I went to pick up the three royal purple (the last, and most important, decision in any PhD process) hard-bound copies of my thesis a couple of hours later, I was smiling again and actually grateful. Getting though that PhD had been the hardest thing I'd ever done. It's a close call now but I think it's still pretty much the hardest thing I've ever had to do. There were so many things that were so hard and so draining about it, but hardest of all had been the realisation that the only way I was going to shift the deadlock with my supervisor and the stalemate with my research was to take full responsibility for everything that had gone wrong. It was no good blaming my supervisor or expecting him to change, if I'd waited for that I'd have waited forever. I'd had to look inside, swallow my pride and find everything I could that was my fault and fix it and I'd felt pretty bad about myself in the process. And then he gave me that little gift of an exchange. Whenever I look back on my PhD years now and start to beat myself up about how useless I was, I always finish by thinking of the stolen box files, and no matter how hard I am on myself I cannot find a way that that conversation was justified or in any way rational. It allows me to lighten up on myself about a

Post Viva PhD celebrations with Dr Mowbray and her lab mates.

whole lot of things over that PhD period. I know it was made harder than it had to be and I know I wasn't totally at fault.

I came back to Cambridge a few months later for my PhD Viva and passed (passed well, actually) but I met my friends in the pub and didn't go back to the lab. I never heard from him again. Whether with a different supervisor I could really have done something very good and been published and gone on to do some great science or whether I would still have found that it wasn't for me and struggled to hold my head above water… it doesn't matter now. I wouldn't change what happens next and if I'd made a single different choice in those years, it would have taken me down a different path to a different outcome. The only way to get where I was going was exactly the way I got there.

I raced December trials in a single and a double. I did OK in both trials. The Nottingham trials hadn't been a fluke.

I eventually tired of the commute to and from Putney and moved to Henley to lodge with Mike Jennings (aka Jenno), who started out as a friend of a friend but soon became one of my best friends.

With the PGCE finished, the PhD finished, a small lottery grant and somewhere to stay less than ten miles from training, I was finally, officially, a full-time athlete and all I had to do was row. It felt pretty good. 'Doing everything I can to get to Sydney' meant getting my diet right too and without the travelling time and getting back so late, I was able to go back to cooking proper meals again. Much reduced was the fattening home cooking of my childhood, and fruit, vegetables and pasta became the basis of pretty much everything I ate. I bought a blender and made gallons of homemade vegetable soups and fruit smoothies. I stuffed peppers and big beef tomatoes with a mixture of pork mince, rice and herbs, twenty at a time so I could heat two or three up for a quick meal when I got home (that recipe was going to be in this chapter, hence the title). I didn't subscribe to the current thinking and advice on a very low fat diet for athletes though. My scientific challenging mindset didn't see any sense in it. Energy is energy and fat is as good a source of energy as carbohydrate, in fact better in some ways. The energy from fat is released more slowly so doesn't spike your blood sugar and crucially fat contains the fatty acids and fat soluble vitamins important in tissue repair and a healthy immune system. It just made sense to me that a little bit of fat was probably a good thing to help you through a British outdoor winter. I didn't eat a high fat diet but never stopped putting butter on bread, dressing on salad and ate a little chocolate and cake most days. I was burning thousands of calories a day; I really didn't see how a little fat was an issue.

The group of Henley friends I cooked for clubbed together to buy me a breadmaker for my birthday (I think they thought it would be a good investment). It's a good one and also has a cake function. Banana Breadmaker cake was my staple and I brought one down to share over breakfast fairly regularly. Rowers have to eat a lot of bananas. It's in the rules.

Mike's training regime was legendarily hard and we were all tired all the time, but again I relished the unaccustomed pleasure of free time and not having to feel guilty all the time about something I should be doing but wasn't. I started to read again, having stopped for years because I'd felt if I was reading it should be one from the pile of academic books or papers accumulating in the corner. I soon bored of daytime TV but watching Watercolour Challenge inspired me (and even instructed me), and I bought myself a small set of paints, a couple of brushes and a watercolour sketch pad and started painting the odd experimental still life (a grand title for painting my pot plants) or pictures copied from photos. They weren't much good but I found it strangely addictive. And that was it for the year; rowing, eating, reading, daytime TV and daytime TV-inspired hobbies. The life of a full-time athlete.

I settled into the Mike Spraklen regime. On training days I'd get up about 6.45am, have a quick first breakfast, then drive to Longridge in time to be on the water by 8am and row/scull 18km (about a hundred minutes). Most rowers do these long sessions at about rate 18 and 70% of their maximum heart rate, but that was not Mike's way. His long outings usually contained five or six pyramid patterns at higher rates and our heart rates would be up at around 80-90% for much of the session.

On Monday morning we'd get straight into our single sculling boats and start the week with two 1500m race pace timed pieces. By 11am we'd be having breakfast, already knackered and already looking through print offs of our current ranking. This may have been the only timed session, but that didn't mean the other outings weren't competitive. We followed each other up and down the river and the whole time we were trying to overtake the person in front and hold off the person behind. On upstream legs where everyone was hugging the slacker water at the side, it was not particularly unusual to run someone up the bank in the fight to get past them without putting your own boat out into the sometimes fearsome stream.

After the first session we'd have a second breakfast together in the Longridge scout camp kitchen. We had a kitty and took it in turns to buy supplies. We ate a lot of cereal and toast, but after a rather shocking diet analysis by our nutritionist where we realised quite how much toast we were eating in a day (and therefore how much butter), a fair few of us switched to porridge. I appointed myself chief cook (for this at least there was no competition) and would do a quick survey of numbers in the last 2k home, then dash to get changed and start cooking. I'd generally get pretty beaten up in the morning session, so the task of making, stirring and serving the porridge helped restore some sort of equilibrium. Then it was back in the boat for seventy-five minutes of the same.

We trained three times a day on Monday, Tuesday, Thursday and Friday. On these days we finished morning training by about 1.30pm but had to be back for a third session in the gym by 3.30pm (usually ninety minutes of weights or ergo), so it was a tight turnaround. Longridge to Henley is about a twenty-five-minute drive so by the time I got home, if I could make and eat my lunch in half an hour I'd have time for a half-hour nap and a cup of tea before I was back in my car. Miriam Batten lived three doors down so we shared lifts most of the time. On Wednesdays and Saturdays the second session was longer (a hundred minutes again) but we'd finish about 2pm and that was it for the day.

Sundays were a day of rest. We'd be hanging out for Sunday by halfway through Monday. By Friday, I'm not sure we were really safe to drive but at least the end was in sight. Saturday morning was often more timed (but fixed rate pieces) and then we were down to that last big 18km (down to the bottom and back twice) session. We put our boats on the water for that last session with no conceivable idea of how we were going to get through it except that:

1. We didn't have any choice if we wanted to come back on Monday and
2. We knew we'd made it every other Saturday.

That last trip back, against the stream, still trying to catch the person in front and not get caught by the person behind, came from that special reserve tank you can only access when you find yourself miles from home with nothing left and no one to save you, and your only two choices are get yourself back or sit there for ever. Two kilometres from home was the travellator. At this point the Thames splits to go round a small island and channels into a bottleneck that becomes a torrent in winter. We'd row into the channel and hit the stream and even though we were still rowing just as hard, we'd stand still (like on the Gladiators' travellator). The only way to get through was to put in a superhuman burst of 20 strokes and inch our way up through the bubbling white water. If we tired halfway and gave up, we'd be pushed back to the start and have to begin all over again.

Once home I'd shower, eat, put a load of washing on, nap, sort the washing and put on a second load, snack, wander into Henley and visit the second-hand book shops in a hazy daze, wander back, eat, watch a bit of telly, sort my washing and go to bed. I'd lie in late Sunday morning, get up, shower, eat, put on a third load of washing, drive to Tesco's to stock up for the week ahead, eat, nap, sort my washing, eat, watch an afternoon film, make dinner for a few friends, eat dinner with friends, go to bed and wake up nervous about the Monday morning timed pieces.

And you can read that and wonder why on earth we'd do it. Why we'd put ourselves through all that, even to go to the Olympics. But if you are even wondering, then it's almost certainly not the life for you, and that's fine. Fortunately there are many ways to live a life and this is just one of them. But some of you who read it will not be wondering why, you will feel drawn to it and excited by it and that's how it was for me. It was tough and I was always tired but I like tough and I'm good at being tired and there was actually a kind of magic to the routine and the grind and the continuous challenge and the intermittent but steady improvement that was above and beyond even the draw of the Olympics. There's a quote you sometimes see on T-shirts at Regattas that says "A bad day on the river is still better than a good day in the office." It was a mantra I played over in my head when I was most tired and most beaten up. Where else really would I rather be? Nowhere, nowhere else – I actually want to be here. I choose to be here. I'm not a victim in my own life. Never be a victim in your own life.

Most of the training was low rate power work on the water, ergo and weights. They require a kind of muscle power I just don't have and would never develop, plus I was sticking to Miles's technique of keeping my stroke length the same no matter what the rate. I also refused to harden the gearing on my blades to give me an advantage in the low rates as many of the girls did, because I knew it would disadvantage me come racing (and I thought the point of all of this was to go fast in racing). I'd often be overtaken or last to finish. But my saving grace was that every Monday morning we'd get that one chance to free rate in the time trials and I'd reliably come in the top three or four week after week. Sometimes the racing pieces would be in doubles and I'd do OK then as well, especially if I was in the stroke seat and in control of the rate.

It was actually starting to annoy Mike. He put a lot of store by his power-based low rate training sessions and believed them to be a true indicator of racing speed. If he'd had his way, I think they would have formed the entire squad selection procedure. He was quite excited about me after my first trials performance, but that all changed after my first 2K ergo test when I didn't pull out the massive score he'd expected. He stopped believing I 'had potential'. I actually saw a shift in his physiognomy around me. He became less and less interested as the months of being rowed over and finishing last on the ergos went on. But then, annoyingly, week after week, I'd defy all his predictions and beat his favourites in the time trial. I could tell my speed did not make him happy, which is a bizarre thing to say about a Head Coach.

Eventually my Monday morning pieces came to more than Mike's attention and became the subject of a breakfast chat. One of the girls said "You rate pretty high in those pieces, what do you go over at?"

"32, 34, maybe higher at the end."

"No way! What did you rate at trials?"

Now remember Miles had told me that all the squad girls rate 36/34/35/38+ and that this was how all international scullers raced. I'd hit those rates at trials so that was what I told them.

"No way!" was the general reaction. And in fact Mike actually said: "There's no way you did that. That's not possible in a single."

"But, I did…" But even as I said it, the doubt had started and I couldn't really be sure any more, even though I'd taken the ratings off my stroke coach and written them in my diary. I didn't argue though. Mike Spraklen is a world-renowned coach who'd taken rowers to Olympic glory and been the first to take British women to any sort of significant medal success in the 1997 World Champs. I'd not done anything. Who was I to challenge him? I'd learnt a lot from my PhD and dealing with my supervisor and I got to this place a lot quicker second time round.

In fact I'd learn to keep quiet about my high ratings in most free rate pieces. The words 'free rate' were deceptive. More than once Mike would accuse me of cheating when I beat his favourites by rating higher in free rate pieces. On one notable occasion on a Banyoles training camp, I was stroking a double with Miriam and we absolutely stormed a win in a competitive free rate, side-by-side piece against a Gillian Lindsey/Helen Raine double. Mike steamed over to us in his launch almost before the piece was over, screaming and furious. "What was that, Alison? What was the point of that? You were way over rating, it was ridiculous. What's the point in sculling so short and scrappy?" He shouted for a bit and then steamed off again, washing us down to go and talk to Gillian's double. As we sculled home Miriam said: "Don't worry, it felt good and it was fast. We beat Gillian, that's why he's pissed off."

I realised that it was an interesting thing, that bolt-out-of-the-blue, second-place, hit-all-the-rates Nottingham time trial.

1. It hadn't been true that everyone sculled at these rates; they all thought it was impossible and they couldn't do it. Mike the international coach thought it was impossible even for international scullers. They all thought it was impossible and none of them could do it.
2. Miles had told me that it was not just possible, but had been and was being done. I had totally and unreservedly believed him as I had no other information to go on and no reason to doubt him. I didn't know if I could hit those rates but I totally believed it was possible and that Miles thought I could do it. I hit them.
3. Once the doubt had entered my mind, from the girls, from Mike and eventually from watching international scullers and seeing that they rarely if ever hit those rates even if they medalled, once the doubt had entered my mind I would never do it again. The only time I would get very close was my last ever sculling race when I really needed to do something special and tried to row with that pure belief again (more of that later). I learnt it's our brains that stop us before our bodies. I think the saying goes, "If you believe you can or if you believe you can't – you're right."

In the last few weeks before final trials, I took a gamble and risked Mike's further disapproval to go back to Thames R.C. and train with Miles again. I'd seen Mike's pre-trials training programme and it was far removed from Mile's programme that had seemed so perfect for me the previous year. Also, I needed practical help and support through trials and it was obvious Mike's would be elsewhere. I was as careful and tactful in explaining to Mike as I could be and he said it was fine, so I left to train with Miles. My gamble seemed to pay off (at least in the short term) and I finished fifth again behind the emerging talent of Katherine Grainger, both Battens and Gillian Lindsey. It was actually a great result for me that put me right up there with the best of British Women's rowing at that time. Miriam and Gillian were World

Champions, Guin had made it to an Olympic final and I'd beaten all the other girls I'd spent the year training with.

Miriam and Gillian were named into the Double again. Cath Bishop and Dot Blackie had won a separate pairs trial and were to be the Pair. The next ranked boat for the 1999 season was the Quad and everyone else wanted to be in it. Guin was the driving force. She had blazed a trail for British Women's sculling in her single but no one seriously thought she could medal in it at the Olympics. Guin was not going to sit back and let her sister take all the medals and glory and knew her best bet was to be in a quad. The logical way to select it was from the trials performances (since that was supposed to be what trials were for) and at least at first that's what happened.

On our first session back, Guin, Katherine, Sarah Winkless (who'd come sixth at trials) and I were told to pick up the Quad and take it for a paddle. As we shouldered the boat and walked down to the landing stage, Guin said cheerily: "So guys, this looks like an Olympic medal-winning crew." I drew breath – I was still struggling to believe I might be able to qualify for Sydney, let alone medal.

Guin was not so cheery when we took the boat off the water. In fact she was noticeably quiet. It was undoubtedly more powerful than our quad last year but no more comfortable. The balance was bad and it was a rough and rocky ride. Naively, I was not unduly worried about the boat or my seat in it. I knew how long it had taken us to get last year's quad moving and I thought that we couldn't have expected much else for a first outing. We'd all been in our singles much of the year: Katherine had trained separately up in Scotland and the rest of us had really been training against, rather than with, each other. And as far as my seat was concerned, I felt safe having beaten Sarah at trials and with enough results under my belt that year to show it hadn't been a fluke. But when I got home that evening Ali Sanders called. "I thought you ought to know that Guin has been going round saying that Lisa should be in the Quad instead of you. She (Guin) has been talking to Mike about it as well. She's trying to get you out and Lisa in."

"Are you sure? I've not seen any of that and she's been really nice to me."

"Yeah well, something's up. We all think it's really out of order. You really deserve your place after this year and after trials. It's not right. I just thought you ought to know, that's all."

I was surprised not just that Guin was doing this but that she somehow felt she had enough right to do it that she didn't even try and hide it. I was confused. I believed Ali but I couldn't believe it of Guin. Within a minute of putting the phone down to Ali, I picked it up again. "Hi Guin, it's Alison." A surprised but perfectly cheery Guin responded: "Oh hi Alison, how are you?" If she was hiding something, she was a much better secret agent than me. "Fine – look Guin. This is difficult, but I'll just come right out with it. One of the girls has just called me and said that you've been going round telling everyone that I should be out of the Quad and Lisa should be in. Is that true?" The moment of stuttering, stumbling and auditory panic on the other end of the line was priceless and 100% incriminating. But then, to be fair, she didn't try to deny it. She stumbled her way through a rather garbled explanation of how it wasn't about me, it was because some of the men's squad really rated Lisa and said it was her stroking of the '97 eight that got them their medal and she (Guin) thought the Quad needed that.

"The men's squad? What have they got to do with it? Lisa isn't even next in line; others beat her in the B final. And why me out anyway? I beat Sarah." I don't remember what I got as a reply, but it wasn't anything that made any sense to me and included a disclaimer that it wasn't her decision anyway it was Mike's (which was true enough). I suppose the truth she may not have wanted or felt able to tell me was that, like Mike, she didn't feel I was Olympic medal material and could therefore stop her getting hers.

I turned up for training the next day and sure enough the scene was set for my trial and execution. My rather arbitrary trial was that I sculled in the Quad for a couple of pieces (on the bendy, stream-filled river) and then I got out and Lisa got in and did the same. Then the five of us sat round the Longridge picnic bench with Mike for the official selection decision. I don't think anyone mentioned the times for the pieces as no one was even bothering to pretend that they had anything to do with selection. Mike couldn't look at me as he told us that the Quad would be Guin, Katherine, Sarah and Lisa. And that was that.

I could have appealed, but even if I'd won I'd have had to row in a boat with an athlete and coach who didn't want me and I couldn't see how that was going to work. Mike's offer was that I either went into the Eight or the Single. All things considered, the Single seemed to be my best bet. I thought my best long term plan was to suck it up this year and use the rest of the summer to improve my sculling and put myself in the best possible place for the Quad in Olympic year.

I can make it make logical sense now and talk about the long game and make it seem like it was a very clear and calculating decision, but behind it all? The truth? I didn't fight for my seat because I didn't really, truly, think I deserved it anyway. This Quad was supposed to be Olympic medal material and I could scarcely even imagine myself at the Olympics. Out loud I railed against Mike, his prejudice and the injustice. Inside, I silently agreed with him.

That night though, Ali and at least two of the other girls called to say how appalled they were and that I deserved the seat and lots of other nice things that made me feel much better. There was always at least one of the girls you'd had to fight against on the water who would be there for you when things weren't going your way.

I wanted Miles to continue to coach me that summer in the Single. This was tricky as Mike and Miles whilst outwardly civil were obviously greatly at odds. However, having dropped me from the Quad, I don't think Mike felt he could refuse me this. And if Miles wanted back into the job he loved at the level he loved, he must have known he was going to have to swallow at least some of his pride and learn to play along.

In the end, my season was pretty damned cool. I discovered that being the GB Single Sculler rocks. Miles and I trained within the squad system and Mike's programme, but found enough freedom to work in a way that suited us both. Miles was also given the Women's Lightweight Pair of Jo Nitch and Melindi Myers to coach. Our two boats were not a bad match for speed and we had our own little squad within a squad going on. Being in the Single could have been quite a lonely affair, but it wasn't at all. Athletes and coaches from both the women's and men's squads, some of whom I'd rarely if ever spoken to, would come and find me before and after races to wish me luck, tell me "Well done" or ask how it was going. The Women's Pair of Cath and Dot (two of the razor sharp girls I'd been most wary of all year) could now not have been nicer. I remember being in a slight state of shock after their first enthusiastic interest after one of my races. I was particularly impressed that Jurgen Grobler, the men's legendary head coach and notorious East German quiet man, would come and tell me "Well done Alison" and talk about my races in a way that showed he must have actually followed them – even though technically I was nothing to do with him. It felt like the time I went to the conference with my PhD material and notable scientists gave me the appreciation my own supervisor had not.

I discovered that there is something very special about competing in the Single at this level. Going out there, on your own, taking sole control of your warm-up, the circulation pattern, getting onto the start on time and racing absolutely the world's best individuals is a uniquely challenging and utterly terrifying experience. The best crew rowers and scullers do not automatically make the best single scullers because there is so much else going on psychologically. The single sculler is a rather different type of beast and everyone else recognises and even, as I was discovering, sort of admires that – even if you are not winning races. It probably also helped that my trials performance and the fact that I was not in the Quad had been noted, and those (including the men's coaches) who could not, for professional reasons, express their disapproval of all things Mike, could at least support me.

My summers at Bedford R.C, racing every tin pot regatta within a forty-mile radius, stood me in surprisingly good stead, but I was still absolutely terrified and almost paralysed by pre-race nerves. Always with insomniacal (if that's not a word it should be) tendencies, I was now getting little or no sleep the night before racing. I also felt physically sick and was unable to eat pre-race, which meant a painful breakfast of trying and failing to get much down. The worry of not being able to sleep and not being able to eat also contributed to my race nerves and since World Cup Regattas are three days long, I'd be in a pretty bad way by the end. The two hours immediately before racing were worst. I used my patented one step at a time approach and focused on my pre-race routine; pre-race paddle, cup of tea, stretch, visualisation, talk with Miles, take my blades down (always myself even if Miles was free), take my boat down, get in the boat and do my set warm-up – and this helped but every minute was still hideous.

Training at the Holme Pierpont centre in Nottingham. Being the GB single sculler rocks.

I played various other mind games to get me through. A favourite, when a sudden wave of panic threatened to overwhelm me, was "It'll all be over in ___ minutes". I'd take the expected time for the race (about eight minutes), add it on to my start time and work back from there. It really helped; maybe just the process of doing the mental calculation was enough to distract me.

And then, finally, there'd be the "ATTENTION... GO!" and the nerves would be gone because now I was racing... and racing... and one stroke at a time racing. And of course, as soon as I crossed the line there was the "Oh my God! That was amazing. I want to go straight back up and do it again."

After my first race, I got a bit of a surprise in the warm-down paddle. Girls from my heat and the previous heat who were still on the water started to chat to each other and call across to me. "Hey, Great Britain. Not seen you before. You new?" This doesn't happen in crew boats, barring the occasional call of "Congratulations" after a hard fought final; everyone keeps themselves pretty much to themselves. But in singles you don't have anyone to share the first few adrenalin filled moments with, so you share them with each other. I quickly got to know these girls, became part of all that and loved it.

And that is pretty much all I remember about my first season in the Single. But I've just been on the World Rowing website to get some actual results and got a pleasant surprise. I remembered I'd had a positive World Cup, but I didn't remember I made the final in my first two International Regattas. I was sixth at both Hazewinkle & Vienna World Cups and am pretty impressed with that even now. At Hazewinkle, Dot and Cath won in the Pair but the Double and Quad were both fourth. Here also was the first senior appearance of U23 Champions Frances Houghton and Debbie Flood as the second GB Double. Knowing how this story pans out, I suspect you'll hear more of them later. In Vienna the Pair and Quad both came third, but the Double didn't even make the final. They came seventh, beaten in placings by both me and Fran and Debbie in GB2.

Looking at the incredibly slow times from Vienna reminds me that this was an outrageously windy regatta that resulted in the unusual scenario of me posting a faster heat time than Greg Searle (my opposite number in the Men's Single), who had rowed later into an even stronger head wind. He wasn't having a good regatta, but at dinner that evening when someone asked him how he'd done, he replied with good humour (and loudly to make sure I'd hear): "Not so good. Actually my time was slower than the Women's single. Alison Mowbray beat me." I always wanted to get a T-shirt printed saying "I beat Greg Searle", but I wasn't sure it was appropriately humble.

Lucerne is traditionally the last regatta of the season before the Worlds or Olympics. Some Nations go to the first World Cup and some to the second, but everyone goes to Lucerne (unless they've got a note from their Mum) so it's the first time you really get to see where you truly stand. For British Crews, a good performance at Lucerne is critical as the 'subject to continued performance' axe is still hanging over your head and Lucerne results determine if you and your crew will be allowed to go forward to race at the Worlds. Lake Lucerne and the town couldn't be lovelier and there is an amazing cookware shop with the best selection of biscuit cutters you have ever seen – but I never really liked racing in Lucerne. I always preferred racing on purpose-built courses rather than lakes. I actually liked downtrodden Hazewinkle and loved Munich with its clear turquoise water. I prefer the way course racing creates the focused tunnel I imagine a 100m sprinter feels.

I came ninth, which didn't mean I'd got slower – just that more people turned up. Critically I was still in the top ten. St. Catherine's in two month's time wasn't just the World Championships, it was also the Olympic qualification regatta and in my event the top ten would qualify. People outside sport don't really realise that it's not good enough to be the best in your country to go to the Olympics – you have to prove you are already among the best few in the world. The least stressful way to qualify for the Olympics (if there is such a way) is to qualify the boats the year before. Even then nothing is certain. You qualify the boat not the athletes so you have to fight to get your seat back in Olympic year, but at least you know there will be seats. If you don't qualify your boat through the qualification regatta, you have to wait another ten months to try for the last couple of places in the 'last chance regatta' and no one really wants to do that.

The Pair and Double were both fourth and the Quad fifth. No medals but we all still got the nod to go to St Catherine's. Not so the demoralised Eight who had struggled all season. They were fifth out of six in Hazewinkle, fifth out of five in Vienna and now their seventh place out of eight in Lucerne meant they were disbanded and just four athletes selected (through more sketchy and controversial seat racing) to go on and race a four at the Worlds.

The last couple of weeks before the Worlds, we all went to Canada and I loved that camp – as I loved the last camp every year. The pressure is building but it was the only real time the men's and women's squads trained together.

We did our key preparation pieces together and were able to compare percentage times with the men's crews. Fran and Debbie, fresh from a second U23s Double win, came out as rowing spares in a pair and I started to teach Debs how to play Scrabble. It was to be a long haul but you've got to start them young.

My parents, now pros at the supporter's game, flew out to St. Catherine's to watch and had another great holiday. Dad had subscribed to Regatta magazine all year, so now knew everything about everyone and was in his element. He kept telling me things about the rowers that he'd read in Regatta magazine. "I know Dad, I see them every day."

It was a tough Regatta. Everyone was chasing those crucial qualifying places, so there were hard-fought battles for every position right down the field. My second race (a Repechage to get through to the semi-finals) was my big race. Only the top two would go through and I'd have to beat at least one sculler I'd not beaten all year to make the cut. Miles and I talked tactics. If I did what I'd done all year I wasn't going to make it, so in this race I was going to have to try something different. My usual race pattern still left me down off the start but for this race Miles told me I was to do whatever it took to be first to 500m. I was to pretend that the race was only 500m long if that's what it took. It was the old London Docks trick again. I knew I was in danger of dying by 600m, but if I was already ahead, and my opponents didn't know I was dying, they might give up just a little.

I was more scared before this race than ever before. It wasn't just the fear of failure, of not making it through, of letting Miles down, of proving Mike right… In this case, specifically, I was terrified of the pain I was going to have to go through and whether I'd be able to hack it. I was terrified of trying to go to this new level and finding there wasn't one. I had no idea what this was going to feel like or do to me. I had no idea if I'd even be able to make it down the rest of the course. After ten years of racing, I was back to the same feeling I'd had in that first ever race on the Manchester canal. I didn't sleep the night before and I certainly couldn't eat that morning. I just drank the amazing syrupy peach juice they served at breakfast. It slipped down easily and, I reasoned, surely contained enough calories to get me through.

I needed a Plan B but there wasn't one – that was the point. I was going to be out there, alone and exposed, and if I couldn't make it past 500m, everyone would see – and I knew enough now to know that it didn't matter if I called it exhaustion or cramp or anything else, no one would care. I'd have 'blown' and whether it was physical or mental that was not the sort of person you ever wanted to race with. So instead I played 'What's the worst that can happen?' "If I race my normal race, the race I know gets me down the course in one piece, I'll be beaten into third or fourth place and not make the Semis. If I go for the new plan, the worst that can happen is that I'll not make the Semis. That's it. It's a no brainer. Stop worrying." An hour and a half before the race, I sat on the floor on my own to go through my pre-race visualisation and only allowed myself to visualise the first 500m as if it was a 500m regatta.

The only piece of racing I can genuinely remember from that whole regatta is that first 500m. I blasted out of the start. Actually it was my normal start – I'm not really a blasting sort of girl (I don't have the guns for it), but after the first 20 strokes instead of settling into a rhythm, I gritted my teeth and upped the rate again. I was doing my last 30-stroke routine down towards the 500m marker. I was really aware of where everyone was and was really racing them, just as I would in the last 500m of a race, and it was really working. I held the other scullers, pushed again into the 500m marker and just got my nose in front. Then I guess I would have allowed myself to settle a bit, but I'd be lying if I said I remember that or any other part of the race.

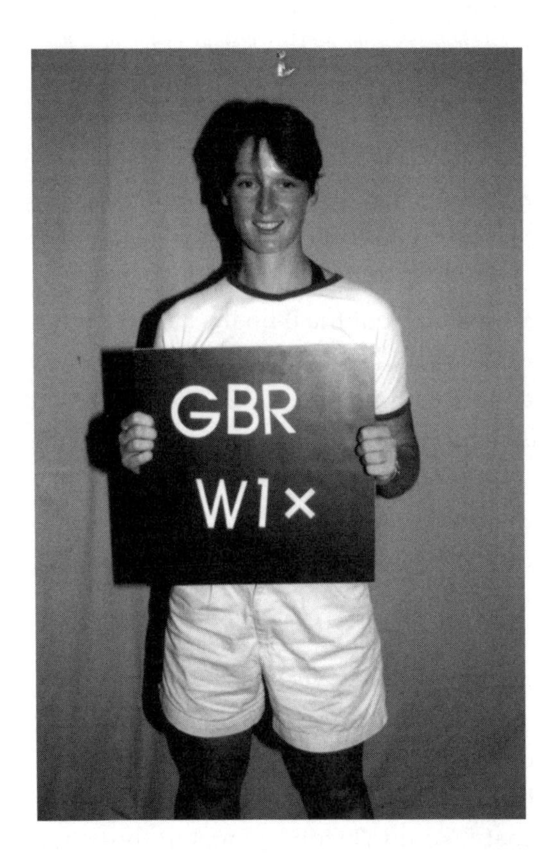

Guilty as charged.

I remember I came second though and made it through to the Semis. I also remember that Miles and I were both totally elated. It was only a Rep and I'd only come second, but I felt like I'd conquered the world. To put it into context, Greg also had a tough Rep to make the Semis and he didn't make it through. He'd ultimately come fourteenth, well outside the Olympic qualification places. The Men's Single was brutally competitive, likely more so than the Women's, but still… this was the level at which I was

World Championships 1999, St. Catherine's, Canada. Last 250m and the Mowbray grin that is really a grimace. I'm not sure if this is the pain of my rep, desperately holding on to a place in the semi-finals, or the pain of my B final two races later, desperately trying to make the last Olympic qualification slot. *(Photo by Peter Spurrier)*

now competing. Technically, in some sense of the word at least, for the second time that season I beat Greg Searle. I really should get that T-shirt made.

It was a step too far for me to make the Final, but the B final was still a tooth and nail fight for the first four places that would secure qualification. I battled hard but came fifth (eleventh overall) in a time of 8.35.52. The Romanian sculler who beat me to that crucial tenth place recorded a time of 8.35.02. There'd been just half a second between me and that Olympic place, a few feet. I paddled in shamefaced and gutted and didn't know what to say to Miles as he met me on the landing stage – it was his Olympic place too. But he just said: "Could you have done anything more?"

"No."

"Well then, there's nothing to be upset about." Technically he was right but actually, as ever, what really made it easier to bear was that I found it far easier to believe I wasn't capable of qualifying for the Olympics than that I was. Looking back it seems hard to reconcile the fact that I didn't really believe I could do it with the fact that I wouldn't stop trying, but those two things really did exist side by side.

The Pair, Double and Quad all qualified their boats but not by much and there were certainly no medals. The Pair finished fifth. Miriam and Gillian, the 1998 World Champions, didn't even make the final and finished seventh. The Quad also failed to make the final and went out to race their B final knowing that they had to win it to get the last qualification place – which they did. The Four of Alex Beaver, Rowan Carroll, Kate Mackenzie and Helen Raine fared little better as a Four than they had in the Eight and came fourth out of five. The Women's Squad was not a happy place to be and there was a distinct feeling of panic setting in. So much had been promised in the summer of 1997 and two years later, just twelve months before Sydney – this. Other nations were coming to the peak of a four-year wind but GB women, who under Mike's tutelage had hit it hard from day one, seemed to have nothing more to give.

We now had four weeks off and then all qualified crews were going to Australia for an Olympic Orientation camp. It happens every Olympic cycle. The rest of the British Rowing Team were going and I wanted to be part of it. I'd held an unspoken expectation all Regatta that a qualification place would get me there. I naively still held a hope that my eleventh place and half second outside of qualification would be enough. Surely I must be seen as well in the mix for Sydney in either the Single or the Quad? In the Single alone there would be at least two more places available through the last chance regatta next year, so technically I was within the qualification standard.

I was very naïve. No one had talked to me about the camp at any point, and as I waited to find out after racing, as we swapped kit with other nations and the boats were packed away, no one would. As I talked to the others, I gradually realised that everyone who was going already knew they were going and had known for ages. The Pair, Double and Quad had all been booked months ago – presumably because it was assumed they would qualify. I'd not been booked – presumably because it was assumed I would not.

I think I was more hurt when I realised this than I had been all year. I'd not had much to do with him but Mike had actually seemed very supportive since I got into the Single. And yet presumably, even as I was making the finals in those first World Cups, the decision had been made that I would not ultimately qualify – even as I came ninth at Lucerne, still within the qualification quota, no one had thought to book me a place. It's one thing to suspect your head coach doesn't believe in you, it's something else to have proof. And it wasn't just Mike. This would have been a management decision. Despite how nice everyone had been to me all season, no one in British

Rowing had looked at me and what I was doing and seen me at the Olympics. In fact, it suddenly dawned on me that that was probably why they had all been so nice.

What I couldn't work out was whether that one place and half a second proved them right or proved them wrong.

A conversation with Miles helped to get my head in a more positive place. "It's actually a good thing for you. They are all basically going on a jolly for three weeks. They'll miss time travelling and there are no boats out there, so they'll just be land training and sightseeing. All that time you'll be on the water. By the time they get back, you'll have a head start." It made sense and I knew he was right. I also rationalised that if I got to Sydney next year, I wouldn't care that I'd not been on this trip. And if I didn't get to Sydney next year… I also wouldn't care. I was ready to start again. Let battle commence.

But first, I'd have a holiday.

Yes, an actual holiday. The first one in… no… wait… I can't remember. I'd rescheduled my return flight to stay out in Canada for a couple of weeks and go hiking. With flights courtesy of British Rowing and my tent for a home, bar hiring a car, this was just about a free holiday – which was good as I was still skint. My sister flew out to meet me and I picked her up at Toronto airport. We both look back now and wonder how this holiday actually happened. She was six years my junior and we'd really had nothing to do with each other all our childhoods, unless you count the occasional argument or taunting. As we'd grown up we'd got past a lot of that and were at least civil to each other, but it wasn't a great deal more than that. She had visited me once in Cambridge and to fill the time we'd spent most of the day walking from Cambridge to Ely along the river and had started to get on. But if we hadn't been sisters, I don't think we'd ever have chosen each other as holiday companions. It was more a case of circumstance. I wanted someone to go hiking with and Mum and Dad bought the flight for Catherine as a graduation present, so she got a free holiday.

For two weeks we walked miles every day with big packs on our backs, camped in the middle of nowhere, skinny-dipped in secluded lakes, drove our free upgrade hire car on long straight roads between National Parks singing "Let's Get Loud" to a J.Lo CD, slept every night in our tent (it didn't rain once), cooked noodles on open fires when in wilderness and ate big meals and drank beer when in town, talked and talked and were comfortable with silence and were absolutely the best-matched holiday companions ever. We started the trip as sisters and finished as friends. It was the first of many Al and Cath adventures.

Al & Cath Adventure Essentials 1999

We finished our first glorious four-day trek in the Canadian wilderness tired…

… but triumphant!

Chapter 11: Surmountable obstacles

"Strangely enough, it turns out well."
"How?"
"I don't know. It's a mystery."

This was it – Olympic year. I came back from Canada very rested and relaxed but still pretty fit after walking six to eight hours a day with a 20-kilo pack and got straight back into training. I brought a bookmark back with me with a picture of a Rocky mountain and the quote: *"The quality of a person's life is in direct proportion to their commitment to excellence, regardless of their chosen field of endeavour." (Vince Lombardi).* I kept it in whatever book I was reading that year.

I joined Leander and enjoyed a few weeks of walking to training and designing my own programme while everyone else was in Australia. I was a bit conflicted as to what to do for the best now. I wanted to trial for the qualified Quad as a priority, but that would mean leaving Miles behind. I met up with Miles and he was not conflicted, "You should be in the Quad for Sydney – you'll make it go faster. Obviously you have to train with Mike down at Longridge."

I asked Mike if I could meet him to review the year and plan for the next, but before I got a word in he started on the attack. "Before we start I have to tell you that if the Quad had needed a racing sub at St. Catherine's, I would have put Fran or Debbie in – not you." It was only shock that made me hold my tongue and not any wisdom. Shock that he genuinely thought that would have been the right thing to do (Fran and Debs would eventually go on to overtake me but I was still easily faster at this point). But mainly, it wasn't about whether he would or wouldn't have put me in, or whether that would have been the right or wrong thing to do. It had not come to that, a sub had not been needed – he absolutely did not have to tell me.

"Mike, I have no idea why you are telling me that now. I actually just wanted to talk to you about this year. I want to be considered for selection into the Quad and to train back here at Longridge with you. Can that happen? Are you saying there's no point?" I felt panicky. Was I not even going to be given a chance?

"Oh… I thought you were going to tell me you wanted to go off and train with Miles this year. I thought that was what this meeting was about." He at least had the decency to sound embarrassed. Now it was my turn to say "Oh" as the penny dropped. So, that was what was going on. It was spite. He'd thought he was about to be dropped and had wanted to get his punches in early. We talked a bit more and he didn't apologise, but he did make nice and said it would be good to have me training with them and he'd like to coach me. I nodded and thanked him because I had to, but I didn't believe him. If I wanted a shot at the Quad I knew I didn't have any choice. My chances of getting in if I trained at Longridge might be slim, but they were non-existent if I didn't. It was going to be a fun year.

It was actually a good first couple of weeks back. Miles had been right; by the time everyone came back from their 'jolly' I was well ahead and not only kept up but even overtook some of the girls, even in the low rate paddling. Even as they got fit again, I still coped better. My summer of sculling had served me well.

It probably also helped that we really did go out in all weathers and the worse it got, the better it suited me. The Sydney course was well known for being windy and I think they'd all seen it looking pretty grim on their orientation visit. No matter how windy it got, the mantra for that year was: "We're going out, it'll be windy in Sydney." And of course, having braved the storms on the Tideway, the rough water didn't scare me anymore. In fact, I came to enjoy the rough days because me and my metronome legs would fair comparably well even into a strong headwind which, as any knowledgeable rower will tell you, favours heavier rowers.

So, I still got beaten up on the water, but perhaps not quite as often or quite as badly. There were a lot of us training down at Longridge and with only three coaches (Mike, Ron Needs and Louise Kingsley) and two coaching launches, we didn't get much individual coaching time – a few minutes a day maybe. But still I concentrated every stroke on how my body felt picking up the water and on trying to keep the tension out of my arms and Lats and connect with my lower back muscles as I'd discovered in that moment of inspiration on the Thames. I found the more I concentrated on getting the feel right in my lower back, of getting my posture and relaxation right, the more reliably I could access 'it'. Then one day, all of a sudden, virtually in one stroke, I felt something different. I felt the point of pick-up move further down, right down into the base of my spine, just above my coccyx. I was able to keep my whole back relaxed. My arm muscles and whole back muscles were still working, but under a relaxed tension rather than a gripping tension, and I felt the boat lift out of the water and run on in a new way. It was a revelation. I thought "Oh my God. This is *it*. This is what *it's* supposed to feel like. What have I been doing all these years?"

My sculling speed and crew boat compatibility were improving. Ergos, however, were a different story. On the long, steady-state ergos, I'd finish long after the others had got up and left. That I could cope with, but the 2k ergo tests were starting to cause me real psychological angst. Last year, my scores had at least been marginally improving as I got fitter and I'd got under the magic seven-minute marker for the first time, but this year I was stuck. I'd thought seven minutes was like the four-minute mile, a psychological rather than physical barrier and once I'd done it I'd be able to take chunks out of my time. But it wasn't like that. Every test, it would still take everything I had to just scrape the right side of seven minutes.

I got lots of technical and strategic advice on ergo tests, but Miriam threw me the only real lifeline. We were still sharing lifts to and from training, and having that time with a double Olympian and World Champion was a real bonus. I saw that she got just as tired and struggled as much as anyone with the training and even with Mike, and she would often have a piece of calm advice. When I was getting most anxious about ergos, Miriam told me: "I used to get myself so wound up about ergos I'd make myself ill and then I thought what am I doing? I'm never going to beat the big girls on the ergo, so what is the point in getting myself worked up? All I have to do is make sure I post a score under seven minutes and then I get to go and beat them on the water. Once I started thinking like that, it's been so much easier. I don't try and beat them anymore, I just turn up and pull around 6.55 and don't worry about it." I'd think about that little piece of wisdom in the run-up to every ergo test for the next five years and it probably saved me from total ergo test meltdown. But, it wasn't a total solution. I couldn't just rock up and safely submit a 6.55 and on a bad day I'd still miss the seven-minute mark.

The intensity of the training ground on and I coped with the sessions, but it was taking its toll. My heart rate was constantly raised. They say you can tell you are getting fitter because your resting heart rate drops and generally this is true (these days my resting heart rate is in the 40's), but only if you are resting. If my heart rate was anything to go by, I was never resting anymore. I was in constant recovery from one session to the next, even if one session finished at 6pm and the next started at 8am the following morning. I'd lie in bed at night and hear my heart beating 70-80 beats per minute in the blood in my ear against my pillow and feel it hammering in my chest. I'd be so exhausted I couldn't move and couldn't keep my eyes open, but still I couldn't sleep. My occasional insomnia became pretty much constant.

I'd lie awake night after night seeing the hours click by to three, four, or even five in the morning, always just getting to sleep in time for the alarm to wake me at 6.45am. We were supposed to record our 'resting' morning heart rate and mine would routinely still be 60-70 beats per minute. I'd drive to training hardly able to keep my eyes open and all I could think of was getting home that afternoon in time for a half-hour nap, but often I couldn't sleep then either. Weekends, when I should have had some free time to catch up with friends and do something nice, were just about trying to catch up on sleep before Monday. And it seemed like I tried everything and there were so many helpful suggestions. I know from experience that, as you read this, at least half of you are dying to tell me, "Oh I know what that's like. I can't sleep sometimes." And then you want to tell me all the helpful tricks you use to get to sleep. I was to learn that there is a real difference between 'not being able to sleep sometimes' and insomnia. I think it's like 'having a few drinks occasionally' is to alcoholism or 'having a bit of a cold' is to pneumonia.

A good friend gave me one of the most massive books I've ever read (even bigger than this one), called *The Promise of Sleep* and I tried pretty much everything. It got so that from about 11am when I'd consciously have my last cup of caffeinated tea, everything I did was about getting to sleep that night. No caffeine after mid-morning, dinner as soon as I got home in the evening, don't watch TV too late or stare at the computer screen, hot bath or shower before bed. Bedtime got earlier and earlier following the recommendations to give myself plenty of time to wind down, warm milky drink, black out blinds, socks on but otherwise make sure I'd not be too warm in bed, low lighting in the bedroom, yoga breathing, read until I felt sleepy (which I always was anyway) – then I'd put my ear plugs in, turn the light off and… nothing, except the sound of my own heart pounding double time in my ears.

Some weeks I'd have to get through several days at a time on one or two hours' sleep a night and we were still training four to five hours a day. A few times it got quite desperate. But if lying awake at home was bad enough, training camps, where we shared rooms, were worse. Lying there hour after hour trying not to move and rustle the sheets and keep my roommate awake was torture.

In the end, after months of this, I gave up. I was sick of it ruling my days as well as my nights. I threw out the regime and mostly I sat on the computer till late and then on the sofa till nearly midnight or later if I felt like it, watching any rubbish on TV, and then, when I was so nearly asleep I wasn't sure how I was going to make it, I crawled upstairs and rolled into bed and… more often than not fell straight to sleep.

It still wasn't ideal. I had to be up at 6.45, so if I didn't go to bed until midnight or nearly 1am that's not a lot of sleep and I was still always tired, but six hours was definitely better than two. I was always really envious of athletes like Sarah and Fran who would say: "I'm really tired today. I'm going to get to bed at eight tonight and get a good ten hours in" and they would. Apparently, that's not how my body works. I did learn to nap in the afternoons though and got really good at that, which is still the best and most useful of skills.

Apart from the lack of sleep, I made it through to Christmas pretty much unscathed. Not so my little sister. We talked more on the phone now that we'd become friends, but had not had time to meet up. It sounded like all was going really well. She had a new job in London that she loved, a new boyfriend that she loved, a good social life with several old friends who were also down in London plus new friends from work. She sounded fine. But there are things you can't see on the phone. One of her best friends called me one evening very worried about her and asked if there was anything I could do.

I met Catherine in Putney that weekend and was shocked by the pale skeletal version of my sister that walked towards me. She was still wearing the same size 12 clothes but they were belted in and hung off her. She'd been depressed and bulimic over her A level period at school but had seemed to stabilise once she left home. I'd never seen her like this before though. We had a girlie afternoon and went shopping and I watched, cold and sick, as she proudly paraded her Belson-like frame in front of the changing room mirrors and slipped easily into new size 8 clothes for up-and-coming Christmas parties. I remember mentally comparing our backs. I liked the way rowing and weight training had made my spine recede into a smooth deep hollow between the long diagonal slabs of toned muscle on either side. My sister seemed equally pleased with her new back where the spike of each vertebra jutted out to form a raised ridge between the diagonal stripes of every visible rib. We talked about the not eating but she wasn't for changing anything. It felt all too familiar.

I felt bad that this had happened while I wasn't looking and kept in touch more, but was otherwise powerless. I actually thought she'd be in hospital before the month was out and at least that would stop it, but she wasn't. While my primary requirement had been to eat enough to complete my Bedford training programme, hers was to eat enough to complete an eight-hour nursing shift. Apparently an apple, a slim-a-soup and a Ryvita will do it. It wasn't much but it kept her from disappearing completely.

A topic of conversation in common was what to do for Christmas as neither of us was going home. Catherine chose to work seven night shifts over Christmas week as her get-out. The previous year I'd been to Jo's family for the day, but this year I thought I should get right away. I knew it would make it easier for my parents to think I had wanted to be somewhere sunny than just that I hadn't wanted to be with them (and easier to explain to other people too). Jo was on for Christmas in the sun and so was Kate Mackenzie, another Thames girls and squad rower we both knew (although a different Kate to the one from my Thames training group), so we planned a trip to Lanzarote.

I'd got to know Mac really well over the course of the last couple of years and she would always be one of my closest friends on the squad. Now, Kate Mac is a detective in the police. She has a degree from Glasgow University, a postgraduate diploma in child forensic psychology and law, and rowed on the British Rowing Team for nearly seven years, competing in the Atlanta and Sydney Olympics. People could look at her life and make all sorts of assumptions about how she got there, but they'd likely get it wrong.

Kate had a violent father. Once he broke her teeth. She was popular at school but often in trouble, didn't really work and left school as soon as she could without any qualifications. Her best friend's father was a pharmacist and he took Kate on to work part-time in the shop. Kate talks about how responsible it made her feel and that it gave her back the self-esteem she had lacked as a child. When it was quiet he used to take time to explain what he was doing and Kate decided that she would like to be a pharmacist. But that meant going to university and she didn't have a single qualification. So she started going to night school and got her GSE's and then took a BTEC, so finally, five or so years later, she could apply to university and eventually chose a Life Sciences degree. I think about this story often. Everyone has a back story and usually we don't know it. I try and remember that I can choose to judge people on how they first appear or I can choose to be the pharmacist.

Kate Mac was twenty-four when she finally went to Glasgow University.

Like me, she threw herself into everything and fell hardest for the boat club. Kate started rowing at twenty-four. Co-incidentally, Jo was up there studying for a PhD (that eventually ended up as an MSc as she didn't have any easier time of it than me) and they ended up rowing together. When Kate graduated, she moved back to London and joined the City of London Police and Thames Rowing Club. In 1996, at the age of twenty-nine, just five years after she'd started rowing, Kate Mac competed at the Atlanta Olympics for Great Britain in the Pair.

The following year (1997) she was selected into the Eight, but then got a bad chest infection that she tried to train through until it was obvious she had pleurisy. Just a couple of weeks before the 1997 World Championships, Kate had to pull out and watch the Eight go on to take a bronze medal and the Four become World Champions without her. Gutting enough, but there's always next year right? Except that 1997 was the year, the only year. Kate made the Eight again in '98 and '99 but, as you've already heard, there were no more medals.

The three of us ended up with a week in a villa in Lanzarote for some reasonably cheap winter sun. Lanzarote has the famous Club La Santa but that was out of our price range, so Mac and I ran for an hour every day in the cratered landscape and dry heat and sweated through body circuits in the living room. I called my parents from a payphone on Christmas Day to wish them Merry Christmas and Mum said "Well *we've* had a lovely day" in a tone of accusation and malice, as if there was no reason for me not to be with them, as if I'd made it all up. I was hurt but didn't retaliate. I had friends and the beach and plans for the Olympics. They had injustice and denial and the knowledge that their daughter was hard and cold, but they were fine.

Then it was back to Longridge and the inescapable feeling that everything was funnelling towards the Olympic selection trials in Nottingham at the beginning of April.

The constant intensity and competitiveness of Mike's training regime had started to kick in, and not in a good way. After three years, the same training that had worked for a year in '97 and lifted so many British girls onto the medal podium was now causing serious damage. The most common rowing injuries of slipped discs, stress fractured ribs, wrist tenosinovitus and over training syndrome would take girl after girl out for weeks, months or for ever. I avoided all these but my training diary records a heavy cold and a bout of tonsillitis. It sounds minor but I rarely get ill, so to come down with anything is significant.

The winter training camp in Banyoles claimed more casualties. I was sharing a room with Helen who was trying for a place in the Quad. Sharing a room with such a direct competitor could have been awkward but you just get used to it. You race against each other and then leave it on the water and share a room as friends. We used to put our Moby CD on and dance around the room on tough days. But then Helen felt a twinge from a rib stress fracture injury that she'd already had time off for that year. She saw the physios and strapped it up and tried to carry on, but it just kept getting worse. She'd often be crying with the pain of trying to get dressed and undressed, but still she kept sculling. She was one of Mike's favoured few (Mike's eyes lit up at the potential of Helen's powerful 6'2" frame and big ergo scores), but knew with an injury all that could change. One of Mike's favourite sayings was that "Injury is just mental weakness." And it wasn't just pressure from Mike. We were just a few months away from Olympic selection and Helen still had a lot to do and no time to be injured. But after a few more days it became obvious she couldn't continue. She flew home and never made it back.

And it wasn't just the physical stress. The smaller girls were not only having to keep up with the same power-based training, but do it under the umbrella of Mike's constant scepticism and disbelief that they were worth bothering with anyway. There is actual research to show that people under stereotype stress have to use extra brain energy that is then not available to them to use for something more useful. It is genuinely tiring and draining and while people might seem to be coping, they will not perform as well as they would without having to fight this mental battle. On one notable training camp, Libbie Henshilwood, a former World Junior medallist and medallist from the '97 Four and Eight, packed her bags and left the squad pretty much under the cover of darkness. We woke up one morning and she was gone. Her good friend Rachel Woolf, also from the '97 Eight, left soon after. They were reliably one of the fastest pairs from that Eight but they were both about 5'10" tall and just 70kg and therefore it seemed in Mike's eyes that their speed was always a fluke and wouldn't last and eventually they would be beaten by his big girls. I believe Mike actually told Rachel that it didn't matter what she did, he would never select her for the Olympics. Suzie Ellis, the '97 cox without a seat in '99 and therefore without funding, also cut her loses and left to get a 'proper job'.

As the Olympics got closer, the squad was shrinking. At some point that year, I don't know when and I don't know how, Miles was asked to try and pull together an Eight for the qualification regatta. It's the kind of project that's right up Miles's street. He accepted and came over the wire.

Meanwhile the selection criteria for the Double and Quad had been decided. Mike set it up that if you wanted to be considered for selection into one of the crew sculling boats for Sydney, you had to compete at trials in a double. There would be no renegade scullers upsetting the system this year. It wasn't just me he was worried about, there were a few others out there. Fran had come inside and was training with us at Longridge (and doing very well) but Debbie was training outside the system with her U23 coach Mark Banks and Rebecca Romero was also going it alone down at Kingston with her coach Ian South. There would be a separate single sculling race at trials and the winner of this race would be able to go forward to race as the GB Single that summer and potentially go on to Olympic Qualification, but would not be eligible for crew boats. It seems bizarre but fairly typical of Mike to view this up-and-coming talent from outside his system as a threat rather than useful. You'd have thought that with the decimation of numbers for the Eight, Debbie and Rebecca would have been useful somewhere.

Anyway, it was new to run final trials in doubles but not a crazy idea. After all, you are staking your claim to be able to move a crew boat. Selection for the rowing boats is always done from a pair's trial, so it wasn't much different from that. It was Mike's method of selecting the doubles though that was unorthodox and contentious. In most rowing systems, the top group of rowers/scullers first compete in a matrix to objectively decide which combinations go fastest together. Athletes ranked 1 & 2 will go on to race together, 3 & 4, 5 & 6 etc. The new crews then have a few weeks to train together before trials, so the result is not a forgone conclusion.

Mike's system was uniquely Mike. If you wanted to race at trials with someone you went and asked them, and if they said "yes" then that was your double. He said that it was in every scullers interest to be in the fastest double they could, so this system would naturally select the right combinations. It sounds persuasively logical, but with the benefit of hindsight, I can say that the lack of any sort of real ranking at this stage in the year would lead to a whole heap of trouble further down the line. If it sounds like I find pleasure in that fact and am eating sour grapes, you are probably right, because of course no one picked me for their double. It was primary school rounders all over again.

I didn't have the courage or confidence to ask anyone to double with me and was not approached. I'm not actually sure how the doubles were decided, but this is what I saw from my vantage point at the back of the rounders queue. I suspect Gillian made the first play. In a bold move after the decline of her double with Miriam, she approached Fran who'd had a storming year at trials and training. Pairing up with the former World Champion was a great offer for the nineteen-year-old Fran and of course she said yes. It was a surprise move but an inspired one, and you could see that it should work well.

With those two out of the equation I'm going to stick my neck out and say that the next most logical combination would have been Miriam and Katherine. Katherine had had another great year and was already showing signs of the total legend she would become. It would have been a good double but it didn't happen. Katherine ended up in a double with Sarah. Actually, I think it was always assumed that Katherine and Sarah would row together. Extremely extroverted and sociable they'd hit it off straightaway in the Quad last year and very quickly became not just the best of friends, but pretty much inseparable. I'm not saying that Katherine wouldn't have wanted to double with Sarah, but I'm not sure Mike's system actually gave her any choice. The advantage of objective ranking systems like a matrix is that it gives you a way of not rowing with your best friend without hurting their feelings. With Mike's system it was really unthinkable that she would row with anyone else.

That left the Battens to form a double. They are quite different those sisters, but with a common agenda as strong as qualifying for a potential Olympic medal-winning boat, they found enough common ground to make a boat move fast for a few weeks at least.

So there you have your top three doubles nicely selected without any need for any awkward trials and looking at it from any angle, everyone could see the Double and Quad in some order, right there. I'd be lying if I said I wasn't at least a little put out. Sarah and I had been very close all year and I'd proved I was capable of beating her. I'm not saying I would definitely have won a trial, but based on the year's results I thought I at least deserved a trial against Sarah (in fact all of them) for a place in the top three doubles. That something as important as an Olympic place seemed to come down to who was your best friend seemed a little rough. Especially as I knew my racing skills were better than my friend-making skills. It was clever though, Mike's system. If I asked for a trial, he'd just say that I could row with anyone who wanted to row with me. And how could I argue with that.

I did have a doubles partner though. There were two of us left after all the cards had been thrown up and come down in pairs and I was with Lisa. Lisa and I really didn't know each other at all until we got into that boat for the first time. But, as I was quickly to learn, if your back's against the wall, you'd want Lisa by your side. Anyone else would have looked at us and what we had to do and thought we were on a fool's errand without a hope in hell. But even before we got hands on the boat, Lisa's talk was 100% positive. She was adamant that we could do this. We had two weeks.

We both lived in Henley and started sharing lifts together to training. With the best part of an hour a day together chatting in the car, we quickly got to know each other. I'd only seen the serious rowing side of Lisa (which can be scarily serious), but I quickly discovered she could be quite wicked and very good fun. It took a few outings and we aired a few cross words in the boat through time-pressured frustration, but we knew we were heading in the same direction and really found a connection. Just a few days before trials, we raced some preparation pieces on Eton rowing lake and as my training diary records, the boat really started to move.

April 8th 2000
3 x 1000M Excellent pieces
34/35 Relaxed

After the pieces, Lisa turned round in the boat and said: "We could *actually* do this". And it's funny because the words and the tone were *less* certain than they had been a week ago but the belief behind them was more so. In Mike's debrief, he too said: "You could *actually* do this" with a tone of slight incredulity and maybe a little anxiety. We were not under any illusions though that this was still a very long shot.

We loaded our boat onto the Squad trailer and drove up to be greeted by the friendly Holme Pierpont wind. It's not ever really a question of whether it will be there, just which direction. The morning of the trials we went for a pre-race paddle and it did not go so well. We were having trouble steering and couldn't work out if it was the crosswind or us or if there was something wrong with our boat. When we got our boat in, we looked at the fin and it did look rather bent – so we tried to straighten it, but when we couldn't, we asked the boatman and also mentioned it to Mike who was very busy checking over Gillian's boat at the time.

I'm not really sure what happened, if anyone checked it, or even if we checked it ourselves again before we boated for our trial. We were so wrapped up in our pre-race plan and what we had to do in the next hour or so and all that it meant and the inevitable pre-race nerves that I think thoughts of equipment just got squeezed out. That's why it's good to have a coach, someone on your side who wants you to win, someone who'll check your boat over before you race.

As we sculled up to the start, there was still a very strong crosswind and the boat felt better and steered straighter. But in our last warm-up start in race direction, the boat veered violently off course and we realised the wind had been compensating and we really had trouble. It was still hard to tell if it was just the wind but it felt too much for that. We were minutes away from the start, we had no one to ask and we didn't know what to do. We had a quick discussion and resolved that there was nothing we could do now so we wouldn't worry about it. In the end we both just said: "It's fine, it'll be fine" and got onto the start. I honestly think we both thought we could will this not to be a problem.

We rowed the whole race practically on one oar. At bow I was responsible for steering and I just called "Left, left, hard left…" all the way down the course to keep us vaguely in lane. Gillian and Fran won, the Batten sisters were second and Katherine and Sarah third. Lisa and I weren't just beaten, we were annihilated.

We paddled in, put the boat back on trestles and looked at it. The fin was bent much more than before. I have no idea when it happened or how it happened, but we had definitely raced with it like that. I have no idea if we could have beaten one of the other crews with a straight fin, but now we'd never know.

If I read this account by any other athlete I'd think they were making excuses for their poor performance, so I'm ashamed as I write this because really there was no excuse. Even if your equipment *is* faulty, it is your responsibility. You check it, you get it fixed and if you can't, you refuse to race until it's sorted. I wouldn't have any sympathy for anyone else in this situation and Lisa and I had none for ourselves. We showed Mike the fin but he said it wouldn't have made any difference. Anyway we knew there was nothing that could be done after the event. And then Lisa and I never talked about it again. I never mentioned it to anyone in any debriefs I had about that trial and when people asked "How'd it go?", I just said "We lost" and left it at that. It still feels like I'm making excuses but I've put it here because it was a learning experience. I'd never be that careless again.

But it wasn't over yet. I hadn't wanted to think about it at all before the trial, but now I had to. I could still get to Sydney but it would take at least two more trials. Lisa was welcomed with open arms into an Eight that was definitely starting to take shape, but had been waiting for more strength from whoever got dropped down from the sculling group. I could have gone that way too but it had less appeal for me than trying the Single again. The Eight was a totally unknown quantity and I knew exactly how close I'd been to qualifying the Single last year. Things would have changed in a year and new girls would be trying their luck for those last single slots, but I still felt it was not only the safest option but also the most exciting. I'd loved my autonomous season last year and have never really been a fan of Eights. Trying to get nine people in the same place at the same time before you can do anything does my head in. And at least this way I'd be responsible for my own fate.

I'd made no plans for what happened if I didn't make the quad, so there were some hasty rearrangements. Debbie Flood had just won the singles race at trials and was officially the GB Single sculler. If I wanted that job I was going to have to prove I was faster than her and that meant another trial. Debs and I had already raced twice that year at winter trials and I'd beaten her in both. On paper I was the faster sculler. But they were 5K head races and this was going to be 2K side by side. Also still relatively new to rowing, Debs was on a steeper part of the learning curve than me and getting faster all the time. There was absolutely nothing to be taken for granted here. The new trial date was set. May 4th. I had three weeks to get ready.

The first thing was to phone my parents. We'd been due to get a couple of days off after trials and I'd actually planned, for the first time in two years, to go and visit them. If nothing else I really missed the Yorkshire Dales and needed a hill fix. I had planned (in my fantasy life, the one where Lisa and I stormed the trial and I got selected into the Quad for Sydney) to jump straight into my car after the trial and continue up the M1 to Richmond. I should have been back that evening for the first time in two years. Dinner was likely already in the oven. But now I was calling to say I was sorry but I couldn't come. I hadn't made selection. I had three weeks until my last and absolutely final chance to make the Olympic team and had cancelled my own leave.

I didn't want to totally disappoint them, so I asked if they would come down to me and book into a hotel in Nottingham for a couple of days since I was going to be training there now. They came down the next day.

I'd already asked Miles if he would take me through the trial. I knew he'd be busy with the Eight and this wasn't a long-term plan, but he agreed to help me out. So instead of driving North, I drove South, picked up my single and some more kit, had one night at home in Henley, then drove back up to Nottingham with my boat strapped to the top of my car. I'll tell you one thing about having to make new plans on the hoof and prepare for a life or death trial. It's a great way to take your mind off a disastrous race.

I met Mum and Dad at the course. Mum handed me an old Quality Street tin. "I'm so sorry it didn't work out. I'm sorry it's all so hard for you. I made flapjack. There's more in the car." Dad opened the car boot. "I couldn't stop her; we had to wait for the last batch to come out of the oven before she would leave." The car boot was full of cake – the cases were on the back seat. Dad started handing me tins with sighs and the occasional raised eyebrow. Mum had filled every old Quality Street, Roses and M&S biscuit tin in the house and then kept going. Dad was now handing out foil wrapped blocks of still warm cake and it just kept coming. It was the old comfort food recipes, flapjack, chocolate biscuit cake and pineapple fruit cake. I could see it all. Mum *had* been sorry it hadn't worked out and *really sorry* it was all so hard for me and was utterly powerless to do anything to make it better. So she'd taken to the kitchen and baked. I knew what it was about. It wasn't about cake. This was Northern code. It was baked love.

I had to go back to proper training for the first ten days or so, back to thirty-minute AT ergos, 20k steady state paddles and heavy weights, as I still had to balance winning the trial in three weeks with the fact that the whole point of this trial was to be fast enough to race at the Olympics in four months' time. I then kicked into my second wind down and race preparation week in less than a month.

The day before the race I've written "POSTURE" and "HANDS INFRONT" in big capitals in my training diary. There is always so much to think about the day before a race, but if it's all going well it usually boils down to two or three things. Apart from what's recorded in my diary I don't remember much about that week, but I remember the morning of the trial. Of course I didn't sleep the night before and couldn't eat breakfast, that much was taken for granted, but I reached newfound levels of pre-race nerves. I had never felt so utterly wretched. This was it. If I lost to Debs today, it was all over. There would be no Sydney 2000, I would have to watch the Olympics on TV, my grant would stop and I'd have to admit that at twenty-nine the Olympic dream was over. This might actually be my last race.

I went for my pre-race paddle and felt sick. I came in, sat around and felt sick. Every time I bent over to pick something up, my blades, my boat, my shoes, I started retching and had to stand up again quickly to stop myself actually being sick. I was hot and cold and felt light-headed. I tried to focus on the one step at a time routine but the wretchedness wouldn't go away, not for a moment. I tried to play "It's all be over in…" But that didn't really help as it reminded me that this time it really could be over for good. Was this all just nerves? It was so bad I couldn't be sure. I thought I might be ill, properly ill. Maybe I had food poisoning? If I'd learnt anything from the doubles trial, it was that you can't ignore all external forces and will everything to go away. If I really was ill, then I didn't have to do the trial today. It would have to be postponed. God, that was tempting. But also awful. I was ready now and if we didn't race today, we'd have to do this all over again at some point. It wasn't going to go away.

But I knew I had to say something this time. I told Miles that I felt really sick, sicker than usual and I thought I might actually be properly ill. Miles said, "Are you sure? If you're ill we will postpone the trial but we have to say now. You know you can't race and lose and then say you are ill, even if you really are."

"I know. But I don't know. Maybe it's just nerves. I think it's just nerves. I'll be OK." I felt a little better just talking about it lucidly like that.

I carried my blades down to the water and went back for my boat. I got in my boat. Miles pushed me off with a "Have a good one" and I responded with my usual "See you later", and I was on my own. I could take some comfort from the fact that it was really windy. The wind was blowing straight down the course; the second half of the race would be rough and after all my training out in the worst of it at Putney – my kind of water.

I couldn't play "It'll be over in…", so I used the Power of Plan B to play "What's the worst that can happen?" My Plan B all year had been that if at any point I got ill or got dropped from the squad, then I'd take myself off and hike and teach my way round Australia (maybe even THE WORLD). I'd kept Plan B alive with a little bit of voluntary teaching at a Henley school earlier in the year and a Lonely Planet *Bushwalking in Australia* book that I now kept under my bed with the *Hamlyn Guide to Birds*. So now, as I tried to calm myself for this, the latest biggest race of my life, I thought: "The worst that can happen today is that I lose and then I pack my bags and within a few weeks I'll be hiking and teaching in sunny Australia." I could picture it and it was a nice picture and for the first time all morning I started to feel like I could face this race.

And I know that sounds weird to some people and you'll get athletes who say you have to focus all your energies on 'How much you want it' and 'What you've given up to get this far' and 'That this is for the Olympics and this is everything' and to 'Leave yourself no other option', but I couldn't think like that. Hiking and teaching wasn't Plan A, it was definitely Plan B. It was a damned good Plan B, but still only Plan B. I couldn't have wanted anything more than to win that trial and go to the Olympics, I knew that; I didn't need to remind myself of it; I didn't need to beat myself up with it. What I needed to do was free my mind of the panic and the sickness and release the race.

Debs and I lined up side by side at the top of the course. Despite the fact that it was just the two of us, it was a proper trial. Mike was there. David Tanner (Performance Director of British Rowing) was there and we had a proper umpire. This was an Olympic trial and carried all the official weight of one.

Thursday May 4th 2000
Race Plan
Put both blades in the water (I'd learnt something from that first trial).

ATTENTION… GO! I released the race.

Stroke 1	*Posture*
	10 Shoulders back/hands INFRONT (WIND)
	10 PLACE (light catch)
	10 QUICKEN (one piece drive)
250m	*LOAD LEGS*
	FINISH INFRONT
	POSTURE

Debs led off the start and was 1.5 seconds up by 250m (about 3/4 of a boat length). Debs and I had never raced each other side by side before so I was not to know, but would soon learn, that this is absolutely Debbie's race style. We are sort of racing dopplegangers, Debs and I. If I'm endurance animal, then Debs is pistons of power. If I'm all about the big finish, Debs is all about the flying start. Debs was a recent convert to rowing from Judo and all that dynamism was being used against me. But I was used to being dropped off the start, so I didn't let her throw me.

500m	*LEGS GO*	*– Heels down*
		– Slow legs – hang off
		– Loose arms – LONG

The times show Debs was nearly two seconds up by 500m. That's about a boat length – I'd have started to lose sight of her. I don't remember much about that race but I remember feeling very calm through that second 500m. I was still sculling well and pushing hard; there was nothing more I could do and anyway I'd been in this situation enough times to know that just because my opponent was out of sight now, didn't mean it would stay that way.

750m	*FINISH INFRONT*	*– one piece through*
		– don't separate hands

Debs still nearly two seconds in front and just out of sight. The times show that she's stopped pulling further ahead but I wouldn't have known that. As it got rougher, my metronome legs kept pushing and I ignored any rubbish strokes and got on with the next one. The rough conditions meant I was not hitting the ratings I often did, but as we came through 1000m still I fought to bring the rate up again and stay light and on top of the water.

1000m	*LEGS GO*	*– lift rate (1-2)*

Still a boat length between us.

1250m	*30 STROKES*	*FINISH INFRONT*
		POSTURE

Debs still two seconds in front as we go through the 1250m mark but for the first time I'm quicker than her this 250m and gain a few feet back – I could just see her again. Then coming through the last 500m as the water gets roughest, I hit my wind for home (did I mention I'm legendary for my big finishes?).

1500m	*60*	*LEGS GO*
	50	*FINISH INFRONT*
	40	*POSTURE*

I got the two seconds back in 30 strokes and at some point I caught her, I was on her and by 250 to go I had my bow ball in front.

1750m	*30*	*SIT UP GO*
	20	*HANDS INFRONT*
	10	*LEGS*

I moved quickly through and crossing the finish line, I had a significant lead. The times would show it was over nine seconds, but at the time I had no idea and I didn't care. I'd won. That was it. I was the GB Single sculler for the 2000 season.

Only one more trial between me and Sydney.

I don't honestly remember what followed, but knowing Debs now I know that she would have come over to say congratulations, shake my hand and probably even give me a wave-soaked hug. It is a blur, but I can picture myself sometime later sitting in the empty locker room showered, changed, relieved and very happy. I sat a while, part savouring the moment and part too exhausted to move. One set of trials takes something out of you, but two back to back is something else. Do you ever feel so tired your face feels numb? But still these are the moments you do it all for.

And I'm having (yet another) crisis of confidence as I write this that says: "Why would anyone want to read all this? Why would they be interested?" This is not the story of how Steve Redgrave won just about every trial and every race for twenty years and five consecutive Olympic Gold medals. I've just recounted a race where I fought to be the lowest ranked GB sculler on the squad and the right, not to go on and win Gold or even a medal in Sydney (not even to hope or dream of that), but just for the opportunity to *try* and be there. And then I remember that actually, that is the point. This is why I'm writing this and why, to my surprise, this story seems to resonate with so many who hear it. Because you don't have to be on the start line of an Olympic final to be so invested in your own future and so exposed that your insides don't want to stay there, and you don't have to win Olympic Gold to feel like you have.

"The quality of a person's life is in direct proportion to their commitment to excellence, regardless of their chosen field of endeavour."

I was happy, not just at the result, but at the conclusiveness of the verdict after last year. At least no one could argue my claim. You'd think, wouldn't you?

As I debriefed with Miles and planned next steps he said: "You should be careful; Mark is going round saying that the trial was unfair, that Debbie was winning but it was too rough at the finish."

"But that's ridiculous, the race wasn't 1000m long, it's 2000m. I'm always down at 1000, but you don't win by being first to halfway."

"Of course, but I'm just letting you know that this is going round."

I felt sick again. A repeat of last year, that horrible feeling that it didn't matter what I did on the water, people would always find a way of talking me out of the boat. But I really didn't believe it. I didn't know Mark at all but I couldn't believe anyone would do this.

I went back to Longridge and started training towards the World Cups. At first I still wasn't convinced Miles had heard Mark right, but every so often, right through the season, some comment from someone somewhere would draw my attention to the fact that the perceived opinion of everyone who hadn't actually witnessed that race, or talked to me directly, was that Debbie had won the trial but I'd been given the seat anyway due to Mike's favouritism (oh the irony). I tried not to let it affect me, but it did niggle and it did hurt.

I don't know whether Mark formally appealed or just gossiped or if he said anything at all, but nothing formal happened that I would ever hear about. I thought maybe I was being paranoid but then one day I saw my name on a thread on an Internet Rowing Chat Room called 'The Tideway Slug'. People posted anonymously and mainly it was harmless, rather boring obsessive rowing talk, but it had been known to get nasty.

- "It's outrageous that Alison Mowbray is racing the Single. Debbie Flood beat her at trials but Mike selected Alison because she's been training with him all year."
- "Yes, I heard that too. It's blatant favouritism."
- "So unfair to Debbie"

Etc. etc. (It was a long thread).

I suppose I should have turned the other cheek but I'm no saint. I logged on and wrote a reply at the bottom of the thread…

- "This is Alison Mowbray. It's crazy that I should have to defend myself on here having done it on the water all year. Debbie is a good sculler and

I've no doubt she will do really well in the future. But, I'd like to make it clear that up to this point Debbie has never beaten me. I beat her at both sets of winter trials and then again by over nine seconds in a head to head trial at Nottingham. I don't know where you have got your information from but those are the facts. I won my place fair and square."

I signed off and checked back a couple of times but there were no more additions. It shut that gossip thread down, but I would continue to hear other whispers all season.

I had three months before the Lucerne qualification regatta and I wasn't actually sure who could coach me. Miles had helped me out for the trial, but really he was on a single-minded Miles mission to get the Eight through Olympic qualification. I wasn't under any illusions about the task in front of me and the fact that I was also going to need someone to be that single-minded about me.

When I got back to Longridge, I noticed that our coach Louise Kingsley wasn't there. That was weird. Like any of the athletes, she was always there. I asked around and the girls said she was still up in Nottingham and hadn't been back since trials. The rumour was that something had happened between her and Mike but no one knew what. It was very odd. She was three-and-a-half years into an Olympic cycle like the rest of us and had been down every day. To leave at this point when she should have had an Olympic crew and a place herself at the Olympics didn't make any sense.

It gave me an idea though. I phoned her between outings that morning. We chatted and she congratulated me and I asked why she wasn't here. She was very cagey and just said it was difficult without giving any specifics. So I asked her if it would make any difference if I asked her to coach me through qualification and to the Olympics if I made it that far. Would she come back then? I think she was a bit shocked but seemed pleased and said she would if Mike agreed.

So, I went and found Mike and said that obviously I'd really like him to coach me, but he was already going to be really busy with the Double and the Quad so I'd also like Louise to coach me if that was OK (which was the way I'd learnt this thing was done here). I never did find out what had been going on with them, but Louise came back and I had my single-minded coach whose one job was to get me to the Olympics. It worked really well. Louise came out with me every session and helped me work on what we'd agree we'd work on and gave me some really useful coaching and totally looked after my boat and equipment and anything else I needed. She also acted as a 'worst of Mike protection shield', which meant I was able to have Mike come out and coach me sometimes to get useful input *and* have Louise take me off down the river or to some far-flung end of the lake and say: "We're not going to do all that's on the programme today and that's fine because you are in the Single and it's harder for you and not necessarily appropriate." She had a very professional knack of breaking from Mike's sacred programme without ever speaking a word against him or even implying that she disagreed with him. And she took input from Mike and was still fine with me talking to Miles and bringing ideas from him without showing a shred of the possessiveness and the "This is my athlete, hands off" you see in most coaches the world over. And I think I was really lucky that Louise was around that year. She was the perfect coach for me at that time.

So, we were into my third World Cup season and my second in the Single. I was starting to know my way around now and it was a wonderful thing to turn up to an International Regatta and feel like I was meant to be there and have scullers from all over the world greet me by name and come up and chat and to be able to do the same.

It was all about those last three qualification places that year and how many non-qualified scullers I could stay ahead of. I had Tim Foster for single sculling company in the first World Cup. He'd injured his hand in a rather unfortunate incident involving a party, a window and some alcohol and was trying to redeem himself and fight his way back into the Four. His good result in the Single did him plenty of favours and he would of course eventually make it back in.

I was doing OK, but was still crippled by debilitating pre-race nerves. In a few weeks I would be facing qualification, the latest biggest race of my life and this time it would be really, really big. I was doing everything I could think of to give myself the best possible chance of getting through, but I was terrified that my anxiety would let me down. Eventually, I think it was Miles who suggested I talk to Dr Babbs the squad doctor and Chris Shambrook the squad sports psychologist.

I talked to Dr Babbs about not being able to sleep before racing. I really hadn't been thinking of sleeping pills because drugs are not my thing, but he suggested the hypnotic Zopiclone as they have a short half-life, only last about four hours and don't make you drowsy the next day. He said even airplane pilots take them they are so safe. I was desperate so I tried them and they worked. It was amazing. If I was hyped up about racing I'd wake up pretty much spot on the four hours, but to get any sleep and not have to lie awake counting the minutes all night before a race was such a relief. They would help me get through both racing and the training load for the rest of my career. I'd try not to take them as a matter of course so as not to become dependent, but if I was ever still awake past midnight, I knew I could take one and be asleep in half an hour and even just knowing they were under my bed would often help me get to sleep without taking one.

I also talked to psychologist Chris Shambrook and not surprisingly he took a more psychological approach. I came out realising that the nerves were real and the not being able to sleep and not being able to eat were real, but I was making myself feel worse by worrying about the symptoms of nerves when really they weren't such a big deal. I only had to race for eight minutes and I wasn't actually going to fall asleep or starve in that time. I still felt sick before racing, but at least now I could think more rationally and stop making myself feel worse. Chris also helped me develop simple strategies like eating my breakfast just before I went to bed the night before racing when I could still eat, rather than in the morning when I couldn't. I knew it would still be in my stomach in the morning, so I no longer felt like I had to force-feed myself and felt a bit calmer.

I also realised, again I think through talking to Chris, that there was a pattern. Every time I felt this dreadful I would actually go out and race really well. It was actually part of what made the difference between the Al Mowbray you'd beat every day in training and the Al Mowbray who'd beat you in racing. Adrenalin is a powerful drug and it will keep you awake at night and make you feel sick and even, weirdly, very sleepy just before you race (you have to watch out for that one). It will pull you apart if you let it but will also make you fly if you know how to harness it, and somehow I did. I literally raced on my nerves and it wasn't pleasant, but it was actually my greatest strength.

And, when I realised that, it made all the difference. The nerves and the sickness didn't go away and I still lay awake (except for the magic Zopiclone four) and couldn't eat and felt unrelentingly awful for at least two hours before every race I would ever do, but at least I now knew there was a reason. Instead of thinking "I feel dreadful, I'll never race well today", I'd think "I feel dreadful, I'm ready." In fact on the rare occasion I didn't feel sick, I'd worry I wasn't ready and would deliberately think about the race until I felt my anxiety levels rise.

The final thing that helped came from a surprising source. I'd somehow thought I had this worse than anyone else. I used to look at the likes of Matt and Steve and think, "It must be so much easier for them, they are up there winning medals and everyone else gets to be scared of them rather than the other way round." Then I watched the first episode of *Gold Fever*, a BBC video diary documentary about the Men's Four in the lead up to Sydney. I watched the first episode just before I went out to the qualification regatta and saw, for the first time, Steve, Matt, James and Tim going through every bit as much pre-race anxiety as I did. The crowning moment was James Cracknell throwing up blue Powerade round the back of the GB marquee at the Hazewinkle World Cup from sheer nerves. It was a transforming moment and I would think about that blue Powerade ever so often for years. I had to stop feeling sorry for myself that day. This was how it was for everybody. It didn't matter how good you got, I could see that the demands and the expectations rose to match and no one, but no one, ever had it easy.

I had another good season and as optimistic a run-up to the Qualification Regatta as I could have hoped for. I've had to look at the database for the results again and again have been very pleasantly surprised. I was fifth at the first World Cup in Munich. My best ever ranking and importantly I beat the Romanian sculler (who'd edged me out of an Olympic place by 0.5 seconds) by nearly two seconds in the final. I had definitely got faster.

I could be pleased, very pleased, with my fifth place. The medal-hopeful Quad and Pair would be a lot less pleased with their fifth places and the Double with their fourth. The new Women's Eight came fourth of the four crews entered, which looks disappointing on the face of it, until you look at the times and see that they were just over three seconds behind the winning Netherlands crew and just over a second (well overlapping) behind the legendary Romanians. It was actually a very good result and put them well on track for qualification.

A similar performance gave me a seventh place in the more highly-attended Vienna World Cup. I was initially disappointed not to make the final after catching my blade on a buoy in my Rep, but I stormed my B final and won! Technically I know I was seventh, but I'd not won anything since I started competing internationally so you take your moments where you find them. The Pair and Double were also both seventh. The Quad won Gold at Vienna, which was nice but a rather hollow victory as the four crews that had beaten them at Munich were not there.

I look back at these results now and wonder how it was that I always felt like the hanger on, the underdog and that that is how I remember it. I know there is a danger that the older you get the better you used to be, but these results shock and even sadden me to look at them now. These results say I was good. I was very good. I *was* World Class. I was every bit as good as Cath Bishop and Gillian Lyndsey and even Miriam Batten and I never felt it, I never knew it. And I still wonder if Mike did that to me or I did it to myself. Somehow in debriefs of these regattas, the insinuation was always that although we'd got the same result, I had overperformed and the other athletes underperformed and both were flukes that would come right eventually.

Mike's squad came home to Longridge in a state of disarray and extreme anxiety. Those girls who had been at it the longest and/or had World medals under their belts were absolutely (and understandably) desperate for an Olympic medal. Mike had his back up against a wall. He'd upset a lot of people in British rowing with his determination to do it absolutely his way and must have known that as much as everyone wanted to see the first British Women's Olympic medal, there were also a lot of people that would begrudge it being done by him.

There was something unusual in the Longridge air when we got back. I became aware that there was talk I was not party too. Mike called a breakfast meeting that first morning and we were all sworn to secrecy (the Eight were training elsewhere). A secret and risky plan was afoot. I could tell from his glances that he was uncomfortable about me being there, but I was technically one of his and he couldn't ask me to leave – so I stayed. I had no idea what was about to happen, but I wasn't going to miss it.

The plan unfolded. It had not gone unnoticed that the newly-formed and unlikely Eight made up of all Mike's rejects, those that had fallen off the bottom of his notice, had been performing surprisingly well. If those bottom ranked girls could do so well in an Eight, what could his top-ranked athletes do if they were all put together in one boat? Maybe the Eights event was not as competitive as the other events this year? Maybe it would be easier to get a medal in an Eight than it was proving in any other boat? The plan he put forward was that the existing Double, Pair and Quad would form an Eight and race at the qualification regatta instead of the existing Eight.

Mike wanted to know what everyone thought of this plan. Well not me obviously – he didn't want me in his Eight, which left me free to sit back open-mouthed and enjoy the beautiful drama. It was really quite something, his plan. Breathtaking in its audacity, Mike's plan would strip the girls in the existing Eight – girls who had raised themselves up from nothing over the past year to put themselves in real contention, girls who were technically also under his care as head coach – of all hope of an Olympic place. If the new Eight qualified, the existing Olympic places for the Quad, Pair and Double would almost certainly go to waste as there was little or no chance the girls from the old Eight would be able to make those boats go fast enough at this short notice (when those who'd been rowing in them all year were struggling).

There was a moment's silence and then Mike went round the eight girls one by one to ask their opinion. I don't remember everyone's individual responses and anyway I'm not sure it's fair to report. I don't actually remember anyone being so bold as to say "Yes, let's go for it", but then I don't remember anyone saying "No, no way" either. Mostly people hedged their bets with "I'll do whatever you think best, Mike." Then it got round to Miriam. Miriam who, having already been disappointed at two Olympics and as the oldest undoubtedly facing her last, would have had more reason than most to go for the desperate plan. But Miriam was having none of it and was the first to actually commit herself either way. "No, no way Mike, it's a really bad plan. I couldn't do it to those girls. It's dreadful. Some of them are my friends and I could never face them again, it's not worth it." There had been a bit of a Gung Ho feel before Miriam spoke. Despite everyone's caginess I think it had been going Mike's way. Then, I felt the atmosphere change. Miriam's comment silenced and shamed everyone.

Everyone but Mike. I'll never forget Mike's response because it turned out to be so true. "Everyone wants to be nice, everyone wants to be liked. But I've learnt that you can't win and still have everyone like you, have everyone be your friend. I know that I've made a lot of enemies along the way but let me tell you this. Those people who have won medals with me, they are always my friends." I saw a couple of nods and thought maybe it would swing Mike's way again and then Miriam countered with, "I don't agree Mike. I think you can be a good person and still win. And if I can't, I don't want it. It's not worth it. And anyway – don't you believe we can win a medal in the Quad? Don't you believe in us? If we're not good enough or we don't believe we can do it, then we don't deserve to win a medal. If we are not good enough, then going into the Eight won't make any difference. There's no such thing as an easy Olympic medal."

I'm not honestly sure how it went after, that but the upshot was that Mike's Eight was not to be. I wasn't the leak, but the whole juicy story got out somehow and the girls in the existing Eight were rightly outraged. This story may rank rather low on the sensation scale compared to football's drunken antics or athletic drug cheats, but this was seriously salacious stuff for rowing.

Anyway… back to me. I had passed all tests and been deemed eligible to go to the qualification regatta. I was to be given one last chance to fight for my Olympic place and I was back to the distraction technique of choosing biscuit cutters in Lucerne.

Final training in Sarnen, Switzerland. At the end of the day, it's just you and your little boat, against the rest of the world.

Eleven girls from the 'rowing developed' countries of Europe, USA and Australia turned up to race off for three last Olympic places available to us. There is a separate Olympic qualification quota from Asia and Africa to ensure the maximum number of countries get to compete, even if they are not as fast as many of those who wouldn't make it through from this regatta. It might sound strange, but I don't think anyone in rowing minds this – I certainly didn't. It's for the good of our sport to help develop new rowing Nations. I raced in the heats and didn't win, so I had to race a Rep. My heat had not been great. I've said before that I never liked the course at Lucerne and I suffered again. I'd lost my focus, missed the 500m marker and dozed through the 750, but this time I realised why. The start at Lucerne is quite close to a tree-lined bank and I felt enclosed and channelled. Then, towards the 250m mark, the lake widens out and my focus had drifted with it. In the heat I'd effectively been going through the motions through the second 500m, until the bank came back down to the course and I realised where I was. That would not do. Every stroke takes focus to keep it lifted and gain every inch from it. You can't afford to miss that intensity for a single stroke and in my heat I'd lost about 30 of them – never again. I annotated the race plan in my training diary.

500m (BE AWARE!) HIT IT HARD. OLYMPICS!
And again at 750m *(BE AWARE!)*

It worked. Two went through from each Rep and I won mine. Technically, I qualified joint third for the final. Joint third wouldn't be good enough. Just three would qualify.

I raced down that final. The latest, biggest race of my life.

BE AWARE! BE AWARE! Every, every stroke.

I came second. I got the second to last place for the Sydney Olympics in my event.

And I stood on the medal podium in Lucerne, the first time I'd ever stood on an International Medal podium, and I had a medal round my neck that basically said 'I can go to the Olympics.'

I de-rigged my boat and walked down to the stands to watch the Women's Eight make their bid for qualification, and I kept bumping into the rest of the GB team who'd just flown out to race Lucerne Regatta proper. They all hugged me and congratulated me. I felt pretty special. Matt Pinsent said did I realise I was actually the first member of the British Rowing Team to have their place confirmed for Sydney. I hadn't, but I did now.

I was nervous for the Eight but they raced brilliantly and qualified. We all had to get a bus back that night to our Sarnen training base, but had a few hours to go out in Lucerne to celebrate first. We all talked about what we'd drink to celebrate and how much, but actually, when we got there, none of us was that bothered. We just didn't need it. Certainly for myself, I didn't want to pollute this feeling or miss a minute of it. I couldn't quite work it out, but it was extraordinary what I was feeling and still there are no words to describe it. It wasn't exactly joy or relief or excitement, but then maybe that's the closest. Thinking about it now I can feel it again, and you know the closest

I can come up with is the feeling of falling in love – that feeling of excitement and optimism and the opening up of a whole new future. We stayed out in bars for a couple of hours but we were all quite fazed and really, really tired, so I don't think anyone minded getting on the bus to go home.

But I didn't sleep for two whole nights because I couldn't believe that someone like me was going to the Olympics. I vividly remember lying on the bottom bunk staring up at the slats above all night. Eyes wide open and not even trying to sleep. And there was no restless tossing and turning and rustling. There was just lying and staring. And there was no way I was taking a sleeping pill tonight; there was no way I was wasting a moment of this. And the cliché would be to say that I couldn't believe it and I didn't want to go to sleep because I was worried it was all a dream that would disappear when I woke up. But that's not how it was. It was the opposite.

Of all the races and moments I've recounted and all I've left to tell, this was the one. This was the big one that would change how I looked at myself and my life and the mystery of how you make it all work out. So, it wasn't that I didn't believe it. I knew it was real. I couldn't sleep because I finally did believe it. I was going to the Olympics. I was capable of going to the Olympics. And more than that – much, much more than that, I'd qualified by myself in the Single. I was suddenly so incredibly grateful that I hadn't made it into the Quad and knew that even if they medalled, I would never have a moment of regret. This might have been the longest and hardest path to the Olympics, but it was so worth it. I knew if I'd qualified in the Quad, I would always have thought (as would everyone else) that it was because I was rowing with the Great K.G or the legendary Batten sisters or Golden Girl Gillian and they had pulled me along. But it was just me. I had been out there by myself and I had qualified for the Olympics. I was good enough.

I was enough.

And you know the thing that kept me awake most? Every time I shut my eyes, I'd think about it again and catch my breath and they'd ping wide open. I kept thinking about how nearly I'd missed it. How nearly I hadn't let this happen. How I hadn't thought I was good enough. How I'd *always* had it in me to go to the Olympics, that there had always been an Olympian inside, but I'd been humbly waiting and thinking that if I was good enough then surely someone else would spot it. And when they hadn't I'd shrugged my shoulders and sighed a bit and maybe moaned a bit, but maybe secretly I was a bit relieved because it took the responsibility off having to make a fuss and push myself forward.

Somehow it's easier if it's their fault for not believing in me, than my fault for not believing in myself.

That was going to have to change. Because I think the answer to the mystery is, that if you always believe there is a way and keep pushing yourself forward, longer than anyone else has the heart for, it usually all works out well.

Chapter 12: Sydney

"Wouldn't it be a shame if I was capable of doing that and I never found out?"

We had a few days off after Lucerne as the last chance before the final run-up into the Worlds or Olympics and I decided that this time I really was going to use them to go up to my parents. It was important to keep it casual with Dad and leave him as little time as possible to get excited, worked up and stressed. Feeling excited, worked up and stressed were three totally justifiable reasons to drink, so I knew the best plan was to just call ahead that morning and get on a train. I'd not been home for two and a half years. It was only two days. He'd know how significant this was, so maybe he'd stay sober for just two days. Significant events were, however, totally justifiable reasons to drink, so I wasn't sure I could count that one in my favour.

It was good to be back in Yorkshire and the ridiculously picturesque Richmond again. I went straight out for my "Hi Honey, I'm home!" run — through the cobbled square, round the castle, drop down to The Swale, past the waterfalls and round by Easby Abbey. Just to know I was back. I ran up Lombards Wynd (surely the steepest paved road in the country), just because I now could. My brother was back from his two years teaching in Poland, so it was good to see him again. It felt good to be back and I had a lot to be happy about. Dad was very happy and he was celebrating. Being happy and celebrating were two more totally justifiable reasons to drink. It all being good and me being happy lasted at least a couple of hours.

"Dad, go away, go to bed or something, I don't want you around. You're drunk."

"I'm not drunk. I've not had anything to drink. I'm just really happy for you."

"I've told you I'm not doing this again. I know you drink. I know you've been drinking. Just don't treat me like an idiot and lie about it."

"But I'm so happy for you. I'm celebrating."

"This is not about you. This was about me but not anymore. I was celebrating; I was happy – but not anymore. *I've* not even had a drink yet, how come you get to be drunk? I've not been home for over two years because you get drunk every time I'm here and I can't stand it. I'm only here a couple of days and you couldn't stay sober. John and I haven't been here together for years and you couldn't stay sober."

"I'm so sorry Alison. I'm such a terrible father."

Now we are into the snotty, blubbing self-recrimination phase. Being a terrible father is not an admission of guilt or responsibility, it's just something else we are supposed to feel sorry for him about. It's also another totally justifiable reason to drink. He continues the script – "But I'm so proud of you."

"I don't want you to be proud of me. I don't want you to boast about this to your friends. You did not do this. It's not your thing. I don't even want you there. I don't want you to come."

"Oh Alison, you can't mean that?"

But I did mean it and I told my mother. "I meant it. I don't want him there."

"I know you did and I can understand it. But you can't do that to him Alison."

And I knew she was right. I'd wanted him to hear it, but I'd also known he would come anyway and that there was no way I would stop him even if I could have done. It would just be too dreadful a thing to do to him. Not so much the not being there (although that was obviously something), but forcing him to stay behind would be the most conclusive and blunt way ever of outing him and his life. Still now, as I imagine him trying to explain to friends, colleagues and patients why he's not at the Olympics watching his daughter compete, I shrivel a bit inside and cannot even complete the imagining. To shatter the fantasy family, the fantasy life illusion everyone in the outside world seemed to believe in… it was, and still is, almost too painful to think about.

If I'd have left him behind, he wouldn't have been there when I came back. He might not have had the guts to kill himself, but he would have drunk himself into some sort of hole. I also knew Mum wouldn't come without him. She'd rarely left him alone since his 'accident' (the accident when he'd got drunk, got in his car, driven onto the pavement, knocked a girl over, then driven home and gone to bed – Dad's 'accident' and Dad's 'illness' are both lovely words devoid of any responsibility) and I don't think ever overnight. She knew he would drink a lot if she wasn't there (even though she didn't believe he drank) and then she didn't know what would happen, but it was likely to be worse than last time.

Katherine, Sarah and I in an airport photo booth somewhere on the way back from one of our many races and training camps pre-Sydney 2000.

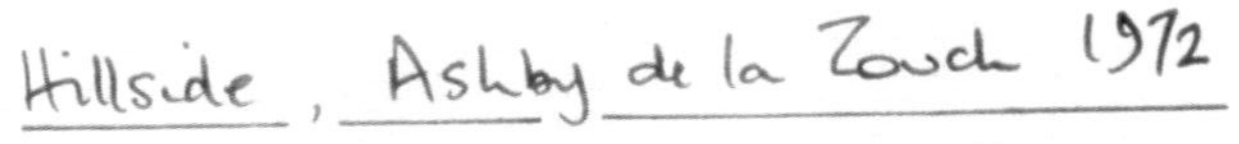

The quest began on Ashby's lawn
With Deb as pair, one sunny morn.
It soon came clear: to win a race
Would not be easy face to face.

East Dilston House 1976

With John, developed simple oars.
Still grounded? What could be the cause?
It must be said, dear son and daughter,
You oughtter go & find some water.

A few pages from a Good Luck photo album Mum made for me. She has a rare poetry talent. Deb is my cousin by the way, she'll appreciate a naked baby photo in a book.

Holiday Cottage, Hornsea 1977

It would take some time, this gruelling quest,
To find a sport to suit you best.
Gymnastics? Yes - fun for a while
But ended in a tangled pile.

Those Early Years began her quest
To find the sport to suit her best
By Liverpool in '89
She knew to Row would suit her fine.

Then Bedford, Cambs & London too
She's strived to make a dream come true
She's given heart & soul & Kidney
(The only word to rhyme with Sydney).

Those years we've shared & hold them dear
Amazed we followed her career
And soon what joy & love we'll know
— Olympic Games, 2 0 0 0!

Pre-Olympic training on the Gold Coast Jurassic Park lake. This was pretty typical of the water, but we went out in everything. "It's going to be rough in Sydney."

Matt Pinsent befriending a snow goose down at the lake. They had a little chat most days.

Dressed in our M & S pyjamas ready for the Sydney 2000 opening ceremony (in our village apartment with the stadium behind us). The fabulous GB Women's Eight who adopted me as one of their own for the night. From left, Lisa Eyre, Ali Saunders, Elise Laverick, Rowan Carroll, Francesca Zino, Alison Tricky, Alex Beever, Charlotte Miller in arms and next to me (in sunglasses) I must apologise for the most unflattering photo of the gorgeous Kate Mac.

Tim Foster and members of the GB Men's team holding up the giant flag at the Opening Ceremony. This was the most entertained we'd been for about two hours.

With my coach, Louise Kingsley, in the grandstands at the Sydney Olympic course. Winks behind us to the left of the picture and Steve Redgrave just behind me (mostly hidden because he's already got enough books written about him).

Great Britain's first ever Women's Olympic rowing medallists. Guin Batten, Gillian Lindsey, Katherine Grainger and Miriam Batten. I stood taking this photograph, and thought "I train with those girls every day. I row with them and race against them and sometimes, in my single, I beat them. Wouldn't it be a shame if I was capable of doing that and I never found out?"

Every rowing autobiog has to have a couple of lone sculler pics and this is no exception. This is me training on the Sydney Olympic course at Penrith Lake at sunrise. (Photo by Peter Spurrier)

Dr Alison Mowbray (left) and Dr Martin Mowbray (right). Richmond named an office block after me in honour of their first Olympian. It's a sureal but very wonderful feeling to know there is something, somewhere named after you.

Women and lightweight men training at Lake Varese in 2001. I was here so often in the next four years it really felt like home. Pretty nice home.

So, he was coming and he would be drunk because it would all be very exciting *for him*. That was how it was going to be.

I also hated the fact that in qualifying for the Olympics, I'd just handed him more material to bolster his story. I knew I couldn't stop him insufferably boasting to everyone. A daughter at the Olympics! What a wonderful man he must be, what a wonderful father he must be, what a wonderful family he must have and what a wonderful life he must have. The hardest thing, when I try and tell people about my dad, is when they say, "Well he can't have been that bad, look at all you've achieved."

And for Dad, other people's reality was his reality. It was more important that other people believed his life was good, than that it actually was. Their admiration was evidence to him that he could drink and still hold it together. He could drink and the rest of the world still thought he was great, so what did his kids know? He was great — his kids just had it in for him (and that was a perfectly justifiable reason to drink). By qualifying for the Olympics, I was effectively colluding and enabling. While I was at home that was what qualifying for Sydney was about.

It was horrible while I was there, but it didn't last when I left. The shine and the excitement came back pretty quickly. I was by now very good at detachment. They were responsible for their lives — I was responsible for mine. The important thing was not to let one mess up the other. Parents may mess with your childhood, but adults are responsible for messing up or fixing their own adulthood. Surely that's what being an adult means.

I couldn't wait to get back to training for the Olympics – in fact I'd not really stopped. I'd run miles and been to the gym while I was in Richmond and now I was straight back in my boat on Mike's full training programme. Miles and Louise said I should take it easy for a while, take a break and then start again, but I didn't seem to need it. I was unbreakable. I'd never felt stronger. I was dreaming of Olympic finals and I knew I could do it if I trained hard enough.

I think that all lasted a couple of weeks and then I started to feel very, very tired. I realised too late that they had been right. There is a reason everyone wants to qualify for the Olympics a year in advance. The Qualification Regatta is a 'Your life on the line' race. You have to treat it like your Olympic final and can't save anything or hold anything back. In fact, the boats had already started their journey by ship to Australia before qualification and I'd chosen to send my old boat and race qualification in my new faster boat, rather than risk staying at home while my lovely shiny new boat got a trip to the Olympics by itself. And it's not just the race, but the months of preparation phase. It's the peak, the summit of your whole season, your whole year. But then if you do qualify, you have to go out and do it all again.

I'd already raced two Olympics that year. I'd raced Debs and then I'd raced qualification and for a while I'd felt great because adrenalin is a very wonderful thing. But now the real Olympics were ahead of me and once I came down from cloud nine, I stopped dreaming of Olympic finals and started worrying I might disgrace myself. I was now about six weeks away from the Olympics and really I could still have taken a break. Rationally, I know now you don't lose nearly a decade of training by taking a week off. I'd have come back fresh and raring to go again and easily got back up to speed in the last few weeks. But full-time Olympic athletes are rarely rational beings, especially when it comes to taking time off. Logic and rationality had been telling me for years that someone like me doesn't get to go to the Olympics and I'd managed to ignore them enough to get this far. So I wasn't going to start paying attention to them now.

Besides we were just about to go off on training camp to Aiguebelette — the final wind in. This was no time to take a break. I had a session with Chris, our sports psychologist, to help reassess my goals before I left. Getting to the Olympics had been not just my goal but beyond my wildest dreams, so what was I supposed to do now I was actually going? What is actually beyond your wildest dreams? People say "Dream of Olympic Gold, why aim for anything less?" But as much as I'm all for the Power of Belief, I can't help feeling it has to be built on *something.* I needed something more tangible. Chris asked me to describe my "Dream Goal", my "Minimum Acceptable Goal" (below which I would be desperately disappointed) and a "Realistic Goal" between the two.

Dream Goal – Make the Olympic Final. It had receded since those first few heady days. I didn't really believe I could do it anymore, but I could just about dream it on a good day.

Realistic Goal – Top ten. Having come eleventh in Canada last year, anything in the top ten would be at least one place better than last year and show progress in a tougher Olympic field.

Minimum Acceptable Goal — Make the Semi-finals (top twelve). It didn't take much thinking to realise that 'Not making the semi-finals' was the tangible form of the ethereal 'Disgracing myself'.

I had my new goals and I felt refocused and a bit better. I like goals even though it's scary making them, because then you have to go and do them or you fail. Setting goals can be scary but I find they help get me off the sofa even on bad days and when I'm really tired, because at least I know what I'm doing it for and I don't like to fail. Of course, the easier way not to fail is not to set goals and stay on the sofa where it's safe. A lot of people watch the Olympics from there.

I was fairly detached from it all, but even I could tell there was something afoot again down at Longridge. I thought Matt Pinsent was just being nice when he said I was the first to have my place confirmed for the Olympics, but it ended up being true. Going through qualification meant my seat had my name on it and no one else could take it. Not so the Quad.

Gillian and Fran had won trials and had chosen to be in the Double, the next four athletes had formed the Quad. The problem now was that although neither crew had had a great season, the Quad did at least look like it had some hope of a medal. I think that having won trials, it was fair enough that Gillian and Fran would feel they should now be in the Quad. I may not have agreed with how the Doubles were selected for trials, but if that was the trial, then that was the trial and it should have meant something. The top-ranked athletes should be in the boat most likely to win a medal. That was surely the point of the trial.

And we needed a medal. Not just Mike and the athletes in the boat, but all of us. We all needed that first British Women's rowing medal. For a start, funding follows medals. The British Women's squad had had proper funding and proper attention for the first time following the medals of '97 and '98. We'd been trading on that despite the disappointments of '99 and been given a chance to redeem ourselves, but we knew that no medals in 2000 would mean a stripping back of all our funding and status. If we thought it was hard now, it would be impossible post-Sydney if there was no Sydney medal. So, it wasn't just those top six who needed Mike to get this right.

Unfortunately for Mike and for all those directly involved, due to the nature of his trials' system and the fact that there was no individual ranking, this was now going to be very difficult. The problem was that if Gillian and Fran went in, the bottom double went out and that was Katherine and Sarah. By this point it was obvious that if you wanted a boat with a chance of winning a medal, no one in their right mind would drop Katherine. Apart from anything else Katherine had the biggest ergo score. There was no way Mike was dropping Katherine.

And Gillian had been a favourite with Mike from the start. A lean, powerful 6″1′, she pulled a good ergo, lifted big weights, moved boats and idolised Mike. She fulfilled all his criteria. Like any teacher's pet I'm sure Gillian took a fair bit of stick from our resident school bullies, but to her credit she always appeared to take it very calmly and professionally and was never less than lovely to me and anyone else who wasn't throwing daggers her way. I like Gillian very much. There was no doubting her single-minded determination though – she was absolutely in this to win a medal. If dropping Fran was what it took, then that was what it took.

Eventually it was declared that there would be a new trial for the Quad. The first I heard was that the decision had already been made that Guin, Miriam and Katherine would stay in the Quad and Gillian, Fran and Sarah would trial for the last place. We all knew Mike's 'gut feeling' Quad was The Battens, Katherine and Gillian but there was no way David Tanner or, I'm sure, Sarah was going to let him do that without at least some semblance of a trial. So, some semblance of a trial was concocted. It was going to be hard at this late stage in the day. If we'd raced in singles back in April there would have been a proper ranking to fall back on, but there wasn't. We could still have rowed a proper matrix now or done seat racing using Debs and I to make up two quads, but we didn't.

Time was ticking on and there was panic in the air. Any time used up in prevarication and trials was time that the selected Quad would need to pull themselves together into a medal performance and no one was underestimating the stretch this was going to take from their current situation. So, instead of a fair trial, the girls were given some semblance of a trial. We would all go to Aiguebelette as planned. Gillian, Fran and Sarah would each get one practice row in the Quad on day one and then on day two, there would be three back-to-back timed 2k races. No allowance made for fade of the three girls who raced three times or any change in conditions. Whichever boat went fastest would go to Sydney. There was to be no further discussion or argument.

Sarah was distraught and livid. She absolutely saw that seat as hers. But there was nothing else she or any of them could do, so she put her race head on and got on with it.

With Guin, Miriam and Katherine having to race three times, the order of who raced with them first when they were fresh was critical. I think there was a draw and I don't know how it happened, but the order came out as Gillian first, Fran second and Sarah third. Everyone just shrugged; somehow it seemed fated. At this point Mike decreed it was important that the races were staged as close together as possible and to this end there would be no re-rigging between races. The boat would be set up for Gillian in the first race and then the rigger heights would stay the same for all three races. Apparently that made it fairer.

David Tanner came over to make this look like some semblance of an Olympic trial. The races were rowed back-to-back and timed. Gillian raced first, Fran second and Sarah third. Gillian's boat was fastest, Fran's came second and Sarah's was third. No one was very surprised. Sarah took her race head off and became very, very distraught and totally livid. She would always, and I think will always, think of that seat and the eventual medal as hers.

The nineteen-year-old Fran didn't show anything at all that I saw. She'd won trials, been in a boat with a former World Champion that had gone increasingly badly and then been dumped. She'd been switched from the top to the bottom boat and faced the rest of the season with a totally demoralised Sarah. Sarah is tough and she did try to rally, but you could see the stuffing had been knocked out of her. Rage is a powerful but not very sustainable fuel.

Guin quite casually told Fran that she (Guin) had pulled harder in Gillian's race because she knew Mike wanted Gillian in and he would be more committed to coaching their boat if she was. Guin didn't seem to think what she'd done was a big deal and it wasn't that she was apologising. But, whatever the rights and wrongs of selection, the Quad was selected and no matter how they got there, no matter how you looked at it, surely no one could ever look at Gillian, Guin, Miriam and Katherine and say they didn't deserve the shot, hadn't worked for their chance.

During all of this, Louise and I were pretty much left to our own devices and I was having a relatively nice time of it. Louise could tell I was knackered and although we'd do the main pieces of work with the team, she'd surreptitiously reduce other sessions when we could get away with it. I was still, and ever would be, exhilarated by the thought that I'd qualified for the Olympics. I spent my spare time writing to all the friends and family I could think of, enclosing a printed list of my forwarding addresses with a note to please write to me. When you are away, there is nothing like finding real post in your pigeonhole.

And each day I'd try and catch my ten minutes. As a full-time athlete, all day every day is scheduled and run by the clock. Training sessions, meals, travel time, physio and massage sessions, crew meetings, stretching, naps, snacks and hand washing your kit in the bathroom sink. The only real free time was a couple of hours in the evening between dinner and bed, but that was no good to me because the sun would have already gone down. My treat, and actually the moments I remember most from that and many training camps, were the ten minutes I could squeeze out of the schedule to slip away for a quick swim and two or three minutes toasting each side in the sun.

Getting a tan (without getting tan lines) is something that most rowers think about, but no one will admit to. Caring about this sort of thing is considered to be a distraction and a sign that you are not being appropriately professional. You'll hear a lot of rowers say "Will it make the boat go faster?" and you are supposed to ask yourself that against everything you do. If the answer you come up with is "No", then you don't do it. That way there are actually very few formal rules because everyone self-regulates. While this is generally a sound philosophy, I disagree with some of its interpretations. What makes *you* go faster is not necessarily the same as what makes *me* go faster.

Swimming in the lake and sunbathing were two things that, while not expressly forbidden, were generally considered not things that made the boat go faster. But I love swimming in cold clear water and as a scientist and microbiologist I had to disagree (although not out loud) with 'expert' Mike that it would lead to cuts and blisters getting infected. Sunbathing is more controversial, but pretty much everyone was surreptitiously trying to get a good even tan – even the guys. It was common practice for the girls to row with their rowing Lycras rolled down and a succession of different shaped bra tops to avoid the dreaded tan lines, while the guys would row with their tops down or half the outing with the left strap off the shoulder and the other half with the right when they thought the coaches couldn't see. But with my fair, freckled skin it didn't matter how carefully I applied the sun cream, I'd always miss a patch somewhere and burn a bit. So I quickly made my own rule that I always rowed with a T-shirt on under my all-in-one and fully sun-creamed up everywhere else, so I'd never have to worry about getting burnt and could concentrate on my rowing. And then in compensation, any day I could manage it, after my five-minute swim I'd have my few minutes drying off, sun-basking in my bikini before floating back to the hotel restored. It was the equivalent of my PhD sunset roof time and I'm pretty sure it did make my boat go faster. I think I overdid it and went a bit pink just once in seven years and one of the girls was very quick to pick me up on it. Still, nothing anyone said or did was missed as an opportunity for comment and judgement.

We had a couple of days at home to turn around and then WE WERE OFF TO THE OLYMPICS! The girl who couldn't even make the school sports teams was getting on a plane to go to Australia with the GREAT BRITAIN OLYMPIC TEAM.

First stop was the Team GB holding camp in Brisbane for our final preparation. This was actually a five-star Radisson country park hotel that had been turned into an athletes' paradise for the pre-Olympic and Olympic period. We were a short bus ride away from a rowing course marked out on a lake surrounded by primeval mangrove swamps. The whole area was wooded and there were always a couple of bush fires smouldering somewhere. The smoky smell hung in the air. It was all rather Jurassic Park, not least because on our explorative rows into the off shoots and channels, we always had to be in sight of a safety launch in case we fell in and had to be hooked out before the alligators got us.

Staying in the holding camp was the first time I met and mixed with athletes from other sports. Different teams were in and out, but there were some athletes, trampolinists and hockey players around while we were there. There was a Rec. room with a constantly-in-use pool table, huge TV and bank of computers for e-mail; rooms for physio and massage; and the all-important outdoor swimming pool. The dining room buffet was set up to cater for our every whim – we were told we could request anything our sport needed that wasn't catered for. When we arrived, they only served porridge every other morning. Rowers have to eat porridge every day (it's in the rules), so that was our request. The athletes were upset by the lack of chips and asked for chips every night for dinner – apparently that was in their rules.

I shared a room with Debbie who'd come out as spare. Even though we were well down in the pecking order, we were somehow allocated an awesome room with balcony views of the golf course on two sides and a huge bathroom with Jacuzzi. Debbie was beside herself with excitement – which I was to learn is just one of the lovely things about Debs (there is no cynical sneering about anything from Debs – ever). We were just starting to get to know each other, so when I came back one afternoon from training she greeted me at the door looking very worried, "I'm really sorry Al – I've made a terrible mess."

"Where?" I said, looking round the room. "It looks fine to me."

"No, in here" she said, pushing open the bathroom door to an Ibiza foam party. Debs (not having read the Jacuzzi instructions which forbade it) had emptied a whole hotel miniature of bubble bath into the Jacuzzi and then left it while she went to stretch. The bathroom was almost completely full of bubbles. She seemed terrified that I was going to tell her off but I couldn't stop laughing and then she couldn't stop laughing and then we had a foam fight, which quite nicely broke the ice. That one little story is as good a way to introduce Debs and describe her to you as I can think of. The only other things you really need to know are that Debs eats more than anyone you have ever met and sleeps more than anyone you have ever met, and very soundly, which always made her the easiest person for restless Al to room with. Once she's asleep, you get the feeling that you could drag her round the room by her ankles and she'd not wake up (this was not something I ever tried). She has the energy and enthusiasm of a puppy and the metabolism of a hamster and anyone who knows Debs will recognise the running round and round on a wheel thing too.

To try and avoid the high winds that were legendary at the Sydney Olympic rowing course (Penrith Lake), the rowing had been scheduled early. We had to be prepared for racing to start at 8am. This would mean getting up at 4am to allow the required four hours for our bodies to wake up and get into a physiological state to race. The Sports Science theory on this goes that in order for this to be OK on race days, you need to spend the weeks preceding the race going to bed gradually earlier and earlier and getting up earlier and earlier until 4am feels like a normal time to get up. Annoyingly enough, this was the one bit of Sports Science Mike did subscribe to. I tried to follow the plan but it really didn't work for me. Still, the only way I managed to avoid nights of complete insomnia was to go to bed as late as possible. The theory of going to bed earlier and getting up earlier is that it tricks your body into switching time zones and it seems to work for most people. But despite my best efforts, my body just wouldn't be tricked. It should have been easier with changing actual time zones and confused body clocks, but it didn't help. My body just seemed to resolutely know what time it was and refused to go to sleep early.

I took my magic sleeping tablets for a few nights to try to get some sleep but even those had trouble knocking me out, and when I tried to stop taking them, I couldn't sleep at all. I'd drift off at about 3-4am, an hour or two before my alarm, day after day. I felt pretty dreadful much of the time. I tried to negotiate for some lie-ins to 7am on the basis that the current plan didn't really seem to be working for me, but I didn't get anywhere. Now, just this once, Mike quoted the science back at me.

I wish I could say it was more fun. Some of it was and I was still very excited about going to the Olympics. But lack of sleep wasn't the only worry. Debs was there as spare and as we were sent out to do the same training and preparation pieces together every day, I still had to beat her every day. It wasn't easy as she was getting faster all the time. One of the last pieces of work we did in Brisbane before moving to the Olympic village was the final 2k race pace piece. The whole men's and women's squad always does this together and then the times are worked out as a percentage of each boat's predicted Gold medal time, so comparisons can be made across all the boats. For instance if the Redgrave four gets 101% and your boat gets 99%, you know you are likely to be going pretty well.

Someone had the sensitivity to put Debs and I in different waves. It was better that we weren't side by side, but then I had to race the whole 2k unsure if my time would be good enough. I tried to tell myself that this unspoken competition with Deb was paranoia and that no one really cared any more. I've noticed how much time we can spend worrying about what other people are saying and thinking about us when the reality, the sad reality really, is that no one is talking or thinking about us at all. Life is usually easier when I remember that.

When the times were printed, I saw I'd beaten Debs by one second. It wasn't much but it was enough to breathe a sigh of relief and think that I could finally put this behind me and focus on the real opposition – those scullers from other countries. Miles said well done on my time and when I laughed and tried to make light of it, saying I'd beaten Debs by a whole second, he got a bit serious on me and said with a meaningful look, "Yes, but you shouldn't underestimate how important that second is. You understand what I mean?" Apparently, paranoia is not paranoia when people really are talking about you.

There was some fun and light relief though. Louise had also been given the Sarah/Fran down-at-heel double to coach, since they weren't medal potential and held no interest for Mike any more. She was the perfect coach for us all at that time. She made an effort to get us all (including Debs) out of the environment that we were finding so difficult and in our afternoons off, she drove us to the beach, local sights or dropped us off at the mall. I have some wonderful and highly-prized photos of us all playing at the beach looking tanned, toned and carefree and I remember that, despite how hard it could be, it was all really a very wonderful part of my life.

We went on mass to pick up our Olympic kit from a local school that had been taken over by the BOA (British Olympic Association). Once you get to the Olympics, sponsorship rules mean that everything you wear must either be unbranded or branded by one of the sponsors – and since they want as much exposure as possible, they provide you with absolutely everything to make sure that for those two weeks (and for as long as possible afterwards) you are a head-to-toe walking, talking advert. We picked up our Olympic rowing kit, two or three different styles of tracksuit, opening ceremony kit, closing ceremony kit, waterproofs, shorts, trousers, more T-shirts and polo shirts than you thought existed in the world, hats, trainers, caps, sunglasses, a watch, underwear (including Team GB G-strings for the girls – presumably for those more intimate sponsorship opportunities), towels, toiletries, suncream, an Olympic cereal bowl (Kellogg's were a sponsor) and it went on.... And then a range of suitcases, holdalls, rucksacks, drawstring and toiletry bags to put it all in. We went from station to station collecting more and more stuff. The older hands already had lots of Olympic kit and were more blasé. But for me, I was acutely aware that this could be it, this could be my only Olympics and my only Olympic kit and I tried everything on and fretted until I got the right sizes for everything. I wasn't the only one.

You can be as cool as you like, as professional as you like and as hard-headed as you like and say the Olympics is about the racing and not about the kit, but really, truly, I don't see how anyone even vaguely human could fail to get excited picking up their Olympic kit for the first time. Tangible proof that we were really there, were really part of it all, especially for those of us that could not hope to medal. We finally got to wear the Olympic rings and feel for the first time like those people we'd always watched on TV. You pick it up and put it on and know wherever you are, forever more, when you wear it, people will look at you through different eyes and say in a tone of disbelief, "Did you go to the Olympics?" And how did we know that? Because we *used* to be those awestruck people. And you know there will always be a few choice pieces stashed in the attic like buried treasure for some unknown generations to wonder and tell stories over. It's a select club and it is forever. You can't buy it in any shop, so there are only three ways to get this kit. 1: You earn it as we did; 2: You are related to it or a very good friend to it; or 3: You sleep for it. Those are the rules. It is our reality and our legacy and it means all that when you pick it up.

I was perhaps most excited about getting my Olympic Suit, which we'd been told was made to measure. I was excited about this as very few off-the-peg clothes seemed to fit any more, but jackets were a particular problem.

Rowers, like swimmers, develop a fantastic shape; broad triangular backs, narrow waists and lean muscular legs. It looks great, but we are certainly no longer off-the-peg people. The guys seem to have fewer problems as athletic-shaped men are not that unusual, but as athletic-shaped women we seem to be way up into a very exceptional percentile that not even sports shops cater for. I'd stopped buying jackets and dresses as I'd have to buy size 16-18 to get them to fit across my back, chest and shoulders, and then they'd be hanging sack-like round my 10-12 waist.

Our suits were supplied by Marks & Spencers and despite us taking the time to go and *be* measured some weeks before, they seemed to think made to measure would be taken care of by giving us different-sized jackets and trousers. I remember the disappointment of being handed my size 18 jacket and size 12 trousers. The only thing vaguely Olympic about it was the badge badly stuck onto the breast pocket with superglue. There were a few seamstresses there who vowed to take the jackets in and let the trousers down for all of us, but by the time we got there they looked rather panicked by the volume of work. What did M&S really expect? We don't live like anyone else and our bodies don't look like anyone else's because no one else trains theirs that hard for upwards of twenty-four hours a week.

Eventually all the kit was collected and the last rowing pieces completed, and it was time to get on a plane from Brisbane to Sydney and go to the Olympics proper.

And the Olympics is absolutely the most amazing, exciting experience. It's everything you think it is from watching it on the TV and so, so much more. We were treated like kings through the airport, picked up the all-important accreditation passes that would now not leave our necks for the next two and a half weeks and walked wide-eyed into the Olympic Village. First stop was an introductory speech by Simon Clegg, the BOA Chef de Mission. He welcomed us to the Olympics and to an elite band. I hadn't realised up to this point just *how* Elite we were. He told us there had been fewer than 3,000 British Olympians, EVER. The *current* population of Great Britain is over 62 million.

I'll try and describe the Olympic Village because it's a place of great wonder and mystery to those who love sport. It's really more like a vast housing estate than a village and reflects the typical homes of the country. Each national team gets their own set of apartments depending on the size of the team and drapes the outside with flags of their nation. Walking round the streets is like walking round the world; neighbouring countries will often have neighbouring apartments; there is reggae blasting out of Jamaica; the Italians are hanging out of the windows saying "Ciao"; you can't see America for stars and stripes; China goes on for ever and the British have a real live old-fashioned red phone box sitting outside that lives in the BOA basement and gets taken out every four years so British Athletes can phone home from a place that feels like home.

We were shown to our functional, rather than five-star, rooms. There are a lot of rooms to temporarily furnish before it's all sold on as residential housing, so to make it at all affordable every expense is spared. Two plain single beds (I was to room share with Lottie, the cox from the Women's Eight), a basic wardrobe and chest of drawers, bare wooden floors and the thinnest possible curtains that would make me very glad I'd held onto my British Airways eye-mask. It could have been any hostel room anywhere, except on the bed was a blue special edition Sydney 2000 quilt (that we got to keep) and hand drawn pictures on the walls from local schoolchildren welcoming us to Australia. There was one picture of rather asymmetric Olympic rings and an Alison stick girl with a very big head, sitting in something that looked suspiciously like a canoe but was definitely winning the race. I was very touched and may even have shed a little tear.

There were enough of us that GB rowing had two houses, with the small GB fencing team living on the ground floor of the girl's house. We also had a living room and I can't remember what, if anything, was in it, because all I can picture now is the huge plate glass window with an unobstructed view across to the Olympic Stadium less than a mile away. We'd be able to see the flame burning once they lit it.

Apart from the houses, the village has everything for the discerning Olympian. Gift shops, grocery store, post office, hairdressers, 50m pool, video games arcade, cinemas, laundry service, cafes and of course the source of all wonder to first and every time Olympians – the food hall. The 24-hour free food hall.

We walked into the food hall on mass for the first time and still we were swallowed up. There are thousands of athletes, coaches and support staff in the village at any one time, all of them have to be fed and every nationality wants the food they are used to at this crucial time. The rowers want their breakfast at 4am before their 8am races and athletes want their supper when they get back from their evening races and 11pm medal ceremonies, so everything is available pretty much all the time. I've heard the food hall described as the size of four football pitches and that seems about right. There were hot buffets all the way round the outside serving pizza, pasta, stir fries, soups, curries (including goat curry if you really have to have it), sushi, meat and fish (grilled, roasted or fried), masses of fresh vegetables and fruit, all the carbs – cereals, rice, potatoes, breads and more pasta of course, a massive salad buffet all the way down the middle, a fruit and juice bar, a hot and cold desserts bar and ice-cream freezers dotted here, there and everywhere, just in case they are an essential part of your training regime. Oh, and in the corner, because they are an Olympic sponsor, there's a 24-hour, free McDonald's (which I promise I didn't visit until after I'd finished competing). There are different coloured banks of seating to help you navigate your way around and find your teammates.

Maybe it's because I so love food that I was so excited by it all, but I think it gets everyone at least a bit like that. Some athletes obviously really struggle and there are understandably stories of athletes from poorer countries being overwhelmed by it all, overindulging and finding themselves barely able to compete. Also stories of athletes sending food parcels home of anything less perishable and vaguely postable. It must be a particular nightmare for weight restricted athletes and those who have to stay particularly light, but we all have to be careful. The point of the food hall is that we can all keep eating the things we are used to, not to go crazy and try everything new. Not until our competitions are over anyway.

And it's not just the food. Because everyone needs to eat, this is where you see EVERYONE. You may well end up eating your breakfast, lunch or dinner across the table from recognisable medallists of any country – those people off the TV. And it's so different when you see them for real. When you watch the TV and see the runners lined up with the runners, the gymnasts sitting with the gymnasts and the volleyball players all on a court together, you are comparing like with like and you can't really see the extremes. But when the Russian female gymnasts troop in behind the US men's basketball team, you can't believe they are the same species. Everyone turns to look, even though, really, we are all part of the circus. I sat at dinner one evening with a group of GB rowers and Steve and Matt were surreptitiously trying to work out the height of a Russian female volleyball player a few seats down. Steve had pushed back his chair and was quietly commenting that her thighbone was a lot longer than his. When the women stood up to go, Steve said to Dot, "Quick, get up and walk next to them so we can see how much taller than you she is." Six-foot Dot was dwarfed, so they reasoned the girl was getting on for 7 feet tall.

I looked and marvelled but it didn't feel like a circus to me, and I was surprised that once I was actually there and I met them, those people off the TV didn't feel like a different species. Actually, for the first time, I felt like I had found my own. It was like my bones settled in and finally found their place. If I'd felt OK at Liverpool because everyone was a top set swot; here, where everyone was a First-class honours student in whatever their chosen field, I felt totally at home. Here, no one thought you were weird to get up at 5am if there was something you really wanted to do with your life. Here, no one called you boring if you worked on it twelve hours a day and refused to get drunk. Here, there were no families or partners, no 9-5 go home and watch the telly routine, no conventions to break and no grains to go against. Here, I wasn't extreme, unusual, exceptional, inspirational, intense, single-minded, tall or strange. Here, I was really rather average.

The whole Olympic Village, the whole Olympic experience, is there to provide everything you need to be at your best, but you have to be very careful or you can get lost in it all. We'd been well warned and it did help. The trick is to somehow let all the hype and excitement give you energy and focus, rather than take it away. You can take two athletes or two teams whose performances have been inseparable in training and competition all year, but when you take them to the Olympics, one athlete or team will feed off the Olympics, raise their game and produce a personal best and the other will freak out and fold.

Eventually when all the orientation was over, we got on a bus and went to the Penrith Lake course for the first time. Most of the others had been last year, but for me it really was my first time. I was glad to see it was a course and not a lake, but apart from it being the Olympic course, it wasn't particularly special or scenic. I do remember being particularly impressed by the shoe collection service though. We boated from one set of landing stages and came in on another. Normally our coaches had to carry our trainers and flip-flops over or we'd have to go round and pick them up, which kept other people waiting. Here, for the first time I'd seen it, they had volunteers who picked up your shoes, put them in a crate with a note of your boat number, watched out for you, and would be ready and waiting on the landing stage with them when you came in. Louise was also looking after the Double and Debbie and wasn't always around, so it really helped me. It was a small thing but bizarrely, in all the pomp and ceremony of the games, having someone look after my flip-flops was the thing that made me feel most like a superstar.

Whenever I hear of pop-stars' outlandish dressing room requirements – "I can't possibly perform unless the room is repainted magenta, there is a constant supply of triple purified water flown straight from Alaska, the food is prepared by my personal chef, beluga caviar on tap, Dom Perignon on ice, separate hand and foot masseurs and I'm bringing my own eyebrow stylist who'll need a separate room so he can prepare himself mentally" I think about how chuffed we all were to have someone bring us our old trainers and flip-flops. I imagine it was a favourite volunteer job too. It's not every day you get to come home from work and say that you've held an Olympic Champion's flip-flops in your hands.

I know I go on, sorry about that. But the Olympics! There are so many stories it's hard to know which to choose and each one leads to another. And there are so many memories. I don't think I've forgotten much. I was making a point of remembering.

The rowing starts on the first Saturday of the Games and with a few days to go, we were all still on the water twice a day. One of the few things allowed (required even) to distract our focus was a Team GB reception at the British Consulate. The Ambassadors' reception no less (and yes, all the usual lame jokes about Ferrero Rocher have all been done). We got all dressed up in our suits and were loaded onto buses to take us there from the Olympic Village. It was another great chance to meet and talk to British athletes from different sports, plus several of my old sporting heroes were walking around in their current guise as BBC commentators. I remember looking around at about 9pm to see that all the worn-out rowers, having eaten the bulk of the canapés, had bagged all the chairs round the outside of the room and were waiting for someone to tell them they could go home to bed. Rowers are not very good at standing up. It's not something we do very much and our backs start to hurt pretty quickly. I noticed that while the rowers were sitting around looking knackered and drinking water, the sailors were holding court in the middle of the room, wine glasses in hand, looking tanned and relaxed and some even disappearing out onto the balcony occasionally to smoke. Several of them would go on to win Olympic Medals later in the week. It was about this time that I began to wonder if I'd chosen the right sport.

I know I'm biased but meeting all those athletes from different sports, I really did start to realise how tough rowers have it. That's not to say that other sports don't train hard, they just train differently (and let's face it, and to hell with diplomacy… not as hard). But really we are proud of being the Olympic workhorses. We know we are hard-core. This mentality may even be to our detriment in some ways as we have a tendency to think that all we have to do to go faster is work harder. Maybe we should have talked to the sailors more; they spend half their time trying to make their boats go faster by actually making faster boats – rowers wash theirs occasionally.

As an athlete you are required to go to the function at the consulate, but, rather bizarrely, the opening ceremony is optional. The problem with the opening ceremony for athletes is that it's the night before the games start, so if you are competing on the first day, you really can't go – and even if you start on the second day you have to consider it carefully. Once you parade in, you are committed to standing around for the whole of a very long ceremony and then you know you'll have to queue for a long time to get a bus back to the village. I was very relieved no one put pressure on me to stay away (not being medal potential had its advantages). I'd been watching Olympic opening ceremonies and those athletes march in and round the track for twenty years on TV, and the thought that I was now going to be one of them was exciting and surreal. The Women's Eight were all going and adopted me for the night so I'd have someone to share the excitement with.

We dressed up in our… well, navy and white pyjamas is probably the best way I can describe our opening ceremony gear, did our hair and make-up (we were going to be on TV darling!) and made our way to the opening ceremony holding pen in the gymnastics hall. If you've ever wondered how they co-ordinate all those thousands of athletes to come out at the right time… this is how. We sat in country blocks all round the gym hall and I have some great photos of the patchwork quilt blocks of colour of different countries sitting in their different coloured uniforms. There was a big screen so we could see something of what was going on but couldn't hear anything, so we amused ourselves. There were several Mexican waves (obviously) and various singing competitions. Mainly, the girls from the Eight and I got envious about how nice other countries' opening ceremony kit was. The German women had lovely little suits that made them look a bit like air hostesses, but still that's not a bad look, and the Aussies had those mad mambo shirts that were all the rage at the time and really well-cut shorts. We were to parade out in M&S pyjamas, which I suppose is quintessentially British in a "We're all slightly mad" sort of way.

I remember being weirdly a little disappointed when I realised I couldn't see what was going on in the stadium and that I was going to miss seeing the opening ceremony for the first time in twenty years. I hadn't thought through how being in it meant you didn't get to see it.

Still it was fun and being G for Great Britain, we didn't have too long to wait. Gradually over the course of the next hour, blocks of teams got up and filed out of the hall. Eventually it was our turn and we filed downstairs to join the back of the procession. Matthew Pinsent was holding the flag (you might remember that), the rest of his crew went upfront with him and then we weren't too far back, mixed in with the tennis players and sailors. Everyone was in high spirits and very chatty and there was lots of pseudo-competitive banter between teams. I stood behind Tim Henman and chatted to him, thinking how small and waif-like he looked next to our rowing guys (and some of the girls come to that). He hadn't looked like that on TV.

We set off walking towards the stadium and I remember it being a fair way, but maybe we were just walking very slowly. Periodically we'd hear cheers up ahead as another team was introduced onto the track and we told each other "That's going to be us." Eventually we walked into the stadium underpass that led out to the track. Teams ahead of us were singing and chanting to make it echo round the tunnel and we added our own. The atmosphere was building and we were buzzing. Finally we were at the front and held in the entrance, while the cheers died down for the team ahead. And then it was us… and then IT WAS ME, walking out into the Olympic Stadium. I was trying to see it and trying to remember it, but now as I write I'm not sure how much I actually remember. I can't really picture it or hear it anymore, but as I type this my heart is racing and there are tears in my eyes so the emotional connection is still there. Of course there was that huge roar from the crowd as we came out and you have to remember how much of a big deal this is for rowers. Footballers and athletes get to compete in this sort of stadium, but as rowers you are generally lucky if there are a few people's mums and a random guy out walking his dog on the bank cheering you on.

Our lap of the track was over far too quickly and then we filed into the middle to take our place. And that was it. I'd always thought the opening ceremony was such a party, but when I got there I realised we were the entertainment, not there to be entertained. We stood and waited in formation for all the other teams to file in and the downside of being only the seventh letter in the alphabet became apparent. And then the rest of the entertainment began, but we couldn't see anything and all the speakers were pointing towards the spectators so we still couldn't hear anything. Kylie was singing but we couldn't hear her. I had to try really hard not to be disappointed.

We stood for several hours. Rowers are not very good at standing. Then there was a bit of fun when a giant Olympic flag the size of the pitch was unrolled over our heads and it was our job to hold it up. I was happier now I had a job and also we got to break ranks and everyone went a bit mental and ran around generally mucking about under the flag (I think I wasn't the only one who'd got a bit bored). We couldn't see anything at all now, but then no one could see us either. And then they took the flag away and it was time to go home, which took a while. I know I sound a bit flat about it now, but still I would not have missed it for the world. It wasn't what I'd expected from watching it on the TV all those years, but I had to be there to know that and I WAS THERE. And really all those hours of waiting were worth it for those few moments of walking round the track waving to the crowd. I was one of those people. I *am* and always will be one of those people.

And then finally, there was nothing left to do but race. Oh, except I had my first ever radio interview to do. Richard Phelps (former GB Men's Eight and my opposite number Cambridge Boat Club President in 1994) was to interview me for Radio 5 Live – live. An advantage of having been the Single for the past two years was the minor celebrity being on my own had brought me. When results were reported in the paper, the others were the GB Double, Quad or Eight, but I was Mowbray (1x). So Mowbray (1x) was getting her own radio interview. I went and sat in the commentary position in the stands and the sound guy put headphones on me and we waited for the countdown to 'live'. Then Richard asked his first question and I couldn't hear anything. I'd not done this before so I didn't know that the sound was supposed to come through the headphones, and that they were not only not working but very effectively blocking out Richard's voice from only a few feet away. "I'm sorry, I didn't get that." Richard repeated the question and again I couldn't make it out. "I'm sorry, I really can't hear you." Was it always this difficult? I was starting to panic as was everyone around me. Suddenly the sound guy twigged and flicked a switch and he and Richard made silent, horror struck faces at each other. Richard repeated the question a third time and this time I heard it.

"So, what I was saying was that there has been quite a bit of controversy surrounding your selection over Debbie Flood. How do you feel about that?" And I must have blanched as the following thoughts simultaneously flooded my head in the second or two while I stumbled to answer. 1. Oh my God! I hadn't been paranoid, people really were talking about this and the common perception was STILL that Debbie had beaten me in the trial. 2. No one would know my headphones hadn't been turned on and to any listeners, it must have sounded like I'd been avoiding a difficult question. 3. Through really bad luck, I'd just missed probably the best chance I'd ever have of clearing this all up because no one was going to believe my answer now after appearing to be so evasive. 4. How on earth could Richard have asked me this as my first ever question on live radio the night before my first ever Olympic race?

I'd love to say that I mastered the situation and coolly and calmly put my case, but I'm sure I sounded as flustered as I felt trying to process all that and speak at the same time. Fortunately, the words I'd written in answer to the Tideway Slug gossip page came back to me and I answered pretty much to that effect. I don't remember any more of the interview, but I don't imagine I shone.

I walked away shattered again. I knew I shouldn't let it upset or affect me, but I couldn't help it. The mental processes needed for forcibly not letting this sort of stuff distract me were sometimes harder work than just thinking about it. It took another monumental effort to get my head back into the right place for my first race the next day.

My alarm went off at 4am the next morning, but I didn't need it. From about 3.30am, for the first time in weeks, I'd been totally and startlingly awake. My heart rate was up but my breathing slow and deep, and my mind totally focused in a way that's near impossible to describe. But maybe I don't really have to because you don't have to race at the Olympics to feel it. Anyone who's ever performed at anything they truly care about will have been there. Now as I write this I'm flicked back to that state and I can feel my heart in my chest and my breathing has slowed and my eyes have actually narrowed. I'm shooting lasers that come up from the bottom of my lungs and out of my eyes, the centre of my vision is tunnelled and simultaneously clear yet blurred, and the periphery is disturbed like the start of a migraine. I move in slow motion with speed and precision.

I knew from that moment that I didn't need to get up early for weeks in advance ever again to trick my body into thinking 4am was morning and it was ready to race. If it was race time, my body would be ready to race. That's how it works. Louise and I went to the food hall for a cup of tea and token gesture breakfast and then caught a bus to the course. I did a 4k warm-up lap with a few full speed bursts, then paddled back in (my flip-flops brought to me even at that time in the morning) and sat around to wait out the next couple of hours. And then eventually it was time and I was heading out to race at my first Olympics. It's still mind-blowing to write that because now, six and a half years on, it's just an ordinary day and I'm sat in an airport waiting for a flight back from holiday surrounded by people – none of whom knows what I'm writing and what I did and they never will because I'm sat here just waiting for a plane and I look like an ordinary person. But I RACED AT THE OLYMPICS. And I will always know that, no matter where I sit.

I raced fine. It was never really about this first race because only the winner went straight through to the semis and I was in a heat with the Bulgarian Neykova, bronze medallist from the '99 Worlds, so with the best will in the world that was unlikely to be me. Still, I raced it out – flat-out – right to the end as Miles had taught me, because truly bottoming yourself out like that makes your body (and mind) more ready to go there again in the next race (when I was really going to need it), not less so as might be expected.

My big race was a couple of days later. The Repechage would decide who would make those last places for the A/B semi-finals. This then, was my goal. This then, was MY Olympic final – again. The third or fourth already that year, I couldn't even really remember. But as Louise and I sat down the evening before to talk through yet again the complicated logistics of getting to the start on time, physically and mentally ready, and talk through yet again the plan for the race on this the eve of the biggest race of my life and everything this year had been leading up to… I wasn't really sure I could be bothered.

"Louise, I'm just so tired. It's been such a tough year already and now I'm finally here, I don't know if I've got anything left to race with." And, from my ME-focused athlete world I might have expected a pep talk or some sympathy, but uncharacteristically from Louise I didn't get either. "I know. I'm so tired too. I wasn't going to say until after you'd finished racing, but I've had enough. I've changed my flight back to an earlier one. I'm not going to stick around after the rowing has finished to watch the rest of the Olympics, I'm going home. I just want to go home."

And I looked at Louise properly for the first time in ages, rather than as just someone who was helping me achieve what I wanted to achieve, and I saw that she did look really tired and really down. I stepped out of my world and my head for a minute and into hers, and thought that if it was tough for me, how much tougher it was for her. She was just a couple of years older than me, for both of us it was our first Olympics, for both of us the man who was paid to lead/help us had been undermining and making things difficult for us for years and yet at least I'd had and still had the rest of the girls on the team to offload to and bitch with and get support from and share this whole experience with, at least I'd still had Louise and Miles. Where had Louise, one place professionally removed, got any of that from? Even within the coaches, as the only female and considered Mike's lackey, I imagine she was isolated rather than supported.

But then as I looked at Louise and thought of what we'd both been through and what had brought us here, I said, "It's pretty cool though, Louise. We're at the Olympic Games. If you hadn't coached me through qualification then I wouldn't be here and if I hadn't asked you to coach me then you wouldn't be here. We got each other to the Olympics." And she looked at me in surprise and brightened. "I'd not thought of it like that, but I suppose you are right."

So we both put our heads back down to the timetables and race plan and got back to work. I did manage to raise my game one last time and recorded a new personal best on that Olympic course to beat scullers from America, China and Tunisia and WIN MY REPECHAGE. I booked myself into the semi-finals and top twelve in the world. It was hardly an Olympic medal and it seemed as if the whole world was winding up to watch Steve try and take his fifth Gold, but it was everything to me in that moment. One of my friends emailed to say a clip of my race had made it into the BBC round-up montage that evening backed by the track *Proud*. You know the one "What have you done today to make you feel proud?" I cried when I got home and watched it, and I cry now every time I hear that track (which can be damned inconvenient because often they play it backing some other video montage just before I'm supposed to go on stage and look professional) because it has such an immediate emotional connection with a year that was both wonderful and draining in equal measure.

The Women's Eight, who'd put in such a fiery and inspired performance at qualification, felt equally drained and were not able to find such fire again. There are only seven places allocated to Women's Eights at the Olympics and it took two rounds (a heat and a Repechage) to cut seven down to the six finalists and eliminate the GB Women's Eight. They were devastated.

And I guess what everyone wants to read in these stories is that I went on to race a blinder in my semi-final, beat several girls I'd never come close to before, qualified for the Olympic final and achieved my dream goal. But it wasn't like that. It was much more realistic and real. I raced well in my semi, but didn't manage to make what would have been a quite extraordinary leap to qualify for the final. Instead I raced in the 'B' final (to decide places seven to twelve). I raced well, beating Sweden's Maria Brandin who'd been the one to beat me in qualification, and came fourth which meant I was tenth overall – one place better than last year in a tougher Olympic field. I was tenth in the world in the Women's Single – tenth in the world at something. I didn't think that was bad for the girl who couldn't make the school sports teams.

I was surrounded by the Women's Eight who'd not made the final, the Fran and Sarah Double who'd come tenth, and the Dot and Cath Pair (1998 World Champions) who were ninth. All were pretty distraught with how their Olympics had panned out. But tenth was pretty good for me, so I was happy and everyone was happy for me. People kept coming up and saying "Tenth! That's pretty good for you, Alison." Mike came up and said, "Tenth! That's pretty good for you, Alison."

And then I came down on that middle Saturday of the Games to watch the finals. I sat in the supporters' stands for most of it with my parents. They were on good form, happy and cheering and having the time of their lives. Here they were surrounded by all the other British supporters in their hotel and at the course. Here they had something easy in common with people. I think it was wonderful for them after having become so isolated at home with really nothing they could share with anyone.

As soon as I saw them Dad couldn't wait to tell me that he'd been talking to Tim Foster's dad the night before, who'd said that I was really very good – untapped potential or something – and that I was going to go a long way. Dad continued, "And he wasn't just saying it Alison, he really knows about rowing. I wanted to call you straightaway last night, but your Mum said we shouldn't disturb you." He was so excited but I couldn't share it, in fact I found it almost annoying. "Dad, of course he'd say nice things to you, you're my parents." It's funny – I remember it now because it never occurred to me that Tim Foster's dad might have been being genuine and that he might have been right.

At some point in the morning, Mum couldn't resist one little comment about how Dad had been overexcited at the airport and had embarrassed her by bounding up to Miriam's husband (who he'd never met) with "It's Alison's coach! Hello Alison's coach!" Never minding that Miles and Miriam's husband are about as physically different as it's possible to get, or spending a moment to consider why my coach (if he had indeed still been my coach) would be at the airport with the supporters nearly a month after I'd gone to Australia, or indeed thinking it would be polite to try and remember Miles's name (if it had been Miles) before he bounded up. I knew my dad well enough to imagine it exactly. A man who had lost any sense he ever might have had of normal social skills and any awareness he'd ever had of a world outside of his own. Mum had to mention it because it was our age-old method of communication, but although it's a vivid image that has lasted and it did make me cringe at the time, it no longer drew me into support, sympathy or debate. She had stayed married to him; she had brought him to the Olympics; she even allowed him to drink; who else did she suddenly expect him to be?

But I'm putting an overly large blot on what was really a nice time for us. To be fair, he couldn't really have won. I hadn't wanted him there, but then what sort of father would he have been if he'd not turned up? And in the times I saw him at the Olympics, he was fine.

It was a calm sunny day (the fabled wind never did blow up for us) and I left my parents to stand by the side of the course with the other British rowers to feel the tension mount before the final of the Men's Four. And I was there to watch LIVE Matthew Pinsent, Steve Redgrave, James Cracknell and Tim Foster win that race by the narrowest of margins. And I was there LIVE, to see that fifth consecutive Gold Medal hung round Steve Redgrave's neck. How many of you got up in the middle of the night to watch that race on TV?

And I thought how lucky am I? Not just that I get to be part of an Olympics, but that it is *this* Olympics and I get to be part of *this* team. Even now whenever I say I was a rower people ask, "Do you know Steve Redgrave?" in a tone which implies I couldn't possibly know such a God, and I can say "Do I *know* Steve Redgrave? I was on his.... he was on my team." We trained together; we rowed on the same water; that evening back in the village, I had dinner sat opposite him and tried his medal around my neck. And I still think that though there was an awful lot of hard work and very little luck involved in my getting to the Olympics, it was pure luck that *this* was my time.

And I went down on the Sunday to watch the last day of finals and I was there to watch LIVE when the Women's Quad of Miriam Batten, Guin Batten, Katherine Grainger and Gillian Lindsey came through to take the Silver medal. The *first ever* British Women's Olympic Rowing medal – we forget that now. We are so used now to British rowers delivering Olympic medals that it's an absolute expectation and we forget there was ever a time, and in such recent history, when the women didn't have one to their name.

I saw those girls race that race. I saw them on the podium with those medals round their necks. And I stood there and thought "I train with those girls every day. I row with them and race against them and sometimes, in my single, I know I can beat them. Wouldn't it be a shame if I was capable of doing that and I never found out?"

I didn't want to say it to myself because as soon as I did, then it was a new goal and a new challenge and I knew I'd have to take it up or be forever left wondering. But it was too late. There was already too much of it in my head. I remember very clearly standing by the side of the course looking at the water as the stands cleared out and the last of the spectators went home. And I thought to myself… "It's like magic this goal-setting thing. I set myself a goal and I don't know how I'm going to do it, but I just keep going and keep going and somehow it happens. I said I was going to get a First and I got it. I said I was going to get a PhD and it took me five and a half years and it was the hardest thing I've ever done, but I got it. I said I was going to come to Sydney and somehow I'm here. How far can I push it?

What if I said I was going to get an Olympic medal? Could I make that happen as well?"

I had a new goal and I had to go after it. Do everything I could to make it happen or I knew I'd never be able to live with myself and the not knowing. So I stayed for the second week of the Olympics and went to the parties and watched as much of any sport as I could and had absolutely *the* most amazing time and totally let my hair down. But by the time I left it was clear in my head.

I'm going to row for four more years. I'm going to go to Athens. And I'm going to get an Olympic medal. Or I'm not going.

It was clear in my head but I've told you where I came from and it wasn't easy to say, even to myself. It was still such a faint and scary dream that I thought that if I told people and just one person laughed at me and said "Yeah right!", then it would disappear (how easy it is to trample over people's dreams). And anyway it seemed such an arrogant thing to say, "I'm going to get an Olympic medal", that I couldn't say it out loud. So when people came up to me and said "Tenth! Well done! That's really good for you, Alison. What are you going to do now? You're twenty-nine, are you going to go and get a proper job?" I just said, "No, well, I'm still really enjoying it and I'm still getting better so I'm going to keep going."

But in my head I was saying…. "I'm going to row for four more years. I'm going to go to Athens and I'm going to get an Olympic medal. Or I'm not going." This was undoubtedly the scariest goal I'd ever set myself and the most decisive I'd been in setting one.

However, before I set off on the next four years, I'm thinking you may be getting a little weary of the perpetual grind and not have the heart for yet more of it. I suspect this because I would certainly have felt the same if I'd dived straight back in myself. So, to help you recharge your batteries for the graft that is to come, I'll take you through a little of what helped me recharge mine.

First, obviously, there was the second week of the Sydney Olympics to experience. Rowing is the best sport for many reasons, but the one that is perhaps least mentioned is that it is the sport best placed *within* the Olympic calendar. Rowers get to race in the first week and not just in the first week but *for* the first week, so we really, truly immerse ourselves in the competition and feel part of The Games. Then, our competition is over and with still another clear week to go, we can watch all the other sports and party. For a whole week that is all we have to do – watch live Olympic sport (free) and party. Oh and eat free food in the 24-hour food hall (and the McDonald's is now not only 'on limits', but weirdly the perfect hangover food). So, here is some advice I've yet to see in any sports magazine. If you are fortunate enough to be very good at several sports and currently wondering which to focus on to see if it will take you to the Olympics, it's placing in the Olympic timetable should really be a major consideration. If it's too late on, you'll spend most of your Olympics hiding out in the holding camp watching events on TV, and by the time you finish competing the fun will be over. White water canoeing first week (good), gymnastics first week (good), women's marathon first week (good), athletics (happen over nearly two weeks so be careful and pick your event), flat water canoeing second week (bad), heavyweight boxing, men's marathon and modern pentathlon all on the last day (very, very bad). The fact I'd been rubbish at every other sport but rowing suddenly became a blessing.

The Olympic Village seems to have a bit of an outside reputation as party central, but that was not how it appeared to me from the inside. There are athletes competing right up until the last few hours of the Olympics and there is a huge amount of respect for that. It would be unthinkable to be drunk and loud in the village while others who might be competing the next day were trying to sleep or still trying to train and focus on their competition. I may have just missed everything (which wouldn't be the first time), but in my experience once your competition is over you can party as loud as you like in the rest of the city but the village is for sleeping and chilling out and being quiet.

And just to dispel one of the most ridiculous Olympic Village myths that gets bandied around by the press every Olympics. The number of condoms taken from the free bowl outside the clinic does not equate to the number of sexual encounters between athletes (we wish). Every year there is some headline about 'Steamy sex village randy athletes go through so many x thousand condoms' and it's all rather ridiculous. Condoms are expensive things and here they are free. People walk past and take handfuls and put enough in their wallets and wash bags to supply years of hopeful nights out. Also I wouldn't be surprised if athletes from some countries send condoms home in the same way that they send food parcels from the free food hall. Besides, where are we supposed to be having all this sex in the steamy sex village? In the narrow beds in our twin bedded rooms while our roommates are sleeping? Obviously where there's a will there's a way and of course stuff happens (in all sorts of places), but the village is mainly for sleeping and chilling out and being quiet.

I settled into a new routine that was all about not missing out on a single opportunity. Not being in the village, the parties were surprisingly hard to find and get to. I'd usually hook up with one or two of the girls from the Eight to go out. We tapped any contacts we had in the Australian team and spent the day asking round to find out what was likely to be going on where and pooled our knowledge every evening. That first night there was a rowing party in the city so at least we knew where to go and after that there were one or two nightclubs that always seemed to be a good bet. But the city centre was a long way from the Olympic Village and every night out involved a bus ride from the village, a long train ride and then lots of walking around searching for 'The Action'. It was worth it though. We had a ball.

Wherever you went it was easy to spot fellow Olympians by the accreditation passes that always hung from our necks, so you could go and chat even if you didn't know them. We didn't dare leave our accreditations in any bags to get stolen as we'd been made very aware of how complicated our lives would be without them. Besides they were a badge of honour and annoying as they were (large nearly A5 laminated sheets) we didn't want to take them off and risk being mistaken for normal people. Most people ended up wearing them with the strap across their chest and the pass under their arm like a handbag – and indeed they could be fashioned into one. We prised the tops apart and stashed a key and cash inside for safekeeping. We met new athletes, drank a fair bit and danced quite literally till dawn. It wasn't a bad recompense for all the hours of training.

Getting home proved the biggest challenge of the night as the trains and village buses stopped way before we were done partying and taxis seemed none existent. After a couple of nights spent walking for hours and dancing for hours more, I abandoned my heeled party shoes and bought some casual trainers that just about passed with my outfits – we all did. We were still athletes at heart and were not going to let our footwear cut short our party performance potential. A couple of nights I ended up taking the train out to the beach to swim in the sea at dawn, so I made sure I always went out in underwear that would double as a bikini and wore a cardigan that worked as a towel. This kind of practical advice is somehow missing from all the official Olympic orientation guides so I include it in case you are someone on your way.

We'd get back to the village somehow, somewhere between 4 and 6am, and go straight to the food hall for breakfast. We'd hang out in a corner (usually the McDonald's corner) well away from any still competing athletes. You didn't want them to have to see you all dressed up in (by now rather worse for wear) party clothes (with seaweed in your hair) while they were still focused on racing. On the way to bed we'd drop by the Team GB headquarters as they opened up to see if we'd got the tickets we'd hoped to get that day and get first pick of any spares. Then I'd go back to get a couple of hours sleep (eye mask on) before getting up to watch the afternoon and evening events I had tickets for. I was lucky enough to get into the athletics stadium a few times. The atmosphere was unbelievable and just like you can't really see the size of people on TV, you also have no idea of the speed they go until you see them run live. Most amazing to me are the long distance 5,000 and 10,000m runners. They float by with such an effortless, relaxed style that when you watch them on TV, they seem to be just jogging. But when they pass directly in front of you in the stands, the speed is unbelievable – it's a sprint, it's anyone else's sprint and yet they keep going lap after lap after lap.

I also went to see GB men play in the first live hockey match I'd watched since school, got to watch diving (although I didn't last long in the hot, chlorinated atmosphere with my hangover) and took the bus out to watch the show jumping. Top, top event though was the gymnastics gala where all the medal winners perform their winning and show routines. Unbelievably, when I turned up that morning to beg for any tickets, there was just that one ticket available.

But eventually, it was time to bring it all to a close. I was wrecked, surviving on Red Bull instead of sleep (not really an adequate substitute no matter what the adverts say) and applying more and more make-up daily to try and paint on colour and even eyes that were no longer there. The athlete saying is that it takes four years of non-stop effort to peak for an Olympics and approximately four days of after-party to destroy the lot. By day seven there wasn't much of me left but I'm an Olympian so I was still fighting hard, and there was still the closing ceremony left to go.

Being part of the opening ceremony had done a good job of lowering my expectations of the closing ceremony, which meant that this time I was less disappointed and more entertained. It was more of a free-for-all in the middle this time, which meant we could at least find our own entertainment. Everyone seemed to have the same idea and after a brief interval of standing to attention and looking the part, someone invented a game using the large Olympic flag we'd been given to hold (a lot smaller than stadium size this time). If a dozen or so of us stood round the edges and held it taut, it made a pretty good trampoline. I wish I could say I'd had the guts to get up there, but me and my low adrenalin threshold would be lying. Dual stars of our personal closing ceremony show were one of the gymnasts who could actually do it and performed whole aerial routines before landing the right way up, and our official big boss man Chef de Mission Simon Clegg who had our respect by just getting up there and didn't need to do anything fancy (which turned out to be a good job). I think Kylie was probably singing again while we were doing this, I'm not sure – we couldn't hear what with the speakers pointing out into the crowd and everything.

I now knew several Olympians from different sports so went round saying goodbye, and then at some point Cesca (one of my best friends from the Eight and party partner extraordinaire) and I broke ranks completely and went to explore amongst the decorative floats and general detritus of the end of an Olympics now scattered around the track. We have some great photos of us posing with 7-foot-high transvestites (a la *Priscilla, Queen of the Desert*), some of whom were wearing even more make-up than I'd had to put on that night.

And that was it. My first Olympics was officially over. It felt like the longest two weeks of my life because to sit down and try and replay all the memories, all the vivid pictures in my head, took forever. People say that life is short but I have a different view. It seems to me that if we measure our life not in years that are passing but in the number of magical moments we can create every day, then our lives slow down and stretch out behind and in front of us exponentially. Of course, on a more practical note, it also helped that I'd barely slept in two weeks so technically it had been more like a month. I hoped I'd be back but if not, at least I'd scraped the flapjack pan of life from this one and eaten it raw from the spoon.

I had a final week of holiday in Australia with Elise and some friends, mainly sleeping on beaches. I hiked a two-day trail in the Blue Mountains, then flew home via a few days in Kuala Lumpur (and another trek) to visit my Malaysian PhD friend Vishna and then that really was that. It had taken four years of non-stop effort to reach my peak for an Olympics, a week of after-party to destroy the lot, and about ten days of sleeping and hiking to rediscover my Karma. Now it was time to start again. Four years to Athens.

Chapter 13: Very many very small steps

"I'm going to row for four more years, I'm going to go to Athens and I'm going to get an Olympic medal. Or I'm not going."

The start of the season, when I could set my own timetable and regulate my own training, were always my favourite weeks of the year. I was still living in Henley at Jenno's so I could just get up, have breakfast, walk down to Leander, put my single on the water and go for a scull. Then I'd have more breakfast down at the club and usually do a second session of weights or ergo in the gym. Preseason training I'd just do two sessions a day, so there was the luxury of afternoons off and not always feeling totally knackered.

It was fun to train down at Leander with the club guys and those few of us from the Squad that were back at it already. During official training the Women's team were segregated down at Longridge reporting for duty and doing what we were told. But here for a while I could train when I liked and how I liked and I really enjoyed it. It was also fun to sit on the ergo and watch the dynamics of who was going to do what in a post-Steve Redgrave GB Men's team start to work itself out.

Steve had retired and the big question now was who would row with Matt. It would be James Cracknell who'd get the seat and I reckon if you ask most people now, they will tell you that the James Cracknell they now know – double Olympic Gold medallist, Polar explorer, TV celebrity and general demigod – was the natural choice and it was always going to be that way. I reckon even by January 2001, most people would have told you that James had always been the obvious choice for that seat. But straight after Sydney I'm not sure that was the case. There were talented guys from the Sydney Gold Medal Eight, Ed Coode from the Pair and Tim Foster from the Four were all still around and perhaps James was not even the most obvious choice at first. James and Matt were both stroke side for starters so James would have to swap sides – a tricky thing to do and really tricky in a pair where the balance is so much more difficult. Swapping sides feels awkward and clumsy to start with, rather like learning to write with your other hand. James wasn't the biggest athlete nor did he have the biggest ergo, and some of the guys from the Eight were nearer to Matt's size. So to start with, it really wasn't that obvious. But what I think I saw from my vantage point on the ergo on those mornings was that James turned himself into the obvious choice. He made it look inevitable.

A very good-looking, fashionable, photogenic guy, James was rather a celebrity after Sydney. Very good-looking, fashionable, photogenic guys with Olympic medals won in spectacular style in races that half the nation gets up in the middle of the night to watch on TV exude natural celebrity. And James rather suits celebrity as we now see. The press and media loved him. He was invited to all the events and parties and went to them all. At one event he met and started dating the Formula 1 racing commentator Bev Turner (who he would eventually marry), so he even had a celebrity girlfriend. But despite all the parties and celebrity, James's goal was to be the best in the British team, rowing with the best in the British team and that meant a lot of training.

But I guess he didn't want to miss a moment either. And fair enough, because as a rower you don't get much attention so when it happens you have to make the most of it. I sat there on the ergo and James would rock up mid-morning looking really rather worse for wear from the night before. I looked forward to him arriving because the first thing he would do (after very little prompting) would be to tell me (and anyone else who'd listen) the crazy, glamorous stories of the night before. A good section of my ergo used to fly by as he talked and then he'd get on the ergo himself, and even though it must have been really painful he'd do a proper full session, have lunch and then do a proper full second session before going home to get changed to go back into London for another party.

He went out every night and made every party but he came back to Henley and trained at Leander every morning, and within a few weeks, by the time everyone else came back to training, somehow it felt like James was the obvious and only choice for the job. He'd pair with Matt for the next four years and they'd both go into a four for Athens where James would win his second Olympic Gold.

I had plans of my own for the next four years. I had decided that my best chance of a medal at Athens was to be in the Quad, so I needed to get myself reliably up into the top four scullers. There are many important factors to making a boat go fast, but I think they can be distilled down to six:

1. Power
2. Endurance

3. Technical mastery
4. Race Head
5. Single-minded determination
6. Team (ability to make your crew mates go faster than they would without you)

If you are a Steve Redgrave or a Matthew Pinsent then you have all six in abundance. But the beauty of rowing is that there are relatively few people with all six, so if you have a good five then you are still well placed to do well and win medals. Since 3 to 6 are about your head and can be developed if you put your mind to it, and everyone is pretty much sure to have either 1 or 2 (it's how humans are built), I reckon anyone can get good at rowing if it's what they choose to spend their time doing above anything else in their lives. In fact, even Steve and Matt would admit that they had so much of five of them that they perhaps did not hone and refine their technique quite as much as they could have done – yet they still dominated the world. You see it in rowing all the time. People of all shapes, sizes and talents win in all sorts of ways.

I had done well on (and would continue to develop) Endurance, Technique, Race Head and Determination. Those I had in abundance. What I was sadly lacking and could never seem to develop was the big number 1. I was not and never would be a power athlete. Power athletes have an anabolic metabolism meaning that when they train, they build muscle. I have a much more catabolic metabolism in that I actually burn muscle as a fuel source during extended endurance training (of which we did hours and hours). For years I'd go to the gym and lift heavy weights to build some muscle, only to go and break it all down again during on the water endurance training sessions. In retrospect I can see now why I was at my strongest the year I won Women's Henley. Then, fitting training around my PhD, I trained a maximum of once a day and did explosive power weights circuits every other day. Occasionally I talked to the physiologists and coaches about doing different training that would enable me to build more power and they were supportive in theory. But in practice this meant I'd have to come off the water sessions after an hour while everyone else was still out there for nearly two, and get off the ergo and walk away half an hour before everyone else. I found I couldn't do it, even during winter training, and of course once I was in a crew we all had to do the same thing anyway.

Whichever way I trained, Power was never going to be my strong suit so

I was already one down, and in the Single there are only five factors – there is no 6, no Team, and Team can be a BIG factor (remember the three-legged races?). It's a rare skill to be able to get into a crew and a) not mess it up and make other people go slower and b) make the others go faster than they would by themselves, but it can be learnt and I thought it was my best route to a medal.

I'd only been back training a few days when I got a phone call. James was getting calls every day to invite him to parties; my one call was slightly different.

"Hello, you don't know me. I'm Head of Chemistry at Wycombe High School."

"Oh?"

"I hear you're a Chemistry teacher."

"I'm more of a Biologist really."

"It doesn't matter, we're desperate."

They needed someone to cover a part-time maternity leave for the start of the new term just a few days away. He'd interviewed several people over the summer, but even though they'd become increasingly desperate, they were not desperate enough to employ any of the applicants. Sarah Lafford, our squad masseur, also taught Biology at Wycombe High so the information about my teaching qualifications had filtered through. I'd been getting a bit anxious that I wasn't doing anything with either my PhD or PGCE and that I would be getting rusty. I had thought I'd volunteer at one of the local schools again, but had never imagined I'd be able to hold down an actual teaching job alongside my rowing. "I'm sorry but I really don't see how I can. I have to train every morning and I also have to go away on training camp during term time."

"We'll sort that out. Why don't you just come down and have a look. I'll show you the syllabus and you can see what you think."

So I drove over to the school and met Malcolm, Head of Chemistry, for an interview. Malcolm was lovely and my interview involved *him* trying to convince *me* that I was up to teaching A level Chemistry. He interviewed well and eventually I said yes.

So for the next few months, I trained once at Leander in the morning then drove the nine miles to High Wycombe to teach my lessons. Most days my first lesson started at 10.30am with an earlier start on Tuesdays, and

Wednesday off. I'd do a second training session after school on the way home. I was nervous about the A level Chemistry but when I opened the textbook to take a look, I was amazed by how much more I understood than when I'd last looked at this stuff over ten years ago. I think ten years of working through my degree and PhD, all the learning, reasoning and struggling had, all actually made my brain work better. I'm pretty sure I actually had a higher IQ.

We tend to think of our IQ as something relatively fixed, at least by the age of eighteen, but I'm not so sure now. I used to talk to the kids I was teaching about the parallels between physical and mental exercise and say that wrestling with problems they couldn't work out was like going to the brain gym. If you go to the gym and always lift the same weights, the ones that feel good, your muscles will stay the same. If you want to get stronger you have to put the weight up and up, and the last weight, the one you can't quite lift… that is the most important one. You have to struggle with that last weight even if you can't lift it, but eventually, one day you find you can lift it – and now the weight below, the one that used to feel so heavy, will feel easy. I wonder sometimes if our intelligence is really fixed by our age or by the fact that we think it's OK to stop putting the weight up as we get older.

But I didn't forget that I used to find Chemistry difficult, which is actually a pretty good place to teach from and I think I taught some good lessons that year. I was surprised that, for the first time in my life, it actually felt OK not to know everything. I think a combination of getting my PhD and going to the Olympics and the positivity of the other teachers gave me enough confidence not to have to be right all the time. We worked it out together. I didn't introduce myself as a rower back from the Olympics, but they gradually found out from one source or another. Every so often a girl would call out "Dr Mowbray? Did you go to the Olympics?" And then there'd be a flurry of questions for a few minutes before I thought we might be slipping into one of those time honoured teacher distraction strategies and I'd stop them and get back to the lesson. In my younger classes the question most asked was "Do you know Steve Redgrave?" and I learnt it wasn't so much a question as an opening for them to tell me that he lived in the same village as them/ their dad knew him/ he'd spoken at their brother's school/ they'd seen him in Waitrose… In my older classes, once the girls hit their teens, I was much more likely to be asked, "Do you know James Cracknell?"

Within about a month of the Olympics, those of us that were coming back were all back to full training, but for the first few weeks at least this was self-regulated. We were all still training by ourselves at our home bases and enjoying the extra little bit of freedom while we waited for our new coaches to arrive.

In a move that surprised many on the outside but almost no one from within, Mike Spraklen – having delivered Great Britain's first Women's Olympic rowing medal – had not had his contract renewed. There are many sides to every story and it depends who you talk to as to what impression you get. Mike was right when he said that many people did not like the way he went about things, but those who won medals with him were always his friends. I'd shared a car with Miriam for enough trips to and from Longridge to know that she had had her fair share of anti-Mike sentiments along the way, but now she'll simply say, "You can say what you like about Mike, and I know he has his faults, but I've worked with so many coaches for so many years and been to two Olympics and never got what I wanted out of any of it. Mike was able to get something out of me that no one else could and I finally got my medal. That's all I know." You'll also not get a bad word about him out of Gillian or Guin. I've not heard a bad word about Mike from Katherine either, but then almost uniquely in British rowing I've rarely, if ever, heard Katherine say a bad word about anyone. If she doesn't have anything nice to say, she tends to keep quiet. Whenever Mike is mentioned around Katherine, she tends to keep quiet.

Apart from that one boat and that one medal, the rest of the Women's squad was pretty cowed and demoralised. Many did not come back and several only did so because Mike was not going to be there. And then there were the ones that had been broken along the way. Of course not everyone makes it through and survives an Olympiad and there are always some casualties and injuries so it's hard to say whose, if anyone's, demise was really due to Mike, but there are several who'll tell you it was.

We had a small squad of returners but at least that left room for fresh new talent. Except there was none. Perhaps the real proof that it was right not to reappoint Mike came from how hard it would be to rebuild a squad from what he had left behind. Mike, in his role as Women's Head Coach, had been technically responsible for finding and developing talent including Junior and Under 23 rowing. But there was none. Just outside the squad, there was Debbie Flood and Rebecca Romero who had been discovered and developed by Mark Banks and Ian South respectively and had remained pointedly on the outside of Mike's system. Apart from them, there was a massive gap between the Squad and the best of the rest. We didn't know it now but in four years' time, all the Squad that would eventually go to Athens (and it would be a much smaller squad) were already amongst the Sydney returners plus Debs and Becs.

I for one was very relieved Mike was not coming back. I cannot think that the story of the next four years would have been what it was for me if I'd had to fight Mike all the way like I'd had to for the last two. I don't know how much longer I could have lasted. I was not alone. We were all fairly battle scarred as we awaited our new coaches.

I keep saying coaches because we were to have two. Marty Aitkin was appointed Chief Coach of Women and Lightweights, and Paul Thompson as Head Coach of Heavyweight Women. Paul had coached the Australian's Women's Pair to a Silver Medal in Sydney. Technically he was my coach and Marty his boss – although with Marty's major role being with the Lightweights, I wouldn't have a lot to do with Marty over the next four years and Paul would increasingly carve his independence.

All the returning women and lightweights turned up at Leander to meet our new coaches for the first time. Paul (aka Thommo) stood up to talk to us and said that this was a four-year plan and a four-year programme, we were going to work hard this year, but it was also the time to get our breath back and regroup. The plan was to build year on year towards Athens, so we would peak when it really mattered.

Already this felt very different. With Mike, there had been little if any sense of a four-year or even a year plan. Most of our focus had been on beating each other that very day, that session even. And the result had been almost the reverse of a four year plan – a strong start with lots of medals in the first year and then a year on year decline as we got closer to Sydney (with that final desperate and debilitating push with the few that remained).

And to back up his intent, Paul said he wanted us to broaden out our lives this year. If we didn't already have them, we were to go out and get part-time jobs or get back into education. Over the next two or three years he actually *wanted* us to make definite and positive steps in the part of our lives outside rowing. "We have to build towards Athens. If you throw everything in this year, where are you going to go? I'm going to put a lot of pressure on you but stay broad as long as you can, and then as we come into the last year or two you can start to cut down everything else and we'll still have somewhere to go."

It would all prove to be more than just a nice opening speech and played out pretty much exactly as he said. He was true to his word though and did put us under increasing pressure as the four years progressed and did not make it easy to hold down jobs and education. Despite the balanced nature of his approach and intentions, Paul could never be described as a soft touch or a pushover. And while there was some flexibility around when and where we could do the training, there was never any around the fact that they all had to be done at some point.

We were left to our own devices for another week or so while the new coaches found their feet and checked out the training venue options available to them. Technically this was none. GB rowing still did not have its own dedicated training facility. Tim Foster once described expecting GB rowing to train on a public river with all the pleasure boats, as like expecting the England football team to train in the park around people walking their dogs. But that's how it was. The men mostly trained out of Leander on the famous and lovely Henley stretch of the Thames, and while the women were not barred from training there, it wouldn't have been in anyone's best interests to have both squads training in the same place messing up the water.

Mike had trained us out of the Scout camp base at Longridge (just downstream of Marlow), which must have seemed laughably basic to our new coaches. It's a rather bendy stretch of water with high stream, no boathouse, boats kept on makeshift racks under the motorway bridge and tiny concrete (rather mildewed) changing room. The whole place was rather muddy, damp and cold. I imagine they must have shopped around for a while not believing this was the best available to them, before finally realising it was. We also had fairly frequent trips to the new Eton College rowing course at Dorney (now the rowing venue for London 2012) when we needed straight flat water for pieces or Longridge was flooded out (as it often is).

So I settled into my new routine of training in the mornings and evenings with the Squad and teaching in-between, and loved the balance of physical and mental stimulation it gave to my day. I'd feel tired from my rowing session when I got to school but when you are on your feet engaging with thirty teenage kids, there is no room for weakness. My physical tiredness would drop away at the start of each lesson and I'd inhabit a new space of heightened awareness trying to keep on top of the lesson plan and thirty kids all doing different things at different speeds. And there were magic moments, just like in rowing, when I felt some or all of the kids shift to a new level of understanding or myself to a new level of competence. Most magic of all were the rare moments when I'd been buzzing round, working hard to get them engaged in some material or task and would suddenly realise that the class had fallen silent and they were all working away productively. When that happens, you don't even want to breathe in case you break the spell. Even the kids seemed to be party to holding the magic because if they needed help, they'd nudge and whisper to their friends or put up their hand and *sotto voce* a question to me when I came round, rather than shouting across each other as was their more usual way. And I'd just stay quiet and revel in it for as long as we could all hold it together, which was never very long – again, much like rowing.

After lessons, I'd sit in the science staff room and finish my work as I gradually came down from the teaching high, at which point I'd feel very tired again. But now I was mentally tired and even though I didn't feel it, I'd have had time to physically recover so I'd use my patented 'No step too small' Bedford RC strategy to get me out of the door, into my car, down to the gym and onto the ergo or weights for my second session.

At some point in that first term, the headmistress stopped me in a corridor and asked if I would speak at the school prize-giving. I said I would but I had never done anything like that before, so I asked her what I should say. "Tell us your story, what you did, how you got there, how hard you had to work, where you are going. Inspire us! Motivate us!" I still wasn't sure so I went to the science staff room and asked the same question in there. Within a heartbeat Malcolm said, "I've sat through a lot of these. Keep it short."

So those two quotes, pretty much verbatim, gave me my opening lines. And as with everything I found that once I got started it got easier and I sat down and wrote the rest. Next I wrote about Greg Searle telling me in a café up in Nottingham how he always gave kids the 'Ordinary People do Extraordinary Things' speech – and how sceptical I'd been that Greg, or any of the Olympians around me that day, could ever have been ordinary, but how training with them for two and a half years and going to the Olympics and meeting dozens of Olympians had taken away some of that scepticism. How I could see it was the things they did every day and not who they were by right that made them extraordinary.

And then I started writing down my story, a brief version of what you're reading here, and I found that reflecting on it and writing it down helped me work out for the first time what I *had* actually done and how I'd *actually* got there. As I wrote I began to get more clarity on how I needed to approach the next three and a half years. I'd been going at such a pace from one thing to the next, I'd never really stopped to take stock. Degree had overlapped with U23s and working in Bedford had overlapped with PhD, had overlapped with PGCE, had overlapped with making the team, had overlapped with getting to Sydney. I'd written brief notes in a training diary most days, but that was just reflecting on the day or at most the week's training. I was used to reflecting, but I'd never done it in such a purposeful and forward-thinking (what can I take from that to take me forward) sort of way.

I wrote about being bad at sport at school, the glory of discovering rowing for the first time and getting my First-class degree at Liverpool. I wrote down my three shortlisted PhD quotes including of course Winston's *"Success is the ability to go from failure to failure without losing your enthusiasm"* and got out my Canadian bookmark to include *"The quality of a person's life is a direct result of their commitment to excellence, regardless of their chosen field of endeavour"* – because I didn't want them to think that this was all, or even at all, about rowing.

I wrote of the repetitive struggle that got me my PhD and then onto the British Rowing Team and writing them side by side enhanced the parallels. I remembered back to my PhD and the dreadful, unrelenting feeling that if I walked away I'd have wasted years of my life and the massive pressure it put me under. And I thought that I never again wanted to feel like I'd have wasted part of my life if a plan didn't work out. Going forward I had to feel every day, regardless of the outcome, that this was what I would have wanted to do. I had to love not just the outcome but the process. Because you don't choose to go to the Olympics, you lay out everything you have and let the Olympics take it – no deals, no bargains, no questions asked, no hope of return. So if it didn't choose me, I had to feel that this was how I would have wanted to spend my time anyway. I had to remember to enjoy it.

And I never wanted to feel like that dreadful second Oxford/Cambridge boat race year when we'd won, but winning hadn't given me any real pleasure because it could not balance the hardship of getting there. So, I knew I had to keep a balance.

And finally as I wrote about standing by the Olympic course at Penrith Lake and my thoughts on the magic of goal setting, it all came together. So when I stood up to speak at that prize-giving, I not only told people for the first time out loud that I was going to row for four more years, go to Athens and get an Olympic medal… I also, for the first time, articulated how I was going to make it happen. "Yes it's important to know what I want to do in four years' time, but mostly that's too scary to think about. More I think, what do I have to do this year… this month… this week… today?" And my new mantra (my very own quote), built on all that had come before became: -

"Today I will have succeeded if I can do one thing better than I did it yesterday."
Alison Mowbray

I didn't have to win an Olympic medal tomorrow; I had over three and a half years left. Tomorrow I just had to take one more step, a tiny piece of it, any bit of it, and do that bit better. Get that bit done. And if I did that every day, did all the bits I could find to do one after the other, then that was all I could do. It was hard but I had to try not to worry about what was yet left undone, because I knew that would drag me down and make me feel like my small steps were not worth taking at all. And then I might stop.

I've worked out that there are approximately 1,400 training days in an Olympic cycle (allowing for the occasional sofa or duvet day where you do absolutely nothing because even Olympians need them sometimes). What couldn't anyone achieve if they took any of their goals and did one small thing towards making it happen pretty much every day for 1,400 days? No goal is too big and scary that we can't at least do the next small step before we give up on it and no step too small that we can't feel good about having done it. It seems to me that as long as we keep moving forward, these small steps can take us just about anywhere.

And that's how I worked for the next four years. I approached each day pushing until I found my one thing. It might just be one small technical improvement I was working on with my coach or to complete today's long ergo just a few seconds quicker, or make it feel easier and more fluid, or to put the weight up on just one of my lifts, or do my stretching and core stability exercises just a little bit better, or to improve my nutrition or get more sleep. And if at the end of the day, when I got home there was nothing I'd done that was better or different, if I felt like I'd wasted a day, then I'd still try and find something. I'd write one email or letter that was on my list of things to do or finish off my marking so it wouldn't be in the back of my mind during training tomorrow. Some days I had to look really hard for something positive and almost, if I'm honest, make it up.

I didn't have the confidence to stand up and speak without notes as I do now, but held onto prompt cards and referred to them often, but still it seemed to work. My opening lines quoting their headmistress and Malcolm got a laugh and it wasn't the only one. I could stand up on stage and be funny – who knew? I talked through my story and articulated my philosophies and felt like I did when I was teaching one of my best lessons or when I was racing.

And when I finished everyone clapped for quite some time while I stood awkwardly on stage not really knowing what to do with myself, but feeling rather like I'd just won a race. A few days later, Lavinia (my head of science) caught me in the staff room at break. She was learning to fly (in a plane – I'm good but not that good) and had had a lesson that weekend with her instructor. She told me how when she'd been up there with all the controls and all she had to learn, it had started to get too much; she'd started to panic and think she'd never be able to do it all. But then she said, "I thought about what you said – that I didn't have to do it all today, that I had plenty of time. So I relaxed and let my instructor worry about most of it and I just focused on getting one thing right and thought that's all I have to do today, just this one thing, and I'll sort something else out next weekend. And it really worked." She eventually passed her test and took me up in her little plane, which was really cool. Not everyone wants to or has to go the Olympics.

My hometown of Richmond was also keen to honour their first Olympian. In fact, it had been a very exciting Olympics for Richmond as there were two of us. Nicola Jackson had been on the GB Olympic Swimming Team and at sixteen was the youngest British Olympian at Sydney. Very little might have happened but for the fact that Mr Harris, my old Biology teacher, was now mayor. But as it was, in honour of Richmond's first Olympians, a new road was called Olympic Way and on it was Mowbray House and Jackson Court. I actually have a building named after me in my hometown (we don't have to mention that it's on the trading estate). Mowbray is not an uncommon name in Yorkshire. There's a Vale of Mowbray, a Mowbray School, a couple of Mowbray Roads and a Mowbray wing of the local hospital amongst others. We got used to seeing our name around us as kids and eventually we even bored of mentioning it and pretending they were ours. So it is quite a surreal feeling every time I drive past and I remember that this one, this particular Mowbray, actually *is* me.

I went up to cut the ribbon to open Mowbray House and Nicola and I were also invited back to turn on the Christmas lights. It may seem a small thing, but Richmond lights are quite famous and people travel from miles around to marvel and ask again "What's with the parrot?" (If that doesn't make sense, you've probably been brought up in the wrong Richmond). Nicola and I joined Santa on a makeshift trailer covered in fairy lights and plywood reindeer and were driven around the market square behind a tractor to wave Christmas cheer to the bemused townspeople perfectly happily going about their own business. There was quite a crowd in the gardens by the time we arrived though. Nicola and I got off first and the crush of confused kids parted silently to let us past, clearly having no idea who we were despite our Olympic suits. Then Santa descended to rousing cheers and was mobbed. It took quite a while before we found him again, dragged him out and straightened his beard, so we could all press a button while someone else pressed the real button that turned on the lights. That then was the summit of my fame.

I'd been worrying about what to do for Christmas pretty much since I came back from Australia, but actually it was my sister who came up with this year's solution. She was still nursing in London and always chose to work Christmas and spend New Year with friends these days, but suggested we all come to her for Christmas this year. At home Dad had his routines and his hiding places, and the stress of still somehow trying to live up to fantasy-conventional Christmas was always a recipe for early disaster. But if we did something where there was no precedent for perfection, then there was a hope he would hold up better.

John was by now back from Poland but living up in Scotland with his girlfriend and nicely out of Mowbray Christmases for a while as Maggie's Mum was on her own – so it was just the four of us. Dad booked us all into a Holiday Inn near Catherine's hospital so she could stay with us when she wasn't working and we set about constructing the most different Christmas we could.

We went and sang midnight mass at Westminster Cathedral and on Christmas morning got up late and met Cath off her night shift. We went to The Waldorf for Christmas breakfast together instead of doing Christmas lunch, then Cath went to sleep as did Mum (because that's her favourite way of spending time), and Dad and I wondered what to do with ourselves for the afternoon. I'd heard a rumour that the Millennium Dome was going to open on Christmas Day and neither of us had been, so we drove through deserted London streets to check it out. When we got there the massive car parks were also deserted and it didn't look very likely, but we wandered around anyway trying to find out if we could get in. We couldn't but it didn't really matter, it was just something to keep us occupied. And it was nice, to spend this time together sober and occupied. I'd let go of most of my angst around Dad and all of my challenge, so I just spent the time being nice. It was false to me, but real to him, and all I had to do to stay being nice was to remind myself that this was the worst part of my life but the best of his and it was just a short time. I was painfully aware that he was holding onto every minute of this time with me being nice to him. It was kind of sad but still kind of nice. It was the nicest few hours we'd spent together in a long while. We had curry for dinner and I went to bed early before anything bad could happen.

These days I try and make sure I'm far away for Christmas, preferably on my own somewhere beautiful in a tent, so I don't have to do any of it.

Christmas – you only do it for the parents.

On Boxing Day, I caught an early flight to go skiing. I'd never been before and reasoned that this was the year to do it. If I broke a leg I'd still have three years to repair myself and make it back. I went with Jo Nitch (one of my lightweight rowing friends) and stayed for about ten days with Ali Gill (ex-GB squad) and Bash, friends of ours from Henley with a chalet in France. We skied all day, but Jo and I knew we'd have to do more if we were not to fall behind. There was a two session a day Christmas training schedule to complete and while skiing all day could count as one, we didn't kid ourselves that it was the same as doing a ninety-minute ergo.

There were just two ergos in the sports centre, so we sat down and set off. I was shocked to find how difficult it felt, my heart rate shot up if I tried to pull anywhere near the scores I'd been able to just a few days before at home. Jo was having trouble too, but we dropped our scores and battled our way through the ninety minutes. It was painful, demoralising and confusing, but when we got back to the chalet we had it explained to us that of course we were at altitude – not very much altitude, but obviously enough. I'd never trained at altitude before, as it had not been Mike's thing.

There are FOR and AGAINST camps in rowing. Jurgen Grobler is strongly in the FOR camp so the men always went to altitude and there are definite physiological benefits to be gained. Training at altitude does increase the oxygen-carrying capacity of your blood, which is obviously a very good thing for a rower. But the AGAINST camp says that training at altitude makes you feel dreadful for quite a while (as I was starting to discover) and the beneficial effects do not necessarily last very long so you have to train at altitude as close as possible to your peak event of the year – and that usually coincides with your key pieces and can mess them up. Each coach balances the factors and makes their call.

Jo and I kept at our ninety-minute ergos most evenings and became rather embarrassed by our monopoly of the only two machines, but not enough to stay away. People started to grumble (under their breaths in the French way) and give us the evil eye when we arrived. They tried to keep the ergos occupied so we couldn't get on, but as none of them could stay on for more than a few minutes we'd always sneak on eventually. Once on we didn't dare get off again to drink or stretch so we rowed straight through reaching down to grab the occasional mouthful of water.

After ten days of skiing all day and ninety-minute ergos at altitude, I came home and did my best ever physiology step test. The physiologists take samples of blood from your ear at increasing intensities on an ergo to check the Lactic acid levels. The lower your blood lactate levels, the bigger your aerobic capacity. It's a good way of checking that the training we were doing was actually working (as well as checking we'd actually done some over Christmas) and enabled us to establish tight heart rate training bands so we'd be able to use our heart rate monitor watches to monitor our own training.

If you are fit most of the steps are not too bad. The top two get pretty hard though and then after the last one at about 90% of your maximum, you have a minute or so off before the dreaded VO_2 max test. It was supposed to be just about pushing yourself to the limit to discover your maximum lung capacity, but we all knew our coaches were far more interested in our absolute scores than in our physiology, so this last step always felt like an ergo test. If you'd had a hard time getting through the steps and were knackered already, the VO_2 max test was start-to-finish agony. You have no idea how long four minutes really is until you've done this test.

I remember this particular session because all my usual steps felt remarkably easy and even the final four minutes was good for me. It was a long time before I met with the physiologist to review the data and when we did it was so good he said he thought it was an anomaly and there must have been some equipment error.

"Oh, are you sure? I remember that test did feel really good."

"Really? Yeah well, I don't know. Don't worry about it."

I was still a bit confused but didn't have the headspace to think it through at the time and I was so used to people telling me that good results were anomalies that I just accepted it. I don't think I really made the connection with training at altitude at the time and didn't mention it. I guess I should have followed it up and I suppose I'm embarrassed that I didn't, but this was already weeks later and we were onto the next phase. I never trained at altitude again and I never saw those results again – they took them off the graph as an anomaly.

Despite the success of my Christmas training plan, I resolved not to go skiing again until after I finished rowing. It had been fun but the whole time I was out there, I'd been scared of hurting myself and my Olympic chances, and it had definitely taken the edge off. You can do everything you want, but not necessarily at the same time; you just have to work out what won't wait. I can ski when I'm fifty; skiing will wait, Olympic medals will not.

My few months of maternity cover at Wycombe High had come to an end. Despite having only been there for a term, the science staff bought me a little present and signed wonderful things on a card I still have – about how much they'd enjoyed having me, my energy and enthusiasm, around. There were a couple of cards from my classes too and I was very touched. I didn't really want to leave and as Malcolm was in charge of arranging cover for absent teachers, we came to a mutually beneficial arrangement. I emailed him over the weekend with my availability for the following week and he emailed me back with when he could use me. Some days he wouldn't know until after I'd left the house if a teacher wasn't going to make it in, so I'd keep a set of work clothes in the car just in case. He used me for any Science cover first, but if there wasn't any then he'd give me anything else. Maths, French, Geography, Latin, Spanish, Art, Drama, Textiles, IT, I've taught them all and I loved it because it meant there was always something new to learn. I'd rush in (hair still wet and eating my lunch) and grab the lesson plans the teachers had left for the two or three lessons I was to teach that afternoon, have a quick look through to see what I'd got and then walk straight into the first class.

The work would always be of the type that the kids could just get on with on their own, but unlike the regular teacher I didn't have any other work to do and I had to do something or I'd fall asleep. Usually, I'd write the instructions on the board, tell them I was really a science teacher and needed five minutes to look through the work and if they could do the same we'd take it from there. Then I had a stab at teaching the lesson. It was more about structure than content and I learnt very quickly that teaching is the skill, not the subject specialism. Whatever else we did, at the end of the lesson I'd ask each pupil to tell me one thing they knew now that they hadn't known when they arrived. Because one thing a day can take you anywhere, right?

I remember it all as a generally easier time without Mike. I think I was doing OK and holding my own. Never at the top, but never quite off the bottom, still improving and still enjoying it. And still evaluating Paul Thompson our new coach, and so far all seemed fine. I was pleased we were back to doing a training programme much more aligned with that which had served me so well with Miles. The volume was similar to Mike's programme but the intensity was down, and whilst I was still tired I generally felt much better on it. Paul seemed to be a perfectly good coach, but for the first few months at least most of my appreciation of him was based mainly on the fact that he wasn't Mike.

In March we went to our Varese pre-trials training camp. If I only wrote about all the grey and black bits you'd be wondering how or why I ever got through all this, but it all has to be balanced against times like Varese. We'd go there once or twice a year over the next four years for about two weeks at a time and stayed in a rather old-fashioned family-run hotel in a little village near Varese. There was no more walking into town on our afternoons off and it had a rather old clanking plumbing system (which kept us awake at nights until Marty decreed that no one was to flush the toilets between 10pm and 6am), but they looked after us really well and the food was wonderful. We ate proper Italian fare; loads of salads and vegetables, delicious grilled meat, fish rubbed with herbs, and the pastas and risottos were the best I've ever tasted. We'd also stop most days at Melomagia ice cream parlour conveniently located on the way home. I'm not generally a fan of ice cream, but this was also the best ice cream I've ever tasted. We ate well, but very moderately actually. We were all critically conscious of putting on weight (like girls the world over) and our male coaches made us weigh in every morning. I never got to a point where I was doing so much training that I could eat as much as I wanted. The more I trained the hungrier I got and the endurance training seemed to put my body in to some sort of stress response where I was more likely to store fat, so I always had to be careful. It was the same for all of us (except perhaps Debs) and always seemed rather unfair.

Paul had been coaching us for about five months at this point and while I thought he was good, there hadn't been anything to really lift him from the rest. But then one day he was coaching me in my single. It was beautiful flat water, but magical boat flow eluded me. Every stroke in rowing is a relentless search for perfect connection with the water. It's an almost imperceptible shift between not quite right and right. There's really nothing to see when you get 'it', but from inside the boat 'it' is unmistakable. From the moment your blades hit the water, your muscles activate in the right sequence in a kind of ripple so no movement is fighting against any other, and despite working just as hard, or even more so, the hard slog becomes almost transcendentally enjoyable.

Because this shift is about something you feel rather than something you see, it's hard for a coach to tell from outside the boat. By this point in my career, there were few things more annoying (and worthy of my distain) than an overenthusiastic coach shouting "Yes, yes, that's good, you've got it" when blatantly every muscle in my body was telling me I had not. Paul was not that sort of coach. For those first twenty minutes of the outing both of us had been equally dissatisfied with the way the boat was moving and we were both working hard on it. Paul called out various things he was spotting from the launch and I changed something small every stroke – searching. Then all at once, within one stroke, the boat shifted and I found 'it'. And on the second stroke, Paul called out "That's it, you've got it! Hold onto that." And ten years on, I can picture exactly where we were on the lake. Most of the rest of those Varese camps blend into one mixed-up memory of beautiful water and mountains and sunning ourselves outside the boathouse between outings and trips into town and good ice cream and risotto. But I can pinpoint that moment because really, while the rest is nice, these are the moments you live for in rowing. All the rest is just a nice holiday and anyone can do that.

That was the first moment when Paul really went up in my estimation. He could not only spot what was wrong (which let's face it is pretty easy – watch any sport even at Olympic level and spot the mistakes, it's not that hard), but he could spot within one stroke when it was right.

The second moment was just before April trials. I met one to one with Paul and he told me that when he'd arrived people (coaches and at least one of the athletes) had had a lot to say about me. They'd told him that I always raced well at trials but that I'd pretty much reached my potential and it wasn't worth wasting too much time on me, that I was 'the cut-off' point at the bottom of the squad, that I was good in a single but not really to be considered for crew selection as I couldn't row with other people. He said he'd also heard that Mike had overlooked me for selection despite beating people at trials. But then he said that he hadn't been listening and it wasn't going to be like that anymore. He said, "As long as you keep doing well at trials, I will keep selecting you."

Varese had shown me that Paul was an excellent technical coach who could really help me and now I knew that as long as I performed he would select me. In those two moments, he'd already done enough to secure my trust and loyalty for the rest of the time we'd work together. He was not perfect and we'd fight a fair bit over the next few years, but if working with my PhD supervisor and Mike had taught me anything, it's that it doesn't really matter how good coaches are at the rest of their job if they have set their mind that you are not worth bothering with.

I don't remember the results of trials that year and they are not in my diary. I definitely made the top five though as I was never out of the final and never last. We went back to Varese to run a doubles matrix to finalise crew selection for the summer. Fran and Debs came out clear first and second, beating Guin by a good margin. Rebecca Romero was fourth, Elise fifth and then me. Only Lisa and Ali Barnes were behind me (Sarah was injured and out for the rest of the season). It was disappointing and put me out of the top four and likely Quad for that summer.

Paul wanted to bring everyone within the system for the summer racing and run a Quad with the top four scullers as the best chance of a GB Women's medal. However, first there was the politics to negotiate.

I'd assumed Guin would retire after Sydney, but she was set for another Olympiad. I remember thinking it would be quite difficult for her as Fran and I weren't the only ones she'd trampled over in her single-minded mission to get a medal. There's an unspoken etiquette in rowing that means it always pays to be careful what you say and do to someone, because at some point in the future you may have to row *with* them again. As it happens Guin had solved that problem at the start of the season by saying that she only wanted to compete in the Single in future, so she was out of the Quad equation.

That left a Quad of Fran, Debs, Becs and Elise, but Mark Banks really wanted Debs and Fran in the Double so he could keep them to himself. Paul did manage to get his Quad to row together for a few sessions and Lisa and I went out in a Double. But the infighting continued unabated and as that's rarely a good recipe for the ultimate team sport, Paul backed down. Fran and Debs would row the Double at least until the first World Cup, and Lisa and I would join Elise and Becs in the Quad.

Elise, Lisa and I obviously already knew each other, but we'd only really rubbed shoulders with Becs at trials up to that point. She'd been quite vocal in her disapproval of what had already happened, but now that this was her crew she seemed to set her mind to it really quickly and there was no more negative talk. It's funny because when you see Becs on TV (now she's so famous), she often comes across as very serious and intense. She certainly has that side to her, which is obviously part of what makes her so good, but what you don't see much of is her almost childlike playful side. Becs can be very dry and direct, but she's also quick to laugh and a lot of fun. If she's sat somewhere by herself, regardless of how she's feeling, her face may well be set in a rather default miserable expression, but we got used to the fact that that was just Becs and she wasn't necessarily miserable. You only had to go over and say "Hi" to have her break out in genuine smiles and start chatting. Over the years we'd get used to people who didn't know her so well saying "Is Becs alright? She looks very serious/miserable" and we'd get used to saying that no she was fine and perfectly happy, she was just Becs.

I'd almost forgotten about that 2001 crew really, but I'm glad to think of it now. Lisa was almost laughably intense and extreme and set herself challenges that sometimes didn't make sense to anyone else, but once she'd set herself them there was no backing down. She'd famously not eaten a biscuit since 1997 when she'd decided she was eating too many and instead of cutting down (a moderate response), she'd banned herself forever (a Lisa response). She had a ridiculously sweet tooth though, so if you could convince her that something was a cake rather than a biscuit, she'd be only too happy to agree with you and eat it. We had lots of debates about this and apparently shortbread is a cake, as are Jaffa cakes, because even though they look like a biscuit, they are of course called cake so that one is really a no-brainer.

Lisa and I ended up being roommates on many training camps. There was more spare time at camp than at home and all of us filled a fair bit of it catching up on those things any self-respecting girl needs to do to keep herself looking good. We brought kit for leg waxing, eyelash tinting, toe nail painting, hair dying and even hair cutting (I was the squad hairdresser in those years), but Lisa always had new 'products' and talked about 'skin care regimes' which was a totally new concept to me.

Elise had to do everything quickly and be ready first for everything. Coming in to the landing stage from every training session, she'd be undoing her shoes and outside gate while we manoeuvred the boat, so she could jump out instantly, undo and stash her blades and then stand there foot tapping saying, "You lot are always so slow." And of course one of *my* many eccentricities is a quite ridiculous competitive instinct, so for the first couple of weeks I rose to the challenge and rushed and stressed to get out of the boat first. I never made it. Elise always won the getting out of the boat race.

We were all such strong determined characters that there were inevitable tensions, but we seemed to really care for each other and caused no deliberate hurt (which was not always the case in our Squad). Generally we got on well and had a lot of fun. We were also united in our mission for it not to be taken for granted that we were a second boat to the Fran and Deb's Double.

Our first run-out was in Spain at the Seville World Cup and GB Women had a great start to the season. Cath and Katherine were third in the Pair, Fran and Debs were second in the Double (albeit a long way down to the legendary Germans), and us in the Quad… we were… wait for it… also second (albeit a long way down to the legendary Germans). It was my fourth international season and my first ever international medal. To have already medalled this early in the four-year cycle was well above my aspirations and step-by-step plan. I was very excited about the possibilities it opened up for the rest of the season. Our Quad started talking about getting in a medal at the Worlds that summer like it was really possible.

Guin was sixth in her single and disappointing for all of us was that the new Women's Eight of Ali Barnes, Bev Gough, Nicole Scott, Helen Fenoulet, Kate Mac, Rowan Carroll, Alison Tricky and Alex Beaver, coxed by Charlotte Miller (Lotty), came fourth out of four.

Seville effectively confirmed the crews for the rest of the season. Fran, Debs and Mark got to stay in their little unit. The Pair of Katherine Grainger and Cath Bishop was coached by Paul, and in the Quad we were joint coached by Ian South (who still came in a package with Becs at this stage) and Paul when he wasn't with the Pair.

The next World Cup was in Vienna and again, for most of us, it was all looking very positive. The Pair and Double both won Gold and we got a second Silver. There was no German Double or Quad though in Vienna, so that had to be taken into consideration. If it seems like I'm a little preoccupied by the Germans, it's not just because they are German. The Germans were not just the reigning Olympic Champions in the Quad, they'd never been beaten in the Olympic history of the event. At this point in time and pretty much in the history of Women's Sculling, the German Women's crew scullers were the top, the best, the idols and the ones to beat. The Germans hadn't just beaten the British girls into Silver at Sydney; no British Quad had ever beaten a Senior German Quad… ever. And it wasn't just the Quad, they regularly had enough top scullers that they could put out a winning Quad *and* Double *and* they had the talent of Katrin Rushchow currently in the Single. Katrin Boron, their top sculler, had already won three consecutive Olympic Golds and was aiming for her fourth at Athens. The Germans were the consistent benchmark against which we could measure our performance.

Guin came fourth in the single but was thirty-five seconds behind the winner Ekaterina Karsten (BLR) (it seems like being called Catherine in some form or other is a good start to being a top female rower, so I blame my parents for getting my name mixed up with my sister's and not giving me this advantage). None of us went to the last World Cup as a decision was made that we would race Royal Henley instead. We raced Henley in our Quad and made it through to the final by beating the Danish National Squad, but were again thwarted by the Germans in the final (by quite a long way).

In the middle of all this, there was more selection drama going on. It had been decreed that the existing Women's Eight was not fast enough to go forward to the Worlds, so the Pair and Double were all now to double up into the Eight and Guin was to give up the Single and also move into the Eight. It was very tough, because of course that only left three seats. It must have been some hard-core and heartbreaking seat racing to get eight down to three, but this time round, even this late in the season, it was done so at least every girl who was dropped knew they'd had a fair shot. It was still heartbreaking though. Kate Mac was at my house in Henley when she got the call to tell her she'd not made it through and she was definitely heartbroken.

Somewhere in all of that, my brother got married up in Edinburgh. I'm ashamed to say that when he called to tell me he was getting married, my very first thought (unvoiced thankfully) was "Oh my God! What if the wedding is the same weekend as a World Cup? What will I do?" I was even a bit angry that he'd not thought to consult me on dates – before I realised that was a little unreasonable. I was completely used to missing all other friend and family weddings, parties, funerals and everything else because they clashed with racing or training, but I'd be screwed if that happened with my brother's wedding. I'd obviously have to go to the wedding (would want to of course) but if I missed a World Cup and someone else subbed in and the boat went better…

2001 crew. Elise, me and Becs hanging out together at Varese Lake between training sessions (I assume Lisa is taking the photo). All the hard work, pain, rain and general grimness of so much of squad training has to be balanced against moments like these.

Thankfully, the dates didn't clash and I was granted an exceptional weekend out of the boat in racing season. It had to be so carefully co-ordinated that Paul had written 'Mowbs Brother's wedding' into the printed Squad training programme for that week. I sent John a copy so he knew how he fitted in. I ran up Arthur's Seat twice that weekend for my training and the wedding was really lovely (maybe I should have written those the other way around).

After Olympic Silver and such a successful 2001 season, expectations were high in the GB women's camp for the 2001 World Champs in Lucerne. At the start of the season I'd have been happy to make the final, but after medalling in both our World Cup races, confidence levels had risen. When we sat down as a crew before the Worlds with Chris Shambrook and our coaches, we set 'To Medal' as our goal.

We raced well and made the final. Suddenly the media got wind of a potential medal and were interested in us. You don't get much attention when you're a rower, so when it happens you make the most of it. The day before the final, the BBC asked to interview me. It was my first interview since the disastrous Radio 5 Live interview in Sydney and my first TV opportunity on the GB team. Let's just say it's a good job this one didn't go out live. Gillian Lindsey was working for the BBC as a rowing commentator at the time and interviewed me down at the lake. We chatted while we waited and it all felt very comfortable. And then we were rolling and Gillian asked her first question, "So Alison, your first World Championship final and you could get a medal. It must be so exciting. How do you sleep at night?"

Again, not the first question I'd been expecting, but at least I knew the answer. In fact, I thought I could even make a bit of a joke. That would be a good opening.

"Ha Ha! Yes. I've got really good drugs."

Even before I saw Gillian's face drop in horror, I realised what I'd said. I'm from a medical family and we used that word all the time for everything from aspirin to antibiotics. But of course in sport, the word has a rather different connotation.

I tried to reel it back in. "I mean, of course it's very exciting and I have trouble sleeping, but I've got these good sleeping tablets…" But it was like trying to explain your way out of a bad joke. Again, I don't remember any more of the interview, but safe to say I didn't make the cut for that night's broadcast.

2001 crew racing in the World Championships in Lucerne. Bow – Elise Laverick, 2 – Lisa Eyre, 3 – Rebecca Romero, Stroke – Alison Mowbray. I'd actually forgotten that I stroked this crew.

(Photo by Peter Spurrier)

And after our final, no one was interested in interviewing us again. We finished a very disappointing fifth behind Germany (obviously) and New Zealand, USA and Australia, none of whom had been to any of the World Cups we'd raced at. It felt like a trick.

The Pair was also fifth and the Double were gutted to not even make the final and finished seventh. Of course there is never any way of knowing how much, if at all, doubling up into the Eight affected their small boat performances, but the gamble did not pay off as the Eight also finished out of the medals. In the end, after a season of such success, GB Women had failed to deliver any World Championship medals.

It was a sobering couple of days for the Women's squad. Paul called us all together before we went home and reminded us that although no one had wanted this to happen, this was the start of the four-year cycle. The whole plan was that there would be somewhere to go each year and there was plenty more to be had. We were to go away, have our four weeks off, but come back fit and raring to go for next year. We would be stepping up and we would get faster.

Chapter 14: Many more small steps

"Today I will have succeeded if I can do one thing better than I did it yesterday."

Three years to go

Paul was right about this being just the first year of a four-year plan, but in that moment few of us were consoled. I remember being devastated which seems out of proportion now. It was the first year of my four-year mission to get an Olympic medal and I'd just won my first ever World Cup Medals and reached my first ever World Championship final. It was a significant step and on balance a perfectly fine result, but I think maybe I wasn't feeling very balanced at the time. The training, selection pressures and racing take a significant physical and emotional toll each year that should not be underestimated but frequently are.

The adrenalin and cortisol produced and the mental strategies we used, helped to counteract increasing physical and mental tiredness as the season progressed. They kept us going and kept us up there. We could keep it all going when we needed to, but for every high there is an eventual low. There are mini lows after each trial and World Cup race, but at the end of the season when you wake up the next morning, there is nothing to counteract the accumulated physical and mental tiredness of the last eleven months and it can hit pretty hard. Finishing racing is rather like shutting off an athlete's antidepressant medication. Of course if you'd done well the accumulation of 'happy hormones' and positive thoughts might keep you up there for a while longer, but it's still likely to catch up with you at some point.

It perhaps hit me harder than expected in 2001 because I'd just not been prepared. In 1999 I'd met my sister to go hiking in Canada and in 2000 I'd stayed on in Australia with Elise and friends. Perhaps because the activity and company had been an unplanned side effect of going on holiday, I hadn't realised how important a part of finishing racing they are. In 2001, I had, in effect, planned the opposite.

I'd been so busy teaching and training all year and we'd been away more than ever on foreign training camps that I'd spent the last few months looking forward to a few weeks of normal life at home in Henley. Time to go pubbing and clubbing with friends, long lie-ins, reading, shopping, watching daytime TV…

But in fact, when I woke up that first morning, early as I had every morning for months, in a quiet empty house after weeks of sharing a room on training camps, with no reason to get up (even though that was supposed to be the point), no one to be with (because my friends were all with their boyfriends or families), with nothing to think about (except how miserable I was at having trained all year just to come fifth) and feeling sledgehammer tired in every cell of my body and brain, my thoughts spiralled down, unchecked by any positive effort on my part to stop them or bring them up again, until eventually I just cried.

I cried for about two days. I did eventually get up so I could lie on the sofa and cry, and occasionally I donned sunglasses so I could wander into Henley and cry, but there was little more I was capable of. Eventually I caved in and against all my better judgement and mainly just because I no longer had the strength not to, I called the blond boy.

I'm a bit behind on this part of my life, perhaps because there's little to say and anything that could be said I'm rather embarrassed about. It's more pathetic than tragic.

The blond boy had got back in touch at the start of my first full year on the squad, towards the end of my time in Putney, and we'd started up long, deep into the night telephone conversations of the type you can only have with someone who knows you inside out and won't take the usual shallow banter you can pass off on everyone else. We made plans to meet up again and I was quite euphoric in the belief that we were going to get back together. This time for good. Then just before we were due to meet, he finally admitted he already had a girlfriend. It seemed the plan was to see us both for a while to find out which he liked best. He certainly didn't want to cut his losses if we weren't going to work out. This plan somehow held a lot less appeal to me and I refused to meet, at least at first. However, after a while, I weakened. It's not that I wanted him back, but I wanted that heart-flipping, all-consuming feeling back. When I first broke it off, aged twenty-three, after we'd been together since we were nineteen, I could reasonably expect that another like it would be along soon enough if I looked hard enough. But now, as each year passed, I was beginning to realise there were no guarantees and after a few attempts I'd stopped thinking I could make anything less work. So eventually I did the obvious dumb thing, met up with him and we started something. He was going to finish with his girlfriend very soon… he just couldn't quite do it yet because they had something on together next week.

I had kept up my role of 'mistress' for a couple of years (there was always something on next week) and bizarrely kept his secret from all but a couple of my very closest friends. With so much else going on in Sydney year, I'd avoided thinking about what was really going on and put off any decisions until after the Olympics. On a good day I could tell myself I was in control and it was fun and frivolous and not doing me any harm. But I'm not very good at lying, even to myself.

When I did get back from Australia nothing changed and it became apparent that he was quite happy for us all to continue indefinitely as we were (cake, eat it etc.). I forced the issue after yet another promised deadline for finishing with his girlfriend had expired after their last holiday and he looked straight at me, and with no hint of evasion or guilt, denied he'd ever promised anything of the sort. He would finish with his girlfriend, but he couldn't do it quite yet. And I can't find any unclichéd description of how I felt when I recognised not a lie but a truth told by someone who believes their own lies. I finally turned over my very own stone of denial and looked at the fossilised pattern I'd been repeating. I knew from experience that we'd keep doing this as long as I'd let him.

He refused to break it off with me though, so in the end I had to do it again. I told him to choose. He said he couldn't. I said if he wouldn't choose, I was leaving, so that was the same as not choosing me. He said it wasn't and if I left, it was my choice not his. I said not choosing is just making a choice without taking responsibility for that choice (I felt I had experience in this field) and left. He chose to let me leave.

I was devastated but had stayed firm for six months. But now, without the mental strength left to even want to list the usual reasons why I shouldn't – I picked up the phone. We talked and he was absolutely, perfectly what I needed him to be, which was why it had been so difficult to give him up in the first place. He was perhaps the only person who already knew I wasn't always positive, happy Al all the time. He was still seeing the same girlfriends but we started meeting up again – I don't remember for how long, some months I think, maybe a year. But it wasn't like before. Before, I'd always thought that it would all work out and that at some point we'd be together forever. But I didn't think like that anymore. I just tried to think about it as little as possible because nothing about it made me feel good about myself.

Anyway, I perked up after a few days of rest, pulled myself off the sofa of self-pity and called round a few friends to see who wanted to go and do normal things with me for a while. Jo Nitch was the best taker. Also long-term single, we formed an alliance to try and break our bad luck. There's a great little speech in *Sex and the City*, which all single girls know. Charlotte says, "We're just not approaching it right. It's ridiculous; here we are, all really successful women in everything else we do but not in this. We make everything else happen, but with men we just sit around and wait for them to find us. We need to approach dating like we approach the rest of our lives, we need to plan it and work at it. Who's with me?" Every so often single girls quote that back, put on their heels, let down their hair and go out and see if they can make it happen. Jo and I both fancied learning to dance and salsa classes were opening up locally, so we thought that was a good start. We also went out into Henley with rules about sitting at the bar and talking to any guys who approached us, rather than sitting in corners talking to each other. I even started internet dating, which is no big deal now as everyone does it, but back then it was still very secret and shameful and only one step removed from sitting in and downloading porn.

So it can't be said that we didn't try, but our efforts were kind of comical. Women outnumbered men about three to one in the Salsa class and the teacher kept trying to make me dance as a man because I'm tall. I've always hated that since they used to make me do it at primary school (and even then I thought it was offensive). But anyway it turned out to be the only way any dancing was going to be done, as any guys paired with me seemed to be so immediately intimidated by my height and stature (despite me doing my best to be friendly and smiley) that they refused to lead me anywhere and just stood around looking rather terrified. Similarly with the internet dating – several promising emails led to rather disappointing dates where I knew within minutes (moments even) that this was never to be and then had to sit it out for the rest of the evening while I'd have rather been back on my sofa.

The nights out with Jo were the most fun of any attempts, but similarly fruitless. We soon learnt to adopt alternative persona as telling a guy we rowed on the GB Rowing Team was instant crash and burn suicide. We went with our real jobs of 'physio' and 'science teacher' for a while, but when even that seemed too intimidating we experimented with 'nurse' and 'primary school teacher', with which we were interestingly more successful (sometimes you really do want to give the guys a good kick and tell them to man up). I did at least get a couple of dates out of our nights out which was a start, but I had to come clean about the rowing at some point and then everything changed. It wasn't that they weren't interested in me anymore, it was more they immediately assumed I'd not be interested in them (even though I'd already agreed to come on a date). "Well it was really nice to meet you and it'll be really cool when I see you on telly to be able to say to my mates that I went on a date with you", while I sat there thinking "Why the past tense? Five minutes ago you were talking about where we'd go on the next date, what just happened?" None of our alliance attempts lasted much past Christmas. Once back into full training, nights on the sofa or sat in the corner of a pub really gossiping with my mates were not only preferable, but also turned out to be more enjoyable and rewarding than bad dates.

Training was much the same, except that it had indeed stepped up a bit and there were more three-session-a-day days. I wrote my goals for the season in the front of my training diary and had a good start to the season.

Distance/Stroke
Sequences
Time Trial – Ruthless
Press out & Over
Write in what I've done to make me go faster

Saturday October 6th 2001 (Longridge)

am 1) *1x* *3.8k Time trial* (being Ruthless)
Blue Bridge to Island corner

1.	*Grainger*	*14.40.15*
2.	*Mowbray*	*14.42.02*
3.	*Batten*	*14.42.91*
4.	*Eyre*	*14.47.12*
5.	*Laverick*	*14.48.77*
6.	*Romero*	*14.54.67*
7.	*Casey*	*14.55.98*
8.	*Winckless*	*14.58.69*
Etc....		

am 2) *90'* *UT2* *8⁰ @ bow*

Saturday November 3rd 2001

am 1) *3.4k Time Trial* (more Ruthlessness)

	Corner to bottom of island	
	Upstream	*R29/30*
1.	*Mowbray*	*14.52.07*
2.	*Grainger*	*14.52.56*
3.	*Laverick*	*15.05.52*
4.	*Romero*	*15.10.41*
5.	*Winckless*	*15.21.11*

Etc….

am 2) *2– Steady State with KG 90 mins*

I was going through a phase of recording weekly totals and we rowed/sculled 138Km that week. I'd forgotten we started the season with so much rowing. Cath Bishop had retired after the disappointments of the 2001 season, so part of it was about seeing whether the best option for Katherine Grainger (KG) was to find her a new pairs partner (2– is a pair) or have her scull and part of it just to try and bring through some more rowers (there were a lot more names underneath both of those results lists). The rowing squad was still moving in the wrong direction. Cath Bishop, Alex Beaver and Rowan had all retired after 2001. Cath (with her PhD in German Literature) went to work at the foreign office, having taken their entrance tests and aced the aptitude in foreign languages section. She would learn Serbo-Croat over the next couple of years in preparation for a posting to Croatia. Rowan had found a large mole on her arm, which turned out to be a melanoma; she was and still is absolutely fine, but wisely decided that a new career less exposed to the sun would be a good idea.

Notably absent in the above list are Houghton and Flood, who were still training in Leander with Mark Banks. Despite some quite serious pressure from Paul to try and get him to bring them over to train with us for just one weekend a month, he wasn't having any of it.

Of course, of all the time trials in all the years, I would choose to reproduce those two. But you must remember I am the hero of my own autobiography so I get to pick which results I display. History is not always written by the victor but sometimes just by those who can be bothered to write it down first. Also, I had forgotten about it, but I do think that win on Saturday 3 November may have been my only one in all my time on the squad, so I'd like us all just to take a moment and look at that result again please.

Up to this point Marty had seemed to touch our world very little, but that was to change this year with the introduction of cycling and cross-country ski camps. Marty was a big advocate of such cross-training ostensibly because of the scientific benefits. In a rowing boat the time limit for single sessions is about two hours, after which your back complains so much from holding the posture and your discs are so compressed you have to stop or eventually do permanent damage. Typically our longest rowing sessions were about a hundred minutes long. However with both cycling and skiing, we could do much longer sessions and hours more training, which of course pleased the coaches. So there was scientific benefit, but we soon understood that mainly Marty was a big fan of cycling and skiing because he was very good at both. He coached us in cycling riding alongside on his bike and in cross-country skiing from his own skis and at least to start with he was faster than any of us and let us all know it.

We all bought new bikes for our first cycle camp in Seville in November and for the first time trained four times a day some days. We'd row, ergo *and* do weights in the mornings and then ride out on our bikes for up to four hours in the afternoons. It was definitely the most I'd ever trained.

It was a cool camp though. Marty taught us to ride in formation in various rotating draft patterns. At first it was terrifying to ride so close to the wheel of the person in front and we stayed well back. But after a few days, sheer exhaustion made us braver and we moved up to cling to the wheel in front like pros, happy to die if it made the ride easier. It was tiring but really quite something to ride for hour after hour through the little villages and near desert and start to get to know our way around this area of Spain that wasn't just the river. People pay a lot of money for that kind of experience. In subsequent camps, Peter Keen from British Cycling came out to teach us yet more skills and drills to make our training safer and faster. I'm no Rebecca Romero, but I'm a pretty good cyclist now and that's not a bad side effect of being on the British Rowing Team.

Our first cross-country ski camp was in January, straight after Christmas. I think Marty would have had us just skiing, but that made Paul edgy and a compromise was reached whereby we based ourselves at the training centre in Sarnen so we could still row in the morning before driving to up to the cross-country ski centres in the afternoon. It was kind of the antithesis of a normal winter training camp where you hunt out warm weather. Some mornings parts of the lake were frozen and the launches had to go out to break up the ice, and on others the freezing fog was so dense we couldn't see anything and rowed side by side to reduce the chance of collision. Even on the mildest mornings any water splashed up onto the decks would freeze in the runners and jam the seats, and when we came in we had to spray de-icer onto our gates to get them open. The bows in doubles would often come in soaking wet and frozen half solid from being splashed by strokes catches.

'Elsie' Lav, Mowbs, Winks and MacG - rowing nicknames had not got much more creative over the years but here no one was 'Big', presumably because we all were. We are wrapped up against the snow and ice of Sarnen. But the problem with rowing and cold weather is you can't actually wear those nice big fleeces to scull in. It just doesn't work. I'm about on the limit of what you can actually move in to scull, no matter how cold it gets.

Katherine Grainger (foreground), Sarah Winckless (middle), me in the background. This looks a lot more idyllic than it feels. Out there it just feels freezing, our hands and feet are blocks of ice and sometimes we'd come to an abrupt stop as ice jammed our runners. I do love this photo though and the way that if you turn it upside-down it still works.

But in the afternoon we went to the mountains and it was beautiful skiing through the snowy conifer woods — I thought I was James Bond (although maybe I looked more *Moonraker*). A couple of times, we skied right down the valley and caught the train back. People pay a fortune for that sort of experience. No one who has been following this story so far will be surprised to hear that I was not the quickest to catch on. I wasn't too bad though, sort of in the middle as for most things. Katherine Grainger and I were closest in speed, so we paired up a fair bit. I enjoyed that as I'd not had chance to spend much time with Katherine before.

As Britain's most successful female rower, I reckon Katherine will be the first of us to write a proper autobiography, but still I'd like to write a little here. Katherine is without doubt one of Britain's most outstanding athletes from any sport. The only female British athlete ever to medal at four consecutive Olympics, it's perhaps only because she is ahead of her time for rowing (i.e. we were still a developing sport delivering Silvers rather than Golds until very recently) that she isn't completely the household name she deserves to be.

Katherine started rowing at Edinburgh University alongside a Law degree and then a Masters in Criminal Law, and then moved down to England to row with the squad. She has since started a PhD (on the criminal law around psychopaths) and it's still ongoing. So far it's taken even longer than mine. On top of all that, almost uniquely in British rowing and perhaps in full-time sport at any level, I have never met anyone who has a bad word to say about Katherine or heard Katherine say a bad word about anyone else. It seems she is so good at what she does, she has no need for either arrogance or pulling other people down to make herself feel more secure. It can be quite hard to get to know Katherine though, which was why I was glad of the chance while we were skiing.

She's very good at asking lots of questions to get you talking whilst revealing little of herself. You can sit down for a coffee or a drink with Katherine and come away an hour or so later thinking that you've had such a good conversation and she is so lovely and interesting, and only on guilty reflection realise you've done all the talking.

All in all, despite being some of the most intense training I'd ever done, it was amazing to effectively be paid to learn to ride and ski as part of the GB Rowing Team. The girls still have cycle camps but the skiing only really happened for two years and they were two of my years.

KG and I mid-ski. We honestly worked hard all the time and were just posing for a very quick photo. Note that we are still totally dressed in rowing tracksuits and waterproofs because it was all we had. No gear, no idea.

I spent that Christmas in Richmond with my parents and took my new bike on long rides up into the Dales. On a memorable ride on Christmas Day, I rode up a particularly high pass between Leyburn and Grinton. The road got icier and icier as I climbed and even though I wasn't sure how I'd get back down and even though a guy on his way down said it was too icy to get to the top, I couldn't stop because the Olympian inside never lets you stop or turn round on a hill until you actually fall off. I stood up in the saddle most of the way weaving through the ice and made it to the top only to look down the other side and then behind me and realise that either way I was well and truly buggered. It was a freezing half hour or so walk down the steep, hairpin bends in my socks (as the cleats on my shoes were too slippy) to get past the ice before I could get back on and ride home.

Christmas was not so bad now I'd given up and was taking Mum's lead as far as Dad was concerned. If you don't follow him, you don't find him and you don't have to fight him. If you humour him and pretend his drunken behaviour is perfectly normal (which it was now anyway), then the days can pass by without any stress or raised voices. Anyway, it was only a few days of my life and it was all of theirs and I was happy out on my bike a lot of the time so could suck it up.

After Christmas, another addition to the training schedule was eighty-minute 'Endurance Weights' circuits. When Mike said we had to go faster, we did more training – but Paul was always reading the latest scientific thinking on training approaches and kept in touch with the Australian Institute of Sport, and when he said we had to go faster we did different training (and also more training). One day he came down with a list of exercises and starting weights for the circuit. It was far removed from the feisty body weight circuits of my Liverpool days and twice as long and less explosive than my self-designed Cambridge circuits, but still I liked circuits so was happy to see them on the programme. We pumped up the stereo, started the clock and picked up the first weights. Very quickly we stalled. No one wanted to be the first to say it, but eventually we all caved. We were supposed to lift 20-30 reps at about a rep a second and these weights were way too heavy for that – some of us would be lucky if we could lift them twenty times even if we had all day. Paul admitted he'd just made the weights up sitting at his desk and they might need a little alteration. We stripped weights off until in some cases they were down to about a tenth and then got going again.

For some reason Lisa had missed that session, but she'd picked up the list from Paul and set up her own circuit in Leander gym later that evening and trained by herself. Chatting to her as we got our boats out to go sculling the following morning, Lisa was talking about how tough the new weights session was.

"But you did know to reduce the weights?" I said.

"Oh no, really! I thought they were heavy, but it was OK. I managed them."

"Seriously! How the hell did you do that? Paul just made those up out of nowhere, they were way too heavy. We couldn't lift them."

"They were the weights on the sheet so I just did them. They were heavy but it was OK."

I remember thinking at the time this was typical Lisa. The numbers on the sheet had represented a challenge and had thereby overridden the part of her brain that should have seen the mismatch between the weights and the *real* aim of the endurance session. There are parallels with not eating a biscuit since 1997. She was very strong so if anyone could lift those weights you might have put your money on Lisa, but still, I was half in awe that she had managed it and half a bit frustrated with her that she had tried. Still, she seemed to have survived.

It may be a coincidence and when you've trained that hard for that many years it's never just one thing, but that session she put her scull on the water and never took it off. Her back had become increasingly stiff during the outing and then 'went' as she was getting out of the boat onto the landing stage. She'd ruptured a disc and had to have months of rest and rehab out of the boat. She made several attempts to build her training back up over the next two years, but each time her back would go again. Perhaps the hardest thing in elite sport is knowing when to take your brain out, follow instructions, ignore pain and push on – and when not to do that.

There were other innovations to our training. We had little impellers attached to the underside of our boats so our rate meters would also display speeds and Paul had tabulated 'Gold Medal Speeds' for every rate. Now even our steady state training was regulated by numbers, not just by racing each other. For the first time, we had a way to race the world (the real opposition, the Germans even) in training rather than just racing each other and hoping it would be fast enough. I couldn't get anywhere near the speeds at first and the 100-minute/18k steady state suddenly went from being a draining but steady session to a total burn-out every time. Within a few days I was absolutely, completely annihilated. It was like going back to Mike Spraklen training. I argued with Paul but he held his line and said our bodies and technique would adapt and we'd be able to do it. Eventually I stopped arguing (although it did take a while) and because I realised it was change or die from exhaustion, I started to look for technical ways I could hit the speeds with less effort and therefore keep my heart rate down a bit. For the first time I really properly started to use the pace coach. Once I got my head round it I actually found it very motivating, because even though I couldn't see how I'd ever achieve the final speeds, I could still find small improvements to write in my diary. *"Today I will have succeeded if I can do one thing better than I did it yesterday."*

One of the biggest speed improvers seemed to be making a big circle and pushing my hands right down onto my thighs at the finish. Many rowers move their hands in and out at pretty much the same height and keep their blades close to the water as this feels safer, but you actually balance much better when the hands are right down. There seemed to be no limit at which this would not improve boat speed. Every single time, in the whole of the rest of my career, no matter how securely I thought this technique was ingrained and how good it already felt, if I challenged myself to push my hands down further I'd find extra speed. I had always slipped back. There's another metaphor in there somewhere.

The speeds started to get better, but it would take a long time, nearly into 2004, to get anywhere near those on the piece of paper at the appropriate heart rates – but in the end we could all do it fairly reliably. So Paul was proved to be right, which would have been very annoying if it hadn't also made me go faster.

Paul had also found a video camera, which was able to send real-time images directly to a pair of video gaming goggles that we wore in the boat. There was only one pair of goggles so if we were rowing in a double or quad, we'd take it in turns. If you were in a single then obviously there was only you with the goggles on, which was interesting since we wore a black woolly hat pulled down over the goggles to block out the light and couldn't see anything except a view of yourself from the side. Paul was supposed to call out directions, but sometimes he'd get engrossed in the videoing and forget and we'd be halfway into an overhanging tree before either of us realised. We absolutely couldn't fall in though as we were wearing several hundred pounds worth of kit on our head.

Video is a hugely important tool in coaching. As an athlete your body awareness becomes much better than the average human being, but still, sometimes it's not enough and your brain will insist on telling you your body is doing something it's not. Often Paul would be saying "You're not getting rocked over enough… still not enough… still not enough…", or "You're in early on everyone else Mowbs… still early… still early…" And I'd be saying, "I'm doing it… I am… I am…" And then he'd give up trying to talk to me and take out the video camera, and when we got in he'd show me a few seconds of film and I'd go, "Oh.,could see it real time, tell our bodies to do something and instantly see and feel the difference. Now I could link a feeling with an image, so all I had to do to row like that again was recapture the same feeling.

We had another sunny, ice cream-fuelled trials preparation camp in Varese at the beginning of April and I didn't have much time for painting my nails. I'd picked up another part-time maternity cover at the school. I had my own classes again which I enjoyed, but it meant I also had to mark their work and I had sixty GCSE practical assessments to get through. They'd changed the whole timetable to fit my lessons around when I needed to train. Teaching science has taught me that if you can get really, really good at what you do, it's worth the effort. Because from that point on you are in demand, you get headhunted, you can call the shots, the world starts to fit round you, and life becomes rather easier. The best people get the breaks – that's just how it is. If you want the breaks – get good. I got to that place with teaching but never really managed it with rowing. I also exchanged papers by fax on my first house that camp, having finally found somewhere cheap enough that I could afford it on an interest-only mortgage.

We got back from Varese, had a couple of days at home and then all drove off to Hazewinkle to race each other at final trials. I came second in the time trial…

Tuesday April 16th 2002

am 1900m Time Trial

Fran	*7.08.97*	*running start*
Al	*7.13.80*	
Becs	*7.15.64*	*Warm Up 20-25 mins*
KG	*7.15.66*	*1 min @ R28-30*
Elise	*7.18.29*	*2 x 10 strokes R34-36*
Winks	*7.21.23*	*1 x 10 flat-out 40+*
Debbie	*7.29.55*	*1 x 20 strokes running start*
Ros	*7.30.88*	
Mac	*7.31.42*	

…and won my semi-final. I've not recorded the result of the final and I can't remember now how I did, but I think I was fourth. It's funny because I'm sure part of the reason I so rarely wrote those results down was that they were so important to me at the time, I couldn't believe I would ever forget them.

We met back in Bisham gym to find out from Paul and Marty what was to happen next in the way of crew trials. Fran and Debs as the top-ranked singles from trials were the Double again and Guin (absent from trials through illness I presume) was the Single. KG had sculled very well at trials and was confirmed into the Quad. Becs, Elise, Sarah and I were to seat race in doubles in two weeks' time for the three remaining places.

That evening Dad called me "for a chat" which was weird because that rarely, if ever, happened. It was strained because we didn't usually do this, but I was nice enough I think – which I'm glad about now.

The following day I trained in the morning, taught my lessons and was on the dual carriageway section of the A404 on my way to Bisham to do my evening ergo when my mobile rang. I could see it was Mum and she so rarely called now that I picked it up. Her voice sounded a little strange so I didn't want to hang up and slowed down in the inside lane to manage as best I could. She told me that Dad had been having chest pain for a couple of days and had just gone into hospital. It doesn't take a medic to put the words chest pain together with my dad's profile of hypertensive, overweight, stressed out guy in his late fifties with a history of heart arrhythmia, sleep apnoea and alcohol abuse and immediately think 'heart attack', but Mum was ahead of me cutting me off at the pass. "You've not to worry Alison; it's not a heart attack. He just thinks it's indigestion, it settles with antacids, in fact it even settles with milk so it must be. He's just gone into hospital for a couple of tests." I remember not just her words, but also the fact that I was driving under the bridge on the A404 when I heard them. I queried, but she told me he'd seen his GP and he'd agreed as well. Who was I to argue with three proper doctors?

I called back later and again the following day, but Mum was out, presumably at the hospital, and the answerphone was not switched on so I couldn't leave a message. I knew she wouldn't realise and would be waiting, feeling aggrieved I'd not called her back and so would not call me again. It would have been useful to be able to call her mobile but Mum had resolutely refused to learn how to use one ("It's just a phone Mum, not a computer!"). Dad had had a mobile for a couple of years now, using it rarely and holding it like some strange foreign object but at least giving it a go. Mum, as in everything, had been happy to let Dad take responsibility. She didn't need one because she'd always be with him.

I remembered the unexpected call from Dad with some unease, realising now that he had called me because he was actually more worried then he was letting on. I trained at Dorney as usual the next morning (Saturday) and when I got home and dug my mobile out of the bottom of my kit bag, I saw there was a missed call from Mum and a short message asking me to call her back. She told me straight away that Dad had died earlier that morning in hospital. An aortic aneurism had blown, it would have been very quick and no one was there. Mum was very calm in that shocked sort of way and I felt rather the same.

My first call was to my sister. I arranged to meet her at a North London train station just off the M25 so we could drive up together in my car. My second call was to Paul to tell him what had happened and that I wouldn't be at training for a couple of days. He said to take whatever time I needed. He didn't mention the trial but it had to be mentioned, so I said not to change any plans at the moment. My third call was to Lavina, my head of science, to let her know that someone was going to have to cover my classes for a change.

I packed a bag, picked up Catherine and continued driving north. Neither of us was upset. We were quite sad, but sad because so much of his life had been so unnecessarily unhappy rather than because he'd died. The only emotion either of us had left for him by that stage was pity. Catherine sums it up best I think when she says that, by the time he died, there wasn't one part of him left that knew who he was or could be himself. Everything was about who he was trying to be to other people.

Strangely though, it didn't feel sad when we got home either. There was no crying. The four of us spent the evening sitting in the living room watching TV together. No one could remember the last time the four of us had all been together. We all stayed around for a couple of days to help plan the funeral and I don't remember any of it being awful like you'd expect. My dad had just died, but I felt like I'd finally got my family back and it felt... better.

With no suspicious cause of death, the funeral could be held quickly and would all be over before the seat racing. It would have been the easiest excuse in the world to use this to pull out, but I knew it wouldn't serve me well in the long run. I was going to have to seat race at some point and having just done so well at trials, I knew I was fit and ready and tapered now. And with the first World Cup only a few weeks away, we *had* to get the boat sorted soon and start training properly again. So I called Paul to say I'd take part as planned and through everything that followed I kept my head in the tunnel, or rather it feels more like a funnel, that narrowed towards racing.

After a couple of days in Richmond, John had to go back to teach at his school and I drove back to Henley to teach my lessons and fit in a few more days' training and race prep before the funeral. Catherine stayed with Mum. I continued to design the order of service and speak to the vicar and relatives about the funeral and plan food and flowers from Henley and drove the 500-mile return trip twice more in the next week or so.

The funeral was surreal and external to me. There was a time in my life when I idolised and adored my dad, but I'd been through my bereavement several years ago and was now just trying to do the right thing and not step on anyone else's grief. Many of his patients came up to me to express their sorrow at the loss of my 'wonderful father', as did a couple of my childhood friends and I just thanked them. Even now, over ten years on, I can imagine I'll be making some people very angry to speak of him as I have. I wasn't grieving in the traditional sense, but in my unguarded, sorry for myself moments, I did feel cheated. Children should have parents they can feel distraught over when they die, not guiltily relieved. Isn't that how it's supposed to work?

But I didn't have much of the anger left for him that I'd felt for so much of my life and I realise now as I write this, that I have let go of it all. I have been to some counselling sessions but writing this book and connecting all the parts of my life has been the real therapy. One more characteristic of children of addicts and alcoholics that I came across in my research is that "they have a tendency to pursue tasks and goals way beyond the point when it makes sense or there is any hope of success." Which I guess puts a slightly different slant on the determination to finish my PhD story and perhaps even more on what is still to come. Quite often, after a speaking job, a parent will come up to me at the end and ask me how they can get their talented child to show some of that same determination – "He could be really good, but he just doesn't seem to want it." So far I've resisted the temptation to tell them that perhaps they (the parent) should drink more.

As the eldest child it felt like my job to speak for him at the service and I wanted to do it. I didn't want to lie or continue the lie anymore, but also this was not the place for any grand exposé or venting of private frustrations. So instead I spoke of him only in the parts I could express 100%, honest warmth. I spoke only of the first ten years or so I'd known him – the half-marathon running, village sports organising, a song for everything, nothing too much trouble, raise the village hall roof with his Elvis, beloved village doctor. I didn't even touch on the last twenty years. It felt like the right thing at the time.

John, who'd been closest to Dad, was perhaps the most visibly upset. John and I didn't see each other much, but once we got past our teens we were close enough. I used to be rather in awe if truth be told. At school my little brother was not just the popular sporty kid I'd always wanted to be, but also an amazing musician. He played his guitar for hours and hours up in his room and wrote incredible songs with lyrics that read like poetry. He had a band at school called Rusty James (with groupies and everything) whose tapes I played in my car until cars didn't do that anymore. He also headed up another band in Edinburgh called Fanatica whose songs are still on my MP3. But actually it's his solo stuff I love most. Catherine and I have confided in each other that we cry a bit from a mixture of pride and envy at his talent when we hear him play live. Things were more strained between us after Dad died though and it would take me a while to work out why.

One reason was that at the same time Mum was telling me Dad hadn't had a heart attack, she'd told John he had. John had rushed to his bedside. I'd not. It was strange that Mum told us different things, but if I'm honest I'm not sure what difference it would have made. I've never felt bad that I wasn't there and in fact I think I'm glad I wasn't. I've still not had a moment's regret we didn't have a tearful bedside reconciliation. People say that alcoholism is a disease, but when you live with it you see it's a lifestyle choice. People who want to can, and do, stop drinking. They seek help, go on programmes, check themselves into addiction clinics – Dad did none of those things and he never once expressed a desire not to drink ever again, even if he was prepared to cut down or stop for a while. He always intended to drink for the rest of his life, regardless of the consequences. In one of our rare honest conversations on the topic, he told me he couldn't imagine never having another drink and didn't think it was necessary anyway. What happened with us was just one of the consequences of his choice.

I know I made Mum feel uncomfortable about her choices too, which was probably why she wasn't so keen on having me around. I used to challenge her about letting him drink and about drinking in front of him. I didn't think it was fair. But she'd also say she couldn't live like that. "I need my wine in the evening Alison, my life is very hard and I don't have much else."

John says, and I believe him, that he never knew Dad drank. It took him until a couple of years ago, some eight years after Dad died, and an accidental conversation with Catherine before he finally realised. He said that when Dad had his 'accident', someone had said something about a yeast infection that made him look drunk and the migraine thing and that's what he'd always thought it was. He'd genuinely thought Dad was ill and that Catherine and I had just been really mean.

John would also spend the next couple of years believing I'd not talked to Dad for the last two years before he died. Again, only an accidental conversation brought it out. He got angry with me for daring to say anything against Dad when "You blanked him and didn't speak to him for the last two years of his life." Apparently that's what Mum had told him soon after Dad died. When I asked Mum about it, she just looked at me and didn't say anything. "Mum, you know that's not actually true, don't you?"

"Well no, I'm not sure I do."

"You used to hand the phone over and we'd talk, you came to visit me many times and we all went out for dinner together. We spent the last two Christmases together. Just me – no one else came."

"Oh, well, I'm glad if you did." I'm glad *if* you did.

"You know John has spent the last two years resenting me because you told him I wouldn't speak to Dad?"

Nothing.

And the most frustrating thing was I could tell it was one of those conversations that wasn't penetrating. This story was now fixed and essential in her world. We had exactly the same conversation again a while later and then I gave up. I also know that if it served some purpose to tell John I'd cut my father off for the last two years of his life, then she'd likely have told other people the same.

Emaciated anorexic Catherine had been on anti-depressants for years (as had Mum and Dad of course – you can change your life or you can medicate yourself to bear the life you lead) and says she would have been incapable of feeling anything very much at the funeral even if there had been something to feel, which she didn't know if there was. Six years behind me, she doesn't have even the nice childhood memories I have of him and there was little for her to miss. By the time she was old enough to have any memories I was about ten, John about eight and Dad was having more trouble impressing us. Little Catherine then, barely able to talk, was an easy target. He adored her and it was never intended to cause harm, but child psychology was not part of his medical training. He teased her, and John and I thought it looked like a fun game and a good way to impress Dad and get one up on each other, so we followed suit – John rather incessantly, mainly I just ignored her. When I look back now, the family meals I so loved were all about Dad, John and I seeing who could be the funniest and smartest often at the expense of something Mum and Catherine had said, until they didn't really speak any more. Working with so many people over the past few years, I've noticed how many eating disorders (both under and overeating) are connected to low self-esteem.

Mum never told us to stop and she and the otherwise isolated Catherine became very close. Co-dependents need needy people. Mum spent my childhood comparing me to cuddly, confiding Catherine and wondering why I was not more like her – more normal. This made me jealous of and even more hateful to my little sister. Psychologists also don't recommend playing one sibling off against another – apparently.

At the funeral Mum was cocooned from reality with us around her, practical things to do and the constant drip of sympathy and attention from friends and well-wishers. Almost happy to be at the centre of her own drama. It wouldn't last and she started to grieve quite seriously within a few days, which I'd somehow not been expecting. She'd been so unhappy when he was there, why was she now unhappy when he was not? I think it was less grief to start with and more a mixture of anger and terror. She'd made a silent deal a long time ago that she would tolerate this half-life for the security of never being alone and never having to read her own bank statements. And then the security and statement reader went and died on her. And eventually it was grief as the story of her marriage was carefully rewritten to something more convenient. When I asked her once how it was possible that she could still be unhappy now after Dad had died, when she'd been so unhappy most of the time he'd been alive, she looked at me genuinely shocked, "I've not had an unhappy life Alison." I should have been happy for her, but I actually felt cheated and angry with her in a way that's perhaps too complicated to explain here.

Mum also says she never knew Dad drank in secret and again she's not lying, it's the truth in her world. When she packed up the house to move a couple of years later, she found bottles of beer and gin hidden in the garden shed and all sorts of corners of the house and was genuinely surprised. For years afterwards, whenever I mentioned anything to do with Dad drinking, she'd join in with her bit of info like it was a new piece to the puzzle, "Yes, and you know that when I moved house, I found alcohol hidden all over the place. The shed was full of it." It didn't matter how many times I told her this was not a surprise, that I'd spent years showing her alcohol Dad had hidden, she still maintained it was a revelation.

Much of this may only make sense if you've lived in a family of addicts, in which case it will all be quite standard stuff. Again the textbooks say we were a typical case.

Co-dependency is a set of maladaptive, compulsive behaviours learned by family members in order to survive in a family system which is experiencing great emotional pain or stress. The system develops in response to alcoholism, mental illness or some other secret or problem that hinders normal development. General rules that lead to co-dependency are: -

- It's not OK to talk about problems.
- Feelings should not be expressed openly. Keep feelings to yourself.

- Communication is best if it's indirect. One person acts as a messenger between two others.
- Be strong, good, right, perfect.
- Make us proud beyond realistic expectations.
- Don't be selfish.
- Do as I say, not as I do.
- It's not OK to play or be playful.
- Don't rock the boat.

These rules can constrict the development of self-esteem and coping. As a result, children can develop non-helpful behaviour characteristics and reactions to situations in adult life. Co-dependency is an unconscious addiction to another person's abnormal behaviour. Co-dependants become addicted to the drama and unconsciously perpetuate the problem to keep the drama going.

Most alcoholics have periods where they stop drinking for a short while and seemingly do well, leading the co-dependent to believe that the problem can be solved. Often people who don't know the alcoholic very well don't suspect any problem and the alcoholic's co-dependent family members do everything possible to hide the problem, preserve the family prestige and protect the image of a 'perfect family'.

Co-dependents often forget about their own needs and desires and devote their lives to attempts to control or cure the drinker. They hide many smaller or perhaps more socially acceptable addictions of their own behind a more obvious addiction in their 'loved one' (textbook inverted commas, not mine). Everything I've read about co-dependants uses the words self-sacrificing. A typical co-dependent usually has many positive characteristics, is a 'giver' of the first order and displays only the highest and finest qualities of character. Typical occupations for co-dependants include the helping and caring professions.

Co-dependents often become Enablers. An enabler is 'a person who unknowingly helps the alcoholic by denying the problem exists and helping the alcoholic to get out of trouble caused by his drinking'. The enabler lies for the alcoholic, thus enabling the alcoholic to continue drinking. Family and marital problems often start because of alcoholism, but spouse and children may contribute to the drinker's habit and make it worse, allowing the drinking to continue rather than deal with family problems.

Denial is essential for alcoholism and family members, who use it to rationalise the alcohol dependency. When family members deny the obvious and refuse to look for help, their behaviours can trigger multiple emotional problems in the children of the family. Part of the history of children of alcoholics and addiction is that it is almost predestined that they will become involved with an addict of some description. Even when the co-dependent person encounters someone with healthy boundaries, they still operate in their own system and are not likely to get too involved with people who have healthy boundaries.

Tick, tick, tick, tick, tick.

Dad was buried in Stanwick churchyard after the service and I've never been back. Never even seen the headstone I helped to design. It's not any grand protest, but I feel I've spent enough of my life forcing myself through the proper daughterly motions and visiting him when he was alive not to have to do it anymore now.

People came back to the house. I'd cooked up a grand buffet (which people thought was wonderful in the circumstances but was all part of my therapy) and we fed and watered everyone. I restocked food and drink, but my head was well down the funnel towards the seat racing that was now just a couple of days away. I made sure I sat down when I could, ate proper food and drank plenty of water. I couldn't actually believe I was going to have to race. Despite all my precautions, there seemed no way I'd be at my best after all this. I knew I had only to say the word and I wouldn't have to, that no one would *make* me race in the same week as my father's funeral and a huge part of me wanted to give in to that. It would have been an immediate relief, but then almost as immediately I'd have had to start thinking about the rescheduled trial and start all over again. When you are this far down the tunnel, you might as well push on through and find out what's on the other side.

I didn't quite know how this was all going to work but as always, the only thing to do was hold my line, keep pushing forwards, keep doing the right things and (repeating *Shakespeare in Love*) let everything else work itself out around me.

This time the mystery resolved itself when Paul called the day after the funeral. Becs was injured and would be out for at least a couple of weeks. The seat racing was off and I was in the Quad for the first World Cup (subject to continued performance).

Before I left, I said I thought we should have some counselling as a family to talk some of the Dad stuff through. Mum was instantly dismissive in her caring sort of way, "We'll talk to each other if we need to", and patted me on the arm. I did try a few times to talk to Mum over the next few years, to challenge the myth and get to some level of real relationship, but each time I faced only either the *nothing* response or once, when I really pushed, she became very distressed and I had to stop. It was more important to look like a perfect family than it was to actually be one at all.

I'm not sure at what point I switched to talking about Mum in the past tense, but I realise I've done it now. She is still alive but has Alzheimer's (an interesting twist in the whole selective memory saga) and I no longer think, as I did when I started writing this book, that she'll ever read what I've written. I've become less guarded. People say it's a tragedy but when John, Catherine and I first realised what was happening, there was a sense of inevitability that we all felt. Yet another perfectly reasonable reason for being unhappy, and she now officially gets to hand over responsibility for her life. My sister, the nurse, calls it compassion fatigue.

That was what happened in April 2002.

But back to rowing.

I rowed with KG, Sarah and Elise for the first two World Cups while Becs recovered from injury, took her university finals and raced in her Single, and then Becs replaced Elise for the end of the season. We came third, fifth and third in the three World Cups, but won the Women's Quad event at Royal Henley (which was very cool).

I generally found it a very tough season in our Quad, whichever combination. On paper, with Katherine and Sarah replacing Lisa and Elise, it was a far more powerful boat than the previous year and if you'd have put the ergo scores side by side (as coaches like to do), you'd have said the 2002 Quad was hands down faster. But it doesn't always work that way.

Temperamentally, we found it difficult to be in a boat together. We all liked each other well enough, it wasn't that. Any one of us could go for coffee and cake with any one of the others and have a perfectly good time (and still can). Katherine, Sarah and Elise all filled their cars with my stuff and helped me move into my new house. We were all friends enough for me to be able to ask them to help me out like that and for them not just to agree, but to be excited for me and make it fun. But it didn't seem to go deep enough for us to be able to row together. I always felt a bit on edge, like I had to watch what I did and said.

We almost always shared twin rooms on training camp and the usual protocol was that the pairings would be allocated at random and we'd share with whoever we were told to share with. It was good for helping us all get to know each other and feel like a squad. In the racing season we paired with a crewmate, but usually swapped pairings each camp, which helped build the crew and prevent cliques. Katherine and Sarah were really good friends and that year they'd already got into the habit of changing their room allocations to share with each other wherever possible. By the time we were all in a quad together it was absolutely accepted practice that if they weren't allocated together, then we'd swap keys so they were. Elise and I, and Becs and I never challenged this and really I think we should have, because it didn't help our crew at all. We spent hours and hours training and working on trying to improve our sculling and yet this simple act of room allocation meant that although we were trying to work as a four, mentally we behaved as two pairs. We hung out in pairs, ate in pairs, trusted and distrusted in pairs, and vented in pairs. And the more we did that, the more we felt bound to our pairs and the less we liked the idea of changing the room allocation.

This is all with the benefit of hindsight and recently gained knowledge, but I reckon one really good, honest, guts out on the table, let's tell each other what we think is really going on here conversation would have shifted that crew more than a hundred hours of training. But no one taught us how to do that bit.

It seems so simple and yet it is complicated and tough in ways you can't really imagine unless you are in it. For about seven months of the year we'd compete against each other daily on the water, on the ergos, in the gym, with smart remarks over the breakfast table and snide asides in team meetings, to establish a ranking for section into the summer crews. Then one day, at some point in April, we went from being competitors to crew mates with less than four months to the World Championships (or Olympics) and just a few weeks to the first World Cup race. But we weren't crewmates as in "This is your crew for the next four months, your unit, your sisters, your team." This was more "This is your crew for the next three-four weeks until the next race… subject to continued performance. If we are not happy with your performance at the next race (or at any point in-between) we'll be dropping whoever we think has been performing least well and put someone else in."

So we couldn't really comment on anyone else's technique because, worried that any faults would get them dropped, they would likely be defensive. And anyway, you weren't really sure you wanted them to get better, because then you might get dropped instead of them and they would also be more likely to beat you next year. And when you were doing something wrong and someone spotted it, it was hard to think of it as an opportunity to make the boat go faster as the textbooks and so many athlete autobiographies will tell you to, but easy to think of it as an opportunity for the coaches to drop you. Sometimes it wasn't the training that was the tough bit.

Henley Royal 2002. A pregnant Miriam Batten, Ali Barnes, Katherine Grainger, Me, Elise Laverick and the Bulgarian sculler Rumyana Neykova (Silver medallist Sydney 2000 and Henley winner). I could invent some sort of story about why I've chosen this particular photo, but the truth is - I want a record for all eternity that once-upon-a-time my stomach was really that flat.

Our World Cup performances meant that despite getting a couple of medals, we'd have had to raise our game to medal against a full field at the Seville World Championships. We didn't and came fifth... again. Fran and Debs had had a good start to the season in their Double, but placed fourth in Seville. The new Pair of Bev Gough and Ros Carslake (who was to be my lovely lodger for the next two years) came thirteenth. Maybe the best result of the Championships was actually from Elise who, after only half a season in the Single, came seventh.

All Paul's attempts to find and develop rowing talent in the early season came to little. They were too far behind and there was too much ground to make up. Sometimes it's easy to forget how good we really were. Although we were getting beaten by the rest of the world, the gap between the squad and the very best of the rest British club rowers was still significant.

So, there wasn't even much attempt to put out an Eight that year. Lisa was still injured and Guin had raced the Single earlier in the season, but was out with overtraining syndrome by The Worlds. Kate Mac was in a Four for the start of the season, but it didn't go well and was scrapped. After her sixth consecutive disappointing season, she finally threw in the towel and retired. It was somehow the saddest thing of all. All her contemporaries had those medals from '97 and most had retired along the way, but she kept hanging on in there, trying and trying and trying to get her medal and that happy ending before she finished, but it just would not happen.

So no medals for GB women, again. Two years down, two to go. It was hard to hold our individual and collective nerve.

Chapter 15: How do you eat a whole chicken?

"A way of life based on the joy found in effort."

Two Years to go

You are probably getting the whole lots of small steps thing by now, but here's another year's worth. And I know the metaphor is supposed to be about an elephant, but although I was eating 4-5,000 calories a day, I didn't ever resort to eating one – one leg at a time or otherwise. Chickens though, I ate a lot of. I cooked a proper meal every evening when I got back from training and any lunchtime I was home. I felt eating properly was as important as anything else I was doing and cooking was never a chore. But the meals had to be quick – typically about twelve minutes. Most weekends I'd cook a chicken and it would then give me several very quick meals. Through the door, kettle on, pasta on, upstairs to dump my bags, veg on, plate up some chicken and heat it in the microwave, drain pasta and veg, add a little grated cheese and a lot of cranberry sauce and stop the clock. I saved all the bones as I went through the week and when there was no meat left, I made chicken broth with lots of veg, lentils and pearl barley as my mother had taught me. Nothing was wasted.

I was better prepared for the end of season lows this time and don't remember it being as bad. I went straight up to Richmond to spend a week or so with Mum as the first block of time I'd been able to spend with her since Dad died. I took my bike and had a great time exploring a sunny, ice-free Dales. Then it was straight back to preseason training and teaching. The Science department had found me my own classes that year and again scheduled them all into the afternoons.

Training stepped up again and Paul was looking for new ways to get ahead. He reckoned core stability training was a seriously neglected area internationally and if we could work out how to do it better then we could get ahead here. His vision of the perfect stroke was of bodies right over, long and stretched out and loose quick catches, and we couldn't really get there, or not sustainably because our supporting core muscles were not strong enough. It takes a lot of strength to be that relaxed. He went through four or five of rowing's top physiotherapists and barely let them finish their first session of the usual Pilates/Swiss ball stuff before he chewed them all out. "I've seen all that before. Everyone's doing that. Normal people go to their gyms and do that sort of stuff. We're trying to get Olympic medals. Show me Olympic medal core stability" – or words to that effect that I've not just made up and were probably less polite.

Eventually, he found someone who he thought could show us something different enough – Lizzie Webb (actually the mother of one of the lightweight guys). Does that name mean anything to you? If you are forty or over, think back to Breakfast TV morning exercise sessions... No! *Not* The Green Goddess! The other one... Mad Lizzie. Well, it was Mad Lizzie who revolutionised GB Rowing Women's core stability programme. She's actually a trained dancer who also choreographed some of the most notable acts of the 80s and 90s, including 'Take That' in their first TV appearance (her favourite story).

Lizzie's first session was immediately different. We did similar 'hold your core stable and lift your leg up exercises', but this time with six-pound lead weights strapped to our ankles. She had us holding various bridge positions until we collapsed, and repeating reverse curl stomach strengthening exercises until we cramped and cried. Lizzie outdid us on all the exercises and said she'd expected more from Olympic athletes. We retaliated that it was alright for her with her tiny little sparrow legs and that she should try holding our great long hefty leavers up and see how she liked it even without the weights. She laughed at us and was not scared. We sniped that it was alright for her arriving fresh and perky when we'd already rowed that morning *and* done weights. She had no sympathy. She'd worked with Robbie Williams; she was used to dealing with divas. Paul was sold and core stability moved from being a sideline activity unless you were already injured to something we all did for between thirty-ninety minutes several times a week. In my training diary it's not called core stability anymore, it's just called *Lizzie*.

I objected as much as anyone at first, but persevered and stopped complaining when I felt it start to work in the boat as well as the gym within a couple of weeks. Lizzie also brought along Dr Alison McGregor (a back specialist) and so it was that the really quite sadistic trio of Paul, Lizzie and Alison came together to concoct a whole new world of core stability pain. As well as the *Lizzie* sessions, they constructed a trunk-strengthening weights circuit (T.S.) to isolate the core muscles in a series of about ten exercises. One particular instrument of torture was made by chaining the ergo handle to the cage. We had to hang off the immovable handle, contract our core, push up through our feet and suspend ourselves about an inch above the seat for minutes at a time. It's pretty much exactly the position and sensation you are aiming for at the start of the drive, so for the first time we could overload and strengthen every necessary muscle in the way we actually use them in the boat.

Three or four times a year, we'd have to drive into London (usually on our afternoon off) to have our progress assessed in Alison's Lab at Charing Cross Hospital. When I say 'assess progress', I actually mean 'test out some ways that assessment could be possible', as this was possibly the first time in the world that anyone had ever tried to get real quantitative data on core strength in this way. In the first non-painful method, we'd lie on our backs on a hospital trolley and Alison would scan our Psoas muscle (a deeply buried band of stomach and back muscle that forms a supportive belt) with the same ultrasound equipment used on pregnant women. We'd concentrate on contracting the muscle in isolation and could see it get shorter and fatter on the screen if we got it right. Alison would then attempt to measure the width of the contracted muscle with a ruler.

The second very painful assessment method involves a machine called Cybex, which looks like a chair from an Alton Towers' roller coaster ride. A bar comes down over your shoulders and another over your legs and you are totally trapped. Then Cybex throws you forward and tries to push you back with increasing force while you press your chest against the bars and use your core to resist, until eventually Cybex wins (and Cybex always wins) and throws you back. Then you have to resist it pushing you forward by pushing your trunk back against the seat until Cybex wins again. There were also similar procedures against the leg bar to test quad and hamstring strength. We did each test several times and Cybex always won.

Eventually the lying around, non-painful assessment method was found to be unreliable and disappeared from use, while the hard, violently painful method was found to produce really valuable data and is still used today – obviously.

It was hard trying to do these new things when I was already so tired. By year three we were training as long and as hard as any of us ever had done. Paul still tolerated it if we had work or study, but there were few allowances anymore and we were now all expected to train together in the same place. I was still teaching four afternoons a week and my days were a logistical marvel timed to the last minute to fit it all in. I'd struggle out of the house with all my bags at 7.10am every morning in my first set of kit and having already had a first breakfast. On a full day, I'd not be back for over twelve hours. I carried with me two more sets of training kit, a complete change of smart clothes for school, towel, wash bag, hairdryer, shoes and make-up, second breakfast including a thermos of porridge if we were training at Dorney (where they only served cereal and toast, which is poor carbohydrate compared to porridge), as many good quality snacks as I had training sessions that day, a tracksuit to change into after the third session, Heart Rate Monitor, training diary, CDs, water bottle, Lucozade sachets and spare food just in case.

I'd drive to the first session planning my moves not just for the day, but until the next point when I'd have a few hours off and didn't need to be somewhere doing something. Sometimes that could be three days away.

We'd usually train twice in the morning; then I had this great routine worked out to get showered, changed and made up in minutes, so I could jump back in my car, drive the half hour and walk into my first lesson seconds before the kids did. I'd then stay behind after lessons to do marking and preparation so it would all be done when I got home in the evening. Finally I'd drive to Bisham to do my third training session. If it was Endurance Weights we'd do it together, but if it was an ergo, I'd usually be by myself as the other girls would have done theirs together in the afternoon.

I actually preferred to do the 16k ergos by myself. Most of the others liked to run the three sessions quite close together so they were done and those who still lived in London could get back, but I was glad to have an excuse not to do that. I was always completely depleted after the second session, and if I did a third too close I couldn't get my heart rate up at all and would be totally useless. Bisham was being converted into the English Institute of Sport (EIS) for most of that year, so we had our own temporary gym set up on a curtained-off indoor tennis court. Mostly I'd have it to myself and grew to love those sessions as I had my solo evening training in Cambridge. I'd get the ergo set up, put Robbie Williams' *Escapology* into the CD player (don't judge), row 8k, get off for half a minute or so to drink, stretch and change the CD to Coldplay (still no judging) and get back on to finish the 16k. About sixty-five minutes in total.

Over the years I'd developed various complicated systems for breaking long ergos down into manageable chunks of time, distance, calories burnt and even, if things got desperate, number of three-minute songs. I was never more than a couple of minutes or a few hundred metres from the next mind marker. I also focused on technique and as with the water work, I was looking for a more efficient way to row and a better feel every stroke so I could keep the speed up and my heart rate down. Always aiming for a new PB, even if only by a few seconds. Despite the hard work I remember feeling both exhilarated and deeply relaxed by the end of most evening sessions. The long period of deep, purposeful concentration on just that one thing is deeply Zen-like (man).

"Olympism is a philosophy of life exalting and combining in a balanced whole the qualities of body, will and mind… Olympism seeks to create a way of life based on the joy found in effort." The Olympic Charter.

I'd text my score to Paul (for the week's published results sheet), stretch, shower and change for the third time that day, drive home, put on a load of washing, cook dinner, eat it, watch TV until about ten, hang out my washing, drag myself upstairs, sort yesterday's dry washing, pack all my bags for tomorrow, get to bed, read a bit and hope to fall asleep.

Annoyingly, the better the evening session and the more energised I felt, the harder it was to sleep. There didn't seem to be any way round this. If I did the third session too early it would be useless and if I left it late enough for it to be good, then it was too close to bedtime. If I was still awake much past midnight, I'd take a sleeping tablet to get my magic four hours, often waking soon after 5am even though I was still exhausted. My two alarms went off at 6.40 and 6.41am (I'd missed a morning session four years before when I slept through an alarm so had set two ever since) and I'd start all over again.

I was always tired. We were all tired all the time. If we'd all said we were tired every time we felt tired, all our days would have been full of people constantly talking about how tired they were – so we didn't really do that. We challenged anyone who did with "Don't mention the T-word". My own personal mantra was *"I'm not allowed to complain about any pain, injury or illness unless it is bad enough to stop me from training and I'm not allowed to mention being tired unless I really am too tired to go on and am asking for time off."*

I lived between the few hours off every three days when I could get home in the afternoon, catch up on a couple of hours sleep and just do nothing. So, it was crazy really that I was still teaching. The extra £500 or so a month was nice to boost my £1,300 a month Lottery Grant (I saved all my teaching money so I'd have something if I was ever dropped from the squad and my grant stopped) and I can say now that I kept doing it to keep Plan B alive. That's partly true. But the real reason I wouldn't stop teaching, even though it all but killed me, was that I just loved it. I loved going to this place where the people I worked with respected and were nice to me. I loved planning new ways to teach the lessons and watching the kids respond when it worked. I loved that I was really, really good at this thing with minimal effort, when I had to work so hard at rowing just to stop falling off the bottom.

I taught GCSE Physics and my class came top in their mocks even though I'd got a D in my own A Level. I couldn't work out why my Year 10 Chemistry Class struggled with valancies until I covered a Year 11 Maths class and discovered most of them couldn't work out +1 + -1 except on their calculators. I realised they were struggling with Maths, not Chemistry, and taught both classes the concept of negative numbers from scratch. I similarly taught all my Chemistry classes how to work out percentages from first principles, so they could work out Molalities (they had a habit of feeding numbers into their calculator and deciding that 50% of 200 was 400). I still remember how rewarding it felt to have a girl tell me "I've been taught this so many times before and it's never made sense but I really understand it now." I drew (hand drew!) a picture of my fish tank complete with its three goldfish swimming around in amongst the plants on a Nitrogen Cycle worksheet for my A Level Biology class. I took advantage of one of the few national exam-free years my little Year 7s would ever have and instead of setting them homework from the textbook, I asked them all to keep a Nature Diary. On homework nights I asked them to go outside, see what was going on, look it up and write about it in their diaries. By the end of the year, we had books full of fabulous drawings and pressed flowers and handwritten notes proudly on display at the open day.

Most fun though was that moment of truth for all Biology teachers – teaching Sexual Reproduction to Year 7s (eleven-year-olds) for the first time. We warmed up by comparing baby photos and telling stories of the funny things their parents said they used to do (which they'd found out for homework). Then I said "Right. Open your textbooks to Page__", and on one side was that classic cross-sectional diagram of female parts and on the other side male parts. They took one look and screamed. I tried not to laugh. I took them through all the 'technical stuff' and then at the end of the lesson sat cross-legged on the front desk in what I hoped was a casual, approachable sort of style, and told them they could ask me any questions they didn't want to ask their parents about sex and I'd see if I could answer them as long as they treated me and each other with respect. They agreed and waited for the first girl to be brave enough to ask.

"Dr Mowbray?"

"Yes"

"How does that artificial insemnination [sic] work? I always thought that the woman swallowed it, but I see that won't work now."

I struggled to keep a straight face and the other girls giggled a bit, but then looked serious and respectful and I did my best to explain as much as I knew and tried not to pull my punches too much since she'd been brave enough to ask. The question that most made me blush was probably, "The book says there is a lot of fluid released with the sperm, but I can't see anywhere for it to go. What happens to it all?"

"Well… what goes up must come down…"

"Eugh!"

Those are just a very few lessons from the seven years I was teaching and certainly not all were worthy of note. I did love it though and I hope I'm not the only one who remembers at least something from some of them. *"The quality of a person's life is in direct proportion to their commitment to excellence, regardless of their chosen field of endeavour."*

So, how much have you thought about rowing in the last ten minutes? And so it was for me. I didn't think about rowing when I was at school because working with the kids took my whole attention. And it was the source of most, if not all, of the fun and humour in my life. Rowing was enjoyable and fulfilling in all sorts of ways, but it wasn't very funny. Rowing made me smile from satisfaction, but it didn't give me the giggles. A bad day on the river may be better than a good day in the office, but a dull day at school is still way more amusing than a funny day on the river.

So I kept it going as long as I possibly could (and probably a little bit longer). Elise was still racing in and out of London pursuing her Law training and we used to talk about our busy balancing act lives and how we made it work. We had a 'Two things rule'. Maybe we could call it the ElAl rule.

The main point of the 'Two things/ ElAl rule' states that, *"You can only do two things well. If you try and do more you will just end up being average at all of them."* You can row and work OR row and study OR row and have a social life OR row and spend time with your family. If you split your time between rowing, work *and* a social life (for instance) that's fine, but don't think you are going to get to the Olympics.

The finer points of the 'Two things rule' go something like, *"You must also know which of the two you want to be really good at and always prioritise this."* For example, ROW and work. *"It's good to have other things in your life, but they can only take up really, really small bits of your time and just fit into the cracks."* For example, ROW and teach and a social life of dinner one night a week with my Henley friends.

That's pretty much it really. There's no judgement if that's not how you want to live your life. It's just as valid to live a broad life and be average at a lot of things (as indeed I am now). But I notice that people who want to be really good at something often run into trouble because they don't understand the rule and spread themselves too thinly. So many things are tempting and difficult to say no to that people end up frazzled and frustrated and sometimes even a little bitter because they have not achieved their dreams.

Incidentally, the ElAl 'Two things rule' also works really well with the previously stated Al theory about working out what won't wait. In combination it goes, *"You can do everything you want and get really good at most of it, if you do it all two things at a time and do the things that won't wait first."*

Towards the end of November we had a Boat/Bike camp in Greece and went straight on to Athens for an Olympic orientation visit. I got to go this time. We viewed progress at the rowing lake (a dirty hole of mud and gravel) and the Olympic Village (a dusty building site of skeletal houses) and received many reassurances that all was going to plan. "This is how the Greeks work. Labour is cheap here. With a few months to go, they'll throw everyone on it and it'll get done."

Back home, my own Olympic progress was more deliberate and systematic. I still concentrated every stroke on how my body felt picking up the water. I found the more I concentrated on getting the feeling of relaxed tension in my lower back, the more reliably I could access 'it'. In my training diary I found this noted as *"Slump a tiny bit in lower back to get the relaxed position. Look down at the stroke coach."* I imaged all my vertebrae stacked perfectly on top of each other with the bones holding my spine in place rather than muscle tension. This posture also naturally kicked my Psoas into action to support and protect my lower back. I now know that this head and neck

James Cracknell shows us round the Athens Olympic rowing lake, about ten months before the Junior Worlds will need to be held here as the Olympic test event. Should we be worried?

Taking inspiration from the ancient Greek Olympic Stadium. Used as the 2004 venue for archery and the end of the marathons.

position are used in yoga to get the same effect. Whenever I hear the statement that rowing is bad for your back (a belief that is often bandied about), I always challenge back that rowing badly is bad for your back, but rowing well strengthens it. The technical advice I was giving myself by this point was contradictory to the more standard rowing instruction of *"Sit up straight and hold your head high."*

I was always open to the fact that there were still more technical improvements and speed to be found, but it never occurred to me that there was anywhere left to go with this relaxation down my body thing. I had literally reached the bottom. Then one day, virtually in one stroke, I felt something different and the point of pick up switched from the base of my spine into my bum muscles. We'd been working on activating these big powerful muscles in isolation from our lower back in the Lizzie sessions and suddenly I was able to do the same thing in the boat. My arm muscles and back muscles were still working, but under a relaxed rather than a gripping tension. I could feel my glutes contract first to pick up the water and then there was a sort of ripple of sequential muscle activity up my back and into my arms and another down through my legs as I gripped the water in a whole new way. It was a revelation. I thought "Oh my God. This is *it*. This is what *it's* supposed to feel like. What have I been doing all these years?"

Meanwhile the jostling for position and Olympic seats became more and more intense. After a year out, both Cath Bishop and Alex Beever had found they couldn't quite leave it and were back. Cath and Katherine still spent a lot of their time sculling, but it was becoming increasingly likely that they would eventually row the Pair. There were finally more rowers starting to come through now but at winter trials they were still a long way behind. We had just two more rowers who were anything near the speed in Ros and Bev, but no one else close enough to form an Eight with them. Basically in the run-up to Athens if you wanted to make it to the Olympics and you weren't Cath or Katherine, you had to be able to scull very fast and make it into the Quad, Double or Single. Everyone sculled most of the winter trying to show they were fast enough to compete at final trials in a single (where there were seven seats available), rather than a pair (where there would be just two).

It was a small core Squad, but there were still not enough Olympic seats for us all. The balance between internal competition that pushed us on and internal competition that pulled us down was finely weighted every day. It was really hard to remember that the girls you raced in training were not the real opposition. We were all on the hunt for medals not just seats, but we had to get a seat to stand a chance of getting a medal. I don't think I would ever have called our squad a team.

Mum and Catherine came to me for Christmas and I enjoyed hosting a first family Christmas in my own home. It was the first Christmas I'd not dreaded for a very long while. I made a Christmas cake on one Sunday off, a Christmas pudding the next, and a few dozen mince pies and almond tarts on a free afternoon. If this was still a cookbook you'd get these recipes plus one for our legendary lemon and celery stuffing. Then I bought a goose from the local farm shop and cooked a roast dinner on Christmas Day. That was it. Christmas – really? What's all the fuss about? The only hitch was that I woke up at 9am on Christmas morning to the smell of perfectly cooked goose. Mum had said she'd get up at 6am to put the goose on and had obviously been unimpressed by my attempts to convince her that it would only take three hours to cook and this Mowbray Christmas ritual was unnecessary. Apparently Christmas has to be hard work or it's not Christmas. She did exactly the same thing the following year after the same discussion. Eventually it took Catherine (the vegetarian) to convince her. "Mum, you know if you get up early and overcook the goose again this year, Alison will go mental."

My training diary records just Christmas Day out of the boat. We went to Seville for a couple of weeks in January (we went so often now we kept a fleet of boats out there) but otherwise trained through another British winter. In April, in the last 2k test before final trials I pulled 6.56.3 – a new PB by about two seconds. It was still slower than any of the girls I was competing with for places, but I tried not to look at it that way and think only that it showed I was stronger and fitter and in a good place for trials.

I had my best ever trials. I came second in my heat, won the Rep and was second in the final. Fran and Elise were injured and didn't race and Debs raced the early rounds but withdrew ill before the final, so not everyone was there. But you can only race who shows up. I was always there and there was always someone missing.

Guin, who had been struggling for months, did not make the final and retired. She'd been in the squad before there was any funding and raced the men at trials back when the girls weren't good enough to give her any competition. Then she'd been part of GB women's first Olympic medal boat at Sydney. It had been a defining career. Lisa didn't make it as far as trials. Her back had gone again during pre-trials training in Varese and she'd finally had to accept defeat, fly home early and call it quits for good.

Over the years I'd not only prided myself on my ability to cope with all the training without getting ill or injured, I'd relied on it. I'd seen how the other girls had peaks and troughs of performance as they got ill or injured, missed periods of training and had to build up all over again. Their peaks might be higher than my current best performances but my improvement graph was a steady, relentless chunk by chunk up with no breaks for injury and only the occasional day or two out if I got a cold. It was tortoise and hare stuff and I always felt my best hope was that if I could pace myself right and stay well in those last couple of years, my final peak might eventually match the best of anyone's. I rarely, if ever, won anything but I was rarely, if ever, totally dreadful. I wasn't exceptional like a KG or a Fran but I began to take pride in the consistency of my performance rather than its brilliance. I never missed a trial or race and I never underperformed.

But as others succumbed to injury I started to worry that having been injury-free all this time, I was really just storing up something big that would take me out too close to the Olympics to be able to come back. When I expressed this anxiety to The Blond Boy (who was still just about around in the periphery at the time), he just said "I don't think it works like that Al. Have you not noticed that it's the same people who keep getting injured and ill? If you have been OK all this time, you'll probably stay OK. I wouldn't worry about it so much." I didn't have to think about it too long to know he was right. There is no rule that says injury had to be evenly distributed amongst any given population, so why had I thought there was? At what point had I lost that faith that as long as I looked after my body it would take me anywhere? It was conversations like that that made it so hard to let him go.

But I didn't believe my good health to be just luck. I was always 'on it'. As well as eating as healthily as I could, **I always ate within twenty minutes of training.** Your body is most immunosuppressed when it's most depleted and its ability to take up glucose and convert glucose to glycogen is highest in the twenty minutes after exercise. I knew I had a twenty-minute refuel window to restore my immune and glycogen systems, so carried cereal bars, cake bars, bananas and dried fruit everywhere with me and ate them while still changing from the previous session.

I always changed. Not just out of cold wet rowing kit but after every session. Sometimes you are warm when you finish a session and it's really tempting to jump straight in the car and get going. But then you get halfway home and hot sweaty clothes become cold damp clothes that chill you to the bone. And while the microbiologist in me knows you don't catch a cold from being cold, if your body is already immunosuppressed and struggling to stay on top of a bug, maybe that will be all it needs to get on top of you. And if you are stiff and cold when you straighten up out of the car, what will that do to a back already pushed to its limit that day?

I always stretched after training. Not always for long. I got it down to about five minutes (ten x thirty-second stretches). People often stretch before training, then can't be bothered when they are tired afterwards – when actually the science tells you to do it the other way round. Studies show that stretching cold muscles before training is of little benefit, but just one thirty-second stretch on a nicely warmed-up muscle is enough to make it longer. And hamstrings are most important for rowers. I reckon that you shouldn't really row unless you can comfortably touch your ankles with a flat back because that is the position you need to achieve in the boat (I still get way past that point). Hunching your back to take the stretch off your hamstrings curves your spine, causing the outside edge of the vertebrae to move apart to form the curve. This gradually, gradually pushes the inter vertebral discs out into the gap until one day, years later maybe, one pops out enough that it won't go back. Poor hamstring flexibility causes life-long, life-limiting back injuries that one minute of stretching a day can prevent. Some injuries are bad luck and some… not so much.

I walked a bit most days and did my trekking. In rowing, if you are not careful, you can sit in the car, sit in the boat, lift weights, sit on an ergo, sit on a bike and maybe even run a bit, but if you add it all up, despite being incredibly active, you might walk for less than half an hour a week. I think you can do all those other exercises wrong and in a way that damages your body, but your body knows how to walk. When you walk straight and balanced, you re-engage your core and reactivate your glutes and all that protects your back.

I listened to my body and found extra rest when I needed it. I'd had a bit of a transformational moment in 2002 after seeing a log of Paula Radcliffe's typical week's training in a running magazine. She had just broken the World marathon record again, but only ever did one or two sessions a day and no more than two-three hours per day. I was shocked and wondered why – if it was good enough for record-holding, marathon-running Paula – we were training at least twice as many hours a week for a six-seven minute race. I understood the additional power and rowing technique work, but still we were doing more endurance training than a marathon runner. In that moment I stopped thinking that the only way to get faster was to train longer and harder, and started thinking of the gaps in training as something equally important. Most of our training was monitored and compulsory, but we were often supposed to do two or even three hours cross-training on our own on Sundays. If I'd had a big week and was feeling bollocked, I would replace it with a half-hour walk and not feel guilty. This is not a mindset encouraged in rowing; in fact I had to keep very quiet about it, because missing a session to prevent becoming ill or injured rather than after the fact, would have somehow been judged to be 'cheating'.

I healed my body with my mind. At least I believed I could. Some days I would feel signs of the most common rowing injuries; more than the usual lower back discomfort, or a hot spot on a rib (pre-cursor to a stress fracture), or a stiffening and slight creak in a wrist (pre-cursor to tenosynovitis) and it wasn't so much that I healed them with positive thoughts but more I refused to give them any attention until they got bored and went away. I simultaneously refuse to acknowledge their presence and did whatever I could to heal myself. Like when you catch sight of someone at a party you don't want to talk to and somehow, without ever looking at them again, take steps to avoid them. I'd relax more, stretch more, eat more, drink more and maybe take a single Ibuprofen before I went to bed a bit earlier than usual, but stay perfectly positive in my mind that there was not a problem. By the morning, it had almost always given up and gone away.

I know it's not good to ignore injury. I'm just saying that this is what I used to do and this is how I used to think and I was one of the few who never got injured. I have no idea if those things are connected.

After my trials performance I had hoped, really hoped, that the Quad would be named top boat and I would be in it. I think a Quad with the top four girls would have been Thommo's preference, but after further Mark Banks' politics, Debs and Becs were named into the Double for the first World Cup and I was in a second boat Quad with Elise, Sarah and Fran. My third Quad and my third combination of crew mates, and again we stepped straight out of competing against each other in our singles to rowing with each other against the world.

We booked a session with Chris Shambrook to 'do some sports psychology' and see if we could accelerate crew formation and head potential problems off at the pass. Elise, Sarah and I were friends off the water, but niggled each other on the water in any combination. And Fran? Well, we all liked Fran, but she'd been rowing with Debs in the Double for the past two seasons, so I for one didn't really know what to expect in the boat.

This crew dynamics thing is a complicated business. I don't really like to talk about it because even now it feels like I'm breaking a contract (the one I'm just about to tell you about). I rarely, if ever, mention any of what I'm going to talk about in this chapter when I stand up and talk, because I don't have time to explain it properly and I don't want people to leave with the impression that I'm being critical of any of the girls I rowed with or that I was somehow above it all. It's just that every year this all could be very, very hard work, much harder sometimes than the training and racing, and if I didn't write about at least some of this stuff then I wouldn't be doing any of us justice. Because the real story, the more interesting one I think, is not that we were perfect teams, but that we were really quite rubbish at it and had to work on it every bit as hard as we worked on our sculling technique. We annoyed each other and irritated each other and even hurt each other sometimes, but always had to come back the next day, smile at each other and get back in the boat to try again. And even for those you couldn't get on with, there was always a level of professional respect. We'd trained together for years by this point and knew that no one had skived or shirked. Everyone turned up and fought hard with everything they had, every single day. And even if you couldn't all be best friends, there was no one you couldn't admire for that.

So the four of us sat in the sun outside Marlow boathouse and talked about our goals for the season until we were all sure we were aiming for the same thing (a medal). Then Chris had us all talk individually about our strengths, which is a weird, uncomfortable, un-British thing to do at first. Then, really powerfully, he had us write down for each of our three teammates why we valued having them in the boat, why we needed each of them to help us achieve our individual goals and specifically why we were glad to be rowing with them rather than anyone else. Finally, he had us talk about our contract. How did we need to behave with each other and to each other over the next five months to give us the best chance of achieving our goal?

Fran said that the Sydney Men's Eight had had a rule that they never talked about each other to anyone outside the boat. If someone had annoyed them or was irritating them, they had to either talk it over with that person, as a crew, or not at all. And once she said it, I could see how totally that had been lived out. They had been a very close team of guys and you never could draw them to speak ill of any of their teammates. I'd always thought they were naturally nice; it had never occurred to me that they might actually have agreed to be nice and have a contract for it. They went on to win Olympic

Gold. Most people outside rowing can't name a single guy from that boat. They weren't individual superstars, they were a superb team.

So, that became one of the rules we agreed to. We also started keeping a crew training diary to write all this in and went out and bought a pretty hardback notebook, because good stationary always makes it official. We sat down together most days as a crew to discuss and write down what had gone well and what we needed to work on tomorrow.

We worked hard at it, but even with *all* of this our Quad was still very hard work and we had a very difficult season. Fran was still injured for the first World Cup so Sarah and I raced in a double and Elise her single. As sculling and temperamental opposites, Sarah and I had a tortured ten days trying to get our double to work in time. I was all about the quick catch; Sarah the power finish. When Sarah was angry and frustrated she showed it, but I prided myself on keeping anger and frustration hidden. I thought Sarah was childish and unprofessional. I imagine she found my calm even more infuriating. Despite both of us coming down each morning all smiles and fresh resolve and positive talk, within minutes of getting on the water we'd be pulling the boat apart in more ways than one.

Sarah and I had a really difficult and humiliating first World Cup. We were tenth, way behind any of the other GB Women's crews. Becs and Debs' Double were also out of the medals in fifth place, but Elise sculled very well to get herself into the final and a fifth place. The Cath and Katherine Pair scored the only medal by coming in second, despite being entered as GBR2 in recognition that they would have to fight for their place back from the 2002 GBR1 Pair of Ros and Bev. Ros and Bev raced well and came fifth, but it was effectively their trial to decide who would be the GB Pair and Cath and Katherine were now it.

After the first World Cup Sarah and I were diluted back into the Quad, but I still found it tough going. Paul had spent the last World Championships taking video of the Romanians Women' Eight doing their steady state training and he wanted us to row/scull more like that. They rowed their steady state with a much exaggerated rhythm – hands much faster round the turn over and up to quarter slide than we were used to, and the rest of the slide much slower than we were used to. Paul started showing us this video pretty much every day and then videoed us to show us how far away from it we still were. I was the worst offender. Video showed me constantly behind the other three and not getting out to the required long angle at the catch. I could just about do it, but only by losing the relaxed postural feel I'd come to rely on to access my power. It felt like a massive, massive change and I had no time to apply my preferred step-by-step incremental approach. Paul wanted all the change now, yesterday if possible.

He'd shout at me about it every time he picked us up on the water. "Mowbs, quicker hands, faster, faster and get your body over; the angles are still short, get over. Come on get over!" And then pick me up on it again via the video when we came in. He kept moving my feet further and further forward in the boat to try and get the angles the same, until I felt like I had no room to spin my hands round at the finish and my blade handles got caught against my body. I wasn't arguing this one though. There were no veiled threats; they were explicit enough. "Mowbs, if you can't do this, I'll put someone in who can." And Alex was going really well so it was no idle threat. As a squad we were two years into an Olympic cycle with no medals. One year could be explained away, two was a worry, but three was unthinkable. For added pressure this summer's World Championships was also the Olympic Qualification Regatta. We were putting ourselves under pressure and then Paul was passing on the pressure he was under as head coach. He had to deliver medals that summer and it's not like football where you can go out and buy better players. We were all he had.

I felt tense and sick most of the time in those intervening weeks. I used to wonder what it would be like if the coaches would just put us into a crew at the start of the season and tell us that we were set and had five months to work out between how to go fast. They wouldn't do that because they seemed to think that without the constant competitive threat, we would get comfortable and complacent and not try as hard. But the problem with constant internal competition is that with the best will in the world and even the best contract in the world, it's impossible to build the sense of trust and team that you really need to make a boat go fast. Far from being upset that I could be making the boat go slower, I think Sarah and Elise were quite relieved that having been beaten at trials, they were now not at the bottom of the pile anymore and the pressure was off them for a while. I would have been the same.

By the time we went to the second World Cup in Munich, I felt I was on trial for my seat again. I was used to being terrified by racing. The non-specific feeling of sick terror still accompanied me from the moment I woke up to the moment the gun went off. But now it wasn't just normal race nerves. Now I was specifically terrified I would get my hands and/or blade handles stuck in my body at the finish because my foot stretcher had been moved so far forward and of the trial by video that would take place after racing using the BBC footage. What if I got my blades caught at the finish and I stopped the boat? What if my hands were caught on camera lagging behind the rest of my crew? What if my blade angles were shown to be short at the catch? I'd probably be dropped, that's what.

Usually, once I came off the start and released the race, it was mostly about racing and whatever good technique was ingrained enough from the hours and hours of training to stick under pressure had to do. The moves are not the dance, the notes are not the music and the strokes are not the race. But in Munich I knew the technique I needed was not ingrained enough to stick and it *had* to be there, so most of my focus was on those two technical points and not in a positive way – more in a negative, terrified sort of way.

We made the final and I raced down the whole course thinking "Finish in front, don't get your hands stuck" and "Get your body over. Oh God what will this look like from the side? The angles have got to be enough."

USA and Germany left us behind but coming into the last 500m we were neck and neck, stroke for stroke, with Ukraine for third place. Crossing the line it was so close that we had to wait for the results to come up on the screen to know if we'd made it. My sense was that we hadn't done enough; I think we all had a bad feeling and unfortunately we were right. We were beaten into fourth place by one tenth of a second, less than a foot over 2,000m. It was desperately close and we were devastated. It had been a hard few weeks, not just for me (although I've obviously been laying it on thick this being my autobiography) and sometimes you just really need a boost. To have got the right side of that 0.1 seconds and been able to stand with our arms around each other on a medal podium and walk around for a few hours with medals round our necks and have a few journalists be interested in us and maybe even get to do a quick happy, smiley, relieved crew interview for the BBC. To have been able to sit down and debrief our race around how we won a medal rather than how we lost one, and have a celebratory drink together at the airport on the way home. To have been able to have done just a few of those things might have made all the difference and might have actually made us feel like the crew we were working so hard to become.

Instead we were the only British Women's crew not to medal. Becs and Debs came second and Cath and Katherine won. Alex hadn't medalled but she'd come fifth in her single, which was also a great result. The Men's crews had done well too. Everyone had reason to be happy and celebrate except us.

We just got to be surrounded by all of it all the way home, while we felt devastated and a bit scared about what this meant for us.

When we got back from Munich, our quad sat in Longridge kitchen to watch the video of our race with Paul. He'd already seen it and I could tell he wasn't happy but as I watched I thought it didn't look too bad. My angles were a little short perhaps but way better than in training. Then as we approached the last few strokes, it was unmistakable – I turned my head towards the camera to look at the Ukrainian crew we were so desperately racing. And Paul called "There! There! Mowbs, what are you doing? That look cost you all a medal."

I was shocked. That was out of order. There is a general principle in rowing that you keep your focus in the boat but it's not a rule. It wasn't in our contract and I probably did occasionally take a look to gauge the distance and the effort required to get ahead, I certainly did in my single. I may have mentioned this once or twice, but I really was legendary for my big finishes. My call to myself in the last 500m was *"If I can see 'em, I can get 'em."* This was not an ergo, this was not a head race or even a matrix. I took the pressure from being side by side with real people and turned it to my advantage in racing. I don't think there has ever been anything I was so in control of, and perhaps even so excelled at, as the last 500m of a side-by-side race.

So to call out that one stroke from 220 in the race and completely disregard anything anyone else might have done in their 220 strokes and say that that one stroke was what lost us the race.... I think that was out of order.

And even if it *was* true, how did it help? We didn't debrief any more of the race or think about how we could go faster because now we knew why we'd lost. I kept quiet and didn't fight my corner. Paul was livid and had his scary eyes in. Something wasn't right in our boat and after the couple of bad weeks I'd had and now this single stroke aberration, I was top favourite for being IT. If I pushed Paul I knew which way he would swing and it wouldn't be in my favour. Fran and Elise didn't say anything either because you didn't speak when Paul was like this, but I got sympathetic looks. Sarah, on the other hand, decided to join Paul in being livid with Mowbs for losing us a medal. She spent the rest of the day radiating indignation and wouldn't speak to me except to throw out a "How dare you say anything when you cost us a medal" when I tried to contribute to a crew discussion.

So Sarah was seriously pissed at me for a day. However, we were professionals. Professionals who didn't know and hadn't been taught how to properly resolve conflict, but professionals none the less and professionals don't let personal emotion and conflict affect the success of the crew. We rarely apologised for anything as this acknowledged fault, which was a dangerous thing in such a competitive system. The usual squad method (the only one we knew) of getting over conflicts like this one was to talk in a sort of code. So on Wednesday morning when Sarah arrived at Longridge, she smiled at me and asked me how I was and was especially nice to me ("You have wronged me but I'm rising above it because I'm a professional and I'm putting the crew ahead of our personal differences") and I was nice back ("I know you still think I'm wrong and are feeling good about yourself by rising above it but I am still right here and I'm only being nice because I'm a professional and am putting the crew ahead of our personal differences").

And it *was* OK. I know it sounds weird but Sarah and I had been here many times before and were used to doing this. We'd known each other a long time and knew each other very well. Despite our differences, we respected and were even fond of each other. We just so often seemed to end up fighting it out for the last seat and that was a hard thing to leave behind sometimes. It wasn't perfect but this was the best we knew how to do and for most of Wednesday, it was enough to get us back on the right track.

Then on Wednesday evening we all did Endurance Weights together. These sessions were generally some of our finer moments as a squad. Anyone who has ever done any sort of circuit training will know that although they hurt like hell, the combination of music, adrenalin and pseudo-competitive banter means they are sort of fun. We chose our own weights and monitored our own progress, so it was one of the few sessions where we weren't directly competing with each other. Katherine had a watch with an interval timer so she called the changes. I had added squad DJ to my roles of porridge-maker and hairdresser, and pre-MP3 playlists made eighty-minute long CD compilations to act as the official stopwatch for our sessions. We'd start quietly enough at first because it was a long haul, but as the temperature rose and the sweat dripped we became more vocal, shouting out encouragement and even the occasional challenge if you thought someone could go faster or get more range. It was sort of fun. What rowers call fun anyway.

But on that that Wednesday evening when the sweat was dripping, the adrenalin was pumping and we'd all got a bit more vocal, I called out a challenge to Sarah (rather unwise in the circumstances) which was not well received. It would all likely have blown over again, but at the end of the session Paul called us all over. "Sarah, I don't know what that was about and I don't care but I'm telling you all. You *do not* swear at your crew mates. Not ever. You need each other and it's totally out of order. I *never* want to hear that again."

I felt sick. How *exactly* did he think that was helping? He'd just blown our overheated little squabble up into a piece of major trouble. I knew I was not going to get away with this one. My suspicions were confirmed when Sarah was sucked up into an animated debrief with Cath and Katherine involving many sideways glances.

Since we'd first started rowing together in the Commonwealth Boat all those years ago, Cath seemed to have adopted it as her own personal mission to make sure I never got above my station. She very kindly made it her job to pull me up when I spoke out of turn (or at all really) or seemed to be enjoying myself too much. I know I can be difficult, but since I left school there have been very few people who have consistently felt the need to let me know it like Cath did. I was not the only one to be on the end of this, but it was by no means universal. There are as many people who think Cath is wonderful as have reason to think otherwise, so this is just my view. Over the past five years I'd kept my head down and done everything I could to stay out of her way, but there was still a constant undercurrent of snipes, jibes, raised eyebrows, significant shared looks and quick put-downs – few, if any, of which were ever significant enough individually to record here. Since Cath had come back, she'd formed a powerful clique with Katherine and Sarah and it was not something anyone wanted to get on the wrong side of.

I was surprised then when Sarah came down on Thursday morning all smiles and niceness again. There was no doubt she was making a genuine attempt to be properly professional and put it all behind us. We rowed twice that morning and I think we were doing OK. It was Ros's birthday, so Bev had made cake and we all had breakfast together with cards and little presents and much singing of "Happy Birthday" and blowing out of candles. And our Quad was moving better and that helped more than anything.

We met again to train at Bisham that night for more Endurance Weights. We'd never done them on consecutive days before but the week had been a bit messed-up after racing. The final piece of unlucky coincidence slotted into place because, for the first time ever, Paul was not able to attend the session. Mostly he was obviously bored out of his mind and sat through the eighty-minutes listlessly texting or writing up training programmes, but he was always there. But tonight, while the cat's away the mice will play. Or maybe – while the top dog's away the Cat will play. Cath basically used the whole eighty minutes to play a coded sniping game at me. Most of those who knew what was going on kept quiet but Cath drew a few in, plus the new girls from the vestigial eight who'd not been at the last weight session and so didn't know what was going on and to who their comments were really directed. They thought this was just a game to pass the time. I just felt sick.

I wondered what to do but couldn't think straight. I was very tempted to leave, but that would have given Cath so much satisfaction. On reflection I probably should have stopped the CD player and had it out, but it didn't even occur to me at the time. My ingrained default position was not to create a scene and I kept my gaze down so as not to catch her eye. I worried that I might not be able to stop myself crying. I know it sounds soft but it wasn't just about that evening. I was already so tired and it was on top of the week from hell, on top of two weeks from hell, on top of five years of drip, drip, drip.

Fran was just ahead of me and at one point lingered by her last exercise, and with her back to the room so as not to be caught (it really was like the school playground), said under her breath "Don't let it get to you. Just keep going. The only important thing is that you finish your training. Don't let her stop you training. Think about the Olympics." I nodded and it did make me feel better. If nothing else, I was relieved to have back up that I wasn't just imagining this game and that someone else felt it was out of order. Fran continued to catch my eye and give me the occasional quiet "Good work Al."

But we all came down the next morning and smiled at each other and were nice and got back into our boats and started training again, because we were professionals and it was the best we knew how to do it.

If I had any final doubts about whether I was being paranoid, they were taken away a couple of weeks later. I was running from a session at Dorney to get to my car to drive to school and found Cath in tears in the corridor. Thommo was by now making it very difficult for any of us to hold down bits of work and he'd torn a strip out of Cath earlier for trying to leave to catch her train into London (where she worked at the Foreign Office in training to be a diplomat). I sort of froze finding her there not knowing what to do, but she initiated a conversation and seemed glad to have a listening ear about how unfair it all was. Being in a similar position I could sympathise and did, and for a few moments we were bound by shared experience. I have no idea how this happened but I actually hugged Cath before I left. It was surreal and I drove to school wondering if the world had turned on its head. It hadn't. The next morning in a squad meeting when I dared to venture an opinion, Cath ridiculed me and took me down in front of everyone. She is so intelligent and quick, it's like being struck by lightning. As the meeting adjourned and we all left, Cath pointedly bumped past me and sneered quietly, "What! Did you think a bit of sympathy and a hug and we are friends now? Did you think I was going to be nice to you now?" No, OK. Finally, finally I got it. I resorted to my tactic of avoidance and made no further efforts.

But our Quad had to go fast at the third World Cup in Lucerne and we managed to put crew tensions behind us. Sarah and I shared a room over the Regatta and genuinely enjoyed each other's company. We all just managed the best we knew how.

The Australian Quad was flying at Lucerne and beat the Germans into second place, but in what seemed to be a full field we were next. We came third! A medal! Hurrah! We had a really good row and got our medal moment and it did make all the difference. Letters arrived confirming our selection for the 2003 World Championships and finally, with two months to go, we were officially a crew.

The Cath and Katherine Pair were also third. Becs, who had trouble on and off with her back for as long as she was rowing, was injured for Lucerne, so Alex stepped into the Double with Debs and they came seventh – a pretty good result on just a few days' training together.

We had two months of summer rowing before the Worlds in Milan and Paul took us to Breisach in Germany for two and a half weeks before we went to Varese for the final preparation phase. Paul likes Breisach because it has the longest, widest, unlocked stretch of river this side of the Nile. You can row for mile after uninterrupted mile without ever having to stop and turn round. As this phase of training was all about getting our endurance base back after the interruptions of racing, it was perfect. We stayed in a lovely old-fashioned grand hotel on the hill and were each given a hire bike to cycle to training, so there was no being shipped around by minibus and we had more freedom in our time off. I shared a room with Elise and we were allocated one of the best rooms I would ever stay in – a large ground floor room with full wall French doors onto our own patio and the garden. I'd just finished teaching before I came out, really finished this time as I wasn't going

Training camp fever. Stir crazy in Varese.

It's a strange thing. At home you spend every minute of the day trying to fit in three training sessions, work, cooking, cleaning, kit-washing, paying bills, driving to training, and seeing friends and family enough so they don't completely forget you exist. Then you come on camp and in the final two weeks, ALL you have to do is row a couple of times a day. How else to fill that time…

Winks to the rescue in an emergency boat washing procedure (maybe). Meanwhile… how many lightweight men does it take to inflate a launch? Four. One to work the pump and three to monitor the tan.

Sarah, the Cambridge graduate, is a word search fiend. She lets Katherine (now Dr Grainger) find the easy ones first.

Becs testing outfits, should she ever be called upon to be a genuine super hero.

back for the final year before the Olympics (the Science teachers gave me a third "We're sorry you're leaving" card and present and I was getting rather embarrassed by this time) and I was so tired I slept for every spare minute of the first three days. Elise kept coming back into the room to find the huge curtains shut and me in bed, "Are you asleep AGAIN!" But after I'd caught up we spent our bits of leisure time sitting on our patio in deckchairs (in the shade obviously), reading and pretending we were drinking cocktails.

We challenged ourselves hard to move on during this time, knowing that our medal in Lucerne was no guarantee of the same in two months' time. We worked a lot on our start, breaking it down and trying to learn from Elise (our fastest starter) to find more speed. In training we took it in turns to call/coach from inside the boat, in addition to any outside coaching, and call anything we thought would make the boat move better. At bow, I was best placed to be heard and gradually took on more and more of this role. I really enjoyed trying to translate into words the feeling I had when it was going well. It was very good for me too because I had to think more deeply and clearly about what was by now almost instinctive in order to be able to articulate them for others. For instance, a common coaching phrase used in rowing right from your first days in a boat is "Rock over and get the weight onto your toes." However, I found it didn't fit with what I was actually feeling. When I got that feeling of perfect relaxed tension, I kept my centre of gravity low by rocking over and feeling heavy onto my heels and then gradually moving up onto my toes as I came forward up the slide – so my call was "Rock over and get the weight into your heels."

By the time we went to Milan for the 2003 World Championships, I was more comfortable with the 'Row like a Romanian' style that had proved so hard for me at first, and there was no doubt that it helped us get onto our feet better and made the higher rates easier to achieve. We'd all moved on well in our technique and crew dynamics and I/we felt more confident of a medal this year than ever before.

Friday August 22nd 2003 – Milan

Agreed crew stroke markers

Loose feeling in lower back

Onto front of seat

Tuck right up. Control

Hands wide apart @ catch

Drive in compact position
Shoulders on early
Sit up at finish
Hands finish in front naturally
Tap down, clean
Move hands away quickly until right over shins
Sit on flaps

Yes, you have read the last point correctly. We all agreed we got a better stroke if we sat angled forward on our seats onto that part of our anatomy than back on our bum bones. This was the best way we found to describe it.

Our teammates all had their finals on the Saturday. Cath and Katherine had an amazing row and won, becoming GB Women's first World Champions since Miriam and Gillian in 1998. The Becs and Debs Double did not have such a good race finishing fourth, a long way down. Still it qualified the boat for Athens. Alex raced well in her Single as she had all season and finished tenth, one place better than I'd managed in the Single four years previously. Cruelly though, the athlete quota for rowing had been further reduced and this time round only the top nine Singles qualified for Athens.

We had to wait until Sunday for our final. Our start practice paid off and we were third to 500m, still well in contention. But then either we had a poor second 500m or the other crews pulled their finger out because by halfway and the 1,000m mark, we were back down in fifth. We threw in *'our 25'* to pull back into fourth place by 1,500m and pushed on into the last 500m. Unbelievably, even though we were in fourth place, we were neck and neck with the Germans in the last 500m, a position that would have guaranteed us a medal in any other year. But this year Australia and Belarus were way out in front. In the last 20 strokes, as we wound for the line, at least part of my usual race head was taken up with the thought "Do not look over. Do not look over. I can't be caught on camera looking across."

We crossed the line level with the Germans and collapsed gasping for painful breaths. The first thing, the very first thing, you do when you cross the line is reach down and scrabble desperately to release your feet from the fixed shoes and free your screaming legs – then and only then do thoughts turn to results. We waited anxiously, watching the scoreboard.

"I think we got it."

"I don't think we did."

"I think we got it."

"I don't think we did."

The results came up and we collapsed anew. We hadn't got it. We were fourth and out of the medals for the third year running.

AUS	6.46.52
BLR	6.48.87
GER	6.49.34
GBR	6.49.65

0.29 seconds. A couple of feet over 2,000 meters. We sat on the water for a long time not wanting to come in and face everyone. As long as we sat on the water, we didn't have to deal with it yet. Sarah called out in anger and frustration and expressed it for us all, "I can't believe we have to go through that all again next year."

Less than one minute after the end of one season and already all we could think about was the work that lay ahead for the next. That is how it is.

Chapter 16: Everything for the last time

"Keep roaring, Tiger."

1 year to go

For the first time as I start this chapter, I *know* I will finish the book. My head is way down the tunnel. For the past two years I've selectively cut down on other parts of my life to create time to write and in the last few months, although working full-time and socialising occasionally, it's been hard to drag my head out and I've often been desperate to get back. It's how I've spent my holidays and most weekends. The 'ElAl Two Things Rule' still applies.

I visualise a shiny hardback book and a launch party and I have even started to imagine that finishing this book will not be the closing down of a story, but the start of a new one. I want *to be* a writer with the same conviction that I wanted *to be* a PhD Scientist, an Olympian and an Olympic medallist. I didn't know that when I wrote the first pages. But I still don't know what will happen to these hundreds of pages and if anyone other than a few close friends will ever read them. You can spend four years training for an Olympic medal and never be sure, not until the last stroke of that final, that you will get it, but the only way to *guarantee* you'll never get an Olympic medal is not to train and never be brave enough to race. And you can spend seven years writing your first book and not know, not until the last word has been written and committed to print, that anyone else will ever see it, but the only way to *guarantee* you'll never get a book published is never to write it and never be brave enough to show anyone what you have written. Confidence comes from success, but we have to risk failure to give ourselves the chance of success.

People sometimes ask me where I get such strong self-belief from and I'm always surprised I come across like that because I don't feel I have very much. I now believe in the process, the repetitive nature of success, so strongly that I don't have to think much about whether I believe in myself or not. I don't have to believe – I just have to not disbelieve long enough to do all the work. The process of proving I can't IS EXACTLY THE SAME as the process of proving I can. Sometimes when I'm really stuck I ask myself "What would I do *if* I had total self-belief?" and then I push myself on to do that. Besides,

Olympians finish what they've started because they know that no matter how unlikely success seems, sometimes crazy things happen, and if you stop before the line you give up every chance of success.

But in summer 2003, with twelve months to go to Athens, sitting on the water in Milan looking at the dropped heads and gasping shoulders of my crewmates, I was lagging behind my current confidence. I had no such conviction that I would finish and see this thing through. Eventually we rowed in, de-rigged the boat and got though those first awkward encounters when everyone you meet knows you are gutted and doesn't know what to say and you don't know what to say back. As soon as I could, I wandered off to sit on the grassy bank overlooking the course so I could cry a bit behind my sunglasses and work out how to stand up and start all over again. I couldn't say "I'm going to row for one more year, I'm going to go to Athens and I'm going to get an Olympic medal, or I'm not going." I couldn't say it, even to myself. I'd not medalled the last three years; in fact I'd not medalled the past six years. I'd never won a Worlds medal. What made me think I was suddenly going to be able to pull it off next year, in Olympic year no less?

So, I sat on the hill looking for something else. This is a story of mindset, not muscle.

I'd had a properly C of E primary school education and one day we'd read the story of Jacob's ladder. There was a very vivid colour print that has stayed with me even though I only saw it that once. The ladder to heaven hung in the sky, the top shrouded in cloud, the bottom hanging in space. The people at the top were smiling and being pulled up the last few rungs by helping hands from above, but the further down the ladder you looked the more desperate it got. People were clawing and climbing over each other to get up the ladder, standing on each other's faces and fingers, pulling off others who got in their way. Some people had lost their grip altogether and were screaming and falling from even quite high up. At ten-years-old I was fascinated by all of it, but transfixed by one particular character. He was right at the bottom, dangling in space and hanging on the bottom rung with one hand. Other characters were hanging onto his ankles and clambering over him to get a foot on the ladder themselves. I looked at him and couldn't believe he was still there, still hanging on. For ages afterwards I would think about that guy and wonder what happened to him. Whether he made it or let go. For years now I'd had the Jacob's ladder image in my head and I was that guy. That's how it felt.

I sat and searched my head for a reason to keep holding on to that rung and keep battling to get a foot onto the ladder. I remembered my PhD, that "Success is the ability to go from failure to failure without losing your enthusiasm" and that if on any one of those mornings I'd chosen to walk away rather than cycle back in and set it all up again, I'd never have found the success that was waiting for me. But it wasn't enough because the full understanding of this magic formula says "If you *know what you are doing is right* and you have the courage to go from failure to failure without losing your enthusiasm, then eventually… success… happens."

By this point I'd seen many people flog themselves like dead horses after dead dreams and you'd look at them and think, "How can they not see that this is over for them and their energies would be better spent elsewhere?", and I wondered if other people already saw this when they looked at me. A medal in Milan would have been no guarantee of a medal in Athens, but it would have given me at least an indication that I was doing the right thing.

And if there was no medal at the end of this, could I really, honestly say that this was how I'd have wanted to spend the next twelve months of my life? I loved rowing, I'd loved it for fourteen years and I'd loved doing what I was doing most if not every day since rowing became my job. But the balance of pleasure versus pain had tipped in the past year and sitting on that grass I thought maybe it had tipped too far. The thought of going through all that again, and worse, with no medal at the end of it – that was a sitting on the grass thought, not a standing up thought. That was a letting go of the ladder thought. Yet twelve months seems such a short time after all that had gone before, that I'm sure many of you will be wondering what all the fuss was about. Why not just go for it?

I was thirty-two. You perhaps have to be a woman in her thirties to realise the full potential of twelve months and that it is certainly not something to be frittered away lightly. I wasn't desperate for kids by any means. I found it hard to imagine kids in my life and didn't have those yearnings after prams that women in their thirties are so harshly mocked for quite naturally having. But I reasoned that this was because I was living such an unusual life and had been since I started my PhD over ten years ago. When I thought about a 'normal' life, the one I imagined I would be embarking on at some point post-Athens (a 9-5 teaching job, coming home to the same place every evening, free weekends, regular holidays), I couldn't think about it without a man and kids in that picture. I mean what else did one do with the next twenty years? I didn't yearn for it, I didn't question it – I expected it. With or without an Olympic medal, that was how the story ended.

I hated and derided the thought of 'settling down' – the very words made me feel rather queasy – but still I expected it as part of life's package. I still believed the legend that 'I just hadn't met the right guy' and rationalised that once I stopped rowing and became a 'normal' person, more normal things would happen to me. You can have everything you want, but not necessarily at the same time, you just have to work out what won't wait. A relationship would wait, an Olympic medal would not. And more than that, *"Why worry, it might never happen. If it does I can worry about it then and if it doesn't then I'll have wasted this whole time worrying about nothing when I could have been happy."*

These were the thought processes in my logical, rational moments. But sitting on the grass in Milan, my thought processes were taking me down another compelling path. I was quite happy to start having kids nearer forty; in fact that was my preference, there was still a lot I wanted to do before I had kids. There is a lot of scaremongering out there about female fertility, but no one seems to mention that lifestyle affects it like everything else. If I stayed healthy and looked after myself, there was still a good chance I'd be OK. But still twelve months IS A VERY LONG TIME. That's a whole year of not meeting someone, of not exploring and travelling the world, of not finding adventure and fun and not seeing what else is out there and what else I could be good at, of not working and actually earning money, before I had to root myself back into the whole new and even more restrictive regime of bringing up kids. That's a big weight to put on one end of the scales. If I couldn't put an Olympic medal on the other side, then I had to find something else. Eventually two thoughts came to me.

The first was that getting a medal that year was actually irrelevant. It was the Olympic medal that was important and a medal in Milan would mean nothing to me without a medal in Athens. The second thought was that in the past two years I'd started to reliably get over the top of Sarah and Elise when it really counted. I really did believe that I could move a boat faster than them (not by much, but a bit). I thought they had slightly less reason than me to keep going and yet they were not giving up. The results from Milan made it obvious that the Quad would be the top sculling boat next year and if I stopped now I would make it easier for Elise or Sarah to get a place in that boat. I only had to let a tiny part of my brain imagine what it would feel like to sit at home and watch Elise or Sarah win an Olympic medal in 'my seat' to realise that there was no way I was giving up. What would that feel like for the rest of my life? It would be unbearable. I didn't know where Elise and Sarah got their self-belief from, but I couldn't stop while they still had enough to keep going. I guess that was the advantage of training in a squad with these girls, even if it was also so hard sometimes. So now I had not one but two reasons to hang on and keep going, and I stood up and walked back.

I didn't have to get started immediately though. I had three weeks to put failure to the back of my mind and recharge before reporting for duty for the last time. First I went and found Aquil, the US sculler. He'd first hit on me at the after-party in Lucerne in 2001 and I'd been rather flattered. He's a minor rowing celeb and a good-looking guy. We'd got on well enough that the same had happened after Seville 2002 and by 2003, we knew each other well enough to know that this year was already a done deal. Only one date a year, but it was as reliable a relationship as I'd had for quite some time.

In-between, despite being the age of email and text, we both liked writing and receiving letters and somehow settled into this as our preferred method of correspondence. There were several occasions when I was at a low ebb about everything. Not only was I rubbish at rowing, but the blond boy was never going to love me so that meant I was totally unlovable and would be forever – and then I'd come home and find a plump letter with a US stamp on the door mat and it was enough to put at least part of my life back into perspective. We met for a coffee down at the course. He'd had an even less successful Championship than me so we could console each other and then he came back with me to our hotel so we could take our minds off losing for a while.

And then there was the Milan 2003 after-party. Worlds parties are immense and if you get it right can carry you through another twelve months of deprivation. Hundreds of physically fit, beautiful people from all over the world, who have all been working harder than you can imagine, have not drunk or been out for months, and are either celebrating or commiserating hard. It's a wonderful thing. It's quite an out of control thing and every year the organising country tried to make the party more low-key and limited, but to no avail. Sometimes, like in Lucerne and Milan, they served only weak beer in an attempt to keep us sober, but they were dealing with professional preparers here and nothing stopped the fun of an after-party.

Seville 2002 hadn't tried any such tricks and had thrown us a proper party in a marquee in town. At one point I vaguely remember they'd had to stop the music to pull a girl down who'd climbed the centre supporting scaffolding and was pole dancing from the top. Apparently that girl was me (I'm a running, jumping, climbing trees sort of girl). I'd taken Becs and Debs under my wing that night and was looking after them (although they claim it was the other way round for some reason). At ten years my junior, these girls had had the misfortune to have studied for their degrees (English and Biochemistry respectively) whilst already training full-time on the team and so had not had a 'proper' university education. I had undertaken a mentorship role in terms of party skills and they were willing and able students.

Seville 2002 World Championships post-race party. This photo is the only evidence I have that the story people tell me about what happened next is true. I have no recollection…

I don't think many of the GB rowing girls made the Milan party. Sarah and Fran were still at the hotel getting their heads around defeat and Elise was going out with Andy Hodge from the Men's team, so I think she was out somewhere but I didn't see her much. But our lovely Men's Eight had won an unexpected but well deserved Silver, so there were plenty of people to help celebrate even if I couldn't myself.

It was a constant source of amazement to me how good everyone's English was, regardless of how much alcohol they had consumed. By halfway through the evening, much of the British team were having a far harder time stringing coherent English together than the Germans, Dutch and Danes. And it wasn't just English they spoke so well. One of the most impressive things I think I ever saw was a Danish guy I was talking to accost a group of Ukrainian girls to ask them the way to the next party, "Hey Ukraine," he said in English, "what do you speak? You speak Russian?" – and having established that they did, he started talking to them in what sounded to me perfectly fluent Russian. I went a little weak at the knees.

At Milan 2003 I partied a fair bit with Lenka Wech, stroke girl of the German Eight who also found it difficult to drag many of her more serious teammates out. Lenka is possibly slightly smaller than me, and with very long, straight blonde hair looks more model than rower, except that she is a brain surgeon in her spare time (no really, rowing women are just ridiculous sometimes). I also always had fun catching up with Sophie Balmary, the crazy French sculler. She was often at a loss for female teammates as she basically was the French Women's team. She'd usually be wearing something that looked like it had come off one of those fashion shows where you go "Well it's all right on the cat walk but no one would wear that in real life" and had dyed red or purple hair or something. Her English was not great but still better than my French, so she'd throw an arm round one of my shoulders to help keep herself up and our conversations generally consisted of shouting very loudly at each other that we were very drunk and should go and get another drink.

The other reliable party girls were the Danish Quad (again usually the sum total of the Danish Women's team), who at least all knew how to party properly and came out together as a crew whatever their result. So again, despite my disappointment, I had the most amazing fun – not quite believing my luck that this place, with these incredible people, was my world and I fitted. I absolutely fitted.

September 2003 (11 months to go)

Then it was back home and it hadn't been hard to plan a postseason blues-beating holiday as my sister was halfway through a year-long trip to New Zealand. It was a holiday but I was also checking in. She'd been incredibly brave to go but was still finding it tough. After feeling nothing at Dad's funeral, she'd taken herself off the anti-depressants with the rationale that she just wanted to feel something again even if what she felt was dreadful. She'd still been skeletally thin and obviously ill, which is actually at least part of the point of anorexia. If you are physically ill you get attention and sympathy, not so if the pain is just on the inside.

Then at some point she'd got bored with the not eating thing and had started to put on weight. "How well Catherine looks!" people would say, "I'm so glad she's 'better', and to Cath "You are looking really 'well'", and I wished they wouldn't because she wasn't well – she'd just put on weight and that's not the same thing. Catherine says that when people say "You look well", she hears "You look fat" and it makes her feel sick. So with all this, it was very brave to go to New Zealand for a year by herself. She got a job as a nurse in a hospital in Dunedin (South Island) and left all her friends and support network behind to go and see if she could 'fix herself' by trying out a new life for a while.

I'd driven her to the airport a few months before and it had been scary dropping her off. She'd even had to lie about the state of her mental health to get a Visa, which was worrying because there are perfectly legitimate reasons why they aren't very keen on people who have been seeing councillors and taking anti-depressants for years leaving all that behind to travel to the other side of the world. I could tell from the little things she said that she'd set herself a deadline of bringing her eating 'back under control' when she boarded the plane. So as I drove her to the airport, I was supportive positive big sister helping her be excited about her plans, but I was still big sister so I couldn't let her get on the plane without at least a bit of a lecture. I didn't really think it would do any good, but big sisters have to at least try. It's in our job description.

"You're going to stop eating when you get on the plane aren't you?"

Nothing.

"Cath, you are doing so well, coming off the pills and going on this trip. It's so strong of you. I really admire you. But I'm going to stop admiring you if you stop eating again. For most people being able to lose weight shows strength, but for you it's the other way round. Eating is being strong. Not eating and losing weight again is being weak."

Nothing.

"Will you please at least try and think of it like that?"

"I will, I'll think about it."

And of course now I'd not seen her for months, so I had no idea what weight she was as she didn't talk about it. I could tell she was finding it tough though.

I got back from Milan, had a day to unpack, wash everything, repack and then I was off again. It was perfect post-race blues therapy. Catherine met me at the airport and I'd forgotten to be prepared to be shocked. She hung back a bit and said later that although she'd been so looking forward to me coming, she'd also been scared because she knew I'd be disappointed in her. She was wearing a big down jacket and loose jeans but I could tell, even from her face, that she'd lost a lot of weight. I guess we both must have stood there for a second before I gathered myself, smiled big and went forward to hug her. I steeled myself not to flinch as I hugged the bones that I knew would be all that was underneath the down jacket. Catherine has always said that I am one of the few people she can relax with because I treat her like a normal person no matter how bad she looks. I would never condone, but if I'd learnt anything from Dad it was that you can't change addicts if they don't want to be changed. I knew Cath was doing the best she could and I always thought that the best thing I could do was to give her a break from herself and help her be happy for a bit, and then maybe someday she'd be happy enough not to need to do this to herself anymore.

Once the ice was broken we were fine and within three hours had climbed to the top of a crater rim overlooking Christchurch and the holiday had well and truly begun.

We trekked through ice caves, lazed in natural hot pools, kayaked in Milford Sound, walked on beaches and ran round lakes, watched penguins hop up very steep hills on ridiculously short legs (how do they do that?), got drunk on Sambuca and played pool with the locals. Catherine did a bungee jump, while me and my low adrenalin threshold and rather snobby distain for 'adventure' activities where you pay very large amounts of money for someone else to *guarantee* your safety and *the only* training and preparation required on your part is not to get pregnant – stood, watched and took photos.

But if I was to recount one adventure that was to perhaps prepare me best for the year to come, then it would be our first hike. A two-day linear 'Tramp' (as they call it in NZ) over Goat's Hut Pass. It was peppered with metaphor. We had a glorious walk up to the hut on the first day but the temperature fell dramatically after dark. It snowed overnight and when we opened the hut door, everywhere was stunningly white in the morning sun. We set off to walk down the other side of the valley, but our progress was alarmingly slow as we had to stop and take our boots off many times to cross and re-cross a stream. I began to fret that we wouldn't reach the road in time to hitch a lift back to our car before dark, so I big sister decreed that we would do it the New Zealand way and there would be no more taking off of boots to cross streams.

Catherine, little sister grumbled at 'being forced' to get her boots wet, but we soon needed our boots on for grip anyway as the stream widened to a fast flowing river. Even so, Catherine slipped and fell at a crossing. She'd brought no spare clothes and I was annoyed until I realised, for the first time, that she couldn't bring them because she was so much lighter and weaker than last time we walked together that she couldn't carry spare anything. The hiking equation is that if you try and carry much more than about a third of your bodyweight, you are not going to go anywhere very fast. I gave her some of my spare kit and went into cold shock at the first sight I'd had of her unclothed body as she changed. Thigh bones and hip bones and a floating rib cage, and I could only think 'Belsen' and that it was surely the worst I'd ever seen her. I plan well and carry spare kit and food, but I really don't worry too much about what will happen if things don't go to plan. Even if I have to walk all night, even if I'm injured and have to crawl for help or sit and wait for days for someone to pass by, I feel secure I can survive on my own reserves and make it out of pretty much anywhere if anyone can. But suddenly it was blindingly obvious that Cath had no such reserves and we were running late, with limited food, few dry clothes and no tent for shelter in a New Zealand winter. I don't think I had ever felt more responsible for someone else's safety.

I put her wet clothes into my pack and we got going again. She fell in at the next river crossing too. "FUCK, FUCK, FUCK, FUCKITY FUCK!" she screamed and just sat in the river and cried. I pulled her out and she changed into the last of my dry kit. I tried to keep it light. "Come on Cath. You'll be fine now. We'll be fine. There's only one more river crossing and we'll send you across that one naked just in case." Because Rule number 1 of rowing in rough water says to *"Remember to enjoy it and keep your sense of humour. If you can feel it's a crazy adventure rather than scary trial that definitely helps."*

The last river crossing was high and fast with snow melt, and if there had been any other way home we would not have crossed here – but there wasn't. I took my pack across, then came back for Catherine's. We both made it and set off a pace. We had a couple of hours left until dark.

There were only two markers left in the track notes. The first was a little wooden bridge that we would pass (but not cross) on our right at about halfway. The last marker just said "Finally walk through the field of cows until you reach the road" and we'd been laughing at that for two days. "You can't have cows as track markers. What happens if the farmer takes them out of the field or they wander off into an invisible corner?" We set off even faster than before. After about an hour, I was checking my compass and the useless sketch map every few minutes and voicing to Cath, "I don't understand. We SHOULD have passed the bridge by now." We walked on and on and I became quite desperate. "Where the fuck is it?" If we hadn't passed the bridge and halfway by now, we were really going to really struggle to make the road before dark. I urged Catherine to walk faster and took yet more kit from her pack so she could. I knew she'd eaten virtually nothing all day, so I took a couple of cereal bars from my spare food bag and handed her one as we set off again. I saw her sneak it into her jacket pocket. I put my big sisterly voice on again – "It won't work in your pocket. Eat it. I don't know how we are going to get out of here, but if you collapse on me we are both stuffed." She ate the cereal bar and we walked faster.

By now I must have been carrying way over a third of my body weight, but whereas my morning pack had felt quite heavy, now I felt nothing. I might be the weakest in the gym or on the ergo, but this then is my power. My back has to be well and truly against the wall to find it, but at least I can be pretty sure it will always be there when I need it. And Catherine kept up so I think maybe she has it too.

But still no bridge and I began to think that all hope was really lost. My head was down and I was looking at my feet. Then I stopped in my tracks. "A cow pat!"

"You what?" said little sister. Now obviously worried that big sister might really have lost it.

"A COW PAT! There are cows! There are cows!"

"Oh my God! THERE ARE COWS!" We jumped up and down and hugged each other.

The field was less than half a mile long with a wall at the end which presumably hid the road – we knew that because of course the field was full of cows, as the track notes had always said it would be. We stopped to take a picture of the beautiful cows and all but skipped through the field, light with relief and already starting to tell the story and find it funny.

"FUCK, FUCK, FUCK, FUCKITY FUCK!" teased big sister.

"It won't work in your pocket. Eat it!" teased little sister in her sternest voice.

That night over hot food and cold beers, we couldn't stop talking through every detail of the story. And it might not have been the most sensible trip for a depressed anorexic to undertake for a lot of very sensible reasons, but for that evening at least, I'm pretty sure she wasn't depressed. I hadn't thought much about rowing for a couple of days either. And it is still our most talked about adventure. Whenever we have a tough time on a trek or just generally in life, one of us is likely to pipe up with either – "Remember Goat's Hut Pass? The tough bits always make the best stories. When this is over, this is the bit you will always remember and tell stories about when all the rest is forgotten."

Or sometimes more simply, "Don't worry; the cows are just up ahead."

October 2003 (10 months to go)

I was actually back and back at training before the end of September. The start of my last ever training diary records my goals for the season.

2003/4 Aims
16K Ergo Av. 2.02
30 min Ergo Av 1.65
2k 6.54.9! eventually

April Trials Go into them with confidence? How?

1. *GOOD START!*
2. *Distance/stroke Rhythm in middle*
3. *Believe* (actually double underlined)

October 1st was the official opening of the English Institute of Sport (EIS) at Bisham Abbey. We were asked to hang around in kit testing stuff out, almost as the entertainment I think. Steve Cram was opening the centre and I was looking forward to meeting him after my childhood days of cheering him round the track at Gateshead stadium. But when I actually stood in front of him and opened my mouth to talk to him, the weirdest thing happened. My mouth went dry, I felt a bit faint, I stuttered and stammered over my words and really rather embarrassed myself. I'd never realised before that being star-struck is an actual, real physical phenomenon – but apparently so.

By the second week in October, we were off on the first of many training camps that year. The day before we left I played tennis with Katherine Grainger to keep her company in one of the few forms of training she could do at that time. In the week before her World Championship win, she'd been suffering from quite severe back pain. The physios had kept her going but after the final she'd been in agony, and a scan back in the UK had revealed a prolapsed disc. Apparently she'd raced the final like that and become World

Champion with a slipped disc. It was twelve months before the Olympics and the very best prognosis was that she would be out of the boat for several months. While I'd been away in New Zealand, Katherine had been recovering under the supervision of rowing's best doctors and physios. Most of her next few months would be spent sweating away on a static bike but tennis was OK too.

While I was over at Bisham, I also dropped by the squad doctor to restock on the Zopiclone sleeping tablets I knew I'd need to get any sleep in the shared rooms on training camp. While he was chatting and writing my prescription, I watched the words on his computer screen saver ping round. Three lines, three statements:

EXPECT NOTHING
BLAME NO ONE
DO SOMETHING

I don't remember who they were attributed to. By the time I'd driven the five miles home, much of my part-formed, homespun philosophy had crystallised into those three phrases. I had an Athens 2004 card I'd bought in Sydney and it had sat on my window ledge for three years to remind me every day what I was doing this for. When I got home, I opened it up and wrote those three phrases inside.

EXPECT NOTHING – don't expect it to be easy, assume it will be hard, assume no one will ever give you a break and you will have to fight for everything. If you see someone else get a break, think that they got lucky and your turn will come – not that "It's not fair." But if no one ever gives you a break, then think that's a good thing because when you get there, you will know for the rest of your life that it was all you. If you get a break it's a bonus and you should make the most of it but don't expect it, don't sit around waiting for it. Don't be one of those people sitting on the sofa expecting life to come to them. Expect to achieve nothing, but do the work anyway.

BLAME NO ONE – don't get to eighty and think that your life has been rubbish but that's OK, it's OK because it wasn't your fault. Don't be one of those people who are happy to be unhappy all their life, as long as they can find someone or something else to blame. And don't blame yourself either because how does that help? Don't be one of those people who spend their life sat on the sofa with anyone who will listen, trying to work out whose fault it is that their life sucks.

DO SOMETHING – get up off the sofa and do something, anything, no matter how small. Doing leads to more doing. More doing leads to a sense of achievement – sometimes just at the doing, even if nothing else has actually been achieved. Achievement gives you the energy and motivation to do more and builds self-confidence. Self-confidence leads to the bravery to do bigger things which leads to bigger achievements and more confidence. People give breaks to confident people who look like they can achieve anything and sometimes other people call that luck.

So I had a new mantra. *Expect nothing, blame no one, do something. What can I do today that's better than I did it yesterday?* After this year, I told myself I may never again spend as much of my life doing any one thing or have as much support. This year may well be the best chance I ever get to find out how good I can be at something. Almost certainly at thirty-three, this is my last chance to find out just how fit and strong it is possible to make my body. And surely the last chance I will ever have to find out how fast I can move a boat through water. This year, everything for the last time and everything the best I have ever done it. No regrets, not ever, not one.

We went to Cyprus for the first time on training camp. It was to be the site of the GB holding camp for Athens and since we wouldn't be going then (as there was no rowing), we got our chance now. It was a combined camp with the men which I always enjoyed. It meant there were people around with whom I wasn't directly competing for a start, but it also meant I had more Scrabble partners. Scrabble had not been the same since Kate Mac retired. Debs was always willing to give me a game, but after nearly four years she still couldn't get the hang of the fact that that big words are not always best and you have to go in at least two directions at once to get a decent score. Dan Ousley and Robin Bourne-Taylor from the Men's Eight gave me a better game and I was frequently beaten. There's no fun in playing if you can win too easily.

We stayed in an amazing beach resort hotel and set up a proper gym in a glass-fronted room overlooking the sea with ergos and weights we'd brought with us by truck.

On the first morning we went for a two-hour, flat-fast cycle ride and I really struggled to hang on, but it wasn't until the 16k second session ergo that I realised quite how much trouble I was in. I struggled after just a few minutes at my usual pace and even after dropping back a lot, getting through the nearly seventy minutes of that ergo was torture. My diary records that my heart rate was around 190bpm for most of that session, but I still only averaged about 2.07 splits. My UT2 threshold (the zone we were supposed to be training at) was about 165bpm, so 190 for over an hour was well over the edge.

It was a big shock. Every other year I'd been back on the water and in the gym a couple of weeks before most of the other girls so I'd at least start the season on the front foot, but this year with my trip to New Zealand that had not been possible. I'd been walking six to eight hours with a heavy pack or running for at least an hour most days so I thought I'd stayed pretty fit, but really nothing is the same as being ergo fit. Plus, I was training with the tail end of a cold I thought I'd shaken.

It was the start of a very tough couple of weeks desperately hanging on in the cycling and gradually, gradually bring my ergos back to something mildly rather than totally embarrassing. I enjoyed the long hilly rides much more. We didn't have to stay together so I could take them more at my own pace and actually on the hills I had the dual advantages of being lighter and from the Yorkshire Dales (home of 1 in 4 and 1 in 3 hills), and put in some good rides to finish near the front.

I was sharing a room with Rebecca Romero (aka Becs), which was always fun and we got on well. Interestingly though she was not our best cyclist, in fact she wasn't out on the roads at all at this point. A repetitive strain injury from our first bike camp had meant she refused to get back on a bike and spent the time we were out on the roads training in the gym. Debs and Elise (our supreme multi-athletes who lay lie to the statement that rowers only row because they can't do anything else) were our fastest riders.

And, of course, if I'd *only* had the training to worry about… but there was also the Bishop factor. Sarah actually felt obliged to sort of apologise for her at one point, "You shouldn't take it personally, she's had a cold and is unfit and is having a hard time keeping up." You and me both, baby.

Physically the flat fast rides were tough and I was always just hanging on in there, but psychologically they were much more draining. We rode in the rotating draft pattern we'd been taught and my anxiety would increase every time I got nearer the front, because every time I got there, within a few seconds there'd be exclamations and abuse from Cath behind. Apparently I always took it too fast, in which case I'd look behind after a few more seconds and find that the pack (controlled by Cath) had refused to follow; or too slow, in which case a shout from Cath would shoot one of the other girls past me to take the front. I'd watch my Speedo as riders peeled off the front and my turn came closer, and each time I took the front I'd concentrate and try so hard and be convinced that this time I could get it right – only to hear the same exclamations. Taking the front without changing pace is difficult because the effort needed changes when you hit the wind resistance, but it took me until nearly the end of the camp to work out that even if I wasn't great at this, none of it was actually about whether I was getting the cycling right or wrong.

I spent a lot of my spare time writing emails and letters to Catherine who was really struggling again since I'd gone. I entreated her to keep moving and keep fighting and to think of herself as a tiger not a mouse. I signed off with "Keep roaring tiger." It wasn't just my sister I was writing to.

After two weeks of camp I'd dragged my body back to some sort of fitness, only to feel another cold starting within two days of coming home.

Cyprus bike training. Another carefully chosen rare moment where I am actually in front. This is because we are going uphill. In the Yorkshire Dales we don't even call this a hill (notice I'm still in the saddle refusing to acknowledge it).

An even rarer photo of Paul (Thommo). You never think to take a photo of your coach. This one is taken by Miles. Paul and Miles got very, very bored driving around for hours and hours as our support vehicle. Their excitement when someone got a puncture and they had to come to the rescue was unseemly.

November 2003 (9 months to go)

By the start of November I was back to full training, but with another cold my 16k ergo scores and heart rates were back to where they had been at the start of the Cyprus camp. All in all, it was not the flying start to Olympic year I'd been hoping for.

But if my fitness and ergos were letting me down, I could still work on my sculling and it was still step-by-step improving. My training diary is peppered with requests to self to 'Stay relaxed' and 'Relax more', to 'Have Patience' and 'Wait', and records of how well I was managing it. The temptation is to grab at the water and jump on the stroke in a very natural attempt to make the boat go faster by getting on with it as soon as possible. But the skill is to separate the 'catch' from the 'push' and be able to get the blade into the water ever quicker (the catch), but then wait for the water to grab the blade and make the connection before you push it away with the legs. Continually working on all this meant that despite my still poor ergo scores (there is no lifting the hands into the catch or waiting for the water to grab the blade on an ergo), I was for the first time reliably hitting the on-water steady state speeds Paul had set as a target over two years ago.

Thursday 13th November 2003 (Longridge)

1. *70' UT2 14k 1x*

Best sculling ever

Speeds all ~ 2.24 best ~ 2.18-2.20

HR 160-165 easy

Speed = TAP HANDS LOW

LIFT HANDS

WAIT

NO FEELING OF PULL OR TUG IN ARMS

2. *Lizzie session (45 mins)*
3. *Strength weights (table in front of diary)*

Massage @ 5pm/Bisham

But then we did a 2k test and I posted a time of 7.02.3. See, how can that make any sense? I was getting the best on-water speeds I'd ever got, comparable with the best of the squad, and yet *still* I couldn't reliably do a sub-7 minute 2k ergo.

Two days later, we flew out to Seville for a combined rowing/bike camp.

Obviously there was a lot of training, but the camp was most notable for this day.

Saturday 22nd November 2003

1. *75' UT2 Session A 1x*
   Watched Rugby World cup final
   !!ENGLAND WON!!
   Eng 20:17 Aus
2. *90' Endurance weights*
3. *12K UT2 ergo (2 x 6k) 2.05.1 HR < 175 (last 10 mins <180)*

Particularly fun because of course both Paul and Marty are Australian. We all sat in a Spanish bar and I watched with a certain sort of fascination the focus with which Jonny Wilkinson kicked. It was so obviously race head. I read in the papers of his marathon after-training kicking sessions when he'd stay behind until he'd kicked x number of consecutive balls clean through the posts and an article in *The Times* comparing Jonny Wilkinson and David Beckham, "Both men are training ground fanatics: lucky men to have such talent, and men who know that the harder they train the luckier they get." It was somehow the first time I'd heard this common and variously attributed quote and I wrote it in the back of my diary. It sounded familiar somehow.

No teaching meant more time to rest, but it also meant I had nothing else going on in my life. I was disappointed to discover that now I might actually have been around to watch it occasionally, *Watercolour Challenge* had not survived as long as my rowing career – poor Hannah Gordon. I started to tinker on my piano a bit but quickly got frustrated with my repertoire, which only ran to the first page of about five pieces, stopping abruptly at the point where the pages became dense with black notes. My belief that small steps can take you anywhere led me to wonder if I could learn to play these pieces, even the black pages, if I broke them down into small enough steps. I started with Debussy's *Claire De Lune*. I'd been able to play the first page since I was about sixteen, but page two is black with huge running cords. I spent nearly an hour practising the first black bar note by note, then slow chord by slow chord, until I could play that one bar full speed without looking at the music. The following day I came back and learnt the second bar the same way. It totally gripped me and there were times I'd drive home from training and couldn't get back fast enough because my muscles were aching to start playing. Often I'd drop my bags and sit straight down at the piano for a few minutes before I even got food. It took me three or four months to learn the whole piece, a bar at a time, but by the end I could play all six pages from memory. It was never note perfect, but I knew that the music is not the notes and I think it sounded OK. People who heard me play had no idea that it had taken me so long to learn hour by hour, bar by bar and often told me I had a very natural talent.

At one point I was being treated by Ashleigh (our exceptional physio from the EIS), for strange, but not desperately serious, shooting pains across my shoulder blades that neither of us could account for. It wasn't until I got back to the piano that evening and stretched out my (freakishly small for such a tall person) hands to accommodate the massive chords and felt the shooting pains again, that I realised this wasn't a rowing injury. I kept quiet about the source for fear of being told to stop and after a couple more weeks of practice, the pain disappeared.

I once heard genius described as 'a weird celebration of mental illness' and it did make me smile.

December 2003 (8 months to go)

By December 17th, my diary records the start of another cold – my third this season. I sculled just two short outings in the next five days to keep my technique ticking over and kept myself on reduced, one session a-day training over Christmas week. It was as worrying as it was frustrating.

I kept up with all my eating, changing, stretching and positive-thinking strategies for staying well, but by this point it didn't seem to be enough. Barring a few weeks after the Worlds each year, I hadn't slept an uninterrupted eight hours' sleep or had a waking heart rate below sixty for years. It's a weird thing that when you are actually supposed to be at your fittest, you feel most dreadful. We all used to joke about how, despite being some of the fittest women in the country, we were so permanently exhausted that we couldn't even run up a flight of stairs without stopping.

Jacqueline, our nutritionist, shared the latest research that protein was also an import part of recovery fuel to prevent muscle breakdown. As one who struggled so hard to keep muscle on during endurance training and looking for anything that might help me recover better and stay well, I latched onto that information. I ate a yogurt with my after-session cereal bar and added nuts to the dried fruit. Milk protein is supposed to be one of the best, so my top trick was to put a few spoons of skimmed milk powder (for protein) and Chocolate Nesquik powder (for carbohydrate) into as many empty plastic bottles as I had training sessions that day and throw them in my kit bag. When I finished a session I'd fill one from the cold tap, shake it up and drink it down. I reckoned they were a lot healthier than the bottles of pre-mixed chemicals that otherwise called themselves protein shakes (and very much cheaper). Another small step.

I finished 2003 in Ireland at Shane's wedding. I trained in the hotel gym in the morning and my training diary records '*DANCIN' THE NIGHT AWAY*' as my second session of the day.

January 2004 (7 months to go)

We were back training together on January 2nd and on the 4th we flew back out to Seville. One of my daily goals since Sydney had been to increase my power/stroke and distance/stroke. Since my body refused to build more muscle, I'd been working on getting better hold of the water and using my core strength. One of Paul's favourite sessions was 'Power Strokes' and he'd line us up side by side and have us race anything from 20 strokes to a couple of minutes at fixed rates of 16, 14 or even 12 strokes per minute. The boats were perfectly matched on rate, so the only way to get ahead was to maximise the power and leverage of every stroke. These sessions couldn't be further removed from the high rate racing I was best at and I was consistently beaten. Then suddenly on this camp:-

Wednesday 7th January 2004

1. *Core stability testing*
2. *75'* *2x* *Power Strokes*

   Me *Becs*

   Alex *Elise*

Alex and I even finished up on some!

Depth of hands and swing up

Tuesday 13th January 2004

1. *75'* *2x* *Me & Becs* *Power Strokes*

Won all pieces against Winks & Debs

2. *60' Trunk Strengthening circuit*

I remember that both boats felt amazing. Like I could lay as much work down as I wanted and we just couldn't lose. Flips sake, it was just good to finish in front and be able to come in and smile and be really happy rather than just fake smile and fake happy. If I could do this at the low rates which least favoured my physiology, what could I now do at the top end?

I managed the whole month without a cold and finally my steady state and thirty minute ergos started to consistently shift the right way. But of course, there were always 2k tests…

Saturday 24th January 2004
2k Erg Test
Oops! Third time lucky
6.57.04!

And actually, considering I'd stopped, got off, had to get back on and start again twice to get through it – it wasn't a bad score for me. I think I probably reassured myself that it showed some physical improvement despite not being a PB. It was the first time I'd stopped on an Ergo test since that one back in Putney though. I think you can probably say that despite feeling more positive than I had in ages, I'd still had just about enough.

Not so the great K.G. Back on the ergo for just a few days and not even back in the boat yet, she laid down an ergo just a fraction outside her PB. And this despite the fact that due to the hours spent sweating away on the static bike, she'd lost the best part of a stone. Her power to weight had actually increased in her 'time off'. Unbelievably, far from months out of the boat wrecking her Olympic medal chances, they seemed to have made her an even better athlete.

And finally, one very apt page from my training diary, which this year featured funny, thoughtful or inspirational quotes from famous people at the bottom of the page.

Saturday 31st January 2004

2 x 2k pieces	*1x*
22/24/26	*24/26/28*
V. V. Rough!!	

"If you are going through hell, keep going." (Sir Winston Churchill, 1874-1965, British Prime Minister)

February 2004 (Six months to go)

On 1 February, I gave myself the birthday present of my best ever 16k ergo. An average split of 2.03.4 at a perfectly reasonable UT2-UT1 heart rate.

I remembered an interview I'd heard with Jonathan Edwards before the Sydney Olympics. He was getting PB times for his sprints, lifting heavier weights than ever before and was the lightest he'd ever been. He said he was faster, stronger and lighter and so it was almost inevitable that he would jump further. He'd gone on to win Gold.

I was also lifting bigger weights and I even looked stronger. When I flexed my biceps I could actually see them. In the same week, both Sarah the masseur and Ashleigh the physio commented that I was leaner and more muscled than when they'd last laid hands on me. They sounded impressed. Maybe one of Thommo's many weight training regimes was finally working for me, or being able get more power down in the boat was building more muscle per stroke, or the protein in my homemade milkshake recovery drinks was doing the trick. Despite the extra muscle, I was only about 71 kg – a kilo or more lighter than I had been for a while. I was faster, stronger and lighter and so it was almost inevitable that I'd be able to move a boat faster. I told myself that a lot.

The first weekend of February I raced my last ever long distance trails – about the 20th of my career having never missed one. I'd had a secret goal this year to win a trial having never yet done so. Having come fourth at December trials, I was running out of opportunities. I have two pages of race plan notes in the back of my diary so as not to lose concentration and miss a single stroke of this last 5k (approx. 20 minute) race, but still finished sixth behind Fran, Debs, Becs, Katherine and Alex, although there were only a couple of seconds between Becs and myself. I was ahead of Elise, Sarah and Cath and the gaps were bigger. It wasn't bad, but I didn't win. I never would.

Two days later we were back on a plane and I was off to Seville for the last time. This wasn't just training, it was an assessment camp. We were to run a full doubles matrix between ten of us for the eight pre-qualified seats in the Quad, Pair and Double – nine different 1500m races over three days. We would still race final trials in singles or pairs, but this matrix would determine who would even be eligible to race off for those places. Cath and Katherine did the sculling matrix, even though we all knew the intention was that they would race the pair. As pre-Sydney had shown, there was no knowing how the season would pan out and which boat types would prove to have the best chances of a medal.

I clearly remember the last paddle in my single before getting into a double to start the trial. I felt as confident as I had before any race. I thought I'd found a new, slightly better way to pick up the water. It felt a little strange but seemed to give me more speed on my stroke coach and I felt confident enough to take the gamble and take this straight into racing.

Three days, two nights of racing; living, eating and sleeping with the girls you are competing directly against for places. All races were time trials, so we would have no idea how we'd done against the other boats and no results would be released until all races had been completed. Three days of racing with no objective measure of how you were doing. *Big Brother* and Bush Tucker trials surely have nothing on this.

Three runs on Day 1 – 9am, 12pm and 1.30pm. Three more runs on Day 2 – 9am, 12pm, 1.30pm. I thought I was doing OK but I started to notice that Paul was avoiding my eye, and I got a tight sinking feeling in my chest that I tried to ignore but couldn't really shake. Three more runs on Day 3.

Later that afternoon, I held my nerve as the result print outs were handed round. I still felt confident – had no reason to feel otherwise. I looked up from the bottom of the list and this time found my name far too quickly. In case you were wondering when we'd get there – this point here, what I'm about to describe, *this* was the worst moment in my six and a half years on the team. Except it wasn't a moment. It would be days, weeks even, before I'd pull myself back.

I was ninth out of the ten. Ahead of Bev, but that was it. The margins were not huge, but I'm not sure I even really looked at the totals – all I could see was the number 9 by my name.

Chapter 17: And everything the best I have ever done it

"If you are going through hell, keep going."

Sick and cold, I kept my eyes on the paper. I couldn't bear to look up and catch anyone's eye. I was embarrassed as much as anything. I had finally felt confident. I'd finally felt good and been quite upbeat and chipper over the past few days. It didn't feel like confidence now. It felt like arrogance. For a few seconds I couldn't think at all, then all the implications flooded in. What did this mean? Did this mean I'd blown it – in one trial after all those years? Had my previous results just been luck? Was I really this bad? Had Mike been right all those years? I'd so nearly pulled it off. So nearly managed to get away with it and make it through without anyone finding me out. Did this mean I'd not get a chance at the Quad or even the Double? Would I be left to try and qualify the Single again exactly like four years ago? Had none of anything I'd done in the past four years made any difference? Of one thing I was certain I was not doing the Single again. If I was going to Athens, I was going to get a medal or I wasn't going. So did this mean it was all over?

Paul said he would see us all individually the following evening to talk about the implications of the results. We were to train as usual the following morning but until then we had free time. Twenty-four hours. More than twenty-four hours before he'd talk to me and I'd know if I even had a chance or if I'd blown it.

I went back to the room I was sharing with Fran. Fran had come top. She had a right to be very happy at this point and there were an awkward few moments where I struggled to get sorted so I could leave her alone to be happy. I congratulated her and meant it and she commiserated with me and tried to reassure me, but despite being the best of friends there was no way to make this moment work.

I changed out of kit, grabbed my purse and sunglasses, escaped and started walking. The training centre is a mile or so from the centre of Seville, so that was a good start and then I just kept going, crying behind my sunglasses. I knew the city pretty well by now after so many visits, but found many new streets and kept appearing in familiar places from unfamiliar directions. "Oh, I'm here!" Despite the nine races in my lactate heavy legs, I walked fast and constantly. If I did that, I could just about manage to keep my mind blank. If I slowed down, it started up again… What did this mean? Did this mean I'd blown it – in this one trial after all those years? Had I just been lucky before? Was I really this bad?

I don't know how long I walked for but I quickly became thirsty from race dehydration, and then very, very thirsty but couldn't stop for water. I walked past shop after shop thinking I should go and buy water, but couldn't stop. And actually the being thirsty and the constant search for water and then not buying it became a way to occupy my mind. I didn't know how I was ever going to stop walking because what would happen then? So I just kept walking.

Momentum gives you balance, so the important thing in rough water is always to keep moving.

If you are going through hell, keep going.

Eventually, I was calmer. I could slow and keep my mind blank. Eventually, I was just too exhausted to think any more. I was certainly too exhausted to walk any more so I went into a bar and bought a bottle of lemonade for the liquid and sugar, and then another. Eventually I suppose I must have walked back to the training centre.

The next morning we all got up and put our singles on the water and went rowing. It was the usual chase each other up and down the river steady state session and as usual I was the cannon fodder. I don't think I even tried to hold anyone off. When we came in and were getting our boats out, I didn't have it in me to fake smile and fake happy and visibly stropped and slammed my blades around. "Fuck it, I've had enough! Every flippin' day I have to go out there and be rowed through and beaten up. I'm sick of it. I can't do it, anymore." Elise was closest and looked at me in genuine surprise, "You've never seemed to mind before. You get beaten every day but you always come in happy and chatty. I just thought you didn't care." So now it was my turn to be shocked – stunned actually. I had always assumed that everyone realised I was upset, but that I'd be getting some sort of courageous Brownie points for remaining upbeat and positive. It had never occurred to me, not for a moment, that anyone would take me completely at face value.

My diary is blank. I didn't care enough to fill it in. I do remember we did a strength weights session, but not only couldn't I be bothered – for the first time ever – to try and put the weights up, I couldn't be bothered to even finish the session. For the first time ever I walked out. I sat outside on a mat in the sun and sulked.

After a couple of minutes, Fran followed me out and sat down on the other end of the mat. We both just sat there in the sun and maybe it felt a little better. But I couldn't help indulging in a bout of self-pity. "I can't do this anymore and what's the point anyway?"

"Al, you'll pull it back at final trials, you know you will. You always do. You're amazing."

So now how was I supposed not to cry? "I don't know if I'll even get the chance. Paul might not let me even trial for the Quad now." And we both knew it was true and there was nothing placatory to say about that, so we both just sat a bit longer. Eventually my anxiety at Fran missing her session grew too strong, so I sent her back. "You'll be OK, Al."

The competition was always intense, but there was always at least one of the girls you'd had to fight against on the water that would be there for you when things weren't going your way.

I didn't go back and finish my session though. "Sod it."

Eventually, finally it was time to go and see Paul and hear my fate. It was uncomfortable as I walked in. It's always so easy to talk to someone who has done well, but what do you say to someone who has blatantly failed at something you know they want more than anything else in the world? He started ambiguously enough. "So, Mowbs, I know you'll not be happy with that." And I couldn't hold it in any more. "No, you know I'm just terrified that I've blown it. That I'm not going to be allowed to even trial for the Quad. I'm not interested in anything else. I want a medal and I want to be in a medal boat. I'm not going to just go to the Olympics again. That's not what I've done all this for." It may have been the first I'd talked to him about it. The first time I'd dared even say it and my chances might already be over.

So I guess what you say to someone who has blatantly failed at something you know they want more than anything else in the world is probably something like this, "Mowbs, I'm not going to lie to you, you've not made it easy for yourself. But I've seen what you do at final trials every year. You pull it out of the bag every time when, and only when, you absolutely have to. Maybe this type of racing wasn't it, but the Olympics is. It's not over for you. I still believe you can do it; you can still get into the Quad." Breathe… "But you are really going to have to prove it to me, the others in the boat and to yourself. It's not going to be good enough to come fourth at trials, I need you to beat one of the top three." We both knew he was talking about Fran, Debs and Becs. "I need you to come at least third to get into the Quad."

When I walked out, I was at least temporarily invigorated. It wasn't over. I had been given my chance. It was a weird thing because if you'd told me a week earlier that I'd have to beat Fran, Debs or Becs to get into the Quad, I'd have been gutted, told you there was no chance and that it was all over for me. These three girls, ten years my junior, had consistently been the top three since Sydney, and except in a rather abstract sense, I'd not given much thought to beating them. I'd been having enough trouble fending off Sarah, Elise and Alex. But now, having spent twenty-four hours really thinking that not only my Olympic dreams but my rowing career was over, I celebrated what just a week ago would have filled me with despair.

The bar had been raised on me yet again, but relief, and perhaps the sense that Thommo wouldn't have set me a challenge he didn't feel I could rise to, carried me through the next two or three days. I started writing sessions and comments in my diary again, but then it stops, and for six days the pages are blank. I didn't miss the sessions but I was not actively present. Again and again I just thought: Five more months of this. For what? I can't do it. I just can't do it.

I was at my lowest ebb and unable to find a positive thought in my head. I sneered at my mantras, none of which seemed up to the task in hand. I didn't expect anything, I didn't blame anyone, but I just couldn't do anything, any more.

Perhaps my only other thought was Elise's landing stage comment. It explained something that had been starting to piss me off. When I asked someone how they were and they said "Fine thanks", I could tell when they meant it and when they didn't. So when they didn't, I'd go back in and say "It doesn't sound like it, what's up?" I'm not saying I was then the best at handling what came out. I was never a great listener (I tried to volunteer at The Samaritans when I was at Liverpool but they rejected me from their training because I couldn't help but try and solve people's problems for them), but at least I'd go back in and ask again. However when most people, even close friends, asked me how I was and I said "Fine thanks" meaning "I'm not really, I need you to ask me again and then I'll tell you", they just said "Great" and left it at that, often going on to talk at length about their own problems since I was so fine. I was mystified, pissed off and even upset at their reaction, when I was sending out such obvious signals. I'd started to get rather resentful in a way that disturbingly reminded me of my dad. But it didn't make any sense because I knew my friends were not uncaring people.

Elise's comment began to make sense of this. Firstly, I was obviously way better at hiding things than I had appreciated and had not been giving people a chance. And secondly, I thought maybe people were somehow not tuned in in the same way I was. I was giving out 'upset' signals I would have picked up on in others. Sometimes I thought I was literally screaming "I AM NOT ALRIGHT, I NEED SOME HELP", but for some reason it was not picked up. I didn't yet understand where it came from, but I began to understand that not everyone had the same intuitive sense.

More recently I now also understand that this is yet another common characteristic of children of alcoholics and addicts. Nothing in their world is as it seems, everything is hidden, everyone spends their whole time saying they are all right and everything is perfect when they never are and nothing ever is. Everyone is lying to you. And while everything can change in a moment, there are always warning signs. Children of addicts learn not to take anything at face value and are constantly searching for the signs and indications of what is real and what is about to change, of what is true and what is lies. I will know when you lie to me. I may let you get away with it because I don't want the confrontation, but I will still know you are lying.

So I could tell when my friends were hurting and covering it up and I really did try to show I cared, even though I wasn't quite sure how to do it. I'd called Kate Mac, Lisa and Gail most days for two or three weeks when they were going through similar rowing and/or boy-related tough patches. I'd been frustrated by my inadequacy to *do* anything to make it better for them, until I finally understood that The Samaritans had been right and just the calls were miraculously something in their own right. I could sit here and wait for them to call me, but I finally understood that if I wanted help, if I didn't want to end my days like my dad, bitter and resentful towards all my friends, then I had to actually stop hiding everything and ask for it. That apparently was how normal people made this thing work.

So when we got back from Seville, I picked up the phone to call Mac, and for perhaps the first time in my life in response to "Mowbs! How are you?" – I said, "Not good actually – not fine. Can I come and see you?"

"Of course!" and I think I actually heard the gratitude at being able to help me and give something back. This really was how it worked then.

So I didn't sit on a hill crying behind my sunglasses trying to work out a way to stand up again, I sat on Mac's sofa talking and crying quite openly. "I can't do it anymore. I've had enough." Trained as a police counsellor, Kate knows how to listen, but she'd also been to all the same places and sitting outside of it now had a better perspective. "Mowbs, you can't give up now. It's only five more months to the Olympics, you're nearly there. You've done three and a half years; you can't waste that for five more months!"

"Three and a half years is already wasted, it's the next five months I can't afford to waste as well." I know I've said all the way through that I was living how I wanted to live and medal or no medal it would never be wasted, and it was true – but I was upset, so allow me a little melodrama.

"I don't understand. It's just a few more months."

But I couldn't talk, even to Kate, who I knew was in exactly the same position except four years older, about the real value of five months to a woman in her thirties because it is such a private thing and yet such a position of public ridicule. There is nothing quite so funny or pathetic as a 'desperate' single woman in her thirties. We all know that.

People on the outside think it's all about cooing over prams and withering ovaries, but it's not. If you have any ambition and spirit, there is just so much to fit into that stage of your life that you can't waste a minute. There is so much to do if you want to get it all done. In my head I was already getting on with my life. I had my boots on, my rucksack packed and was on my way to the airport with my Lonely Planet guidebooks. The only half bearable alternative to racing for a medal in Athens that summer was to be camped up somewhere beautiful in the middle of nowhere, miles from the nearest TV or newspaper, pretending it wasn't happening and that I'd never have to go back.

"If I'm not going to even have a chance of a medal, I can't give up the next five months of my life. It's too long and I'm too tired. I can't do it." It didn't matter where we went with the conversation, I always came back to that.

But then eventually, after several more cups of tea and at least a bottle of wine, a realisation. "I can't row for five more months but I don't have to. It's only two months to final trials and if I don't come third, then it's all over anyway. I can't row for five more months but I can row for two. I don't have to decide if I'm good enough or not. I just have to do everything I can, put in all the work, race the race and let someone else decide. Then at least when I'm eighty, I'll not have to look back and wonder if I could have done it." Or something like that that I haven't just made up.

So, two months I could do. I'm not saying I was suddenly better and motivated Mowbray all the time again. I was still very up and down, but I could see a way through and start moving forwards again. But if I was going to do it, I had to do everything so there would never be any regrets. That then, more even than the medal, was the goal.

But for the first time, I didn't think about doing more hours training or pushing myself harder in the hours I did. Paula Radcliffe had shown me I was doing all I could there, perhaps more already than was really useful. I could also look in the mirror and be happy with my commitment to improve my technique (my one consolation during this time was the thought that the 'new' technique I'd used in the matrix was not representative of me at my best), my nutrition, my core stability and flexibility – and even the way I rested, played the piano and managed my downtime. So instead, I looked not at the areas where I was already pushing the limits and more work might conceivably give me the fractions that might take me past Sarah, Elise and Alex, but the neglected areas where a little attention might give me the big steps and seconds worth of speed I needed to beat Fran, Debs or Becs (for the first time in over three years). Where were the gaps? What still was I missing? I came up with three things.

1. **My equipment** – I was sculling in a soft old boat with soft old blades. Stiff new equipment transmits more power straight to the water.
2. **My self-belief** – I thought I'd been doing so well with this, but the impact of getting that one bad result had shocked me. My first thoughts had been that I'd been caught out and that *this* result was the real one. After over fourteen years of continuous physical and technical progression psychologically, I'd been catapulted straight back to being the girl who couldn't make it onto any of the school sports teams and only won because the real athletes went the wrong way.
3. **I didn't have anyone on my side** – I'd had my best trials performances working pretty much one to one with Miles. I didn't have that anymore and several of the other girls did. Paul was my main coach and most of the time I wouldn't have had it any other way, but he was head coach, so around trials it was his job to find the best people not to get the best out of me. He would give me my pre-race pep talk, but I'd know that actually he didn't really care if it was me who made it through and he'd go on to say just the same thing to Sarah and Fran. Not having anyone who was just for me was a definite gap.

Expect nothing, blame no one, do something. What could I do about any of that?

1. My equipment

I'd known for ages I needed a new boat and blades, but the extra effort of sorting it out had taken a backseat to daily training. But when I actually got down to it and *did something* it wasn't so hard. I picked up one of the many *Regatta* magazines that were lying around, found the number for the Concept II blade supplier and gave them a call. ONE phone call and a couple of hundred quid and I had new stiff blades delivered within twenty-four hours.

Getting a new boat was rather trickier. I had to make twice as many calls.

My boats were made by WM which is basically one guy in Switzerland and I'd actually done most of the hard work months ago. Weeks of emails and phone calls had gone unanswered well into the New Year before I finally tracked him down and made him promise to build me a new boat in time for April trials. The boat was now built, but was sitting in his workshop in Switzerland and he seemed even less interested in delivering it and getting his money than he had been in building it. He didn't do deliveries and I didn't have three days off to drive across Europe, so the boat had just sat there and I had fretted and complained about it for weeks but done precisely nothing.

But now I was *doing* stuff so I picked up the phone again. I was starting to get the hang of this asking people for help thing, so I called The GB Rowing Team Boat Men. They are not paid to have anything to do with our singles (which we have to buy ourselves), however I was discovering that people sometimes quite like helping others anyway.

"Mowbray! Good to hear from you. How can we help?"

They couldn't, as anticipated, drive across Europe to pick up my boat, but they gave me a number for Paul Willis who imported boats from an Italian manufacturer. I called Paul and he said he was going over to pick up a load of boats in a couple of weeks. WM was a bit out of his way, but if I bunged him £50 to cover the extra fuel he'd be happy to help.

TWO phone calls and £50 quid and something I'd been putting off and getting me down for months was sorted. I would have felt rather stupid if I hadn't felt quite so pleased with myself.

Doing leads to more doing and more doing leads to a sense of achievement and improves self-confidence.

2. My Self Belief

One of my goals for the 2003/2004 season had been to do some individual work with a sports psychologist, but again I'd put it off because it took time out of the usual day to day grind. And again, I knew if I didn't sort this, it would be something I'd look back on and regret if I didn't get my medal. How could I expect anyone to put me into a medal boat or row with me in a medal boat if I didn't at my core believe I was as capable of it?

Again, help was easily available and I'd practically been pushing it away. Chris Shambrook was paid to work with the rowing team as a sports psychologist. He'd run several team sessions for us over the years and always offered individual sessions, but to my knowledge no one was actually taking him up on the offer. So now I finally gave him a call and he practically bit my hand off for the opportunity. When you are in the middle of it, you think you are bothering people and forget *who* you are and that the people around you would love to support you in achieving your goal. Leading sports psychologists want to work as closely as possible with Olympic athletes to help them achieve Olympic medals. That's what gets *them* up in the morning.

So one day after training, instead of heading straight home to maximise my rest and recovery, I stayed behind for an hour to talk to Chris. Firstly, as it had been with Mac, it was good just to talk. It was good not to have to hold all of this in and be brave all the time. Specifically though, I talked to Chris about how to fundamentally build the core of my self-belief and confidence. He had me do something quite simple – something I use with individuals and groups all the time now to help them do the same thing. He had me write, in a blank page of my training diary, a list of the reasons I had to be confident. The concrete results and achievements that made me who I was and could give me reason to believe that I was firstly a real athlete and then at least a potential Olympic medallist.

Because the biggest and most damaging fallacy in sport and life is that "You are only as good as your last result." It's not true. We are as good as the whole sum of everything we are and everything we have ever done. And it turns out that *this,* exactly *this* is the mindset of people with stable high self-belief – those who are seemingly unfazed by the odd knock and whose confidence rides high in the face of what to most people would be a devastating blow. If we think we are just as good as our last result, then we are setting ourselves up for huge short-term swings in our self-confidence because there will always be short-term swings in our performance.

An ergo score is the sum total of every stroke, not just the score for the last stroke.

CONFIDENCE BANK

1. *Seville power strokes (2x with Alex + Becs)*
2. *Boston trials – ahead of Sarah, Elise. V close to Alex*
3. *Best step test*
4. *Every singles trial I have ever done*

It wasn't a long list to start with. It didn't need to be. I was already thinking straighter. The 'Best step test' refers to the latest physiological assessment. By now it was all high tec. and run at the British Olympic Medical Association labs. We had to do the whole thing wired up to heart rate monitor sensors and in a face mask with tubing attached to a machine that measured our breathing rate and the absolute volume of air we could get into our lungs.

I'd been even grumpier than usual when I turned up for this test. I was still feeling fragile and had good days and bad days. "What really is the point?" I said to myself and probably the poor sports scientists as well. "I already know from my steady state ergos that either my improved technique or physiology means I'm going to record one of my best step tests. You'll measure my skin folds, but I and anyone who sees me already knows I'm leaner. And we all know that despite all of this, I will still record the lowest scores in the squad. I don't need this now. I'm doing the best I can to stay positive and convince myself I have what it takes to do this. I do not need to do something that will tell me, yet again, in black and white that I shouldn't be able to."

But I had to do it anyway. And, surprise surprise, as we sat down to go through the results, it was my best step test. The physiologist (I think it might have been Craig) was happy and happy for me – helping Olympic athletes get their best ever step test in Olympic year is the stuff that gets them out of bed in the mornings – so I don't think he could understand why I was grumpy.

"Because, what is the point?" I said in my most arrogant strop. "I'm still one of the weakest athletes. How is it helping to know that?" And he looked at me with genuine surprise. "Why do you say that? We don't think of you like that? Why would you think that?"

"Because of this," I said pointing to the comparative VO_2 max column, which showed I did indeed have one of the smallest lung capacities on the squad.

"Oh," he said with dawning realisation. "But we don't look at that column. We look at this one." And he pointed to an adjacent column I'd never even looked at before. It was headed VO_2 max/Kg and when I looked down the numbers for the squad, I can't explain the shock and turning of the whole world upon its head that happened in that moment. My VO_2 max/Kg body weight ratio was one of the highest. I think it might even have been *the* highest. I had slightly smaller lungs than most of the other girls and could take in less oxygen per minute, but I also had significantly less body mass (over 10Kg in some cases) that needed to be oxygenated. My ability to take in and transport oxygen around the body and muscles *I actually had,* to operate aerobically rather than generate lactic acid and to re-oxygenate any lactic acid I did produce, even while still rowing flat-out, was scientifically, in black and white, phenomenal. My peak power was not and never would be as good, but that was no longer the whole story. I'm not just psychologically strong and technically good at the end of a race, it turns out I am physiologically and almost freakishly built for endurance.

But it was rather a shock how much of me *didn't* want to hear that information. What has this story been about if not one of someone with little or no natural talent battling through despite the odds? And not just the rowing story. How many times have I told you that I'm not really that intelligent, but I got my school exams, my First-class degree and even my PhD because I worked harder than everyone else? Even now I was hesitant to write about that VO_2 max/kg result because it's not really the story I want to tell you. To find out I actually had any sort of natural advantage feels a bit like cheating.

It's worrying how much we can attach ourselves to an identity and what we pride ourselves on even when it's not helpful to us. I had to work very hard for a long time,and even now, to remind myself that there is not more honour in pulling yourself up from nothing by your boot straps than in fully utilising your natural talents. And it didn't mean I could get away without doing any of the training, it didn't invalidate my effort. I may have been born with big lungs, but my fifteen years of endurance training had also expanded them (my chest circumference had increased by over 6 inches in fifteen years). At this level, natural talent is never enough. THERE IS NO SUCH THING AS AN EASY OLYMPIC MEDAL.

They had not been flukes then, all those successful races. I was not a pretender waiting to be found out. I had a real right to be here competing for an Olympic place and an Olympic medal.

I also wrote my First-class honours and PhD into my confidence bank. They reminded me that it wasn't just my lung capacity I had to rely on. I could always get up and go and do it again and I could always peak and pull it off when it really counted.

Chris was also surprised I'd written so little about team. "I've seen you in crew boats for years and each time you do something to make them go faster. I don't know quite what it is, but it's like you have the x-factor. I wish I could bottle it and give it to other crews." And the world flipped over a second time. I was used to coaches thinking of me and talking about me as a negative force in crews, certainly not a magical x-factor. But Chris had worked with me for nearly seven years. He was not a rower so he was not talking technically, but he was a psychologist, so there must have been something he'd heard and seen in our crew meetings and on-and-off the water dynamics that had led him to form that opinion. It was really important to me because as much as I wanted to secure a place in the Quad, I only wanted it if I really was the best person for that seat in every sense. So 'being the x-factor' went in my bank too and it was probably about that time that I realised I'd also filled the third and final gap. I was the only one of the girls using Chris for individual sessions so I was likely the only one getting this sort of help and feedback. Chris therefore was the person I had on my side.

I worked with Chris over the course of three or four more sessions. I talked about how hard it was to get beaten all the time in training and still believe I could beat the same girls at trials. And he just asked, "How do you think the other girls feel when they have to race you?" And I swear, from my self-centred, pity-me position I'd never thought about it that way round. "Oh my God! It must be really hard. They must know by now that it doesn't matter how many times they beat me in training, on the ergo or even in a matrix, in a side-by-side race I can still beat them. Even if they are ahead all the way, if I'm anywhere near them with 500m to go, they must know I'm going to go through them. I've been doing it for years. *They* must look at *me* on the start line and be worried!" Chris just nodded rather smugly.

I went back to look at the seat racing results again and actually with the benefit of perspective, they were not that bad. I was, as always, a consistent performer and there was nothing shocking about any of my rows. It's just that a second behind here and half a second behind there starts to add up. I had a great row with Debs to come second just behind a Houghton/Grainger combo and finished second in a Bishop/Mowbray combination ahead of Laverick/Grainger in one of my best rows of the three days – who'd have predicted that? If you'd looked at just two of those races, you'd have definitely wanted me for your crew.

I had more reasons to be confident than I had ever realised and I knew I needed to use it more – needed to project it more. I needed to be the one psyching others out come trials and I needed my eventual crew to be able to take confidence from me, not the other way round. It didn't feel natural to bound around declaring how good I was, so we worked on how else I could do it. It turned out that the old trick of standing tall, pulling my shoulders back and sticking out my chest was enough. I definitely felt different.

That was what happened in the twenty-nine days of February. It was a good job 2004 was a leap year.

March 2004 (5 months to go)

March was so cold that Dorney Lake froze and we moved our boats to the running water of Henley for a while. It's funny when the lake freezes because you always crane for a first glimpse of the water as you drive in and it's exciting to see it looking glass smooth. Then you think it's odd how the trees are moving but the water is not. *Then* you realise it's frozen.

We dream of flat water, but row in all weathers and go out in all waters. The first thing you are aware of as you wake up is what it sounds like outside. Can you hear the wind? Is there rain lashing against the window pain? Then you pull back a curtain to take a look.

In rowing we say that, "The weather you get is the weather you want." So when it's raining you say, "Great, I love rowing in the rain, it's like wearing blinkers and it really focuses me", and on windy days – "Great, I love rowing in rough water, its fun and I'm better at it than anyone else. Besides, it's going to be rough in Sydney/Athens." On race days you look for the flags down at the course and if they indicate a tail wind you say, "Great, that's really good for me as a lighter athlete." And if they indicated a head wind you say, "Awesome, I love a good head wind, I can keep my rating higher than the other girls. I have the advantage." If it's a crosswind, you just don't look any more and ignore it as you would someone at a party you really don't want to speak to.

I found cold very difficult though. I'd get hot and sweaty from working hard, then sit and freeze each time the coaches stopped us to talk. Dexterity and grip is all important so you can't wear big padded gloves like other winter sports. Many people row with bare hands all winter, but I wore thin black cotton gloves which I bought for £5 a pair from M&S. Even so, my fingers alternately froze, then screamed as the blood flow came back. My feet were even worse. I'd squeeze a couple of pairs of socks inside the fixed shoes but it was never enough, especially if it was also raining and they got wet. My toes froze solid every single winter outing.

Second outings were worse. We'd come in, shower to try and warm up, pile all our dry clothes on, then sit in the kitchen drinking tea and eating porridge, shivering and watching the clock tick by – wondering if we were going to warm up in time to take our layers off and go back out there and do it all again.

But of course, I'd rather have gone through any number of hours of that than get on an ergo for seven minutes.

My last ever ergo test.

I really, really wanted to beat 6.56.6 and get a PB. Perhaps even hit the 6.54.9 that I'd set as my goal for the year. My diary says my prep had been good, but when I turned up that morning my head was not in a good place and I couldn't make it go anywhere more useful. Take all the sickening nerves I felt before every race and about quadruple it. If anything, the environment in which I had to do this had got even worse over the years. We used to book individual time slots, but now we lined up in waves of five or six athletes and set off together. The up-and-coming rowing girls did their test at the same time. They were getting bigger and taller every year and arrived with bigger and better ergo scores as recruitment and development got more and more specific. They couldn't touch me on the water but most, if not all, of them would be quicker and finish before me on an ergo. I arrived that morning to all the shouting, sweat and adrenalin of a previous wave, and had to sit down on a practice ergo to do my warm-up while I listened to another.

Mostly by this point after the Seville races I was managing to stay positive, but still the challenge ahead of me to make the Quad was huge and daunting. There were a few things I just wasn't strong enough to cope with and this turned out to be one of them. I sat down on the test ergo alongside five other girls, all of whom I knew would finish between ten and thirty seconds before me even if I pulled a PB. I almost made it to halfway, but as soon as it really started to hurt, as soon as I really had to struggle to keep the average score down to something that would scrape me, yet again, just under seven minutes my will started to fade. "What really, truly was the point?" And then without any real conscious thought, I stopped. The second you stop it's an amazing relief and then the very next second it's horrific, because you know the only options are to go through it all again or walk away for ever.

If you are going through hell, keep going.

I quickly got off the ergo and out of the way so as not to distract the other athletes, but I was truly distraught – panic-stricken really. It was Seville results day all over again and just like Seville I had to get out. I jumped in the car, drove the couple of miles into Marlow and parked up. Marlow is on the way home but I couldn't make it any further. This was a big moment. If I went home it was all over, no more medal, no more Olympics, no more rowing.

I walked into the park and sat on a bench. I think I called Mac and maybe even a couple of other friends, but no one picked up. Eventually I called Mum. "Mum, I can't do the last ergo test. It's all too much. I'm sat in the park. I'm not going back. I'm giving up. I'm not going to the Olympics. You'll have to sell your tickets."

"Well if you really think that's the right thing to do, then I'm sure you are right. It doesn't matter to me you know. I couldn't be any more proud of you anyway. I only want it because I know it means so much to you." It was the right thing to say in a situation when there are no right things to say. I imagine I may even have heard her start to get the flapjack-making kit out.

I don't really know what we talked about, but (just like The Samaritans training had said) it was good to have someone on the end of the phone.

Eventually I calmed down a bit and called Paul. I knew all the ergo tests would have finished, but he'd still be there. "I'm sat in the park. I'm not coming back. I'm giving up." I can't really remember what he said, but he didn't try and talk me out of it. But when I put the phone down, I thought again and the final turnaround thought was this. "Is this really going to be what ends it? An ergo test? How stupid is that. I know I row faster than I ergo. Am I really going to give in and let an ergo test decide my fate?" So, I called Paul again. "Stay there. I'm coming back."

I got back on, warmed up again and all on my own, with just Paul watching – which would have been much my preference anyway – I started again.

Saturday 20th March 2004
2K ERGO TEST
6.57.6 Av. Split 1.44.4 R33

It wasn't my goal of 6.54.9, it wasn't even a PB, but I finished, got under seven minutes and was allowed to go on to compete at final trials in an actual boat. Paul would not stop teasing me, "I'm sat in the park. I'm not coming back!" I'm nothing if not a drama queen in a good crisis.

My new boat was delivered just in time to take to Varese for our pre-trials training camp. I gave Paul Willis his £50. It didn't seem nearly enough for the massive difference it made to me and my Olympic chances, but what was? I thought about bunging him an extra £50 but it almost seemed an insult and I couldn't afford any more, so I made him a tin of my Mum's flapjack and chocolate biscuit cake. He seemed much more pleased with that than the money. He emailed me to say it was the best he had ever tasted and I should be selling it because you couldn't get anything like it in the shops.

The first time I raced a side-by-side flat-out 500m piece in that new boat and put all my gradually acquired new connection and power through my suddenly acquired stiff new boat and blades, I absolutely flew. In the first ten strokes, I all but shocked myself to a standstill with the increase in bite and power (I can still feel it now) and got out in front. When I was still level at 250m and still well in contention at 500, I think maybe I wasn't the only one to be surprised. Through the line I was second only to sprint queen Debs, a whole second faster than Becs, two seconds faster than Fran and Elise and three seconds ahead of Sarah. Whole seconds, not just fractions of seconds. I was now actually good at getting started. I could now win low rate power strokes *and* flat-out power sprints from a standing start. So many demons conquered. The whole world turning on its head.

'500M piece in Varese' went into my growing confidence bank. I also added very good 2k, 1000m and 1500m pieces from that camp, consistently getting myself above Elise and Sarah, if not Fran, Debs and Becs. There's no record of Alex in any of these races, who I assume was ill or injured.

I rated 39/35.5/37.5 for that 500m piece. I was back up practising the high ratings. Finding things to put in my confidence bank had made me reflect on some of my best ever races and I thought it was odd and rather frustrating that despite all my technical and physical improvements, my best ever result was probably my first Nottingham trials. I knew those same performances would not be good enough now – everyone had moved on, the whole world had moved on – but still they had been something special. They were the first and only times I'd hit those high rates. Since people had told me they weren't possible, I'd not been up there again.

I wondered if it was possible to row with that same pure belief. I set myself the goal of racing final trials at 36/34/35/36+ and told myself often that no matter what anyone else said or did, I'd done it once and I could do it again.

But it wasn't just the new boat and blades. I was sculling really and consistently beautifully. Paul came and found me one evening, "Look at this Mowbs", and showed me maybe just a minute worth of video of me in my single that afternoon. I remember it looked very casual really – a pleasant scull on a sunny day on a beautiful lake in Italy. No skin-tight racing Lycra; I was just wearing rowing shorts, a loose singlet top and a cap, but I was tanned, lean and lightly ripped. I looked like an athlete. I sculled along steady state – long, loose, relaxed, perfect. The blades buried in minimal frames while I was still tucked up on front stops having wasted nothing of my leg drive. It didn't matter which frame you stopped on, it still looked… well… perfect. And then, at a call from Paul, I kicked into a full-rate burst and nothing but the rate and the speed of the boat changed. I was still long, loose, relaxed. My shoulders were down and finally, finally even my face remained relaxed with no more sign of the characteristic Mowbray grin that was really a grimace.

There was actually nothing more for Paul to say except – "Scull like that at trials Mowbs and you'll do alright."

It wasn't just my single that was going well. Trials were important, but less than five months away from the Olympics, we spent a lot of time in crew boats that camp so they'd be ready to go when we were finally selected. Twice I got to row in a quad with Fran, Debs and Becs and it just flew. It was without doubt the fastest and most beautiful boat I had ever rowed in. I gained more confidence that I deserved to be there.

And finally I had a secret advantage that I was keeping all to myself. I always bought copies of *New Scientist* and *Scientific American* at the airport to keep up with a bit of science. On the way out to the Varese camp, I found an article written by a physiologist who was also a keen amateur runner. He described running in a marathon where he'd thought he'd used up everything and then something happened (I can't remember what) and he found he could keep going and finish the race. He went on to explain the evolutionary physiology of this apparently common phenomenon.

As human beings, we are actually perfectly adapted for running all day. Before horses, range rovers and guns, it's how we used to hunt our prey. Believe it or not, we can run down pretty much any animal. We won't necessarily beat them in a sprint, but if we track them and keép going and keep going and don't let the animal stop to rest or eat or drink, eventually the animal will fall down exhausted while we are still running. But this is only half the story. What happens if after running all day to catch dinner, when you are walking slowly home completely and utterly spent, you yourself are chased by a lion and you have to sprint to get up the nearest tree? Those that could do it survived, those that could not were eaten by lions (this is the usual oversimplified view of evolution, but you get the point).

So we have an evolutionary lion-defence reserve tank of energy our brains hold us back from using. No matter how hard we try and how much we think we have pushed ourselves, we cannot make ourselves access it unless we are actually chased by a lion (or a metaphorical lion). Reading this article, I remembered that Commonwealth trial at the Docks when I'd raced flat-out to 1,500m, only to find it was a 1,750m race and still gone on to hold my lead and win. I'd been completely and utterly spent and then within one stroke, when I discovered I had to go on, I found I could. And I thought that even Catherine and I speed-hiking Goat's Hut Pass against the clock with panic setting in was it. It's hard to use this knowledge because the whole point is that if you have any idea that you have further to go, your brain will hold onto your reserves. However, I thought that just knowing I had a spare tank, no matter how spent I felt, must be useful to me somehow. This then was my secret advantage.

In order to see if I could force myself to access it, I made a plan to move my whole race forwards by 250m, just like I had unconsciously done in that docks race. I would do my 1,000m lift at 750m and my last 500m flat-out sprint between 1,250 and 1,750, and hope that if I told myself all the way down I was only racing to 1,750m, my body and brain would be fooled enough to really bottom out and open up the reserve tank for the last 250. I didn't try it in Varese because I was saving this advantage for trials, and anyway, you can't trick your brain and body too often. They are smarter than you think. Sometimes smart might just beat fast.

April 2004 (4 months to go)

We travelled back to the UK and did our final preparation on the now defrosted Dorney Lake. Trials were to be on April 13th and 14th in Belgium.

Thursday 8th April 2004

SORE THROAT – missed the 1000m pieces

1. *6k paddle*
2. *Lizzie class – 75 mins*

I drank lots of fluid, rested and tried not to worry. But if I was ill and missed the trial it was over for me after the Seville results, so it was hard not to be a little concerned.

Friday 9th April 2004

1. *10k paddle + bursts*
   V. good bursts
   – contracted glutes all the time. Helped time the connection and drive.

This was a good day. I remember Paul caught me at the end of the last lap and said "Mowbs! – that was very nearly quite good" – which from Paul was really quite something.

Ros's mum volunteered to drive both of us and Bev to Hazewinkle, Belgium for the trials and come along as a supporter. We were halfway to the port before she clapped a hand to her mouth in horror. "I've forgotten my passport!" There was a moment of panic. There was not time to fetch the passport and make the ferry. "Never mind" she said, "I'll play the batty white-haired old lady and they'll let me through." Ros's mum is indeed very white-haired, but not in the least batty. I wasn't convinced that even if she pulled it off, port controls worked like that, but since we had no alternative we kept our fingers crossed and kept driving. When we got to the ferry we handed over our passports and from Mrs Carslake, "Oh officer, I'm such an idiot. I completely forgot that I even needed a passport. And I have to get these girls to their Olympic trials. I don't know what they'll do if we can't get on the ferry. I will have ruined their chances of going to the Olympics. I'm such a terrible clutz." They waved her through.

We had a short paddle that evening and a couple more the next day to stretch out after the long drive and then it was time. I walked round holding my head high and my shoulders back and it did make a difference to how I felt. All those thousands of tiny steps and hundreds of technical improvements were now focused into four last points. BACK, LEAVE IT, SQUEEZE and PUSH. Get my BACK right over from the finish, blades in quick, then LEAVE IT and let the water take them, SQUEEZE with the legs rather than jump on the catch, PUSH with my core to make a solid finish, then straight BACK over again. If I got those things right, then everything came right. I wrote those four words in black marker pen on the metal frame of the wing rigger of my new boat (positioned just above my feet), so they'd be the last thing I'd see as I took off to race.

The first challenge was to make the final. There were the seven of us, plus two up-and-comers Annie Vernon and Helen Austin, who were allowed to race the singles trial even though no one really expected them to be a serious challenge at this stage. Seven of us and only six places for the final meant that the seeding for the semis was more important than usual. One semi was going to be tougher than the other. The results of the time trial would decide who went in which semi, based on the FISA rules.

Ranking	Semi No.	
1	1	
2		2
3		2
4	1	
5	1	
6		2
7		2

I raced an OK but not stunning 1,900m time trial at 10am on April 13th.

1.	Fran	7.18.22
2.	Becs	7.21.46
3.	Winks	7.21.68
4.	Mowbs	7.22.80
5.	Elise	7.23.89
6.	Debs	7.24.90
7.	Alex	7.27.15

Crucially and luckily I was fourth, which put me into the favoured semi. I ate at the course, then had about an hour back in the hotel to take an alternate hot and ice-cold recovery shower and rest in preparation for the semi at 15:12. By some perhaps rather sadistic twist, Sarah and I (undoubtedly the closest rivals for that last Quad place) had been allocated to share a room. We were both utterly pleasant to each other, but I think we could both have done without having to manage that dynamic on top of everything else. Sarah was in the shower when Paul rang. "Mowbs, I've got the line-up for the semis", and innocent as anything he said, "Tell Sarah she's in Semi 1 with Fran, Elise, Annie and Helen. You're in Semi 2 with Debs, Becs, and Alex."

"How do you work that out? I thought 1 and 4 were supposed to be in the same semi."

"Mowbs, that's how it is. Get used to it."

I put the phone down. So that's really how it is. Paul had switched Sarah and I round to favour Sarah. Despite all his positive talk to me over the past few weeks, he wanted to give Sarah the best possible chance, even if it meant breaking the rules. I was right to think that when push came to shove he wouldn't be on my side, but I'd been wrong to think that as head coach he would remain impartial. Again, it wasn't Sarah's fault, but this was an almost Spraklenesque move. The only thing I couldn't figure was how David Tanner had allowed it. He was usually a stickler for the rules. That was his job.

But as Paul said – this was how it was and I'd better get used to it. Expect nothing, blame no one, do something. Don't ever expect the easy ride, don't waste time and energy blaming anyone, do something instead. I decided to take it on the chin as my due for having messed up the Seville matrix. I quickly turned it round in my head and told myself that I had to beat Alex at some point anyway, and if I was going to be fast enough to beat either Debs or Becs (Fran was flying), I should be able to beat her quite easily without it taking too much out of me for the final. Plus, Miles had always said it was a good thing physiologically to stretch yourself in a good hard race in a heat or semi, as it made you race better not worse in a final. And, on top of all that, the final was not until tomorrow. If I couldn't race two races in two days, what had all this training been for? Throw it at me then. See if I care.

I told Sarah as neutrally as possible and she received it as neutrally as possible – both of us pretending this was all perfectly to be expected. I had my shower and as I got out the phone rang again. It was Paul. "Mowbs, there's been a change of plan. You and Sarah are to swap semis."

"Oh really?" I said innocently. "Why's that?" I knew full well why that.

Paul had been trying to sneak this off under David's nose, but David had seen and wasn't having any of it.

"It doesn't matter. That's how it is."

So I had to tell Sarah and I saw her take a deep breath, then turn it round in her head too, "OK then." I'm the hero of my own story, but I'm not trying to pretend I'm the only one or that it is the only story.

I was second to Fran in my semi, beating Elise. Sarah was third to Debs and Becs in hers, beating Alex (perhaps not fully recovered from whatever had been ailing her in Varese) by a good margin.

So now we were six. That was the Quad and the Double right there already, but I don't remember even registering that I'd just moved past having to try and qualify the Single again. It was top boat Quad or bust for all of us.

Wednesday 14th April 2004

FINAL

6.00am	*bus*
6.30-7.00	*pre-paddle*
7.30	*Visualisation & loo*
7.45	*by boat*
8.00	*on water*
8.30am	*race*

To be honest I don't really remember much of what happened before I got on the water. I will have set my alarm for 4.30am so as to be up for four hours before the race, but I can't imagine I needed my alarm to wake me up. You can imagine Sarah and I getting up and getting ready in the same room.

I can't remember much of that morning but when I think of it now I feel a deep sense of calm, like the morning of my university finals. The calm that comes from knowing that no matter what happens; you have done everything, absolutely everything you can and there can never be any regrets. And actually a large part of me just wanted it all to be over. If I wasn't fast enough then so be it. At least it would all be over.

I watched my 'perfect' Varese sculling on the screen of Paul's camera and then a visualisation was always the most fixed and critical part of my routine. I visualised my way down the race making all the moves 250m early and stopped the visualisation at 1750m to try and convince myself that was the end of the race today. Then, mind, body and breath in perfect balance, I interacted with people as little as possible so as to maintain the state I knew would let me access 'it' as soon as I hit the water. The only mental picture I have before I got in the boat is of walking in front of the lake and making a conscious effort to lift my head, pull my shoulders back and stand tall. I was ready.

I put my boat on the water. Paul pushed me out, "Have a good one."

"See you later" and I started the mental countdown. "Thirty-seven minutes and no matter what happens, at least it will all be over." I did my warm-up and got onto the start with about six minutes to go and just… waited…

"Fourteen minutes and no matter what happens at least it will all be over."

And I know I said it's not true that you are only as good as your last race but that's just what you have to remember for yourself, for your confidence bank and self-esteem. At some point, whatever we do, we always face a final trial and in final trials other people *will* judge us on just that last race and we *will* have to accept that the verdict determines the direction of the next part of our lives – but only the direction.

Lane 1 – Elise; Lane 2 – Becs; Lanes 3 and 4 – Fran and Debs (winners of the semis); Lane 5 – me; Lane 6 – Sarah. Sarah on my right, everyone else on my left. We were called forward to row, buried our blades and used the power of prayer to keep our boats straight. My last ever final trials. My last ever race in a single. Everything for the last time and everything the best that I have ever done it. Third or bust. BACK, LEAVE IT, SQUEEZE & PUSH.

ATTENTION… GO!

My new start in my new boat kept me in contention in the first 250m. For the first time I'd not left myself a mountain to climb in the second half of the race. I settled onto 36 and kept pushing it up there all the way to the 500m mark.

500m – Up & In, LEAVE IT. I settled onto 34 and let the boat run out. With only 250m of this to recover I had to maximise relax and flow. My time to 500m is the only one missing from all the splits on the official results sheet, so somehow there is no record of my best ever first 500. With no times recorded I can't be sure, but I have an image of Elise dropping back on my far left, Becs, Fran and Debs slowly moving ahead on my left, and being side by side, stroke for stroke with Sarah on my right.

750m – Up 1. 25 strokes. LIFT OFF. SQUEEZE. I mentally gritted my teeth, physically relaxed and bringing my 1,000m push forward, lifted the rate back up to 35. At some point in that lifted 500m I went through Sarah. And then well through her to clear water. By 1,250m, I was fourth.

1250m – MY last 500. 60 strokes. I started counting them down in tens (plus one for luck), lifting the rate each time. 36+. *PUSH*. Becs was several lanes across to my left and difficult to see, but at some point, I can't be sure when, I was aware she was back in sight. I lifted again for MY last 20 strokes, trying to believe it, trying to leave nothing and totally empty the tank. Into MY last ten and the only concession I'd made with myself for this not really being the real end was that I didn't go into my usual shortened, fit as many strokes in as you can, boat jumping out of the water, leg annihilating wind. But still I pushed on and I can't really be sure at what point it happened, but it did happen and quite quickly once it started. I went through Becs and was third.

All that remained was to stay there.

I finished *my* last 500m, then passed the 250m to go marker and started again. I lengthened out, relaxed and called in my head – *30 STROKES, 10 STROKES GO!* And it was there. I could keep going. Sarah and Becs were not coming back on me. They didn't know I'd wound early. They would still be expecting the Mowbray big finish – how could they ever expect to catch me now? Into the last 20 and Debs was back in sight.

Into the last 10 and I jammed the blades in and went for my final wind. The boat jumped and kicked its way in the last 10 like the big guys jump an ergo across the room when they sprint. I was taking chunks out of lactic acid queen Debs. I took nearly three seconds out of her in the last 500m and nearly four out of Fran. After all that, it was *still* there. I got nearly half a length overlap on Debs, but didn't pass her. Becs came back on me a bit in the last few strokes but it didn't matter. I crossed the line just over a second ahead of Becs and nearly two lengths ahead of Sarah.

I was third. Whole seconds, not just fractions of seconds.

It's like magic, this goal-setting thing.

Sometimes when you've put so much into something and it finally pays off, all you feel is relief and really rather deflated. This was nothing like that.

I was completely exhilarated. Yes at coming third and securing myself a place in the Quad but more, much more, than that. This was that same primal joy of that first race in Manchester when I had no idea how I was going to do it, but did it anyway.

Fourteen and a half years after getting into a boat for the first time and rowing still had the power to surprise and delight me. I *was* my own ongoing science experiment to see what else my body might be capable of – to find the things it would do for me. "Oh my God! My body will do THAT?" Because the glorious thing about rowing is that sometimes if you hang on in there long enough and hard enough, smart might just beat fast.

And finally, more than that, much more than any of that – to feel that perfect connection each and every stroke, the water accept the blades, the contraction of your glutes and core against the water like there is nothing in-between, the ripple of muscles firing and relaxing, the sensitive stability, the float and run, the relaxed tension. To be so at one with this little sliver of a boat that it feels more part of you than something to fall out of. To so lose yourself that there is nothing in the world but this feeling, nothing but this race. To feel that. To feel that for even just a few minutes. This is what you do it for, for this, for this feeling. To race the best race you have ever raced and row the best you have ever rowed exactly when you need it most. To have that for the rest of your life. This then is payback for everything that has gone before.

A clay pot will always be a clay pot while it sits in the sun. It has to go through the white heat of a furnace to become porcelain.

I sat there on the water breathing heavily and exalting in it. We shouted congratulations to each other across the water. Then Sarah called across, "Well done, Al. My legs were shot though after racing Alex yesterday." And I felt the first small cold hand of fear cut through the euphoria – a sickening feeling of inevitability. This then was the story Sarah was telling herself. If this was the story she told when she got off the water or if anyone else – Paul in particular – already thought this, then everything could change. I quickly reassured myself that I was safe. Thank goodness I'd beaten Becs – who was in effect now a buffer. If Paul wanted Sarah instead of me, then he'd have to race Becs as well and risk her seat on another trial. I couldn't see him wanting to do that. It made me a little sad though. Was I going to have to race another Olympics with a behind the scenes whispering campaign over the right I had to my seat?

My doubts lasted no more than a few seconds. I WAS NOT thinking like that. I could not think like that. I didn't have the strength. The trials were over. Now, finally, I got to focus on the Olympics. I pushed the bad thoughts away and was happy again.

I de-rigged and loaded my boat. I pulled my phone out of my bags and already there were congratulatory texts waiting from friends following the results on the British Rowing web page. One from Kate Mac. "Two months ago, crying on my sofa saying you were going to give up. What are you like? I told you so!" As I wandered up to watch the last of the racing, Paul pulled up in the car he was using to follow racing. I ducked my head towards the open window to talk.

"I did it! I came third!"

"Yeah, well done Mowbs." His words were positive, but his tone was strained and he avoided my eyes and looked away as quickly as possible. I remember it exactly because again the fear caught me. I didn't need any sensitive intuition to pick up that all was not well here. He wasn't pleased. Why not? Why couldn't he look at me? As he drove away I felt for the first time that even though he'd said in Seville I could turn it round at trials by beating one of the top three, he may never have actually believed I could do it. I thought, "He doesn't actually want to select me and now my result is going to cause him problems." The same sickening feeling of inevitability. But again I pushed it down. I couldn't think like that. I'd spent the last two months aiming for this point; all that had kept me going was that no matter what happened it would all be over. I'd crossed the line and my head had come out of the trials tunnel. I was celebrating now. There was no going back to racing, it was too late. I pushed the feeling down and made it go away. I was happy again.

We packed up and Ros's mum drove us back to the ferry, blagging her way back across without a passport. Seriously, she should be a drug runner or something. Ros and Bev had been beaten by the Cath and Katherine pair in their trial, which effectively ended their Olympic dreams, so I tried to keep a lid on my excitement. I'm not sure how well I managed it though and bless them, they were both so sweet.

I got home, picked up a second bag that was packed and ready, jumped in the car, drove to the station and just made the train I was booked on to go to Edinburgh to see my brother's family. We had two days off in a row which hardly ever happened, so I hardly ever got to see them as Edinburgh is not a one-day trip. I'd raced at 8.30am in Belgium and by late afternoon I was on a train heading up to Edinburgh – slick work.

I was that weird combination of exhausted and hyper that doesn't really let you rest and friends were still calling and texting. A few hours in and I settled down and started to doze. My phone rang again and it was Thommo.

"Yeah, well done again Mowbs. I'm calling to talk about what happens next."

"What happens next?" A query of his statement, not a question.

"Yes, so Fran is in and you, Debs, Becs and Sarah will seat race in doubles on Tuesday."

"No, no, no, no, no. What seat racing? You said if I came third at trials, that was it. That was the Quad."

"I never said that."

"You did, in Seville. That's what you said. That's what I've been aiming for and that's what I've done. You can't change your mind now."

"I've not changed my mind. There was always going to be seat racing."

"No, there wasn't. There can't be. I'm on a train to Edinburgh. I'm going to be sleeping on my brother's floor for two nights. I wouldn't be doing this if I'd known there was going to be seat racing. I'd have stayed at home to rest and train. You know I would."

"Mowbs, there was always going to be seat racing. We start training again on Saturday and you'll race on Tuesday. That's how it is."

I sat there and perhaps only you who have read the story of the past two months can know how I felt in that moment. I tried to play back my conversation with Paul in Seville to see if I'd misinterpreted. And then I remembered the gut feel I'd had from the exchange in the car after trials and it all fell into place. That's why he'd not been able to look at me – embarrassment and guilt. I think he'd known he was going to go back on what he'd said to me in Seville. He hadn't planned any seat racing because he'd assumed I'd come fourth or fifth, and either way he'd be covered to take Sarah after my Seville result. It was perfectly reasonable that there should be seat racing in Olympic year, I accepted that, but I was sure it had not been planned and that I was right not to have expected it. Paul was a meticulous planner and we always got our training programmes and dates in advance. Every other year we'd had dates reserved in our diaries for possible seat racing if it was needed, but not this year. If he'd planned seat racing, we would have known about it. My brother's wedding was written into our training programme for God's sake, I don't think he just neglected to inform us about a set of Olympic trials. I really think Paul had not expected this and I had forced his hand.

It had happened again. I was so furious I couldn't let it go, not this time. I was violently in denial. No trials were going to happen. I wasn't worried because it wasn't worth worrying about. I called Paul back. "You can't spring more trials on us like this, it can't happen." But of course there was no backing down and after a few more minutes of to and fro (frustratingly interrupted by several signal cut-offs and call backs) I finally had to accept – there were going to be more trials. There are always more trials. It is never over.

So I switched tack. Now I just wanted him to admit why he was doing this. I was still absolutely furious. "There's no way you planned this. Just admit it. Would we be racing if I'd come fifth and Sarah had come third? Would *I* be getting another chance if *I'd* had to go through the other semi? You didn't believe I'd do, it did you?"

"Alison, it's perfectly reasonable that you should have to seat race for a crew boat. The other girls are all having to race and no one else is making such a fuss. I'm not arguing with you anymore."

"I just want you to admit that you didn't plan this until I pulled it off at trials."

"I'm not going to admit that because it's not true. You can come to the trial or you cannot, it's up to you, but that's the only way into the Quad."

I don't really know what happened next. I think I was still angry and spitting, rather than defeated and crumpled. And you know only as I write this have I realised something. I stood up for myself. I believed I deserved my place. I created a scene. I'm quite proud of that.

But eventually I ran out of anger fuel and I did crumple. I couldn't do it. I couldn't get my head back into the trials tunnel and do it all again. I was completely and utterly spent.

But I sat a bit longer until very gradually, I found I could. I thought I'd used the lion-defence reserve tank but apparently not. Or maybe there is yet another reserve tank that physiologists haven't discovered yet. "Fuck it!" I'd beaten Sarah at every other trial for years apart from Seville, I could do it again. And maybe it was a good job. After what happened at Sydney, I didn't want any doubt, any rumours, anyone to think I'd had an easy ride, anyone to think it wasn't fair. If anyone thought that Sarah had been disadvantaged even a little bit by her semi, then let me put them straight once and for all. I've always believed that at the end of the day you can't talk your way into a boat, so sometimes you just have to stop talking and show what you can do on the water. That hadn't been the case with Mike but it still was here. I might be made to do trial after trial, but at least they would be fair trials. A tiny, tiny voice said, "But what if this is one trial too many, you push your luck too far and this is the one Sarah beats you on?" But it was only a tiny voice and the voice that said, "Line 'em up. It doesn't matter how many times you make me race. Seville was the anomaly, the other results, those are the real ones" was much stronger. My self-belief had moved on as much as my boat speed in the last two months.

I thought about getting off at the next stop, turning round and going home but I didn't. I needed my break and there was still time. I completed my journey and had a lovely relaxing day and a bit playing with Nell, my one and a bit year-old niece, going on gentle walks and eating a lot. My only concession was to book into a B & B to get a proper bed. By the weekend I was back at Dorney and training again. It's a mark of the anxiety that everyone feels about the regression of fitness over an extended trials period that we did a full session of weights on Saturday and a 16k ergo on Sunday (although I don't suppose I pushed either very hard). On Monday we rowed 3 x 6k in each of the three possible doubles combinations for racing the following day. This was not to be the same as Seville though. This was side-by-side seat racing, not a matrix. This was much more me. We wouldn't know which combinations would go out in advance and there would only be as many races as was necessary to get the results they needed. Everyone has to think that they might be raced to ensure they push to their max in every row, but I don't think anyone really thought that Debs would face a seat race. She'd done enough already but we needed her to make up the numbers. I had a strong hunch that Sarah and I would be raced first and if Sarah beat me that would be the end of the races, but I'm not sure where that feeling came from (that was sarcasm by the way, in case you missed it).

Tuesday 20th April 2004

SEAT RACING 1500m free rate – running start

1. (Stroke) Debs — Becs

(Bow) Me — Sarah

When Sarah and I were put into the bow seats of the two doubles, it pretty much confirmed that we were to be raced first – but of course you can never be sure. Debs and I had an OK but lacklustre start and Becs and Sarah got ahead. Maybe I was struggling to get my head back in the tunnel. Approaching halfway, Becs and Sarah were nearly a length up although they never broke clear. Then I think Debs and I must both have thought at once that it was just not going to happen this way. I probably called a push, but all I really remember is that within one stroke something changed. I dug in and Debs dug in, but it wasn't just that we applied more power – our blades connected with the water in a whole new way and suddenly, even though we were nearly a length down, I knew there was no way we were going to lose. And I know I keep on about it, but these truly are the moments you live for in rowing. I can picture exactly where we were on the lake and still feel the difference in my hands. It's like the timing is so perfect, the blades fold themselves into the water. You have never worked so hard and yet it has never felt so easy. I've had it in a single and it's wonderful, but when you both get it at the same time in a double, the effect is multiplied a ridiculous number of times. When Debs and I got it, our boat picked up and flew and this race turned from a trial into just so much fun.

We slid through the Becs and Sarah double like a proverbial hot knife through butter and my diary records that we *won by about 1 length.*

Unsurprisingly, Sarah and I swapped places for the second leg of the seat race and we rowed back to the start of the course.

2. *(Stroke) Becs* *Debs*
   (Bow) me *Sarah*

There was really no doubt by this point that Sarah and I were being raced, but it remains fair because this race might form the first leg of the next seat race, so everyone still has to pull for their own sake and not just for ours. How it works is that Sarah would have to make her double with Debs go more than a length faster than Becs and I to prove that she could move a boat faster than me. We lined up level and were set off again. This time we were pretty much side by side, stroke for stroke the whole way down the four-five minute race. The two boats finished…

Exactly level.

Nothing is ever said while you are still in the middle of racing, but it was more than clear that I had beaten Sarah in our seat race by at least a length. As I predicted, racing was therefore not over. We sat on the grass and waited for a decision on the next combination.

But then Becs said she was feeling ill and, after a brief discussion between the coaches, racing was postponed until further notice. We were all to go home and await further instructions. It was a real pain but couldn't be helped. I was relieved to at least have won my most crucial race, but also still worried. It seemed almost inevitable that after all that had already happened Paul would use Becs's illness to declare the seat race invalid, and Sarah and I would have to race again at a later date. I went home with a feeling of fatalism that Paul would find reasons to keep racing Sarah and I until she beat me, at which point *that* would be declared the fair trial.

I sat on the sofa at home that afternoon, looking at my mobile on the table, waiting to hear what would happen next. My head still in the tunnel. I completely assumed there would be more racing at some point and I was just waiting to hear what and when. Then the phone rang and it was Sarah. "Hi Alison, I'm just calling to say congratulations."

"What? I don't understand. Congratulations for what?"

"For getting into the Quad."

"I'm in? How am I in? How do you know?"

"Paul's just called to tell me."

I was confused and disbelieving. There was so much interference in my head not daring to believe it was true that I couldn't think what to say in proper response to Sarah's very gracious call. After I put the phone down, I sat there in shock looking at my phone and waiting for it to call again. Not making the mistake of taking my head out into celebration, not again. I actually have no idea whether Paul called me or I gave up and called him, but when we spoke he confirmed that I'd been selected into the Quad. Sarah and Elise would race the Double. I called Sarah back to apologise for being so useless when she called me and thank her (which was such a difficult call). So in the end, after everything we'd been through, it was Sarah who called to congratulate me even before Paul got round to telling me. Like I say, I'm really not trying to pretend I'm the only hero or mine is the only story.

At the bottom of that rather full April 20th 2004 page in my diary records:

!SELECTED INTO QUAD! (Subject to continuing performance etc. etc – until Poznan)

Becs – Stroke

Fran

Debs

Me

The tough bits always make the best stories. The trick is to remember that before you see the cows.

Chapter 18: Awesome girls

"The starting point of all achievement is desire."

After nearly four years of work I was in exactly the boat I wanted to be in, with exactly the girls I wanted to be in it with. The four of us put our boat on the water at Longridge the day after the seat races and rowed our first 20k/100-minute session as the selected Quad. I'd been in quads for four years and straightaway this one felt different. The boat balanced and flowed and for the first time in a very long, while I felt truly comfortable in a crew.

We sat at the picnic bench after the session with Paul and Mark Banks (who were to be our two coaches) and set our goals towards Athens. And I think it was Fran (who had won trials and could have rowed in pretty much any boat she wanted) who spoke first, "I want to win Gold, I want to be an Olympic Champion and the reason I'm in this boat with this crew is that I think this is the boat and this is the crew that can make it happen."

Fran has crept into this story and didn't get as much of an introduction as some others. I'd like to put that right. If Debs is perma-puppy, then Fran is whatever the opposite of that is. There is something about being a tall child and especially a tall girl that shapes you I think. People always assume you are older than you are so you are fast-forwarded through your childhood, held responsible for your peers, assumed to be the most confident and made to be the leader. This develops qualities that are culturally less valued in girls and grown women than in boys and grown men, so as a tall girl the adults in your world create a curious tension. I was always 3-4 inches taller than my peers and I'm sure it shaped me. Fran was 6 inches to a foot taller than hers.

Fran's rowing story is very different from my own. Her school had a boat club and she was great at it. She was one of the cool kids on the school team; it meant her height was something to be envied and I think it helped her in the way I thought it might have helped me if I'd had it. When she was sixteen, an ex-pupil who was training with the GB team and aiming to get to the Sydney Olympics, spoke at their boat club dinner. Fran was inspired. She took her dinner menu and wrote on it, "I am going to do everything I can to get to Sydney", signed it and then made her friend sign it as witness. You perhaps have to have worked with kids and even adults to know just how unusual that statement is and so how unusual a kid Fran was. When you ask most kids and even most adults what they aspire to, what their dream is, they will tell you, "I want to go to the Olympics", "I want to be a Premiership Footballer", "I want to be a pop star", "I want to get promoted", "I want to retire at fifty".

Fran is the only sixteen-year-old I've ever heard already know the difference between what you can and what you can't control, and to understand that that is how dreams become reality. "I'm going to *do* everything I can." The guy who spoke at Fran's dinner never made it to the Olympics, but Fran celebrated her twentieth birthday the day she raced her B final in the Double at Sydney. I'm ten years older than Fran, but I think it's just taken me at least ten years longer to get everywhere. I cannot even imagine where she will be and what she will be doing by the time she is forty, but it makes me sort of envious just to think about it.

So Fran made her statement and we all sat back and took a breath. Certainly for me, who'd just spent the best part of four years aiming for a medal, any medal, and had not even realised that yet – talk of Gold was a new prospect and took a little getting my head around.

But then I think we just thought, "Why not? Fran is right. What else are we going to aim for over the next few months?" And buoyed by our outing and Fran's confidence, I signed up. We all signed up. But we didn't actually know how we were going to make it happen. There was still no model for this in the GB women's team, no heritage of Olympic Gold medallists to follow and pace ourselves against. If we made it, we would be the first (assuming the Pair hadn't pipped us to it the day before). So we sat there, talked about what we'd learnt from being in crews the past few years and made our own rules. I got out our 2003 crew diary and we read through it, so we could learn from and build on what had gone before. In the end, above all, we resolved to "Train like Olympic Champions and behave like Olympic Champions and see if we can make it happen." And I bought a new crew diary because having good stationary makes everything official.

But ours wasn't the only contract. There had been open animosity between Paul and Mark over the years, including at one point a rather unfortunate text about Paul that Mark had meant to send to someone else but had somehow arrived in Paul's inbox. So when Paul and Mark said that they would be co-coaching us, they added that they had already talked it through and agreed to behave themselves. Apparently, it's not just athletes who should remember that it pays to be careful what you say to and about everyone. You never know when you might end up on the same team.

And as for Paul and I? I'd felt some resentment over the trials, but had let it go pretty quickly. I was sculling faster and better than I had ever done in my life. I'd made a jump in performance that had needed to happen but I'd never known was there. Paul had been a crucial part of making that happen whatever his methods and motives. Besides he wouldn't be the first coach to lose sight of me behind Sarah's statuesque potential; I couldn't blame him for that. I'd lost myself there enough times.

We got back in the boat and started training – three sessions a day most days now. It had taken nearly four years to get this boat selected and we had just sixteen days between our first outing and our first International Regatta. Almost no one I talk to realises that this is how it works.

It felt so different though this year and it wasn't just the rowing. My selection letter arrived with its usual proviso, but for the first time those words didn't keep me awake at night and I didn't carry them with me into the boat. For the first time I felt that instead of fighting against each other for a ranking in case one of us was dropped, we were fighting together to be a crew that no one would want to split up. Final trials and seat racing may have been a furnace of tension, but I had truly been transformed. I had no doubts this year about the legitimacy of my position and knew no one else could have either. I never had had any doubts about Fran, Debs and Becs in any capacity. Here finally, I could talk without check and balance, say what I wanted and be an idiot sometimes, and when they laughed it was because I amused them and they liked me for it (and vice versa because I don't think I was the only one who had been shut down). Also, this was it – everything for the last time. There would be no more trials and no more getting back into singles to race these girls again next year. I had everything to gain by making them go as fast as possible and nothing to lose.

I'd hate to give the impression that it was all plain sailing as soon as we formed our Quad though. We might have made our contract about the big important things, but it's often the little things that trip you up, and times and timings seem to cause as much friction as just about anything else in life. Rowers guard against this by using a carefully devised and relatively simple system (relative to the solar system). Rowing involves so many people, so much equipment and takes so long to get going that you actually need several start times to work out which part of the process you are talking about. It's pretty straightforward when you get the hang of it, but in case you are not a rower and feel inspired to take up rowing after reading this book, here is all you really need to know.

At the boathouse (ATB). An ATB time tells you what time you should rock up at the boathouse. It's OK to still have sleep in your eyes and be half-dressed, but it's wise to have had at least some breakfast. An ATB time assumes that everyone will get themselves to the boathouse; if this is not the case, then an earlier 'at the bus' (not abbreviated to avoid confusion with ATB) will need to be quoted. Control freak coaches may set an even earlier 'Wake up' time, but rowers who can't get themselves up usually deselect themselves at an early stage so this is rarely used except for crucial races.

Hands on. If a 'hands on' time is quoted, you are expected to get yourself to the boathouse, dressed, warmed up, carry your blade or blades down to the water and be by the boat opposite your rigger by the stated time. In a crew boat there will usually be a crew chat at this point where the coach will let you know how hard they intend to work you and whether you can hope to get back before dark. Then someone (the cox if you have one) will call "Hands On" and everyone puts their hands on the boat and picks it up. This will usually be fifteen-twenty minutes later than an ATB start time, but if a hands on time is stated, it is rare to also give an ATB time as people decide for themselves how long they need to get ready. Rowing is an empowering sport.

On the water (OTW). This is most usually used for club or squad training sessions. If an OTW time is given, it is up to the individuals or individual crews to decide what time they need to be ATB and 'hands on' to be ready OTW to meet all the other scullers/crews to start the training session. An OTW time is usually twenty to thirty minutes after an ATB time and about ten minutes after hands on.

Start Time. For pieces, racing and private matches. If a Start Time is given, it is up to scullers and crews to decide on their ATB, hands on and OTW times in order to give themselves time for a proper race warm-up. A crew will usually give themselves twenty-five to thirty minutes from being OTW to being on the start.

That's it. So if you've got all that, then you are good to go.

It is perfectly acceptable when a time is stated to ask for clarification as to whether that is 'At the Boathouse', 'Hands on' or 'On the water'. In fact, it's practically another rule that someone has to ask. Usually the same person always asks and everyone else rolls their eyes, as in 'Not again', but then enough heated debate almost always ensues to make it clear that it really had not been clear and it was a good job that someone had asked for clarification.

This system generally works very well. Rowers are a pretty disciplined bunch and rarely late. However, the problem with being an old hand is that you start to get rather fixed in your ways, make all sorts of assumptions and stop checking. That's generally when the problems start.

I've been keen to point out that my story is not the only story and my view is not the only view. With this next section, I'd like you to scrap all that and remember that in this I was definitely right all the way through and there is no other version of the truth.

As we parted that first morning Paul called out: "See you at quarter to eight tomorrow morning." And because we were all old hands and knew the ropes, no one felt it necessary to ask for clarification. I was the oldest hand down there (having trained at Longridge in the Mike days) so I knew that quarter to eight had always meant ATB for 'Hands on' at 8am. It had meant this the previous year when I'd rowed with Fran, Sarah and Elise, so I don't know where the problem suddenly came from.

We moved our boat to the 2k course at Dorney in preparation for the first World Cup. Fran came from London and would usually arrive a bit early to avoid the traffic and because she liked to stretch a lot. Debs came from Henley and Becs and I both came from Lane End. Becs and I would sometimes be a few minutes later than 7.45 if we got stuck behind traffic as we are both night owls, hate getting up early and refused to set our alarms a minute earlier than necessary. Anyway, there didn't seem any point as I'd always done this and there had never been a problem before.

Straightaway though, this year it was different. Whatever time the last one of us wandered into the gym, Fran would be twitching and stand up and start to hustle us out and down to the boat. The first couple of mornings I asked "What's the hurry?", but Fran brushed it off and wasn't talking. I could tell she was angry and her attitude annoyed me. After just a few days, this one thing started to polarise our happy Quad every morning. Finally, over a week later (half of our sixteen days), it all came to a head. Becs and I got held up in traffic and both rushed into the gym just after eight. Fran was rigid with rage. As we pushed off for our outing, we saw Sarah and Elise in their double going round for their second lap already. I said, "Wow, they're out early."

"No they're not," Fran retorted. "They were here at 7.30 and on the water at quarter to eight." Then it all finally came together in my head and as we got off the water, I finally said, "Fran, what time do you think we are supposed to be on the water?"

"Quarter to eight! Quarter to eight!"

So finally, finally, when we came in that morning, we had a proper conversation about start times and worked it out. And there were no more arguments not being had every morning and I was totally over it and let it go – as you can surely tell.

It's not by accident that ex-rowers end up being pretty successful at whatever they end up doing next in life. It's because they are some of the very few people in the world who've already worked out that there are always at least three start times for everything and you'd better make sure you are all talking about the same one. Approximately 80% of world conflict could be avoided by people not pissing each other off by being late (or some such figure I've not just made up).

May 2004 (3 months to go)

The boat was moving very well considering we'd had so little time together. My diary also shows that my 16-18k ergo splits were still coming down, I was getting new PB's more often than not and getting very close to the 2.02 target I'd set myself at the start of the year.

In early May we travelled out to the first World Cup in Poznan, Poland. Gillian Lindsey was over as part of the BBC commentary team and while we were down at the course, she stopped to chat and congratulate me on my trials result, "Third! Well done! That's a bit of a result for you isn't it?" And I was just about to agree with her and be my usual self-effacing, self-deprecating self, when my new self-belief kicked in just in time for me to remember… "No, not really, I was second last year."

"Oh!"

Why does no one ever remember? Why is it always a surprise when I do well? I'd been doing well at trials since my Bedford days and still everyone is always surprised. But then so am I aren't I? I finally realised that people forgot because I let them. If you walk around telling people you are not very good and recede into the background, you can hardly be pissed off if people believe you and leave you there. Everyone has their own lives to lead, their own self-belief demons to battle and precious little time and energy to pander to yours as well. We do not have the right to expect other people to have more faith in us than we have in ourselves. So if I'm good, I'm putting it out there. It's not arrogance, it's common sense. Those who push themselves forward get on. Those who don't, get bitter.

It was a small field with no World Champion Aussies or Olympic Champion Germans to test ourselves against. But you can only race who turns up. We had a really good row and…

WE WON! WE WON! WE WON!

1. GBR
2. DEN
3. CHN
4. NED

This was my seventh season on the team and my FIRST EVER INTERNATIONAL WIN. If anything else was needed to bind us as a crew, this was it. We were unreservedly, unashamedly, childishly, happy. We jumped around and hugged each other as we got off the water (in fact we tried to do it on the water but it is a little tricky), got to stand in the centre spot while they put the (at least Gold-coloured) medals round our necks and were the media centre of attention for the few moments that anyone is ever interested in you if you are a rower – even if you win.

It had not been possible to book flights back that night, so the four of us would get an evening together to celebrate before we went home. We had a day and a half out of the boat and I was determined to really enjoy the next thirty-six hours and celebrate what we had already achieved before thinking about the next step. What if one of us fell over and broke something? Or Becs's back went again? Or any one of us got ill? I swear – by this point, if you could wrap each other up in cotton wool and live in those germ-free bubble rooms, you'd do it. Guin used to say that for two months before a Worlds or Olympics she wouldn't even breathe in a lift if there was anyone else in there. We all washed our hands more like surgeons than sportsmen and held the handrail when we walked downstairs. And even if we all stayed healthy, did everything we could over the next three months and raced the race of our lives in Athens, we could still get beaten. I was all too aware that this could be it, our one moment together, my one win in seven years.

Besides I reckon a bit of celebration doesn't do any harm and is vastly underrated. Coaches can be very quick to jump on you as soon as you get out of the boat from a good race and talk about "the importance of not being complacent." People are OBSESSED with this 'not getting complacent' thing, so that on top of all the worry about whether you are fast enough, you also have to worry about whether you are worried enough about whether you are fast enough. And if you are not worried enough that really is cause for concern. But at the end of the day, what is the point of any of this if it doesn't make you happy? And I think it makes you go faster too. Just because I'm smiling doesn't mean I'm not deadly serious. It's all part of the strategy.

So as we got on the team bus to the hotel I was enjoying the moment, but I was a little careful as not everyone had done as well as they'd hoped. Sarah and Elise had come fifth in their Double, which was actually less disappointing than it sounds as the first three doubles across the line had all been from Germany. We would obviously have to face a quad selected from some of that talent eventually, but in the meantime Sarah and Elise's loss had effectively been our gain. In the Men's team the Four had won, but the Silver medal-winning Eight from last year's Worlds had come fifth in a small field. Despite their obvious disappointment, they were lovely and congratulated me and asked about our race as I had done for them the year before.

I got separated from my crew as we got off the bus, so ended up catching the lift up to my room by myself. The lift doors had nearly closed when they pinged open again and there were Cath and Katherine. I think we all just froze for a moment before we collected ourselves and they came in. I had my warning radar up. It was encounters like these that I tried my best to avoid these days, but Katherine was lovely as usual. "Hey Al! Well done! That was awesome."

"I know! Thank you! You know that's my first ever World Cup win. My first win at all since I got on the squad! I'm very happy and excited."

"I know," said Cath, no mistaking her tone, "I think the whole bus got that."

And even in the moment, I hated that I let her do it to me – but my happiness just drained away. I stopped feeling the warm glow of being on a bus talking with friends who were helping me celebrate and all I could hear was my own voice inappropriately loud and overexcited being humoured by teammates who were too nice to be rude. I could hear and see my father's daughter and that one line activated pretty much all my insecurities. How did she know how to do that? Every time. And I didn't doubt why she had felt the need to do it. Their Pair had come second to the Romanians. A close second and an amazing race considering Katherine had been out all winter, but still we'd got the win and all the attention that went with it.

It all went very quiet. Eventually, finally, the lift stopped and they got out and I carried on for one more floor. I was sharing with Debs and let myself in. "I've just been Bished!"

"Oh no Al! How? You were only gone five minutes."

"I got trapped in the lift."

"Oh Al!" – laughing because I had been drama queening it up for her amusement. But then I sat down on a bed and got serious for a moment. "Debs, you've got to tell me the truth. Was I over the top on the bus? Did I piss everyone off?"

"No Al, no. You were fine. You were really fine. You mustn't let her do that."

"I know, I know. I just had to check."

We got changed and went and found Becs and Fran and had dinner and a couple of drinks together in the bar. I felt better with the comfort blanket of my crew, but still it had gone, the carefree joy had gone. I got maybe a couple of hours of my thirty-six.

We were back to training on Tuesday with just fourteen days to prepare before we flew out to the second World Cup in turquoise Munich. Now was the time to think about how to step up and we sat down and analysed the video and split times before we even got back on the water. There is so much to do between recovering from one World Cup and winding down for the next. Long, steady endurance sessions and short, intense power-building sessions in the boat, on the ergo and in the gym, analysis of racing and training video, meetings about goals and progress, core stability work, stretching, massage, physio, unpacking, washing, sleeping, eating, paying bills, general life admin, repacking and the occasional friend or family birthday or wedding (because people will insist on continuing with their lives even in an Olympic year).

We'd spend forty-five minutes or so at a time (when we were too knackered to do anything else) in the slack water behind the island at Longridge, perfecting roll-up exercises to help us achieve perfect synchronicity and balance while the boat was all but stationary. We could work for half an hour or so and never take a stroke. Momentum gives you balance so it's important in rough water to keep moving, but as any practitioner of yoga or Buddhism will tell you, the real art of perfect balance is in being able to stay absolutely still. Think about the cycling analogy again. Billions of people can ride a bike, but only the really top riders, those totally at one with their bikes, can balance and stay on while going nowhere at all. And the tightrope analogy too – if it wobbles you want to run to the other side, but how much more skilful to stand still in the middle and regain your balance. And if you can balance when stationary, then how rock solid will you be when you up the pace – and how much more stable now when the going gets rough, than all those who spend all their time going fast?

So it is in rowing (and life obviously). The roll-up exercises break rowing down into its simplest constituent elements so you can practice each bit and get it right, and get it right together. We'd all sit at 'back stops' with our blade handles up into our ribs and the spoons square and buried in the water – the boat stationary. Then we'd just sit, and sit, and sit until we felt there was no tension in the boat, no one was leaning and no one was holding on and we'd all found our own centre, our own balance. And then one of us (we'd take it in turns) would call "Ready… Go" and on the "Go", we'd tap our hands straight down – nothing more. If the caller had felt it right and we all moved exactly together to exactly the same point – the boat would still balance in this new position with the blades out of the water. And it had to feel and even sound just right or it was not acceptable and we'd all call "Yes" or "No", because the important thing was that we all learnt to feel it the same.

I learnt, from those hours of sitting still, how to hold myself without holding on. A relaxed feeling in my lower back, all my vertebrae stacking one on top of each other. On the in breath I'd imagine the vertebrae moving apart, elongating and separating, and on the out breath I let the muscles relax and flow down my back. In… and out…, in… and out…, deep diaphragm breaths into the pit of my stomach (French horn training) until my back was holding itself up, my shoulders were down and heavy in their sockets, and my hands were loose and heavy on the handles. A position of minimum energy.

When we were happy with that we'd move on to 'Hands away', then 'Bodies Over', 'Quarter', 'Half' and 'Full-slide' (all with four possible variations of square or feathered blades, above or into the water). Any roll-up to blades into the water also has a whole new element of making sure the catch feels and sounds just right too. The sound we were aiming for was a sharp "CHCK" (like you make by expelling air sharply with your tongue behind your teeth) and you can only get this if your hands have been right down in the boat and you lift the handles from your big powerful lat muscles. If you try and put (or place as it's sometimes called) the blades into the water using your arms and hands, it will be slow and you won't be rewarded by the noise. And you want the noise because when you get the "CHCK" together as one, you feel it immediately – the water sucks itself onto the blade which is now loaded and primed and almost moving itself through the water.

Quarter-slide is the critical 'Row like the Romanians' position. It's traditional to talk about and think about the 'back stop' position of the stroke as the 'finish', but this is an unstable place to stop. The natural 'finish' of the stroke is about quarter slide (actually little more than an inch or so up the slide). If you arrive here right and stay relaxed then you can balance your single or crew boat pretty much indefinitely whether the boat is moving or not. The Romanian Rhythm we were looking for is one continuous flow out to quarter, then a tiny moment of pause while we all came together and waited for the boat, before we'd glide up the rest of the slide under more control. As you get further and further up the slide, the blade angles get closer and closer to the boat and you lose more and more of your tightrope counterbalance pole. If you lose your nerve and throw your balance at anything more than about half-slide, then there is nothing to save you and I've occasionally seen whole quads or even eights roll straight over practising these roll-ups. We never rolled our quad but I've certainly rolled my single practising this.

After twenty-thirty minutes, when we'd been through every roll-up position and felt like the boat was rock solid and had got just the right noise at the catch, we'd allow ourselves to take one stroke. We'd do the full roll-up to the 'CHCK' then pause again, eight blades braced against the water but waiting, holding our relaxed balance here in this the most difficult and dangerous of positions. Then on a second "Go" from the caller we'd push on all eight blades together straight back to the quarter slide 'finish' position and glide, like that, balanced with the blades off the water pretty much indefinitely. It's easy to think you are pushing together when you are rowing along stroke after stroke, but doing just one from stationary highlighted all the little discrepancies and the boat would let us know by twitching and sometimes very nearly rolling over. Eventually we'd take two or maybe three strokes at a time, then scull back continuous rowing feeling for every position together – Romanian rhythm. Always and reliably the most beautiful sculling we'd ever done.

I might have gone a little crazy if I'd only thought about rowing and thought about it in this depth, but I still had the piano. Having learnt *Clair de Lune* I'd worked though Synding's *Rustle of Spring* in the same way, bar by bar, and had now started on Chopin's *Raindrop Prelude*. I'd learnt the first page of both pieces in my teenage years and then given up on them. Every time I play 'Rustle of Spring', I can still hear my piano teacher laughing at me and my first attempt at hammering up and down its scales and arpeggios all those years ago. "That's more like a hurricane than a rustle!" I was rather put out at the time, but got her point. I started thinking about the music and practised touching the keys as lightly as I could to still get a note. So now as I practised I kept the first arpeggios rumbling and earthy as the hidden activity of the bulbs and seeds germinating underground, and then I think you can hear in the music (and even see it on the page) when the shoots are growing up and up towards the light, so I'd gradually increase the pressure and volume and try and play with the same sense of direction and anticipation. And finally there is a definite moment when the shoots burst up into the light one after another and grow taller and taller and uncurl into flower.

Pianists call that interpretation and touch. Rowers might call it piano feel. It's amazing what you can practise when you think you are practising something else.

And there was one more thing to fit into those two weeks between Poznan and Munich (because otherwise I would obviously have got bored). I went into London for a training day on marking Year 9 Science SATS papers and then a couple of days later, well over a thousand of them were delivered to my door. Even in the years I was teaching, a lot of my classes stopped over the summer because the kids were on home study/revision time and I had less work to do and less income because I was paid on supply. So to balance this, I'd been marking SATS papers every summer since 2002. I could mark the papers and earn money from home, but what really sold it was that sometimes, it was just really funny (much, much funnier than even a very amusing day on the river). About twenty papers into my first ever batch, I was marking a question on human reproduction and again there was that cross-sectional diagram of male parts that my Year 7s had so screamed at. One of the questions was:

Q: Sperm are released in a sugary solution. What is the sugar for?

As most of the kids knew, the sperm have a long way to swim so need the sugar to give them energy to help complete the journey. But one bright spark thirteen-year-old lad had written:

A: To make it taste nice for the woman.

I had to mark it wrong (for more reasons than one), but it made me laugh. I texted the question and answer to the rest of my crew (Winks, KG and Elise that year) and it made them laugh too. After that it was the highlight of my day and a good bit of crew bonding to text these off-the-wall answers on any topic (not just sex) to my crew over the next three summers.

At the end of every page I'd add up the marks per page and then do some rapid mental addition as I flicked through the pages totting up their final score. I got very quick at adding up numbers between one and twelve in my head. It was in the contract though that every paper had to be checked, preferably by a second person. Most other markers used their partners or children, but I just had teammates, so two or three mornings a week I'd bring down a stack of marked papers and a tin of flapjack as payment and during our morning break, various girls would pick up a batch of papers, check the addition and find any errors. There were always some willing volunteers and it was a bizarrely fun thing to do together. Sarah and Katherine were my best and most enthusiastic checkers even in the years when we weren't in the same crew. Sarah in particular is lightning fast at mental arithmetic. I think it helped us all to have something else to think about.

We raced some excellent final pieces producing percentages comparable with the M4- (the Men's lead boat containing Matt Pinsent) and our World Champion W2- and my diary records our "*Best steady state yet – Really lovely*". And then it was time to head off to the second World Cup in Munich. Here we faced a fuller field; there were eight quads including a German Quad containing their top scullers from the Poznan Doubles. There was still no sign of Boron in any boat.

The morning of our first heat (Thursday 27th May), I came down to breakfast sick with nerves as usual but tried to eat something and not look too wretched. Unusually we were in single rooms so I don't think any of us had even missed Fran, until one of the coaches came across to tell us she was sick with some stomach bug, maybe food poisoning, and would not be racing today, if at all this weekend.

Emergency plans swung into action. The medical staff rushed to Fran's aid to see if there was any way they could make her better in time for any of the races and Sarah was requisitioned to double up into the Quad as well as the Double. World Cup racing is rather condensed, so Sarah was going to have to race at least twice every day for the next three days. In our first race, we were drawn into the same heat as the Germans. It was a good row but my diary records that the *"Germans beat us quite comfortably"*.

We had to race a Rep on Friday to qualify for the final. We wanted to win it and did, but it was very close.

> *Video analysis* *More hand speed*
> *Leave it out there*
> *TOMORROW* *REALLY EXAGGERATE*

Sarah was doing a great job of juggling both boats and seemed to be quite enjoying it. It was the media story of the weekend and she was the hero of the hour jumping from one to another (if you think I sound a little envious, you are probably right, but I was trying not to be). It was a different story for us in the Quad. I'd filled my hand luggage with as many SATS papers as I could carry and sat and marked, occupying my time and mind AND earning money in the dead time. When any of the rest of the squad (women or men) needed a distraction, they'd come and check them for me.

The Saturday finals were very close together. The Double's final was first and Elise and Sarah had an awesome row to take Silver. They were well beaten by New Zealand's formidable Evers-Swindell sisters, but they BEAT a German double by a second and a half. Sarah then jumped straight into the Quad from their medal ceremony as we rowed up to the start.

We raced and came second by a couple of lengths – 7.99 seconds behind the Germans. My diary records – *"Good race, good row but pesky Germans too far away. Good pushing on to 1,000m though."* A decisive defeat and you could waste hours and go crazy trying to figure out the Sarah v Fran factor to work out how close our complete Quad might be to that German Quad – so we tried not to do that.

But we did know we'd just beaten three more crews we'd likely face at the Olympics, including Belarus (Silver medallists from 2003), even without Fran. Potentially there was only Australia (current World Champions) to add to that mix. We were looking good for an Olympic medal of some colour. Shame then that we'd decided some colours weren't good enough anymore.

June 2004 (2 months to go)

We flew home, had a day off and then there were sixteen days left before the flight to Lucerne for the final World Cup. I don't think anyone had anticipated Fran's stomach bug being quite so severe and she was out of the boat for seven of those sixteen days. The rest of us spent more time than we would have liked in the gym and borrowed Sarah or one of the spare Lightweight men to get out on the water occasionally. Still, as soon as we did get Fran back, we had a great row and I had two of my best consecutive days – perhaps ever.

On the Monday I got a new PB for my thirty-minute anaerobic threshold ergo and on Tuesday I got a new PB for the 18K steady state ergo, hitting both of the targets I'd set myself at the start of the year.

The lactates recorded in my diary were low indicating that they were not even particularly painful sessions. I've just been looking through some old notes and found a record sheet for a 30 minute ergo dated 6/11/01 where I averaged 2.03.2. I could now average 2.02 for my 18K, faster than three years ago for well over twice the distance and time. At thirty-three, I was still getting better and faster and even enjoying it again. It was all coming together at just the right time.

But no one was complacent (heaven forbid). There was a lot to do in the eight days left to us before we went to Lucerne. Paul sat us down in front of the Munich race video and we watched the first few strokes off the start several times in slow motion. We knew Sarah was in for Fran and we'd not really practised starts together, but still it was blatantly obvious that what we were doing would not do. We started with the traditional two ¾ length drawn strokes to get the boat up and moving and while we were at it, the Germans set off with five short wind strokes to our two and took the best part of half a length out of us. We obviously had to get more strokes in.

We took our boat to the straight measured course at Dorney and spent a whole session experimenting with just the first 100m off the start pontoons. Paul and Mark timed us, then we'd spin the boat, row back up and do it again trying something different. By the end of the session, we thought we'd found something punchier and faster.

We also had another technical break through that week. We were knackered so had taken ourselves away onto the river behind the Dorney course. There was no coach with us, so after we'd worked our way to full slide roll-ups and taken our single strokes, we were experimenting a bit. One of us, I think it might have been Fran, said, "What if we did two roll-ups one after each other?"

"You mean two strokes?"

"No, two roll-ups."

"OK?" We'd never tried this before so had no idea what would happen. "Fran you call it."

"OK… Backstops… Two full roll-ups to blades in the water… Ready… Go…" – one full perfect roll-up to blades in the water, 'CHCK' and wait. "Go…" – push off together and squeeze one perfectly balanced stroke, then keep going past the quarter-slide position into the second full roll-up, lats up, blades in the water, 'CHCK', then…

"Wow! What happened there?"

"I don't know, I'm not sure, I couldn't stop my blades in the water."

"Me neither, the handles just came back at me and I couldn't stop them I thought we were going to fall in!"

"It was like the stroke took itself."

"It *was* like the stroke took itself."

"I think the stroke *did* take itself."

"Let's try it again, and this time don't stop the blades, just put them in and see what happens."

"OK. Don't take the stroke though, just put them in and leave them there."

And we did it again and this time we didn't fight the blades, we just held onto them lightly and let them take their own path – and without doing anything, the blade handles shot back towards our bodies and the spoons through the water. We tried it again a couple of times, then sat on the water and talked about it and this is what we worked out. When you put the catch in clean and right, the momentum of the boat moves the blades through the water without you having to do anything. The blades move that fast and powerfully off the momentum of one single stroke in a slow moving boat, so it's going to be a lot faster when the boat is skimming along rate 18 and impossibly fast at race pace. At race pace, the blades will start moving themselves through the water faster than you can ever grab hold of them and move them yourself. Therefore any work you do trying to get hold of the water at the catch and accelerate the blade is wasted. Worse than that, if you take hold of the handles too early, your work will actually get in the way and slow the blades down.

Those of you who row might be thinking that you know all this – that you know to leave the blades out there and have patience at the catch. We thought we knew this too. There was about thirty-five years of rowing experience in our boat, a lot of it to the highest possible level, but the extent of this was new to us all. We'd been told not to jump on the catch, but we didn't really understand why until we felt what we felt that day. Our coaches had told us to be patient at the catch, but I think perhaps they were just saying it because their coaches had told them and it was accepted practice – I'm not sure they had ever felt this before either.

We were excited and went into another standard rowing exercise that we'd all been doing since we started rowing, but perhaps hadn't really known what we were doing it for. We put the blades into the water and let the handles drift through and then just pushed the last quarter of the stroke. Then drift for half – push for half, drift for quarter – push for three quarters. We'd always done this and it does make the boat run better, but now, because we knew why we were doing it, we took it a stage further and caught the boat earlier and earlier until we thought we'd found the exact point after the free speed, but before the handles started to decelerate. Picking the boat up in that fraction of a moment when it was ready to be moved on. Not following anyone, not even Becs at stroke, but each individually feeling the boat and finding it and using that to bring us together.

Once we found this new thing, we gripped the water in a whole new way and felt the boat lift out of the water and run on. It was a revelation. I thought "Oh my God. This is *it*. This is what *it's* supposed to feel like. What have I been doing all these years?" But I was reassured because this was a revelation for all of us. If Becs, Fran and Debs had never found this before, then I thought there couldn't be many people in the world who knew this even existed. And we had to concentrate really hard at first to keep hold of it and sometimes it would disappear for a while and we'd have to start right back over, but by the time we went to Lucerne we not only had our obviously new start, but this tiny almost imperceptible thing that gave us at least as much.

A week before Lucerne Regatta proper, Alex Beever flew out to try and qualify the Single for the Olympics in the 'last chance regatta'. I've looked for Alex's results in the previous two World Cups but she wasn't there, so I can only assume she was ill or injured after trials and this was her first race back. I remember being convinced she would qualify. I thought if I'd qualified four years ago, then Alex could do it as she was at least as fast. It was a close run thing but she didn't make it and after three years of making this her life, she would not go to Athens. People forget that this is how it is for so many.

But now I was at my last ever World Cup regatta and my last ever Lucerne. I'd arranged for Mum to come out. She used to love the GB supporters' team buzz of coming to watch racing with Dad, but hadn't been to anything since he died. She'd booked to go to Athens with Catherine (as usual the supporters had to book their tickets before any of us even knew if we were selected) and I thought she'd feel better about that if it wasn't the first time without Dad. Ros was rowing in a Four at Lucerne, so I asked Ros's independent and practical mother if she'd mind if my rather less independent and practical mother tagged along. They got on famously I think and had a ball.

This was the last race before the Olympics and everybody was there including Australia – the reigning World Champions. They raced in the first heat and were beaten by the Ukrainians who'd come seventh at Munich. That was good to know, although we knew they were likely to be rather jet-lagged and would have more speed come the Olympics. We were drawn into the second heat and poised ourselves on the start, side by side with the Germans (you should hear dramatic music whenever they are mentioned by now). We blasted off with our new sequence, found our magic new flow and… well the words I wrote in my training diary that night probably say it best.

Friday June 18th 2004 Lucerne
HEAT – Led to 500m in a flying start then were rowed down by GER as we struggled in a massive head wind and terrible water. BUT KNOW we can beat them now.

The Germans beat us by three and a half seconds, about a boat length, but still it gave us that confidence and there was a real change in all of us. Before the race we had told ourselves and each other that we could do this and thought we believed it, but I don't think any of us realised how much was missing until we found real belief from that race. We'd led the Germans to 500m; we'd never led the Germans before – no British Women's Quad had ever led the Germans before. It had caught us by surprise. We hadn't known what to do with it, that's all. We knew now.

The following day we won our Repechage and booked our place in the Final. Even with the extra race of the Rep, there was still a lot of time to fill with something other than obsessing about racing and beating Germans. When I retired from rowing I was going to be 'trekking, camping girl', so I occupied myself and my brain for a free hour or so both days finding just the perfect combination of Swiss Army knife blades and gadgets that I thought I would actually use from the mind-blowing choice. I also bought my last selection of biscuit cutters from the world's best biscuit cutter shop.

Eventually, Saturday turned into Sunday. Quite wonderfully the quote at the bottom of my diary page for Lucerne Finals day page reads: *'The starting point of all achievement is desire. Keep this constantly in mind. Weak desire brings weak results.' (Napoleon Hill, 1883-1970, American investment writer).*

We boated for our final in rain that got heavier and heavier during our 'warm-up'. Sometimes I had to wish I'd discovered I was good at table tennis or billiards or something. We sat on the start, trying to stay relaxed before the call over and it stopped raining… and started to hail. But the weather you get is the weather you want right? I thought of this and tapped Debs on the back. She turned round and I said, "Great British weather. We've got the advantage." She smiled at me and nodded and then maybe because I knew that Rule No. 1 of rowing in bad weather is the same as Rule No. 1 for rowing in rough water, I said "Pass it on." Debs smiled, leant forward and tapped Fran on the back. Fran smiled and leant forward to tell Becs. And then we all looked forward in the boat and waited, happy in the hail. The umpire started the call over and we all came forward and sat in our new, shorter positions. We were ready.

If I was recounting this race from memory, as I have done many times, I'd tell you that we had a flying start, got ahead in the first 10 strokes and were out to a length lead by 500m. So it was rather a shock to look at the World Rowing results data base and find that the Russians beat us to 500m by 0.24 seconds and we only led Germany by inches at this point. I think it just felt so good and so in control that I had the confidence of being a length up, even though we weren't. Now that I know differently, I can picture us side by side, just inches up for most of this race, but still I always felt like we had it. By 1,000m even the data base says we were in the lead, but not by much. 0.2 seconds ahead of the Russians (a foot maybe) and one second ahead of the Germans – all six boats still overlapping.

Only in the third 500m did we start to split the field. We moved further ahead but still couldn't shake the Germans. By 1,500m they'd moved into second place and we were now 1.5 seconds up, still less than half a boat length. But the Germans had no precedent for being beaten by the British (not at this game anyway) and didn't know it was possible. In the last 500m my memory does serve me right and I remember their charge and the sense of them moving through us foot by foot, stroke by stroke, of their bow girl moving up alongside me and then of just burying ourselves in the last ten strokes and no memory until the "BEEP.BEEP… BEEP.BEEP" across the finish – very little time between those first four places and no time at all between the first two.

Gasping and grappling desperately to release our feet, still in the pouring rain, we twisted to look to the scoreboard. The results didn't come up immediately, which meant it had gone to a photo.

"Did we do it?"

"I don't know."

"I think we did it."

"I couldn't tell."

"Aghhh!"

Lots more gasping.

I think you get the best sense for these things at bow and I had a different sense to the photos I'd sat though in Munich and Milan the previous year. I thought we'd done it with the same vague feeling that I thought we hadn't in Munich and Milan, but none of us wanted to allow ourselves to feel anything until we were sure. We grabbed bottles from the water boat, desperately thirsty despite the conditions and turned the boat, but still no results came up. The longer it took, the closer we knew the photo was. We rowed down to the grandstand and Becs shouted across to the press and media, "Did we get it? Did we get it?" And there is a brilliant series of photos where you can see, still through the torrential rain, Becs asking the question, her hands raised and all our faces turned to the stands, pained, confused, expectant and then the transformation in the next frame as we hear back, "Yes, yes you got it!" and the still moment of half delight, half not daring to believe as we wait for confirmation to come up on the scoreboard. And then the picture of pure joy across our faces as we watch the results come up.

1. GBR 6.23.77
2. GER 6.23.85
3. USA 6.25.10
4. RUS 6.25.67
5. AUS 6.31.22
6. UKR 6.33.25

0.08 seconds. Easy!

"Al, did we get it?"
"I don't know… I couldn't tell"

"Did we get it? Did we get it?"

"Yes! Yes, you got it!"

Photos by Peter Spurrier

And it was pure joy. We rowed over to the medal pontoon and for the first time ever, a GBR Quad got to stand in the centre spot while the Germans took second place. We were given yellow bibs to show that we were not just Lucerne winners but Women's Quad World Cup winners 2004, and then we stood while they put the (at least Gold–coloured) medals round our necks.

This was the story of the regatta; we were the only British winners in an Olympic Boat class. The Double had come fourth, but it had been another deceptive result as the Germans still had more talent than they had seats and had put out two Doubles that came second and third (you are only allowed one boat per event at the Olympics). The Pair, with at least as much desire for Olympic Gold as ourselves, had fallen further down the field into third place, six seconds behind Romania and five behind Belarus. The Men's Four were back in third place and the Men's Eight had an even worse time and didn't even make the A-final. I've completely neglected to talk about the Lightweights in this story as I haven't time for everyone's tale. Approaching the Olympics it was not looking good for them, but the best of the talent at the time was the Helen Casey/Tracy Langlands Double (the only Women's Lightweight event at the Olympics so it is crazy competitive) who came fifth.

But back in the media stand that day, we were the ones everyone wanted a piece of. Still soaking wet and now shivering (Debs rather uncontrollably), we did our interviews wrapped in blankets that had miraculously appeared from somewhere. Microphones were thrust into our faces, "How was the race?", "How does it feel to be Olympic favourites?" Fortunately I'd got a lot better at this interview thing over the years and said some quite sensible stuff. We had a great time and enjoyed the attention while we had it. But in the back of our heads we were already thinking, "It's not going to be as easy as that." All we'd done was stick the knife in and make the Germans a bit angry. There were eight weeks until the Olympics and they'd be watching videos of us off the start now. And critically, what we'd already seen and already worked out was that the legendary, three-time Olympic Gold medallist Katrin Boron had finally made an appearance in a Double with Kerstin El Qalqili-Kowalski (Olympic Champion from the Sydney Quad) and they had been beaten by a street by the Evers-Swindell sisters. So it doesn't take a genius to work out that if you are number one and two and you have been beaten by clear water in the Double, and meanwhile your teammates have been beaten by a few centimetres by some rookie British Quad… well… you are going to want in to that game, aren't you?

With Mum and the yellow bib that would soon be hers.
Not quite sure which of us is most happy about our win.

We couldn't know for sure and we'd not know until the start lists were published just days before the Olympics, but for the next eight weeks we had to assume that the German crew we'd face at the Olympics would contain Boron (the German equivalent of subbing in Matthew Pinsent) and El Qalqili-Kowalski, and be stronger and faster than the one we'd just, just beaten today. When we talked about it, which we did just once or twice before we put it away and didn't talk about it again, we agreed that that was what we'd assume and that it was a good thing because it would force us to raise our game again and make sure that we never got… complacent. And if it didn't happen, it would be a bonus. Expect nothing.

But in this moment, we were absolutely buzzing. This in itself, whatever else happened, was an historic moment. I got the other three girls to sign my yellow bib and kept it safe to give to Mum as a trophy. We each received a small but really lovely block of engraved glass saying that we were Lucerne winners in the Women's Quad and then there was just one, small cut glass goblet engraved with 'World Cup Winners 2004', which I secretly coveted. This would be my only World Cup win ever and while I knew I didn't deserve it any more than the other girls, I couldn't help but want to keep it. As we finally rowed back to the pontoons towards warmth and dry clothes, I didn't say anything except perhaps to wonder out loud what we would do with only one trophy when there were four of us, and perhaps there might have been a slight tone of something in my question that only those who knew me really well would have heard. We carried the boat in and when Paul appeared with the trophy boxes, Fran, Debs and Becs disappeared off to the side in a huddle for a moment. When they came back Fran took the little glass goblet and gave it to me, "We've all agreed that we want you to have this Al, it's your last World Cup – we'll have other chances."

"No really, I couldn't." But it was only a token protest and I was already taking the trophy. Awesome girls.

Saturday June 20th 2004 Lucerne
FINAL. We Won!!
Beat GER by 0.08 secs in the best race of my life.
Hail stones @ the start but kept our heads – led @ 500m and held off final charge.
Felt comfortable!

'The starting point of all achievement is desire. Keep this constantly in mind. Weak desire brings weak results.'

Chapter 19: The final furnace

"Train like Olympic Champions and behave like Olympic Champions and see if we can make it happen."

July 2004 (6 weeks to go)

Mathematicians amongst you will have noticed that I've gained a couple of extra weeks in moving from months to weeks, but that's OK because six is a small enough number. Besides, by this point I was glad of the extra weeks. I'd gone from desperately counting them down to wondering if there would be enough. I was enjoying it again now and there was a lot still to do. We had twenty days in the UK between getting back from Lucerne and flying out to our penultimate training camp in Breisach. Once we went to Breisach we'd only have a couple of days at home before the Olympics, so this was our time to fit everything in.

In our traditional three days off after Lucerne, I went up to Richmond and fitted in a couple of land training sessions in the gym of The Scotch Corner Hotel where I used to waitress. It was over two years since Dad had died and for the first time I started to notice a change in Mum. Grandpa (her father) lived about fifty miles away over the Pennines in Alston and Mum drove over every other weekend to see him. All our lives it had been common knowledge that Mum did not like driving and wasn't much good at it. Dad liked driving and Dad did all the driving and Mum just pottered about locally avoiding big roads. Dad always drove Mum up to Alston because "it's a very tricky road." When he was serving his driving ban, they cut down on driving trips, and when they did have to go somewhere and Mum drove, Dad still did all the looking and judging when it was safe to go at junctions and agreed that it was probably best she just didn't try and overtake. After Dad died, when I went to Richmond, I'd always volunteer to drive Mum anywhere we went to give her a break, even though I was tired and had just driven over 200 miles. I thought I was helping. But this time when I offered to drive her up to Grandpa's, she said: "Oh, but I quite enjoy it – I was going to drive you."

"No, it's OK..." I started, then reeled myself back in as I noticed the change. "That would be great. Thanks." So Mum drove. And I noticed the satisfaction and pride with which she did it, stopping along the way to show me the field where she always got out to look for Black Grouse. And I sat enjoying the slow but perfectly safe drive, taking care to make sure I sat back at junctions and said or did nothing to undermine this new confidence.

And when we got home I came into the kitchen to find her with a screwdriver in her hand trying to work out how to put a new plug on a lamp. My hands automatically moved to take it from her. Mum didn't fix things. Driving and fixing things were tricky, important jobs and Dad did those because Mum wasn't capable. And she gave the plug up, but there was a reluctance. So I checked myself again and handed it back and casually sat at the kitchen table to chat as if this sort of thing happened every day. And again I noticed the pride and satisfaction of a task achieved, of acquiring a new skill and of being able to show me that she could do it. And for the first time, I started to see that Mum might not be who we'd thought she was all our lives. Because if doing something, anything, no matter how small leads to a sense of achievement (sometimes just at the doing, even if nothing else has actually been achieved) and achievement gives you the energy and motivation to do more and builds self-confidence – then maybe we should all have thought more carefully about who we were really helping when we took over and 'helped'. In another year or so, the woman who hadn't known how to read a bank statement or pay the car tax would sell the family home and buy a new one – all by herself.

Our short break over, I went straight back to a press conference in Leander where the Olympic team was officially announced. Less than six weeks before Athens, I was confirmed into the Quad and could finally start telling people I was going to the Olympics.

It was not downhill all the way home though. It was like our Lucerne result increased rather than released the pressure. Straightaway and constantly, people were on our case about not being complacent. Everyone seemed desperately worried in case we somehow, inconceivably thought we'd done enough and could just cruise out the last few weeks. It wasn't enough to be continually trying to move on, we also had to get stressed about whether we were moving on fast enough – or we obviously weren't worried enough.

We moved our boat to Pangborne, a stretch of water Mark knew and he took us there supposedly to take us away from the pressure during crazy Henley Regatta, but I remember it being the opposite. Mark and Fran seemed particularly highly-strung and there was lots of tension and picking holes in things and worry and stress and no one else around to disperse it with. I respected both Fran and Mark and tried to think that it was good to have people around me to push me and make me want to do it better, but I stopped enjoying it again. I was learning Scott Joplin's *Maple Leaf Rag* by this point and my memory of our time at Pangbourne is of stress and tension and playing *Maple Leaf Rag* over and over in my head. It's a happy piece.

We decided we would race Henley Royal Regatta, but train through and use the initial races against college and club crews more like practice pieces. We made it through to the Final without doing anything very wrong, then beat Ukraine by 2 ¾ lengths. It was a very fun day and winning a Henley medal is a big deal. In some circles it will get you as much respect as an Olympic medal and many club athletes (still working full-time) train very nearly as hard to get one.

Mid-July we took an evening off, shook out our ball gowns, put up our hair, slapped on the slap and drove into London for a night of glamour and (one glass of) champagne at the BOA Gold Ball. I'd made it my mission (particularly since I met Steve Cram and rather messed it up) to try and meet my Olympic heroes and this was the place to get a few in. Debs was too

A couple of moments of glamour in a not very glamorous life. Winning the Princess Grace cup at Royal Henley and a rare night out at the BOA Gold Ball.

young to remember any of my favourite Olympians first time round, but she agreed to come and 'do fan club' stuff with me. Sebastian Coe was an obvious first target and Debs at least knew who he was. We had him spotted for a while and grabbed him when he finally had a minute to himself. I did better this time (maybe the glass of champagne helped) – "Hi, you don't know me but I just wanted to say 'Hi'. I used to come and sit on the grass banks at Gateshead stadium and watch you run. I felt like I knew you when I cheered the TV when you won your medal. And now I'm an Olympic rower." Seb chatted to us for a while and Debs and I had our photo taken with him.

Then I spotted Allan Wells. I was on a roll now and didn't feel I needed Debs, which was a good job and she wasn't even born at the time I was idolising "Alan who?" – I went over, apologised for interrupting his evening and said my line. Then he surprised me by turning it straight back round. "I know who you are. I watched you on the TV win that race in Lucerne in all the rain. Congratulations, it was fantastic!" In the end, we talked for ages about running and rowing and the Olympics and he seemed just as pleased to talk to me off the telly as I was to talk to him off the telly. I just came away thinking that he'd seemed like a really nice guy when I used to see him interviewed on TV and I'd been right. He was really just an ordinary, lovely superhuman.

And finally the last thing to fit in was to go and pick up our kit. We headed to Earl's Court at our appointed time and it was quite literally a military operation as the army were involved in distribution. There was a lot of kit, at least a suitcase and a couple of holdalls full each, and most of us wanted to try it all on and get it all right. Getting free kit when you are an athlete is very exciting. In fact show me anyone who doesn't like getting free stuff, regardless of how much money they have, and I'll show you someone who is… unlikely to be from Yorkshire.

Again I was excited by the promise of a 'made-to-measure' suit. They were nice suits from Ben Sherman made from specially manufactured cloth with 'Going for Gold' written into a subtle pin stripe. But still, despite having taken our measurements, they were decidedly off-the-peg sizes and we were still not off-the-peg sized people. It seemed the only way they'd thought to get legs and arms long enough was just to give us really big sizes. When enough of us complained, we were told we could come back into London for a re-fit on another day. At which point they had to be reminded that this was

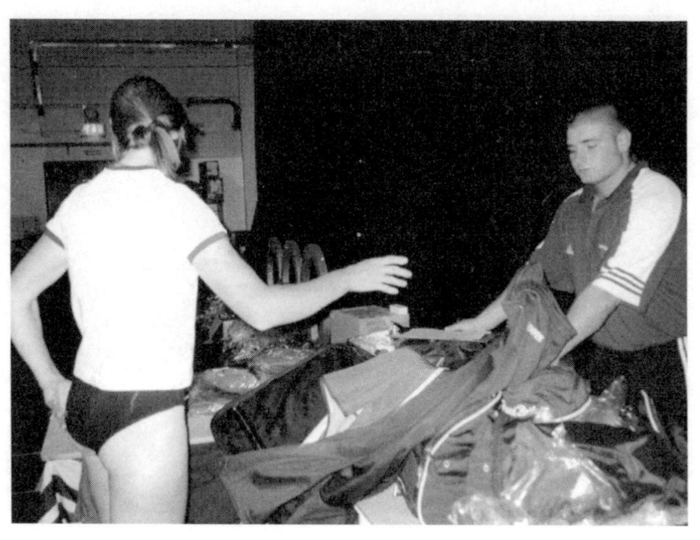

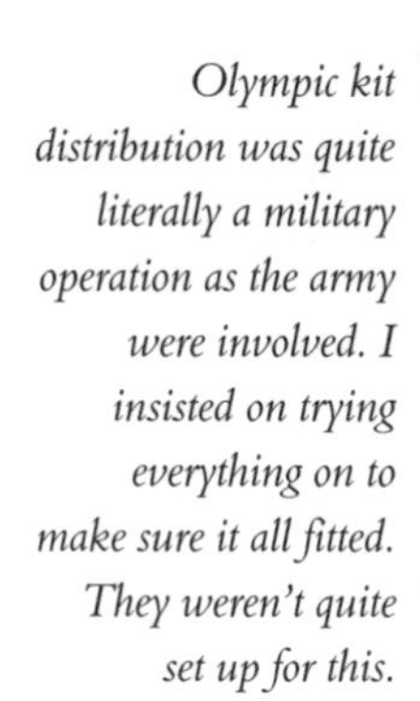

Olympic kit distribution was quite literally a military operation as the army were involved. I insisted on trying everything on to make sure it all fitted. They weren't quite set up for this.

the Olympic team they were supplying and we didn't have another day because we had that training thing going on.

So they sent a tailor out to us at Dorney when both the men's and women's teams were there and over half of us brought our suits back. The tailor arrived and we could tell he was a tailor because he had a tape measure around his neck, but that did seem to be it. Cath stood there first and he folded the waist of her trousers over an inch or so and then let it go and then pinched in the sides of the jacket a bit and just said, "Yes, so we can just take that in a bit and it'll be fine." And we all just stood there politely while he held onto the tucks and looked vaguely down the line, "Ah, I didn't expect there to be so many of you." Eventually I could stand it no more so I asked as gently as possible, trying not to sound like I was teaching him how to do his job, "How are you going to know how much of that to take in when you get it back to the shop?"

"Hmm," he said, like I'd raised an interesting point.

"Perhaps you could pin it?" This was about the extent of my tailoring knowledge but it seemed a good start.

"Ah yes" – but still no movement.

"Well, do you have any pins?" with slightly less patience. He patted his blatantly empty pockets, then told us they were in the car and disappeared off. He was away absolutely ages and eventually returned with about half a dozen pins stuck into the lapel of his jacket. By this point I really wanted to say: "You've just been scrabbling round the floor of your car looking for those haven't you?" but held off. We also had to find him a pen and scraps of paper

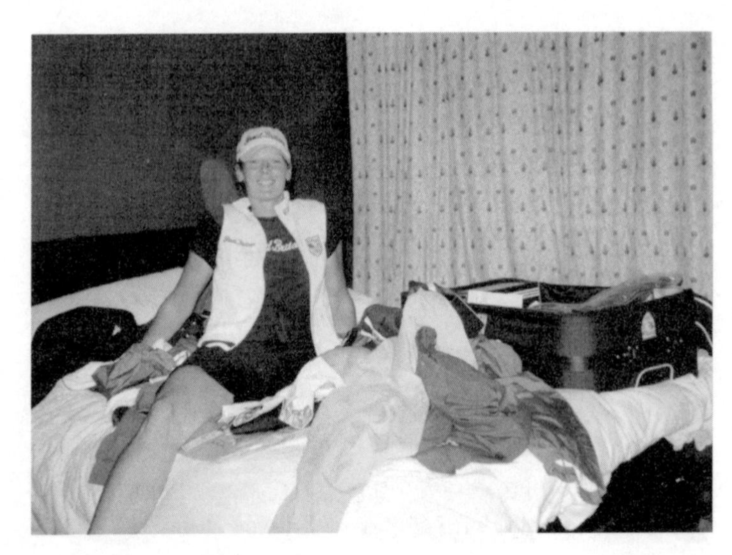

Happy as a Yorkshire girl in free kit.

to write our names on and put in the suit pockets to identify them. He'd not got those either. Just because you tailor some Olympians does not make you an Olympic tailor.

But then we went to Breisach, my last Breisach, and any and all of those distractions were taken away. Paul's primary aim of these sixteen days every year is to make amends for the constant wind down and recovery pattern of summer racing and basically to beast us into supreme fitness. He hopes to do through Breisach what Jurgen does when he takes the Heavyweight men up to altitude at this point. I don't actually know which is the best or the right way, I've only ever done it the Mike and Paul beasting way. I trusted Paul though. He read all the research and listened to all the latest stuff; if he thought there was a different or better way to do this, we would have been doing it.

Monday July 12th 2004

Day 1 Breisach

1. 22k UT2 115 mins 4x

2. 20k UT2 110 mins 4x

Whoomph! Breisach has landed.

I always liked Breisach – the hotel, the river, cycling round on our hire bikes, the fact that it was fairly reliably hot and sunny and that there was a wonderful grand piano hidden away that I could use without attracting too much attention. It was all as good as it could possibly be considering I knew I was going to be dragging my knuckles across the floor tired after a couple of days. I did my last ever thirty-minute and 18k ergos, my last ever eighty-minute endurance weights circuit and my last ever 5½k Tank Emptier.

We only did one Tank Emptier piece a year and it was designed to improve our physiology and race confidence. We set out rating 24 and built the rate two pips every 500m until the last 2k. Then with 3½k of hard work already under our belts, we'd race 2k flat-out finishing with a wind for the line. The thinking was that once we knew we could race our 2k when already exhausted, we'd never fear it again.

Even by itself it was the hardest training session we ever had to do and we'd do it when we were already knackered. I remember getting a small sense of the same dread I'd got in my first ever races when I wasn't sure if I'd even be able to finish. I guess that was the point – to push through any remaining areas of self-doubt. We were supposed to push ourselves hard right from the start rather than pace it. Normally, as in any race, there is no way of telling if you are 'cheating', so how hard you push yourself is a question of trust. But this year we rowed the Tank Emptier with the strain gauge blades, a special set with sensors inside that fed a pressure profile from each blade to a computer that Paul could both watch real time and download for later analysis. Technically all eight blades should have the same profile and we'd used them before to help correct discrepancies between our left and right hands and to bring all four of our stroke profiles closer together. Here though I think we were all aware they were being used for a different purpose. It had not previously been possible to measure the pressure each person in a crew applied each stroke and compare them against each other. It was now.

Saturday 17th July 2004

1. TANK EMPTIER 5.5k Piece

Made all the rates and kept the boat moving but bit disappointed we didn't get a better rhythm early on.

2. 75' T.S.

'Nobody notices when things go right'. Zimmerman's Law of Complaints

Perhaps another perfectly placed random quote in my diary. I was still finding sculling in our Quad rather more stressful than I thought it had to be, mostly due to the above Law. Fran and I seemed to move temperamentally further and further apart as Athens moved ever closer. I knew she liked and respected me as much as I liked and respected her, so it was rather a shock to find myself getting so irritated. It felt like every time I found something to comment on that was going right, Fran would go "Yes but…" And find something that was not. I'm more than glass half-full girl; if there is even a drop in the bottom, I'll need to focus on how good that drop is to keep me going. Fran seemed to be the opposite and needed to focus on every drop that was missing. There were several post-outing debriefs when I thought we'd had a great outing and really moved on, but Fran still found the drop that was missing and I found it pretty difficult to cope with.

Fran never picked us apart; mostly it was herself she was dissatisfied with, or something general to do with boat feel without any indication of blame. So every day I told myself that we were all successful and we'd all found our success in different ways, so there wasn't a right or wrong way to do this. Fran was the fastest sculler in our crew and for all our sakes, I needed her to keep doing whatever kept her feeling confident and sculling well. It just wasn't the way I needed to be and I had to try and protect myself. Debs was stuck in the middle in-between us in the two seat – a happy, friction absorbing buffer. Debs and Fran have been rowing together so long they are more like sisters than friends or teammates, so Fran would sometimes off-load more frustration onto Debs than she would ever dare with me. Sometimes I worried for Debs but she seemed to be fine. But I was sharing a top floor, sun-trap balcony room with Becs and I saw that even serious-minded, mega-focused Becs was starting to get worn down. Still, despite the perhaps inevitable niggles, we were an increasingly close and supportive crew and on our off time we enjoyed each other's company. We also absolutely stuck to our contract and talked about even this within our crew rather than offload on anyone else outside. It kept the trust between us regardless of how difficult it got sometimes.

I really wanted my last ever ergos to be new PBs. I sweated and gasped my way through a last 18k ergo the day after the Tank Emptier – the ergos crammed into a tiny back foyer of the hotel with only the skylights and a couple of fans for air – but in the end found my poor scores more amusing than distressing. If the goal of the camp is to work yourself to destruction, it's probably not wise to also have goals to hit personal bests. Also I'd have been doing something wrong if I had had anything left after the Tank Emptier – it does what it says on the tin.

Then that's it for my individual diary. There are no more entries. The four of us spent half an hour together most evenings looking at video from the day's sessions and coaching ourselves and each other from it. Then we'd get out our crew diary and sit in one of our rooms, or rather sprawl over the beds too tired to sit up, discuss the day and take it in turns to write up our thoughts on the sessions and what we needed to do better tomorrow. After all that I found I decreasingly had the time, inclination or need to repeat the exercise individually.

In one of our last full squad meetings in Breisach, I dug out my *Scientific American* article to share the 'secret advantage' of understanding your body's reserve tank. I was never going to race these girls again so I didn't need any secret advantages and I wanted them to carry this with them into their Olympic finals like I would carry it with me. They all listened but I remember being surprised that it obviously didn't have the same impact on any of them. They didn't believe it like I believed it.

And finally, if I had one more Breisach tale to recount, it would be the source of the only story that most people who have ever heard of me have heard of me for. We had a *Daily Mail* journalist come out for a couple of days. I don't quite know what she was expecting to take back for her readers, but despite sitting down with most of us for quite some time, I don't think she found it in the tales of Degrees, Further Degrees, PhDs and professional careers on hold she found here. She sat in on a final squad meeting and at some point, for some reason, I joked about being ten years older than the rest of my crew. Suddenly her ears pricked up and she was straight in, "Are you really? How old are you?" and before I could reply Sarah responded with a light-hearted, "Yeah, Alison's the Grandma of the crew."

Straight away the journalist came back with, "They call you Grandma! Do they really call you Grandma?" I think Sarah was actually a bit taken aback at her enthusiasm and tried to reel it back in. "No… it was just a joke." But the woman was off. This was more interesting than degrees and jobs and hard work. "They do, they do! They call you Grandma. That's brilliant!" And I just sat there with my mouth slightly open thinking, "Is there a way to respond to this?" I had never heard the nickname before and didn't think it was true, but to deny it at this point would have sounded like I minded, which I didn't. So I just smiled and half laughed and left it.

And that was the story, wasn't it? By the time I got to the Olympics 90% of journalists who interviewed me over the next six months (and about 80% of anyone new I met) would start with the line, "So, your crew call you Grandma don't they?" Every time they would think they were original and funny, and every time I'd have to try and think of a way of deflecting it without sounding like I hated the name and was being defensive – which I didn't and wasn't. At one point, when I read it yet again, I thought I might be going rather crazy and asked the girls. "I really don't mind if it's true, but *do* you call me Grandma?"

"No Al. No! Really we don't. We never think of you like that. It's so ridiculous. You are the young one."

I wouldn't have objected to my crew giving me the name, but I really did object to some stupid journalist, who'd missed every single interesting real story about all of us, reporting on one made-up one. Just because you interview some Olympians does not make you an Olympic journalist.

We had two days at home to turn ourselves round before going to Varese for our final pre-Olympic camp. My last ever training camp. We'd go straight from there to Athens so everything had to be sorted at home for another extended time away, plus the complicated packing of training, competition and 'post competition' (aka party) gear into one 25 kg bag plus hand luggage. We worked out that we could take our suit bags as extra hand luggage, so all 'casually' walked in carrying bulging suit bags normal mortals would have struggled to lift.

I stayed in the family hotel in Varese for the last time and shared a room with Fran. Sharing with Fran was always an easy, relaxed pairing as we're both quite quiet and like our own head space. When Fran and I shared, I always felt rather like we were the grown-ups with Becs and Debs the kids next door. Fran and I watched episodes of *The West Wing*, read and drank cups of tea. Becs and Debs had designer hot chocolate topping-making competitions and called us in to "Quick! Come and look! Come and look!" and jumped up and down on the beds with excitement.

Our sessions moved away from the Breisach beasting so we could start to recover. No more weights, ergos or circuits – just rowing and the still crucial 'Lizzie' sessions. We spent nearly as many hours training, but the focus had shifted to more technique and speed work. We were still chasing just one more technical improvement, just one more shift in boat speed, just one more, just one more. Always the sense that our competitors were on the water somewhere still moving on and we had to stay ahead. Always the knowledge that the Germans with Boron would be faster than we had been in Lucerne and we had to find more, we had to find more.

For nearly two years, Paul had been trying to get us to use our big lat muscles to get the catch in. I started this rowing story with the idea that SEPARATION is a big word in rowing and it was still with me every day. Every day trying to bury the catch in an ever quicker, ever more forceful "CHCK!" from the lats, SEPARATED completely from the shoulders and arms which stay loose – a meter of muscle to switch off between the source of power and the point of connection with the water. And simultaneously a second SEPARATION between the lats and the legs so the lats put the blade in, but our thighs stayed pressed against our calves. All eight blades totally buried before the legs had even start moving. Lats power the blade in, legs power the stroke – SEPARATE them out. And then a final SEPARATION as you wait for the handles to come back towards you before you pick up the push. GO-WAIT-GO. Like a sprinter trying to be first out of the blocks if they also know they have to be first to stop.

We'd been working on this for two years and had made progress, but not enough to satisfy Paul. Every session he coached us he was on it and when he was with the Pair, Mark picked up the theme. We all knew we were running out of time. We couldn't know what it would feel like until we got it, but we knew it wasn't quite right yet. It was beautiful how our boat was moving but it could yet be more beautiful.

And then one day, about halfway through an outing, we suddenly got it. The catch sharper, harder and looser than we'd ever got it, the fraction of float more free than we'd ever had it and the push more perfectly timed with the boat and with each other than we'd ever felt it. And it's like you daren't move a muscle (even though everything is moving) and you daren't even breathe (even though you are reaching for air) because everything must stay like this, just like this, for as long, as long as possible, until you've had a chance to ingrain it and activate the right muscle paths to form the new habit. Like trying to hold a complicated puzzle together in your head for long enough that the pieces will remain fixed when you open your eyes. A level of concentration unparalleled by anything I have ever known.

It came and went a bit in the rest of the outing, but now we really knew what we were aiming for and if we concentrated we could get it back. We finished the session exhausted and exhilarated, put the boat away and stood in the boathouse to debrief with Mark. We were buzzing and I was primed and ready to enthuse. We waited for Mark to lead the discussion.

"That was really good today, you've really moved on. So tomorrow morning when we come down, we need to think about the next step. We can get it even harder and sharper from the lats. More…" and he raised his hands in front of him in the movement Paul had demonstrated time and time again.

And my confused head just went, "No… hang on… wait! What just happened there? Not moving on, not yet, what about today? I've got all this energy and enthusiasm for today. What do I do with that?" The energy of my happiness switched to energy of frustration (being two sides of the same hyperactivity coin). "No Mark, wait! We shouldn't be thinking about that yet."

"But you've got to move on, Alison."

"Yes, but not yet. We've been trying to get that for two years, it's all we've thought about every session for weeks. We got it today, really got it, but it was on and off, maybe ten minutes in the whole outing. I don't want to think about the next step yet. Tomorrow we should be thinking about going out and getting it for maybe half the outing and then 80% of the outing, then getting it rate 24, then 34, then 44. I think if we could get that and reliably get that racing at the Olympics, it would be amazing. I think maybe it's all we've got time for. We can't keep finding new stuff, at some point we have to get good at what we already do." (Or something quite like that, that I've not just made up).

"You've got to keep moving on, Alison. You can't be complacent."

"Arghh! I AM NOT BEING COMPLACENT but we've not got this right yet. I just want to keep working on this."

"Well maybe we just have to agree to disagree."

"We can't, we have to agree what we are all working towards tomorrow."

"Alison, why do you always have to have the last word?"

"I don't!" OK, maybe he was right with that one. I could see that arguing was not helpful though and his comment did shut me up. But later that evening, Mark came and found me.

"Alison, I didn't want to say anything in front of the other girls, but I was very surprised and disappointed with your attitude today. It's not the attitude of an Olympic medallist. You've got to keep driving for more and want to keep getting better. You are good, but you can't afford to be complacent."

I don't remember exactly but I think I might have used the 'nothing' response to this one.

But it is confusing. Am I successful in what I do because I manage to see and celebrate the small positive steps or could I have been even more successful if I'd pushed myself harder and been more miserable? I still consider that question often. There are certainly plenty of very successful

Plank it until your arms collapse from under you. Note Mark Banks in the background getting a hand massage from physio Pam – stopwatch RSI?

This one's a killer. Balance on the side of one foot, lift your hips and rotate your body so your arm goes through the gap. Many times.

Bow pair always in sync (nearly).

Extreme Lizzie. One arm, one leg, ankle weight on, hand behind your back. (Don't try this at home unless under expert supervision.)

Winks looking rather close to the edge.

Our core stability programme devised by 'Mad Lizzie' off the telly. In my training diary, it's not called core stability – it's just called Lizzie.

people around who are constantly hard on themselves and never happy with what they achieve. I am prepared to accept that I may be wrong and limiting myself but somehow, I still feel in my gut, that I am right on this one. It is a balance, but I do think that there comes a point, a few days before a 'final' performance, when it is the right and conscientious thing to do to stop looking for 'the next big thing'. That it is not complacent to allow yourself to believe, just sometimes, that *what you already have will be enough*. That at some point you get more from the confidence and enjoyment of what you already do, than from the constant search for what you still can't. The theory is not the lesson, the notes are not the music, the moves are not the dance and the strokes are most definitely not the race.

But I think at the time I was confused enough and ashamed enough that I kept quiet, and next outing we pushed for more.

But these were the small things. The BBC came out to interview and film all potential medal crews on and off the water for footage to show before the

A final training outing in Varese. See this is what I'm talking about. Arms loose, shoulders down, catch thrown in with the lats, blades buried, shins still vertical, no leg drive lost, nothing else moves, wait for the boat to come to you. God we were good.

finals we hardly dared even think about yet. I love that I have film of us all sitting together in the sun in the hotel garden in Varese, answering questions almost with one voice, our answers overlapping and reinforcing, the same language, the same mind and of some of that beautiful paddling on that beautiful lake with the mountains in the background. Paul lost the footage of my 'perfect' pre-trials single sculling so that exists only in my mind's eye now, but I still have that of us in the Quad. Long, loose, sharp and flowing – I can still feel it when I watch that video and my body still aches for it.

I report this as a positive time and it really was. I was still quite desperately tired though. I don't mention it all the time because it would be boring and it was just sort of my natural state by this point. I called it 'terminal tiredness' because even after a day off and a long lie in, even after the three days off and three lie-ins after Lucerne, it never really went away any more.

During Varese, we had to start getting up earlier and earlier again in preparation for early racing (our final – assuming we made it would be at 9.30am). I'd learnt my lesson on this at Sydney and argued my case with Paul and the physiologists that people's sleep patterns were different, and getting up at 5am for weeks did NOT necessarily mean we'd all feel fresh as a daisy for a 9.30am race time. Fortunately, I had Becs as back up on this one who was even more adamant and we kept the morning wake-up time to something reasonable. I think we probably got up about 6.30ish and maybe closer to 6am by the time we got to Athens as a bit of a compromise.

I could feel myself physically recovering and I felt springy and powerful for outings, but in-between I was permanently sleepy. I lived for the afternoon nap, which I'd limit to thirty minutes so as not to be drowsy for the afternoon session (and anyway there was rarely time for more). And this was not a new feeling, I'd felt like this for years, as long as I could remember really. I tried not to take my sleeping tablets at home, but had long ago given up trying to get to sleep without them when I was sharing a room on camp. Too stressed by my efforts to lie still to ever drift off naturally. I did sleep when I took them, so I couldn't understand why I was always so tired. Much later I would discover that Zopiclone are from a class of drugs called hypnotics, which induce a sort of trance-like state that is not actually the same or effective as deep REM sleep. I don't think I'd have stopped taking them even if I had known as it seemed the only way to get any sort of sleep and I wasn't about to start taking something more serious and addictive. It was a short-term fix, never a long-term solution. The long-term solution was retirement – I just needed to last that long.

Some of my tiredness was also because I never slept through the night. We still had to piss into a pot every morning and take it to the physiologists to put it into their hydration level machine (even though I could now work out my osmolality to within a fraction just by its colour) and the only way for me to be hydrated enough to not get told off was to drink so much in the evening that I'd have to get up in the night, and then it might take me a couple of hours to get back to sleep again. I tried to argue that even if my urine was a little yellow in the morning, I was sure I could drink enough in the first hour of the morning to be fine all day and that would be worth it to sleep through the night, but I was told that this was the only way it could be done. Apparently pissing in a pot was more important to my athletic importance than sleep. I'd fought for 6.30am 'lie-ins' so I didn't fight this one. It was funny though. In my whole time on the squad, my two biggest physiological drains were: 1. Insomnia/sleep deprivation and 2. Period Pain. And despite all the massive physiological attention to detail in so many areas, these two points were never discussed and never seemed to be considered relevant.

We spent years chasing fractions of a percentage and yet if I'd had to race on the wrong day of my cycle, it would have taken chunks out of my performance (20%ish is my rough estimate from experience; it would definitely have cost us a medal) and yet no one ever mentioned it and it was left to chance that we would all manage it ourselves. I took the pill my whole rowing career and ran packs together during racing season and stopped for breaks when I thought I could risk a couple of muscle-weakened, painful stomach-cramping days. I assumed that was the best/only thing to do but I didn't really know. Obviously, it even affected hydration results. For a couple of days a month my morning 'sample' would be rather yellow and I'd get told off for being dehydrated, even though I knew that actually my body was super-hydrated and just not letting any of it go. It coincided with a kilo or so increase in body weight (rather than the decrease associated with dehydration) so it shouldn't have been too hard to make the connection, but when I tried to explain, it was dismissed as irrelevant. I didn't understand how I seemed to be the only person to work this out. No more than A level Biology surely.

Amazingly this whole topic does not seem to fall into sports science training and I know I was not the only one to struggle. If I did a PhD now, it would be on the effect of the menstrual cycle on women's sport as there doesn't seem to be any information and research – or if there is, it's not out there with those who need it.

August 2004 (10 days to go)

So I got on the plane and flew to Athens as part of the GB Olympic team. And I can't remember if I mentioned it, but the Olympics is just the most amazing, exciting experience. It is everything you think it is when you watch it on TV and so, so much more. Still there was the excitement of four years ago, but I did feel different. Four years ago I couldn't believe the girl who'd struggled to make the school sports teams was part of the Olympic team, but now it felt right. I never stopped thinking it was incredibly special, but by now this was my job, this was what I did – this was me.

There were just eight of us in the GB Heavyweight Women's Olympic rowing team in 2004. Polite journalists call us 'Open weight', but I don't think any of us really minded the title Heavyweight. I mind much, much more when anyone tries to call us 'GB Ladies' or our sport 'Ladies' Rowing'. Titles do carry connotations and if you think I'm making a fuss, then I'd like you to try calling the Men's team 'GB Gentlemen' or their sport 'Gentlemen's Rowing' and see how that fits.

Of the dozens that had trained and trialled, hoped and dreamed, frozen and sweated over the past four years, just the eight of us had made it. Most of the others sent cards and 'Good Luck' messages. And by this stage, it is OK to start hoping for a bit of luck. You spend every minute of every day for years and years trying to control everything you can control, but as Paul was very fond of saying, "You do everything you can to prepare and you race your best race, but on the day it still takes the sun, the moon and the stars to all line up in your favour to make Olympic medals – especially Gold ones."

The course was too far from the village to travel for training and racing each day, so David Tanner had sourced and booked a beautiful beachside hotel closer to the course. An advance party had set it all up for us. Our nutritionist had worked with the kitchen staff on the menus and extra-long beds had been brought in for some of the extra-tall guys. There was no pool table in the rec room, but we did have a large screen TV with live BBC feed so we could watch the Olympics and computers for internet access (still hardly any of us had laptops) – and there were Olympic posters everywhere. We would all be able to move to the village after racing for the second week, so it was all kind of perfect.

My first experience of Olympic Athens was of driving in through the final panic preparations. It would be ready, but just as they'd said four years ago, last minute was how the Greeks worked. We drove to the course in our minibus that first afternoon and got stuck behind one truck that was marking the blue line on the road for the Marathon, and another that was shoving plants into dry and dusty verges and dribbling water over them. The Greeks really did a great job and everything worked and was finished on time, but the venues were covered with dry dusty soil that one imagined they'd planned to turf or properly plant but in the end just had the odd flower stuck in looking rather desperate for a drink. The rowing course was finished and ready for us though and impressive with its mountain backdrop.

My second impression of Athens was of the shimmering heat. It was noticeably several degrees cooler out at the rowing lake than in the village and central venues, but still it was hot enough to suck moisture from your breath and energy from your body. "It's going to be hot in Athens" had been as much a stock phrase as "It's going to be rough in Athens" and we'd been preparing for both for years. Our drinks sponsor Lucozade had designed a special high electrolyte, lower glucose drink powder that used to arrive in

Above: Katherine and Sarah trying to look like turning up at the Olympic rowing lake is not such a big deal.
Right: our Team GB apartments in the Olympic Village, complete with genuine working red phone box (we went to take a look at the village, but wouldn't move in until after racing as the course was too far away).

plain tubs straight from the lab and I don't think was ever available commercially. We had spent a lot of our time training in hot sunny venues and while the discomfort of doing our ergos in that small non-air conditioned room in Breisach may have seemed basic, it did actually have acclimatisation advantage that a more comfortable and sophisticated venue did not. It's important to be heat acclimatised, but research also shows that keeping your body as cool as possible during training and recovery means you get the most from the sessions. GB Olympic kit had been specially designed with heat in mind and counter-intuitively on the hottest, sunniest days, we put clothes on (often soaked in lake water) rather than took them off.

Paul had sourced gel-filled, 'ice jackets' (that look like a cross between a life jacket and one of those flexible, ridged ice packs) that we'd been using since Milan 2003. One of our jobs after each session was to soak them to refill the gel, then stash them in the section of the hotel freezer purloined for our use. We picked them up before each session and carried them down to the course in cool boxes to wear during the outing. After racing, our coaches would run down to the landing stages with the cool box and we'd put the ice jackets on for our cool-down row (this had not been felt to be necessary in Lucerne).

And it's amazing how these details totally filled our days. We just trained twice a day now and they were relatively short sessions but still, by the time we'd got up, pissed in a pot, had breakfast, got our ice jackets out of the freezer, driven down to the lake, got sorted and briefed, rowed our session, debriefed, snacked and stretched, driven back to the hotel, sorted out our jackets, showered, changed, had lunch, taken a nap or caught up on emails (rarely time for both); it was time to pick up the jackets again, drive down to the course, do a couple of press interviews or even a bit of filming (being a potential medal crew was very different from my single interview Sydney experience), get sorted and briefed, row our session, debrief, snack and stretch, drive back to the hotel, sort out the jackets, shower, change, have an early dinner, meet with Paul and Mark to watch the day's video and plan logistics, goals and say 'yes' or 'no' to potential media requests for the next day and then meet again, just the four of us to write up our crew diary – it was pretty much time to go to bed again.

I started a routine of going for a twenty-thirty minute walk along the rocky beach on my own before I went to bed. There wasn't much time to myself all day, but by this point in the evening there was nothing more I should be doing. It was really beautiful down there and I just walked by myself in the dusk and found the still quiet place in my head I'd learnt to find at exam time and in my PhD. I'd walk until I found it and then I'd sit on a rock and look out at the sea, and just sit for a minute or two before I walked home. Momentum gives you balance, but the greatest balance of all comes to those who can just sit.

The only thing allowed to disrupt the routine of our last few days was the ambassador's reception in the beautiful rooftop courtyards and vine-covered walkways of the British Embassy. We donned our (now better-fitting) Olympic suits and mingled with the rest of the GB team, especially welcome as we had missed out by not being able to go the Cyprus camp or stay in the village. The BBC presenter team were there including Brendan Foster and Sue Barker and I had that weird experience of wanting to go and chat to them, but feeling like they were too famous and then remembering that they were actually here to present on me. I plucked up the courage to say my "I used to watch you at Gateshead stadium and cheered you on the TV" line to Brendan Foster, who was typically self-deprecating. We ended up talking about both being from the North East and The Great North Run.

Because we weren't staying in the village, getting to and from the opening ceremony would have been even more of an effort than at Sydney and it was decreed that none of us would go. Medal potential (including ourselves) and Group A athletes (racing the following day) would likely have elected not to go anyway, but still that left a few athletes who I think should have at least been given the choice. I'd found the Sydney Opening Ceremony a bizarrely disappointing experience but still I was very glad, at this my second Olympics when I was focused on a medal, that I'd gone to the opening ceremony the first time round when just being at an Olympics was everything.

Even in four years, things had moved on and you weren't really allowed to say any more – that just being at the Olympics was everything and enough. Anyway, whatever the rights and wrongs of the issue, no British Rowers were going to the opening ceremony. We were however encouraged to gather in the rec room to watch it together on TV, and Debs and I came up with a plan. We started by trying to encourage people to wear their opening ceremony gear to watch the TV – then, in the hours leading up to the opening ceremony, the beady-eyed might have noticed that posters were disappearing from the walls and that one of the Union Jacks had vanished.

That evening the whole team gathered round the TV to watch the Nations

The usual suspects. Someone forgot to tell Fran that she wasn't actually on Crimewatch.

I'd got pretty good at this by now and journalists actually sought me out for quotes and interviews. I still think I'd have been pretty good at being famous.

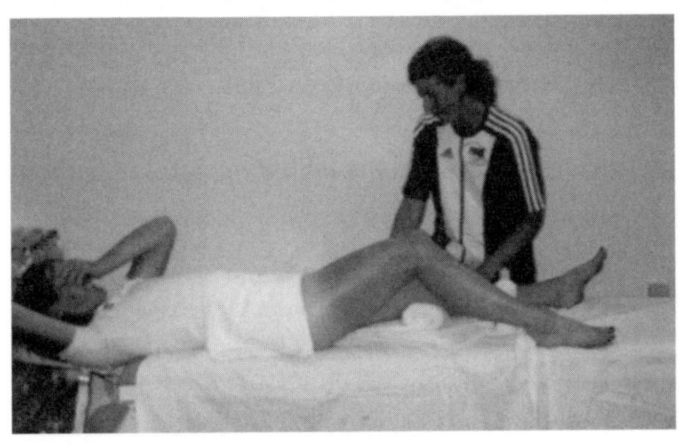

A relaxing post-race massage.

Physio Jackie strips the lactic acid from my quads and releases my IT bands. Sometimes it's more painful than the race itself – as you can see.

parade into the stadium. Several of us were dressed up and there was a really good feel and much excitement even without being there. At around about D for Denmark, Debs and I slipped out; then, as Team GB paraded into the Olympic Stadium, Debs and I marched into the TV lounge in our full opening ceremony outfits, carrying the Union Jack on a homemade flagpole made of rolled-up posters stuck together with physio tape. Our efforts were applauded and a few people even joined us for a lap of honour round the outside of the hotel (to the amusement and cheers of the other hotel guests), while the rest of Team GB completed their lap of the stadium.

Our makeshift ceremony was enough for us to feel we had really arrived, with the added advantage of being able to sit straight down again with a cup of hot chocolate to watch the rest on TV before taking the lift to bed. Sometimes the Olympics is about making the most of the moments it gives you and sometimes it's about making your own moments (and I'm going to say that thing about how much of what I've learnt about life I've learnt from rowing just this once more and then I'll try not to say it again, because I don't want to overdo it).

Then really, truly, there was nothing left to do but race.

It had been no surprise when the crew lists came out that Boron and Kwalski had moved into the Quad. If we'd been holding onto any small hope that this particular star would align in our favour and they'd stay in the Double, it was extinguished. It would have been a bonus, but as it was it didn't disrupt our focus. Everything was as expected.

The Germans were seeded into the first heat. The Germans won their heat.

We were seeded into the second heat. We won our heat.

We were both straight through to the final the following Sunday without having to meet.

Everything was as expected.

The rest of the quads had to race again on Tuesday in the Rep to make the remaining four places. They went to USA, Russia, Ukraine and Australia (who had got over their Lucerne jet lag and improved their speed, but still lost to Germany in their heat). Denmark, the same crew who'd been Silver medallists in 2002 when we'd been so gutted to come fifth, didn't even make the final.

Meanwhile, we had a whole week to wait. In our preparation we'd decided to take a bit of a gamble and assume we could still win our heat at less than our peak, so we were now actually into our final taper and preparation pieces. We filled the week as best we could and actually, with still two outings most days around racing times and all our pieces and processes to fit in, it never felt like too much time.

The closest I ever got to being a flag bearer. A 'Blue Peter' flag made of rolled-up posters and physio tape. I'm treating our makeshift ceremony with the gravitas it deserves.

On our way out to race our heat. The tape on our riggers is because it was quite rough that day and there was a theory circulating that this would stop some of the splash into the boat that makes you take on water. We wouldn't need it for the final. Mostly I like this photo for how incredibly low and relaxed my shoulders are. The bump on my left shoulder is from an A/C joint dislocation when I fell head-first off my bike coaching on the towpath in Cambridge some ten years previously. I must have bust the ligaments because the collarbone still pops up when I reach forwards. It's a good party trick.

We watched some of the Olympics on our TV. Team GB medals started to roll in and this winning medals thing that we'd been dreaming about for so long started to become very real. And there was still racing going on around us all the time. Some British crews had semi and even quarter-finals to race and those that did not make it straight through had their own last chance Repechage to deal with. Most days there'd be another crew that hadn't made the A-final to try and have just the right conversation with, and by Thursday/Friday they were all racing in their B, C and even D finals. Everyone races a final in rowing, everyone gets a ranking and even in the D finals, people are fighting tooth and nail for the difference between coming nineteenth and twentieth.

I met my mum and sister down at the course. I was surprised and quite choked when I saw Mum squeezed into the signed World Cup Winners yellow bib I'd given her. I thought she might frame it or something, but had never imagined she'd wear it. It looked a little ridiculous but she didn't care. If she could have had 'Alison Mowbray is my daughter' tattooed across her forehead, I think she might have gone for it.

I couldn't quite get my head around the fact that this was my last ever week. I'd looked forward to it all being over for so long, but now I was enjoying it again and definitely still getting better. It had been my commitment to myself for as long as I'd been rowing to keep going as long as both those things were true, so I wondered if I was being hasty in my decision. I thought in particular about the progress we'd made in timing the separation at the catch and I wondered how that would feel if I took it into my single. I wondered how much faster I could still go. I even wondered if I could finally win a trial. But every time my head started to go there, a dozen reasons why not started to flood in and in the end I just cut short my thought processes with one line. "I'm not thinking like that. I don't want even the slightest thought in my brain that there will ever be another chance if I don't get it right on Sunday. Everything for the last time, this time."

After our heat Chris Shambrook gave us an A4 sheet entitled **GB W4X Athens 2004, Mental markers for the week**. There are five points and they are all good, but maybe the one I like most says: *As athletes you want to know how good you can be – your excellence so far has given you the chance to find out how good you can be in the most exciting context possible… the Olympic Games. Be excited that you are going to find out just how good you can be when it most counts, and know that all the choices you have made before now have paid off and given you the chance to take the ultimate step up to the highest level. An opportunity to thrive on! Step up and relish the opportunity YOU have created.*

Opportunity rather than threat. If ever I felt myself start to feel worried or anxious during the week, I would catch myself and turn it round in my head. This was '*The best opportunity I would ever have to find out how good I could be,*' that was all. I was well practised; I'd been doing it a long time. My school PE jumper was the wrong colour and I might be picked on for being different, but I could get to sleep if I thought about how much warmer it would keep me than all the other girls.

We met to discuss our race plan. A question non-rowers often ask is who makes the decisions during the race and who does the talking since we don't have a cox. The answer is mainly that we have a race plan and we have talked it through for weeks before we race, so we don't need to do much talking on the water. One command from one person triggers a whole chain of action. Every word has to be discussed and agreed because just like there are at least three possible interpretations of "We'll meet at 9am", when you just say a command like "Sharp catches" or "Harden on", it can mean different things in different people's heads and here it had to mean the same. Debs made most of the race calls, but Fran called the last 500m into the line as lactic acid queen Debs did not have breath by that point. Bow often does the race calls as they are facing the right way to be heard, but I'd never been given this role, even to try. Paul always phrased it that the girls in the middle of the boat were in a better position to be heard, but I knew that despite doing most of the calls during training, Paul still had it in his head that I was easily distracted and liable to go off on my own if I was given anything to do but row.

We'd developed our race plan over the season and were happy with most of it, but still looking for how we could get more in the final. None of us had ever been in an Olympic final before, but we were aware of two things.

This might be it. Our one and only Olympic Final (certainly the case for me). One chance to get it right. There was no chance to practise, no way of knowing what it would be like until we were there. No real comparison with our heat or Lucerne or even World Championship Finals because…

…in an Olympic Final, everyone raises their game. People and crews do things differently; they are braver because they feel they have nothing to lose. Everyone in that final thinks they have a chance at a medal, but know they will have to up their game to get it. At least three crews think they have a chance at Gold, but know they will have to up their game to get it.

What could we do in our one-shot Olympic Final to up our game and give ourselves a fighting chance? I talked again about our evolutionary 'lion escape reserve tanks' and about how the best races in my life had been when I'd moved my race forward by 250m. We all said that our best crew race had been when we'd been bravest in the Lucerne final and gone for it without any real thought about how we'd last the distance. I can't remember where the reservation came from, but we couldn't quite agree to shift forwards by 250m and agreed on 100m. Our usual plan and everyone's usual plan is to lift and race it home from halfway. We agreed to try to be first to 500m as we had in Lucerne, then shift our whole race plan forward by 100m and race our LAST 1,000M from 900m to 1900m and then… well, it was an Olympic Final. We figured we'd find something from somewhere to get us through the last dozen strokes. That was our new plan.

Our last 24 hours

The middle Saturday of the Games was Finals day for Group A crews. We'd rowed an early session that morning before racing, then sat in the TV lounge to watch the finals. We watched Elise and Sarah win an amazing Bronze behind New Zealand and Germany, then Cath and Katherine take Silver two seconds behind the Romanians, which felt slightly more mixed. Amazing for getting a Silver medal, but we knew, like us, they had been aiming for Gold – and for KG, this was a second Silver. Even at the time I remember thinking how cruel and strange it is that a Silver medal could make you and everyone around you unreservedly happy one year, but then just reservedly so four years on. Both results upped the anti for us. It was an unbearable thought that all our teammates would go home with medals and us not. And of course, the opportunity of going one better and being the first ever female British Olympic Champion rowers was still up for grabs.

We left for our second outing before we had time to watch the Men's Four but heard by phone that they'd won as we travelled to the course.

And then from that moment really, us walking in as they were all walking out, it was all about us. As the only British crew from Group B to make a final, there was only us left to race.

We walked past the fence of reporters on our way in. I'd intended to ignore their calls and walk straight past, but then I heard Martin Cross call "Ali, Ali, over here" and I went over. Really he just wanted to wish us all the best, but he did start to ask a few questions. I started to answer, but very quickly it felt all wrong. I felt myself being drawn out of the tunnel and cut it short and said goodbye. As I walked to the boathouse I was cross with myself for allowing myself to be distracted and then I realised I was now distracted by being cross, so I tried to let it go. I visualised the race and by the time I got in the boat, I was really back in. But that was it. No more interviews, no more talking to anyone except my team. Talking about winning isn't the same as doing winning.

We rowed just two laps that afternoon, finishing with a start-out-of-the-blocks race visualisation down the course – always my favourite session. We started at a rate 18 paddle, but made all the calls at the right markers and felt the response in our bodies. Debs called the big 20 stroke push at 900m – 100m early – and I felt the commitment in the water together even at 18. We didn't mean to, but by the end of the track there was so much adrenalin in our system that the rate had lifted to a very easy 24-26. We couldn't help ourselves, our focus was absolute, and it was probably the best paddling we had ever done. We came off the water buzzing, but absolutely calm, absolutely in sync and absolutely ready.

We had an early dinner together in a rather empty hotel restaurant. Having finished racing, most of the other rowers were off out somewhere finally spending time with their families and friends. They'd be back though. We didn't have formal rules, but it was generally accepted that your competition was not really over until the last team member had raced. If there were champagne bottles around, they were not in our sight; everyone we saw was quiet and calm and anyone who was around dropped by our table to wish us all the best and tell us they knew we'd be brilliant tomorrow. If anyone was late back tonight, we certainly wouldn't hear them and everyone would be down at the course in time to watch us race. All this went without saying. I know other Olympic teams have all sorts of codes and rules and make their athletes sign behavioural contracts and set curfews and some even send people home immediately after racing so they won't disgrace the sport, but not rowing. Sometimes, often, I'm very proud to be a rower.

All the support staff were around somewhere, keeping out of our way if we didn't need them, but all still around. I was aware of the whole combined force of British Rowing quietly aligning itself behind us in one last team effort push to help get us over the line, preferably in first place. Everyone knew we were going for Gold and absolutely how close it was going to be. It could have been extra stressful to be the sole focus of all those people, the last boat to compete, the only Sunday finals crew, but it didn't feel extra stressful. It made me feel very special and that I was capable of *doing* something very special. It made me feel like I might be one of the Other People.

After dinner we stayed in the dining room with the sea view since we were the only ones left there anyway, and Paul and Mark joined us for a final meeting. A well-oiled machine now, we got out the timetables and working back from the 9.30am race time, wrote down wake-up, breakfast, drive to course, hands on for pre-race outing, pre-race chat, hands on to race, push-off and on the start times. We discussed everything and if anyone was unclear about anything they asked and no one rolled their eyes and got impatient, because the first important thing was that tomorrow everyone would be in exactly the right place at exactly the right time so no one would irritate anyone.

We talked through the race plan one last time and then really, really talked about all the possibilities of what might be happening around us and how we should think and respond in each case. Because it's not like you can stop in the middle to chat. Plan A was to race the hardest, fastest start we'd ever done, be first to 500m, and then be able to watch from the front for the rest of the race. But we talked about how this was an Olympic final and there wasn't a crew out there who didn't have exactly that plan. Everyone was going to go out harder and faster than they'd ever done in their lives. But we said, without being complacent, that apart from this new German combination, we'd already beaten all the other crews out there this season – so whatever happened, however far they managed to get ahead in the first half of the race, IF WE WERE ROWING WELL, as well as we knew how, then they could not stay with us in the second half. We were the better crew. We just had to keep our heads and believe that. Whatever they did in the first half of the race to try and break us psychologically (because that would be their only hope and almost certainly what they were talking about in their team meetings tonight), we wouldn't let them.

IF WE WERE ROWING WELL, whatever else happened, in the last 500m it WOULD BE BETWEEN US AND THE GERMANS.

But the Germans were a different matter and not just because they were Germans. We had never raced this crew before. Our status and seeding had meant we'd avoided them in heats, which should have been an advantage, but it also meant we hadn't had the practice row against them we'd had in Lucerne. Paul pulled out a graph he'd made comparing start ratings and times in our heat with the Germans' start in their heat to try and give us some of the information we'd missed by not racing them. He said that the Germans had been quicker off the start because they'd kept their rating and boat speed up higher for longer than we had. I looked at his graph and the difference between the German start and ours appeared quite shocking – our rate and speed dropping far, far quicker than the Germans. We were all a bit shocked. But then the scientist in me noticed that the points on our line graph were closer together than on the German line graph, "Paul, the difference is not as pronounced as your graphs suggest. You've drawn the two graphs on different scales; if you'd drawn our data onto the same scale as the Germans, it wouldn't look as bad."

"Alison, I'm just telling you that you need to rate higher and go harder off the start if you want to keep up with the Germans."

"Yes, I get that and we will, but you can't draw a graph like that. That's all I'm saying." I wanted to tell him that I admired his innovation and thought processes, but I'd have had to mark him wrong in his Year 9 SATS for that graph. By this point Becs (who was ultimately responsible for the rates) had worked it out too and joined in. "Yes, the scales are completely different – you can't say what you're saying from that graph." Paul put his scary eyes in and I could tell he was rallying for a fight, but then I could also see him remember where we all were. He picked up the graph and put it away. "It doesn't matter, forget about it. I just thought it was helpful."

"Paul, it is helpful, it's just the graph…" I really can be most annoying.

"It doesn't matter Alison, just leave it." So I did. But it seems there was more than one misunderstanding from that interaction that I'd like to clear up. I've heard second-hand that somehow Mark left that meeting thinking that Paul had told us to pace ourselves off the start and he is still aggrieved about it. I don't know if that's true, but all I want to record is that whatever way he went about saying it, Paul was very clear that we were going to have to go harder and faster out of that start than ever before to stay in touch with the Germans, and all four of *us* were very clear about that.

We all calmed down and started talking about how to beat the Germans. Plan A was to stay high and fast off the start and stay ahead like in Lucerne, but we all thought it would be wise to have at least a Plan B. We said that the Germans could do anything. That was what we could expect. And certainly one possible way that this could pan out was that they would get ahead off the start. If that happened, then we would just have to keep our nerve and fight to stay as close to them as possible and take them back on our 900m push. I asked the girls if they wanted me to call if the Germans started slipping away as I would be closest to them. They agreed that I should.

Paul: "But not too often Alison, you mustn't get distracted."

So we had a Plan B.

But what if Plan B didn't work?

We talked about it and said that the Germans could do anything. That was what we could expect. If nothing we did at 900m and in the third quarter worked and they were still ahead coming into the last 500m, then we could still get them. Gillian Lindsey had told us that whatever boat you were in, it was always possible to make up a length in 500m, so even if you were a length down you should never give up. I also said that in my single coming into the last 500m, I always told myself "If I can see 'em, I can get 'em" and it almost always worked. We had practised our finish into the line a hundred times and knew it was good. Even in Lucerne, under all that pressure, after all that front-ended work, we'd still held it absolutely together and held off everything that anyone could throw at us. We decided that the final plan, if all else failed, was that even if we were still down with 500m to go, we would still all believe that "If we can see 'em, we can get 'em". We all believed, really believed, we could make up a length in the last 500m.

So that was that, and Mark and Paul left us to it. We'd booked Chris Shambrook to continue with us and while we waited Becs and I argued about sunglasses. Oakleys had given us several free pairs and Becs wanted us all to wear the gold ones tomorrow because "it will look really cool on the podium when we win." We thought we'd covered everything that could cause disharmony but this was the one thing, THE ONE THING, we hadn't discussed. I couldn't talk about it, wouldn't even discuss it and Becs couldn't understand why. So many problems but how to explain? Talking about winning is not the same as doing winning. The arrogance of going out in gold sunglasses. We can't give that fuel to our opposition. If we win, the conceit of standing on the podium in our glasses looking like we knew we'd had it all sown up. And if we lose in gold glasses? Inconceivable! But how to explain all this when already just thinking about it is shifting my head to a place it shouldn't be. "Becs, I'm sorry. I can't talk about this. Please wear whatever glasses you want, but don't talk about it with me anymore." But she wouldn't leave it and in the end, just to make her stop, I agreed to hand my gold glasses over to put into the cool box with the ice jackets, so we had them if we won and wanted to wear them. I still have no idea what happened and whether they were in there and I never had any intention of wearing them.

Then Chris joined us having missed all the fun (psychologists are like policemen, there is never one around when you really need them) and we got to work again. Point 1 of his **Mental marker for the Week** sheet had asked us to be prepared to share with each other why this chance was so important to us and why our commitment was going to be at its highest ever in the Final. I don't remember what the other three said and I'd be doing them a disservice if I tried to make it up. I remember that it worked though. As each person shared their very different WHY behind this one same goal, I felt my own resolve harden and belief strengthen. It was important to hear each other's, but actually that week I'd found it important even to think about it for myself. If you are not careful, this thing you do becomes just something you do and then just something you have to do because the Olympian inside won't let you do anything else. But WHY REALLY was I doing this? This, to the best of my recollection, was my WHY.

"I remember watching my first Olympics on TV and seeing the athletes win races, and even at the age of nine I thought how amazing it must be to know you were the best in the world at something. I decided then that I wanted to be the best in the world at something. I liked the idea of being best in the world at a sport and tried tennis and netball and even ice-skating, but I wasn't even the best in my class so I didn't think I could be best in the world. I thought it might be something to do with music for a while but I was second horn and again, not even the best in my school. Then I thought it might be something to do with science for a long while. I was best in my year at university, but when I tried to take it on to the next level I couldn't do it. Somewhere amongst all of that I actually forgot or lost heart with trying to be the best in the world at something. I haven't thought about it for a long while. With rowing, I've always just tried to be the best I can be and it's brought me here.

But I realised that this is it. I actually have a real opportunity to be the best in the world at something. If we do this, then for the rest of my life I'll know that I was once the best in the world at what I do. How many people can ever say that? And more than that, this is almost certainly the best, perhaps the only opportunity I will ever have. I'm retiring and I can't imagine ever working so hard for so long on any one thing again. I can't imagine ever having so many people around me to help. I find it scary to think that if we don't do this tomorrow, if I/we let this slip by and don't win, then that will be it. I can't see how I will ever get an opportunity like this again. I'm sick of being very good but not quite the best. I'm sick of being plucky runner-up and smiling and making the best of it. That is what this means to me. I want to be the best in the world at something and finally, this is it."

Then there was just one thing left. Chris had given us all a piece of paper the day before and asked us to write a few lines about each of our crew mates. He'd produced a single sheet of A4 for each of us with individual and crew photos and the comments from each of our teammates under the heading **'Your place in creating history'.** I don't have the other girls' pieces of paper, but this, as far as I remember, is what I wrote for each of them. It's still what I remember them for anyway.

Becs – *Even though it's your first Olympics, you shoulder all the responsibility of stroking and steering and take it all absolutely in your stride. You have the most single-minded focus of anyone I've ever met. You don't say very much in crew debriefs, but when you do choose to say something we all listen because what you say is usually different and always right. Your insights have been fundamental in helping bring this boat together and keeping us moving on.*

Fran – *You are an amazing friend and have helped me personally in some of my toughest moments over the past few years. You challenged me to set the bar even higher on my dreams and aim for Gold and it's your confidence that has given me the confidence to believe that that is what I should be aiming for. Your absolute attention to detail and refusal to ever accept that what we do is good enough has been* *tough, but an essential balance to my positivity. You are the fastest sculler in Great Britain and having you in the boat gives me confidence that we can take on the best in the world.*

Debs – *You are the sunny peacemaker in the crew. You seem to be a sponge that absorbs anyone's anger and frustration and have kept us all calm and happy. You are the most powerful sprinter in the boat and at the start of a race, I just sit behind you and feel your power. I know you give us a massive advantage off the start.*

I've just spent three hours looking for my sheet of paper and found it in the last box of memorabilia. I've not read it in nearly seven years, but this is what it says:

GB W4X. Athens Olympics 2004
Your place in creating history

Al, your years of experience in raising your game and performing on the day when it counts most means I know you will raise your game and lift your performance higher than anyone else in the field and in doing so once again (as you always do), you'll surpass any conceived expectations of the sum of your parts.

Perspective – you always know how much better we are than any previous GB Quad since 2001, so we can trust and believe you when you say even our worst rows are still better than any previous quad's best – ***Fran***

You provide absolute consistency in your performance. You have sheer racing drive which makes you overcome/exceed people's perceptions of your ability. You find a positiveness out of anything or anybody (you balance Fran on the +/- continuum!). Your positiveness has at times kept the crew from sinking quite low in attitude or enthusiasm – ***Becs***

You always find something positive in what we are doing, no matter what. You are the most consistent at keeping calm in the boat. And you give a damn good haircut! – ***Debs***

Alison's mental strength is that she is always looking for positives on almost any situation – a great quality to have in any crew. Technically, the speed the blade grips the water defines your excellence – ***Mark***

Alison's DETERMINATION is second to none. Gritty, tough and extremely positive – ***Paul***

We all sat quietly and read our sheets and tried not to cry. Imagine having a sheet of paper like that in a drawer somewhere for the rest of your life. Becs put hers down and just said: "Thank you all so much. You've all said such amazing things. I never knew you all felt like that about me or that anyone thought those things about me. I know I look like I'm going to cry but I am really happy. Reading this is the most amazing thing that has ever happened to me. I almost feel like I don't care what happens tomorrow anymore, it's already been worth it for this… don't take that the wrong way or anything… I mean obviously I do still care what happens tomorrow… "

"Becs, it's OK! We get it!"

And then Chris gave us one last sheet of paper and left us to it. This is some of what it said:-

DEFINING YOUR FUTURE

You have a defining day approaching – a day that will alter how you think about yourself from here on in. We know from athletes that have gone before you that as a result of rising to the occasion and taking control, they think of themselves as:

- *Carrying an immense amount of inner pride from that day that does not diminish.*
- *Being someone who found out everything they could about themselves and are not left thinking 'if only' or 'what if?'*
- *Being hugely satisfied that they found a way to push themselves physically and drain every possible ounce of effort from themselves.*
- *Knowing that they have the mental fortitude to excel in the future – whatever the context.*
- *Motivated and inspired every time they think back and reflect upon how well they stepped up to the challenge and took it on when they most needed to.*

CHOOSE how you are going to influence 'forever' … on YOUR DEFINING DAY THAT YOU HAVE CREATED FOR YOURSELF.

Debs and I went upstairs to the room we'd shared all week and packed our race bags. We set our alarms for 5am and I suspect Debs probably went to bed at that point as there really is no limit to how much she can sleep, but I went for one last beach walk. I walked a bit further than usual, partly because this was my last chance to explore what was round the next corner and partly because I just needed to walk a bit further that evening. I came across a house. There was lots of noise coming from the garden, so I peeked over the gate to take a look. They had a tarpaulin rigged as a big screen in the courtyard under the vines and half a dozen Greeks were sitting drinking wine and watching the day's Olympic highlights projected onto the makeshift screen. They saw me looking and ushered me over saying something in Greek that sounded more welcoming and friendly than, "Hey, you nosy parker, what you looking at?" – so I opened the gate and went in. They welcomed me quite literally with open arms and a glass of wine. I didn't speak any Greek and they no English, but I shook my head at the wine, pointed to the Olympic rings on my T-shirt and to the screen. They got that I was an athlete of some description and I got that they were all very pleased with this. They were obviously asking "What sport?" so I did the rowing action with my arms and mouthed "ROWWWIIING" very slowly like you do when you think it will help, and they went "Yes, Yes, Yes!" and made the rowing action too. I knew that they almost certainly thought I was a canoeist because no one ever knows the difference, but I thought that was probably close enough.

I sat down with them for a short while to watch the Olympic highlights. If they had been British or spoken English they'd have been making me talk about stuff I couldn't talk about, but as it was they let me just sit there and somehow it was the easiest place to be. It was all rather surreal and by the time I'd walked home, I sort of wondered if it had really happened – like it was one of those points in scary films where the protagonist goes back the following evening to show a friend and nothing is there.

I helped myself to cereal and milk from the table of snacks that was laid out for us 24/7, taking it absolutely as my due that the world (well this world anyway) absolutely revolved around me and everything I needed would be available without me even having to ask. And sat alone in the silent dining room eating the breakfast I knew I wouldn't be able to get down in the morning. Then I went to the room I shared with Debbie, safe in the knowledge that I could have dragged her around the room and she wouldn't have woken up (this was not something I actually did), which made her the perfect roommate for restless Al the night before her first and last Olympic Final. I took my sleeping tablet, attached the essential accreditation pass to my bag so I couldn't forget it tomorrow and went to bed for the last night before my last ever race.

Ten thousand tiny steps.

Chapter 20: 4 hours, 36½ minutes and it will all be over

"The successful warrior is the average man with laser-like focus."

Our alarms go off at 5am to make sure that we are really awake by 9.30. I wake up wired. I am nervous but not scared. I have never been more ready, more prepared for anything. This is the biggest opportunity I will ever have to show anyone what I can do. We breakfast as best we can and Paul drives our minibus down to the course. The girls always let me sit in the front as I feel travelsick even on days when I'm not about to race an Olympic final.

We put our boat on the water for our pre-race paddle and row just one 4k lap including another call over visualisation down the track. It is good. I keep my focus in the moment so although I'm absolutely aware that this is a defining day, I can cope. It's feeding rather than draining me. Every nerve and muscle is alive so I feel my skin can't contain them. I want it to be over though, like I always do. I want it to be over, so I never have to feel like this again. I've put myself through these unbearable hours so many times and have learnt to accept that it can never be any easier or anything other than this, because if I didn't feel this I wouldn't be ready. I can gauge how ready I am by how bad I feel. Too good and I'm not ready and I must think about the race, side by side with the Germans, just for a few seconds to make it real again and bring back the sickness. I have to do that a few times because I find it alarmingly easy to start thinking of this as the stuff of legend and tell the story in my head before it's even complete. But then after a few seconds the sickness comes back and I have to stop thinking about the race and focus on what I am doing now, in *this* very moment.

I would give anything, ANYTHING, for racing to be postponed so I could be released from this for even a few minutes. But every time my head goes there, I have to pull it back. Even on rough days you don't let your head go there and today is a beautiful day. I pull my head back, stay in the tunnel and bear it because this is where I have put myself. This is where I have to be today and this is what I have to do. Athletes talk about choices but this doesn't feel like a choice. As hard as it is to stay in – if you took me out, I would be destroyed.

We take the boat off the water, shower, change and go sit in one of the rest rooms to occupy the next collection of minutes stretching, trying to eat and pretending to read. Becs, like many athletes, listens to music on headphones, but that's not something I've ever wanted to do.

At some point we all independently take out pens and write three words or phrases on the triangle of skin between the forefinger and thumb of our left hand. This part of our hand will be turned towards us when we scull and our left hands will be on top so the words will always be visible. In the last few weeks we've been narrowing down and narrowing down, until we each arrive at three points which act as anchors for our whole stroke. Three things that make everything else fall into place. Each of us has three different points because we have different things we need to focus on to all scull exactly the same. I write BACK OVER, HANDS UP, WAIT.

Get right OVER from the BACK of the stroke. I still, despite all the practise, need to stay conscious of this and speed my hands away from the back a little quicker and rock over a little more than feels totally natural and comfortable. If I focus on this, then I get to the quarter-slide balance position with the other girls and we get to feel that beautiful fraction of a second where we wait for the boat to move under us before it takes us up the slide.

Then I must focus on HANDS UP because the catch can never be quick enough or hard enough. I've written HANDS UP, but those words connect to a pathway in my brain that activates my lats. If I get this right, then my whole body will remain under 'relaxed tension' as I connect. My core will contract to hold the blades against the water and my thighs against my calves. Not the big six-pack stomach muscles (which I do have by the way and very fine they look at this point of my athletic peak), but the lower, deeper muscles that hold my whole back strong and firm without having to hold it in tension. Then the temptation, especially if we are rating 45+ off the start, or are half a length down on a crew and putting in a big push, is to jump on the blades so I must consciously…

WAIT. Even in those extreme moments, I must be patient enough for the water to accept and suck onto the blades and for the movement of the boat to start to bring the handles back towards me faster than I could ever grab hold of them myself. Only then can I push and my Glute muscles will contract automatically to start the stroke. My legs will go down, my back will open, my hands will flow in, down and round, and I must force myself…

BACK OVER. And I must do all of that every stroke for over 35 strokes a minute for six and a half minutes. A level of concentration unparalleled by anything I have ever known.

With two hours to go before start time, there are no more idle minutes because I start my pre-race routines. I'm on the clock now until the starter says 'Go'.

I take myself to a quiet corner, orientate myself in the same direction I will be when I race and sit on the floor in a loose approximation of the rowing position – my legs bent up and elbows resting on my knees. I close my eyes, relax my breathing, put myself into the boat and attach the boat to the start pontoon. I inhabit my body, but sometimes I look out of my own eyes and sometimes I see myself from the side. I can switch. My crewmates know what I am doing when I do my visualisation and know not to disturb me, but it's not something they do. I've done this before every head race, long-distance trial, heat, rep, semi and final, every single race since Ron Needs taught me how to do this over ten years ago before my first Boat Race, clicking his rate watch at the right stroke rate and calling out the 250m markers so our cox could call out the commands.

I've learnt to do it by myself now with no rate watch and to count the strokes to each marker and hit the rates so closely, that even with my eyes closed I'll finish my 'race' within seconds of the predicated race time. Each year I ask my new crew if they will try this with me. But each year, after a couple of attempts, they tell me it doesn't work for them and they'd rather do something else if that's all right. I'm not sure that any of the rest of the women's squad did this – except Elise maybe.

So I put myself on the start, focus on Debbie's back and call myself an 'Attention… Go'. I visualise every stroke and every call down the course, feeling it through every muscle, my body twitching slightly with each stroke. I love this part of the morning. This is the only six and a half minutes between 5am and 9.30am where I don't feel sick, because I'm racing and I feel good when racing. Some athletes talk about visualising different scenarios, but I don't do that. I'm always aware that there are other boats around me, but they are never fully formed and never in any particular place. I always look exactly how I want to look and feel exactly how I want to feel in my body and that's all that matters. I always have to push all the way to the line, but feel confident every stroke that I will achieve whatever I have set out to achieve. Today I cross the 1,900m mark in the lead, then stop because I am trying to convince my body to give everything it has by that point.

I breathe hard in the final minutes of the visualisation and when I finally open my eyes, I don't quite open them all the way because I am in 'the state'. This is the difference between the Al Mowbray you beat in training and the Al Mowbray who'll beat you in racing.

"The successful warrior is the average man with laser-like focus." Bruce Lee

I stretch again, just lightly, and do some warm-up exercises, more to keep me awake than anything else as adrenalin is a weird and dangerous drug.

We gather ourselves together, sort out everything we will need (which isn't much), check our bags in and go to the loo for nearly the last time. Then we meet Paul and he gives us his final words of wisdom. He reminds us of all the training and preparation we have done, that nothing has been left undone, that this crew is exceptional and we are exceptional, and that he truly believes that if we go out there and row the best that we are capable of then it will be enough. Paul is also a big believer that the notes are not the music, so he talks about that too.

We routinely then have a quick conversation about whether we have time to go to the loo again and generally we do, because if we need to go once we get on the water then we will just have to hold it in. There is always an anxiety about how long the queue will be and whether there will be time. That's OK though because it's quite a low level of something to be anxious about considering the circumstances. We will all need to go again by the time we get to the start anyway. That's partly because we are in such a perfect state of hydration that our bodies cannot actually hold onto any water (we have been pretty much perfectly and constantly hydrated and never been more than an arm's length from a water bottle since we last let ourselves not care the week after Sydney) and partly because defining moments have a habit of shrinking your bladder to the size of a small walnut.

Finally, there is nothing left to do but pick our blades up and take them down to the pontoon. There are lots of people hovering in the wings who would love to take my blades down for me, but I must do it as part of my ritual. And anyway how else would I fill those three minutes? We stand by the boat which is on trestles and has been checked and polished to within an inch of its life by Olympic boat men in the couple of hours since we last saw it. I call "Hands on!" and "Lift!" and the boat is balanced on our shoulders and we are carrying it down to the water for what I have to assume will be the last time we will ever row together.

"Above Heads!" and "Down!" and we roll our boat down to make that satisfying 'smack' when it hits the water. I walk the couple of paces across to pick up my blades and as I straighten up, I am facing the direction of the grandstands – and I see, several hundred yards away, behind the tall wire fencing that separates the athletes from the friends and family spectators, a wide yellow shape and a rather taller bare mid-riffed stick and I realise that my mum and sister have come to wave me off, as is our family tradition.

I raise a hand in acknowledgement and they wave back and that's all I'm going to do, and then the track that's playing over the tannoy changes to J-Lo "Let's Get Loud". It's the anthem from our first Al & Cath adventure in Canada five years ago. My heart lifts a bit and I feel it must be one of those signs I don't believe in. I look across to Catherine, put my hand to my ear, then raise it to point at the music. Even from that distance I can tell she is shrugging and looking confused. I feel a bit irritated that she does not understand, that she does not just hear the music and make the connection and I repeat the mime rather more emphatically. Still nothing. It suddenly becomes incredibly important to me that she gets it before I get on the water and I am very annoyed at her little sister slowness. I point to the air again and start to do a little hip wiggle dance on the landing stage to try and make my point and then I catch myself and freeze, deadly guilty. What am I doing? Where is my head?

I go back to the boat and really, really try and focus on just putting my blades in the gates, but still I feel distracted and out of the tunnel. I feel angry for allowing myself to get distracted, then realise that that is another distraction so I try and let it go. Rule 4 of rowing in rough water: *Accept that a fair proportion of the strokes are going to be rubbish because you are doing something very hard. If you row a rubbish stroke accept it and forget about it and just think about how you can make the next one good. This is particularly important when racing. Then, for every rubbish stroke you do, remember that your opposition will be finding it just as tough and rowing at least as many rubbish strokes. The less time you can spend worrying about the rubbish stroke you've just done, the more time you've got to think about how to make the next stroke not rubbish.*

But I'm struggling, really struggling now. I stay calm and keep trying though. I get in the boat, narrow my eyes and control my breathing. With thirty minutes to go before our start time, Paul takes hold of my blade to push us out. "Have a good one".

"See you later." The ritual helps.

We start the warm-up we have planned and executed so many times and again the ritual and routine helps draw me back. I catch myself a couple of times still thinking of my little dance and feeling annoyed, but I push it away and pull in the sensation of my lats lifting into the catch, the sound of the catch hitting the water and focus absolutely on picking up the water as low and deep as I can find in my body.

Fran makes the calls but here on the much shorter, narrower warm-up lake, it's my job to look over my shoulder to keep us safe from other crews and call when to stop and turn. The responsibility of my role helps and somewhere between Paul pushing us out and us pulling off to the side to stop and do a few roll-ups, I must have slipped back in because I wasn't thinking about it anymore to remember that I should have been forgetting.

With fifteen minutes to go, we gather by the bridge with the other Quads and wait for the marshals to allow us onto the course proper. I'd be lying if I tried to claim I was so focused I wasn't fearful. "What if I catch a blade off the start, catch a crab and stop the boat in front of everyone? What if I do that and ruin the chances of my crew? How will I ever live with that?" But I have to push that thought away, because thoughts like that make you hold back and be cautious off the start – and if you hold anything back, then you may be less likely to mess up but you will already have lost. No one else will ever know it was you who lost them the race like they would if you messed up publically, but you will still have lost and you will always know it was you who lost it.

And then there is the less specific dread of taking myself and my body to a point of pain I know only too well and then onto somewhere it has never been before. A huge part of the mental battle and exhaustion in these last few hours is in the split between the instinctive, reptilian, life-preserving brain that tells you "No!" and the far too highly-evolved human part that you own and have to constantly make say "Yes" against all logic and reason.

We row across and into our central seeded lane, Lane 4. We straighten up and come forward for our final practice start. I call it and we power off for 12 strokes, then wind down and spin in our lane to come back up. We all have watches attached to our shoes and are all trying to stay calm about time, but there is always an anxiety. We want to cut it as close as possible so we are not sat too long on the start where every spare minute feels like an hour, but similarly to cut it too fine runs the risk of receiving a false start penalty. That anxiety makes us feel rushed and the final minutes disappear in seconds. The difference between too long and not enough time is probably about half a minute.

We paddle back up to the start pontoon, spin again and back the boat down so the stake boat boy lying prone on the pontoon can take hold of our stern. We are attached with about seven minutes to go. All crews are attached and everyone is looking at their watch wondering, "Are we OK?", "Are we on time?"

We take off the white long-sleeve tops that have been shielding us from the heat of the already quite powerful early morning sun and pass those, together with our water bottles and anything else we are not actually wearing, forward to Becs who puts it into a bag marked GBR W4x in the somewhat optimistic hope that we might ever see it again. The stake boat boy pulls us back so he can reach the bag from Becs. Then all that is left in the boat is us, our stroke coach and a rigger jigger spanner (with 13mm and 10mm ends) attached to Debs footplate, because we have all independently learnt that lesson at some point along the way.

The stake boat boy keeps us back a bit at this point because the umpire calls "Arm the start mechanism" and there is a warning horn and then a great whoosh behind us as the start buckets rise out of the water. The science of man has taken over from the power of prayer in keeping boats straight on the start of major events these days, and we align and tap our bows into the plastic cup that will hold us level and straight and drop back into the water as the lights turn green.

The umpire calls "TWO MINUTES. TWO… MINUTES" with the exact same pacing and booming intonation that every umpire always calls it. And there is absolutely nothing left to do but wait. The race has already taken over from any other thoughts or feelings of dread and I am calm and anticipatory. It can sometimes feel rather isolated here in the bows, but Debs turns one final time to smile at me and reaches back to squeeze my foot. I smile back and reach forward to squeeze her hand and know that we are both excited rather than scared.

For all four of us, our first Olympic Final.

Everything I've ever done has led to this point. Everyone who has ever done anything for me or to me. Everyone who has ever believed in me and everyone who has not. If one thing had been different, it would have taken me down a different path to a different place and I wouldn't have emerged here on this start line – today. Don't regret your past; change your future.

The umpire starts the call over. "LANE 1 – USA." We all come forwards into our start positions. "LANE 2 – UKRAINE." We square our blades in the water. "LANE 3 – GERMANY." I am aware of them on our left – reigning Olympic Champions. Katrin Boron my opposite number at Bow, going for her fourth consecutive Olympic Gold. "LANE 4 – GREAT BRITAIN." I've been rowing for fifteen years, this has been my job for seven years and I've been working towards just this, every day for four years. And it will be over in six and a half minutes. But all that's in my head is the first three strokes. Not the finish line, not the medal, not the cameras, not the Germans, not anything but the first three strokes. I sit there and visualise them over and over – because this is what I can control.

And I don't think about my crew either. Because perhaps the true mark of an exceptional team is that in the performance moment, you don't have to consider them at all. I am so totally confident that they will do their jobs right that I don't have to waste a single thought even thinking about how much I trust them.

And when the camera pans across from Boron to me you can see me look back left and right to CHECK I'VE GOT BOTH BLADES IN THE WATER. Because I've learnt something in seven years.

"LANE 5 – RUSSIA" Reigning Olympic Bronze medallists on our right.

"LANE 6 – AUSTRALIA" Reigning World Champions, they'd beaten us by a street the year before. We are surrounded by medallists when none of us has one. Everyone will take a risk at some point in this final and Australia's is immediately obvious. They are the same scullers from last year, but they have raced this year with a different girl stroking to when they became World Champions. They were beaten by Germany in the heat so in the days between the Rep and this Final, they have swapped to put Amber Bradley back at stroke. It's a risk, but if they don't take it they have lost anyway. We must all think like that.

All crews are sat forward and ready. There is a pause of an indeterminable number of seconds.

"ATTENTION…" I contract my glutes and lower core muscles against the water to take up the slack like a sprinter pressing into their blocks.

Everything for the last time and everything the best I have ever done it. That more even than the medal is the goal.

"GO!" Lights turn green, buckets drop and we jump on that first stroke together, punching it through the water. It's good, and the next, and the next. In those first 20 strokes you don't look outside the boat, you don't think of anything except the catch and the finish and keeping the blades high, clean and safe off the water. In the body of the race you rate 35/36 strokes per minute, but off the start you're up at 45/46 strokes per minute. It's so fast, it's so furious – six crews in a desperate side-by-side battle, fighting for advantage. One tiny slip and it will all be over.

At about 20 strokes, I let my vision and focus widen for the first time to take in the other crews. All boats are still side-by-side except perhaps the Germans who have already slipped us by a couple of feet. I bring my focus back in to try and do something about it. BACK OVER, HANDS UP, WAIT. We stride out to a slightly longer rhythm, down through 250 metres and onto the minute. Around one minute is a critical point. After about 50 seconds of sprinting, you have used up your creatine and anaerobic energy capacity. Lactic acid levels are already critical. This is the point where you see 400-metre runners look like they have literally hit a wall and their bodies are being pressed back by something solid. Runners will tell you that running the 400m is the most pain an athlete will ever feel. Rowers beg to differ.

Only practice and racing through this again and again will tell you that this point is not the end. If you can live with this pain, with lactic acid poisoning and tying up every muscle, and push through the minute, then your body will concede defeat and your aerobic system properly kicks in. Now the hours and hours of aerobic training for this six-and-a-half-minute race pay off, now the slaying thirty-minute ergos at anaerobic threshold come into their own. Those who do not trust their bodies or cannot live with the pain through the minute pull back a bit and wait to recover. They lose races. Those who have learnt to embrace this point as the defining moment of any race press on and may yet win.

We press on. But all crews press on. We are all the very best in the world at what we do.

400m. 500m. A quarter of the way already. Again I let my focus widen to check where we are. We are primed to expect the unexpected and it's a good job because this is truly unlike any race I have ever been part of. Usually by 500m, the crews will have started to separate and there will be clear water between the stern of the leading boat and the bows of the last. But not in this race. Here, all six crews are still on top of each other. USA on our far left have dropped back a few feet and Germany by my left shoulder have moved a little further ahead to sit maybe half a length up, but everyone else is within that frame. At the 500, Debs makes the planned call and I add "Germany half a length, stay with them" – and I take the leap of faith and reach inside to see what else might be there. We all reach for it and it's unbelievable, because each time you'd swear you were already giving it everything and you are, but in those moments if you trust and leap there is almost always more. The boat lifts and we push on into the second quarter. I have no quiet calm feeling of inevitability like I did at this point in Lucerne, but I can do nothing except keep bringing my focus back in and checking "How does this feel? Is the boat moving the best I know how to make it move? Am I really committing everything and holding nothing back? BACK OVER, HANDS UP, WAIT."

600m. 700m. "GERMANY STILL MOVING, STAY WITH THEM". It's about 10 strokes per 100m and all we can do is press out each one. The water is miraculously flat and calm despite all our plans and expectations otherwise. Without wind and waves to deal with, there is nothing to separate the crews except their flat speed. I don't see the very Greek, dry, green/brown mountains on my left because they are outside the range of my focus, but I am aware of the way they enclose the course and hold me in and that that is how I like it.

800m. Approaching our planned 900 metre move now. And not a moment too soon. Just before 900m, I let my focus widen to judge the race again. USA have dropped well back now – but in this moment as I position ourselves in the field, my sense is that even though we are still in contact, everyone else is just 'there', behind my shoulders, sitting up on us and looking back with all the advantage. And the Germans? I can't even see them any more so they must be at least a length up. And in that moment I think…

"We're fifth. Again."

What do you think in this moment? What goes through your head approaching halfway when you are back in fifth place? And for one stroke I thought it. "Shit! Never mind the Gold, how are we even going to get a medal out of this?"

And then a second stroke. "How could I bear it if Elise, Sarah, Cath and Katherine all go home with medals and not us?" But by the third stroke I am thinking: "I know we are every bit as good as them. Maybe better. If they can do it, we can do it. We talked about this before we came out. We said to expect anything but IF WE ARE ROWING WELL, we know that except for the Germans, NO ONE CAN STAY WITH US." And I brought my focus back in to feel the boat, and it was good. WE WERE ROWING AS WELL AS WE HAD EVER DONE, so I had to stick with it and keep the belief that this would all work out because we had all agreed that that was what we would do.

And if that sounds like a lot to think of within three strokes, then it would have been but I didn't have to think it all. We'd talked about this so often and I'd thought these thoughts so many times that I could shortcut them. I could start a thought and then leave it and move onto the next, because this was a script and I knew what the final thought would be.

So at 900m as Debs calls "10 in – GO!" – any moment of doubt had gone.

We all stick the blades in a bit early and jump on them a bit harder for a couple of strokes to lift the rate, and then settle onto a yet higher plane. And at this point it is *everything* you have ever learnt. You finish what you've started. Success is the ability to go from failure to failure without losing your enthusiasm. Expect nothing. Blame no one. Do something. And DO IT NOW. What can *I* do *this* stroke that is better than the last stroke?

BACK OVER. HANDS UP. WAIT.

Always pushing, always positive. Our first 10 strokes take us through the Russians and as we go through the 1,000m marker, the results that flick onto the TV screen for you at home say we have also gone through Ukraine and are already in third place. Maybe we did briefly, but by the time the camera cuts back to the boats, Ukraine have pushed again and we are back in fourth.

At 1,000m, Debs calls "10 out – GO!" and we lift again to push out of the thousand. In 2001 it hadn't been enough, in 2002 and 2003 it hadn't been enough, but here, in 2004, we have finally between us banked enough small steps. Now when we push we really do go through Ukraine and this time they are not coming back. This time we are really in third. Bronze medal position. But I'm not sure that even registered.

900m to go. 800m. And now we are vying with World Champions Australia on our right. It's difficult to tell on the TV pictures because of the angles, but if you line the bow balls up with each buoy line across the course, you can see we are just behind… less behind… less behind… and NOW, *this* stroke we are dead level, and by the next stroke and 700m to go, we are through. By inches in that stroke, but once we are through, they have nothing left and within 10 more strokes we are all but clear.

On the TV pictures it looks like that, it looks like we are side-by-side racing the Australians for those 200m – but I was barely aware of them. As soon as we were on them and moving like this, moving so well, I knew we had them and my focus was on the real goal. On the Germans and Gold. Not a distraction now but using it to pull me forwards. I'd marvelled in '97 how Miriam and Gillian had scorned Bronze to keep pushing themselves to destruction for Silver, and again in 2000 when the Sydney Quad had done the same. I'd wondered at myself and doubted that if I had been there in those boats that I would have had the drive to keep pushing for more with a certain and unbelievable medal already secure. But I should never have doubted – we should never doubt. What I discovered this day, perhaps my defining moment is that whatever we do, as long as we do not let belief hold us back, there is an Olympian inside that will not let us settle and cannot let us rest. So, we do not have to worry that we will be unable to push ourselves hard enough. The tape in our brain will always want to tell us that we are not good enough and that this cannot be done, but when we switch this off we are released to find out for ourselves what is really possible. You don't have to believe in yourself, you just have to not disbelieve. And preferably put in fifteen or so years of dedicated practice.

600m to go. Fran calls our first 10 into the line early as we'd agreed and we all lift again.

500m to go and it is exactly as we said it would be. We have clear water on all four of the trailing crews and have left them for dead. With 500m to go, it is BETWEEN US AND THE GERMANS. "If we can see 'em, we can get 'em!"

500m, 60 strokes left – *a minute and a half* left of my rowing career. I'm at the back of the boat and I'm closest to the Germans.

And I can't see them.

If I can't see them, they must be at least a length up. And I can't look over my shoulder even a little in case it's caught on camera, so I can't really tell if they are just on our bows or if they have a length or even two of clear water. But my sense from the noise and the puddles and just my bow girl feeling is that they are well clear.

But at this point, I'm convinced it makes no difference. We'd talked about it before we came out. The Germans could do anything. This is what we expected. This then is still plan… I'm not sure if it has a letter, I'm not even sure there are enough letters. Maybe we were just down to hoping it would all come good. Hoping doesn't really count as a plan, but sometimes in the final moments it's all you've got. And anyway the Olympians inside have taken over and wherever we are it makes no difference to how hard we push. Lifting on each 10 and finding more and still finding more. How? How is that possible when at every point in this race I've been convinced I was absolutely on the edge. It's a mystery.

"10 strokes" – 50 strokes left. Can't see them.

"10 strokes" – 40 strokes left. Can't see them.

"10 strokes" – 30 strokes left… and suddenly as we come into the last 250m, the spectator grandstands finally start and I suppose it gets really noisy – but I honestly don't remember. Because suddenly, as we come into the last

250m, I'm aware we are on them. And in the next 10 strokes, we take chunks out of them – with each stroke Debs will see them, then Fran, then Becs until we have nearly half a length overlap.

WE ARE FLYING AND THE GERMANS ARE DYING.

And the last 20 strokes are like the first 20. You don't look outside the boat, you don't think of anything except the catch and the finish and pushing your screaming legs down harder and harder. Back up to well over 40 strokes a minute now. And I can't tell you where we are or anything about those last 20 strokes, because in the end, all you care about, all you are trying to do, is absolutely empty the tank. All you care about is that when you cross the line you will have ABSOLUTELY NOTHING LEFT THAT YOU CAN EVER RECRIMINATE YOURSELF FOR. That there was not one single stroke where you could have done more.

Eight strokes.

Five.

And as we cross the line, there is a "BEEP… BEEP"

And I know absolutely in that moment. I don't have to wait for any results and certainly not for a photo because I know absolutely in that moment.

That the Germans have won.

And we've lost.

And that's what it felt like. The video replay shows that they held us to about half a length and if you let the video roll on, you can see the slow motion Chariots of Fire footage of the Germans throwing their hands in the air, their mouths open in roars of celebration. And then you see us, bent over and crumpled, our mouths open in the agony of exertion that you feel only if you lose.

It was like that for about a minute, gasping and groaning and no one saying they wanted to go back up and do it again, until finally I lifted my head. I heard the noise of the crowds and I was suddenly, for the first time since we put the boat on the water, aware we were being watched. And I thought about how this must look. I thought about my mum and sister in the grandstand and how they must feel watching me now like this. And I thought about all the people watching on TV, who could only ever dream of the Olympics and what they would think of me now. I had a flash picture of the Bronze medal-winning GB Men's Four stood on the podium in Atlanta – Tim Foster beaming and looking happy, the other three grim and sulky.

And I thought I still had one choice left to make on this day. Do I choose to think of this as a failure for the rest of my life, or as a success? Who do I want to be? So I turned it round in my head one final time and I thought, "Hang on a minute. Four years ago back in Sydney. What did I say I wanted to come here and do? I said I wanted to WIN AN OLYMPIC MEDAL and what have I just done? Oh my God! I've actually gone and done it! I'VE ACTUALLY JUST WON AN OLYMPIC SILVER MEDAL." And I thought that back then, standing at the course in Sydney, if you'd told me I was going to have this moment I would hardly have dared believe you. I would have taken this Silver in a heartbeat. And I thought about myself as the eleven-year-old school kid who was no good at sport.

And my next thought was "Hang on a minute. I'm only ever going to do this once and I've just wasted a whole minute of it. What am I doing?" I sat up and looked forward in the boat and saw the other girls pulling themselves together in the same way. I saw Becs raise her right hand in a weary but unmistakable salute that somehow gave me permission to do the same. And I sat right up and raised both hands above my head, fists clenched in celebration and shook my head to get rid of those negative feelings (you can see it on the video). Because we are all competitive people and we will all keep pushing ourselves on and on, and that is a wonderful, if rather kind of crazy, human thing. But I think it's also important to recognise WHEN YOU HAVE ACTUALLY GONE AND DONE IT. And that sometimes it is OK to stop and just enjoy what you already have.

And I decided that this was that point for me. I cleared my head and looked around and let the realisation of what I had just done flood into me and from that moment, it felt incredible. I leant forward to try and hug Lactic Acid Queen Debs, who had by this point fallen backwards over my feet. These celebratory moments in a boat are really rather ungainly, and extremely sweaty. She smiled and gasped: "Well done Al! We've got a Silver medal." Because she is Debs.

Never giving up. Chasing them down…

And down….

Photos by Peter Spurrier

We put our feet back into the boat and rowed over to the media pontoon as per instruction. We were first there, the other medal crews still out on the water and Paul and Mark no doubt pushing their way through the crowds, and I think we were all aware that we had just a few moments left together. We hugged each other as we got out of the boat and then stayed in a locked circle, heads almost touching, still gasping for breath while we tried to get this straight. We'd all committed to go for Gold. If we'd won, what to think now would be easy. But as it was we needed a moment to get back on track and realign our heads. We needed to know what we were all thinking, so we could make sure it was all still the same.

I think we were thinking the same thing, but perhaps Fran voiced it first. "We had to think like that all season. We had to believe we could get Gold and train for Gold and we had to go out there today and really believe it. Because today at 900m, when we were back in fifth place, if we hadn't trained like that and believed like that and raced like that all season we would not have come back through." And I remember exactly that she said: "This Silver medal is a direct result of aiming for Gold all season." And I knew she was right. We all knew she was right. I said: "Maybe when we go back and watch the video we'll see something we could have done better, but if we spend the next few hours worrying and wondering about that and then find out there wasn't anything, then we will have wasted all this. If there is something then we can worry about it later, but not now; we have to enjoy all of this now because this next hour will never happen again." And then we all had to say a few times to each other "It's amazing to have a Silver", "It's still the best that any female British rower has ever done", "We did absolutely everything we could out there", "We did absolutely everything we could all season", "This is an amazing thing." Because when you really do believe and you really do want something, it is hard to get your heads round accepting something else. It takes a bit of work, but it can be done. It can still feel incredible if you let it.

Then finally we saw Paul and Mark making their way down the slip to the pontoon. And we all pulled ourselves back a bit from the better place we'd got to. Because this wasn't just our dream, we'd taken the responsibility for theirs too out onto that water. So, I remember feeling nervous and maybe even a little guilty as they approached. But then they reached us and Paul came straight over and hugged us and said, "Well done! That was a fantastic race. You did absolutely everything you could out there. I'm very proud of you." Which is all you can ever say. Mark was a little behind; he wanted to congratulate us too, but he was carrying the cool box and thought he might still have a job to do. "Well done girls. That was awesome. Do you want the ice jackets?"

"No Mark! No way!" Laughing from all of us. Four years building ourselves to our peak and paying attention to every detail and we had a week in which to destroy all that, starting from now. Those are the rules.

Then they left us because we were being hassled to go and do media. We started to walk up the ramp, but I turned to look at my exhausted and still rather struggling crew and it wasn't quite right. I had another flash of the Atlanta Four and I remembered how disappointed I'd felt and almost angry watching the other three and how I hadn't been the only one. Fellow rowers had talked about it for quite a long time. We were equal us four, my ten extra years counted for nothing except perhaps in this. I had watched two, maybe three extra Olympics on TV and several dozen more medal ceremonies. So I stopped us again and brought us back to our heads-together huddle. "OK, we are going to walk up there and be live on camera. How we are in the next five minutes will be how people will remember us. We're rowers, we won't get more than this." And everyone was quiet for a moment, then Fran said "OK Al. How do we need to be?"

"We are happy. We are happy to have the Silver. We did everything we could out there and we've done everything we could all season. People will be watching us who have dreamt all their life about just going to the Olympics. People will be watching us who have worked just as hard as us for this and not got a medal at all. They will not understand if we do not look happy. We got an amazing Silver medal. We are happy aren't we?"

"Yes Al!"

"OK, smile then and let's go."

And we walked smiling, really smiling, up the ramp towards the world's media, stopping on the way to hug and congratulate The Germans.

We did a good job of our interviews – still, nearly fifteen minutes after our race breathing so hard, we couldn't finish our sentences in one breath. Debs held up by Fran. The same words and thoughts coming from all our mouths – still absolutely a crew.

And as I was being interviewed, I said, "It's amazing. There are eight of us in the women's heavyweight rowing team and we ALL got medals. We are ALL going home with a medal" and as I spoke I saw Sarah and Elise and Cath and Katherine smiling and waving at us behind the interviewer and I pointed to them. The interviewer turned and spotted them and beckoned them over. So the eight of us stood there together for a moment, our arms round each other's shoulders. Eight women, nine Olympic medals (with Katherine's from the Olympics before), eight degrees (three achieved in this last Olympiad alongside their training), two PhDs, one Masters, one PhD student, one Law student, one professional musician, one diplomat, one teacher, one marketing professional, two fluent foreign linguists, one baker of the world's best flapjack. Eight women. Show me any such eight women. British rowing had never had eight such women who could stand shoulder to shoulder, and I don't think it ever will again. It will have more successful Olympians. It will have Gold medals. But I can't think it will ever have eight women such as stood there that day. There is no such thing as an easy Olympic medal, but now there is World Class start talent spotting and early funding, now there are sponsorships and a dedicated 2000m rowing lake and training centre at Caversham, now there is real belief from everyone that British rowing women can win Olympic medals and that they should probably be Gold. Now there are women who take just three and a half years to go from first getting in a boat to getting an Olympic medal, not fifteen. But those are not the only reasons. Debs and I are both too short to have been picked up by the current talent spotting criteria. Coaching and selection bias is now basically another rule. But that day the eight of us stood on the shoulders of those women who had gone before, who had just as much talent and worked just as hard but, without a system to support them, never got medals. Just as those women who come after will stand on ours.

And then the four of us got back in the boat and rowed over to the medal pontoon in front of the friends and family grandstand. In rowing, there is no podium and all medallists stand on the same level. And we stood there while Matthew Pinsent in his IOC role put our Silver medals round our necks. He told us that he'd been allowed to choose two medal ceremonies and he'd chosen us as one of them. That in itself was pretty cool. I started to cry a little as he put the medal round my neck and he told me off – "Not you too!" – so I stopped. And then he left and everyone else left, so it was just us twelve medallists standing side-by-side on the pontoon. And the four of us stood there with our arms around each other, our medals round our necks and watched the Union Jack go up the flagpole, while they played… the *German* national anthem.

Photo by Peter Spurrier

And people always want to know: "What does it feel like to stand there on an Olympic medal podium with an Olympic medal round your neck?" because so few people ever get to find out. And I'm sorry but like so many Olympic Medallists, I don't really have an answer to that question. There are no words to describe that feeling except that it *is* pure emotion. It was extraordinary what I was feeling. The words happiness and joy don't really cover it, don't really come close. And alongside whatever that feeling was, I felt a deep sense of ending and closure, but also of loss that I was going to stop doing this thing that I loved. But I fought, as I had done all day, to stay in the moment, not to think "What next?" but to see everything and hear everything and feel everything as it was in that moment. I don't know what it was, but it was a truly awesome and totally overwhelming feeling.

I wanted to remember, but in truth I remember very little. The pictures I have in my head are all from photos or video rather than from life. I have the most wonderful profile shot of the four of us watching the flag rise up the flagpole (cover photo) and you can see everything I'm trying to describe absolutely in my face. And I thank the photographer Peter Spurrier for capturing that moment, because I have no picture of it from my own eyes. I have no real memory of anything between Matt telling me not to cry and some point much later, although still on the pontoon, when Fran weirdly asked if she could look at my medal, took it off me and passed it to someone behind her. I remember thinking it was all rather odd, but my brain was operating in treacle – until Becs and Debs grabbed me under the arms and Fran picked up my startled feet, and in time-honoured fashion for the celebration of the end of a rowing career, they threw me in the lake. Which freshened me up rather quickly.

So I have no visual memories, but there is a deeper emotional memory that is triggered every time I watch one of those Olympic montage videos – most times I stand up to tell this story and often in the writing of this book. Also, fairly reliably whenever I recognise that same emotion in others wherever they have found it, and sometimes just from running to glorious music in a beautiful place. In these moments, even eight years on, I am flooded again with that feeling. It rises up from my chest to my throat and sometimes (if I'm not anywhere too public) forces its way out in great chocking gasps and running tears. I suppose it is the feeling that people have when they think they've found God. I don't subscribe to any religion since to class myself with any group or school of thought is the antithesis of all that I am, but I suppose people would call me Humanist when I say that I believe the reason this feeling is so powerful is that it comes from within ourselves and we do ourselves a disservice when we attribute it elsewhere. It is the excitement of finally believing, if only for a moment, in *our own* power and unlimited potential. The whole world opens up.

I can't adequately describe that Olympic medal moment, but I don't have to because – and I know it sounds like a cliché but I really believe it to be true – *everyone* can get to feel that moment for themselves. Because it's not about winning an Olympic medal. When you have been brave enough to set yourself a goal and work so hard for something for so long and it *finally* pays off, *that's* what it feels like, *that's* your Olympic medal moment. It doesn't matter what it is. I'd had flashes of it before and I've had flashes of it since in other things I've done, but *nothing* as intense as this, because *nothing* I'd ever set out to do has been *so* scary or been *so* hard or taken *so* long. But everyone can have that feeling. And I know I'm right because people I speak to so often come and tell me what their Olympic medal moment has been.

When I came back from the Olympics, someone told me there are more people in Britain who have won the National Lottery than have won an Olympic medal. And the scientist in me went, "What are the odds?"

The odds of winning the National Lottery are about 1 in 14 million and I had *less* chance of winning that medal. Who'd honestly have put money on me as that eleven-year-old schoolkid, not even making it onto the school teams, to be the 1 in 14 million to make it through. The first one ever from my school. Yet how many people when you ask them how they are going to change their lives say "I'm going to win the Lottery" – and then sit on their sofa and wait for their 1 in 14 million. Well good luck to them I say (and don't stop playing the lottery by the way because it paid my 'wages' for long enough). So you can sit on your sofa and wait for your 1 in 14 million or you can get up and start reducing the odds. When we sat on that start line for our Olympic Final, you *could not* get odds on us not winning a medal. It was almost inevitable. But it's too easy to watch someone else's final and think they've had it easy when you've not followed them day after day reducing the odds and reducing the odds until they *make it* almost inevitable.

Another question people ask is "How long did it take? How long were you working for that?" – and again I don't have a simple answer. Because it wasn't just the few months I was rowing with that amazing crew or the four years that I held it as my dream or the seven years I was on the British Rowing Team or even the fifteen years since I first got in a boat back in Liverpool. Again, it's a cliché but it's true, this medal is the sum total of everything I have ever done and particularly and especially everything I've ever done that was hard and everything I've ever done that was difficult. That was what getting dropped off the school sports teams was for and getting through my PhD was all about, long after I'd given up on becoming a great scientist. That's even what learning how to be the child of an alcoholic was about and making the most of the advantages it has given me in life. I don't believe in fate or that anyone had a plan for me or that anyone gave me these trials for a reason. I believe that by getting through them and taking the learning from one thing to the next, I gave them reason. I have made it all make sense.

So, I often finish my talks by saying you could have had Steve Redgrave here with his five Gold Medals or Matthew Pinsent with his four but firstly… well, I'm a lot cheaper. And secondly, when you meet those massive guys in all their size and glory, you somehow can't help but think "Well of course they did, it's a great story but what's that got to do with me?" But I feel like I've written this as living proof that it's not who we are, or what we are, or the things that we're born with. It is the things that we do EVERY SINGLE DAY that make us and shape us and can take us just about anywhere.

So do have the courage to go after your dreams. They won't be the same ones you've had since you were six, things change. But go after them on a daily basis because doing leads to more doing, while stopping leads to more stopping. And remember that no matter how hard it gets and how pointless it seem at times, *nothing* you ever do that's hard and *nothing* you ever do that's difficult is ever wasted. You just don't yet know when you are going to need it.

The starting point of all achievement is desire; finish what you've started; success is the ability to go from failure to failure without losing your enthusiasm; a clay pot will always remain a clay pot while it sits in the sun; no step is too small if it takes you towards your goal; life is a crazy adventure, not a scary trial, enjoy it and keep your sense of humour; float over the top, rather than plough through the middle; accept that a fair proportion of strokes will be rubbish because you are doing something hard; don't let perfection get in the way of a good performance; keep moving in rough water; momentum gives you balance; if you're going through hell, keep going; relax harder; the greatest balance of all comes to those who can just sit; trust in your lion defence reserve tank and the Olympian inside; expect nothing, blame no one, do something and do it now; what can I do today that's better than I did it yesterday. Empty the tank. Everything the best you have ever done it.

Be legendary for your big finishes.

What will be your story when you are eighty?

No regrets. Not ever. Not one.

Epilogue Part 1: What happens next?

"What's the worst that can happen?"

And that is where the story usually ends. The athlete holds their medal high, cameras flash, dreams are achieved and all is well with the world. A full stop. But this is now, nearly nine years on. So what happens next?

"What do you do when you've achieved everything you wanted to achieve? Where do you go from there?" People asked that a lot at first, genuinely intrigued as to what great things I'd be doing next with my life. After his fifth Gold medal Steve Redgrave famously set himself the new goal of raising £5 million for charity in five years, but I had no such grand plans. I didn't want a new goal. I was very tired. I'd pushed myself through my degree, then my PhD, and that had overlapped with my PGCE and simultaneously getting onto the squad, then I had followed the goal of getting to Sydney and then of getting a medal in Athens. And in fact even before all that, there had been my eight hour a day O level revision schedule and the battle to recover myself for my A levels. There had always been a goal, something to drive myself on for next and I kept after them because I instinctively felt it was taking me somewhere necessary. I was never really sure where it was, but I was sure I would get there at some point and it would all be worth it. And I think I thought (although I'm not sure I thought about it in concrete terms – it was more an unspoken understanding with the world) that when I got there, then I would be happy just where I was and be allowed to rest.

This, I thought, was that point. I had done 'it'. Now I could relax, reap the benefits and enjoy the ride. For the rest of my life? I think I thought so. Or at least, I reasoned, until some other goal grabbed me with the same force. This was the first time in my life that a goal hadn't been immediately obvious, but it was natural enough to assume one would materialise fairly soon if I wanted one. Only not too soon, I hoped, because I really needed a rest.

It was hard to stop though. Even in those first few hours, I kept having to talk myself through it. I was enjoying rowing again and I was still getting better. What if a Gold medal was out there waiting? Was it cowardice not to keep pushing forward and see if I could make that happen too? I thought it might be cowardice because I did feel afraid at the thought of keeping going. Afraid of the now very successful medal-winning U23 and Junior Women's teams that were coming up behind me. I'd just won an Olympic medal and was streets ahead of them in every trial, but I didn't feel like that and I didn't know if I could go back to hanging onto the bottom of my ladder while people pulled themselves past me again. Afraid of competition even between us still – if I wanted to be in the Quad in four years time, then I would have to continue to defend my seat against Olympic Bronze medallists Elise and Sarah. But all these things were not quite enough to stop me, because I knew they were limiting beliefs and it was cowardice to give in to them. There was one thought that stopped me more than any other though.

Athletes say that if you do the same thing, you cannot be surprised when you get the same result. I'd been on the British team for six and a half years and I'd been single for six and a half years. If I rowed for another four years, there was no reason that that would change. The best possible outcome of rowing for another four years was that I'd get a Gold medal. And yet when I thought of myself stood on the medal pontoon with a Gold medal round my neck aged 37½ and still single, with just a couple of years left to do all the other adventurous things I wanted to do in my life – find a 'mate' and start on the bottom of a career ladder with no money before I had to have kids or not at all. It was too much. It was too much to leave undone. Even a guaranteed Gold medal did not balance all that, and of course there could be no guarantees.

But STILL, even balanced against all that, it was so hard to stop this thing that I loved. But I knew I needed a rest. My heart rate was constantly about 20 beats per minute above 'normal' and had been for years. I'd barely slept an unbroken eight hours sleep in a similar length of time and most of any sleep had had to be drugged. Just because I'm my father's daughter didn't mean I wanted to be him or my life to be like his. So I rationalised that I didn't have to be so final about it. I could take a break for a year and still come back if I wanted to.

So as we rowed back from the medal pontoon, as the lake water dried off me in the increasingly hot sun, I looked forward to a new life. I'd made myself a promise in that last year when I was so totally single-minded and saying "Yes" only to rowing and "No" to everything else, that when it was done, medal or no medal, I was going to say "Yes!" to everything that came my way for as long as I could. So as we rowed back together for that last time, it was all about saying "Yes!" There were some GB supporters and flags in the far stands calling us over and we said "Yes!" and broke the rules a little to go and see them. Friends waded into the water to hug us and bedeck us in flags. A Liverpool rower friend (known only as Sheepy) gave me the Union Jack umbrella that provided the backdrop for one of those wonderful, spontaneous photos that capture a moment of perfect happiness. We took as long as possible rowing back in. Stopping for photos, stopping for water, stopping just for the hell of it, stopping just to hold onto these last few moments together in this crew. We were by this point unreservedly and rather frivolously happy. Not something any of us got to feel very often.

We did rowing media and met family and then we were driven into Athens to the BBC studio overlooking the Olympic Stadium. When Sue Barker and Brendan Foster finished their link into the next live broadcast, Brendan got up and bounded over to shake our hands full of genuine excitement. I'm not sure if he remembered meeting me at the embassy or if his words were an accident, but in a lovely mirror as he grasped my hand he said: "I watched you race. I was shouting at the TV!" We all sat on the studio sofa with the Olympic flame as a backdrop and got our second five minutes of fame. You only have to watch a few seconds of either of those interviews, even with the sound down, to see my genuine excitement and happiness. I'm proud of all the interviews I did that day. I still think I'd be quite good at being famous.

We went back to our hotel for a late lunch and, having already been up for over ten hours and wanting to go out BIG that night, tried to get a little kip. But no way, every nerve still alive and singing. We gathered in front of the TV with other rowers to watch the start of the women's marathon. "COME ON PAULA!" Even before we left to walk up the road to see them pass all was not looking great, but we held firm in our belief. Coming out of the hotel though, the shocking afternoon heat hit us rising up from the road – I know we'd just raced an Olympic final, but it sapped us even in that short walk and it seemed unbelievable that anyone could run even a few minutes in this, let alone a marathon. I think we all had a sense of doom as we waited, but we were not happy to be proved right as the leaders came past with no sight of Paula. She appeared some way back and we cheered ourselves hoarse – "COME ON PAULA! WELL DONE!" – in the somewhat vain hope that it would help. Then we 'rushed' back down the hill on Olympic Final legs to re-join the TV pictures only to watch her stop, and then see those classic, soul-destroying shots crumpled and crying on the curb.

It went quite quiet in the TV room, but not as quiet as in our corner. I think very few of the millions of Britons who watched Paula that day were quite so emotionally placed to so absolutely feel it. I was thinking it but then, as so often happened, Fran actually said: "It just makes you realise doesn't it how incredible it is that we won a medal at all. We really can't waste a moment regretting Gold: I feel so lucky now to have our Silver." And it was the most perfect flush out of any last feelings of what maybe could have been. All week, if ever I felt any regret about Gold start to come back, I quickly countered it with "Remember Paula."

It's a funny thing the Olympics. It's the combination of competition and time boundedness that make it one of the greatest personal challenges on earth. One of the Olympic Sailors I got to know commented (perhaps a little scathingly) on Ellen Macarthur: "You'll notice how she does challenges, not competitions. She sets herself up to be the first to sail across here or round there but never racing anyone else anymore, and it's always a first so she's not trying to break a record or do it faster than anyone else. As long as she keeps going, she can't really fail." I thought it was harsh, but it did get me thinking and I've been rather observant the past few years. More and more people are setting themselves wonderful personal challenges – run x number of marathons back-to-back, kayak round the coast of Britain, cycle round the world, climb Everest… I'm not being scathing, I really do think it's wonderful. But they have generally removed the elements of competition and time and as long as they have the mental strength to keep going (and the weather holds out and they don't get injured, which are external factors so they can't be said to have 'given in'), they can't really fail. And we are evolutionarily built for that as humans. We are built to run for days and days and keep going and keep going. It's actually our natural state rather than otherwise and as these people will tell you, it makes you feel amazing because actually it's a much more *natural* way for us to live than our 'normal' existence.

But the Olympics is different. The equivalent would be to say that people can only start climbing Everest on one day every four years. And in order to even qualify you must have climbed the other six highest mountains within the past four years within a qualification time. Then, even having qualified, if you are ill or injured or not quite ready on that day, then I'm sorry but you'll have to wait another four years and do all the qualification mountains again before you can come back. And only the three fastest teams past a point will be allowed to go up to the actual summit; everyone else must go back down and wait for another four years and do all the qualification mountains again, even if they have been within sight of the top. And even then only the first team to make it will be allowed to the very top so they can wave their flag for the photo while the others stand on either side, just a foot or so down.

I'm not saying that climbing Everest or any other mountain or any other challenge should be done like this or that the Olympic way is in any way better. I'm just trying to help people understand how different the Olympic way is and the peculiar stresses that the combination of competition and time puts on people. Because I don't think many people really, really understand. And it is important to me that you understand. Because otherwise how can you understand or believe me when I tell you that it is entirely possible to hold the joy of getting a medal of any colour side by side with the disappointment that it is not Gold. That even in the midst of joy at the achievement, there can still be a touch of disappointment, but it doesn't have to take away the joy. That these two emotions are not opposites that cancel each other out. Only when you've been through it can you really understand that the odds of not getting injured and beating the vagaries of selection and being consistently fit on all the critical days needed for qualification, of no one in the crew getting ill in the final weeks and pulling out our best race just when it mattered (the crews we beat in Lucerne by fractions of a second we beat by whole seconds in Athens), are so low that you have to feel immense gratitude for beating them to win a medal of any colour. Even if that also sits alongside the disappointment that on that one day we were not able to find just a bit more speed or that the top Germans couldn't have held their nerve and stayed in the Double, or that the sun, the moon and the stars couldn't have lined up just a little more in our favour and delivered us Gold.

I settled into my Olympic routine of all-night parties, dance until dawn, swim in the sea (every morning this time because most of the nightclubs were on the beach), 24-hour food hall breakfast, couple of hours sleep, afternoon events, evening athletics, then party again. Making the most of what I knew was my last Olympics. I'd brought dance all night shoes, bikini underwear and towel cardigans with me as I'd learnt to in Sydney, but had not been prepared for the fact that everything I now wore must have a medal pocket (as I wouldn't trust it in a bag), so a couple of little dresses didn't get worn. Medals are currency because they get you into all the best parties that week, so we carried them everywhere even though it was rather scary that we somehow had to be responsible for these irreplaceable items while under the influence of more alcohol than we'd drunk for a very long time. I was in the stadium to watch Kelly Holmes win her second Gold and the Men's 4 x 100 relay win theirs. I have even more Athens than Sydney stories, but this is already so long that I'm just going to select my favourite story (perhaps ever).

I was in the athletics stadium with Debs and Fran to watch Paula try for the 10,000 metres. We were going to cheer hard to see if we could help her out. As we sat chatting the guy in front turned round and said: "You are from Great Britain?" He was sat with his wife but she didn't speak much English, so she'd asked him to tell us this story. I think they were Portuguese but I can't remember for sure. His wife was a marathon runner so she had raced on that same day as our final. The marathon had finished with two laps around the ancient Panathenaic stadium and the husband had been sitting there waiting to cheer her on. The stadium had been pretty much full of British supporters waiting to cheer Paula to victory. As they all sat waiting, the husband got chatting to the Brits on either side and told them that his wife was racing. Of course to the Brits, sitting next to someone related to someone racing was almost as good as sitting next to her themselves, so with various nudges and excited pointing of fingers word spread that "That man there, his wife is running in the marathon." So they all sat there and waited for Paula and of course she never showed up. Then at last, some way down the field, never in medal contention, the Portuguese runner appeared. She entered the stadium and her husband stood up to clap and shout her name. By this point all those Brits within about a hundred seat radius felt like they knew them both personally and also got to their feet and clapped and cheered and shouted her name. Further round people were going: "What are they saying? Who is she?" "I don't know but who cares. Look, someone to cheer! Finally we get someone to cheer!" And right round the stadium, thousands of British supporters took all the energy and enthusiasm they'd been storing up for Paula – that with another nation or another

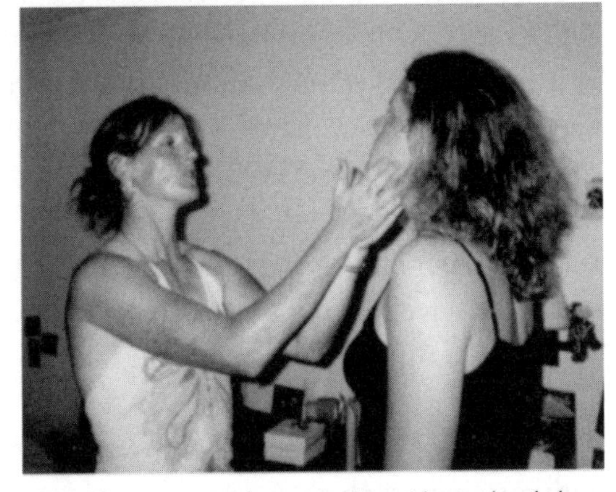

In addition to my roles as squad porridge-maker, baker, DJ, aerobics instructor (not even had time to mention that one) and hairdresser, I was also occasionally called upon as crew make-up artist.

sport may have ended up in anger and frustration – and thought "What the hell!" and stood up and clapped and shouted her name so loudly that she could hear it on the track. She ran the last two laps of her marathon to the sound of her name resonating round the stadium.

That was how this woman, who had likewise given over everything she had to the Olympics to finish halfway down the field, got her Olympic medal moment.

And the reason she had wanted her husband to tell us this story? She had come to the track that night to cheer on Paula, firstly because she was her hero, but secondly as her way of saying thank you to the British supporters who had cheered her on. It made me feel quite proud to be British. I also noticed how many of the stadiums in Athens were half full of British people that week. They'd seen the empty seats while shouting at the TV at home in the first week, spotted the opportunity, bought tickets and flights and got themselves there to cheer live. Those two stories made me realise what an incredible, unprecedented Olympics a British Olympics would be. So when I (finally) came back from Athens, I spoke at an almost endless succession of London 2012 bid events and at each one I told those stories, particularly in response to the almost inevitable challenge that we wouldn't be able to afford to do anything as slick as Sydney or as showy as Beijing and our Olympics would be poor in comparison. I told those stories and promised that the half-empty stadiums of Athens, and later the bussing people in from the country to fill Beijing stadiums, would not happen here. Most athletes only get to go to one Olympics and they never get a medal. But I promised that in London 2012 every Olympic and Paralympic athlete from every sport would compete in front of a packed and enthusiastic stadium and get their Olympic medal moment. That even matches between countries we've never heard of in a sport we never knew existed would be full of people going: "What is this and who are they? Never mind it's sport and it's the Olympics! Yeah! I'll cheer red and you cheer blue!" And so, when 2012 tickets finally went on sale, sold out and could have sold out twenty times and everyone got rather annoyed about that, I had a different perspective. I felt very proud of us again.

I had a lot of fun that second week in Athens (and I had particular fun with my single status, Olympic parties are one time you really do not want a boyfriend hanging around) and this time the party wasn't over when I got home. Team GB came into the packed arrival hall at Heathrow to a hero's welcome. Tess, my housemate, picked me up from the airport and I got home

Celebrating with my mum and sister in Athens.

I had to put this one in because caught on camera is our team doctor, Dr Babbs (white top, sunglasses on head) tucking into a free McDonalds in the Olympic Village food hall.

to find my neighbour Maggie had decked the front of the house out with banners and silver balloons. Half my street came out to toast me with champagne and cheer me through the door.

I was fairly low down on the list of Olympic celebrities but still the party and function invites flooded in. I noticed that quite often they came very late with just a day or two notice, so I knew the organisers had been down the list of Gold, then Silver medallists in more noteworthy sports and been turned down, before they started to invite Silver and Bronze medal rowers. But I didn't care and said yes to everything I could possibly fit in. I did the 'Welcome Home' bus-top tour of London that ended in Trafalgar Square and then we all went to the Palace to meet the Queen. We all got rather tipsy on the quite ridiculously strong gin and tonics they serve there, but managed to maintain a decent level of respect and decorum and no one was sent to the tower.

One story I don't often tell for fear of it being misconstrued is that Kelly Holmes stole my bra. After the procession, we were taken to a gym to change out of our tracksuits and into our Olympic suits to go to the Palace. Kelly Holmes was there saying: "Oh my God! I've forgotten to bring a white bra to wear under my shirt and this one will show through." So I said: "I have got

My homecoming (note my very cool car; I loved that car). Becs lived in Lane End too so later the village gave us a proper celebration, hired a limo and drove the four of us round the streets and to visit a couple of local schools. We so loved the limo that we rehired it to take us to Sport's Personality of the Year.

With my mate Chris Hoy (although I may be over exaggerating the relationship and I'm not sure a photo of me made it into his autobiography) at one of the many after-parties when we got home. I think this one was in Hamleys.

a spare one but it's going to be much too big." I still had a rower's back and Kelly Holmes is very petite (although I know she doesn't look that like on the telly lined up with other athletes).

"No, that's great. Please can I borrow it?"

"Of course, but look I know it sounds really mean, but I really must have it back. It's a 40A and no one makes them that size. I had to order this especially from M & S and it'll be a real pain to get another one."

"No problem, give me your address." So I did, but I never got it back. So that is the story of how Kelly Holmes stole my bra. Although for legal reasons, I should probably mention that I'm sure it's been an oversight and sending it back is still on her 'To Do' list.

After a few weeks, athletes started to go back into training for the next Olympic cycle or those that were retiring started proper jobs. I wasn't doing either so I kept saying "Yes" and it became quite funny because there ended up being a group of Silver and Bronze medallists from rowing, canoeing, sailing and swimming who were in a similar situation to me (i.e. not famous, not training and not working so could still say yes to everything) and we saw each other everywhere and became good friends. It was an amazing time.

And I was still saying "Yes" to everything when my goddaughter's mother (Janet Mowbray of Chocolate Puddle Pudding fame) contacted me to say that a friend of hers who taught at a school near Blackburn had asked her to ask me if I would come up and present some prizes at their Sports Evening. So I said "Yes", even though I had no connection to the teacher or the school and it was a 400-mile round trip. When I got there the teacher said they'd looked me up on the internet and found out that I was a teacher. Since I was used to standing up and speaking to people, would I mind also saying a few words as well as presenting prizes? I said "Yes" even though it was a very scary prospect with no preparation. I spent the majority of the evening (during everyone else's speeches) surreptitiously writing notes on my programme. But when it came for my turn to stand up, I put down my notes and for about thirty minutes I just told the story as it came into my head in that moment – much as I have told it to you here, spurred on by an audience that laughed in all the right places and had tears in their eyes at the same points I did. And when I finally stopped talking and stood, rather shell-shocked, there was a brief pause and then the clapping began and people stood up to clap more and I hurried back to my seat, not really knowing what to do. I sat down next to one of the Blackburn Rovers football players, who was also there as a guest but not entrusted to speak, and

Athens Team GB on a truck ready to be driven through the streets of London in the homecoming parade.

Eking out my final moments of fame in Trafalgar square at the end of the parade.

under cover of the still loud applause he said: "I'm so embarrassed. I had no idea you guys did all that. I don't do anything like that. And how much do you get paid, I bet it's not much is it?" I told him and he said again: "I'm so embarrassed. I had no idea."

And afterwards, kids and adults alike came and talked to me about what they'd taken from my story and how it had helped them think about their own challenges and goals. It was as it had been after the Wycombe High School speech but I'd forgotten. It was almost confusing. Mine had been such a personal mission; I'd done it all for myself in a single-minded, almost selfish, way and yet people talked to me as if I'd been very generous. This was the point at which the woman with cancer thanked me for helping her. It was a very strange but amazing thing. And then the head teacher came up and said: "That was fantastic. Will you come back and do it again and we'll pay you next time?" – and I realised that this was actually a job.

I did go back and they did pay me. I joined a speaking bureau, but didn't get any work for a while because it's not enough to have a good story if no one knows who you are and your biggest claim to fame is that Kelly Holmes stole your bra (which is anyway not really a story for school prize-givings). But this was also the point when I started working as a London 2012 bid ambassador. As with the parties, I was way down the list, but continued to say "Yes" to everything they asked me to do and got sent to all the most unglamorous locations including numerous North London and East London schools where there was little or no publicity to be had for anyone more famous. A couple of times though I did stand up and speak alongside Ken Livingston or Seb Coe and even at a couple of parliamentary launches in the Houses of Parliament. I wasn't considered famous enough to go to Singapore for the vote or even Trafalgar Square, but I did get sent to the East End again and was standing on a stage in the Excel Centre when the verdict was announced. And though I didn't get paid, it was a great experience to turn up at all sorts of places with all sorts of people and not only have to stand up and speak to them as an audience, but get round as many individuals as I could and try to connect and make a difference in just a few minutes.

And I learnt that that, for me, is the main point of my visits. One of my favourite interactions was with a fifteen-year-old lad. I'd done the formal speaking bit and we were now just chatting together, and at one point he stopped me with: "This is really weird. A few months ago I watched you on TV winning an Olympic medal and now I'm just talking to you like you are an ordinary person."

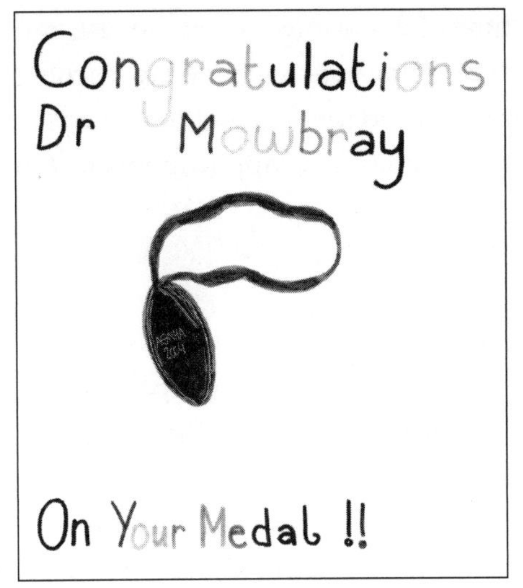

A handmade card from some of my schoolkids. The comments inside are even more lovely.

"I am an ordinary person."

"Yes, I see that now."

So for a while, I really felt like I had it all. I had finally arrived. Everything I had done so far in life had been worth it and rewarded; my future stretched out before me, uncertain but sure to be happy and wonderful; I was invited to parties and was popular; I had a three-month 'pension' continuation of my rowing grant and a part-time teaching job at the school where Jo taught, so money was not a worry and I could keep my savings for the long-planned trip to Australia. I even dated one of the Olympic Sailors for a while. He was small and dark rather than tall and blond, but for a first time in a long while I felt the flip.

I remember saying to myself most days, "I thought I couldn't have everything I wanted all at the same time. I didn't think that was possible, but it is. I have it all. I have everything I want all at the same time."

It was wonderful, but of course that crazy phase of heightened reality could not last for ever. The invites slowed and actually I was glad because I'd become rather tired of having that same, first five-minute conversation with new people you meet, then moving on knowing you'd never see them again. My body eventually went: "No! No more! Stop this madness!" and gave me flu to make me lie on the sofa like a normal person for a few days. And of course, it all went very bad with The Sailor. I hung on for a while until I recognised so much quicker this time the familiar pattern and what it was that had likely made my heart flip in the first place. It hurt, but it didn't take ten years to leave it behind this time.

I'd finally hit the post-race, crying on the sofa slump phase. But it was OK because even though it didn't feel any better to know what it was, I did know what it was, and also because it was finally – after seven years – time for Plan B to swing into action.

My sister was by now in Australia, picking up nursing work on a working holiday visa and having a much better time of it. I wanted to get the visa and an open-ended ticket, pack my boots and camping gear and take my teaching qualification, barmaid and fruit-picking skills and see where it took me.

I logged onto the Australian Working Holiday Visa application site. On the first page, there was one question.

"Are you under thirty years of age?"

"No."

"Fuck off then." And it shut down the site.

I was furious. This was the first time anyone had ever told me point-blank that I was too old to do anything without at least giving me a race or way of proving otherwise. I thought about visiting embassies and writing letters, but I was too tired to fight anymore and scaled down my plans. I reckoned my savings would last about three months so I booked a return flight and headed off in January 2005.

Mum had beaten me over there as I'd put her on a plane before Christmas for her first ever solo flight. I think we'd both been a little scared but she had more than coped. The three of us just hung around together in Sydney for the first couple of days and it was lovely, but those treks in that 'Bushwalking in Australia' guide had been patient for a very long time. Cath and I hiked a two-day coastal walk that started just a train ride away from Sydney and walked back in through the Royal National Park. It was stunning. Cath had been anxious about leaving Mum behind, but I'd said she'd be fine (which Jo, who knows me too well, has named 'The typical Mowbray response') – it seems heartless, but I genuinely don't see the barriers other people see and it has its advantages as we'll see more than once before the end of this story. Catherine and I walked back into the flat glowing, excitement coming off us like radiation, and were met by Mum in pretty much the same state. She'd got the bus into Sydney by herself and walked round the shops and chatted to people and then found the restaurant on the front that she'd last visited with Dad and had a lovely lunch watching the ferries come in and out. "It was quite an adventure really." Not everyone wants or needs to get an Olympic medal.

Then we had a cool ten-day 'Girls on Tour' driving holiday up the East Coast together but by the time we got back to Sydney, I was restless again and eager to get on with my retirement plans. One of them was learning to scuba-dive and another was learning to sail, so I caught a flight back up the East Coast to Airlie Beach. I checked into a backpackers and went out for my first solo wander feeling odd and strangely anxious. I imagined Cath and Mum getting ready to go out for dinner in Sydney and I thought how lonely it would be to sit there by myself this evening. I thought, "What have I done? Why do I always have to make it hard for myself? Why couldn't I have just done the easy thing for once and stayed in Sydney where there are people I know? What made me come all the way up here by myself and think it would be alright?"

But I was here now, so I played 'What's the worst that can happen'. I was booked onto a five-day dive course and then a sailing course, so the worst that could happen was that I'd just be by myself in the evenings and I could always make dinner in the hostel if I couldn't face sitting in a restaurant by myself. OK, that was it and that wasn't so bad. I walked back to the backpackers feeling slightly better. A girl was sitting on the benches outside and asked if I knew when they opened the office. Her accent gave her away as Scottish and I sat down to chat. Her name was Heather and Scottish Heather had been at this a few weeks longer than me, so knew it was perfectly acceptable to end a ten-minute conversation with a fellow solo traveller with the words "Do you want to meet up later and go for dinner?"

And that was that. I went from scared and anxious to perfectly fine within ten minutes and for the next two and a half months, while I toured my way round Australia, sometimes by myself and sometimes with Catherine, I was absolutely fine. I was more than fine. I felt bold and adventurous; the fist of excitement expanding in my chest, day after day after day. And I remembered why it is that I always have to make it hard for myself. It's because scientifically speaking, from my empirical experiments, the sense of exhilaration is in direct proportion to how prepared I've been to scare myself half to death.

I loved the diving and the sailing course on a little boat with a genuine sea-dog, grey-bearded, barking captain, but decided that both sports were rather low energy for me at this point in my life. I actually missed the feeling of exertion and specifically my lungs actually started to ache for the feeling of total expansion and reaching for air. I ended up running on the beach and swimming in the lagoon in my spare time and found them at least as, and possibly even more, wonderful, which was a good thing to know as they are a lot cheaper. I went back to Sydney for a few days to pick up Catherine (Mum had gone home by this point) and we headed to Tasmania to hike more trails from my book including The Overland Track. Eight to nine days of *'Australia's most famous walk; Cradle Mountain; serene glacial lakes and windswept*

Snorkelling off a dive boat on the Great Barrier Reef. I had to put this in. Just to record again, that at one point in my life, my body really did look like this. It took a lot of work though.

plains.' We did it in about six. It was our longest, hardest walk yet and our biggest adventure carrying everything we needed for a week on our backs. It felt more like the sort of thing I should be doing now with my Olympic rower legs while I still had them.

Then Catherine left to return home for good and I was truly flying solo. But by this point I'd started seeing a rather nice New Zealand guy I'd met at a party in Sydney, so made Sydney my home base but headed off for a couple of weeks at a time – learning to surf and windsurf, swimming and running on beaches, hiking more trails from my book (including a very cool solo hike pushing past the cobwebs on the practically unused trails of beautiful Frazer Island while all other adventurers paid very large amounts of money for four-wheel drive tours). I'd been wondering how fit I wanted to stay but decided I always wanted to be fit enough to run for an hour without any trouble, because if I could do that I'd be fit enough to do pretty much anything I wanted to do in life now competing at the Olympics wasn't on the list.

Plan B was everything I'd hoped it would be. I had achieved everything I wanted and was not yet striving for anything more. I had everything I needed and wanted in my life and had the same hopeful optimism about the future, even though I had no idea what it would be, that I'd felt as that Liverpool student. I felt like I was balanced, frozen in time, just for these few weeks, before I had to head home and start working out how to live a new life.

Which eventually I did.

I came back to work which was good, as I also came home skint. I'd spent all my savings and at thirty-four I had no money. In fact, it was worse than that for a while. Wycombe High School had emailed me while I was away to offer me another part-time maternity cover that started as soon as I got back; I also started doing some speaking work for a Leadership Development Consultancy called Lane4 that takes sports psychology into business (Greg Searle works there and got me involved) and for a charity called Sporting Champions that goes into schools. I'd been booked for my first job through the speaking bureau Creating Excellence (which paid the same for a two-hour lunch slot as I'd previously got from a month's grant), but all of these paid one to two months in arrears so I got nothing for a long time. This PhD Olympic medallist survived on an overdraft and the bit Jenno paid me for doing his garden for over a month. But actually it was still a wonderful time. The important thing was that for the first time, ever really, I was time rich. I had WEEKENDS, like WHOLE WEEKENDS, from Friday afternoon to Monday morning, and I didn't have to sleep half of it anymore – and more than that, I had WHOLE DAYS OFF DURING THE WEEK. And because I didn't have any ambitious life plans, when I had a weekend or a day off, they really were free. There was nothing I *should* be doing and so I could do whatever I wanted.

In the summer of 2005 I supplemented my income with more exam marking, coached two weeks on my first Eton Rowing Course (the best job ever) and then I was part of the on-course commentary team for the rowing World Cup at Eton Lake. I wanted to do a good job and worked as hard as for my finals, researching and making notes on every athlete until the early hours each night, then getting up a few hours later to cycle in and do the commentary. I truly loved it but had a couple of weird moments. Driving to the lake two days before the regatta started, it wasn't the first time I'd been back, so I had no expectation that when I arrived at the course and saw – for the first time since my Olympic final – a rowing lake all decked out in flags and grandstands and the tents and boat racks and paraphernalia of racing that it would make me cry. It was so unexpected I didn't even realise what was happening until I realised I couldn't drive anymore and had to pull over. There was no mental processing or thought involved, it was a purely emotional reaction that left me rather shattered. It was the first point in a whole year that I even realised there was any grief for giving up this thing I loved. I think I'd just done a very good job of keeping busy and pushing down any thoughts of rowing when they surfaced.

I pulled myself together, drove in, started work, worked hard, loved it and was fine again. Then on about day two, I was walking around the boat area looking for athletes from different countries to get stories for my commentary. In particular there wasn't much online information about the Paralympic rowers, so I interviewed as many of them as I could find. I was determined to have something to say about every rower there if chance arose. I ran into the German coach. She recognised me and asked why I wasn't racing, was I having a year off? And I answered quite lightly, almost jokingly, as I had all year, that no, I'd retired, I was getting old and I'd quit while I was ahead. But unlike every single other person I'd done that to all year, including my own coaches, she didn't laugh. She continued looking at me very seriously, puzzled even, and said: "Why? No? Surely not." I laughed and shrugged and walked on, but as soon as I left her it hit me what had happened. Her tone was unmistakable. She would have watched video of me for years when we were watching the Germans. She didn't know my ergo score or what I lifted in the gym. She only knew what she saw in the boat and this coach, who I perhaps respected more than any other for what she had done, had respected and rated me. I thought that maybe she would not have let me retire without a word.

It was the first point that I really realised my 'tester' year was up. I'd always said to myself that I could come back if it felt right even if I'd told no one else, but the year had so flown by that it felt like nowhere near long enough. But still I thought I should test it out. My boat was under wraps somewhere, I wasn't even sure where, so I went to the gym thinking I would start training properly again for a couple of weeks and see how I felt. I exercised (I didn't call it training any more) most days and knew I was still fit, so I sat down to do a ninety-minute ergo. I wasn't at all worried about the score and didn't look, but after about fifteen minutes I just stopped. I couldn't be arsed. It felt very strange that for the first time ever I actually had a choice about this. For the first time ever I didn't feel utterly compelled to finish – so I stopped.

I was further put off when the new GB Women's Quad of Becs, Sarah, Fran and Katherine became World Champions a few weeks later. I was pleased for them but felt like that was it for me then. My time had passed. They didn't need me. I'd never get back in there, even if I could be bothered to train for it. The thought of turning up at winter trials and having to answer the question "What are you doing back here; I thought you'd got a life?" – and then coming way down the field made me squirm. And even the thought of having to pull myself up from the bottom again with no grant, while I worked to make ends meet, under the still constant scepticism of those who thought my Silver was absolutely the summit of any realistic ambitions, made me feel so tired. I'd thought I could maybe come back if I wanted but it felt like the door had been slammed shut. So I just picked up all the other strands of my life again and pushed down any thoughts of rowing if they surfaced.

The new term started and I went back to part-time teaching around my other bits and pieces. As there were no vacancies and no maternity leaves in the WHS science department, I'd assumed I'd stop teaching for a while and invest more effort in getting my still vestigial speaking career off the ground while I still had some currency. But in my last week, the kids were just awesome. I think I was doing some pretty good teaching and as I thought about leaving, I realised I didn't really want to. So as I passed the deputy head in a crowded corridor and he shouted: "Thank you and good luck" across heads, I found myself shouting back: "I know there are no science jobs but I'm really loving it at the moment, so if anything else comes up, bear me in mind." We'd just passed shoulders and he barely skipped a beat to turn back and say: "How's your drama?"

So I added part-time drama teacher to my CV and I learnt a lot that helped me in my emerging co-career as a Leadership Development Consultant for Lane4. The basis of my work with Lane4 was, and still is, coaching; the central premise being that people have the answers within them and you are facilitating that discovery process rather than passing on knowledge. Since I didn't actually know anything about drama, this was a pretty useful philosophy – and when, at the end of the first term, my kids showed the incredible mini-plays they had put together (some so powerful they made me cry) I thought this thing really must be true.

I was only teaching part-time and as the paid speaking jobs were few and far between, I still had more time than money and wouldn't have had it any other way. I was still earning more than I'd ever done in my student/rowing years and as I knew how to live cheap, it felt like plenty. Mainly I started going out on my bike, a few hours at first and then whole eight-hour days like I'd not done since my Yorkshire school holidays. I discovered I still loved it just as much. I started noticing and following cycle route signs, and when I looked into it, I found they were SUSTRANS (Sustainable Transport Network) cycle routes. When I looked at the website, a map of Britain came up completely networked by these routes – many of them away from the road on canal or purpose-built tracks. I looked at the map and thought that you could cycle pretty much anywhere you wanted to go on these tracks. I called Catherine.

"I've got a plan!"

"Oh dear."

So we got out maps and planned a 1,300-mile route on SUSTRANS trails from Land's End to John O'Groats, that criss-crossed the country so we could stay with family and friends or just in places we liked the sound of. You can do it on main roads in about 850 miles, but we thought that looked rather dull. We reckoned we'd need to average about eighty miles a day for sixteen days to get it done in the time Catherine could take off work, so we started training and trained long and hard – whole days, then whole weekends. We planned to do it late summer so had about eight-nine months to train.

I had created a wonderful new life but still at the start of 2006, I started to feel strange. I couldn't really explain it even to myself except that I felt 'weird'. I started to feel rather resentful towards those people who had teased me all those years I'd been rowing that I should "get a life". I was out there now earning money, buying things, doing the rounds of Saturday night pub and club crawls and weekends away and holidays that 'getting a life' seemed to entail, but I couldn't help thinking "Is this it? Is this what you were trying to tell me I was missing out on when I was rowing? It's fun for a bit but it's not a patch on what I had. Have I really given up rowing for *this*?"

I still said "Yes" to as many things as I could and lived as full a life as I could, going walking or cycling in new places, meeting interesting new people, getting good at my new jobs and learning new things. I ran the London Marathon and surprised myself by completing it in a time of 3:39. Over twenty minutes faster than my first one when I'd been ten years younger. I coached on the Eton rowing courses again that summer and had another wonderful time. I loved so many parts of it, but I was still living a kind of half-life. This world I had entered, this 'normal' life of regular working days, free evenings and weekends and holidays seemed set up to cater for the regularity and security that family life and the raising of children require. The benefit of not having family is total freedom, but if you don't have a partner and children to be home for in the evenings and weekends and you don't actually need the security of regular income and savings, then it seems to me you are accepting all the restrictions and constrictions of this life without any of its benefits. It is still a half-life.

Catherine and I kept training for our big trip. Catherine was still very anorexic, so Mum took me aside at one point and said, "Are you sure this is a wise thing for Catherine to be doing? All that exercise when she's not eating?" Mum's point had really not crossed my mind so I said, "She'll be fine. She'll have to eat or she won't make it. She'll be fine."

And I guess Mum's understandable conventional attitude, and all I know that follows from not taking it, is why I want to write this next section – even though in a more conventional autobiography it might be considered a distraction.

Late July 2006, Catherine and I met in London on our bikes to get the train down to Land's End. Bottom to top is supposed to be best because you are with the prevailing wind most of the way (and contrary to gut feel, it's not uphill to Scotland). We set off and put in a couple of wonderful but very tough eighty-mile days along the crazy up and down west coast of Cornwall roads. Catherine ate fine, not loads, but more than I'd seen her eat in a long while. But then her heel started to hurt, and by halfway through the next day she was off her bike and in pain by the side of the road. I felt the heel and when she moved it, I felt the diagnostic creak I'd been used to feeling in rowers wrists. "You've got Tenosynovitis in your Achilles. You can ice it and take anti-inflamatories, but it's not going to get better unless you stop."

We put her seat down a bit which I thought had caused the problem; she took Ibuprofen and we stopped at pubs on the way for ice and she very, very painfully creaked her way into Cheltenham where we were staying with Nicky (a family friend who used to be so close we thought we were cousins until the age of about ten). We did all we could for Catherine's ankle that evening and worked out a fifty-mile next day (which was the least we could do and still hope to make it in time), but we were realistic and talked about nearest stations and putting her on a train to go home so I could continue on my own if she couldn't make it. That had always been Plan B. But when Nicky went to bed, Catherine collapsed on the sofa crying. "It's so painful. I don't see how I can do this, but I'VE GOT TO DO THIS. I've told all my friends and everyone at work I'm doing this. I can't go back after four days. This is more important to me than anything I've ever done in my life. This is the first time I've ever really said I was going to do anything. And I've done all that training. This is more important to me than my job; this is more important than not eating. I'VE GOT TO DO THIS. But I don't know how. It hurts so much."

I froze a bit inside. Up to this point, I'd been treating the whole trip pretty lightly. It was a cool thing to do but it was just a fun way to spend the summer and although I'd trained and prepared well, I was never really worried I'd not make it. I knew by now my body would not let me down. I'd been sure Catherine could do it – she is actually one of the few people I know who can match me for endurance – but I'd always just thought that if she got injured, she'd get the train back. But now this was different. From her words and statements I absolutely recognised what this was. She had scared herself half to death committing to this and dared to set a goal where she might fail. And yet still she'd been brave enough to tell everyone that this was what she was going to do. It no longer felt like a choice. As hard as it was to stay in, if you took her out, if this injury took her out, she would be destroyed. You don't have to be on the start line of an Olympic final to be so invested in your own future and so exposed that your insides don't want to stay there.

Land's End to John O'Groats was her defining moment and she didn't have the whole of British Rowing aligned behind her to help her across the line. She just had me. For the first time I realised the challenge I'd set myself that summer and it was nothing to do with whether *I* was physically capable of cycling the length of the country. I had to step up and take the front for the whole of the rest of the trip, which significantly increased the work load for me, and there were days (notably our longest 120 and 100-mile days up the Northumberland and Scottish coast, when the wind forgot it was supposed to be prevailing in the other direction) when I was absolutely floored, lost all power like I'd not done since that Bedford training day, and had to stop for pies again (a seriously underrated athletic energy food). But I was all the time aware that this trip was no longer about me.

Catherine stepped up like I'd never seen. The morning after the crying on the sofa, she walked gingerly downstairs, "It's painful but it's OK, not as bad as last night. I can ride." So we got on our bikes and rode our fifty miles, stopping for ice at every pub. By the end of the day, she was all but crying in pain again, but over dinner that night there was no defeat. She just said, "It's going to be OK. It's going to hurt all the way but I'm going to be able to finish. I can't imagine any more pain than I was in last night, but I still made it today. So no matter how bad it gets, I know now I'll always be able to get up in the morning and keep going."

Heard that before anywhere?

I was trying to be supportive and kept asking "How is it?", until Catherine came back with "You don't have to ask anymore. It's going to hurt all the way, so there is no point in asking. I'm going to finish the ride anyway, so there's no point in talking about how much it hurts all the time."

That sounded familiar too somehow.

We could have shortened the trip and gone a more direct route, but I don't think either of us wanted that as then it wouldn't have been the same trip and we wouldn't have truly finished what we'd started. I've made it sound a bit grim, but although it had its moments, it really wasn't. We had some fabulous scenic sunny days and Cath just put up with the pain and enjoyed the adventure anyway. We went through so many places and saw so much. Our favourite ritual was that every time our track went over a motorway bridge, we'd look down at the queues of cars below and yell "SUCKERS! SUCKERS!" as we cycled on our unimpeded way. All we had to do every day for over two weeks was get up and ride. It was straightforward and liberating. The uncomplicated feeling of freedom was amazing and we'd not even left Britain. In the final few days we both grew very tired, but our legs were by now so strong we made short work of the Scottish hills.

Catherine at John O'Groats. We made it!

We made it and Catherine made it on an ankle that creaked and screamed with every peddle push. She still says it's the best thing she's ever done in her life and it's right up there for me too. And she was truly transformed. Not immediately on the outside, not so you'd notice. She was still very anorexic for maybe another six or so years. But when she got back to Cambridge, she was not Cath The Anorexic anymore – she was Kitty The Mad Cyclist. She said that people always used to ask "How *are* you?" when they saw her, but now friends and friends of friends alike (because word had spread) greeted her with "OMG! You're the one who cycled Land's End to John O'Groats. That's amazing. You are totally mad!" She finally had some self-esteem and a new identity and gradually, gradually became happy enough not to have to do that to herself anymore.

I got home with two days to update my notes and then I was back on the on-course commentary team for the 2006 World Championships at Dorney. I also took on organising and running the post-Worlds party. I'm proud to say it was utter carnage and considered to be one of the best ever. I'd lost no weight cycling ten-hour days the length of the country, but lost nearly half a stone in one night as the only sober person trying to hold that party together and make sure no one actually died. There was blood, but no one actually died.

Once the summer was over I was OK in parts, but still felt weird, increasingly so now. I realised with some shock that two years had all but disappeared since Athens and there were only two more to go to Beijing (I still, and I think always will, measure my life in Olympiads). Despite what I'd told everyone, I'd never myself made a definite, purposeful decision that I would retire from rowing for good. I'd always had it in my head that I could just wait and see how I felt after a break. Two years in was the crunch point. If I was coming back, it had to be now or never. I'd been feeling very anxious for a while that I'd not been out in my boat, not even seen it for two years (I imagined it all broken and mouldy under the cover). I'd never meant to stop completely, but once I'd stopped competing internationally, Leander hadn't really wanted my boat around – so it had got shipped around a fair bit and my new blades vanished very quickly, never to be seen again. It was also not really possible for me to row out of there now, I'd have to join a 'proper' club to do that. It all seemed rather hard work to organise and again the very thought made me feel very tired. But I did locate my boat on an outside rack and thought I could just go for one scull to get me started before I moved it to another club. Even then, I knew it was a cop-out – going back to rowing, just because I'd not managed to adjust properly without it.

I was quite scared of what I might have let happen to my beautiful new boat, so it took a ridiculous amount of 'one step at a time' energy to go down and take the cover off. But when I did, I smiled; it still looked beautiful and perfect and I felt some of the old excitement. Why hadn't I done this before? I rigged it and took some borrowed blades down to the landing stage, then slid my arm underneath to throw it onto my shoulder in the still familiar move. But I stopped and slid my hand back, turned it over for the first time, and there, in the bottom of the hull, was a big tear and hole right through where someone had obviously dropped and dragged a rigger through it at some point in the past two years. I wrapped it back up, put it on the rack, put the blades back and drove home. If I'd been old motivated Mowbray compelled by Olympic ambition I'd have called someone that night, had it fixed in a couple of days and been back on the water within the week, but now it all just seemed too hard and I did nothing. That was my one attempt to restart my rowing career and I could do no more. What was wrong with me?

But I didn't know what else to do. I still, whenever I tried to motivate myself to do anything significant to move forwards, felt incredibly tired. I'd so loved my time in Australia that when I'd come back I'd planned to see if I could find a way to get a working visa and go again for longer. I started to try and make that happen but it seemed the only way was to get a job in a school and root myself in one place, which was not the freedom I craved. I knew there must be a way, there is always a way, but I was too tired to find it. I was surprised at how tired I still felt over two years after Athens. Still terminally tired and I resented it; I'd not given up rowing to still feel this tired. I found myself increasingly wanting to just stay in bed or on the sofa if I could make it that far. But I felt the danger of this and kept trying at life.

I'd come to a bit of a crunch point with teaching and Lane4. If I was going to continue teaching, I really had to get a proper job with a proper contract. Up to this point I'd always insisted on working on a supply contract so I didn't feel tied down and could still take a day off for the occasional well-paid speaking job. I loved teaching but the thought of doing it full-time 9-5 made me feel panicky with claustrophobia. I'd also come as far as I could go working the one day a week or so I was with Lane4. If I wanted to continue to develop and get more work, I needed to do more. They wanted me to work full-time for them, which was incredible really – consultant jobs there are very sought after. But again I couldn't even bring the thought into my head without panicking. I'd always worked hard, academia and rowing, more hours, later into the evening, no weekends and fewer holidays than either of these jobs were offering me, and all for virtually no money. But I'd always been free, accountable only in the end to myself, and it appeared I couldn't give that up for any money. What I knew I should be doing was going it alone and marketing myself properly for the speaking work. I saw how others were doing it. But again, I just didn't have the energy and again I beat myself up about that. WHAT WAS WRONG WITH ME?

In the end Lane4 agreed to take me on a 4/5ths contract, which effectively gave me an extra fifty free days a year on top of my holiday. I had a couple of sleepless nights over even that amount of restriction, but it was a good compromise and I took it. Six years on and I'm still there, still working 4/5ths and it was definitely the right move. I have loved it. As I taught people the importance of listening, I learnt to listen; as I explained the benefits of expressing your emotions and feelings, I started to give it a go. I discovered that from my varied background, there seemed to be almost no situation for which I didn't have a short story to help people make sense of their own world and I learnt when to tell that story and when it was best to keep quiet and let them tell their own. I discovered that my enhanced intuition enabled me to feed back to people I'd just met truths about their lives they'd not told me, rarely if ever told anyone else and sometimes barely recognised themselves. And I somehow also knew when it was OK to tell them and when to hold back. I found that my inability to see barriers in life freed people from their own. And, almost purely by accident really, I seem to have found work that I am perhaps not just more suited to than any other, but also, as I continue to learn (and I know it sounds an arrogant thing to say), more suited to than most other people in the world. I'm developing my own brand around it with adults and kids alike – and I think, eventually, I could be one of the very best in the world at this job that I do, that I never even knew existed and can't even really describe.

And it wasn't just the work. We had a Lane4 team day and as part of it I sat with the people I worked most closely with and we wrote one word feedback for each other. And as I opened my piece of paper, I can't describe the turning over of the whole world that happened in that moment. Amongst the nice but usual words like passionate, inspirational and gifted, three people had written the same word – 'caring'. I looked at the paper and tried not to cry. I'd never seen that word and me associated before and when three people I'd known for less than a year had had just one word to describe me, they'd chosen that one. When I was eleven-years-old and struggling to make friends, to know how to do that thing, my mother, in a moment of high irritation at my non-compliance with her world had told me: "You're so hard and cold Alison. It's not a criticism, I'd quite like to be more like that sometimes but I can't be – you are just so unlike me. I've got friends I've had since my school days, we've been friends all our lives, you will never have that because people don't mean anything to you. People and friends aren't important to you." It wasn't the only time my parents expressed their annoyance with me in this way and I had thought all my life that this thing – this hard, uncaring coldness – was somehow part of me, fixed and imprinted in my genes, and all I could ever do was try and be as nice to people as possible to try and hide it. I even wondered for a while if I had some autistic or Asperger's tendency. But from that day I stopped thinking like that. I've still got the piece of paper.

But life still felt like a struggle. I knew I had to keep moving to stop sinking. On the surface, my life looked wonderful. In my 1/5th time plus holiday, I got just about the coolest job ever as an academic tutor for British swimming for when they took the younger swimmers out of school for training camps. I got a two-week, all-expenses-paid, paid trip to Auckland and supervised their study for the few hours a day they weren't swimming. I ran and swam every day when I was out there and in this training camp environment, I felt at home and happy. I came back and enrolled Catherine and myself on a winter skills course in The Cairngorms and learnt how to use crampons and ice axe so we could climb mountains even in the snow, and took control of Christmas by booking a cottage in Aviemore and saying that that was where I was going to be and if anyone wanted to join me that would be great. John and family came for a few days and Mum and Cath for the whole time. Catherine and I climbed a snowy mountain on Christmas morning and then came back to cook Christmas dinner with Mum. I loved every minute and felt happy and free.

But for New Year 2007, I made the mistake of coming back and going to a party in London. Colliding back with real life and real people, I felt dreadful again. Two and a half years in and there was the very real possibility of sitting watching the Beijing rowing on TV, of my ex-teammates winning medals (probably Gold since they were current World Champions), from my sofa – still single, still with no prospect of children and still no idea what I would do with the rest of my life if I didn't have them. And as for the prospect of going through the rest of my life like this, single, without 'the guy'? Unthinkable – again it wasn't that I was desperate for it, just that it was really impossible even to look forward and see what that might look like. A thought that never even crossed my mind in Athens was that I could give up this thing I loved and change my whole life around and still be single in four years time. I'd never even thought of that. So for the first time in my life I couldn't look further forward than tomorrow and with no purposeful sense of direction, I felt… dreadful. Dreadful had by now taken over from just feeling weird

I loved the work and was getting good at it. I was starting to get more speaking jobs and I'm not kidding when I say that if you've never been in an Olympic final, I can take you there. I spoke at one business dinner and at the end a guy came up holding his contact lenses in his hand. He said he'd been so engrossed in the last ten minutes he'd forgotten to blink and they had dried up and popped out onto the tablecloth. The workshop facilitation and one-

A mini Al & Cath adventure walking holiday in the UK. The Cannon is instantly identifiable to all who know it, so I'm going to let them feel smug in their knowledge and not tell you where. Catherine would like me to explain that her profile is created by her jacket inflating on a very windy day and not by too much cake. Note that I am still dressed head to toe in rowing kit. For years I wouldn't let myself buy any walking or cycling kit while I waited for it to wear out and then gave up. I still can't throw a lot of it out though, it took so much of me to earn every piece.

to-one coaching was a whole new skill, but I was amazed that when I listened to these people and asked them a few questions, they actually came up with lists of things they could do to make their work/life better, not just a list of reasons why nothing could change. And more than that they went away and did them, actually changed their lives for the better. It was exhilarating. I was exhilarated and almost on race high as I left the sessions, but then I came down. I was working a fair bit in London and as I walked back to the station, I'd slow and sink and feel bone-crushingly, face-numbingly tired. I used to look at the railings by the side of the pavement and wonder what would happen if I just sat down there and stopped. Didn't move and didn't talk to anyone. I thought that eventually someone would have to pick me up and if I refused to speak or do anything anymore, someone or some system would have to look after me.

But I just kept putting one foot in front of another and dragging myself off the sofa – weekends walking in the South Downs, Lakes and Wales with Catherine or on my own; 120 ferociously hilly miles of my first cycle sportive in the 'Etape du Dales'; and I tried to recreate the joys of the previous summer by going cycling with Catherine again at Easter, this time in France (it was good but lacked the exhilarating purposefulness of going end to end); getting made up and dragging myself into London for nights out with Kate Mac and Cesca. But while my friends held court and socialised in the pubs and cocktail bars, I'd do my best for a bit then have to escape to the loos or outside to stand by myself, practically hyperventilating from the pain of it, for as long as I thought I could reasonably stay away, before taking a deep breath, forcing a smile and going back in until it felt unbearable again. Annoying people tell you to stop when you feel like this and ask you what you are running away from. They don't know that if you stop now, you will fall off the cliff and then there is no way back. I want to say; OK then, if I stop (which actually I'm longing to do) and fall in a crumpled smashed-up heap at the bottom, are you going to pick me up and look after me? And always be there to look after me because I won't know any other way? No? Well then.

By summer 2007, I knew something was really wrong with me and I thought I knew its name. I talked to Catherine a bit but wouldn't let her tell Mum. I knew if either of us had told her she'd have been on the phone and then straight down to visit me and take care of me (as she had always wanted to), but I wasn't having it that way. Mum and I had two standard conversations. I called her about once a week and every so often, at the end of the call, when she said: "It was lovely to talk to you", I'd say: "Well if it was then maybe you'll call me next time. You never call me you know." And she'd say: "I don't like to, you are always so busy." So I'd say: "I'm not busy all the time and if I miss you, just leave a message and I'll call you straight back. I'd really like you to call sometimes." And she'd say: "Oh, OK then." But she wouldn't, or maybe once but not again and then a while later we'd have the conversation again. Same words, pretty much exactly. I quoted them back to her once, both sides of the conversation as I've just written it here, and she still looked at me non-plussed and said: "But you *are* really busy." We had the second type of conversation every couple of months when I visited. She'd say: "It was lovely to see you." And I'd say: "I'd like you to come and visit me sometimes, you never visit me you know." And she'd say: "Well I don't like to, you are always so busy." So I'd say: "That's why it's better if you visit me. It takes me a day to get here and a day to get back. You say you are lonely and don't have anything to do, so it might as well be you spending the time on the train. It would be easier for me and I'd like you to come down and stay with me. We could have fun." Usually the conversation would end there with an agreement that she would call me to book a date, but sometimes she'd extend it with: "But you don't need me." So I'd say: "It's not a case of needing you Mum, I'd just like to see you. Don't you want to see me?" But whichever way the conversation ended, there'd be no call and no visit.

I know it was contrary, but I somehow wasn't going to let her be the mother she needed to be until she started being the mother I wanted. I found the immediate suction whenever I expressed any distress, sort of distasteful and recoiled. I didn't want to *have* to be ill for us to have a relationship. I didn't understand the terms and conditions of co-dependence at the time so didn't have words to describe it, but still I knew it didn't feel right. I think perhaps I always had.

I also didn't want to talk to her about this thing because I knew she'd use the word Depression and suggest drugs. She had taken anti-depressants on and off since her early 20's, self-medicating once she had a licence, never seeing another doctor and never getting counselling. I think that first doctor who gave her a label in a tough final year at university (that she could then apply to herself for the rest of her life) did her a terrible disservice. Dad had prescribed himself anti-depressants on and off in the last twenty years of his life and they'd given them to Catherine from an early age. I didn't think I was Depressed; I thought I was depressed, as in unhappy. I think Depression is when everything is OK in your life but your brain is physiologically incapable of making the 'happy chemicals'. Treatment for Depression involves taking the 'happy chemicals' as anti-depressant drugs. I think depression is when something is wrong or missing from your life and your brain is not making 'happy chemicals' because you are unhappy. You can take the 'happy chemicals' as drugs and feel better, but whenever you stop taking the drugs there will still be something wrong or missing from your life and you will still feel depressed. You can change your life or you can medicate yourself to bear the life you lead.

Catherine and I went trekking in Iceland for our summer holiday. I was very tired and trekking/camping usually fixed me for a while. Just before we left, I had a call from a friend to let me know that one of our close ex-rower friends had had some sort of breakdown. None of us had even remotely seen it coming. I was shocked by what had happened to her and took it as a warning. This thing, this falling off the cliff, could really happen and I knew she wasn't the first ex-rower to fall. But what shocked and warned me most was my first reaction to this news. My first gut reaction was envy. She was being looked after now, no more decisions, no more picking herself up every day. All that had been taken away.

So our trip to Iceland was supposed to help. But if anything, it made it worse. I know I said Catherine was getting better but although she weighed a little more, she was still, at this point, totally obsessed by food and ate very little. My unsettledness and general unhappiness had triggered some of the same body dimorphism and obsession with weight it had in Bedford. I was a world away from anorexic, but ate less and was lighter than I'd been for a long while – yet still felt fat. I could usually rationalise it but when I saw myself next to the model-skinny (rather than Belson-skinny) Cath, I felt gross, literally sick at the sight of myself. And I felt food guilt every time I ate a perfectly normal-sized meal as Cath picked at a salad or as I tried to enjoy a cake while she turned her nose up and went out for a smoke. Normally I could cope, but I wasn't feeling normal. On about day two we went on a warm-up day hike before our first big trek and I talked it all over with her, told her I didn't have the energy or strength to support her at the moment and in fact I really needed her to adapt to me for a change. I asked her to eat more normally around me just for a couple of weeks. I don't know what I expected but it wasn't that she'd say, in a very matter of fact way, with no hint of apology, "No, I can't do that." Over the next couple of weeks it was really hard to accept that it wasn't that she wouldn't help me, but that she couldn't.

She did her usual trick of drinking the soup and leaving all the noodles from our trekking/camping dinners (while I ate all mine feeling like a pig). Then she'd wake up at about 4-5am starving and because breakfast was the one meal she could eat and enjoy, she'd get up to eat it. Unzipping her sleeping bag, unzipping the inner tent, rustling in bags for food and cloths, unzipping the outer tent, zipping up the inner, zipping up the outer – and way before any of that was finished, I'd be awake. Deathly tired but awake. Then, after a few of days of this, when I'd tried rationalising and then begging her to eat dinner or even to eat her breakfast before she went to bed so she would sleep and not wake me up, and she wouldn't/couldn't, I was so intensely angry even by the first zip that there was no way I could get back to sleep.

It came to a head in the middle of the second week when I heard the first zip at about 3.30am. Just four hours after we'd gone to bed. I lay there thinking I would literally explode and then I did. I got up and found her sitting outside in the dark, smoking and eating her breakfast. There was no more patience and control. I shouted: "What are you doing? It's 3.30am, its pitch-black, it's NOT morning. I begged you to eat more just a few hours ago so you wouldn't have to get up and wake me again and you wouldn't. I told you I was totally exhausted and needed to sleep. How dare you! If you won't eat and are starving, then that's your problem. You should just lie there and be starving and have at least some consideration. At least TRY to behave like a normal person. You don't even try."

I went back to the tent fuming and furious. Expecting her to follow me, tell me how out of order I was and fight. Instead, after just a couple of minutes, the tent unzipped tentatively and quietly, and a person half the size of my sister crept in, crying. "I'm so sorry, Al. I'm so ashamed. I can't help it." And so I had to feel ashamed too. But as I lay there I knew I couldn't do this anymore, not at the moment. If a breakdown could happen to my friend, it could happen to me. So I detached. In the morning I was calmer and more rational, but still I told her that I wasn't in a fit state to cope with her any more on top of coping with myself and that this was the last holiday we'd go on together until she was eating properly. We'd still talk and visit obviously, but there would be no more Al & Cath adventures. I expected her to be upset but she wasn't. "Yeah, you know we've probably just been together too much this year. Every holiday and lots of weekends. It would be too much for any sisters. And this trip has been so difficult because it's rained all the time. I think you are right. We should just take a break." The self-centred nature of her illness still wouldn't let her acknowledge that there might be anything wrong with me.

We still did some wicked things on that trip and I have good memories and photos. Iceland is a freakishly awesome place, even in the rain, and in the end we gave up on the trekking and spent most of our time wallowing in the thermal hot pools and swimming in the heated, outdoor pools with incredible views that even the smallest town seems to have. But still I came back more tired and lower than I'd started. Trekking trips were a banker to fix me and I wasn't fixed.

I came back and continued my descent. I stopped dragging myself into London to go out and stayed on the sofa watching DVDs. I stopped going away for weekends and stopped planning holidays since I couldn't do them with Catherine anymore and my 'going without a proper bed and hot shower for several days at a time' adventures weren't the type of holidays even my fittest friends appreciated. I started to worry about what I would do for Christmas and New Year, always the worst time. Work was still going well, but I found it harder and harder and started to feel like a fraud. I cut the end of my speaking slot sometimes because I didn't feel I could, with all integrity, stand there and say that the hard and difficult bits were the important bits and nothing was ever wasted. I sort of still believed that was true. I still believed I'd pull myself out of this somehow and would eventually learn from it, but I knew I could never again be the same happy optimist who believed I was heading somewhere wonderful and would eventually get there. This had stripped me of something I'd never get back and I resented that.

I'd always wanted to be a 'normal' person but now I was, I felt so boring. I'd lost the energy and excitement for life that expanded my chest and surrounded me with a Ready Brek glow. I knew now I shouldn't have stopped rowing. You can do everything you want, you just have to work out what won't wait – and it had taken me three and a bit years to work out that everything I was now doing would have waited. I remembered that maybe I didn't have to do this all by myself and tried to share how I was feeling with three or four of my closest friends. I tried to explain and cried on their shoulders a bit, then waited for the phone to ring for them to check in with how I was. But it didn't and more than that, next time I saw them they didn't ask and there was awkwardness in their interaction. It was like they thought I'd embarrassed myself and they were doing me a favour by pretending it had never happened. No one would let me say that I shouldn't have stopped rowing. This seemed like too terrible a conclusion to have reached about my life. Everyone just told me again and again all the wonderful things I'd done since I stopped and didn't want to hear that they would have waited. I stopped calling my friends and wondered how long it would take for them to realise I'd disappeared and give me a call. No one called.

But I thought that just because I felt boring, I didn't have to look boring. I thought of myself as that tanned, glowing, beach tousled-haired adventure girl that had come back from Australia and as we girls often do, thought that at least a good haircut would help. I had a good hairdresser but I think I caught her on a bad day and, anyway, it maybe wasn't fair to expect half an hour work with her scissors to turn round my whole life. She cut a foot off my hair and when I looked in the mirror at the end, I had a shoulder length bob with a three quarter fringe – like about a third of the women out there at the time. I thought she must have cut that hairstyle several times a day. She saw my distress and tried to salvage it with a few layers, but it was too late. I was even more boring.

On the way home, I could still sort of laugh at myself for feeling like the haircut had JUST RUINED MY WHOLE LIFE. But still I felt it. Boys will not understand at this point. Girls will nod in sympathy. By the time I got home and looked in the mirror again, I was in actual physical pain. I couldn't bear myself, any part of myself. I didn't want to be here doing this, but there was nothing I wanted to do, nowhere I wanted to be. Couldn't even bear to lie on the sofa. I almost took scissors to my own hair but knew that at the moment, feeling like this, that could never end well. This is the point in other athlete autobiographies where they take those scissors to their arms, but that's not my way. I have never thought like that. There was only one thing I could think of to do and I put on my trainers. I didn't want to go for a run, but still I knew it had the power to make me feel better if I would let it.

I ran out of the house and onto my usual beautiful field and woodland route. I pushed myself on but every so often I would just find myself walking. I walked for a while but walking didn't have the power to stop me thinking, so I'd somehow pick my feet up into a run again. I ran/walked out of the wood, over the style and into the last field and then on the side of the hill I just stopped. Absolutely where I was. Didn't move another muscle. There was nowhere I wanted to be and nothing I wanted to do, so once I'd stopped there was no reason to move again. I was outside myself looking in and felt quite calm. My outside self was wryly amused and I thought I would have little sympathy for anyone else being this melodramatic, but I didn't try and stop it or move myself on. I looked at the grass and thought, quite calmly, that I could sit down, but that would have involved moving and I didn't want to do that. So I just stood. I don't know how long I stood for but it was a long time. The bullocks came over, but you know about them. The light faded and it got quite cold, but still I stood.

Epilogue Part II: And what happens after that?

"If there is something I want to do, I'm going to have to do it by myself or it might never happen."

And then, eventually, quite calmly, I decided to move my muscles again and ran on. Like you always have to do when there is no one to save you and your only two options are get yourself back or stay there for ever. I still felt dreadful as I ran/walked home and I still felt dreadful when I got home. It was a strange physical pain that made it hard to breath. But I somehow knew that this was the bottom. It would not get any worse. I had decided to move again.

I called Catherine to cry down the phone a bit and she was sympathetic and didn't try to suggest I did anything, which was just what I needed and made me feel rather ashamed because I knew that's still not how I would have been able to be with anyone who'd called me in the same state. Now I was a bit calmer I got out my scissors and cut my own hair and although I couldn't make it longer again, I did make a better job of it.

Fortunately I think, I was working in Frankfurt that week for a few days one-to-one coaching with some people from one of the German Investment banks. It was just before things started to go so wrong for these banks and they had put me up in a beautiful, expensive, family-feel little hotel for the three nights I was there. I had a beautiful, big, comfortable room and bathroom, and there were chocolates on the pillow and fresh fruit in a bowl and both were constantly restocked – so every time I left I came back to more. I felt very cared for. This, plus the absorbing, focusing one-to-one sessions, seemed to help so that although I still felt dreadful at times I found that if I waited it would dissipate. On the second day, one of the trading guys I was coaching rushed in a bit late saying he was very sorry but all hell was breaking loose on the trading screens – the crash was literally happening in front of his eyes and he couldn't leave. I arranged to come back after close of trading for just an hour. And I know we all knock self-serving bankers and especially arrogant traders, but that's not what I've most usually seen. This guy was a quiet, thoughtful, self-aware, modest, young German and he was shocked and distraught. He described getting to be a trader and what it meant to him in the same way I described getting to the Olympics.

I worked with him for just that hour on how to handle pressure and build and maintain belief. I listened and asked questions, and then let him sit back while I told him the most relevant story that came to me. He left calmer and more confident and I thought that I wouldn't have known how to do that even a year ago. I realised that I hadn't got what I'd expected from the past three and a half years, but I'd not got nothing. Life is not a bank account.

I went swimming on my way back to the hotel. forty-five minutes of trying to slip quickly and seemingly effortlessly through the water, reaching for air at the ends. Forty-five minutes of searching for it every stroke, nothing else but this in my head. It was like meditation and I floated home at least temporarily restored. I could think straighter for a while.

I knew, from what I'd learnt at Lane4, that I was in the pit of the Nike tick of transition. Life as a full-time rower on the left and life post-rowing up the mountain to the right. I had thought that a partner and kids was up the other side (you don't have to read many sports autobiographies to know that this is the usual way out), but I couldn't even seem to get started. I had been dating. Some had lasted a few weeks, a few months even, but they'd all ended one way or another – some painfully and some not. But there had been nothing and no one I thought I could be 'rest of my life' happy with. And anyway, I wasn't so sure that was the answer now. I didn't feel envy when I looked at my friends' lives with kids. I felt anxious and panicked by the restrictions and seemingly perpetual round of activities and weekend parties. I think I'd finally realised how far out of sync I was when Catherine described a couple she'd met who were cycling round Europe for a few years. The guy had a buggy on the back of his bike so he could carry their two young kids, and the woman had a trailer on the back of hers so she could carry all their camping gear. At the same time as Cath had said, "How can you bring kids up like that?" I'd thought, "OMG! That's brilliant. I could have kids if I could do it like that!" No wonder I was having trouble finding a guy with a similar enough mindset and outlook on life. What really were the chances there could be anyone out there who will make my heart flip, feel the same about me AND want to live like that? But still I was stuck, holding onto some semblance of the traditional dream. And those helpful people who said, "The man of your dreams could be just round the next corner" didn't help, because they were trying to pull me back to a place of denial and waiting rather than letting me find a way to accept a different kind of life and move on.

I knew that going back to rowing wouldn't help, it might just delay the inevitable for a little while but I would still have to go through this at some point. And I realised that this finding the guy thing might never happen; it might, but it might not, and if it didn't happen then what was Plan B for a happy life? What else is up the other side? I'd never had a Plan B for this, had not been prepared to contemplate one. I'd broken one of the rules of my own life. I have very few rules for my own life but it's amazing how often, when I'm having a tough time, it comes down to the fact that I've broken one of them. Always have a Plan B.

The second rule for my own life is *Expect Nothing, Blame No One, Do Something* and I realised I'd been breaking that too. I *had* been expectant. I had expected that after pinnacle of the Olympic medal, life would be easier, that I wouldn't have to work so hard, that I would be given at least some happiness for free. That's what the guy and kids had been about, that and the comfortable certainty of the future. I'd thought that when I had them, there would be people around to give me happiness and I wouldn't have to get up off the sofa every day and find it for myself. People with kids say that getting up all hours of the night and chasing round after them is hard, but they've forgotten how much harder life is when there is nothing and no one to get up for or chase round after except what you make for yourself every day.

It made me very tired to think that this was how life really was and it took me a long time to get my head round it. Perhaps the hardest thing of all to accept was that I was always going to have to work hard at being happy. But was I always going to have to have some PhD or Olympic medal to be chasing? Did it really have to be that hard? I thought about all the amazing things I'd done in the past three and a half years, all the places I'd been, the new friends I'd made and how happy they had made me in the moment. But then how unhappy I'd been in-between because I didn't know what I'd be doing for the rest of my life that would guarantee some sort of permanent happiness. I thought about how the last ten-fifteen years had been nothing like I'd expected or imagined when I left Liverpool and yet they'd been wonderful. Really, unbelievably wonderful. I could not have predicted, even at twenty-two, that I would compete at two Olympics, let alone win a medal, or that I would now be earning good money doing a job I loved but hadn't even known existed. So I started to wonder why I was so worried that I didn't know what the next ten-twenty years would bring. Anything could happen.

I could do, literally, anything, and if the past was anything to go by it was likely to be pretty damned good. I was still the same person.

So I started to get a bit excited about the future, even though I had no idea what it would be. And I thought that I didn't need to change my life, I needed to change my philosophy on life. I needed to move from *'I'll be happy when… '* to *'If I'm happy now, I'm happy.'* (I realise this is not a new philosophy but it was new for me) and more than that *'If I'm happy now I'm happy and if I live to be eighty and most of my days have been happy days, then I will have had a happy life.'* I thought that in the past three and a half years if I'd have had that day at a time philosophy and not worried about the future, then I would have had a very happy time and probably not have ended up stuck in a field looking at cows.

I worried for a little while longer about not having kids because so many people said, "You have to have them in case you regret it when it's too late." I thought this was an even worse reason than, "Because I don't know what else to do with my life" – but I did worry that they might be right and I might regret it. But then I had a revelation when I asked myself the simple question "Why do they have to be mine?" and realised that they don't, there are no rules about that. And if they don't actually have to have my genes (which I'm really not thinking is any great advantage), then I've found a way through. I can spend another ten years doing all the adventurous things I want to do with my life while my body will still do them and if, when I get to fifty or so, I think I would really like kids in my life, I can foster or adopt. I had found a new way forward – a Plan B. I decided that if I'm going to be single and childless, then I'm going to really use my freedom, have fun and adventures and be *Sex and the City*, make-everyone-envious single, not pity-the-spinster single. There are only these two options as a single woman. That's just how it is.

We all need purpose and to feel life has meaning, so we all create it to get through. Some people create children and some people create a God. Some people create both and get to feel very smug about the meaningfulness of their life. Culturally, we tend to believe that those things are 'real' and anything else is just made up to compensate for not having them. You hear such statements about childless people, especially childless women all the time. But I don't think that's very fair. We are all just making it up. We're all just getting through the best we can.

I realised that even in the absence of an all-consuming goal, I still needed purpose, to start setting small goals again and keep planning small adventures. When I'd run the 3.39 marathon, I'd immediately thought that with better preparation I could go even faster. Sub-3.30 maybe. That was exciting. Sub-3.30 is not fast for a real marathon runner, but it's fast for a normal person. I opened up my laptop and applied for the Paris Marathon in late April 2008 – just over six months away. When I got up the next morning to go running, it immediately felt better. I wasn't just running around in circles in the park anymore, I had Paris in my head and was training towards sub-3.30.

When I'd gone into my online bank account to pay for the marathon, I'd had a shock. There was money in it – a lot of money – for the first time ever. I realised part of the reason I was so tired was that I'd been working so hard earning all this money. The student/rower in me was still chasing up and down the country after a couple of hundred quid and still not realising I had any to spend. I still had lots of my fifty free days left that year. I didn't know much about my future, but I knew it certainly didn't include dying before my time, knackered, with lots of money in the bank (like a certain person I'd once known). Two things had to change. 1. I had to start turning some work down and working less hard and 2. I had to start spending some of this money on things, really great things, rather than just £3 cups of coffee and £7 glasses of wine in London. I thought I could afford to go away somewhere really cool (or actually somewhere really hot) for Christmas, but that would mean going on my own now. I realised that this was another thing I'd been expectantly waiting for. When I came back from my Australia travels, I remember saying to myself that I wanted to do more of that, but not on my own next time. I'd find 'the guy' and travel with him next time. I had to stop waiting so I invented a new mantra that said, *'If there is something I want to do, I'm going to have to do it by myself or it might never happen.'*

I didn't quite have the confidence to go off completely by myself yet, so I started the booking process to go to a Spanish language school in Mexico for three weeks over Christmas and New Year. I figured that this way I'd have somewhere to stay and something to do and people to be with at least part of the day and the worse that could happen was that I'd spend the afternoon on my own on the beach and eat by myself in the evenings. It was scary and exciting – a feeling that experience told me was usually rewarded.

And finally, the last thing I did in those so productive three days in the lovely hotel in Frankfurt was that I found something for after the Paris Marathon, so I had yet more to look forward to. I booked onto 'The 5-Dale

100' – a 100-mile cycle sportive that started in Richmond five weeks after the marathon. I decided I could afford a new bike but knew nothing about them, so I emailed a bike-mad guy I'd just met twice and within a couple of hours he emailed me back with half a dozen good options and said he'd meet me in London sometime if I wanted some help looking them over. I thought: "How nice!"

Almost simultaneously Gail texted me having seen my 'bad hair day' Facebook update. So even though I was in Germany, I gave her a quick call and model Gail gave me good advice about bad haircuts and made me laugh. As I put down the phone, I thought how it hadn't been fair to expect my friends to be counsellors and therapists. They didn't have any more idea about that than I did. If I wanted that I should pay someone qualified (which eventually I did) and be happy to take from my friends what they did have to give. I counted my best friends up on my fingers and even if I just counted the really, really good friends I almost didn't have enough fingers. That seemed like a lot (especially to the girl whose mum had told her she'd never have any).

The turnaround and recovery wasn't immediate. I think it took me about two years to really pull myself out. I had good days and bad days and good hours and bad hours within a day for quite some time, but it helped that I could now look at each hour or day on its own merits and understand that a bad day was just a bad day, not a bad life, and remember that the good day yesterday still counted.

And once I'd started investing in my life again, life started giving it back, almost immediately. The following day, even before I'd left Frankfurt, I had an email from British Swimming asking if I would go with them on training camp again as a tutor for two weeks – this time to Perth, Western Australia. Then a couple of days later I got another email from Ricochet, a TV production company. I'd answered an advert some months before for a Channel 4 programme that was looking for "Physically fit women to take men on in the last bastions of male-dominated physical work to see if girls can do it." One of my colleagues at Lane4 had forwarded the email with a note – "This sounds like you Al!" Ricochet thought it sounded like me too and invited me in for an interview and screen test for their programme *Dangerous Jobs for Girls,* and I got it. I was to go back out to Australia for three weeks in February. I began to feel the excitement of the months ahead. This was no half-life.

On the way back from Frankfurt I bought a book in the airport called *Food is better medicine than drugs*. I'd been more than a little worried for years about my mother's poor eating habits and reliance on an increasing number of drugs and, as the book was written by a proper doctor, I wondered if she might believe him more than me. But on flicking through, I noticed there were sections on being low in energy and low in mood, and as a result I started to seriously cut down on the carbohydrates that had been recommended to me when I was rowing as 'good' carbohydrates (pasta, bread, cereals, rice etc.), realising that they release their energy very quickly and would not help my energy/mood swings. Mainly I replaced them with even more fruit and vegetables. I think it helped me feel more stable and balanced and formed the basis of a nutritional philosophy around healthy eating/healthy life that I started to develop for myself.

On the last day of my Australian coastal trek – the flies were terrible and lacking a cork hat, I had to get quite inventive.

I went to Perth with the swimmers and stayed on to hike an amazing five-day coastal trail. On the last night, I slept out on the beach under incredible stars when there was nowhere to pitch my tent, scared but exhilarated and repeating often, *'If there is something I want to do, I'm going to have to do it by myself or it might never happen'* – because surely everyone should sleep a night out under the stars at some point in their lives. I came back, worked a bit and flew to Mexico. I'd been

In Playa del Carmen, Mexico with Natalie and Frederique, two of the wonderful girls I met on that trip.

prepared to spend a lot of time on my own, but the school seemed to be full of fun, adventurous girls in their thirties, escaping the confines of a traditional Christmas. I went scuba-diving in the blue ocean on Christmas Day with one and then to an all-night live reggae band beach party for New Year with several others. A very lovely Mexican drummer from a rock band spotted me at the party and pursued me quite charmingly for two days, before I thought "What the hell" and gave in for the remaining time I was there. Every evening I'd meet up with the girls to go for dinner, cocktails and dancing, then gradually we'd disperse and meet back at 9am (after maybe a couple of hours sleep) for breakfast in the gorgeous courtyard before class, sharing stories of who had been where and done what with whom the night before. It was *Sex and the City*, pretty much exactly.

In February, I flew out to film *Dangerous Jobs for Girls* with the two other girls on my team. Nic was a university lecturer and mother of two, who had been UK kick-boxing champion, then half of the UK's top all-female rally-driving team and was now half of the UK's only all-female power-boating team. Jo was the UK kite-surfing champion and about number six in the world at the time. Between us we 'manned' a commercial fishing trawler in the South Australian Ocean for eight days, the last forty-eight hours on our own, pulling

the nets up every four-six hours for all eight days and landing over 21 tonnes of fish. We completed the task, but the real success for me was that when you watch the four programmes with four sets of girls doing different jobs (they are still on Dave sometimes), we are the ONLY team of girls who don't fall out and bitch about each other to camera. And that was because before we ever got in front of the camera (and in secret because obviously the production company wanted the conflict), we sat down and talked about our 'contract' just as I'd learnt to do on the rowing team. We included the 'we'll sort things out between ourselves and never talk about each other to anyone else' clause and stuck to it even though they tried to set us up a few times.

And through all of this I had Paris and sub-3.30 on my mind and kept training. While I'd obviously not done as much as I'd wanted on the fishing trawler, I'd still banked a dozen or so runs between 2 and 3.15 hours in the last six months, plus the dreaded sprint sessions needed to get up to speed. When I got back off the boat, my running was further impeded by a swollen knee. I ran anyway, stiffly and in pain, until a couple of weeks later I noticed a little lump appear, and after digging around in my knee joint with my pen knife extracted a long, sharp fish spine. I ran better after that.

Into the home straight of the Paris Marathon. You can take the girl out of the Olympics…

Then one weekend in April, I caught the Eurostar to Paris with Jenno as my support team. I woke up early on the morning of the marathon, sharp with race-head like I'd not felt for a very long time. Excited and a little nervous, but gloriously not sick to the stomach. I wanted to get under 3.30 but my future didn't depend on it. I walked down to the start, warmed up and squeezed into the sub-3.30 start gate, feeling very tall and female compared to most of those around me. There was music playing and a minute-by-minute countdown on the speakers and the air buzzed with our shared anticipation. The fist of excitement swelled in my chest and brought tears of familiarity at this almost-forgotten pleasure to my eyes.

The gun went and I clicked my watch as I ran under the start gate and got into my running. To get my sub-3.30 I had to run every km just a couple of seconds under five minutes and despite all the training and the couple of practice races I'd done, I actually had no idea if I could do that. As I ran past the 1km marker I clicked my watch again, took a deep breath and looked down – 4.57.90. Bang On! Then kilometre after kilometre, I knocked them out. Running freely and easily, intensely focused on my internal state, not just for minutes as in rowing but for hour after hour after hour. Keeping my posture relaxed, my breathing quiet, slowing my pace if I registered too many seconds under five minutes. Letting people pass me, savouring every easy kilometre and still on target – until at about 2½ hours I recorded a five-minute kilometre for the first time and had to start pushing to keep it under. I started to struggle but with less than an hour to go, I knew that was OK. It was always going to get hard at some point and I knew well enough how to suffer for an hour if I had to. Jenno popped up to cheer and a few seconds passed more easily, then back to the increasing pain. Into the last few kilometres and now I felt I was sprinting – flat-out, lactic leg sprinting, but still registering over five minutes every kilometre. I tried to calculate how many seconds I had to spare, but the numbers on my watch stopped making sense, stopped even telling the time to my oxygen and glucose-starved brain, let alone arranging themselves into the calculations I'd been carrying out kilometre by kilometre up to this point. So in the end, in the last 2.2km, I had no idea. I stopped looking at my watch and just ran. "The faster I run, the faster this is over…" Jenno popped up again with a "Come on Al!" and I manage a smile but not a wave.

I saw the finish and finally *my* finish kicked in and I was really sprinting. Passing guys in droves but not racing anyone but myself, not even the clock. Apparently you can take the girl out of the Olympics, but you can't take the Olympic spirit out of the girl. I nearly ran over the top of the last official cameraman crouched on the ground, sprinting and sprinting and I'm through. I click my watch for the last time and take a look.

3.29.12

Six months of training, 26.2 miles and three and a half hours of running and I was inside my goal by just forty-seven seconds. It's like magic, this goal-setting thing. There's this bit at the end of my 'Inspirational Speech', when

I'm building up to my legendary big finish and I say "And it doesn't seem to matter what it is, when you've set yourself a goal, worked so hard for it and it finally pays off, then this is what it feels like, this is your Olympic medal moment. And I truly believe that anyone can have that, that anyone can feel it." I'd almost stopped saying it, almost lost faith in my own rhetoric. But I definitely had another Olympic medal moment that day despite finishing 5,769th. And I knew I had to keep setting myself goals, even if there was never another of Olympic medal proportions and even if I sometimes had to sort of make them up.

The buzz carried me for weeks, right through to the 5 Dales 100 where I rode for just over seven hours, pretty much non-stop, up and down the ferocious Yorkshire hills on my gorgeous new bike and was fastest woman home.

That all took me well into 2008 and there have been over five years since then. But that's pretty much how I now live my life. Never considering myself too old or too untalented to try something new and spending as much time as possible doing the things I love. My mantra has shifted from *"What can I do today that's better than I did it yesterday"*, which I still think is an essential Olympian mindset, to *"What can I do today that's better, different or I've never done before"*, which is rather more balanced. I focus on living, not just achieving. But I still have the Olympian inside and know I will never be complacent; I will always drive myself on and do my best – I don't also have to beat myself up about it.

Six more marathons, an Ironman triathlon, hundreds of miles of incredible trekking, many new countries, a dozen or so snowy mountains, and about five years ago I found a great new joy when I finally found dances where the guys are taught to lead and have spent the intervening years learning to dance

Image @ Jerry Lebens 2013

Modern Jive (Ceroc) and more recently the gorgeous, complex and meditative Argentine Tango. Now when I go abroad for work or trekking, I take my tango shoes as well as my running shoes and have danced all over the world. I could write a whole other book about the things I've learnt about life from learning to dance (and probably will), but actually I've found it just as interesting to discover the things I already knew about dancing from learning to row and play the French horn. I have taken to it like a swan to water. I can go dancing and after just a few minutes find the same quiet peaceful energy that it previously took me until morning three of a trek to find. In my first Tango lesson, that guy summed me up after ten minutes with "You're not very good at doing nothing are you?" – but now the guys I dance with comment on my stillness and 'quiet energy'.

I've developed my nutritional and healthy life philosophy into something very practical and now run workshops on it myself. It is a whole other book (probably the next one). I recently had an email saying "THANK YOU!" from a guy who was at a session I ran about ten months ago. He went away and by following my advice on what to eat and doing a lot of exercise, he says he's lost 27kg and is fitter than he's been since he was 18.

I've also started running sessions on 'Yogic Sport, Yogic Business & Yogic Life' in which I try and teach kids and adults the idea of 'The search for it'. Writing this had made me realise that the crucial difference between most of the Olympians I know and a good club athlete is their constant self-determined search for improvement, every stroke or every step. What I call 'The search for it'. And I thought: "Who is teaching the kids that? Or even that's it's out there and they should be looking for it?" So I started running 'Yogic Sculling' with the kids on the Eton Rowing Courses. We do postural, breathing and body consciousness exercises, then get on the water at dusk and row up the lake to try and find 'it'. I tell them it's out there somewhere. When I ran World First Yogic Rugby with a team of twelve-year-old lads, they wrote to me afterwards: *"Thank you for the session, it was great and I learnt a lot about using your mind to make better passes and stuff. It really worked."* And when I ran World First Yogic Business, I had several hundred suited and booted people standing up, eyes closed, breathing and finding inner flow.

In the summer of 2008, I was invited to accompany a group of London 2012 hopefuls to the Beijing Olympics as their mentor (it's really not a bad life). I was able to see some events including a day of rowing. The Quad,

Yogic Sculling stage1: This is not a very exciting photo. We are trying to focus on our breathing and posture to 'get in the zone' and access 'flow', so we can all be successful warriors whatever we choose to do in life. Bruce Lee would understand.

Yogic Sculling stage 2: Then we go out on the water and I take them through some boat and body movement and awareness drills before we scull up the lake into the sunset in search of 'it'. All that's missing is the yoga mats.

which still included Debs and Fran, having been World Champions for three consecutive years, came second to a freak appearance Chinese crew. It was Katherine Grainger's third consecutive Olympic Silver. This time they were all devastated. And of course Becs did get that amazing Gold and in cycling no less. It felt weird to sit there just watching. I still felt like I should have found a way to continue at least for a while, at least until I had stopped getting better and had discovered my true limits. I could not have continued as I was, but with fifteen years of endurance training under my belt and the highest VO2 max/kg on the team, it might at least have been worth exploring a less exhausting and more sustainable way to train (although realistically I'm not sure that would have ever been compatible with British Rowing). But despite this realisation, I still had no regrets. I'd had to stop and have the four years I'd had to realise all this. I'd had to stop and 'get a life' to find out that it would after all have waited. You can't regret what it takes hindsight to learn.

But once Beijing was over, it was easier for me. Whatever my ambivalence about stopping rowing between Athens and Beijing, I can't think of any circumstances under which I would have continued after that – so post-Beijing, it was just not a question to bother my mind any more. Life has continued to become more free, more adventurous and more tranquil. My resting heart rate is low and although I keep some magic sleeping pills for emergencies, I rarely need them and sleep unbroken nights. I couldn't compete in an Olympic final, but I still hardly ever get ill and feel as fit and healthy as I ever have. I can run up a flight of stairs without stopping. Catherine and I spent three glorious days cycling coast to coast through the Northern Lakes, Wolds and Moors last summer and she ate at least as much as I did. Al & Cath adventures are back but have become Al & Kit adventures because, like I said, she has found a new identity.

Every year, as my birthday approaches, I compile a list in my head of things I've done, places I've been, things I've learnt and friends I've made in the past year that have made it worth getting a year older. By the time I finish, I never mind the extra year on my age. And then I start thinking forward to the year ahead and making plans for what will be on next year's list. I have a little more idea what the future will bring, but not much.

But as I've pulled myself back up, my mum has slowly sunk and it's not been easy. She looked for and bought a new house and the purposefulness of that did her good. She went back to work part-time (one of the nurses in the clinic where she worked has told my sister that our mum was "probably the loveliest doctor I've ever met") and was great for a while, but once she'd moved and retired that seemed to be it. No more purpose. No reason to get up anymore. The three of us kids became increasingly worried about her lifestyle. We'd been trying to get her to do some exercise for about twenty-five years, but she just laughed at us like it was something people like us did but not something she needed to bother with and rarely even walked anywhere. Her diet was poor and she still drank a lot more alcohol than is recommended for a long and healthy life. And then there was the general purposelessness about her life and the amount of time she spent sleeping. She'd sometimes spend two weeks at a time in bed. When I asked about her plans for the rest of her life, even just the small plans, she said, "I can't see anything ahead except decline" (which is worrying because goal setting works both ways).

The three of us would have long conversations with each other discussing strategies to try to encourage her to do some exercise or eat better, but nothing we tried made any difference. I spent hours listening and sympathising, but she was a sympathy sponge and seemed to absorb as much as I had to give without it ever making any difference. She said she was Depressed and I understood that, but although she would let me sympathise for as long as I could, she didn't want to listen for one minute to the research saying that people who don't exercise and eat badly are almost bound to be depressed or that happiness is hard work and you have to keep getting up to find it. Eventually Catherine and I realised we'd been here, exactly here, before with Dad and we'd best save our energy. It took John some time longer as it was his first time.

And then Mum started to become more than usually confused and forgetful. It took me just a few minutes of Google research into Dementia and Alzheimer's to discover the unbelievably unpublicised fact that they are both thought to be mainly lifestyle diseases with the same risk factors of poor diet and lack of exercise as we'd associate with cancers and heart disease. Lack of 'brain stretch' (learning new things) later in life also contributes. One mental health website said that only 10% of Alzheimer's was genetic and another had it at just one case in 100. Either way, it didn't take a medical genius to put Mum's lifestyle together with her increasing symptoms and see what was happening and what was ahead. We all tried to reason, cajole and coerce for a while, but to no effect. The nothing response was very prevalent. When I talked to Mum about the link between lifestyle and health, I spoke in Martian. If you get ill there are drugs and if there are no drugs you are screwed, but that's OK because it's not your fault – apparently.

I really tried to help. I took a week off work and went back up for ten days, emptied out the fridge and we went shopping for fruit, veg and fish. I explained why and gave her the articles I'd printed out on lifestyle and memory loss, which she 'filed'. I got her up every morning and we went for a good long walk to get our 10,000 steps in and even went to aqua-aerobics a couple of times. It was lovely to see all the women there chatting and laughing and having fun and I wanted Mum to be part of that. And there was no depravation; she really enjoyed herself and we ended most walks in the café for coffee and cake (where I also picked up leaflets on local walking groups and tried to get her interested). Mainly we ate fruit, veg and fish, and loads of it, so she was never hungry and came downstairs shocked but delighted after about six days saying she'd lost half a stone. I was actually a bit worried at her reaction though. She seemed to think the new lifestyle was about weight loss rather than memory loss and nothing I said or did would make her connect the two. If she had let this thought penetrate, she'd have had to change her lifestyle or take responsibility for what was happening to her and she didn't want to do either of those things.

We had an argument at the top of the stairs one night when I 'caught her', after we'd had a lovely healthy balanced day that had included wine for dinner, going to bed with a large tumbler (about half a pint) of wine. I was very angry that I was taking this time to help her and she wouldn't help herself, but she told me that she didn't care about her health because since Dad died, she'd not really had anything to live for anyway and there was no point in doing anything to extend her life. I finally went very hard line and explained that I wasn't just here for her, I was here for me too, because if she kept doing what she was doing she was going to need looking after pretty soon and the three of us were going to have to do it.

"YOU WILL NOT ALISON! I WILL NOT HAVE THAT. You will not be looking after me."

"OK, fine. But someone's going to have to pretty soon if you keep up with this. So what's your plan?"

Nothing.

When I left, she continued for a while eating the food I'd stocked the freezer with and went to aqua-aerobics one more time before she said the 10am start was too early and she was not good in the morning. When I came back next time, there was nothing fresh in and everything was back to 'normal'. She said she didn't see the point in continuing with the 'diet' now that she'd lost over a stone. I finally gave up on trying to change her and just started adopting strategies to minimise my own stress and frustration. I brought my own food with me and spent a good amount of time out on my bike. I'd been here before.

A year later, she had a diagnosis of dementia and Catherine and I were beating up and down the country trying to keep her company and look after her. John did too but he was looking after my two young nieces for me, so it was even more difficult for him to find time. After another year or so, it became obviously impossible. Catherine spent ages setting her up with homecare and day centre visits, but Mum's dementia made her paranoid and within a week she'd told the carer she didn't need to come back and stopped going to the day centre. Within another month, she was living on the psychiatric ward of the local hospital so they could stabilise and assess her. After a couple more months, she had a diagnosis of Alzheimer's. She was sixty-five. Life expectancy from diagnosis is an average of seven years. The first thing Mum said to Catherine was: "Well at least if it's Alzheimer's, we know it's not my fault." Catherine snapped rather. I'm glad I wasn't there.

I know it sounds heartless, but no one really gets it. The closest I can think of is that it's like watching a parent smoke all their life, begging them to stop and then have them develop lung cancer. None of us could know how it would end or that it would end with this, but we could all tell it was never going to end well.

Mum needed 24-hour care so never went home and is in a lovely care home now. The three of us visit and do the best we can. I'm proud of how this has brought us together rather than pulled us apart as it does many siblings. I find it impossible to do much sympathy but have stopped all challenge, push and irritation that she should do anything herself to make her own life better and just do kind, patient and jigsaws. I've learnt new skills. For a long time she was rarely happy and even in a place full of people, she said she was lonely and was often distressed. It was distressing. I kept trying to change things to make her happy, before I finally realised nothing did that, nothing had ever done that. My new mantra became *"I've got to stop trying to make her happy, she's never been happy, even when her life was up to her she wasn't happy. Her unhappiness doesn't suddenly become my fault now she has officially quit responsibility for her life. She's just not a happy person."* It's quite a long mantra. It's quite a difficult situation sometimes.

At the moment Mum still recognises me as someone she likes and wants to spend time with, but she doesn't know my name much less that I'm her daughter. She has no short-term memory at all and people say talk about the past, but she has no long-term memories either. It's not like it is in the movies. It's hard to understand, but the thing that makes most sense when I try and interact is the science that says her brain is being destroyed by sticky brown 'plaques' of decay. Because Mum has no two connected thoughts, there is no two way conversation, no matter how hard I try, and actually it distresses her to try, so we do jigsaws together and I either chatter or just stay quiet. She seems calmer now and almost content sometimes, but for several years I had to repeat my mantra and remember the top of the stairs conversation when I was trying to leave and she was crying and begging and sometimes even screaming at me to stay. For a while I became terminally tired again and developed the first severe back pain I'd ever had. It stopped me running and dancing and even walking at times. I linked it to anger and frustration, but as with Dad I've found there is actually no way to make this all make sense and it twists me up inside if I try and trace it back through the generations to find out who's to blame. So I stop myself doing that now. It is what it is. It is just sad. Stop looking for reason and blame and detach. Blame no one. It stops with here, with me. Choose awesome.

And it is awesome. I guess the final piece of my current life fell into place about three years ago when I realised that since I work everywhere I can live anywhere. I decided I wanted to live by the sea. I looked at a map and seeing that Brighton was the closest sea to London (where I had more regular work than anywhere else), I went house-hunting there. But the first day it just didn't feel right. I went for a run and running west with the sea on my left, the coastline was all built-up and before too long I was running through industrial estates. I was already over the idea. What was I thinking, planning to move at this time when everything with Mum was so uncertain and I was having to learn to take control of her finances and think of selling her house? I turned round to run back and pack. Facing east I saw white undulating cliffs in the distance and I had a flashback to two or three years ago (when I was nearing the bottom of my tough time) and a walking weekend with Catherine. We'd been walking over the Seven Sisters Cliffs on the South Down's Way and I'd looked at the expanse of undulating rabbit-trimmed green, edged with white cliffs and blue sea and felt an intense desire to break into a run. I remembered saying to Catherine, with no hint of premonition: "I think if I could run along here most days, that's pretty much all I'd need to be happy". I ran back to Brighton, got out my map and it turned out they were the very same cliffs.

So I took my search a few miles east, found a house the next day and within three months I'd moved to Newhaven to live with a view of the sea.

The Seven Sisters, plus my sister and her Rocket Dog

When I was house-hunting, the estate agent asked for my criteria and I said my top one was to live within five minutes run from some clifftops. He looked confused and said he didn't have a box he could tick for that. I have no TV, two ovens so I can feed all my friends at once when they visit, am up a track with no road noise, but just twenty minutes to Brighton and dancing – and did I mention my view of the sea?

When I'm away, I miss my house and life by the sea like I'd miss a partner and think I'm the most content I've ever been when I'm here. I run on the cliffs and swim in the sea and sit and look at the view and that's usually all it takes for the excitement and love of life to return even if it's been hiding, which isn't very often now.

I've got my Ready Brek glow back and I think it's brighter than ever. I can really feel it. Sometimes I'm sat quietly somewhere and I hardly know what to do with it I'm lit so brightly from the inside. And people can really feel and even see the glow. They comment on it very often.

I found a quote from Nelson Mandela's inaugural speech. *"Our deepest fear is not that we are inadequate. Our deepest fear is that we are powerful beyond measure. It is our light, not our darkness, that most frightens us. We ask ourselves, "Who am I to be brilliant, gorgeous, talented and fabulous?" Actually who are you not to be? Your playing small does not serve the world. There is nothing enlightening about shrinking so that other people won't feel insecure around you. And, as we let our own light shine, we unconsciously give other people permission to do the same. As we are liberated from our own fear, our presence automatically liberates others."* It resonated so deeply it had me in tears, because I recognised that this has

Cooling off on about day 3 of a trek in the Pategonian Lakes. Photo taken by Elaina, another solo trekking girl I met at the top of a mountain the day before. We were both gibbering rather at the terrifying sheerness of the scree descent we had to get down to reach our next campsite. We agreed to walk down together. We walked together this day as well before we parted ways. We are still in touch through the wonders of Facebook.

turned out to be so true. I think that I'd spent most of my school life and a lot of my rowing life trying to shrink so as not to make other people feel insecure. I certainly did it a lot when I came back from Athens and even stopped telling people about my PhD and Olympic medal for a while. I'd tried to dim my light in an attempt to fit in better, but it just made me feel ever more out of place and awkward. But now I find the more I am brave and brilliant and let my light shine by sharing my adventures in spoken or written stories… the more I am just the best of myself, the more it really does free those around me to do the same. Not to go and do the same adventures, but to be the best of themselves. Kids and adults alike come up to me glowing, telling me of the things they are now going to do and sometimes send me emails when they've done them.

The Edmund Hilary quote for why climb Everest was "Because it's there". But I don't feel like that about the mountains I climb or the trails I hike or the marathons I run or even the dancing. It's not because it's there, it's just because I can. Because I couldn't and now I can. Because I'm over forty and I still can. Because at any point I could get ill or injured, so I do it while I can. Because I'm still conducting my scientific experiment to find out *if* I can. Because I can.

Last year I took a sabbatical from work to spend two months in Argentina to tango, trek and practise my still terrible Spanish. It is a close-run thing as to which felt the bravest: trekking for ten days on my own in the Andes (four consecutive days and three nights of which I didn't see another human being) or walking solo into my first traditional Milonga (tango dance hall) in Buenos Aires. But they were two of the most wonderful experiences of my life. I have never been so effortlessly happy as in those two months and I know that this is how I must continue to live a large part of my life.

So now I'm not just trekking girl, I'm Tango Trekking Girl and I don't reckon there are many of those in the world. That feels different enough and definitely not boring.

And finally, to close the loop, I volunteered as a Games Maker for London 2012 Olympics and Paralympics at the rowing lake, which honestly made me about as happy on a daily basis as anything I've ever done. I felt nothing but joy and pride to have played at least some small part in its history when British women (still under the leadership of Paul Thompson and David Tanner) finally won their first Olympic Gold medals for rowing, especially

Gamesmaker Al and Paralympic rowing Champion Alla Lysenko of Ukraine. A wonderful woman and legend of the lake in 2012. She lost both her legs in an accident aged 39, took up rowing at 40 and 3 years later won Paralympic Gold (in full make up and glorious headscarves). She weighs 90 Kg. I use this picture in my healthy lifestyle talks to head off at the pass those people who would like to list the reasons they are not suited, or their lifestyle is not suited, to exercise. Never be a victim in your own life.

when Katherine Grainger got Gold at her fourth time of trying. I felt no envy. I realised I wouldn't swap my little Silver Athens medal for one of those big Gold gongs even if I could. It's so part of me now. I love it even more than when I won it because of all that it has given me and taught me. Gold would have taken me somewhere different to here. And I really love here. Debs and Fran, who'd also invested everything they had in another Olympiad, came away with nothing as tangible as a medal this time and were devastated again. Eight years on we are still close and my old crewmates feel more like sisters than friends. I was devastated for them, but still relieved I didn't have to feel devastated for myself. I describe my London 2012 Olympic experience as "All the joy of an Olympics without any of the terror." I've started learning Portuguese so I can volunteer or work at Rio and plan to take two months every four years for the rest of my life to go wherever the Olympics takes me.

And all the time, I've been writing this. It really did start out as just a collection of recipes, but at some point, a few years ago, I did a couple of really well-received speaking jobs in one week, one especially to an audience of several hundred thirteen to eighteen-year-old schoolgirls. At the end I was literally mobbed by these girls, wanting my autograph and just wanting to talk to me. I felt like a pop star. And from one girl, "You've got killer legs, I'm going to take up rowing if it gives me legs like that." I laughed, rather embarrassed. I never intended to be inspiring or a role model and I don't really want the mantle. But I couldn't help thinking that it's not such a bad thing if girls find something to aspire to in my size 12, well-muscled, running,

Some people wonder if I ever actually do any work. This is to prove that I do, I just don't talk about it very much because there's always a lot else going on.

As you see I work hard and put a lot into it. The quality of a person's life… etc.

dancing, hill-climbing, cycling, will-carry-me-anywhere, rower's legs, rather than size-six, starved, lipo-suctioned, air-brushed, glossy-magazine legs. So on the way home, I started to think that maybe I was missing something and when I got back I opened my laptop and started to rewrite my recipe book, meaning just to add in the words I spoke when I stood up to speak… and then it just got a bit out of hand to be honest.

And so, without me even really realising it, this book and becoming a writer has become the next big thing – the consuming purpose. Whenever life gets complicated and stressful, I ask myself two quite stark questions. 1. If I found out I only had a year left to live, what would I want to spend it doing? And 2. If I got knocked over by a bus tomorrow and was lying on the curb breathing my last, what would I regret I'd not done? And then I sort my life out to do more of the first thing and get the second done. For several years now, the answers have been 1. Trekking and Tango and 2. Finish this book. So I've increasingly made more time for my treks and dancing and I've GOT THIS BOOK DONE.

So I really must finish this now… writing and lying on the sofa in my house by the sea. It's my solitary haven. There is often a guy around in some part of my life, but I would still describe myself as single. Spanish does this better because it has two verbs for 'To be'. Most people would describe themselves as 'Estoy soltera' as in 'I am single at the moment', but I feel 'Soy soltera' – 'I am a single person', a whole, complete, single person. Like a rich, dense, marzipaned fruitcake. I love this life, but it's not all easy. There are a lot of guys who lie and cheat and it's still my default to find them more attractive than I should. It's helpful that I can at least tell when they lie and I call it out pretty quickly these days and don't hang on. The benefit of being a whole person is that you are not so desperate for someone to complete your life that you have to be in denial about such things. But even when you are a whole person it's painful to be lied to by someone you were trying – despite all that has come before – to trust.

But there have been some good guys too in the past few years who ice and decorate my life for a while and I'm not averse to the possibility, and even like the idea, that one might eventually decorate it for at least a very long time (I can't seem to say 'for ever' about anything). But as I've approached the end of this book, I've felt a disinclination that that would be how it would end. I know if I'd been able to finish this with "And reader we were married", so many people would have sighed with relief that I had finally come over and complied and was traditionally happy, but I'd have felt rather a traitor to my many beautiful, intelligent and courageous 'Soy soltera' friends and the many, many more beautiful, intelligent and courageous single people I know are out there. Because almost no one talks about or writes about us. People who have already read this book have said I'm brave for writing as candidly as I have and indeed the thought of people reading all this feels very scary. I have put it all on the outside. History tells me that this feeling is usually rewarded, but I can't help but fear that this time I may have pushed it too far. I suppose time will tell. I didn't mean to write all this when I started writing about flapjack but having done so, I can't take it out. Because I think I actually know as many women like me as not like me and I've never read a book about us.

The wonderful Kate Mac (who has found her own, rather similar way through) put it best. "It's difficult. It's hard being single when everyone else is coupled and familied up, so you need people to understand. But you can't really talk about it because the last thing you want is pity and all you get is pity." It's hard sometimes in the same way that making relationships work and being a parent is hard sometimes, but there are lots of books written about those things. The only books on being single are about how to not be. Almost no one tells you how you could actually make it work.

But I have found something I never even knew existed and I don't think I've heard anyone else try to describe. The life I have was definitely Plan B, but now I have it I don't think I would/could swap it for a traditional Plan A. I have created a life where there is almost no 'have to' or 'should' and anything is possible. The freedom is exhilarating. I get up most days and think "Anything could happen, absolutely anything could happen" and very often it does – the fist of excitement still, at forty-two, expanding in my chest day after day. People talk about the love for their children and what it gives their lives and I do get it, even if I can't feel it. I'm not saying that this is any better, just that this is also incredible and it is out there. And if you have a partner and kids, you can't have this too, can't even imagine it – in the same way I can't even imagine the love you feel for your kids.

The thing is… I have no fear.

Not of the future, because even though I don't know at all what it will be, I am excited rather than scared by that. Anything could happen and even if it's not enjoyable for a while, I know I can cope. Not of being alone, because 1. I actually love it and 2. I am never on my own except when I want to be and don't see why that should change as I get older like people seem to worry it will. I have vague plans to take up horse riding and choral singing in my fifties, golf and water-colour in my sixties, archery in my seventies and crown-green bowls (or maybe rock-climbing) in my eighties. And anyway, it seems to me that it's the married people with kids who have more trouble as they grow older and their kids move away and their partner dies, than those who have had to be self-reliant and make new friends all their lives.

Not even afraid of dying, not at any time, because, even though I plan to last well into my 80s and hopefully beyond, now I've finished this book there is really nothing left undone and I really do have no regrets.

It doesn't mean I'm never afraid, about real things, like walking into strange tango halls and trekking in the wilderness on my own. And that's important because that type of fear keeps you safe. But not too safe. I wrote my Argentine trekking and tango adventures as a sort of blog for my work colleagues and the wonderful Justin wrote back that I was… "never bonkersly without a care, but never held back by irrational fear" which I think I would like on my tombstone, whenever I get there.

So I'm finishing this book not at the end, all tidily sown up but sort of in the middle. A pause before the next crazy chapter begins. After all, if I really do live into my eighties, then I'm barely halfway there. And I'm finishing here because I think every book I've ever read about a woman or by a woman has finished either with the traditional happy ending where she meets the man of her dreams or with the traditional tragic ending where she doesn't. But I don't think I have ever read a book about a woman or by a woman that finished just with the words...

I am enough.

"Success is a finished book, a stack of pages each of which is filled with words. If you reach that point, you have won a victory over yourself no less impressive than sailing single-handed around the world."

Tom Clancy

Key to the Second Colour Picture Section

1: Athens 2004
Top left clockwise: Savouring our last moments together as a crew. Debs & I dancing the night away after our final. A favourite crew photo in the Olympic stadium and last known sighting of a Mowbray bicep. My Scrabble crew – Robin Bourne-Taylor, Josh West, Dan Ousley & Ed Coode – on our way back from a late night Scrabble game (probably). A photo of me with someone famous.

2: Fitting so much in
Top left clockwise: Christmas in Patagonian Chile 2008 (day 3 of a 10 day solo trek). Crab fishing on 'Dangerous Jobs for Girls' (2008). Top of Cairngorm in the Scottish Highlands on a flippin freezing day in December 2008. Christmas Mexico 2007 – diving in The Cenotes, Playa del Carmen. Well on my way to finishing a 130 mile cycle sportive on a beautiful English summer's day (July 2013). Lago Azul, Patagonian Andes (March 2012), two full days hard walking from anywhere and it's all mine (I didn't see anyone for four days) – I sometimes wonder if fewer people see these sights than see Everest.

3: Dancing
Top left clockwise: Ceroc weekender – dance until dawn Friday, Saturday & Sunday nights (several times a year, every year). Dutch tango festival (2013). Working it out in a tango workshop with David in Hove. Tango in Buenos Aires (2012). Bringing in 2013 on a beach in Mexico. The ultimate tango shoes from Comme il Faut (Buenos Aires), my current favourites in blood red – I am insanely tall in these and I just don't care. Closer to home in a gorgeous Brighton Milonga.

4: Sitting
Top left clockwise: Make tan while the sun shines – Patagonia 2012. Top of the world - Patagonia 2012. Christmas in Mexico 2012. Christmas in Hawaii 2010. Sydney coastal walk 2005.

5: Family
Top left clockwise: With Mum & Catherine, Loch Morlich near Aviemore (Christmas 2006). A brace of Mowbray sisters. Al & Cath adventures inc. – at the start of 'The Way of the Roses' Sustrans coast to coast cycle route (summer 2011). Dancer Nell & Runner Lily (could just as easily be the other way

round). John with Baby Nell. Being Auntie Al. Another snowy mountain in Scotland with Catherine.

6: Friends

Top left clockwise: Batty old birds up mountains, with Jo Dowman in The Brecon Beacons (2010). Brighton dancing amigas Claire & Rachel at Lisbon Tango Festival 2013. Mac n Mowbs, Olympic Stadium Anniversary Games (2013). Visting Cesca (party partner extraordinaire) in Hong Kong (2010). 2013 Iron Maiden training partner Moyna (last seen training together in an Liverpool Uni boat over 20 years ago). With Gail – 40 years old and friends for over 30 of them (2011).

7: London 2012

Top left clockwise: At Wheelchair Rugby – this Arena is going to Rio "Take me too!" Last of 19 Olympic and Paralympic Gamesmaker shifts at Eton Dorney Lake. Olympic cycling with Kate Mac. Paralympic Athletics with Debs. Capturing a spirit of London 2012 moment at the rowing course – all the spectators wanted a photo of them sitting on the Olympic rings and every day they spontaneously organised themselves into an orderly queue and a couple of Gamesmakers spontaneously took it upon themselves to act as the 'official' photographers. All British Olympic Medallists invited to the Olympic Opening Ceremony. Clocking on for a typical morning Gamesmaker shift (after cycling 15 miles to get there). Rowing the Olympic Flame on its final stages in Glorianna on the morning of the opening Ceremony.

8: Promise me

Top left clockwise: Coaching beginners at Eton Rowing Courses summer school, The youngest lad in the red top tugging at my sleeve on the way home after day two "Alison, Alison, how is it possible that rowing can be SO MUCH FUN!" More ERC. Yogic Rugby. With Lily after her first 'Mini Mile' at the Edinburgh Marathon. Engaging the community with the Olympic Spirit as a London 2012 Bid Ambassador. Yogic Sculling.